CHRISTOPHER HART

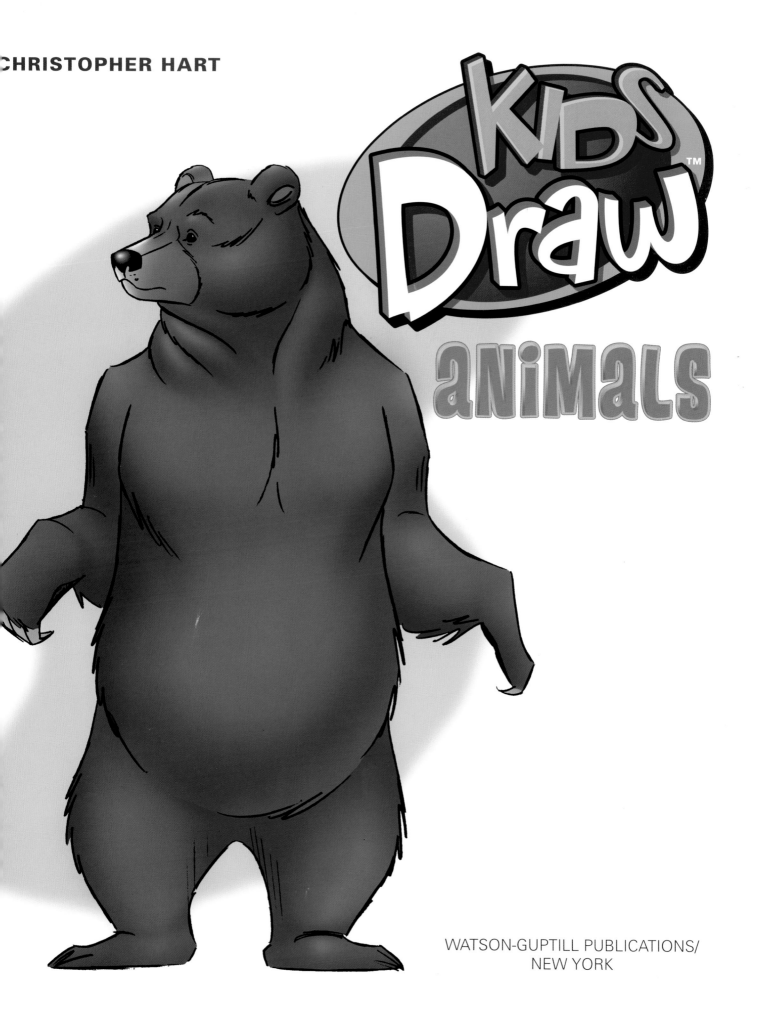

KiDS
Draw™

aNiMALS

WATSON-GUPTILL PUBLICATIONS/
NEW YORK

No animals were harmed in the making of this book, and one was even fed.

For my daughters, Isabella and Francesca, two of the best artists I know.

Special thanks to Julie Mazur for suggesting this subject.

Senior Editor: Julie Mazur
Designer: Bob Fillie, Graphiti Design, Inc.
Production Manager: Hector Campbell
Text set in 12-pt Frutiger Roman

All drawings by Christopher Hart.

Cover art by Christopher Hart
Text copyright © 2003 Christopher Hart
Illustrations copyright © 2003 Christopher Hart

First published in 2003 by
Watson-Guptill Publications, an imprint of the Crown Publishing Group,
a division of Random House, Inc., New York
www.crownpublishing.com
www.watsonguptill.com

Library of Congress Cataloging-in-Publication Data
Hart, Christopher.
    Kids draw animals / Christopher Hart.
            p. cm. — (Kids draw)
Includes index.
Summary: Explores how to look at an animal, such as how it stands and
walks, and provides step-by-step instructions for drawing animals from
the jungle, savannah, farm, forest, and sea.
    ISBN 0-8230-2631-0
1. Animals in art—Juvenile literature. 2. Drawing—Technique—Juvenile
literature. [1. Animals in art. 2. Drawing—Technique.] I. Title. II. Series.
    NC780 .H26 2003
    743.6—dc21

                                        2002151435

Printed in China

First printing, 2003

11 /14

www.kidsdraw.com

SEE YA THERE!

CONTENTS

INTRODUCTION

What's your favorite animal? Dogs? Cats? Horses? Or maybe it's penguins, or the humongous Galapagos turtle? Whatever it is, chances are this book will show you how to draw it!

We'll start by learning some basics about animals—how their bodies are put together, how they stand, how they walk. Then you'll draw all kinds of animals, from gorillas and grizzly bears to camels and crocodiles. Best of all, you won't be just copying, but really learning how to draw as you practice and have fun.

So is your pencil sharpened? Is your paper ready? Then let's start our journey through the wonderful world of animals. Just don't feed the lions!

THE BASICS

L et's start with a few basics. The more you know about how animals stand and move and walk, the better your drawings will be.

How Most Mammals Stand

Many of the animals you'll draw here are *mammals.* Mammals are animals like horses and dogs, who feed their babies with milk and have skin that is more or less covered with hair.

Most four-legged mammals have skeletons that are pretty much alike. Two that *don't* are the bear and the elephant. Believe it or not, their back legs are arranged more like people's!

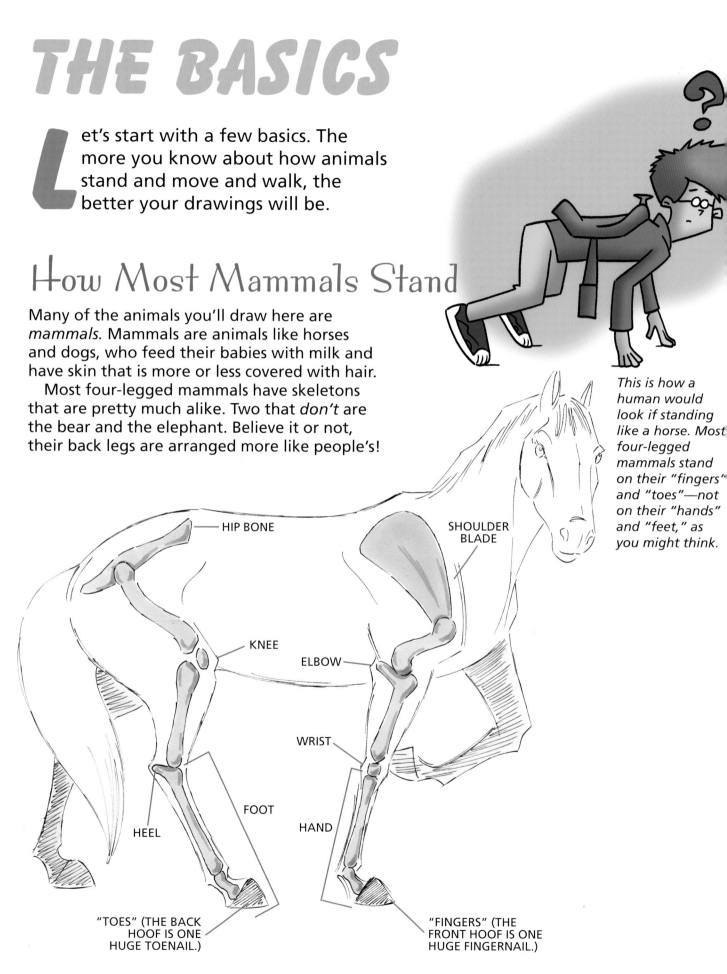

This is how a human would look if standing like a horse. Most four-legged mammals stand on their "fingers" and "toes"—not on their "hands" and "feet," as you might think.

HIP BONE

SHOULDER BLADE

KNEE

ELBOW

WRIST

FOOT

HAND

HEEL

"TOES" (THE BACK HOOF IS ONE HUGE TOENAIL.)

"FINGERS" (THE FRONT HOOF IS ONE HUGE FINGERNAIL.)

6

Many other types of mammals have this same basic skeleton. See how the skeleton creates "bumps" in each animal's outline?

BUMPS

WOLF

LIONESS

BIG-HORNED SHEEP

How Animals Walk

Animals with four legs walk in very specific ways.

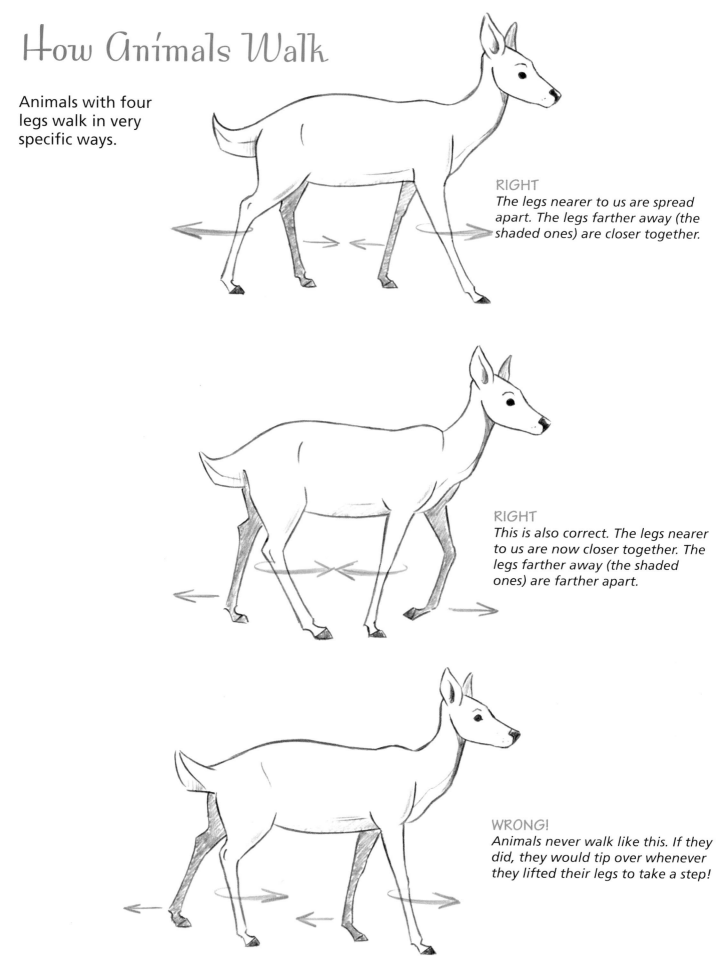

RIGHT
The legs nearer to us are spread apart. The legs farther away (the shaded ones) are closer together.

RIGHT
This is also correct. The legs nearer to us are now closer together. The legs farther away (the shaded ones) are farther apart.

WRONG!
Animals never walk like this. If they did, they would tip over whenever they lifted their legs to take a step!

Tips and Tricks

Here are a few tips for making your drawings look more realistic.

Make the nearer legs a little longer than the farther legs. This is because of a rule in art called perspective. Perspective says that things closer to us look larger than things farther away.

Shade in the arms and legs that are farther away. This helps the closer ones stand out.

To draw an animal on all fours, draw a box around the feet. This will keep the pose lined up right. (See how the front of the box is wider than the back? This is because of perspective.)

9

AFRICAN ANIMALS

It's time for the fun stuff—drawing animals! Let's start in the wild jungles and savannas of Africa.

Proud Lion

The lion has a massive skull. The forehead is small and the chin is big. Its forearms are thick and powerful. To make the lion look proud, push out its chest.

LONG "TEAR STAIN"

Leaping Lion

Here's another lion. Even though its neck is under its mane, you should still draw it. This will help you get the right length for the neck. Just erase it after you've added the mane.

Growling Lion

Is there anything scarier than a growling lion? The eyes get beady and narrow...the forehead creases... the nose crinkles...the teeth are bared.... Yikes!

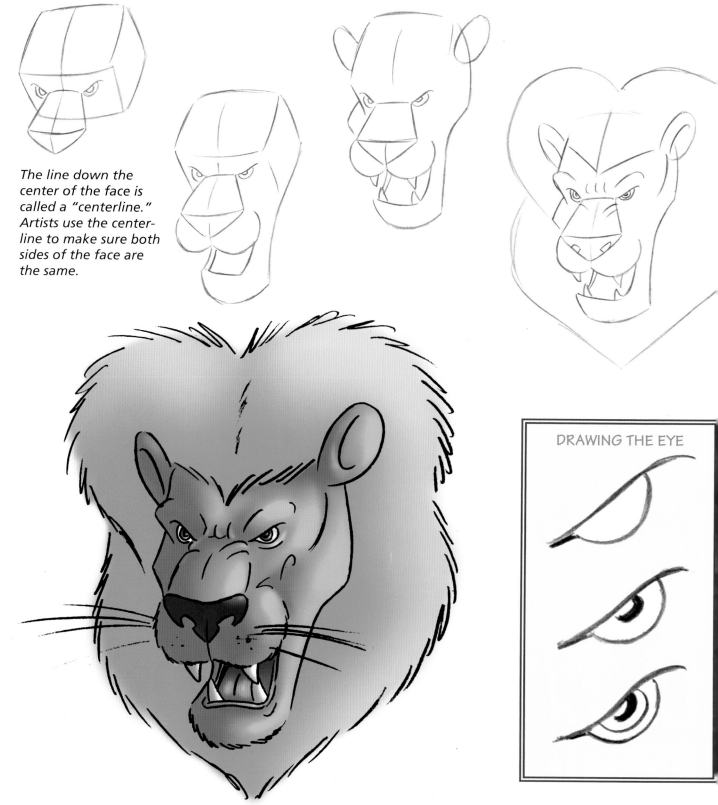

The line down the center of the face is called a "centerline." Artists use the centerline to make sure both sides of the face are the same.

DRAWING THE EYE

Gorilla

Gorillas are strong but they can also be very gentle, especially when caring for their young. Every group of gorillas has a male who's in charge. He's called the "silverback."

Use curving lines to draw the body.

Old World Monkey

The monkey's arms are longer than its legs. It also has long, thin fingers and toes for holding onto vines.

Draw the tail early on. If you wait too long, you might run out of room on the paper!

Rhinoceros

Rhinos have heads that look like saddles, bulky bodies, and tiny legs. Even though rhinos are huge, they can charge their enemies at very high speeds.

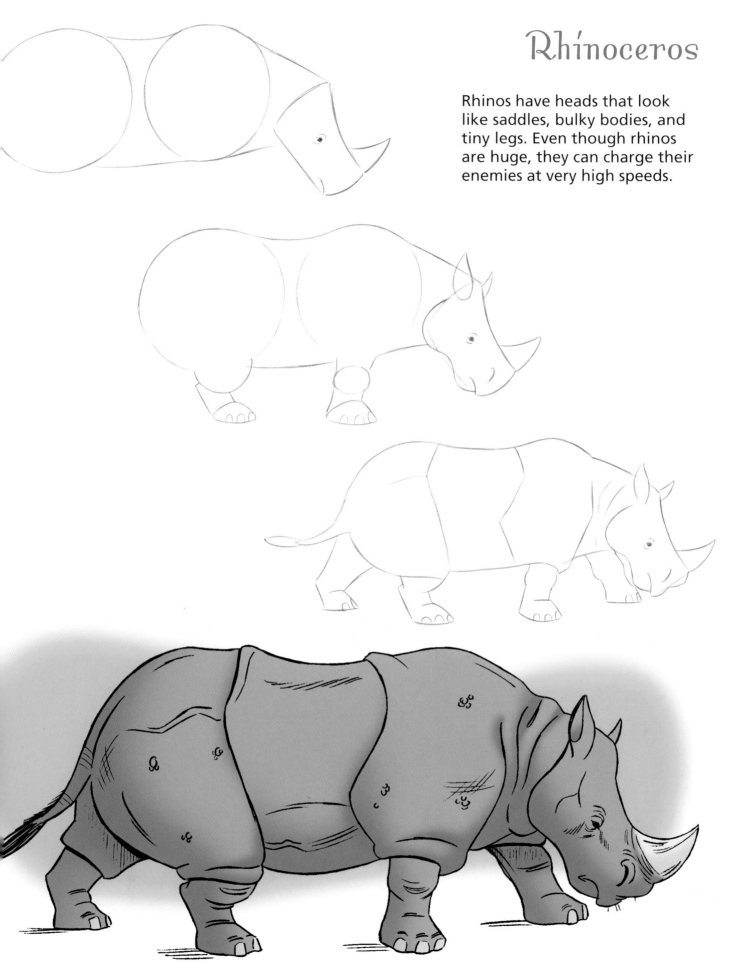

Giraffe

As everyone knows, giraffes have long necks. They also have huge chests and shoulders, but tiny hips.

The coat has big patches of brownish-red with tiny bands of white in between.

Hippopotamus

The hippo's body is easy to draw, but its head is tricky. To make it easier, draw the head in two parts. Then bring them together to finish.

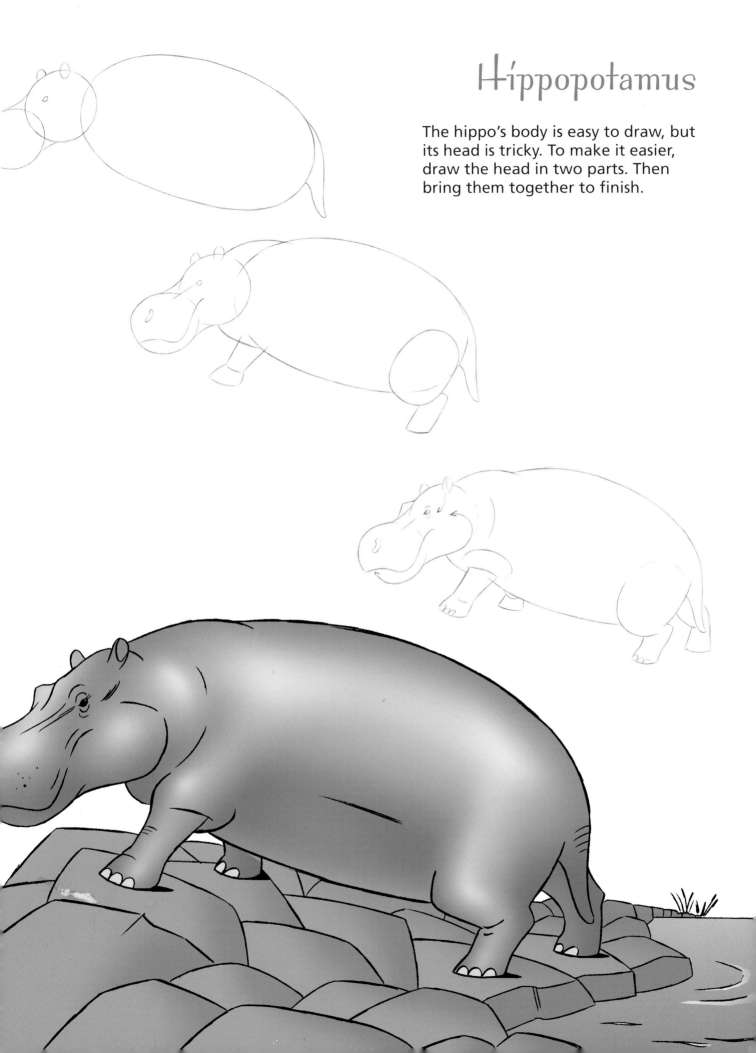

Elephants: African Versus Indian

Let's look at the differences between these two types of elephants.

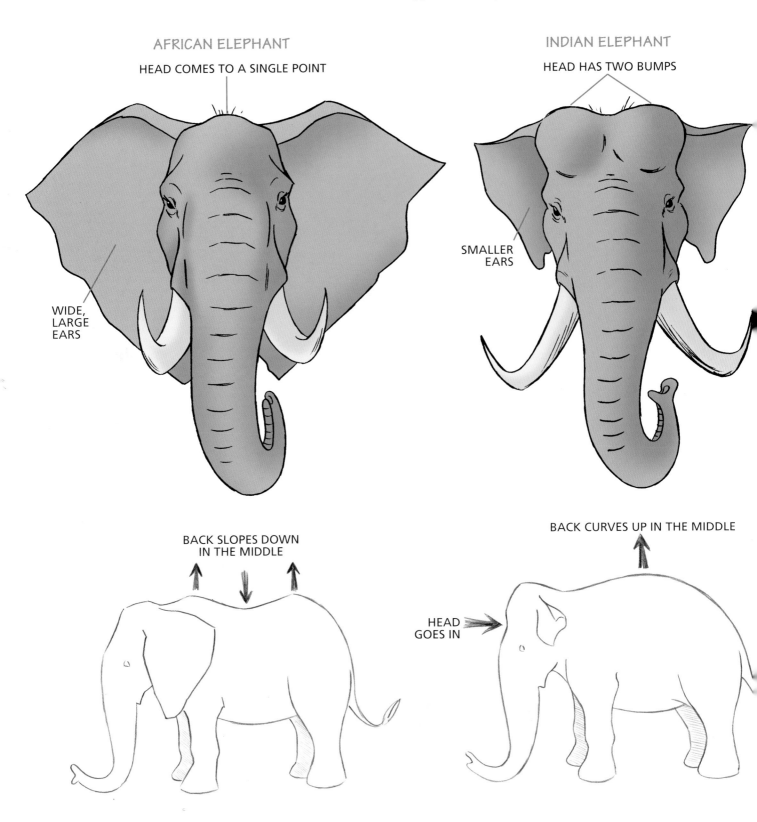

AFRICAN ELEPHANT

HEAD COMES TO A SINGLE POINT

WIDE, LARGE EARS

INDIAN ELEPHANT

HEAD HAS TWO BUMPS

SMALLER EARS

BACK SLOPES DOWN IN THE MIDDLE

BACK CURVES UP IN THE MIDDLE

HEAD GOES IN

African Elephant Taking a Dirt Bath

African elephants are my favorite. Here's one flinging dirt on itself to get rid of insects and pests.

Baby African Elephant

Baby elephants have big foreheads and even bigger ears. Their bodies are round, but thinner than an adult's. This makes their legs look longer and less sturdy. And their feet look too big for their bodies, just as puppies have big paws.

Cheetah

The cheetah is the fastest animal on land. It can run up to 70 miles per hour! It can only go that fast for a quarter of a mile—then it runs out of energy.

Cheetahs are built for speed. They have thin legs and narrow waists, which keeps them light. But they also have strong muscles in their thighs and shoulders.

ADD MORE CHEST

BEARS

Bears are very popular animals. They're the stars of cartoons and picture books. They're on candy and cereal boxes. And, of course, teddy bears make the best cuddle dolls ever! But not all bears are alike. Let's draw a few kinds.

Grizzly Bear

Grizzlies are massive animals with big bottoms. Their paws are thin but their legs and arms are thick and powerful. (In this pose you can't see the tail.)

Draw a bigger circle for the rear.

Grizzlies are excellent at catching fish.

25

Standing Grizzly

Bears can also stand on two legs, like humans.

Black Bear Cub

Baby bears have heads that are big for their bodies. They have poochy little tummies and small chests. Their snouts are short, and they've got big eyes. This cub is a black bear. Black bears are the most common type of bear. They are smaller than grizzlies.

The tummy overlaps the back legs.

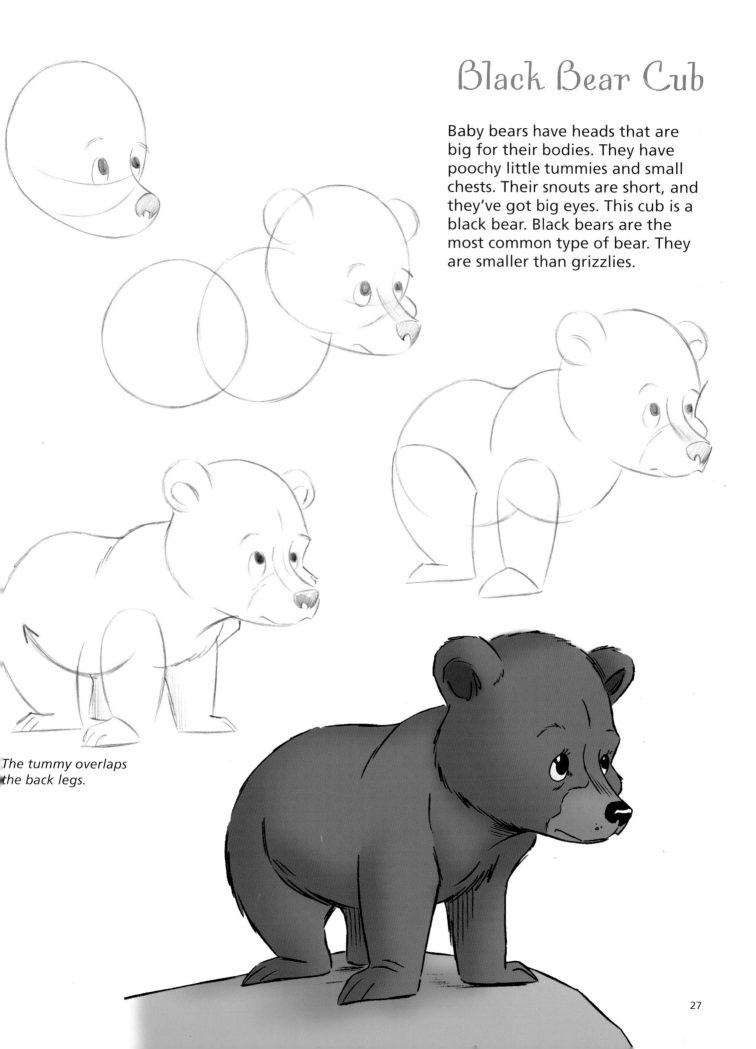

Polar Bear

Polar bears are great hunters that live in cold
northern climates. To catch their prey, they have
to get into the freezing cold waters of the Arctic.
So it's no surprise that they are excellent swimmers.

Polar bears have
huge paws!

Panda Bear and Cub

Here's a playful panda mom and her cub. The pandas' distinctive black and white markings are what make them so popular. Outside of zoos, these bears can only be found in China. Sadly, this beautiful bear is an endangered species.

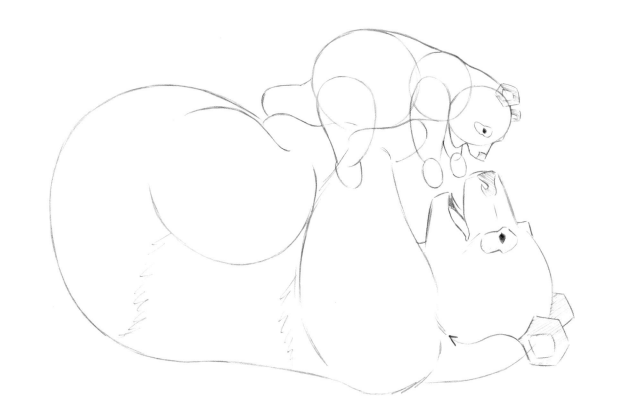

HORSES

Artists love to paint horses because they are such strong, graceful animals. Let's start with the head, then try a few poses.

The Horse's Head

The horse's head is very wide at the jaw and thin at the nose.

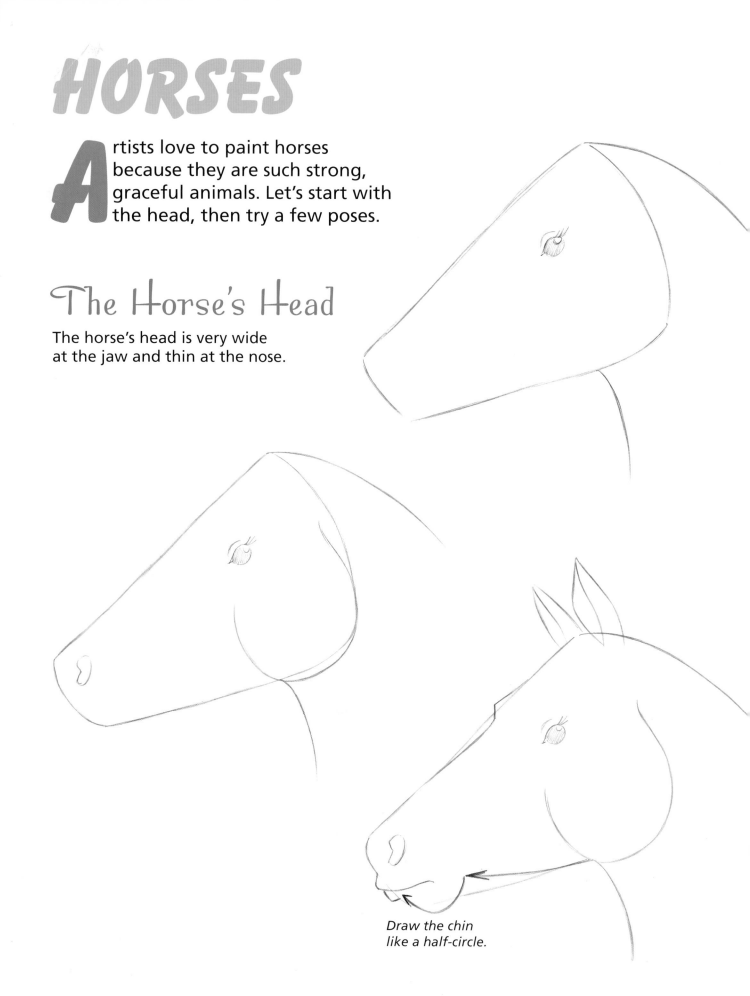

Draw the chin like a half-circle.

Standing Horse

Horses are proud, mighty creatures. Sometimes I watch the horses near my house. I always try to remember how they look so I can draw them later.

TAIL GOES OUT AND THEN DOWN

HIPS SLOPE DOWN

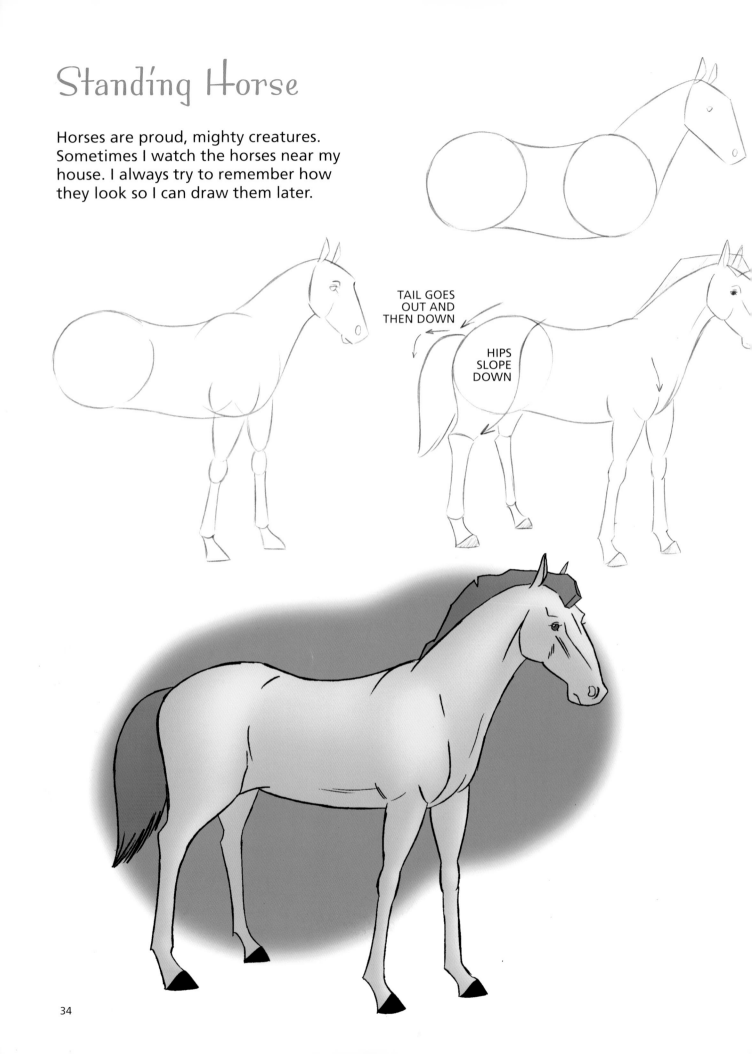

Rearing Horse

When a horse is spooked—by a bee, for example—it rises up on its two rear legs and waves its forearms.

3/4 View

The first two drawings you did were "side views," as if you were looking at the horse from one side. Now let's try a 3/4 view. This is something between a front view and a side view.

Notice how the body is shorter in this view? This is because the horse's front is hiding part of its rear.

Horse Drinking Water

The horse's neck is so long it can drop its head to drink water without bending over. The horse is a very muscular, lean animal. You can see the outlines of bones and muscles underneath its skin.

'S SLOPE
WN

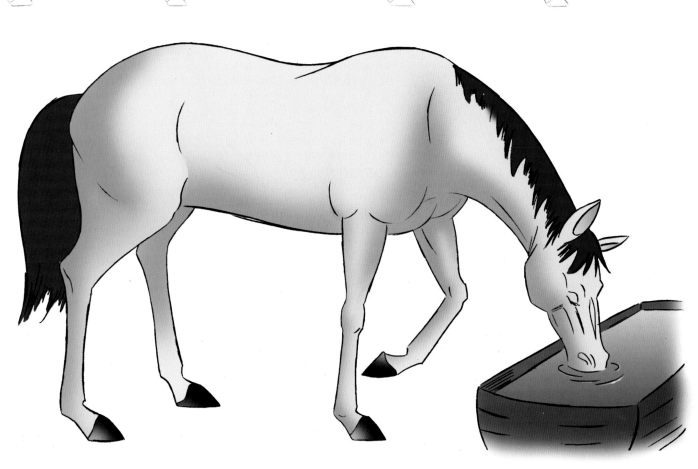

BIRDS

Some birds fly, others swim. Some hunt during the day, others hunt only at night. Some live in the tropics, others live in the Arctic Circle. Wherever they live, whatever they do, birds continue to fascinate us.

American Bald Eagle

Look at the eagle's sharp, hooked beak—this tells you right away that it's a hunter. Eagles have amazing vision. This is where the term "eagle eye" comes from. They use their sharp claws to snatch fish from lakes and streams.

Owl

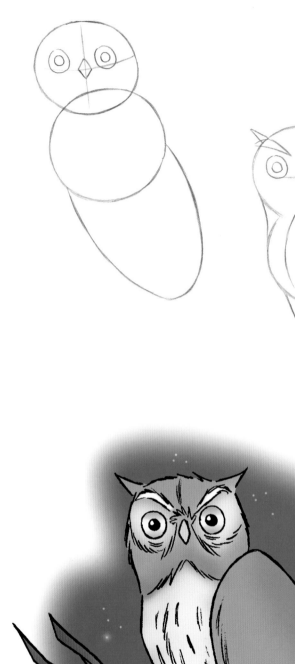

Owls sleep during the day and are active at night. Their large eyes help them see in the dark. Owls might make you think of haunted houses, but they're actually very helpful animals. They eat unwanted pests, such as mice. The beak is small but it's hooked. This tells us the owl is a hunter.

Hawk

The hawk's hooked beak tells you it's a hunter, like the owl and the eagle.

Toucan

The toucan is a lively, friendly looking bird that lives in the tropics. Its beak is almost as long as its body. The upper beak is much thicker than the lower beak. And check out those stripes!

Penguin

Penguins have plump bodies, small heads, and sharp beaks. You might be surprised to learn that their wings are really quite long. Baby penguins look furry, unlike their smooth parents.

REPTILES AND EXOTIC ANIMALS

These are the cool animals that most American kids don't see around much. This might make them seem harder to draw. But with a little practice, even a Galapagos turtle is easy!

Crocodile

The "croc"'s body is simple to draw—it's just one long shape. But the head is kind of tricky. Here are three tips to remember:

1. The eyes bulge up above the forehead.

2. The tip of the nose gets bigger.

3. The mouth starts up high, near the eye.

Indian Cobra

This snake can spit poison into its enemies' eyes, blinding them on the spot. Check out the cobra's "hood." And have fun with those markings!

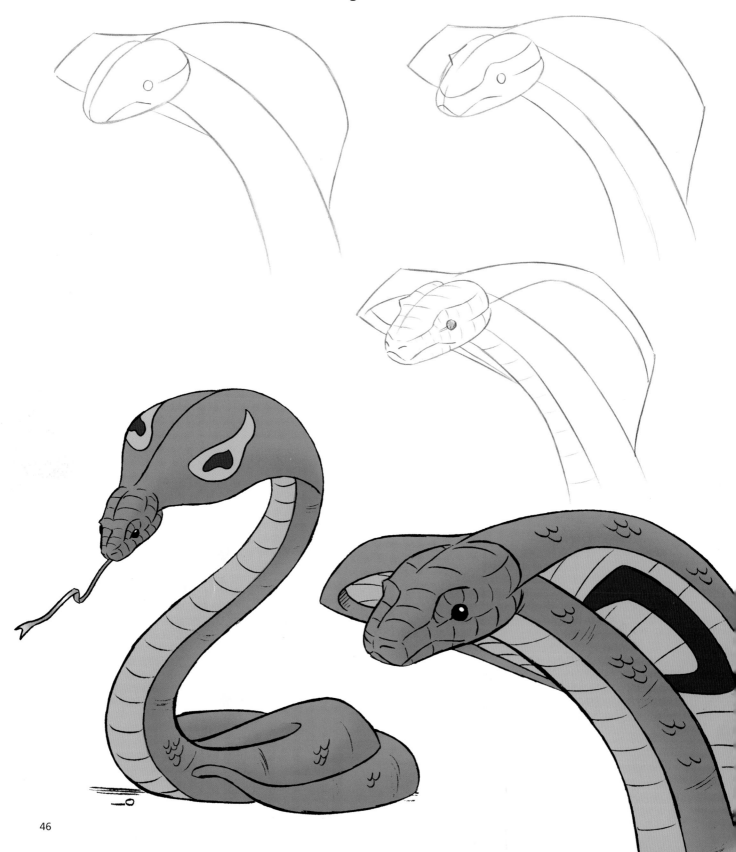

Galapagos Turtle

The Galapagos turtle isn't actually a turtle at all, but a *tortoise.* Its flat, elephant-like feet tell you that this big fella can't swim. It's strictly a land animal. It's got a tiny head and huge arms, which it uses not only to walk, but to dig. The Galapagos can weigh more than 500 pounds!

Camel

The most famous thing about the camel is its hump. Many people think the camel stores water in its hump, but this isn't true. The hump is really a big mound of fatty tissue. When food is hard to find in the hot, dry desert, the camel uses this fat for energy.

Kangaroo and Joey

Here's one of the "wonders from Down Under" —Australia, that is. The baby kangaroo is called a "joey."

Kangaroos have long tails, strong legs, and tiny arms. When they're not hopping, their long feet lie flat on the ground.

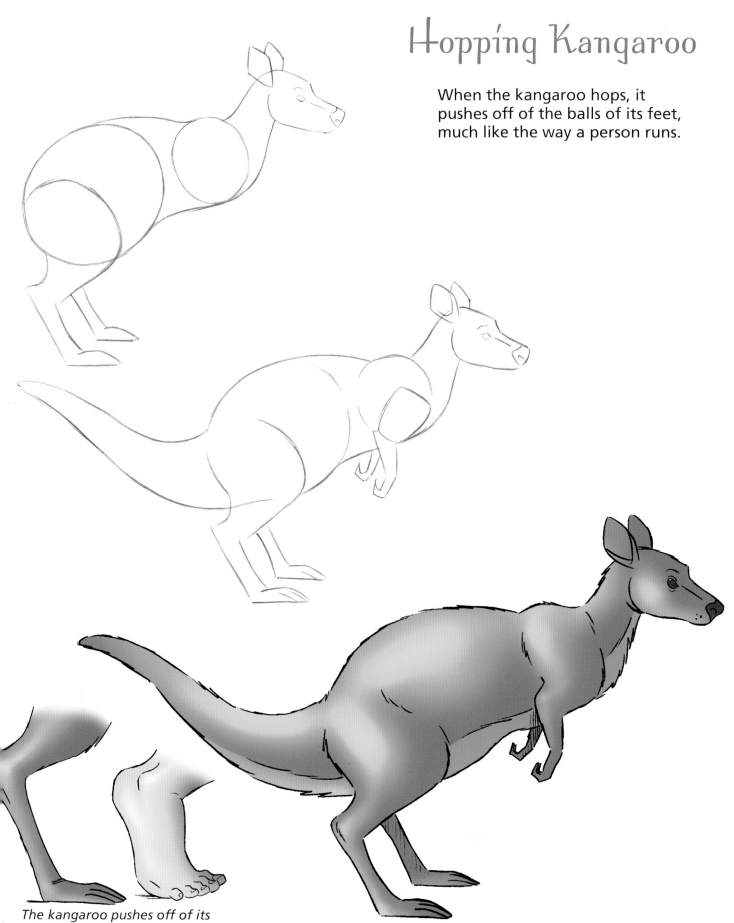

Hopping Kangaroo

When the kangaroo hops, it pushes off of the balls of its feet, much like the way a person runs.

The kangaroo pushes off of its toes, just like we do when we run.

SEA CREATURES

Get your scuba gear on, because we're about to take a dive! There are some cool, some cute, and even some terrifying creatures that live in the ocean.

Dolphin

The friendly dolphin is easy to draw. It's got a large, rounded forehead and a rounded body with stiff flippers. Its mouth makes it look like it's smiling.

Shark

The shark has many rows of small, razor-sharp teeth. (You can't see them all in this pose.) In case you didn't know, that famous fin on its back is called a "dorsal fin."

Here's a tip for drawing the eyes of sharks or any other fish: Never show eyelids. Leave the eyes wide open.

Swordfish

The swordfish is a deepwater fish. It is long and leaner than the shark, with long, graceful fins. Its head goes gradually into the shape of a sword—try not to make it look as if a sword has just been "stuck" onto its face.

Sea Lion and Pup

The head of a sea lion looks a lot like the head of a dog, but without the long ears. Its neck is wide and its chest is proud. A baby sea lion is called a "pup."

CUTE CRITTERS AND PETS

This book just wouldn't be complete without a few cute critters—and of course our best friends, cats and dogs!

Beaver

This little fella is all work and no play—a few beavers can build a dam in no time. Beavers have big noses and small eyes. They also have chubby arms and legs, but skinny hands and feet. Beavers are so cute, it's hard to believe they're in the rodent family!

Bunny Rabbit

The bunny rabbit always sits with its back arched. Can you guess why? It's all coiled up so it can jump at the slightest danger.

TAIL
TURNS UP

Pig

Did you know that pigs are very smart animals? You might also be amazed at how big a pig's body can get. Some weigh up to 400 pounds! But no matter how large a pig is, its legs are always tiny.

Piglet

A piglet's belly looks higher off the ground than an adult's. Its legs are long compared to its body. And its ears are quite big.

Raccoon

Raccoons are always getting into things. If I leave my garage door open at night, I can be sure the trash bags will be torn open by morning. And we all know who did it!

Raccoons have wide faces and pointy noses. Their "bandit" eye-masks and striped tails make them easy to spot.

Dog

I couldn't create a book about animals and leave out "man's best friend," could I? Here's one of the most popular breeds: the lovable Labrador retriever. Other types of dogs sit this same way.

Welsh Springer Spaniel

This is my dog, Rusty. He's a Welsh springer spaniel and has rust-colored markings. Rusty is always energetic, devoted to his family, and loves children. I'm glad he's part of our family.

Cat

Even under all that fluff, the cat still has a solid body. Draw the body first, then erase most of it. Just leave some sketchy lines for the fur.

When a cat leaps, its body str-e-e-e-e-e-tches out, long and lean.

Index

ADULT

DEVELOPMENT

AND AGING

■

BERT HAYSLIP, JR.
University of North Texas

PAUL E. PANEK
The Ohio State University at Newark

1817

HARPER & ROW, PUBLISHERS, New York

Cambridge, Philadelphia, San Francisco,
London, Mexico City, São Paulo, Singapore, Sydney

To our wives, Gail Hayslip and Christine Franklin-Panek,
and our children, Stephen and Patrick Hayslip and Rachel and Rebecca
Panek

■

Project Editor: Lenore Bonnie Biller
Text Design: Keithley and Associates, Inc.
Cover Design: Delgado Design, Inc.
Text Art: Vantage Art, Inc.
Photo Research: Cheryl Mannes
Production Manager: Willie Lane
Compositor: ComCom Division of Haddon Craftsmen, Inc.
Printer and Binder: R. R. Donnelley & Sons Company
Cover Printer: Phoenix Color

ADULT DEVELOPMENT AND AGING

Library of Congress Cataloging in Publication Data

Hayslip, Jr., Bert.
Adult development and aging / Bert Hayslip, Jr., Paul E. Panek.
p.   cm.
Bibliography: p.
Includes index.
ISBN 0-06-045012-6
1. Adulthood.   2. Aging—Psychological aspects.   3. Aging.
I. Panek, Paul E.   II. Title.
BF724.5.H39 1989
155.6—dc19   88-15465
                                                      CIP

89 90 91 9 8 7 6 5 4 3 2

▪ BRIEF CONTENTS ▪

• DETAILED CONTENTS •

Chapter 3   Research Methods in Adult Development and Aging   86

Chapter 4   Sensory and Perceptual Processes   114

Chapter 7   Cognitive Processes II: Learning and Memory   226

Chapter 11   Work, Retirement, and Leisure   396

Chapter 12   Death and Dying   434

Chapter 13   Mental Health and Psychopathology   472

▪ TO THE INSTRUCTOR ▪

We wrote this book in response to our need for a text that could be used in courses taught in departments of psychology and in courses in the behavioral social sciences, which are often composed of students with diverse academic backgrounds. We wrote a text that would engage the student at the outset by presenting in a readable manner the major issues and facts in the field of adult development and aging. We believe that a broad research base and scholarship are important qualities that define our text. However, we also feel that the everyday relevance of the knowledge generated by this research is equally central. Consequently, we have strived to place an equal emphasis on both the basic issues and applied aspects of adult development and aging, so that students can appreciate the relationship between the process of research and its usefulness in better understanding adults of all ages.

ORGANIZATION

The text is organized topically rather than chronologically, since some of the topics we discuss will be equally relevant to both older adults and younger adults. Aging is best thought of as an ongoing process, not easily segmented into discrete stages that are mutually exclusive. Yet there are some aspects of young adulthood, middle age, or late adulthood that are unique and need to be understood in the context of biological change and/or psychosocial factors that are distinct to each life period. For these reasons, our discussion of issues relevant to adults and aged persons varies both within and between chapters.

We believe that organizing the material topically also helps the student understand adulthood in a more integrated manner, making it more likely that topics in different chapters will be seen as interrelated rather than as independent. The chapters are also arranged so as to lay the groundwork first for the student's thinking about adult development and its research methods, and then to proceed to deal with basic psychobiological processes (i.e., biology of aging, sensation/perception), followed by topics that are distinctly psychological (i.e., learning/memory, intelligence, and personality). The later chapters are predominantly psychosocial and/or clinical in their orientation (i.e., work/retirement, death/dying, mental health/psychopathology, and intervention/treatment). This chapter organization reinforces the text's dual emphasis on basic and applied research.

COVERAGE

Reflecting the diversity of research in adult development and aging, we also provide up-to-date coverage of many new, emerging, high-visibility topics in the field, such as elder abuse, minority aging, Alzheimer's disease, adult learning (Elderhostel), and dual-career marriages. Moreover, we have devoted entire chapters to such high-interest topics as death and dying, and work, retirement, and leisure to enhance the text's readability and appeal.

PEDAGOGY

At each chapter's beginning, questions are raised regarding the most important issues in that chapter in order to structure and guide the student's learning at the outset. Following each chapter a summary, and a list of key terms and concepts are presented to cue the student again to the most important issues in that chapter.

Boxed inserts in most chapters target the student's attention to noteworthy developments in the field. A glossary at the text's end assists the student in defining terms throughout the text.

An Instructor's Manual containing test items and a variety of classroom activities is also available.

It was our intent to write a text that is scholarly yet applied in its orientation to provide the student with a well-rounded, integrated view of adulthood and aging. We feel we have achieved these goals and think that both you and your students will find the book to be not only interesting and informative, but also enjoyable.

We would like to acknowledge the efforts of the following persons whose critiques of the manuscript at various points in its development were most valuable:

Mark Byrd, University of Kansas
John C. Cavanaugh, Bowling Green State University
Andrew C. Coyne, The Ohio State University
Armin Grams, The University of Vermont
Lillian M. Grayson, Simmons College
Laurence H. Harshbarger, Ball State University
Irene M. Hulicka, State University College at Buffalo
Janet W. Johnson, University of Maryland
E. John McIlvried, Indiana Central University
David B. Mitchell, Southern Methodist University
Russell J. Ohta, West Virginia University
Carlton Parks, Texas A&M University
Sandra M. Powers, The University of North Carolina at Greensboro
Charles E. Streff, Fitchburg State College
Thomas Tighe, Moraine Valley Community College
Beatrice B. Turkoski, University of Wisconsin—Milwaukee
Mary Ann Watson, Metropolitan State College

Additionally, thanks are extended to Jan Nelsen, Joyce Spencer, and Pam Gutowski for their patience and expertise in typing the manuscript. We would also like to thank Judy Rothman, Leslie Carr, Jeanne Hess, and Bonnie Biller at Harper & Row for their constant support and most helpful suggestions throughout the process.

Bert Hayslip, Jr.
Paul E. Panek

This text deals with the field of adult development and aging, which is a relatively new one not only in psychology, but also in other behavioral sciences, such as education and sociology. Despite its infancy, we hope that you share our enthusiasm for the study of adults of all ages, so that your own lives, as well as those of your children, grandchildren, parents, and grandparents, may be enriched by what you learn.

We have presented the issues and facts of adult development and aging in a clear, readable fashion and stress the applied, everyday implications of these facts wherever possible. We feel that presenting information in this manner and pointing out its everyday relevance, regardless of your major or training, will help you not only to enjoy but also to understand more fully the material in each chapter.

Understanding adult development and aging requires an appreciation for basic research findings and their applied, everyday value. We present the facts of adult development with this in mind. At the text's outset, we discuss adult development and aging in an overall sense, followed by a discussion of research methodology. In this way, you will have a sense of the many approaches to adult development and aging and the methods by which the facts about adults of all ages are gathered. This sensitivity will help you put the many dimensions of adult development into a broader perspective and evaluate them as they apply to you personally. While some chapters deal with basic biological and psychological processes (e.g., sensation, perception, learning, memory), others are distinctly applied in their orientation (e.g., work and retirement, death and dying, mental health and psychopathology).

In order to understand the developing individual's behavior, one must recognize that he or she is affected by many interacting factors of a biological, interpersonal, psychological, and cultural-environmental nature. Given the complex nature of human development, it is important to realize that the processes of development and aging do not occur in a vacuum. For instance, declines in sensory functions may have a marked effect upon intellectual abilities in many adults. Thus, human development is best understood and studied in holistic terms.

One implication of this holism is to see the developing person as embedded within the environment, acting upon that environment as well as being acted upon by it. Consequently, we see individuals not just as passive receptors of information in their environment but also as active processors of that information.

The text is organized topically rather than chronologically; some issues have greater relevance to older adults, whereas others are more relevant to younger adults. Consequently, our discussion of issues particular to young adults, middle-aged persons, and older adults will vary both within and between chapters.

We feel that learning about adult development should reflect both the continuities and discontinuities in life that we all experience as we age. While we do not "suddenly" change when we wake up on our twenty-first or sixty-fifth birthdays, in many ways our lives are much different than they were when we were younger—that is, as adults, we are much like we always were in many respects but in other ways, we may have changed a great deal. Being sensitive to this issue of change and stability in our lives is the key to a realistic, yet balanced sense of the life cycle—where we have been, and where we are going.

At each chapter's outset, a number of questions will be presented that you should be able to answer after reading the chapter. Following each chapter a summary is presented and key terms and concepts are listed in order to cue you to the most important issues within that chapter.

We have also put together a glossary to provide you with quick, accessible definitions to terms throughout the text, and we have included a variety of real-life scenarios and boxed inserts in each chapter to enhance your learning and enjoyment of the material in this text.

We believe that these features will not only make learning easier and more effective but also make this learning more personally meaningful to you.

Growing and changing throughout life are realities for us all. Understanding these changes and being able to see that they can help us adapt more effectively when we or others important to us experience them is our major goal. We sincerely hope that you enjoy reading this text!

Bert Hayslip, Jr.
Paul E. Panek

After reading this chapter, you should be able to answer the following questions:

- What are myths and stereotypes about development and aging? How do they develop? What are their harmful effects?
- Why is it difficult to classify individuals into specific periods of life on the basis of chronological age?
- What are developmental tasks? What role do they play in development during the life cycle?
- How do cultural ethics affect an individual's views of society and others?
- Why is it important to consider individual differences at all points along the life cycle?
- What are the seven major issues that theories of development must address?
- What are the major models of human development? What is the position of each with regard to the above seven major issues?
- What are the three major influences on developmental change?
- What is meant by "person-environment interaction"?
- What are Birren's three Types of Age? Why are they important?

ADULT

DEVELOPMENT

AND AGING

▪

In our rapidly changing, highly technological culture, it is rare not to be reminded of its impact on our lives. Consider the following events and changes that many of us have been exposed to within the past decade:

The Challenger disaster	Obsolescence of occupational skills
The AIDS epidemic	Euthanasia (mercy killing)
Computer technology	Cocaine and alcohol abuse
Surrogate mothers	Three Mile Island
Raising the age of	Alzheimer's disease
mandatory retirement	Test-tube babies
for federal employees	Artificial hearts
to age 70	Crisis in social security
The sexual revolution	

While this is certainly not an exhaustive list, it brings to light the impact of cultural changes of many varieties on people at various points in their lives, regardless of age. In many cases, these events are particular to persons at particular points in their life span. In other instances, their effects cut across age.

These cultural events, as well as more personal experiences such as birthdays, marriage, illness, divorce, parenthood, job changes, and death, sometimes cause us to reflect on our past and future. Depending on our own unique life histories, these events may mean different things to each of us.

In the following chapters, we will explore a variety of biological and psychosocial issues as they affect our development at all points in the adult life span. These cultural and personal changes may or may not reinforce an assessment of our lives as happy or successful relative to the time we feel we have left to accomplish the personal, social, or vocational goals we have set for ourselves.

This internal sense of individual time (Neugarten, 1973) often compels us to structure our lives relative to our age peers. That is, we make comparisons between ourselves and our age peers in terms of the quality and quantity of our experiences. For many of us who are young, the prospect of growing older or dying seems distant. This psychological distance is reinforced by the system of age norms and age constraints (Atchley, 1975; Neugarten, 1973) that often serve to reinforce us for behaving in age-appropriate ways (and that implicitly punish us for violating these age norms). Another important consequence of this age grading is to isolate us further both physically and psychosocially from those who are either older or younger than we are. Thus, persons who are distinctly older or younger are perceived as different from us—they seem to manifest different thoughts, feelings, and behaviors *because* of their age. Not only does this create more social-psychological distance between persons of varying ages, it also lessens the chances of our testing and challenging beliefs about the aging process.

Our misconceptions are inadvertently reinforced by selective exposure to older persons in certain well-defined situations, such as nursing homes or retirement communities. As a consequence, we may come to define our expectations about others in terms of what they are capable of or what attitudes they hold on the basis of their age. We exclude such other important information about them such as their childhood experiences, education, socioeconomic class, gender, race, ethnicity, occupational history, health, or personality makeup.

In the chapters to follow, we will learn that the study of adult development and aging rests on two very central assumptions. First, many important forces of a biological, psychological, and cultural nature create changes in our lives. Second, chronological age (experiences that are actually correlated with one's age) is but one of many determinants (causal variables) that account for our behavior. It is for these reasons that we have organized our study of adulthood and aging topically (for example, learning and memory, sensory processes) rather than chronologically. Doing so puts changes in a variety of behavior domains into a larger perspective so that we begin to see the aging process in a *relative* light. In other words, we want you to view chronological age on par with other factors as an indicator or predictor of behavior. We do this with the hope that you can then appreciate the aging process in the context of other influences that make you a unique individual at any age, be it 25 or 75.

Given our society's concern with chronological age as a predictor of behavior (Hagestad & Neugarten, 1985), a topical approach helps to desensitize one to the aging process by breaking down the social or psychological barriers that we often create or are created by others to separate persons of varying ages. These barriers reinforce our thinking, "Well, I might like to get old, but I would just as soon not *be* old!" Consequently, moving over these psychological hurdles enables us to see both the positive and negative aspects of being young or old. Chronological age loses its potency, and we begin to understand others as unique human beings who *happen to be* a given age.

Additionally, through this desensitization process, we can also understand the roles of age-related factors that do make us different from others who are older or younger than we. From our new perspective, an individual's chronological age becomes a *necessary, but not sufficient* criterion for (predictor of) developmental changes experienced during the adult years of life.

We hope that through the study of adulthood and aging you can more fully appreciate the similarities and differences between individuals who vary in age. Holding such views about development in adulthood has many advantages. Whether you are a professional who deals with adults, a child caring for an aging parent, or a parent or grandparent, viewing the aging process in *relative* terms can enhance the quality of your own and others' lives. You may come to see your parents or grandparents in an entirely different light, be a more effective and compassionate professional, or view your own aging in more realistic, balanced terms. The myths of the aging process can be separated from the facts, which in our age-graded culture are often difficult to disentangle. Whenever possible, we will present comparative findings about younger and older adults. We urge you to view these findings in a relative

Younger and older persons have much to teach one another; this emphasizes the continuity between life periods.

manner. That is, relative to young adults, older adults behave or do not behave in a certain way.

Our society is rapidly becoming more attuned to the unique problems adults of all ages will face. This realization becomes all the more apparent given demographic changes in our population. As Figure 1.1 indicates, birthrates and death rates have stabilized over the last ten years, while infant death rates have declined. Moreover, life expectancy has increased from 70 years in 1970 to 75 years in 1984 (Statistical Abstract of the United States, 1986). As we will discuss further in Chapter 2, improved health care, better nutrition, lower mortality associated with serious illness, and perhaps an increased awareness of taking care of one's health (e.g., smoking, obesity, exercise) are each in part responsible not only for the lowering of infant death rates, but also for the increase in life expectancy over the past 20 years. These data collectively indicate that in the future, more people will be surviving into their seventies and eighties. Thus, demands on caregiving will be greater for future cohorts of younger persons. Recent estimates (Statistical Abstract of the United States, 1986) suggest that in 1985, approximately 12 percent of persons were aged 65 or older. In fact, the percentage of older persons has risen steadily over the last 20 years and is projected to exceed 20 percent by the year 2000. Moreover, between 1960 and 1984, numbers of persons aged 75 and over doubled (5.6 million to 11.5 million). While persons over the age of 45 exceeded 30 percent of the total population in 1985, that percentage is expected to reach 36 percent by the year 2000 (Statistical Abstract of the United States, 1986). If persons between the ages of 25 and 44 are included, these figures increase to nearly 65 percent. Figure 1.2 clearly indicates that the

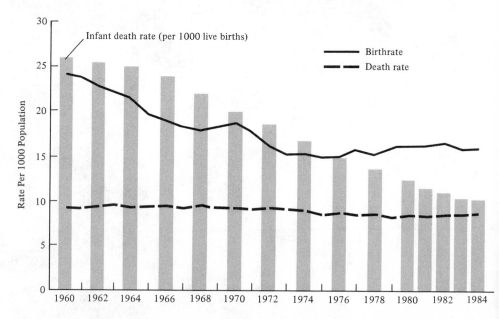

Figure 1.1   Birth- and death rates: 1960–1984. Rate per 1000 population. *Source:* U.S. Bureau of the Census, *Statistical Abstract of the United States: 1986* (106th edition) Washington, DC, 1985.

relative balance of younger versus older persons in our society will shift even more dramatically in the future. While the numbers of persons aged 44 or younger have already or are projected to decline, those over 45 will become more numerous. Thus, concerns that affect all adults will most likely assume more importance in the future and have an increasing biological, psychological, economic, and political impact on many aspects of our lives.

Despite these obvious changes in the makeup of our population, views about later adulthood and the aging process continue to be clouded by misinformation. Indeed, most of us have little preparation for the experience of having to deal with being older in our society (Rosow, 1985). In contrast, many Eastern cultures, such as those of Japan and China, treat their elderly with an attitude of reverence and respect (Butler & Lewis, 1981; Palmore, 1975a, 1975b) to the extent that the old are not "strangers." So prevalent are misperceptions of the aged and so powerful are the effects of damaging stereotypes about older persons and the aging process that many elderly come to believe such myths themselves (Kausler, 1982), often making adjustment more difficult and survival less likely (Bennett & Eckman, 1973). Sadly, it is no wonder that older people have often been found to hold the most negative views of old age (Thorson, Whatley, & Hancock, 1974).

One very important goal of this text is to examine and hopefully dispel

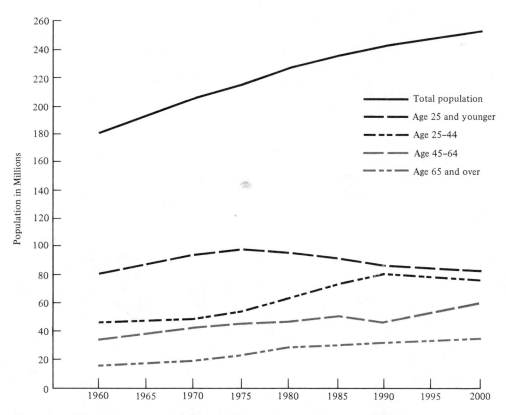

Figure 1.2   U.S. population by age: 1960–2000. *Source:* Adapted from U.S. Bureau of the Census, *Statistical Abstract of the United States: 1986* (106th edition) Washington, DC, 1985.

many of the **myths** and **stereotypes** that surround the **aging process** and the aged. What purposes might be served by dealing with such misperceptions? Kalish (1975) suggests three important reasons to study later adulthood, which can also be treated as benefits to be realized from a discussion of the false beliefs many hold regarding the aging process and the elderly in particular. Kalish has labeled these reasons as **service, insight,** and **theory.** Service relates to providing resources for today's elderly and those who will be old in the future so as to make their lives—and ours—more fulfilling and satisfactory. Insight can be thought of as coming to a better understanding of others' aging and our own aging process. Such a gain in understanding will effect a change in attitudes (and hopefully behavior) toward those elderly persons with whom we interact and enable us to see our own aging in a more realistic, positive manner. The last reason to study aging, according to Kalish, relates to theory—putting later adulthood "in perspective" and seeing human development as a "lifelong process" (Kalish, 1975, p. 2). Thus, reducing misconceptions of what it is like to be old and to grow old has many advantages, both for the professional dealing with the elderly, and for lay persons whose contacts with older persons are likely to be less extensive. We will again deal with this question of attitudes in later chapters.

AGING AS PART OF THE LIFE SPAN

Most contemporary thinking about human development treats the life span as an integrated, contiguous set of age-related events from birth to death with which people cope in a variety of ways. Behavior thus becomes organized out of experiences that encompass the entire life course (Birren & Renner, 1977). Simply put, this means that one's experience in any broadly defined life period (childhood, adolescence, early and middle adulthood) cannot be viewed apart from the events (and one's reactions to those events) preceding it. Therefore, in studying human development, continuity in adjusting to life's problems should be stressed. Despite this, it is also important to realize that some discontinuity does, however, exist when studying specific segments in the life span (such as later adulthood). While age-related problems or developmental events may change over time, one's mode of adjustment to such occurrences is predictable; people do not "suddenly" change just because they reach a specified chronological age, for example, 65. In our discussion of adult development and aging, it is important to understand the myths and stereotypes about the aging process and older persons and that later adulthood cannot be truly separated from other segments of the life span; they are interdependent. We will explore attitudes toward aging and older persons more extensively in Chapter 9. Why then, do we raise such issues at this point?

We feel that the perspective you bring with you about almost any issue affects your assessment and reaction to those issues. To put it bluntly, what you see is often what you do get. In other words, we feel that you will learn more about adult development and aging if you are relatively free, or at least aware, of your own biases about younger and older people. Through such a self-examination, you can evaluate the facts of adult development as they apply to you personally as freely and as fairly as possible.

As our above discussion implies, both describing and explaining human development are complex tasks. Human **aging** is affected by many biological, psychosocial, and environmental factors. In some cases, these factors affect everyone; in other cases, their influence is more specific. Throughout our discussion of adult development and aging, the influence of both sets of these factors (and their interactions) on our lives will be emphasized.

While our culture is perhaps preoccupied with age as a valid indicator of one's personality or capabilities (see Hagestad & Neugarten, 1985; Maddox & Campbell, 1985) professionals in human development often have difficulty in deciding not only which specific chronological ages define the limits of stages of the life cycle, but also what such age ranges *mean*—what do they tell us about human behavior? Consequently, it should not surprise you to learn that there is dissatisfaction with chronological age as an indicator of human behavioral change and as a research variable (Hagestad & Neugarten, 1985; Wohlwill, 1970b). Indeed, the concept of developmental stages is a controversial one among adult developmental professionals (Lerner, 1986).

In order to understand adequately adulthood and aging in the broadest sense, it is important to first discuss concepts and theories of development, since they provide an effective means by which we organize information about the course and process of development along the entire life cycle and affect the assumptions we make about whether people change. Moreover, they help us to understand why people change. Therefore, we will not only present, but also compare and contrast the major ideas and theories about development so that you can clearly recognize and understand their similarities and differences. In doing so, you should realize that different theories about development and aging do start off with different assumptions about people and thus are difficult to *evaluate* in a relative sense.

Theories of development help us organize and interpret the many diverse facts we accumulate through everyday observation as well as through careful, systematic research. Moreover, they can stimulate research on nearly endless topics by allowing us to formulate working hypotheses about how our facts relate to one another, or whether they are related at all. In light of the evidence that accumulates pertaining to a given theory, that theory may need to undergo change or be dismissed entirely (Hall & Lindzey, 1985; Lerner, 1986; Reese & Overton, 1970). Thus, theories are more or less *useful* in light of the evidence supporting their ability to help us make sense of what we know about development.

For example, many professionals in the field of adult development and aging once believed that intellectual functioning clearly declined with increasing age and assumed biological factors to be behind such a decline. In light of evidence to the contrary (see Chapter 7) our notions of whether intelligence declines have been fortunately revised, and we now realize that such losses are not inevitable, and when they occur, they can be remediated in many cases.

To cite another instance where new facts lead to the revision of "facts," many professionals at one time believed that when older persons experienced symptoms such as disorientation or memory loss, such symptoms were a reliable indicator of an organic disorder (see Chapter 13). More recent evidence, however, suggests that such behaviors might just as easily be attributed to depression, which is highly treatable.

WHO ARE ADULTS? WHO ARE THE AGED?

Given that people do not suddenly change when they reach a given age, one of the most difficult tasks within life-span developmental psychology is deciding what chronological ages define life periods within the life cycle, such as adolescence, young adulthood, middle age, and later adulthood. Furthermore, the term *age* can have different meanings to individuals at different points along the life cycle.

For instance, 6-year-olds may view their 15-year-old siblings as adults, or maybe even aged! Fifteen-year-olds may consider themselves as adults while their parents may still consider them children. Most 30-year-olds consider themselves as adults, yet a 20-year-old may view the 30-year-old as middle-aged or even old. Likewise, many 60-year-olds may see themselves as middle-aged, reserve the term *old* for someone who is 75 or 80, and address the 30-year-old as "son." Therefore, in everyday life, *old* is a relative term—depending upon one's point of view. For example, a recent poll (*USA Weekend,* 1987) of nearly 1000 adults of varying ages regarding their chronological estimates of "old" suggested that for 18- to 22-year-olds, 65 was old, while for 65-year-olds, 72 was old. It should be apparent that there is no easy answer to determining who is an adult, who is middle-aged, and who is old. It often depends on whom one asks, as well as that individual's particular age (or *perception* of his or her age).

Professionals not only fail to agree on the wisdom of characterizing adulthood in terms of stages, they also have differing opinions on how to label or characterize stages or life periods along the life cycle, as well as about which chronological ages define the parameters of each stage. As indicated in Table 1.1, there have been various schemes proposed to define the "stages" of adulthood and aging. These designations are often arbitrary and, as we have pointed out, not absolute or distinct, thereby contributing to uncertainty (Lerner, 1986) regarding the value that developmental stages have for the adult developmental researcher.

As individuals proceed along the life course, entrance to and exit from these purported stages is gradual. According to D.J. Levinson (1986) (as indicated in Table 1.1), early adulthood theoretically ends at about age 45, and middle adulthood begins at age 40. The five-year span (ages 40–45) serves as a midlife transition period during which the stage of early adulthood draws to a close and the stage of middle adulthood begins. Similarly, beween the stages of middle adulthood and late adulthood is a five-year span (ages 60–65), the late-life transition period.

As a matter of convenience, we shall structure our discussion throughout this text using the classification system of D.J. Levinson (1986): *early adulthood* (17–45 yrs), *middle adulthood* (40–65 yrs), and *late adulthood* (60+ yrs).

TABLE 1.1

**VARIOUS THEORISTS' CONCEPTION OF THE STAGES
OF THE ADULT LIFE CYCLE**

Theorist	Stage	Age Equivalent
Birren (1964)	Early maturity	17–25
	Maturity	25–50
	Later maturity	50–75
	Old age	75+
Bromley (1974)	Early adulthood	21–25
	Middle adulthood	25–40
	Late adulthood	40–60
	Preretirement	60–65
	Retirement	65–69
	Old age	70+
	Senescence	Terminal illness & death
Havighurst (1972)	Early adulthood	18–35
	Middle adulthood	35–60
	Later maturity	60+
D. J. Levinson (1986)	Early adulthood	17–45
	(Midlife transition)	(40–45)
	Middle adulthood	40–65
	(Late-life transition)	(60–65)
	Late adulthood	60+

Further, the stage of late adulthood is often separated into "young-old" age (60–75 yrs) and "old-old" age (75+ yrs) (Neugarten, 1976). For reasons that will soon be obvious, this system needs to be seen as serving a *descriptive*, organizing function.

Problems with the Use of Chronological Age As a Causal Variable

Though persons are often classified to specific stages of the life cycle on the basis of their chronological ages, as we noted earlier, there is some dissatisfaction with the use of age in this regard (Birren & Renner, 1977; Wohlwill, 1970a). When we assume someone's age *causes* that person to respond in a certain manner, we are ascribing age the status of an **independent variable**. That is, we should be able to independently assign individuals to be a given age when investigating the effect of age on behavior. Obviously, this is not possible! One cannot arbitrarily designate a 20-year-old as one of a 40-year-old group of individuals. Thus, age is widely regarded as a nonpsychological, **dependent variable** (Birren & Cunningham, 1985; Wohlwill, 1970a, 1970b). We will have more to say about independent and dependent variables in Chapter 3 on research methods.

In many respects people remain much the same as they age,
while in other respects they exhibit great change.

   In both everyday and laboratory situations, we are often interested in
what it is about individuals (such as personality traits, physical characteristics, behaviors, experiences) who happen to vary in age that makes them
different from, or similar to, one another. Thus, while age, which is simply
the passage of time from one's birth to the present, cannot itself *cause* people
to change, experiences or events that are *age-related* (correlate with age) in
nature may explain *why* they change. Therefore, it is better to view age as an
index of change, just as inches are an index of a person's height, rather than
a *cause* of change.

   Consequently, though the use of chronological age or developmental
stages may help us to organize our knowledge about people and their behav-

ior, it does not allow us to explain the how and the why of that behavior. For example, using chronological age to index differences in political attitudes toward defense spending between 20-year-olds and 60-year-olds may be useful for discussion and comparative purposes. However, this classification of individuals on the basis of chronological age does not explain how such attitudes came about or why individuals of varying ages maintain or give up these attitudes.

BIRREN'S THREE TYPES OF AGE

Birren (1964, p. 10) and Birren and Renner (1977) suggest there exist three types of age meaningful in describing individuals: one's **biological**, **psychological**, and **social** age. Each index of aging is thought to be independent of the other. That is, persons' biological age does not necessarily affect their psychological and social ages, and vice versa. In reality however, for most individuals, they are somewhat related.

Biological age has two aspects. First, it can be considered to be the relative age or condition of the individual's organ and body systems. For example, does the 80-year-old individual's bodily processes (e.g., cardiovascular system) in fact function like those of an 80-year-old? Since it is possible for an 80-year-old who is physically active (a runner) to have the heart or lung capacity characteristic of someone younger, and vice versa (perhaps that person is a couch potato or a heavy smoker), biological age would not be synonymous with chronological age. Likewise, being 8 years of age, yet suffering from progeria (accelerated aging), where one only expects to live to be 12, makes that person biologically older than an 8-year-old whose likely life span is 70. The other aspect of biological age refers to individuals' present position relative to their potential life span, which varies from species to species. Flies have a potential life span of days, dogs 15 to 20 years, and humans 100+ years. For this reason, a given chronological age has different meanings for different species. Fifteen years to a dog implies the later stages of its life cycle, adolescence for a human, and late childhood for an elephant! Thus, chronological age carries a very different meaning from species to species.

Psychological age refers to the adaptive capacities of the individual, such as coping ability or intelligence. These are usually inferred from the person's behavior in everyday situations or on the basis of interview or test data. Psychological age also refers to persons' subjective awareness of their adaptive skills or performance level. Psychological age may be related to both chronological and biological age but cannot be fully described by their combination. Though an individual may be chronologically 90 years of age and bedridden with severe arthritis, that person may still be quite alert and talkative, keep abreast of current events, behave assertively, and have sound reasoning skills. Moreover, this individual's behaviors reflecting these skills may be similar to or exceed those of individuals in their twenties.

Social age refers to the social habits and roles of the individual relative to the expectations of society. This includes many observable manifestations of social age such as the way one dresses, one's preferred activities, or one's attitudes toward specific issues. As with psychological age, social age is some-what related to chronological, biological, and psychological age, but is not completely defined by them. For instance, someone who is chronologically 80 years of age may share similar attitudes and prefer leisure activities typical of persons in their thirties (they both voted for Reagan and enjoy bowling). While these indices of age vary within and between persons, they do, how-ever, interact to a certain extent to ultimately determine the individual's functioning. For example, someone who is critically ill (leukemic) will most likely be less adaptive and be restricted to certain types of activity in accord-ance with our lessened expectations (regarding independence or responsibili-ties) of persons who are very ill.

OTHER TYPES OF AGE

The following types of age are often also used when discussing individuals as well as the aging process.

Legal Age Perhaps the most widely used definition of age in the United States today is the **legal** definition. This interpretation defines age in terms of governmental laws and mandates as to who is a child, who is an adult, and who is an older person. For example, prior to recent court decisions (see Chapter 5), the legal definitions of old in the United States were age 65 for males and age 62 for females. In many states, the legal drinking age remains 18, while in others it is now 21. These age designations are mandated by law and are usually related to some external factor such as accessibility to Social Security benefits. Though the legal definition lacks scientific precision, it does mandate a specific criterion or reference point for making decisions about people. The legal definition of old varies from country to country, but the concept remains the same. That is, society's rules and regulations set the standard for what is considered old or young, child or adult.

Functional Age The concept of **functional age** is becoming very popular today, but it is still in need of refinement as both a hypothetical construct and as an applied and experimental concept before its usefulness can be fully determined (Birren & Renner, 1977). Though there are many views or defini-tions of functional age, what they share in common centers on the assumption that one's functional age is an index of one's level of capacities or abilities *relative to* those of others of similar age. Such skills can range from job per-formance to the condition of various organ systems.

There are two types of views of functional age, each with its own research tradition. One type closely parallels Birren's (1964) view of biologi-cal age and is illustrated by the work of Fozard, Nuttal, and Waugh (1972), who analyzed a large number of varied measurements of 600 healthy men, ranging in age from 20 to 80 years. They were able to derive six preliminary aspects of functional age: blood serum and urine; auditory functioning; an-thropometric descriptions (observable physical characteristics, for example, grip strength); verbal, perceptual, and motor abilities; personality; and sociological assessments. In brief, Fozard and his associates postulated that how individuals perform on these various measures could be used as an index of their functional age. An individual may be chronologically 65 but be able to discriminate tones or have the hand speed of someone 40 years of age. Therefore, that person's functional age would be 40 years.

A second line of research is exemplified by the work of Dirken (1972) and McFarland (1973). In this case, functional age reflects one's standing on a composite index of a number of biological and behavioral measures of job performance and work capacities. The main goal of this approach is to find a replacement for chronological age as a marker for hiring, firing, job rotation, and retirement; this perspective clearly suggests that it is possible for a worker who is 60 years of age to perform as adequately on the job as a person who is 20.

At present, each conception of functional age is limited in that it still is in part defined by chronological age. We will discuss the implications of functional age regarding the assessment of work performance in greater detail in our section on industrial gerontology (Chapter 5).

Normal Versus Pathological Aging

While for the most part our discussion of adult development and aging will center on what can be considered normal aging, it is nevertheless important to recognize the distinction between a "normal" as opposed to a "pathological" aging process. For example, making a decision that someone is aging abnormally may signify a "problem." As a consequence, that person is labeled (by self and others) as different. A number of things may then happen, ranging from others avoiding this problem person to that individual's being institutionalized. Normal aging involves changes—biological, sociological, or psychological—that are inevitable and occur as the natural result of maturation or the passage of time (Drachman, 1980). These should be distinguished from pathological aging, that is, changes that result from pathology or disease and are not part of the inevitable aging process. This fact is important because all too often, as we will see, many laypersons and professionals alike view the aging process from a pathological-decremental (loss-oriented) perspective that conveys negative attitudes, stereotypes, and unrealistic images of aging and older persons. Such biases about elderly persons are referred to as **ageism** (Butler, 1969, 1975).

As one ages, the manifestation of underlying physiological changes, such as gray hair or hardening/calcification of one's bones or nails, are part of the normal and inevitable aging process, not the result of pathology or disease processes. On the other hand, such things as heart attacks, cataracts, and deficits in concentration due to brain damage are pathological and due to disease processes that are *not* part of the normal and inevitable aging processes. This distinction also has a great deal of importance for counselors and clinicians, in that what might be pathological in one context (aggression in public) could be normal and quite adaptive in another (a nursing home) (Gurland, 1973). Both normal and pathological aging processes will be discussed in greater detail in our chapters on biological aging (Chapter 2), mental health and psychopathology (Chapter 13), and intervention and therapy (Chapter 14).

Developmental Tasks

Given the general dissatisfaction with the use of chronological age in explaining human development, many theorists prefer to assign individuals to stages of the life span on the basis of **developmental tasks** (Havighurst, 1952, 1953, 1972, 1973)(see Box 1.1). Developmental tasks, then, are concerns, expectations, goals, events, and/or behaviors that individuals are expected to encounter and resolve at specific times during the life cycle for normal development to occur. Our resolving these developmental tasks is thus often viewed as especially critical to later development. Examples of various theorists' conceptions of developmental tasks or critical issues for specific stages of the

BOX 1.1

DEVELOPMENTAL TASKS

All societies and cultures distinguish between individuals who "are" or who "are not" considered adults. Anthropologists often discuss and describe **rites of passage** or rituals that pertain to people when they move from preadulthood to adulthood. These rites of passage usually differ as a function of the person's gender. For instance, in primitive (nonindustrialized) cultures, the rite of passage from preadulthood to adulthood for females may be the ability to bear children. For males, it may be the ability to hunt independently.

In industrialized cultures, these rites of passage are usually called milestones or developmental tasks. They are defined by activities or events such as graduation from high school, obtaining a driver's license, voting, and living independently from the family.

According to this approach, as you progress through the life cycle, you are constantly developing and mastering new skills or tasks pertinent to each stage. At each particular stage, there are behaviors, activities, skills, or milestones that you are expected to accomplish.

A developmental task, then, is a situation or life adjustment task enabling individuals to cope with the "demands, constraints and opportunities provided by the social environment" (Havighurst, 1973, p. 10) relating to family, school, peers, or community.

Each set of developmental tasks is specially timed,

based upon what Havighurst terms a "teachable moment . . . when the body is ripe, and society requires, and the self is ready to achieve a certain task, the teachable moment has come" (1972, p. 7). Havighurst's developmental tasks (and, as we shall see in Chapter 10, Erikson's notions of psychosocial crises) are thus both founded on the notion of "critical periods" (Scott, 1962) in human development—the idea that certain aspects of the organism (person) have their own special (or critical) time in which to emerge or develop. If we are not properly stimulated and nurtured at this time, our growth will be harmed. Furthermore, we will not have a second chance at these critical learning experiences; they are part of the maturational plan governing that organism's development (Lerner, 1986). Three principal interactive factors help to define developmental tasks (which have been organized into *sets* of tasks from early childhood through old age): (1) biological (maturational) change, (2) cultural-societal expectations, and (3) the values/goals of the individual. All of these influences present the individual with new challenges, opportunities, and threats and, in addition, structure the sequence of social roles the individual is expected to play throughout the life span, as well as those specifically encountered in the adult years. Their solution is, by definition (Havighurst, 1952), deemed to be healthy; failure leads to unhappiness, social disapproval, and difficulty with future tasks.

life cycle are presented in Table 1.2. While developmental tasks are often seen in normative terms, they may vary as a function of factors such as cultural change, socioeconomic level, ethnicity, race, gender, marital status, educational level, and occupation. Thus, issues defining these developmental tasks and norms for behavior or activities are always *relative* and never absolute. That is, they may vary from culture to culture, or as a function of historical change or individual life circumstances (K. F. Riegel, 1977a, 1977b).

Many of the topics that will be discussed in the following chapters *cut across* developmental tasks particular to younger or older persons. For example, courtship and marriage are equally relevant issues to young adults and to never-married and/or widowed persons who are older.

The classification of persons into any stage of the life cycle must be done using a combination of criteria: chronological age, completion of developmental tasks, and the achievement of a certain degree of psychological maturity (Whitbourne & Weinstock, 1979). Given the complexity of this task, it is difficult to classify individuals neatly into life stages. It must always be kept in mind that while our discussions will in many cases concentrate on *normative (average) trends* in development, there are major *individual differences* in *when* and *how* specific individuals experience many of the issues and changes we discuss.

Developmental tasks are not permanent or fixed; they vary from cohort to cohort, as a function of many cultural, environmental, and social factors. While they may serve as a viable starting point for descriptive purposes, as explanatory concepts regarding development they have definite limitations. At this point, you may find it helpful to list what tasks you feel are appropriate for you and contrast them with those of your parents or grandparents to appreciate more fully the cultural (cohort) specificity in how these tasks are defined.

CULTURAL ETHICS

Yankelovich (1981a) speculates that prevalent cultural attitudes in the United States during this century have affected the attitudes/beliefs, goals, and behaviors of individuals who matured from childhood to young adulthood at different times during this century. These prevailing attitudes of society are called **cultural ethics** (McIlroy, 1984) and, to some extent, determine how individuals view their relationship with society and others at all points in the life span.

During the 1950s, the major cultural ethic of the United States was that of denial, which encouraged Americans to put the needs of others ahead of their personal needs, that is, self-sacrifice (Yankelovich, 1981a, 1981b). For example, parents spent their savings on their children's education rather than on personal items such as new cars or vacations. Individuals were encouraged to be *other-oriented* rather than *self-oriented.*

During the 1960s and 1970s the ethic of self-denial was replaced by the ethic of self-fulfillment. At this time, Americans searched for creativity, autonomy, self-actualization, and pleasure over material gain and the needs

TABLE 1.2

EXAMPLE OF DEVELOPMENTAL TASKS/CRITICAL ISSUES ENCOUNTERED BY INDIVIDUALS DURING ADULT LIFE AS POSTULATED BY VARIOUS THEORISTS

Life Span

Birth ———————————————————————————————————— To Death

Chronological Age in Years

15	20	25	30	35	40	45	50	55	60	65	70	75	80+

Stages of Life

? —— Young Adulthood —— ? —— Middle Adulthood —— ? —— Late Adulthood —— ?

Theorists:

Erikson (1963)	Intimacy vs. isolation	Generativity vs. stagnation	Ego integrity vs. despair
Gould (1972, 1975)	Independence from parents Career development Starting a family Questioning of self	Attempting to attain life's goal Settling down General mellowing	
Havighurst (1972)	Courtship and marriage Adjustment to marriage Beginning a family (parenthood) Child rearing Family responsibilities Career development Social relationships Civic responsibility	Helping children Adult social and civic responsibility Satisfactory occupational performance Development of leisure activities Accepting and adjusting to physiological changes Adjustment to aging parents	Adjusting to declining physical strength and health Adjusting to retirement and reduced income Adjusting to death of spouse Anticipating one's own death
Sheehy (1976)	Independence from parents Further identity formation Career and family involvement Adult responsibility	Midlife transition or crisis Reestablishing or renewing self-concept	

of others. This is often referred to as the "me generation," which is character-ized by egocentric thinking—putting our own needs and desires above those of others.

During the 1980s, American society is thought to be moving toward a new social ethic of commitment. This new view of the importance of a commitment to others and society is often referred to as the *us* generation, as opposed to the 1970s' *me* generation.

The above ideas suggest that developmental tasks relevant to adoles-cence and young adulthood are dynamic and changing, this change being the result of many sociocultural forces. For this reason, developmental tasks, and their relevance, vary from cohort to cohort.

These sociocultural factors may also have different implications and relevance for individuals, as a function of their age (Neugarten, 1968). For example, periods of economic uncertainty and high unemployment have greater relevance for adults, since they must worry about paying bills and keeping a job, than they do for older individuals who are retired, or for young children who are years away from the job market. Oerter (1986) has even suggested that Havighurst's developmental tasks may need to be redefined along a continuum of breadth, that is a broad (life-span tasks) to narrow (interpersonal relationship–specific tasks particular to individuals) focus. Moreover, the individual's own unique values and goals as well as the active support of others are important factors defining developmental tasks for persons of all ages. Thus, conflicts between what society expects and the individual's behavior may not be harmful to one's development.

As we indicated earlier, since certain developmental tasks or critical developmental issues are more important than others at specific periods dur-ing the adult life span, the depth of coverage of these issues within chapters will vary depending on the topic (see Table 1.3). We will again raise the issues of stages and developmental tasks when we discuss stage theories of person-ality development in Chapter 10.

TABLE 1.3

SUSPECTED CHANGES FOR VARIOUS PROCESSES DURING YOUNG ADULTHOOD, MIDDLE ADULTHOOD, AND LATE ADULTHOOD

	Young Adulthood	Middle Adulthood	Late Adulthood
Sensorized perceptual processes	Stability	Minor change	Significant change
Cognitive processes	Stability	Stability	Stability?
Physical condition	Stability	Minor change	Significant change
Socialization processes	Stability	Stability	Stability
Personality processes	Stability	Minor change?	Significant change?
Occupational processes	Stability	Stability	Significant change?

Note: The question mark (?) indicates suspected change or stability still in question.

Individual Differences/Interindividual Differences

You have probably noticed by now that we have begun referring to the process of human development and aging as one and the same. Simply put, this is because from the moment we are born, we are aging. As our discussion to this point implies, development and aging both imply change. Therefore, when we use the term aging process, we are not specifically referring to older adults but to changes across the entire course of life span development and aging. The aging process proceeds at different rates among different people. As we can imply from our earlier discussion of development, aging takes many different forms as well. This is consistent with the large number of differences *within* and *between* individuals at all points along the life cycle. For example, some individuals may begin to lose their hair during their late twenties and become bald, or have white hair by their mid-forties. Others, however, may not lose any hair, or their hair may not turn white until their late sixties. Therefore, while we may discuss topics such as psychomotor ability, intelligence, memory, attitudes, and so forth in general terms regarding individuals at any point along the life cycle, **individual differences** in such abilities or characteristics are nevertheless great, and moreover increase with increased differential experience across time (Krauss, 1980). Not all individuals at a given point in the life cycle will share the same attitudes or evidence similar abilities or performance levels. We must constantly be aware of the fact that there are vast individual differences among persons at all points along the life cycle (Hoyer, 1974; Maddox & Douglass, 1974). For example, each person's uniquenesses are important in designing skill-training programs or educational curricula to meet the needs of participants (see Chapters 6 and 7).

Individual differences or **interindividual differences** refer to differences *between* persons on any trait, behavior, ability, or performance skill at a given point in time (P.B. Baltes, Reese, & Lipsitt, 1980; Huston-Stein & P.B. Baltes, 1976). For example, suppose you and your roommate are of the same age, gender, have the same hair color, come from the same socioeconomic background, and are enrolled in the same course. On the first test in that course, you receive a grade of A and your roommate receives a D. While you both are similar in other respects, this difference in test performance is termed an individual difference between you and your roommate that may determine whether one of you drops the course. Our task then, having described such differences, is to explain and modify these differences (P.B. Baltes, 1973); that is, *why* did your roommate do poorly and *how* can he or she improve?

Intraindividual Differences/Intraindividual Changes

Intraindividual changes refer to changes *within* an individual *over time* on any trait, behavior, ability, or performance skill. **Intraindividual differences** refer to differences *between* traits, behaviors, abilities, or performance levels *within* that individual *at any one point in time* (P.B. Baltes et al., 1980; Hoyer, 1974; Huston-Stein & P.B. Baltes, 1976). How your intelligence changes over time would be an example of an intraindividual change. The differences between your grades (performance) among your various courses this semester would be an example of an intraindividual difference. For instance, you may be receiving an A in this course, a B in mathematics, and a C in English Composition. Maddox and Douglass (1974) have reported that individuals tend to maintain such intraindividual differences on a number of social, psychological, and physiological measures over the life cycle. Moreover, it is not uncommon for interindividual differences to become greater with increasing age (Krauss, 1980; Maddox & Douglass, 1974). That is, greater variability in performance is observed between individuals with advanced age. Additionally, they may become more variable, *relative to themselves* earlier in time (P. B. Baltes, Reese, & Nesselroade, 1977). The issue of variability with age is illustrated in Box 1.2.

BOX 1.2

INTERINDIVIDUAL DIFFERENCES AND AGE

What do we mean by interindividual differences becoming greater with increased age?

Below is a list of test scores for 30 students enrolled in a college course. Let's suppose 10 of these students are young adults, 10 are middle-aged, and 10 are older adults. From examining these data, a number of points about development can be illustrated. First, the average test score appears to lessen with increasing age. However, variability between persons (interindividual differences) becomes larger

with increasing age. In view of this fact, focusing on average scores may not be desirable. This variability can be observed by looking at the standard deviation and range of scores for each of the age groups. This variability increases across levels of age. The standard deviation and range are two "statistics" that are used to describe the variability of scores. The larger the standard deviation and range, the greater the variability of scores.

Test Scores

	Young adult individual	Middle-aged individual	Older individual
	80	100	57
	95	65	100
	100	78	57
	100	99	89
	85	87	100
	99	95	94
	95	92	83
	93	81	72
	84	76	78
	96	87	91
Average score	92.7	86.0	82.1
Standard deviation	6.81	10.56	15.13
Range	80–100	65–100	57–100
N	10	10	10

Finally, it must be noted that aging and development are universal characteristics of all living organisms and thus entail change. Dialectically speaking, change is normal, expected, and characteristic of persons who are acted upon and influence their environments (K. F. Riegel, 1977b).

MODELS AND THEORIES OF DEVELOPMENT

In order to understand changes in our behavior, performance, attitudes, personality traits, and processes along the life cycle, we must first acquire some knowledge regarding the various theories that attempt to organize the facts of development as well as to explain the course of development and aging. Theories provide an effective method for organizing information, data, and speculations about the course and process of development along the entire life cycle (Lerner, 1986). Theories vary in terms of their breadth. They may be relatively narrow and concern questions such as: How are abilities developed? How are our abilities related to each other? Do they increase or decrease, and why? Alternatively, broader theories may be needed to explain how individuals cope with cultural change or with distinct classes of life events.

Prior to discussing the major broad approaches that incorporate more narrow theories of human development, a number of points regarding theories must be kept in mind. First, theories are considered hunches or educated guesses. Theories of human development do not have the same specificity as those in such physical sciences as physics. Second, many of the ideas and concepts presented by these theories are considered **hypothetical constructs**; that is, they do not have any physical or material existence outside of the theory. Thus, these constructs will be difficult to measure, observe, and validate accurately. A good illustration of this point can be made if we think of the construct of self-concept, which we discuss in Chapter 10. For instance, while we may all have a personal idea of what self-concept is, we cannot directly observe it. We may say a person has a good or poor self-concept based on some observable evidence such as that person's general attitude toward life, number of friends, or participation in clubs or social organizations. As this example illustrates, self-concept does not exist as a physical entity that can be observed directly. We must infer self-concept from some other evidence, such as a person's behavior and attitudes.

Third, theories guide or limit which behaviors, traits, and abilities are observed and explained, as well as what types of research procedures are employed. For example, let's suppose Theory X proposes that one's traits, behaviors, and abilities are determined by genetic makeup. Therefore, researchers who support this theory would tend to downplay the effects of environment, experience, and learning and concentrate on research procedures that imply a genetic cause. For example, they might examine the influence of patterns of inheritance on coping ability using family histories or study identical versus fraternal twins. On the other hand, suppose Theory Y proposes that traits, behaviors, and abilities are the result of environment or learning experiences. Researchers who support this theory would downplay the importance of heredity and concentrate on research procedures that involve the manipulation of the environment or the accumulation of experience. For example, they might study the impact of divorce on subsequent coping skills, personal adjustment, or life satisfaction.

Finally, many theories tend necessarily to view human development as though it occurred in a vacuum and were not affected by factors such as social expectations or norms, diet, socioeconomic status, or social class influences. In all fairness, given the complexity of human development, it is quite difficult for any theory to explain adequately all aspects of human development by encompassing every potential causal factor. Developmentally, one of the most difficult tasks for a given theory or theories of human development to accomplish is to be able to account for both the stability and change in individuals' behaviors during the entire course of the life cycle.

In order to understand *why* major theories of human development differ, we introduce a number of issues, which these theories must address and often disagree on. Understanding each of these issues will help you more clearly separate what various theories have to say about development and aging.

DEVELOPMENTAL ISSUES

There are a number of major issues that all theories of development must address in order to explain adequately the course of human development (J. Langer, 1969; Reese & Overton, 1970). While we present these issues as extremes, in reality they are end points along a continuum. They are not clear-cut dichotomies. Moreover, as we will soon see, many approaches to development and aging encompass each extreme along a given continuum, and theories differ in terms of the emphasis they place on each extreme regarding development. Again, clearly understanding these issues will help you more fully appreciate each model's unique contribution to organizing our knowledge about adulthood. These issues are (1) the issue of **developmental stages**, (2) **qualitative versus quantitative change**, (3) **active versus passive role of the organism** (person), (4) the influence of **nature versus nurture**, (5) an **elementist versus holistic approach to development**, (6) a **structure-function vs. antecedent-consequence analysis of behavior**, and (7) determinism versus nondeterminism. A particular theory's position or stance on these issues will determine how it views the course and process of human development.

Issue of Stages The position a theory takes with regard to stages of development is related to its view toward the quantitative versus qualitative nature of development. For this reason, our discussion of stages should reinforce the distinctions inherent in the issue of qualitative-quantitative change.

This issue revolves around the question of whether higher order behaviors and activities, such as motor skills or cognitive skills, develop in a manner incorporating earlier (preceding) and simpler forms of behavior (stages of development). While stages themselves are by definition qualitatively different, achievements in earlier stages do lay the groundwork for later stages. Alternatively, theories that deemphasize developmental stages see the change in abilities or skills as the result of the continuous growth and development of separate and specific systems (ability, trait). Stage theories view the development of abilities and skills in terms of building blocks—one ability is based on another ability to the extent that there is an *organizing principle* governing the development of each stage as well as how individuals progress (or regress) from one stage to another (Lerner, 1986). Theories that do not accept the conception of development as occurring in a series of stages view all behaviors, abilities, and traits as developing for the most part independently of each other.

For example, let us use the higher order behavior or activity of running. Since many theories of development view all developmental processes as the result of previous simpler behaviors, running would be seen as evolving from walking (yet qualitatively different from it), which in turn evolves from standing, which evolves from crawling. This is considered a stage theory. Examples of such stage theories that most students have come in contact with are those of Sigmund Freud, Erik Erikson (see Chapter 10), and Jean Piaget (see Chapter 7). An assumption central to the stage theory perspective is that in order for development to proceed to a higher stage, the organism must have successfully completed or acquired the behaviors or activities of the previous stage (you cannot walk before you stand). As this example implies, stage theories also generally suggest maturational timetables for abilities and skills that change qualitatively and advocate discontinuity of development. Such qualitative, discontinuous changes are based upon an underlying maturational process or principle that links each qualitative stage and specifies how persons move through each stage. Of course, stages also imply that most persons' behavior within stages is logically consistent, and that such stages apply to most individuals (J. Langer, 1969; Lerner, 1986).

Other developmental theories that stress learning experiences take issue with the assumption of stages. These theories suggest that each behavior or activity evolves, for the most part, separately and independently from all other behaviors and activities. That is, crawling ability evolves and develops independently from running ability. Implicit in this view is that even an individual who has never crawled would still be able to run. Such behaviors are often rooted in experience. Therefore, growth and development are quantitative and continuous, and in this case running and crawling may be under the control of separate experiential factors.

It should be stressed that stages should not be considered or viewed as having a physical, material existence but are hypothetical constructs that are used more meaningfully to describe behavior and development.

Qualitative Versus Quantitative Change   This issue is concerned with the question of whether behavior change is the result of the continuous accumulation of small improvements in similar behaviors or processes (quantitative) or the acquisition of new processes or behaviors (qualitative). Consequently, development in adulthood could be understood from the quantitative viewpoint as an extension of what occurs in one's childhood. Basically, the quantitative position considers all behaviors to be the result of continuous improvements of the same behaviors or associations. With the passage of time, appropriate reinforcement, and trial-and-error experiences, the individual acquires a huge number of associations that are added to each other to form a large repertoire of habitual modes of response (J. Langer, 1969). In a sense, the more we practice a behavior or skill, the more it improves. Therefore, very complex behaviors (driving a car) are the result of the accumulation of improvements in simple behaviors (shifting gears, learning to steer, pressing on the brake). Understanding how older adults learn by studying younger adults illustrates a quantitative approach to development. According to this view, while older adults may learn less quickly, fundamentally they learn in basically the same way—the underlying mechanisms of learning are similar in each case.

On the other hand, the qualitative approach does not consider complex behaviors and abilities to be the result of the continuous accumulation of simple behaviors. That is, complex behaviors such as fine motor control do not simply evolve from improvements in gross motor control—they are said to be discontinuous. Complex behaviors are the result of the development of different processes. From this point of view, older adults might learn differently than would younger adults—different underlying factors would explain learning in each case. Stage approaches to development typically emphasize qualitative change.

Let us briefly discuss another example to highlight these differences. Improvements in higher-order behaviors involving fine motor control (throwing a curveball) may or may not be related to gains in lower-order skills of gross motor control (arm movement) or simple reflexes (shifting one's body weight to avoid losing balance). If we view such changes as quantitative, each skill could be acquired independently of the other through appropriate training and experience. Qualitatively, the acquisition of these skills would be under maturational control and therefore be age related. Thus, each skill would be qualitatively unique, yet organized by some underlying principle; for example, gross motor skills may precede the development of fine motor skills (Werner, 1948).

Gains or losses in weight with age may be quantitative (they can be measured in the same units (pounds) or qualitative (resulting from glandular malfunction, diet, or exercise). Many aspects of developmental change in constructs such as personality or intelligence are both quantitative (varying in level) and qualitative (varying in kind—the underlying reasons for change vary across age).

Active Versus Passive The central focus of this issue is whether the developing organism plays an active or passive role in its own developmental process. In many respects, this issue transcends the field of human development but nevertheless has important implications for the study of adulthood. The passive view assumes the organism plays an inactive role in the development process, and thus development results from stimulation impinging on the person from the environment. In some respects, our abilities, reaction times, personality traits, and behaviors are the result of learning or stimulation from the environment. That is, individuals are relatively passive while the environment molds or shapes them. Consequently, if we want them to change, we must provide those experiences that we feel will facilitate this change.

On the other hand, the active position suggests that individuals take a direct role in their development. Individuals initiate their own actions to deal with the environment and continue to acquire knowledge from the environment in this way throughout life. Individuals thus seek out, construct, and initiate their own development and experiences. In this sense, if we are helping someone change, we might focus on that person's feelings, values, skills, etc. and use these as a basis for life-changing choices that person makes. Rather than make decisions for this person, we would use this information to enable the individual to formulate his or her own choices.

Nature Versus Nurture   This issue is perhaps the most familiar to you since it is usually discussed in courses on introductory or child psychology. It is also known as the heredity versus environment issue. Basically, this issue is concerned with the question of whether development is the result of genetically determined hereditary forces (nature), or of learning and/or other environmental influences (nurture).

Elementarism Versus Holism   The major concern of this issue is whether all aspects of development and behavior can be reduced to an observable stimulus-response connection (elementarism), or whether, to understand behavior and development, we must view the total situation (holism). For instance, suppose we observe in a nursing home situation an older resident striking a staff member. The elementarist position would suggest that in order to understand and change such behavior, we must concentrate only on that observable behavioral event—the resident's striking the staff person.

The holist position, in contrast, suggests that in order to understand an observed behavior, one must look at more than just the observable evidence. Specifically, one must try to determine the overall meaning or reasons underlying that behavior, or the context in which it occurred. For example, the observable striking may have been intentionally motivated by anger, retaliation, or frustration, or it could have been accidental. Basically, the elementarist approach assumes that in order to understand behavior or development, we must reduce it to its most basic observable units, while the holist position views development as an overall process involving the organism embedded in the environment.

Another example of the elementarist versus holist position can be found in the health care profession (nursing and medicine), where the distinction between traditional and holistic medicine is often made. The traditional medical model and medicinal treatments concentrate on dealing with a specific symptom, illness, or organ structure, while the holistic approach is concerned with the well-being of the whole individual in a social and environmental milieu. For instance, consider an individual who has ulcers. The traditional approach would concentrate primarily on the surgical treatment or the chemical (drug) control of the ulcer. The holistic approach, in contrast, would concentrate on both the treatment of the ulcer and the recommending of changes in the individual's diet, life-style, working environment, and so forth. Holists would argue that in order to treat patients effectively, one must observe and treat *all* aspects of individuals and their environments.

Structure-Function Versus Antecedent-Consequence Analysis of Behavior   Another major issue over which theories of development disagree is whether they analyze behavior and development in terms of structure-function or antecedent-consequent relationships. Developmental theories that take a structure-function approach attempt to identify what function a particular behavior or activity serves for the organism, as well as what system or structure within the organism is responsible for that behavior or activity. For instance, think of the ability to use language. Theories from the structure-function perspective may attempt to explain the course of language development on the basis of what social or emotional function language serves for the individual and the identification of what underlying cognitive or biological structures are responsible for language development. Often, theories from this perspective attempt to link an observable, quantifiable behavior (language ability) to an unobservable construct (cognitive functioning). For example, Piaget's theory (Brainerd, 1978) might link language development to the ability to internalize one's experiences (language is a symbol system to represent reality).

The antecedent-consequence approach attempts to explain development on the basis of observable events: immediately causal factors that can be identified. That is, the environmental stimulus or cue causes the individual to emit a particular response or behavior. Using our previous example, this approach attempts to explain what observable (a parent's reinforcement) antecedent has led to a particular verbal response (say "ma-ma")—a consequence of the parent's attention to the child. Therefore, theorists from this perspective often attempt to link observable, quantifiable behaviors (language) to another observable stimulus or cue (verbal stimulation from another) in the environment.

Determinism Versus Nondeterminism   A final issue on which theories of development differ is whether behavior at a given part of the life span is or is not determined by biology or past experience. This distinction has important implications for older adults in the workplace and in the classroom. If we view an individual's behavior (e.g., one's ability to learn a new skill) as determined by biological makeup or certain experiences (i.e., upbringing), we may conclude that that person is not capable of being retrained or educated to acquire a new skill. In other words, the individual is a prisoner of health, physique, upbringing, or past work record. The nondeterminist position would suggest that the individual's present level of skill, motivation, work record, etc. must be considered in making a decision about whether this person should be retrained. For example, to continue to view older persons in biological (loss-oriented) terms, emphasizing how they may have been when they were younger, or by comparing them to younger persons, is to espouse a deterministic view of aging. The nondeterminist might consider such persons in the context of their present skill levels and deal with them as unique, changing individuals who must be understood in light of numerous factors, independent of past experience or background. Determinists generally emphasize the qualitative nature of aging (an emphasis on biological determinants) and consequently tend to be reductionistic. Moreover, they emphasize man's passive nature, where behavior is a function of forces over which one has little control. Thus, an older person's inherent inability to learn would prevent him or her from profiting from new experiences. Fortunately, the evidence dealing with the cognitive skills of older adults (see Chapters 5–7) does not bear out this deterministic viewpoint.

DEVELOPMENTAL MODELS

In this section, some of the major organizing ideas about human development will be presented and discussed. These are called *models* of development. Each model might encompass several specific theories, which we will discuss on a chapter-by-chapter basis as appropriate. In each instance we will present each model's position on each of the developmental issues we have raised.

The models or general points of view that will be discussed are termed **organismic, mechanistic, psychoanalytic** (J. Langer, 1969; Lerner, 1986), and **life-span developmental** (P.B. Baltes, 1973; P.B. Baltes et al., 1980). Their positions on each developmental issue are highlighted in Table 1.4.

Organismic Models   Theorists within the organismic model view the course of development as being genetically programmed, leading to a natural unfolding of behavior and development. For this reason, organismic theories stress the importance of "nature" in development. Further, development is seen as qualitative and progresses through a series of discontinuous stages.

Theorists from this perspective believe organisms (persons) play an active, assertive role in their own development—they actively seek out knowledge and information. Finally, organismic theories suggest that in order to understand and investigate development, one must take a holist perspective and analyze together the structure and functions of human behaviors and activities.

Organismic theories imply that development can be characterized by both progressive and regressive changes in behavior, though development does seem to follow a fairly fixed and predictable course for the most part. This assumption implies that the course of development is difficult to modify,

TABLE 1.4

COMPARISON OF MAJOR DEVELOPMENTAL MODELS
REGARDING ISSUES OF DEVELOPMENT

| Issue | Developmental Models | | | Life-Span Developmental |
	Organismic	Mechanistic	Psychoanalytic	
Qualitative vs. quantitative change	Qualitative	Quantitative	Qualitative	Both
Active vs. passive organism	Active	Passive	Both	Both
Nature vs. nurture	Nature	Nurture	Nature	Interdependence between nature and nurture
Elementarism vs. holist	Holist	Elementarism	Holist	Elementarism within the context of the whole
Stages	Stages	No stages	Stages	No formal stages
Structure-function vs. antecedent-consequence	Structure-function	Antecedent-consequence	Structure-function	Both
Determinism vs. nondeterminism	Determinism	Nondeterminism	Determinism	Both

in that structural/organizational changes have already occurred. For this reason, training, education, or intervention strategies would be of little value if the organism's current stage of development did not permit it to be ready or functionally able to deal effectively with those experiences. For instance, the organismic view might argue that young children may not be able to learn a particular problem-solving strategy because their logical reasoning skills have not developed to the requisite stage, while older adults may be unable to learn that same problem-solving strategy because their logical reasoning skills have changed qualitatively (regressed) and no longer permit them to acquire the problem-solving strategy.

In conclusion, theories within the organismic model view the course of human development as a sequence of discontinuous qualitative changes in abilities from childhood through late adulthood, with progressive decreases in abilities beginning in middle age based on an assumption or regression to an earlier, less mature stage. A particular weakness of organismic theories for our purposes is that they underestimate the effects of training and experience on behavior. For example, Piagetian theory predicts poorer performance among older adults on many logical reasoning tasks (see Chapter 6). Yet researchers have found that this apparent decline is really a manifestation of a *qualitatively* different type of thinking (see Chapter 6), important in its own right.

Mechanistic Model   As can be seen in Table 1.4, theorists within the mechanistic camp stand completely opposite organismic theorists on all comparison dimensions. Mechanistic theories are often referred to as the S-R (stimulus-response) or behavioral (response-stimulus) model. The core assumption of this model involves the influence of learning and reinforcement on development.

In this case, human development is seen as a progressive, continuous, quantitative change in the level of abilities and behavior. Therefore, the development of abilities results from training, learning, and experience (nurture). The goal of research is to study the observable and quantifiable antecedents (stimulus) and consequences (responses) of behavior at its elementary level (reductionist). That is, we look at the behavior itself, independent of the function that it serves for the individual.

These theories look upon development as a continual process. Therefore, they generally do not take the decremental view of aging, as does the organismic model (assuming regression to a less mature stage later in life). Mechanism is a popular alternative among developmentalists, being the basis for social-learning explanations of personality (see Chapter 10) and intervention approaches to learning and memory in later adulthood (see Chapter 7). The major weaknesses of the model are (1) the assumption that almost all human abilities can be improved through training, reinforcement, and experience, and (2) a tendency to overlook the broader person-environment context in which the behavior occurred.

Psychoanalytic Model   Though the psychoanalytic approach shares many of the characteristics of the organismic model and is often considered as a theory of human development (J. Langer, 1969), it is, however, somewhat more narrow and is primarily concerned with personality development and socialization processes, incorporating one's parents as the primary agents of such socialization.

The psychoanalytic model views development as biologically based, progressing through a series of discontinuous stages that are qualitatively different. These stages are termed *oral, anal, phallic, latency,* and *genital.* Each stage has a psychosexual connotation, since the energy required to progress through the stages is sexually and maturationally determined and in fact is relocated (the locus of one's satisfaction changes) so that one's needs can be satisfied.

The organism is thought to react as a whole, and developmental changes in behavior and modes of relating to others are explained on the basis of the interactions among specific hypothetical structures: *id* (instinctual), *ego* (reality based), and *superego* (ego ideal, conscience). The psychoanalytic model views the individual as in a state of constant conflict (Maddi, 1980) involving opposite forces (e.g., life and death forces within the personality). That is, the individual attempts to remain passive but, due to pressures from each component of personality, must actively deal with this conflict in order to revert back to a passive state or, in other words, maintain a psychic balance (homeostasis). In conclusion, in terms of normal development, psychoanalytic theory focuses upon the transformation of irrational processes into rational ones and upon the maturation of psychosexual functions (Hall & Lindzey, 1985). More recently, it has evolved into a theory emphasizing psychosocial functions (Erikson, 1959, 1963) (see Chapter 10) where greater ego control over the pressures of the id and the superego is emphasized.

The major weaknesses of psychoanalytic theory *as a theory of human development* are that (1) it views development as being fixed by late adolescence, after which there is no further (qualitatively new) development, and (2) it concentrates primarily on explaining personality and socialization processes, overlooking other important environmental/contextual or cultural influences on development. Extensions of the psychoanalytic model into adulthood will be discussed in greater detail in Chapter 10 on personality.

Life-Span Developmental Model   The life-span developmental approach (P.B. Baltes, 1987; P.B. Baltes et al., 1980; P.B. Baltes & Willis, 1977; Huston-Stein & P.B. Baltes, 1976) integrates aspects of many of the above models, incorporating the work of K.F. Riegel (1975, 1976) on the dialectics of development, though in the strictest sense it is incompatible with both mechanism and organism. According to Riegel's **dialectical** theory (see also Chapter 10), internal factors (genetically preprogrammed instinctual behaviors, traits, characteristics, physiological states) and external factors (aspects of the physical environment, cultural components) continuously influence and are influenced by each other. Basically, internal forces interact with external forces. Both affect the course of development, and both are constantly changing and being changed by each other. Therefore, there is an *interdependence* between internal and external factors throughout the course of development. For this reason, theorists from the life-span developmental perspective suggest that an eclectic model is required to adequately explain development, since development is quite complex, affected and being affected by many mediating or moderating factors. These include inner-biological factors (health or illness), the physical or cultural aspects of the environment (outer-physical and cultural-sociological factors) and *individual-psychological* influences.

According to Riegel, developmental change is a given, varying in terms of the extent to which these factors are working at cross-purposes with one another (i.e., they are out of sync) (K.F. Riegel, 1976). For example, one may wish to marry but not find a suitable would-be mate; illness may interfere with one's career plans; one may be forced to retire due to poor health or company policy. For persons who are adapting well to these changes, there is more synchrony, though a certain "out of syncness" is to be expected given the interdependence among these factors.

According to K.F. Riegel, a "crisis" is a matter of degree, since crises stemming from asynchrony (events that are not in sync) are normal and unrelated to age per se. Stability (no crises) is the exception (K.F. Riegel, 1976). Crises can be disruptive at any point in the life span depending upon how one copes with change (a given), and thus the often-used term *midlife crisis* (Golan, 1986; Jaques, 1965; D. Levinson, 1978) is inaccurate. As Neugarten (1973, 1977) notes, for some individuals, "off-timeness" (with reference to the **social clock**—expectations about appropriate shoulds/should nots at certain ages) that should induce a negative crisis is actually beneficial. These persons may even *plan* for such off-timeness (for example, delaying having children until one's late thirties or early forties, or retiring at age 55).

According to the organismic and psychoanalytic viewpoints, complex developmental change lessens once adulthood is reached, and thus behavior/ development is *unidirectional* (proceeds in one direction); it either increases *(grows)* or decreases (declines). Figures 1.3 and 1.4 illustrate how the life-span developmental model views development as both **multidimensional** (there are many types of development) and **multidirectional** (change can take on many forms) at all phases of the life cycle. Some forms of change are age irrelevant, and others are specific to certain parts of the life cycle (see Figure 1.4). In effect, development is **pluralistic**—it can take many forms, of which increments and decrements in specific behaviors are but one type (see Figures 1.3 and 1.4), at all points in the life cycle. As Figure 1.4 illustrates, many different types of abilities or behaviors have different courses of development in terms of *onset, direction, duration,* and *termination* (P. B. Baltes et al., 1980).

In this chapter and throughout this text, we consistently refer to a variety of changes in behavior that may or may not occur as a function of the aging process. To the extent that they correlate with chronological age, they are termed *age-related* changes—they are often assumed to be the result of the aging process. As we discuss at this chapter's outset, in reality such changes in behavior, traits, abilities, and so forth can be attributed to other factors rather than age (the passage of time) per se.

In fact, P.B. Baltes, Reese, and Lipsitt (1980) suggest that, to understand adequately changes in the context of adulthood and aging, one must consider three types of influences that result in change. These are termed **age normative, history normative**, and **nonnormative** in nature.

Age-normative influences are factors that are general to development, are highly related to chronological age, and affect persons of a given age in a particular manner (though their timing may vary for different subgroups of

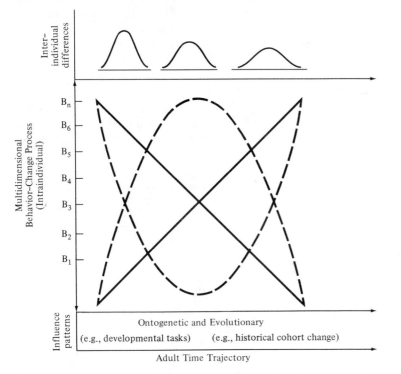

Figure 1.3 Examples of multidimensional, multidirectional but systematic behavior-change processes. While some changes are incremental, others are decremental. Still others involve both growth and decline. As age increases, differences among persons also become greater. *Source:* P. B. Baltes & S. L. Willis. (1977), *Handbook of psychology of aging* (p. 137). New York: Van Nostrand Reinhold. Used with permission of the publisher.

persons). These age-normative factors can be biological or physiological in nature (such as the onset of puberty) or social-environmental (such as retirement or the legal age at which one is considered an adult).

History-normative influences are factors or events that occur at a specific point in time (day, year, month) and theoretically affect everyone in that society or culture. These events, however, have an impact of a short-term nature and may in fact have different effects upon individuals of varying ages. For instance, if a war were to be declared, the most pronounced effect of this event would be on individuals of draft age. History-normative factors also include influences that are particular to a given **cohort** (generation) (the Great Depression of the 1930s) that are more long-term in nature—values toward hard work, politics, or economics may have a lasting influence on you if you grew up in the Depression years.

Nonnormative influences are factors that are not related to age or history, but still affect specific individuals during the life span. In a sense, these factors cannot be attributed to the normal process of development or to the impact of environmental, cultural-societal events. Accidents are commonly deemed examples of nonnormative events. Each set of influences is ongoing and interactive in their influence across the life span (see Figure 1.5).

Each of these factors exhibits different levels of influence upon the individual at different points along the life cycle. For instance, age-normative influences are often considered to be the result of maturation and are under genetic control; therefore, they have the most pronounced effect during childhood and old age. History-normative influences are most pronounced among adolescents and young adults, and nonnormative events increase in significance with increasing age (Danish, 1981). (See Figure 1.6.)

In conclusion, groups of theories, otherwise called models, suggest a single type (growth or decline) of life-span trend for all abilities, while the life-span approach suggests multidirectional change and differences among

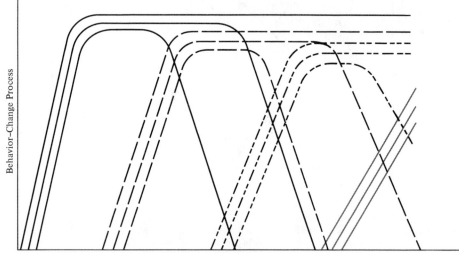

Figure 1.4   Examples of diverse (pluralistic) behavior changes. Each type of change differs in terms of onset, duration, and termination across the life span. *Source:* Adapted from P. B. Baltes, H. W. Rees, & L. P. Lipsitt. (1980). Reproduced, with permission, from the *Annual Review of Psychology,* Volume 31, © 1980 by Annual Reviews Inc.

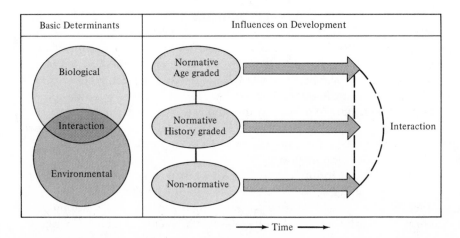

Figure 1.5   Influences that regulate life-span development. *Source:* P. B. Baltes, H. W. Reese, & L. P. Lipsitt. (1980). Reproduced, with permission, from the *Annual Review of Psychology,* Volume 31, © 1980 by Annual Reviews Inc.

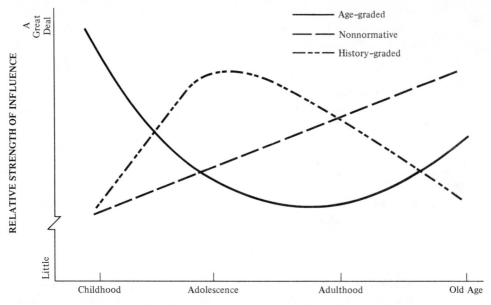

Figure 1.6   Prototypical profile of life-span influences. *Source:* P. B. Baltes, H. W Reese, &
L. P. Lipsitt. (1980). Reproduced, with permission, from the *Annual Review of Psychology,*
Volume 31, © 1980 by Annual Reviews Inc.

separate abilities or behaviors in terms of life-span trends. Such an approach
is pluralistic—it is concerned with the *description, explanation,* and *modification* of
intraindividual changes in behavior and interindividual differences in behavior changes from birth to death (P.B. Baltes & Goulet, 1970; P.B. Baltes et al.,
1980; Huston-Stein & P.B. Baltes, 1976). At this point, you might wish to
review Table 1.4, which presents a summary of how the organismic, mechanistic, psychoanalytic, and life-span developmental approaches view each of
the developmental issues we have discussed. Each is unique in its point of
view; each contributes something to our knowledge of adult development.

Each of the previously discussed models has attempted to explain
human development. Though each has its limitations, as well as its advantages, the one that appears to be most appropriate given the complexity of
human development is the life-span development model. This model stresses
the dialectic, dynamic nature of development during all phases of the life
cycle as opposed to models that stress progressive increases or decreases with
increasing age. Further, the life-span developmental approach highlights the
importance of individual differences in behavior and the ongoing interrela-
tionship among individuals of particular cohorts and their environments
across the life span.

PERSON-ENVIRONMENT INTERACTION

In order to understand the importance of individual differences in development and abilities during the life cycle as a function of the person-in-context,
it is important to discuss **person-environment interaction**. This topic will

also help illustrate how changes associated with the aging process have many implications for our everyday interaction with the environment. All aspects of behavior and performance can be conceived of as a result of the interaction or transaction between individual and environment (Pervin, 1968). Therefore, a match or "best fit" in terms of abilities, skills, and performance levels of the individual to the environment expresses itself via high performance, satisfaction, and little stress in the system (the individual), while a mismatch leads to poor performance and stress (Jahoda, 1961).

For successful performance and adaptation, individuals must match their ability levels to the demands of their environment. This fact is of great importance in understanding how people cope with change. Lawton and Nahemow (1973) view the aging process as continued adaptation to both the demands and pressures from the external environment and to the internal changes in physical and cognitive functioning that take place during the life cycle.

Lawton and Nahemow suggest that the individual's internal representation of the external world mediates this person-environment interaction. By internal representation we mean how a person conceives or views the environment, or what Lawton and Nahemow call "environmental cognition." Environmental cognition is affected by memory processes, perception, and cognitive style. In order to describe how the aging individual interacts with the environment, Lawton and Nahemow present what they call the **transactional model**, which has five components: (1) *degree of individual competence,* (2) *environmental press,* (3) *adaptive behavior,* (4) *affective responses,* and (5) *adaptation level.*

Degree of Individual Competence   Briefly, the degree of individual competence can be conceived of as the diverse collection of abilities residing within the individual. These include sensory processes, intelligence, learning abilities, and perceptual-motor speed. Further, the factors differ among themselves and vary over time between minimum and maximum limits that are specific to each person. In other words, each of us has particular strengths and weaknesses. These skills are different from one another, and our levels of each skill are different from those of our peers.

For example, recall our previous example regarding you and your roommate in terms of academic course work. Each of you has specific skills that enable you to do well in some of your courses and perhaps not well in others. You may do A+ work in English, A work in psychology, B work in biology, and C work in Speech, while your roommate may do A work in Speech, A+ work in biology, and C work in all other classes. Again, this highlights the importance of considering individual differences in understanding developmental change along the life cycle.

Environmental Press   Environmental press is defined as those forces from the environment impinging upon and affecting the individual. Examples include other individuals, the demands of a task, driving a car on the freeway, taking a test, and taking part in an activity. Simply, environmental press refers to any stimulation from the environment that comes in contact with individuals and places demands upon them.

Adaptive Behavior   According to Lawton and Nahemow, adaptive behavior can be considered the outer manifestation of individual competence and one *result* of the individual-environment transaction. Adaptive behavior is often observable as performance on a task, such as a test grade, golf score, or number of years driving without an accident.

Affective Responses   Affective responses are the inner (unobservable) aspects of the individual-environmental transaction that include the individual's evaluation and emotional reaction to the environment (e.g., a task, situation, event). Basically, affective responses refer to our subjective self-evaluation and assessment of our performance on a task. If we feel we performed poorly, we may feel distressed and consequently change our self-view.

Adaptation Level   **Adaptation level** can be considered the process whereby individual receptor processes (hearing, vision) tend to function at a comfortable level relative to external stimulation, so that stimulus of a given magnitude is perceived as neither strong nor weak (Helson, 1964; Lawton & Nahemow, 1973). Wohlwill (1966) has suggested the term *optimization principle,* an extension of adaptation level theory (Helson, 1964), to describe how stimuli that deviate in either direction from the adaptation level will be experienced with positive affect up to a limited point. Beyond this comfort zone, positive affect then decreases and again becomes negative as the stimulus increases beyond the adaptation level (Lawton & Nahemow, 1973).

You might think of adaptation level as the level at which you feel comfortable receiving stimulation from the environment. For example, the loudness level at which you normally listen to your stereo is your adaptation level. If the volume is either too low or too high, you feel uncomfortable. Your adaptation level may be different from that of your roommate or your parents.

The transactional model of Lawton and Nahemow (1973) and the work of Wohlwill (1966) have a number of significant implications for the everyday interaction of individuals with their environments at all phases of the life cycle. For instance, with regard to adults and the middle-aged, Barrett (1976) has presented a new approach to job design—the congruence model, which postulates that there is an optimal match or congruence among abilities, preferred attributes of a job, and the complexity of the job that results in maximization of one's resources in terms of individual productivity, work satisfaction, and organizational tenure (remaining with the same company). With regard to older adults, as Lawton and Nahemow (1973) state, one of the major tasks in planning environments for the aged, whether regarding institutional settings, the design of transportation systems, or that of housing facilities, is creating those environments to match the needs and competence levels of the older person.

In conclusion, regardless of our age, in order to deal effectively and competently with our environment, we must deal with environmental demands and tasks that match our ability levels. If stimulation or tasks above our ability levels are encountered, stress and poor performance may result. We might define our performance under these circumstances as indicative of **functional age**.

ADULT DEVELOPMENT IN CONTEXT

Many times thus far we have referred to the developing individual in the context of biological, psychosocial, and cultural-environmental changes or influences. What do we mean by this? Figure 1.7 illustrates adult development in the context of historical change and a variety of more narrowly defined factors that influence our behavior. While the assumptions inherent in our model are not new, we hope that this working model will help you to understand adult development more completely.

To the extent that there is something that is systematic and age-related about our behavior, the *age continuum* serves as our individual time line, which begins at birth and ends with death. We emphasize age continuum because, as Riegel's dialectics suggest, change in human development is the rule, rather than the exception. To *not* change or fail to cope seriously interferes with our development. This age continuum also serves as a focus or basis for the

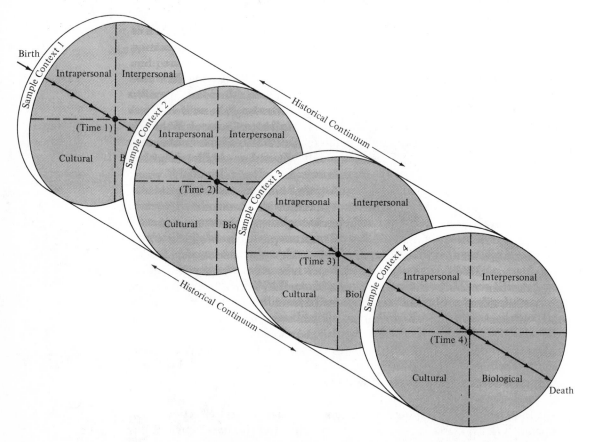

Figure 1.7 Adult development in context. Development occurs at both individual and historical levels, which interact with one another. Moreover, dimensions within individuals are in constant change, affecting how the individual reacts to the historical context and to life events. In order to understand adequately individual development, many samples of the individual's behavior in context must be studied.

interaction of what might be termed various sectors, arenas, or dimensions of influence. The *intrapersonal* dimension deals with our feelings, goals, abilities, or attitudes—in short, how we *internally represent* (at present, in the past, with respect to the future) our experiences. The topics of learning, memory, intelligence, personality, and sensation/perception are all quite relevant to the intrapersonal dimension of development.

The *interpersonal* dimension reflects our relationships with others in a number of contexts or situations—as workers, parents, children, or spouses.

The *biological* dimension most directly relates to topics such as health and illness, death, longevity and sexuality, while the *cultural* dimension not only encompasses issues of socialization, attitudes toward aging, work, and retirement, but also relates to questions of mental and physical health care.

Because we do not develop and age "in parts," each of the above dimensions or sectors of development overlaps with and affects the others. It is for this reason that dashed lines indicating boundaries that are somewhat fluid or fluctuating have been placed between our sectors in Figure 1.7. For example, our health *(biological)* is affected by and affects (1) our *knowledge* of the importance of eating a balanced diet or exercising *(intrapersonal)*, (2) our prevailing attitudes *(intrapersonal)* toward and access to health care *(cultural)* as well as (3) our relationships with others who provide this care or are affected by our own ill health *(interpersonal)*.

Figure 1.7 also suggests that each of these dimensions is itself changing, (hence the slight change in their shape) consistent with historical time (Neugarten & Datan, 1973), along a historical time (T) continuum. Each point in history serves as a larger context for our development. Besides changes in individuals, we must also consider changes in our culture that vary with the ebb and flow of historical changes that help to define the context of development. These cultural changes affect us at each phase of the life cycle. We label this historical continuum *contextual time.*

While we might draw several *samples* of a person's behavior at various chronological age points in time, each must be considered as a small slice of the individual's life in the context of (1) the influence of intrapersonal, interpersonal, biological, and cultural factors; (2) how that person represents relevant experiences at present; (3) the influences of experiences in the individual's past; and (4) those experiences that the individual can anticipate in the future. Therefore, numerous samples of behavior (e.g., sample context 1, sample context 2) could (and should) be taken to understand more fully this changing individual. Moreover, each sample of our individual's behavior in context is influenced by how each of our sectors is itself changing as a function of the passage of contextual time along our historical continuum. Hence, historical contexts change along a dimension of *contextual time,* as do individuals, who also change along *individual life time* (Neugarten, 1973), marked by the age continuum that begins with birth and ends with death.

We can use the transactional model of Lawton and Nahemow to understand the relationship between the developing individual and this changing, multidimensional context. Hence, one's competence, adaptive behavior (intrapersonal, biological), and environmental press (interpersonal, cultural) all interact to produce affective and behavioral responses that should, if development is to proceed, allow for and be a result of the individual's coping adaptively (reaching a comfortable adaptation level) with various aspects of the environment.

As you read about the various sectors of adult development and aging that we have arranged topically, try to think not only in terms of their relationship to one another and their influence on our development but also try to envision how these sectors have themselves changed over the last decade, for example.

Understanding adult development in this way will help you realize that while the topics we discuss are presented as if they were separate issues, in reality such dimensions of change are necessarily interwoven with one another and interwoven as well with changes in our culture. These influences change individuals and are being changed by them. As we first pointed out, your own development and aging can be understood best in *relative* terms, that is, relative to how each of the sectors or dimensions is interacting across the life cycle and relative to changes in each sector across contextual time.

SUMMARY

There are a number of problems associated with classifying individuals into specific segments of the life cycle in terms of chronological age, as well as with the meaning of such age periods. An overemphasis on one's age as a predictor of behavior, in combination with selective exposure to individuals varying in age, can lead to unrealistically positive and negative ideas and expectations termed *stereotypes* of the aging process and older persons. Equally important is separating normal and pathological aging. There are vast *individual differences* among persons at all points along the life cycle, as well as *intraindividual differences* within individuals at all points in development.

Though many definitions of age exist, it is thought by many researchers and theorists that the functional age concept provides the future direction for defining and discussing the effects of the aging process.

The major models of development are *organismic, mechanistic, psychoanalytic,* and *life-span developmental.* These models differ in terms of seven major issues that each approach to development must address: (1) *qualitative versus quantitative* change, (2) the *active versus passive* nature of man, (3) *nature versus nurture,* (4) *reductionistic versus holistic* development, (5) the issue of *stages,* (6) a *structure-function versus antecedent-consequence* interpretation of change, and (7) a *deterministic versus nondeterministic* approach to development. At the present time, all theories of development are somewhat limited, though the life-span developmental theory appears the most adequate relative to our present state of knowledge. According to this view, developmental change is both *multidimensional* and *multidirectional* and explained by *age-normative, history-normative,* and *nonnormative* influences.

The concept of *person-environmental interaction* suggests that for successful performance or *adaptation,* an individual must have ability levels matched to the demands of the environment. This *transactional model* assumes that a match in terms of abilities, skills, and performance levels of the individual to the environment expresses itself in high performance, satisfaction, and little stress in the system (the individual), while a mismatch leads to poor performance and stress. This assumption has numerous implications for the design of environments conducive to the *optimization* of functioning in adulthood.

A contextual model for understanding adult development was presented that incorporates *intrapersonal, interpersonal, cultural,* and *biological* factors. Each set of influences interacts to account for individual developmental change along an *age continuum* of *individual time.* These influences and their interactions are being changed as a function of the larger historical context in which they are embedded. They change along a *historical continuum* as a function of *contextual time.* Adult development and aging is therefore best understood in *relative* terms, emphasizing a changing individual in a changing environment.

KEY TERMS AND CONCEPTS

Stereotype

Myth

Aging

Aging process

Developmental tasks

Rites of passage

Biological age

Psychological age

Social age

Legal definition of age

Functional definition of age

Cultural ethics

Individual differences

Interindividual differences

Intraindividual differences

Intraindividual changes

Multidimensional change

Hypothetical constructs

Qualitative versus quantitative
change

Active versus passive role of
the organism

Nature versus nurture

Reductionist versus holist
development

Developmental stages

Structure-function versus
antecedent-consequent analysis of
behavior

Mechanistic model

Psychoanalytic model

Organismic model

Life-span development

Age-normative influences

History-normative influences

Nonnormative influences

Multidirectional change

Person-environment interaction

Adaptation level

Pluralism

Transactional model

Dialectics

Social clock

After reading this chapter, you should be able to answer the following questions:

- What are some of the major biological and physical changes experienced by most individuals during young adulthood? Middle adulthood? Late adulthood?
- What are the implications of changes in one's biological and physical condition for individuals of varying ages?
- What are some of the stresses of middle age? Old age?
- Why do some individuals reevaluate their life and goals during middle age?
- What diseases are responsible for the deaths of the majority of older adults?
- What are some of the major structural and functional changes in the brain as we age?
- How has life expectancy changed from ancient to modern times?
- How and why have trends in life expectancy changed in the United States and other industrialized nations since 1900?
- How do intrinsic and extrinsic factors affect life expectancy?
- What are the implications of increased life expectancy upon our economic system and institutions? Political and legal systems? Educational system? Health care system? Housing and transportation services?

CHAPTER 2

BIOLOGY OF AGING AND LONGEVITY

▪

INTRODUCTION

For many of us, the significance of development and aging lies in the age-related changes we experience in our physical or biological functioning, whether such changes are mild in nature (aches and pains, stiffness) or severe and life threatening (heart disease, cancer, stroke). Moreover, many persons are fascinated by the thought of living a long time or, for that matter, remaining ever young.

While such ideas reflect a belief in the physical or biological basis for the aging process, we learned in Chapter 1 that such factors are but *one* set of antecedents that contribute to development and aging. Nevertheless, they are a reality for many persons. They are not only important for research purposes (in ascertaining what the contribution of biological change is regarding one's ability to learn new information), but also in understanding that the biological aspects of the aging process can aid in separating fact from myth. Consequently, this sensitivity is an important determinant of our attitudes toward self and others at various points in our life span (J. F. Fries & L. M. Crapo, 1981). Adjusting and coping with physical change in themselves or in others is indeed a concern for adults of all ages. Biological and physical events can greatly affect our mobility, our relationships with others, and our own self-esteem. It is with these thoughts in mind that we discuss the inevitably related topics of the biological processes of aging, that is, aging at the most basic, cellular level, and longevity, the outcome of these underlying cellular changes.

The focus of this chapter is on the biological aspects of aging and longevity. In discussing these issues, we emphasize the implications of biological changes with aging on the body systems as well as the psychosocial effects of these changes. For instance, changes in physical appearance such as wrinkles or gray hair may lead to changes in self-concept for individuals who highly value their physical appearance.

We will also present specific biological and physiological theories that have been suggested to explain the aging process. For example, one popular theory suggests that the processes of aging are genetically preprogrammed. When this program "runs out," many bodily systems decline, and our lives soon come to an end. Finally, factors that relate to longevity, or how long we will live, will be presented and discussed, to the extent that these factors may either speed up or slow down the aging process and affect longevity.

As discussed earlier, the topics to be elaborated in this section will clarify how the course of biological development from birth to death is under the control of various biological/physiological processes. These processes play a significant role in how long we live, how quickly we age, and the observable physical changes that we experience as we get older. First, however, we will highlight some of the major biological, physiological, and physical changes that affect individuals at each major segment of the life cycle.

YOUNG ADULTHOOD

As we discussed in Chapter 1, the period of young adulthood is usually considered to be from approximately age 17 to the early forties. Though there are substantial differences among individuals, at this time in life most biological and physiological functions are now at their peak or most efficient level. By the middle-to-late twenties most of the physical growth and development of muscles, internal organs, and body systems has plateaued. In fact, most individuals in their twenties and thirties view themselves as being at their peak regarding health, life-style, sex life, and physical condition, a belief that is supported by research (Sinclair, 1969; Timiras, 1972).

The cardiovascular and pulmonary systems do begin to undergo slight changes, but these do not result in noticeable decreases in heart and lung functioning until about age 40. However, some definite changes do occur in the structure and function of the nervous system. For instance, the number of cells in the central nervous system decreases and the size of the brain decreases (Sinclair, 1969). We will have more to say about the brain and the aging process later on in this chapter. With proper activity, life-style, and diet, however, most functional (behavioral) declines can be avoided, and for the most part, one's peak condition can be maintained throughout the forties and fifties.

Regardless of one's diet, exercise, or activity level during this period of the life span, the body and organ systems do begin to change. For the most part, however, these changes are internal and are not generally felt or observed by the individual or others. Therefore, with regard to biological functioning, the period of young adulthood gives the illusion of being a stable period.

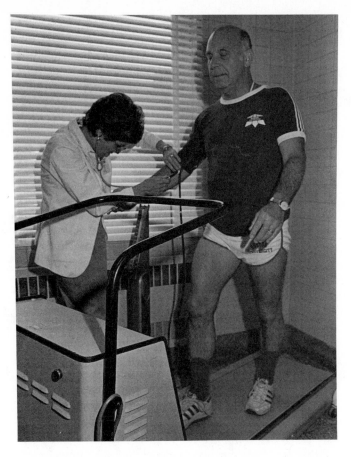

Keeping fit and taking care of one's health are keys to a sense of well-being in adulthood.

MIDDLE ADULTHOOD

The period of middle adulthood usually refers to that phase of the life cycle between the early forties and the early-to-middle sixties (D. J. Levinson, 1986). It is a period characterized by many biological, sensory, and perceptual changes. These changes, moreover, often have tremendous psychological significance for some persons. As we noted in Chapter 1, there is a great deal of interaction among the various dimensions of change in adulthood. Interestingly, though many of these changes have a profound impact on the middle-aged person, until recently, theorists and researchers have generally overlooked this stage of the life cycle.

For some individuals, middle age is a difficult time of transition, change, confrontation, and crisis. S. B. Sarason (1977), among others, suggests that middle age can be viewed as a time of confrontation between the realities of one's present life and situation and the myths and dreams of one's youth. During middle adulthood, individuals may begin to compare the "realities" of their occupation, family, and achievements with the myths, goals, and dreams of adolescence and young adulthood. Middle adulthood has popularly been perceived as a time of introspection and assessment of actual accomplishments in relation to previous goals. The greater the discrepancy between the current situation and the goals of young adulthood, the greater the potential for stress and crisis during middle adulthood. While this introspection may occur during middle adulthood, it is not unique to persons in their forties and fifties (M. Romaniuk & J. Romaniuk, 1981) and, in fact, it can occur at any point in the life cycle.

In general, however, the process of seeing oneself growing older is gradual and often begins in one's thirties but this perception is affected by such factors such as one's health, social class, gender, race, educational level, occupation, or personality.

Biological and Physical Changes

Perhaps the most noticeable of changes occurring at this stage of the life cycle are biological or physical in nature, since they are usually external and observable. They may trigger, for some persons, an assessment of the "time past" versus "the time left to live." For example, the *skin* begins to lose elasticity and wrinkles appear (Roseman, 1980). In her review of physical aging, Whitbourne (1985) notes that for both genders, the *hair* begins to lose color and luster and starts to fall out (see also Wantz & Gay, 1981). Regarding the *skeletal system,* longitudinal research suggests that, on the average, all the skeleton within the body has been transformed to bone by age 18, at which time we achieve our maximum height (Roseman, 1980). Thereafter, due to increased loss of calcium, increased porosity, and erosion, the *bones* become more brittle, and the articulating surfaces begin to deteriorate. This process contributes to arthritis, which, as reported by Wantz and Gay (1981), is increasing in frequency, especially in females during young adulthood. Further, due to settling of bones within the *spinal column,* changes in body curvature and a shrinkage of the intervertebral disks and vertebrae, individuals may "shrink" 1 to 2 inches in height over their life span, usually beginning during their fifties (Garn, 1975).

The *muscular system* begins to change noticeably during middle adulthood. Maximum muscle mass and strength reaches its peak by the early twenties and begins to decline in the thirties (Roseman, 1980; Wantz and Gay, 1981; Whitbourne, 1985). Further, *muscle tone* changes, and there is a redistribution of fat and subcutaneous tissue. Therefore, if persons are not careful about their diet and do not exercise, a "middle-age paunch" may "suddenly" appear in their late thirties or early forties.

In terms of the various *organ and bodily systems,* there are also some reliable changes that occur during middle adulthood (Bromley, 1974). For example, there are changes in the nervous system that begin after the cessation of neural maturation and growth, usually between 18 to 25 years of age. Vogel (1977) reports the central nervous system to reach its peak in terms of functioning neurons by age 30 (approximately 20 billion neurons).

During middle adulthood, the frequency of heart disease, cardiovascular failure, and hypertension begin to increase. Whitbourne's (1985) review of the evidence pertaining to the aging of the cardiovascular system suggests that though the structures within the cardiovascular system show some signs of change and degeneration with age, these disorders are highly dependent upon environmental factors such as smoking, stress, diet, and relaxation (see also Elias & Streeten, 1980; Wantz & Gay, 1981).

Finally, there is some decline in the secretion of gastric juices and the metabolism of proteins and fats. Since the digestive system does not work as efficiently as it once did, it is not uncommon for individuals to begin to noticeably gain weight, even though they are careful about their diet and exercise. These changes in bodily condition and physical appearance can have a pronounced effect on our life-style, self-concept, occupation, personality, and social relationships.

EFFECTS OF BIOLOGICAL AND PHYSICAL CHANGES

Think of the potential effect that these changes have on individuals whose self-concept, identity, and occupation hinge upon their physical appearance, such as actors and actresses. Sontag (1977) believes the physical changes that become evident during middle adulthood may be particularly difficult for some females, since our society traditionally views it as important for women to be beautiful and youthful in appearance. You might observe television commercials for beauty aids (such as creams to smooth the skin and lessen wrinkling) to validate this assumption about cultural standards for beauty. For some women, the physical consequences of aging may decrease their value and self-esteem, due to their accepting the myth that decreased physical beauty implies something negative. Fortunately, however, this view is changing.

Another physiological change that is apparently particular to women (since in males there are no sudden changes in the reproductive system characteristic of the climacteric) at this period of life is **menopause**, which is the cessation of the menstrual cycle (or end of the reproductive phase). For many women, menopause can be frightening and troublesome, while for others, it presents few, if any, difficulties. Menopause usually occurs during one's late forties or early fifties. Menopausal characteristics or symptoms of a physical nature include nausea, headaches, "hot flashes," and dizziness. Whitbourne's (1985) review of the literature suggests that there are often many negative psychosocial effects related to menopause (frequently stemming from a lack of accurate information about menopausal changes), such as decreased self-esteem, changes in one's identity, and depression due to the inability to produce offspring. For some women, menopause may create a sense of urgency—that time may be running out. It is important to note, however, that not all women experience negative symptoms associated with menopause, and in fact, menopause may be looked upon as positive in the sense that it frees the woman from the worry of becoming pregnant.

This potentially stressful period for the middle-aged woman is sometimes further complicated by the departure of the last child from the home, which is often referred to as the **empty nest**. Seeing one's children leave home may reinforce an awareness of time being limited. It should be noted that instead of having a negative, depressing effect upon mothers and fathers, the empty nest may have positive effects. It relieves the parents of financial, social, and temporal burdens. They now have the free time and available money to do the things they have always wanted to do. Perhaps they may take a cruise, return to school, pursue a career, or develop new personal interests.

One difference between the significance of such biological and physiological changes for the individual during young adulthood as opposed to those during middle age is that during middle adulthood the person is often all too aware of the changes—such as seeing the first gray hair. During young adulthood, we are seemingly unaware of these changes, whether they are occurring or not. If they are noticeable, they are often dismissed, due to the fact that they do not signal impending decline. Later on in life, individuals often come to the realization that youthful physical appearance and related activities are a thing of the past and there are now limitations in terms of their abilities and physical capabilities (McIlroy, 1984).

In addition to the observable changes in physical appearance during middle adulthood, health may begin to become a major concern. Individuals or their peers often begin to experience chronic health problems such as obesity, cancer, cardiovascular disease, hypertension, or digestive disorders (ulcers).

Observation of ourselves, our peers, and our parents aging physically and eventually dying, as well as observation of our children growing up and entering adulthood, often results in persons coming to the realization that they are in the middle of their life cycle. Consequently, death, once vaguely in the future, is now seen as inevitable. Jaques (1965) feels that we all will experience a **midlife crisis** in some form, as a result of the self-realization that we will eventually die. On the other hand, some researchers report that middle age is viewed as the prime of life (Borges & Dutton, 1976; Newman, 1982). In a series of studies, Cameron (1972, 1975) and P. Costa and McCrae (1978,1980) found *no* evidence of negative moods, feelings, or dissatisfaction among middle-aged males and females. Given the inconsistency of the research in the area, it would be clearly inaccurate for us to suggest that all middle-aged individuals experience a crisis. Seeing middle adulthood as a time of crisis can literally lead to a crisis of sorts if we fail to experience a middle-age crisis!

The Concept of Time

Often, if anxiety or a crisis is experienced as a consequence of menopausal changes or a perceived end to one's parental role, middle-aged individuals may change their **time perspective** and begin what is called **existential questioning** to deal with a crisis. This anxiety may be a cause or an outcome of such questioning (Kalish, 1985). For example, Neugarten (1976) reports that in middle adulthood, some individuals begin to view their lives in terms of "time left" as opposed to "time since birth." This is called a shift or change in *time perspective.* In fact, during middle age many individuals develop a sense of time urgency (Gould, 1979). They may feel that they are running out of time to complete the goals they set for themselves during young adulthood.

Interestingly, research suggests there are gender differences in relation to the shift in time perspective during middle age. For example, Baruch, Barnett, and Rivers (1983) that found middle-aged women do not usually measure their actual accomplishments against their personal expectations and do not generally express a concern that time is running out, as do men. McIlroy (1984) and Baruch et al. (1983) suggest this gender difference in time perspective may be due to differences in socialization throughout life with regard to career goals or personal goal orientation.

Perhaps as more women enter the work force, and current cohorts of female children are socialized toward career goal attainment, this difference between males and females may disappear. Another potential explanation for the observed gender difference in time perspective may be the fact that women live longer than men, which often results in women worrying about living too long and not being able to function independently, as opposed to not living long enough (Baruch et al., 1983).

A common theme during middle adulthood is existential questioning. Existential questioning involves reflection, introspection, self-analysis, and questioning about one's life and activities. Again, this may be brought about by biological changes or by changes in one's family. For example, both Gould (1972) and Neugarten (1976) emphasize how during middle age, individuals begin a process of self-reappraisal of their lives, their values, and themselves. In a sense, they may ask, "Who am I?" or "Where am I going?" If one has emphasized physical vitality, for example, perceived losses associated with menopause, the empty nest, or with the aging process may bring about such reassessments. It is important to point out that consistent evidence for such a crisis during one's middle years is lacking (P. Costa & McCrae, 1980).

LATER ADULTHOOD

As we noted in Chapter 1, later adulthood was defined as beginning at between 60 and 65 years of age. There are numerous biological, physiological, and physical changes that accompany normal aging at this point. Some of these changes include reduced muscle strength, loss of lean body mass and increase in body fat, impaired coordination and agility, reduced joint mobility, lessened cardiorespiratory endurance, loss of bone mass, and reduced oxygen intake (Pardini, 1984).

The magnitude of these changes varies considerably among individuals, but may be more substantial for the "old-old" (75+). Many of these changes can be remediated or postponed through diet, activity, and fitness programs well into one's seventies and eighties.

As we discussed earlier, the number of older Americans has increased substantially during the present century and will continue to grow. For example, the number of individuals 65 years of age or older in the United States has grown from 4.1 percent in 1900 to 11.9 percent in 1984. It is estimated that by the year 2000, this number will be 13 percent and may increase to 21.2 percent by the year 2030 (American Association of Retired Persons, 1986). Consequently, the above physical changes affect a significant number of persons. As we shall see later, these changes can have a substantial impact on older persons, their families, and on those who provide health care to the aged.

EXPLANATIONS FOR THE AGING PROCESS

The internal and external changes that occur with normal aging are considered to be under the control of various biological and physiological processes. Given the complexity of the human aging process, it should make sense that there is no one single theory or hypothesis that adequately explains all the factors involved. In the next section, we present examples of biological and physiological theories, in some cases more adequately considered hypotheses, that attempt to explain the normal aging process. The fundamental assumption of all biological and physiological theories is that the life span (how long a member of a species will live on the average) of any organism is ultimately determined by an inherited genetic program. As we shall see, there is no shortage of ideas about why we age.

Biological Theories

Biological theories are usually divided into two major categories: (1) **genetic**, which concentrate on genetic structure, formation, and processes as explanation for aging, and (2) **nongenetic**, which focus on changes that occur at the cellular and tissue level with age after cells have been formed (Finch & Hayflick, 1977; Shock, 1977). In each case, we will highlight one or two specific approaches within each major category to give an example of the general assumptions about aging.

GENETIC CELLULAR THEORIES

General Genetic Theory   The basic assumption of this theory is that there is some genetic program that sets the average upper limit of the life span for all species (all cells reproduce for a specific number of times and then die). This upper limit differs from species to species. For example, while the mayfly has an average life span of only 1 day, the rat's life span is 2 or 3 years, the dog's life span is 12 years, the horse's life span is 25 years, and the human's life span is 70 $^+$ years (Comfort, 1964; Shock, 1977). Also, in humans, it has been observed that individuals who have long-lived parents and grandparents live on the average longer than those who do not.

   This explanation makes common sense and is supported by the literature (Shock, 1977). This literature suggests that (1) there is a genetic program that sets the upper limits of life span in a species, that (2) there is some familial characteristic that influences differences in life span among individuals of a single species, and that (3) the expression of the basic genetic program can be altered by environmental factors.

Hayflick's Aging Clock   Hayflick (1965, 1977) and his associates have demonstrated that normal human cells will survive and reproduce in a culture for a certain period but will eventually enter a state of degeneration and then die. Human cells will reproduce themselves almost 50 times ($+$ 10 times) before they die. Therefore, on the basis of normal rates of metabolism, Hayflick has estimated that the full potential human life span is no more than 110 to 120 years. This means that if Hayflick is correct, and even if all pathological causes of death were eliminated, a human would eventually die as a result of the expiration of the programmed life span of the cells.

Though the aging process and the potential life span of all species is significantly related to genetic inheritance, other factors such as diet, exercise, and environment can affect both these factors.

Other examples of genetic theories are: (1) the *DNA* (deoxyribonucleic acid) *damage theory,* which assumes that damage to the cellular DNA results in death to the cell, (2) the *somatic mutation theory,* which suggests that as the body ages more and more of its normal cells are replaced by "mutant" (abnormal) cells; when sufficient quantities of these mutated cells are present, the external and internal characteristics of aging will appear, and (3) the *error theory,* which assumes that aging is the result of errors that may occur in the structure of DNA molecules or information transferred to messenger RNA.

NONGENETIC CELLULAR THEORIES

In general, all nongenetic cellular theories of aging assume that with the passage of time changes take place in molecules and structural elements of cells that impair their effectiveness to function *after* these cells have been formed.

Wear and Tear   This theory is based on the assumption that living organisms behave like machines. That is, when things get old, they wear out and finally become unusable. In general, this theory views human aging as analogous to the aging and deterioration of a car, a television, or any other machine or appliance (Shock, 1977).

This theory assumes that as a result of use (wear and tear), various parts of the human machine (organs) finally become worn out. Though this theory appears to be "good common sense" and easy to understand, the machine analogy is not adequate. Basically, unlike machines, which cannot repair themselves, living organisms have developed many mechanisms that permit self-repair, such as new skin tissue replacing old tissue.

Accumulation Theories   Cellular aging has also been attributed to the accumulation of deleterious (toxic) substances in the aging organism (Shock, 1977). There are two explanations that are considered accumulation theories: one involving changes in the body's ability to eliminate metabolic waste, and the other pertaining to changes in **collagens**.

The *metabolic waste theory* suggests that aging occurs as metabolic waste products, which are considered injurious, gradually accumulate in the cells of the body. One such waste product is **lipofuscin** (age pigment), which begins to accumulate in various organ systems with advancing age. After many years of accumulation, lipofuscin becomes manifest as liver spots on the skin. It is assumed that the deposit and accumulation of lipofuscin results from age-related changes in the body's ability to metabolize or effectively process certain nutrients. Therefore, metabolic waste accumulation appears to be more of a symptom of aging rather than a cause.

The *collagen theory* is based upon the established relationships between changes in the body's fibrous proteins (collagen and elastin) and aging (Shock, 1977; Whitbourne, 1985). Basically, collagen and elastin fibers are quite abundant within the body. In fact, they are the two most common proteins in all connective tissues. These fibrous proteins are found in muscles, joints, and bones. Research has demonstrated that with increased age these fibrous proteins become thicker, less elastic, and less soluble (Whitbourne, 1985). They tend to mass and replace existing tissues. Age-related changes in collagen and elastin fibers are associated with various external signs of growing older such as wrinkling of the skin (exacerbated by exposure to sunlight), sagging muscles, and slower healing of cuts and wounds. Although this theory is plausible, it still can be considered only a tentative explanation for aging and must await further experimental verification.

In general, nongenetic theories appear to explain internal and external changes that are associated with the aging process, such as liver spots, but do not adequately explain the *cause* of the aging process. Other nongenetic theo-

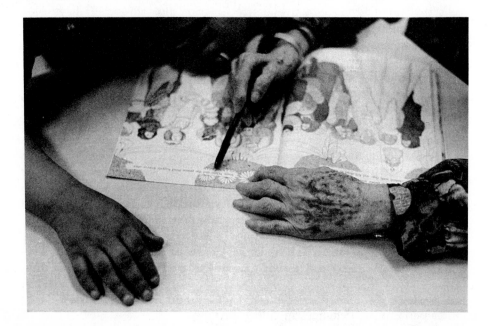

One common physical manifestation of the aging process is the accumulation of lipofuscin, which appears as liver spots on the skin.

ries are (1) the *deprivation theory,* which assumes aging is due to deprivation of essential nutrients and/or oxygen required by the cells of the body, (2) the *free radical theory,* which suggests that cell death, and subsequent aging, results from the damaging effects of the formation of "free radicals" (unstable atoms of the cell), and (3) the *cross-linkage theory,* which postulates aging as the result of the formation of cross-linkages (bridges) between the protein molecules that form the intercellular material in the body.

Physiological Theories

Physiological theories attempt to explain the aging process and the life span of organisms either (1) on the basis of a breakdown in the performance of a single organ system, or (2) in terms of impairments in physiological control mechanisms. Generally, physiological theories of aging have focused attention on a single organ system in order to explain the total effects of aging and are therefore often referred to as single organ system theories (hypotheses) (Shock, 1977).

Single Organ Systems　Failures in a number of specific organ systems have been proposed as the cause of aging. For example, since failure of the heart and blood vessels represents a primary cause of death among the aged, failure of the *cardiovascular system* has often been regarded as a primary cause of aging. Another theory from the physiological perspective assumes aging can be attributed to the slowing of metabolic processes at the cellular level. Since the rate of cellular metabolism is regulated by the *thyroid gland,* aging is thought to be due to the inability of the thyroid gland to supply adequate amounts of hormones. It has also been suggested that since the *pituitary gland* plays a central role in the control of the adrenal and thyroid glands, aging could be caused by a failure of the pituitary gland to carry out its functions appropriately.

Physiological Control Mechanisms　The human immune system protects the body not only against microorganisms that invade the body but also against atypical mutant cells that may form in the body. Basically, the immune system carries out this protective function by generating antibodies that react to foreign organisms by forming special cells that engulf and digest these foreign cells and substances. The aging process has a marked impact on the capabilities of the immune system. Production of antibodies reaches a peak during adolescence and then declines. Research indicates that this decline is so dramatic that, in some species, senescent (old) animals retain only one-tenth of the immune capability of younger ones (Shock, 1977).

　　This approach is referred to as the *immunological theory* of the aging process. There are several variations of the immunological theory of aging. The first type is based on the assumption that the basic impairment in the immune system is a loss in the ability to recognize slight deviations in molecular structure and cellular characteristics. Therefore, cells that have undergone mutation and would have ordinarily been destroyed by the immune system are no longer recognized and are permitted to grow and develop to the detriment of the organism.

Another variant of immunological theory suggests even though the immune system of the aged organism recognizes these deviations and foreign substances, it is unable to produce an adequate supply of antibodies to destroy them (Shock, 1977).

Finally, the *autoimmune theory* of aging (Blumenthal & Birns, 1964) suggests that aging results from the development of antibodies that destroy even the normal cells in the body. That is, the autoimmune antibodies function in a self-destructive manner. Further, various organ systems may begin to reject their own tissues. The variety of theories about the aging process at the biological level are summarized in Table 2.1.

The exact trigger or underlying factor for the aging process is still to be determined. Current scientific thinking emphasizes the roles of genetics and biological processes in the aging process. Until recently, some scientists thought a good method of studying the genetic/physiological aspects of the aging process was to examine individuals with a rare but fatal disease called **progeria**.

Progeria is a strange, incurable disease that rapidly turns children into aged individuals. For instance, a child with progeria may be eight years old chronologically but have the physical appearance and bodily condition of someone 85 years of age. Victims of this disease lose their hair, suffer heart attacks, and become arthritic. At the present time, the cause is still unknown, and there is no cure. The onset of symptoms usually occurs in late childhood, and death usually occurs in one's teens.

Though it was once thought that by studying this disorder scientists would learn more about the aging process, this line of research has proved fruitless since the overall resemblance of individuals with progeria to older adults is quite limited. For instance, researchers have found that individuals with progeria rarely suffer from diseases or disorders that are usually associated with the normal aging process, such as cataracts and cancer.

TABLE 2.1

THEORIES OF BIOLOGICAL AGING

Genetic Theories	Nongenetic Theories	Physiological
Genetic program	Wear and tear	Cardiovascular system
Hayflick's aging clock	Accumulation of toxins	Thyroid gland
DNA damage	Metabolic waste (lipofuscin)	Pituitary gland
Somatic mutation	Collagen	Breakdown of immune system
Error in DNA	Deprivation of nutriments	Autoimmune (self-destruction of normal cells)
	Free radical theory	
	Cross-linkage of proteins	

See N. W. Shock. (1977). Biological theories of aging. In J. E. Birren and K. W. Schaie (Eds.), *Handbook of the psychology of aging* (pp. 103–115). New York: Van Nostrand Reinhold.

The Brain and the Aging Process

Without a functional central nervous system, it would indeed be difficult to do most of the things that we do on an everyday basis. Our ability to think, reason, and act in response to incoming information from the environment depends on the integrity of our central nervous system (brain and spinal cord). So, too, is our emotional response to what we or others think, do, or say. Implicitly, we might assume that in the absence of other causal factors, changes in the structure and function of the brain would help to explain a variety of the behavioral changes discussed throughout this study of adult development and aging. It is for this reason that we will examine some of the major changes in the brain with the aging process.

Bondareff (1980, 1985), R. D. Adams (1980), and Whitbourne (1985) discuss the major normal structural changes in the human brain that accompany aging. In most cases, our information about such changes comes from studies of animals, or from postmortem studies of individuals who have given their permission for such analyses. Whitbourne (1985) emphasizes the difficulty in getting accurate information about age-related changes in brain tissue. Autopsies may not be done quickly enough, and death itself may cause changes in the brain. Moreover, if persons die, they are probably not "normal"—if either disease or injury has occurred, it may alter the structure and function of the brain. A last concern relates to the wisdom of studying animals to learn about human beings; there may be important species differences that limit the validity of certain information about brain function gleaned from animal research. Because we cannot at present routinely study aging changes in an individual's brain function while that person is alive (although newer computerized brain techniques can be used in vivo) (see Carlson, 1986), our studies are limited largely to cross-sectional comparisons of autopsied brains from different individuals of varying ages.

As with psychological or behavioral change, the aging of the central nervous system occurs at different rates for different persons. Moreover, different regions of the brain seem to age differently. As a general rule, however, changes in the brain do occur in a very gross anatomical sense (Whitbourne, 1985).

Relative to younger brains, older brains are smaller. From the ages of 20 to 90, the brain loses between 5 to 10 percent of its weight. The extent of this loss varies with the individual's health and with the region of the brain studied (Whitbourne, 1985). Brain volume also declines with age (especially after age 50) by approximately 15 to 20 percent. As the volume of brain tissue shrinks, the brain's appearance also changes. The *gyri* (swellings) of the brain become smaller, and the *fissures* or *sulci* (valleys between the gyri) widen. Again, such changes vary with health status. With age, the volume of the ventricular fluid increases, compressing adjacent tissue (Bondareff, 1980), leading to increased ventricular size, due as well to the loss of brain cells.

The central feature of the aging brain structurally is the loss of *neurons* (nerve cells) that receive and transmit information. The brain is very complex and contains more than 20 billion neurons and even more (120 billion) *glial cells* (nonneuronal brain cells that serve a nutritional and supportive function)

(Carlson, 1986; R. F. Thompson, 1975). The interconnections between these neurons are nearly infinite. While some neurons degenerate and die (dying neurons are not replaced), others do not. When a neuron dies, all its connections (actually a small space between neurons referred to as *synapses*—there are thousands per cell) with other neurons die as well. Synapses (which also help integrate information from various parts of the nervous system) occur on the *cell body* and the *dendrite* of the neuron. These aspects of the brain cell (cell body, dendrites) are the site of the neuronal electrical and chemical activity characteristic of brain function. With age, these cell bodies change in appearance (become more irregular) and accumulate the yellowish pigment lipofuscin, which interferes with neuronal function (protein metabolism). Additionally, the fluid surrounding the nucleus of the cell body develops spaces (vacuoles).

Extending from each cell body are dendrites, whose function is to receive incoming information from other neurons. While they are normally intricately intertwined, with age this organization becomes more simplified, and eventually the cellular dendrites disappear altogether, meaning that less information is received by each neuron (Whitbourne, 1985). Consequently, less information can be transmitted via the *axon* to other neurons, or to muscles and glands. Also, with age, within the cell body, **neurofibrillary tangles** are more likely to develop, where nerve fibers in the cell body and dendrite increase in number and become interwoven, pushing the nucleus aside and interfering with the functioning of the cell body (R. D. Adams, 1980; Bondareff, 1980). These neural tangles are found in normal brains but are especially prevalent in the brains of persons with certain forms of **dementia** (see Chapter 13). Neuronal structures may also degenerate due to a reduction in cerebral circulation, either from normal changes in cardiac output, heart disease, a progressive narrowing **(atherosclerosis)** and hardening **(arteriosclerosis)** of arterial walls, or the shutting off (produced by *infarcts* of varying sizes) of blood flow gradually (or all at once, as with a major stroke). There are many (see Whitbourne, 1985) who believe (with some support) that regular aerobic (oxygen-generated) activity—running, swimming, tennis—can slow down this degenerative cardiovascular process. Bondareff (1980) suggests that changes in the volume of the fluid surrounding neurons (and its composition) may also contribute to neuronal loss.

With age, and especially in certain forms of dementia, **senile plaques** are more likely to form. Senile plaques are abnormally hard clusters of damaged or dying neurons, present in specific areas of the brain (see below), whose presence interferes with neuronal function. As neurons die, certain types of glial cells also increase in size. Glial cells may also perform their function of providing nutriments for brain cells less adequately with age.

Thus, we can observe a number of structural changes in neurons with age. Such changes may be caused by a *critical loss* of a certain number of neurons especially important to the storage and reception of information (termed pacemaker neurons) (Whitbourne, 1985). Such changes occur throughout the brain, but we emphasize critical loss because there is a great deal of redundancy (duplication) of function in the *cerebral cortex* (Whitbourne, 1985).

The cortex is the part of the brain mediating more complex behaviors, and is organized into *hemispheres* that function somewhat independently of one another. These hemispheres appear to mediate different functions. For example, the *left hemisphere* primarily controls speech/language or verbal ability, and mathematical/symbolic skills, while the *right hemisphere* primarily controls spatial and complex perceptual abilities (Carlson, 1986; R. F. Thompson, 1975). With age, right-hemisphere functioning appears to decline at a greater rate than does left-hemisphere function (Klisz, 1978).

In addition to the above structural changes, the concentration of *neurotransmitter substances* that make possible synaptic transmission appears to decline with age (R. D. Adams, 1980; Whitbourne, 1985). Thus, synaptic transmission and coordination is impaired.

Various *functional* areas of the cortex controlling sensory experience are differentially subject to neuronal loss with age, particularly the *occipital* (visual), *parietal* (skin and muscle senses), and parts of the *temporal* (hearing) and *frontal* (motor control) lobes (see Figure 2.1). The loss in the various areas of the *associative* (nonsensory or nonmotor) *cortex* (R. F. Thompson, 1975) that control higher cognitive (thinking) functions (e.g., long-term memory, abstract reasoning, symbolization) as well as coordinate the sensorimotor cortical areas is less severe (Whitbourne, 1985). With appropriate stimulation or experience, the associative cortex appears to show a great deal of **plasticity**. Neuronal connections may be regenerated or neuronal loss may be less (Lerner, 1984; Whitbourne, 1985) due to the neuronal redundancy in this area

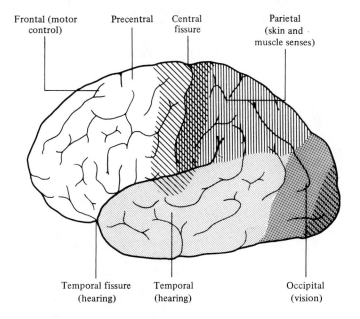

Frontal (motor control)   Precentral   Central fissure   Parietal (skin and muscle senses)

Temporal fissure (hearing)   Temporal (hearing)   Occipital (vision)

Figure 2.1   Major subdivisions of the brain in relation to fissures (sulci). All remaining parts (noncrosshatched) of the parietal, preoccipital, temporal, and frontal areas that are not sensory or motor in nature are termed *association* areas (higher mental process.) *Source:* R. F. Thompson. (1975). *Introduction to physiological psychology.* New York: Harper & Row. Reprinted by permission.

of the cortex (resulting in more frequent activity by fewer cells or more constant activity by healthy cells) that makes such plasticity to a certain extent possible (Whitbourne, 1985) (see Figure 2.2). Transmitter substances in these areas remain relatively constant, and thus wisdom (use of experience), abstract reasoning, judgment, foresight, or long-term memory may be relatively unaffected by aging (Bondareff, 1980, 1985).

In addition to neuronal loss in the cerebral cortex, evidence for such degeneration is found in certain areas of the *brain stem,* which connects the cortex with the spinal cord. Neurotransmitter deficits in certain areas of the brain stem seem to be linked to disturbances in sleep patterns, short-term (secondary) memory deficits, and overarousal (R. D. Adams, 1980; R. F. Thompson, 1975; Whitbourne, 1985). Changes in fine motor coordination, large muscle control, and both visual and auditory function, however, seem to be linked to age-related changes in various cortical areas (see above).

We do see some reliable evidence for neuronal or transmitter substance deficits in certain areas of the cerebral cortex, while due to overlapping neuronal connections, other functions seem to be less sensitive to aging deficits and demonstrate a great deal of plasticity due to increased experience or stimulation (mental or physical exercise). Furthermore, declines in brain

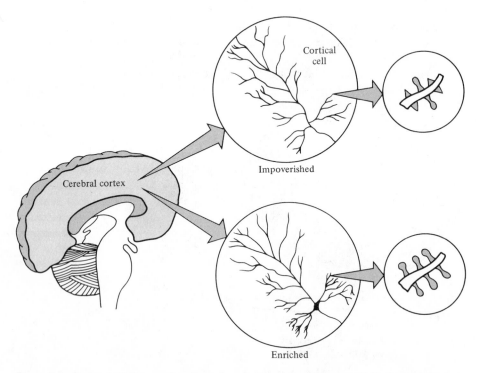

Figure 2.2 Brain plasticity as a function of environmental enrichment. Cells from cerebral cortex of rats put in an enriched environment show more numerous branching of dendrites that stretch out to other brain cells and more fully developed dendritic spines, which receive chemical messages from the other cells. *Source: New York Times.* (1985, July 30). Copyright © 1985 by The New York Times Company. Reprinted by permission.

function vary both within (by cortical or subcortical area) and between persons, and such changes are highly subject to, and confounded by, disease. While these alterations in brain structure and function do occur, many older persons can compensate for behavioral deficits in memory, fine motor coordination, or the learning of new information by relying on their experience, planning, and organizational skills to maintain effective functioning on an everyday basis.

LONGEVITY/LIFE EXPECTANCY

As we noted earlier, theories of aging explain the aging process at a biological (molecular) level. **Longevity** is a term indexing how long we live. One necessary but unfortunate outcome of living long enough to experience aging-related changes we have discussed is that when these changes are disruptive enough to interfere with vital functions, we die. Thus, how long we have lived when we die (or how much of our potential life span we achieve) has been defined as **longevity**. As discussed before, a number of researchers and theorists suspect that there is an upper limit to the life span for each species that is based on a genetic program for that species (Lansing, 1959; Shock, 1977).

Closely related to longevity is **life expectancy**. Life expectancy refers to how much of the *maximum life span* for that species the individual organism attains, or the *average* length of life for a member of that species. This distinction between average length of life and the maximum length of life for a species is illustrated in Table 2.2. As this figure indicates, currently humans (in the United States and other industrialized countries) usually have a life expectancy (longevity) of 70 to 80 years, though they have the potential to live 110 to 130 years (maximum life span). For purposes of our discussion to follow, we will use the term life expectancy.

TABLE 2.2

LENGTH OF LIFE FOR SELECTED ANIMALS AND INSECTS

Organism	Average Length of Life (in years)	Maximum Length of Life (in years)
Human	70–80	110–130
Domestic dog	10–12	34
Domestic cat	10–12	26+
Fruit fly	—	37 days
Worker ant	—	5 years

Source: Adapted from J. E. Birren. (1964). *The psychology of aging* (pp. 57, 58, 59). Englewood Cliffs, N.J.: Prentice-Hall; and A. K. Lansing. (1959). General biology of senescence. In J. E. Birren (Eds.), *Handbook of aging and the individual* (pp. 119–135). Chicago: University of Chicago Press.

HISTORICAL, CURRENT, AND FUTURE TRENDS IN LIFE EXPECTANCY

Human life expectancy has exhibited a phenomenal change from the time of the ancient Greeks to the present. For instance, life expectancy at birth in ancient Greece was 18 years (500 B.C,), 25 years in ancient Rome (A.D. 100), and 35 years in thirteenth-century England. It is estimated that the median age in the Colonies just prior to the Revolutionary War was 20 years of age. From 1775 to 1900 in the United States, the average life expectancy increased from about 15 years to 35 years.

The major increase in life expectancy on a worldwide basis, from ancient times to the beginning of this century (1900), can be attributed to factors such as improved housing, sanitation, and the development and use of antiseptics. Since 1900, life expectancy has increased due to the passage of public health laws and codes, better sanitation and hygiene, immunization for childhood diseases, improved medical care and medical practice, and improved nutrition (Strehler, 1975).

It is important to note that the basic increments in life expectancy with each subsequent year have been relatively minor since the 1940s; the most significant increase in life expectancy in the United States occurred between 1900 to 1940. This is due to the fact that the major causes of death in old age are diseases that have no known cure at the present time.

Health

Older adults tend to have more chronic diseases than the young, older adults have about twice as many hospital stays as young adults, and their stays last almost twice as long (T. Hickey, 1980). However, the majority of older adults report themselves as being in "good" or "excellent" health. This is contrary to the stereotyped view of the physically infirm, disabled, sick older adult. Interestingly, research suggests that while the self-perception of health and health status are not identical, these self-assessments of health by older adults are quite accurate (Siegler & P. T. Costa, 1985). For example, LaRue, Bank, Jarvik, and Hetland (1979) found self-reports of health to provide a reasonable and valid means of health assessment when compared to physicians' ratings of older adults.

Additionally, as reported by Cockerham, Sharp, and Wilcox (1983), individuals of both sexes over age 60 tend to perceive their own health in a significantly more positive manner than do younger age-groups. Cockerham et al. (1983) suggest this positive evaluation by older adults is due to adjustment to or living with the acquired medical or physical conditions common to the elderly. That is, they have learned to accept such conditions as arthritis and high blood pressure. The major difference between subgroups of aging persons in health status appears to be between whites and nonwhites: 70.2 percent of whites report good to excellent health, compared to 56.2 percent of nonwhites, while only 28.8 percent of whites report fair to poor health, compared to 43 percent of nonwhites. Perhaps this difference can be attributed to the greater availability of medical care and services to whites at early points in their lives.

In general, physicians tend to give low priority to the medical needs of older adults for two reasons. First, it is assumed that being sick is a necessary part of being old, and second, many elderly believe that symptoms of illness are normal and inevitable results of aging and therefore do not seek help. For example, D. K. Harris and Cole (1980) report a study conducted by the University of Illinois based on 900 older adults who were homebound. It was found that many of the individuals were too ill even to walk to the door and had gone for months without seeking medical aid; they thought that because they were old, they were supposed to be sick. Also, physicians tended to write off reported symptoms as "normal" in the elderly person. Often, routinely treatable illnesses, such as heart attacks, viral infections, and even appendicitis, may go undiagnosed!

Another explanation for why physicians give low priority to the needs of the elderly rests with their medical training, which primarily emphasizes acute illness. Since older adults are more likely to suffer from chronic illness, often with no known cure, the situation becomes frustrating and depressing to many physicians. Geriatric medicine has received little, if any, attention in the U.S. medical schools, a situation that creates a void in the physician's knowledge about caring for and treating older adults. In a survey conducted in 1976 by a committee of the United States Congress, only 10 medical schools out of 104 indicated that they had or were planning to include geriatrics as a specialty area. Therefore, physicians in most instances are not adequately trained to deal effectively with the medical problems of old age, though this situation will likely change in the future. Indeed, recent discussions of geriatric medicine (Rowe & Minoker, 1985) reflect this emerging sensitivity to the unique health care needs of older adults.

LEADING CAUSES OF DEATH

Data from government sources (U.S. Public Health Service, 1981; Statistical Abstract of the United States, 1986) and other sources (T. Hickey, 1980) suggest the leading cause of death for older adults to be chronic disease. The ten leading causes of death for persons age 65 and over, for both genders in the United States, are (in rank order): (1) diseases of the heart, (2) cancer (malignant neoplasms), (3) stroke (cerebrovascular), (4) influenza and pneumonia, (5) arteriosclerosis, (6) diabetes, (7) accidents (motor vehicle and others), (8) bronchitis, emphysema, and asthma, (9) cirrhosis of the liver, and (10) kidney problems.

With regard to this ranking, heart disease, stroke, and cancer account for three-fourths of all the deaths of older adults. These chronic illnesses have no medical cure and have often been called the "companions of the aged," since they are so prevalent among older adults. However, while 80 percent of older persons have at least one chronic condition, for over 50 percent of these same individuals the condition does not interfere with or restrict their activities. Additionally, these chronic conditions tend to vary by gender. Older women have higher rates of arthritis, diabetes, high blood pressure, and

BOX 2.1

OLD, BUT NOT SENILE

The following article was written by Margaret E. Kuhn, national convenor of the Gray Panthers.

There is a theory of health-cost containment in vogue in Washington and among certain members of the medical establishment that suggests that good old supply-and-demand principles can reduce not only what it costs to treat the elderly and the poor but also the whole cost to our society of health care.

The theory goes like this: If sick elderly and poor people are forced to pay a larger share of the costs of treatment, they will shop around for less expensive care and the marketplace of health providers will be so fearful of losing money that it will respond by finding new and less costly ways to attract "buyers."

This theory is worse than just utter nonsense—it is an insult to the intelligence of Americans and a cruel attempt to shift the burdens of runaway health costs onto the shoulders of our most vulnerable citizens: the old and the poor.

This punitive approach is one of many put forth in the urgent attempt to finance Medicare and Medicaid into the next century. In addition to cuts in both programs by the Reagan administration, the latest proposal would require the elderly sick—regardless of means—to pick up part of the cost of the first 60 days of hospitalization. This may sound reasonable for those with adequate incomes, but it does not make sense for a person on Social Security with only $284.30 a month to live on when the average cost of a day in the hospital is $245.

Can anyone seriously believe that an elderly person who falls sick will be able to shop around for less costly health care? Where? Another community hospital? Another family doctor? Does the president really think that elderly sick people can do what others have failed to do—confront the obscenely high costs of medical care in this country?

The current plan does one thing and only one thing: It allows the government to run out on its commitment to the health of older citizens—and it does nothing whatsoever to contain the greed of the health care industry. In effect, it says to the elderly that our government is too cowardly and ineffectual to deal with this hot issue, so older people must bear the burden.

Here are the dimensions of that burden:

Hospital costs last year rose three times faster than the inflation rate, and there has been an alarming 450 percent increase in the hospital day rate since 1950. Further increases will occur with the closing of community hospitals and the emergence of large chains of hospitals operating for profit. And health care for the elderly costs four times what it does for other Americans. Social Security provides the total income for more than a third of our nation's population over 65. Medicare is the only health insurance that most of the 26 million older Americans have. Even with that, Medicare covers only about 45 percent of their total day-to-day medical expenses.

The administration has proposed a "trade-off" with older citizens: in exchange for cost-sharing of the already bloated medical costs of the first 60 days of hospitalization, the government proposes to pick up the total cost of care after that period. What they fail to point out is that most hospital stays average about 11 days and that less than one percent of the hospitalized elderly would use the "catastrophic illness" coverage. I believe the government should provide both kinds of coverage and could finance both if it would find the courage to address the real problem.

The administration has said it wants to increase everyone's consciousness of health care costs—from patients to hospital administrators. It seems to me that the very last people in this country who need a lesson in cost awareness are the elderly, most of whom count pennies in the supermarket, deny themselves even the most modest pleasures, and even avoid seeking proper medical care because they fear the costs.

Let the administration direct its message to those who have the primary power to cut medical costs: hospital profiteers who abuse the Medicare system by adding phony charges and inflating legitimate costs, doctors who ignore "reasonable charge" levels and bill whatever they please, proprietary nursing homes that continue to charge unconscionable rates despite one of the most shameful records of abuse in the history of modern medicine, physician teams

(continued)

who refuse to accept Medicare assignment and order unnecessary tests, drugs, procedures, and in-hospital stays.

And let the message be heard by politicians who mistakenly believe that once people reach age 65 they lose their right to decent, affordable health care and their ability to fight for it. Older Americans have contributed much to this society and will continue to contribute to the well-being of future generations. The issues of age challenge the whole society and are the levers for change.

Source: Margaret E. Kuhn. (1983, July 31). We're old, not senile, Ronald. *New York Times.*

vision impairments than do men. Men have higher rates of asthma, chronic bronchitis, hernias, ulcers, and hearing impairments.

Also, health condition is related to economic status at all stages of the life cycle. A good illustration of the relationship between health and economics in older adults, as well as the difficulty of their situation, is illustrated in an article taken from the *New York Times* (1983) by Ms. Margaret E. Kuhn, national convenor of the *Gray Panthers* (see Box 2.1). This article nicely demonstrates the difficulty older adults have with obtaining adequate health care and the relationship between economic conditions and health. Moreover, L. W. Gerson et al. (1987) have found impaired physical health to relate strongly to lessened mental health among the aged. When older persons could not engage in everyday activities, mental health was impaired as well.

Since health condition is related to a number of behaviors and activities in older adults (personality, mental health, learning and memory, skilled performance, and intelligence) (Siegler & P. T. Costa, 1985), it is important that researchers take a more active interest in the health disorders of old age. But as medical science makes new discoveries regarding these diseases, for example, cures for cancer, heart disease, organ replacements, the increments in life expectancy may again become substantial. K. Davis (1985) notes that mortality among elderly persons has dropped substantially over the last decade due to improved treatment of heart disease and cardiovascular disease, though this increase is not as dramatic as it might seem.

This fact is illustrated in Table 2.3. As indicated in the table, for white

TABLE 2.3

LIFE EXPECTANCY AT BIRTH, BY SEX AND RACE, FOR SELECTED YEARS

Sex and Race	Cohort		
	1900	1950	1978
White males	46.6	66.5	70.2
Nonwhite males	32.5	59.1	65.0
White females	48.7	72.2	77.8
Nonwhite females	33.5	62.9	73.6

Source: *Population Bulletin.* (1980). Vol. 35, no. 4, p.16. Washington, DC: Population Reference Bureau, Inc.

males, during the 50-year period from 1900 to 1950, predicted life expectancy at birth increased by approximately 20 years (46.6 years to 66.5 years). But for the 28-year period from 1950 to 1978, predicted life expectancy at birth only increased about 4 years.

A life expectancy table is presented in Table 2.4. This table was developed by Woodruff (1977) and lists ages and predicted life expectancies for the ages of individuals most likely to be reading this text. The data indicates that, for example, if you are a 20-year-old Caucasian male, you are predicted to live to be 71.4 years of age. It should be noted that the figures presented here are theoretical approximations, as well as norms and averages. There will be many individual differences regarding how many persons your age will reach or exceed this prediction. Additionally, many factors affect these projected life expectancy figures, and these will be discussed shortly.

Life Expectancy in Other Countries

How does life expectancy at birth in the United States correspond with that in other nations? The answer to this question can be found in Table 2.5. As observed here, life expectancy in the United States is greater than in many

TABLE 2.4

LIFE EXPECTANCY FOR SELECTED AGES BY SEX AND RACE

Age	Caucasian		Black		Oriental	
	Male	Female	Male	Female	Male	Female
18	71.2	78.6	66.1	74.6	73.2	80.6
19	71.3	78.6	66.2	74.6	73.3	80.6
20	71.4	78.6	66.3	74.7	73.4	80.6
21	71.5	78.7	66.5	74.7	73.5	80.7
22	71.6	78.7	66.6	74.8	73.6	80.7
23	71.7	78.7	66.8	74.8	73.7	80.7
24	71.8	78.8	66.9	74.9	73.8	80.8
25	71.9	78.8	67.1	74.9	73.9	80.8
26	71.9	78.8	67.3	75.0	73.9	80.8
27	72.0	78.9	67.4	75.1	74.0	80.9
28	72.1	78.9	67.6	75.1	74.1	80.9
29	72.2	78.9	67.8	75.2	74.2	80.9
30	72.2	79.0	68.0	75.3	74.2	81.0
31	72.3	79.0	68.1	75.4	74.3	81.0
32	72.4	79.0	68.3	75.4	74.4	81.0
33	72.4	79.1	68.5	75.5	74.4	81.1
34	72.5	79.1	68.6	75.6	74.5	81.1
35	72.6	79.2	68.8	75.7	74.6	81.2
36	72.6	79.2	69.0	75.8	74.6	81.2
37	72.7	79.3	69.2	75.9	74.7	81.3
38	72.8	79.3	69.4	76.0	74.8	81.3
39	72.9	79.4	69.6	76.1	74.9	81.4
40	73.0	79.4	69.8	76.2	75.0	81.4

Source: D.S. Woodruff. (1977). *Can you live to be 100?* Boston: Chatham Square Press.

TABLE 2.5

LIFE EXPECTANCY AT BIRTH FOR SELECTED NATIONS

Country	Year	Male		Female
Mexico	1975	62.8		66.6
Denmark	1977–78	71.5		77.5
Norway	1977–78	72.3		78.3
Haiti	1972	—	*44.5	—
Ethiopia	1968	—	*38.5	—
Japan	1970	69.1		74.3

*Estimates for male and female combined.

Source: Adapted from United Nations. (1980). *Demographic Yearbook, 1979,* 31st ed., pp. 450–471. New York: United Nations.

nations, but not as high as in others such as Japan and the Scandinavian countries. As one would expect, life expectancy at birth is greater in the developed, industrialized nations and substantially less in underdeveloped, Third World nations.

FACTORS AFFECTING LIFE EXPECTANCY

How close we come to meeting, exceeding, or falling below our life expectancy depends on a myriad of factors. These factors can be considered as *related* to life expectancy but have not been demonstrated empirically to be *casual.* Therefore, caution is urged in overgeneralizing their importance as causes of life expectancy.

In discussing factors that affect life expectancy, we must first distinguish between **intrinsic or primary** and **extrinsic or secondary** factors. Intrinsic factors are those that contribute directly to life expectancy, such as genetic inheritance, gender, and race. Extrinsic factors affect how long we live in an indirect manner; such factors include exercise, diet, and interpersonal relationships (Timiras, 1972). Simplistically, the intrinsic/primary factors set certain limits for an individual's potential length of life, and the extrinsic factors influence whether that potential length is achieved, exceeded, or missed (Fries & Crapo, 1981; Timiras, 1972; Wantz & Gay, 1981).

Intrinsic/Primary Factors

These factors are assumed to set certain limits or define the parameters of the life expectancy of the organism, since they have been repeatedly demonstrated to be related to life expectancy in a number of species (Timiras, 1972). They are generally considered fixed, or determined, since they are inherited from our parents or are related to universal biological and physiological processes. Again, it is important to keep in mind that though these factors have been demonstrated to be *related* to life expectancy, they cannot be considered *causal.* In many cases these factors have been linked to life expectancy by studies of lower animals, and there are inherent problems in generalizing data obtained from lower animals to humans. Finally, there are vast individual differences in these factors since humans do not develop in a vacuum, nor do these factors function in isolation.

The major intrinsic factors related to life expectancy appear to be genetic inheritance, gender, race, and health condition.

Genetic Inheritance Numerous studies of life expectancy in humans and other species have reported associations between the life spans of individuals and that of their immediate ancestors (Birren & Renner, 1977; Timiras, 1972). This relationship is thought to be due primarily to heredity. Simply put, long-lived parents tend to have long-lived children. This relationship, though significant, is quite complex. Generally, how long you will live in relation to your parents' life span will depend upon interaction of the other intrinsic/ primary and extrinsic/secondary factors (e.g., diet, exercise).

On a related topic, as suggested by Timiras (1972), there have been some reports that parental age at time of birth is related to life expectancy of the offspring. That is, offspring of younger mothers live longer than off-spring of older mothers. However, investigations on this relationship have been based primarily on lower animals, such as fruit flies. Therefore, generalization to humans is extremely difficult. Moreover, findings for humans have been equivocal.

In conclusion, while there is a genetic program that sets certain limits for the potential life span of a species (Shock, 1977), this expression of the basic genetic program can be altered by many internal and environmental factors.

Gender and Race Research indicates that there are some familial characteristics that influence differences in how long one lives among individuals of a single species. For example, Omenn (1977) reported numerous differences in life expectancy of different strains of mice.

In terms of our discussion, the major acquired (inherited) familial characteristics that affect life expectancy in humans are gender, race, and health condition (the inherited susceptibility to certain diseases or disabilities). For organizational purposes, we will discuss race and gender together and health conditions separately.

As previously demonstrated (see Tables 2.2, 2.3, 2.4, and 2.5), there are definite differences in life expectancy as a function of gender and race. Basically, in the United States and in most nations in the world, females live longer than males (Timiras, 1972; Wantz & Gay, 1981). Generally, females live 7 to 8 years longer than males born in the same year (Birren & Renner, 1977). The difference in life expectancy for males and females has increased since 1900. For example, statistics indicate that, for males and females born in 1900, females outlived males by approximately 2 years. For males and females born in 1960, females are expected to outlive males by 6.5 years; and for those born in 1975, women are expected to outlive men by approximately 8 years. We still do not know for certain whether this sex difference is due to genetic inheritance or other factors. For example, females may have a genetic program for a longer life, or females may be the stronger or healthier members of the species and therefore live longer. Their greater life expectancy may be the result of other primary or secondary factors.

The fact that females live longer than males of the same cohort has significant implications regarding interpersonal relationships during late adulthood. Given the fact that the majority of females marry men who are older than themselves, the chances of them outliving their husbands by 10 or 15 years are quite likely. For this reason, females should acquire the skills necessary for independent living, such as bill paying, simple home mainte- nance, and driving a car, since it is quite likely that they will need these "independent living survival skills" after the deaths of their husbands. Fur- ther, during adulthood, women should begin to develop friendship networks independent of those associated with their husbands, in order to have friend- ships that will be maintained after the deaths of their spouses. Finally, women should begin economic planning, such as building a credit history, since it is likely that they will have to support themselves after the deaths of their husbands.

With regard to *race,* whites generally tend to live longer than members of minority groups (Timiras, 1972, 1978; Ward, 1984) in the United States. Recently, experts in the field of population statistics have begun to report what they describe as the **cross-over effect** (A. N. Schwartz & Peterson, 1979). This refers to the fact that, for recent cohorts, it is predicted that black females will have a higher (longer) life expectancy than white males born the same year. The cross-over effect pertains to cohorts born in the late 1960s and early 1970s. Specifically, prior to this time (the late 1960s to early 1970s), the predicted general rank order for life expectancy at birth from shortest to longest was black males, black females, white males, white females. After this time, the predicted rank order was black males, white males, black females, white females. In other words, black females and white males changed rank order (crossed over).

We still do not know if these differences can be attributed solely to genetic inheritance, to other primary or secondary factors, or to an interaction or combination of these factors.

It is important to note that in the United States there are ethnic and racial minorities that have life expectancy rates substantially lower than those of black and white Americans. For example, life expectancy at birth for native Americans is approximately 47 years, and for Hispanic Americans, it is 57 years.

Health Condition   It is not surprising that the better the health condition in which you remain (or the better your access to health care; see Davis, 1985) at all points of the life cycle, the more likely it is that you will live longer (Siegler & Costa, 1985; Timiras, 1972, 1978; Wantz & Gay, 1981). However, many individuals overlook the fact that a number of the major diseases or causes of death (for example, heart disease or diabetes) occur at *all* points along the life cycle. This may suggest a familial pattern of incidence, for example, an aged father and his middle-aged son both having heart disease. Again, we do not know if these relationships have a genetic basis or are due to other factors in common, such as diet, stress, and shared environment. Further, a number of diseases or disorders (several forms of mental retardation, Tay-Sachs disease, sickle-cell anemia) have a demonstrated familial or racial inheritance pattern and are related to a shortened life span. For example, only blacks develop the blood disorder called sickle-cell anemia, and only Jews whose families came from Eastern Europe get Tay-Sachs disease, a disorder that leads to nervous system deterioration and death in childhood.

With some disorders, such as heart disease, many of the potential negative affects can be remediated with early diagnosis, proper medical care, drugs, exercise, and dietary intervention.

The factors we have just discussed have been demonstrated to be related to life expectancy in humans and other living organisms. They are referred to as instrinsic or primary because they are thought to play a significant role in determining the longevity of the organism. Further, these factors are thought to be relatively fixed or unchangeable since they are the result of biological and physiological processes that are genetically inherited or determined.

Before concluding this section, the authors wish again to stress that you keep two facts in mind. First, though these factors have been reported to be related to life expectancy in humans, they are not causally related, nor is the relationship a simple one. Second, though we discuss these factors separately, in reality they do not function independently or in isolation. That is, they interact in a complex manner. Therefore, at the present time, it is impossible to determine or predict exactly how long you will live by assigning numbers for yourself along each of these factors or dimensions to arrive at your exact predicted length of life.

Extrinsic/Secondary Factors

These factors are assumed to modify the limits projected for life expectancy by the primary/intrinsic factors. Research indicates the expression of our basic genetic program can be altered by many environmental factors (Shock, 1977). Further, the effect of these extrinsic/secondary factors can be positive or negative (they can enhance or lessen life expectancy).

Research (Birren & Renner, 1977; Shock, 1977; Timiras, 1972, 1978; Wantz & Gay, 1981) has repeatedly reported relationships between a number of extrinsic/secondary factors and life expectancy. These factors are referred to as extrinsic, since they are not inherited at birth per se and are the result of environmental, social, or psychological conditions and events. Usually, individuals do not have any "control" over the primary factors, while to some extent, individuals can manifest some control over the secondary factors.

The major extrinsic/secondary factors related to life expectancy appear to be nutrition/diet, climate/physical environment, exercise and activity, medical care, stress avoidance, interpersonal/social relationships, work and work satisfaction, education level and economic status, cognitive/intellectual factors, and personality. Again, our decision to discuss these factors independently is for organizational purposes. In reality, these factors often interact and in some cases are dependent upon each other. For example, individuals with high educational levels and economic statuses have the economic resources available for improved nutrition, high quality medical care, and work satisfaction.

Nutrition and Diet   The foods and substances one eats can affect physical appearance, size, and life expectancy in both humans and lower animals. For instance, Omenn (1977) reports on the relationship of nutrition to longevity, as well as to a number of physical and physiological traits, in mice.

Research indicates that the avoidance of obesity and a diet low in animal fats are both related to life expectancy (Wantz & Gay, 1981). Though dietary restrictions that lead to low blood-cholesterol levels may not be related directly to longevity, they are related directly to high blood pressure and cardiovascular disease, which may shorten life. Therefore, dietary and nutritional factors have an indirect effect upon life expectancy.

It is important to note that nutritional factors are related to more than just life expectancy, especially in older adults. As reported by Eisdorfer and Cohen (1978), chronic nutritional deficiencies in older adults (and in young adults as well) can lead to vitamin deficiencies, which in turn may have negative effects upon various organs and organ systems in the body. These deficiencies can eventually lead to disorders that produce an often-reversible dementia (see Chapter 13). Individuals with this dementia-like condition manifest rapid and sudden cognitive dysfunction, high levels of anxiety, and even delusions and hallucinations (Eisdorfer & Cohen, 1978); thus, it may be confused with psychosis.

This is particularly relevant for individuals who work with older adults living alone in the community who may manifest these behaviors. When one visits older adults, especially those that live alone, one should attempt to make some assessment of their dietary intake. That is, are they eating at all, eating junk food, or eating a balanced diet? Often, individuals of all ages who live alone do not eat nutritionally balanced meals. Instead, they tend to eat meals that are expedient and quick. One major reason for this is that the process of eating is a "social event" in most cultures, even our own. For example, everyone in the family gets together to eat and talk during evening dinner, and many dating situations involve going out to eat dinner, a hamburger, or a pizza. From childhood on, we often associate eating with interpersonal situations. For this reason, we do not like to eat alone, since it may lead to feelings of isolation and loneliness. Rather than cook a big meal or go out to get a balanced meal when we are alone, we may find it easier either not to eat or to eat something quickly.

Finally, dietary or nutritional intake is significantly affected by economics at all age levels, since it may be difficult to eat nutritious meals if one does not have the money to purchase such food. This problem is particularly relevant for older adults who, as we will discuss, often have many economic difficulties (Chen, 1985). For this reason, many communities and agencies sponsor meal programs for the elderly to provide meals that are free, or at greatly reduced cost to the individual, based on the person's ability to pay. These projects serve two important purposes: first, they provide elderly persons with a nutritious meal; and second, they provide an opportunity for social interaction.

In conclusion, dietary/nutritional factors have been found to be related to life expectancy and certain aspects of mental health at all points along the life cycle, particularly for older adults (Siegler & P. T. Costa, 1985).

Climate and Physical Environment   Research suggests that the climate and physical environment in which we live and work is related to life expectancy and many medical or physical disorders (Wantz & Gay, 1981). Each species has specific requirements in terms of temperature and climate in order to sustain life. For instance, tropical birds cannot live for a prolonged time in a cold climate. It should be noted that other factors within a specific climate or physical environment, such as exposure to chemicals, noise levels, and pollution, can affect life expectancy directly or indirectly.

For example, if you work on a job in which you are repeatedly exposed to dangerous chemicals and live in a city with a high pollution level, both these factors have the potential of either reducing your life expectancy or contributing to disease.

Quality of Housing   The most obvious aspect of the physical environment for older adults is housing. Due to a number of reasons ranging from poor health to a lack of physical mobility, older adults spend an increasingly larger proportion of their time at home. Housing plays an important role in their lives and covers a large spectrum (Lawton, 1985).

Statistics indicate that about seven out of every ten community-living older adults own their own homes (Chen, 1985; Lawton, 1985). Since these homes were usually obtained when their owners were young, they are generally older, located in older neighborhoods, and more likely to be substandard in terms of conditions. Though the neighborhood may be deteriorating and the houses have more rooms and space than their owners actually require, many elderly persons prefer to remain in their own homes, since the surroundings are familiar and living alone provides a feeling of independence.

The remainder of community-living older adults (30 percent) live in rental properties. These range from apartment units and public housing facilities to single-room occupancies. Due primarily to economic reasons, older adults are unable to compete with younger persons for adequate housing. Many older adults who rent live in older apartment buildings located in run-down areas of the city where rents and services are low and crime rates are high. A number of these older adults live in inner-city hotels and rooming houses in which they have single-room occupancy (SRO), usually with a shared or community bath and no kitchen unit; these single-room units are also found in small and rural communities (Lawton, 1985).

Exercise and Activity   Numerous researchers report the positive relationship between exercise and physical activity and psychological and physical well-being at all points along the life span, as well as their relation to life expectancy (Buskirk, 1985; Whitbourne, 1985). Regular physical exercise throughout life is thought to have many positive physical and psychological effects. These include such effects as improved cardiovascular and respiratory-system functioning and increased muscle tone. In terms of psychological functioning, it is assumed that the better your body "feels," the better your feeling of well-being. A general relationship between regular (long-term) exercise and physical activity and life expectancy is well documented (Timiras, 1972; Wantz & Gay, 1981; Whitbourne, 1985), though consistent empirical data are lacking. It is likely, however, that a program of physical exercise in combination with a clearly designed diet regimen will contribute to less weight gain, lower blood pressure, and lower cholesterol levels. Such persons lower their risk of heart attacks and strokes, both leading causes of death in our country. In fact, running is often prescribed as a treatment for depression. We will have more to say on exercise and activity in our chapter on retirement and leisure.

Education and Economic Status   Research indicates that educational level and economic status are related to life expectancy (Bengston, Kasschau, & Ragan, 1977; Chen, 1985; Pfeiffer, 1970; Rose, 1964). In general, the higher one's educational level and economic level, the longer one is likely to live.

As would be expected, educational level and economic status are highly related and are correlated with the majority of other secondary factors linked to life expectancy. For example, being highly educated and making a comfortable salary usually implies work satisfaction, good medical care (Shanas & Maddox, 1985), a nutritious diet, and a safe physical environment, while the opposite is true for individuals of low educational levels and economic status. Though education level and economic status are not causal factors in life expectancy, they are directly related to many other secondary factors that affect life expectancy.

In terms of education, with successive cohorts or generations, there has been an increase in the mean years of educational attainment for members of that cohort (Bengston et al., 1977). For example, in 1975 the median years of formal education for individuals of both genders under age 25 was 12.3 years; for individuals of both genders over age 65, it was 9.0 years. Within all cohorts, females tend to have slightly more years of formal education than males.

In most cases the difference in total years of formal education between young and old individuals reflects the ease of availability of education for younger cohorts (Ansello & Hayslip, 1979). Individuals over 65 did not have transportation such as school buses to bring them to classes. Additionally, economic conditions were somewhat more difficult for older cohorts. Often, they had to leave school at an earlier age in order to help with the family finances.

Finally, it is impossible to talk about comparisons of educational attainment between young and old in absolute terms, because 12 years of education today is not identical to 12 years of education for individuals over age 65. Those individuals over age 65 with 12 years of education would be considered an elite group, while for those under age 25 the same number of years would put them at the median.

In conclusion, older cohorts generally have fewer years of formal education than younger cohorts, but the differences can be attributed to a number of factors such as economics and availability of opportunity.

Also, in terms of economics, we are often led to believe by the media and the popular press that most older adults are wealthy and live a life of affluence. This is far from the truth. Though there are some affluent older adults and the economic position of older adults has improved in recent years (Chen, 1985; *Wall Street Journal,* 1983), many are poor or just "getting by" financially. In fact, some older adults are in such a disadvantaged economic position that they constitute a major social problem within our society today. Statistics indicate the economic condition of older adults is affected by factors such as gender, race, marital status, and previous occupational or socioeconomic level (Soldo, 1980).

The most frequently used method of describing a particular group's economic handicap is with reference to the United States Social Security Administration's **poverty level** or **index**. This is the official marker of poverty in the United States. The index is set at different levels for different types of individuals and/or families, such as single, nonfarm, and so forth. Individuals and families whose incomes fall at or below this index are considered not to have the necessary economic resources for adequate daily living (Chen, 1985).

Data reported by the American Association of Retired Persons (1985) indicates that about 3.3 million elderly (65+ years) were living below the poverty level in 1984. This is approximately 14.7 percent of the elderly population. This same data indicates another 2.4 million (9 percent) were classified as "near poor." As reported by the Special Committee on Aging of the United States Senate (1985) and by Chen (1985), poverty rates increase sharply with age and gender. For example, older women and the oldest old people are most likely to be poor. Further, elderly individuals living with their children have the highest income levels, followed by married couples. Elderly people living alone, both men and women, have the lowest incomes. These same statistics illustrate how poverty varies among subgroups of older adults. For instance, according to the American Association of Retired Persons (1985), approximately 11 percent of elderly whites were considered poor in 1984, while 32 percent of elderly blacks and 21 percent of elderly Hispanics were considered poor during this same year.

Older adults often face difficult economic hardships during periods of high inflation, since they are primarily on fixed incomes. The most significantly affected older adults are individuals who worked at lower-level occupations their entire lives, earning minimal wages (A. J. E. Wilson, 1984). Since social security and pension benefits are closely tied to earnings, they receive low levels of benefit payments. Since these individuals earned just enough to "get by" when they were working, upon retirement and the reduction of income, they now experience poverty for the first time (A. J. E. Wilson, 1984).

Medical Care As one would expect, the quality of medical care received by an individual is related to life expectancy (Shanas & Maddox, 1985). As medical care and technology improve, life expectancy in a society increases. For example, medical science has developed vaccines to prevent diseases that in the past killed people during childhood or early adulthood, such as whooping cough and polio. Further, as medical care and knowledge progress and cures, vaccines, and treatments are discovered for diseases and/or pathological conditions such as cancer, life expectancy will also likely increase (Davis, 1985).

Work and Work Satisfaction   Numerous investigations document the relationship between work and work satisfaction and life expectancy (Palmore, 1969; Rose, 1964). For instance, working in hazardous conditions, such as exposure to pollution and dangerous chemicals, increases the probability of a shortened life span. Also, the type of work we do is highly related to economic level and other secondary factors related to life expectancy.

Individuals who have high work satisfaction tend to have higher self-esteem and a more positive outlook on life than those who are dissatisfied with their work. In general, though both work and work satisfaction are not related to life expectancy in a causal manner, except in occupations that are highly dangerous, they are related to many of the other secondary factors connected with life expectancy. We will have more to say on these topics in Chapter 11 on work and retirement.

Interpersonal and Social Relationships   Research suggests the positive relationship of interpersonal/social relationships, such as friends and spouse, to many psychological factors such as self-esteem or life satisfaction at all points along the life span (Kahn & Antonucci, 1980), as well as to life expectancy (Bengston el al., 1977; Timiras, 1972; Wantz & Gay, 1981). The presence of others makes us feel worthwhile and reduces feelings of isolation, loneliness, and depression. That is, "others" provide necessary and beneficial psychological and social support for us. In Chapters 8 and 9, we will have more to say about interpersonal relationships and the functions they play in adulthood.

As many of us have experienced from time to time, if these social support networks are not available to us, we may experience feelings of loneliness, isolation, or depression. The chances of this occurring increase substantially as we get older due to the deaths of friends, relatives, and spouses.

Interestingly, some researchers (Lawton, Moss, & Moles, 1984; B. M. Levinson, 1972) have suggested that animals as pets can facilitate psychological well-being in people. However, this research area is highly controversial and lacks a definitive data base. Though we cannot say with a great deal of certainty whether pets can or cannot facilitate psychological well-being, an ever-increasing body of literature suggests that animals do provide many positive effects for both younger and older individuals (Cusack & Smith, 1984).

Personality/Stress Avoidance   Research has suggested that an individual's personality type, particularly in terms of how that person reacts to stress, is related to life expectancy (Siegler & P. T. Costa, 1985). For instance, Friedman and Rosenman (1974) investigated the relationship between personality type and incidence of coronary disease among men. Their research suggested there were two personality types, **Type A** and **Type B**, and there was a significant relationship between Type A behaviors (personality traits) and coronary heart disease. Basically, Type A individuals can be viewed as having a stressful personality type, since they tend to respond to every situation in such a manner that stress has become characteristic of their normal everyday functioning. That is, they see stress in everything they do. Persons with Type A traits are hard driving, highly competitive, impatient, always rushing, and striving to accomplish more than is generally possible. On the other hand, Type B individuals are more passive and relaxed.

Of specific relevance from a life-span perspective is the work of Selye (1976) on stress, since stress and our reaction to it have been found to be related to medical conditions such as ulcers and hypertension and to life expectancy (Eisdorfer & Wilkie, 1979a, 1979b; Shock, 1977; Siegler & P. T. Costa, 1985).

Day-to-day stress and coping with stress in our lives is a normal part of life. Stress may be found on the job, at home, on the highway, and in our personal life. There are vast individual differences in the perception of stress as well as individual reactions to stress. However, the more we age the more we are likely to encounter those situations likely to be perceived by a majority of individuals as stressful. These include death of a spouse, retirement, change in health, and the death of close friends. As demonstrated by Selye (1976), the prolonged and repeated exposure to stressful situations and events encountered by individuals as they age may contribute to a number of psychological and medical/physical problems in old age, such as ulcers during middle age and heart disease in old age.

Selye conceptualized the effects of repeated exposures to stress upon the organism in a theory of stress referred to as the **general adaptation syndrome**. This theory postulates three stages that the body goes through in reacting to stressful situations.

General Adaptation Syndrome. Stage one, the *alarm reaction,* is characterized by a general mobilization of the body's physical and psychological resources in order to deal with the perceived stressful situation, that is, to attack the source of stress, defend oneself, or retreat from the situation. During this stage, certain bodily systems increase or accelerate, such as hormonal secretions, heart rate, and respiration. Though a stressful situation may be the same (death of a spouse), there are individual differences in the reaction to the situation. For example, one individual will appear to become immobilized and sit motionless while another may express high anxiety and tension (Eisdorfer & Wilkie, 1979a, 1979b).

If the stressful situation continues or new ones emerge, the second stage, called *stage of resistance,* begins. During this phase all physical and psychological systems of the body continue to function at a high level of strain in order to cope with the stressful situation. Selye believes this reaction to prolonged stress can lead to psychological and/or physical problems including high blood pressure and depression. Continued exposure to stress will eventually cause the bodily systems and processes to become depleted. Further, as the system becomes depleted and the stress remains, individuals may begin to take drugs and medications, on which they may become dependent in order to cope with the stressful situation.

According to Selye, if stress continues to persist, the individual's bodily systems move into the third and final stage, the *stage of exhaustion*. During this stage, the bodily system becomes exhausted and can no longer help the individual cope with the stress. This may lead to feelings of resignation, mental and physical breakdown, and even death.

The theory of Selye has many implications for how individuals cope with change, especially older adults. That is, as we develop, we are repeatedly encountering stress that eventually weakens our psychological and biological systems. This repeated exposure to stress may lower the resistance and adaptive capacities of the individual. With increasing age, the chances of encountering high stress events (Holmes & Rahe, 1967) may increase, such as death of close friends, death of a spouse, retirement, and being a victim of crime (Eisdorfer & Wilkie, 1979a, 1979b). These events potentially have a more pronounced effect on an already weakened individual's ability to cope. Therefore, it seems ludicrous to look upon old age as a serene, tranquil period with little or no stress. As suggested by Lawton and Nahemow (1973), if we experience a decline in our capacities and abilities with age, previously nonstressful events and tasks, such as climbing three floors of stairs, now become stress-producing events or tasks due to our decreased physical abilities (cardiovascular efficiency, arthritis).

It is important to develop appropriate coping mechanisms early in life and to maintain them throughout life, because stressful situations obviously do not disappear as we get older. M. A. Lieberman (1975), for example, has developed a model of coping with institutionalization that incorporates a number of factors (perception of stress, existing coping skills, resources, personality characteristics, extent of change as a stressor). While an in-depth discussion of coping and stress is beyond the scope of this text (see R. S. Lazarus & Delongis, 1983), we will discuss the issue of coping with change again in Chapter 10 on personality. Thomae (1980) has argued that personality is a factor that mediates one's *perception* of stress and is critical to illness. That is, what is stressful to some persons will not be stressful to others (Eisdorfer & Wilkie, 1979a, 1979b). Moreover, one might respond ineffectually to a stressor, which creates a secondary source of stress for the individual (Eisdorfer & Wilkie, 1979a, 1979b). For example, coping maladaptively with the loss of another person through death by isolating oneself from others is itself stress producing and contributes to the difficulty in coping with this loss (see Chapter 12). Individuals who fail to cope with stress or change may demonstrate symptoms of *helplessness* (Seligman, 1975): depression, anxiety, or decreased cognitive functioning. They may also begin to attribute their failure in coping to their own lack of ability, rather than to the nature of the stressor itself with which they must cope. One major form of coping with stressful situations involves developing satisfying leisure activities. Leisure competence will be discussed in another chapter (Chapter 11) in this text.

Though not directly related to life expectancy per se, the topics of crime and elder abuse are relevant to our discussion of stress.

Crime.   The severity of the crime problem for older adults is a controversial issue. Some researchers believe crime against the elderly to be a major problem of which we are just becoming aware. That is, the aged are prey to all forms of crime such as street crime, fraud, abuse, and robbery, while others believe that the idea of a high crime rate against the elderly is a "myth" (Janson & Ryder, 1983). Data suggests that older adults have an extremely high fear of crime (they consider it a major problem) (Lawton, 1985). If one looks at the actual crime statistics, the aged emerge as a low crime *rate* group (Lawton, 1985). Regardless of which point of view one holds, one criminal act against anyone, regardless of age, is one crime too many. Moreover, *fear* of crime may be more harmful than victimization (Lawton, 1985). Since crime comes in many forms, we shall discuss how these forms affect older adults.

In order to answer accurately the question of how prevalent crime is against the elderly, one must look at individual types of crime. Regarding street crime, the most common crime of this type against the elderly is purse and wallet snatchings. Such crimes are also highly related to the nature of one's neighborhood; that is, poor, run-down areas tend to have a great deal of street crime against individuals of all ages.

Though we often feel that older adults are prey to violent street crimes, such as assault and rape, the actual statistics do not support this assumption (Lawton, 1985). Data appears to indicate that when older adults are victims of violent crime, the assault usually takes place in their home or apartment, rather than in the street.

We have already discussed a number of reasons why older adults are potentially susceptible to crime. Generally, they are perceived as vulnerable. Moreover, most elderly are women, and since they are poor, they tend to live in run-down or older neighborhoods and thus be doubly vulnerable.

Crime has more of an effect upon the victim than just losing a purse or a wallet. Crime involves potential physical and psychological injury: the loss of important cherished possessions and the creation of excessive fear to the point where one is afraid to go out. Being victimized is a blow to one's self-esteem, and if one is poor, lost money is not easy to replace.

Research indicates the fear of crime is widespread among the aged to a much greater degree than the actual crime rate; this fear is still, however, "real" to the person (Lawton, 1985), limits mobility and interactions with others, and causes the individual to be constantly anxious and fearful.

Perhaps the most common form of crime committed against the elderly is fraud or misrepresentation. It is a nonviolent form of crime and includes such activities as mail-order fraud ("our product removes all wrinkles"), insurance fraud (paying for policies that are not needed), and medical "quackery" (a miracle cure for cancer). These types of crime are very common against older adults and are used to swindle money, property, and possessions from a vulnerable group of individuals.

Elder Abuse As a Form of Crime.   One type of crime against the elderly that has received a great deal of recent attention is **elder abuse**. We are just beginning to document cases where the elderly are being abused both physically and passively by their adult children, caretakers, or institutional staff (S. Powell & Berg 1986). In most cases, these instances of abuse go unreported, so there is great difficulty in documenting them (Salend, Kane, Satz, & Pynoos, 1984). A common form of elder abuse consists of actions such as tying an elderly person to a chair and leaving that person in a bedroom or an activity room all day without even the opportunity to go to the bathroom. Crouse, Cobb, Harris, Kopecky, Poertner, Edwards, Ham, and Sophos (1984) surveyed selected counties and municipal areas in the state of Illinois in which they asked various professionals, such as lawyers, physicians, nurses, and mental-health workers, to provide an "estimate of the reports of elder abuse they become aware of in the average month." Crouse el al. (1984) found that 12,000 total cases were reported from among the selected counties and municipal areas by the professionals. Results indicated approximately two-thirds of the cases were characterized as passive neglect (ignorance of the elder's needs) and verbal or emotional abuse (humiliation, yelling at an elder). These investigators suggest the prevalence of elder abuse is similar to the incidence of child abuse, though each is likely to be underreported. We shall have more to say about elder abuse as an indication of family dysfunction in adulthood in Chapter 8.

Factors Related to Fear of Crime.   Concerning fear of crime among the elderly, four factors appear to be related to the severity of this fear: gender, race, social class, and community size. In other words, females are more afraid than males, black elderly are more afraid than white, those from lower social classes are more afraid than those from higher classes, and residents of larger cities are more afraid than individuals residing in smaller towns and rural areas.

What can be done to reduce crime against the elderly? There are a number of alternatives that have been suggested to make older adults less vulnerable to crime. These include neighborhood crime patrols, self-defense programs, greater police protection, and keeping guard dogs, to name a few. Each can be effective to some extent, but the greatest deterrent to crime is the development of greater personal awareness, using good judgment, and caring about our neighbors (see Box 2.2).

Cognitive/Intellectual Factors and Life Expectancy.   Numerous research investigations have linked cognitive/intellectual factors with life expectancy. Basically, this research suggests that individuals with better or higher cognitive/intellectual abilities live longer, often referred to as the **wisdom factor** (Birren & Renner, 1977). For example, Fozard, Nuttal, and Waugh (1972) demonstrated an individual's performance on a number of verbal, perceptual, and motor tasks as one of six measures of the individual's functional age; other measures were blood serum and urine, anthropometric descriptions, personality, and sociological assessments (friends, "significant others"). Greater functional age related positively to life expectancy.

One major thrust of the research in this area has attempted to link life expectancy or survival to sudden and dramatic declines in cognitive/intellectual performance from a few days (Kleemeier, 1962; M. A. Lieberman, 1965) to a number of years prior to death (Jarvik & Blum, 1971; Jarvik & Falek, 1963; K. F. Riegel & R. M. Riegel, 1972).

An example of this type of research is the work of Kleemeier (1962). Kleemeier administered an intelligence test on four occasions, at 2- to 3½-year intervals during a 12-year period, to 13 older adult males. Kleemeier observed, even though the performance of all participants decreased over the 12-year period, that there were substantial individual differences in the magnitude of the decline. Further, soon after the last retest, 4 of the participants died, and it was observed that the decline of the test scores was more rapid and of greater magnitude for those who died than who survived. This decline was labeled **terminal drop**. That is, impending death is often preceded by a terminal drop in cognitive/intellectual functioning. More recently, numerous investigators have examined (with some success) the ability of specific measures of intellectual or memory functioning to predict terminal decline and terminal drop (Botwinick, West, & Storandt, 1978; Palmore & Cleveland, 1976; Siegler, McCarty & Logue, 1982).

Terminal drop is a controversial topic, due to a number of methodological problems associated with the research in this area (Siegler, 1975). For instance, the poor health of the individuals who died may have been responsible for the decrease in test performance.

Overall, there is some support for the relationship between cognitive/intellectual performance and life expectancy, but again, the relationship is not causal. Further, the relationship between cognitive/intellectual performance and life expectancy could be significantly affected by other secondary factors

BOX 2.2

WIDOW DEFIES MUGGERS

A grand jury Tuesday dropped charges against an elderly Alabama widow who defied eight muggers with an unloaded pearl-handled revolver and then was arrested for illegally carrying a gun.

Roberta Leonard, 67, of Sylacauga, Alabama, said she bore no grudge against her attackers.

"I used to be haughty and mean, but my heart is melted down now," said the gray-haired widow, a devout Pentecostalist, after the grand jury decision. "I'm so happy, I thank the Lord."

She had been charged with illegally possessing an unregistered gun and could have been sentenced up to a year in jail if tried and convicted.

Authorities meanwhile dismissed charges against four of her attackers because they lacked evidence. Two others were held on weapons charges and two teenagers still must appear in Family Court.

Wearing a green polka-dotted dress and sunglasses and leaning on a cane, Mrs. Leonard went to the grand jury hearing in Criminal Court Building in Manhattan on the arm of her lawyer Judd Ryan.

Source: *Charleston Times-Courier.* (1983, August 17).

such as educational level and economic status. These factors will be discussed further in Chapter 6 on intelligence.

The factors we have just discussed have been demonstrated to be related to life expectancy. These factors are referred to as extrinsic or secondary because though they are not causal factors, they do interact with the intrinsic/primary factors to the level where they do exert some effect upon life expectancy. Further, many of these extrinsic/secondary factors are highly interrelated, for example, educational level and economic level with quality of medical care. As opposed to the intrinsic/primary factors, which are considered static or fixed, the extrinsic/secondary factors are quite dynamic and modifiable; that is, they can be changed for better or worse.

Self-reflection regarding how each of us stands on these factors may lead to positive and happy feelings for some or to negative and pessimistic feelings for others. But, as suggested by Woodruff (1977) and Wantz and Gay (1981), it is never too late to begin to alter our current position with regard to these factors. That is, we can watch our diet or begin an exercise program.

In the next section, we shall discuss a number of cultures that purport to have many "long-lived" individuals. Researchers study these cultures in order to try and determine what factors are contributing to this purported longevity.

LONG-LIVED CULTURES

In this section, we shall briefly discuss cultures that are thought to have a fairly large proportion of the general population living to advanced old age (100 years+). The two most highly cited cultures of long-lived individuals are the Vilcabamba of Ecuador and the Abkhasia of the Georgia region of the Soviet Union. We will present some background information on each of these cultures in order to observe what factors may be contributing to their assumed long life.

Abkhasia is a small republic in the Caucasus mountains of the Georgia region of the Soviet Union. Individuals from Abkhasia are known for supposedly good health and long life. Reports (Leaf, 1973) suggest that according to the 1970 census, 194 individuals from a total population of approximately 100,000 were over 100 years old. Well over 1500 were over 90 years of age, and some were reported to be over 140 years old.

Vilcabamba is a village high in the Andes mountains in Southern Ecuador whose residents are also known for being long-lived. Of the 1971 population of Vilcabamba of 819, 9 of the individuals were over 100 years of age. Further, the proportion of the population over 60 years of age for Vilcabamba was 16 percent (approximately), which was substantially higher than for all other sections of rural Ecuador (approximately 6 percent) for that same year (Leaf, 1973).

Table 2.6 illustrates information regarding the characteristics of Vil-

TABLE 2.6

CHARACTERISTICS OF ABKHASIA AND VILCABAMBA ON EXTRINSIC/SECONDARY FACTORS RELATED TO LONGEVITY

Abkhasia	Vilcabamba
Diet	
Avoid being overweight	Meager daily caloric intake, averages 1,700 calories, which is approximately ½ the amount eaten by the average American daily.
Do not drink coffee or tea	
Do not eat butter, and eat very little meat. Meat eaten is either broiled or boiled, and cooked only to the point where the blood stops running.	Eat very little meat
Eat many vegetables	Eat many vegetables
Climate/Physical Environment	
High altitude, mountainous	High altitude, mountainous
Exercise/Physical Activity	
Work and rest in moderation	Engage in strenuous daily activity
Remain active until advanced old age	
Education/Economic Status	
Agricultural Society, on collective farms	Agricultural Society, most are poor by U.S. standards
Medical Care	
Primarily folk medicine; modern medical care is virtually absent.	Modern medical care is virtually absent.
Work/Work Satisfaction	
Regardless of age, individual performs functional activity.	Enjoy work, looks forward to work
Work in moderation	Work until advanced old age
Interpersonal Relations	
All individuals are made to feel part of the family or group throughout life. Therefore, strong social support.	All individuals are made to feel part of the family or group throughout life. Therefore, strong social support.
Personality/Stress Avoidance	
Noncompetitive	Avoid stress and anxiety
Avoid stress	
Cognitive/Intellectual Factors	
Not studied	Not studied

cabamba and Abkhasia on the extrinsic/secondary factors we have discussed that are assumed to be related to longevity. After you observe their characteristics, see what statements could be made about you for each of them.

Studies of long-lived individuals in other cultures have identified a number of factors in common among these varied cultures. These are daily physical activity, a diet low in calories and animal fats, avoidance of obesity, low blood cholesterol and triglyceride levels, and the absence of high blood pressure and cardiovascular diseases.

It should be noted that reports of extreme life expectancy in these and other cultures are being challenged and called into question by some researchers (Palmore, 1984). Specifically, these researchers suggest reports of extreme longevity are erroneous, since they are self-reports that often prove to be inaccurate. Since many of these cultures are not modernized, they lack accurate record keeping of birth dates and birth certificates. Further, as reported by Palmore (1984), in the case of the Abkhasia, there is a general proneness to overstate one's age, since old age is revered in that culture. Therefore, whether there are specific cultures that have sizable proportions of long-lived individuals is still an area for scientific research and documentation.

In the next section, we will discuss the implications of increased life expectancy upon a society, with particular emphasis on the United States. Increased life expectancy, especially when large numbers of individuals are reaching advanced old age, can put a severe strain on economic, housing, transportation, and medical resources within that society.

IMPLICATIONS OF INCREASED LIFE EXPECTANCY

As we have previously discussed, life expectancy has increased substantially since ancient times on a worldwide basis. With regard to the United States and most industrialized nations, the greatest increases have occurred during this century (since 1900).

One of the most important statistical facts about life expectancy is the great increase this century in the number of individuals over age 60 in the United States, with a concomitant decrease in the number of individuals under age 18 (which indicates a low birthrate) (see Chapter 1). Specifically, the United States is rapidly becoming an "aging society." Data reported by Soldo (1980) and the United States Bureau of the Census (Statistical Abstract of the United States, 1986) indicates that in 1900 the proportion of the total population over age 60 was 4.1 percent, and the median age was 22.9 years, while in the year 2030, the proportion of the population over 60 will be 18.3 percent, and the median age will be 38 years. Similar trends are found in most industrialized nations. Therefore, it is projected that in the future, the percentage of adults and older adults (especially the old-old, 75+) will increase, while the percentage of children and adolescents will decrease (see Chapter 1). These demographic shifts have many implications for our society's economic system, political and legal systems, educational institutions, health care systems, and housing and transportation systems. As a consequence of these changes, our perceptions of our own and others' aging will likely differ from those held at present. Moreover, changes in the family related to caring for older members are likely.

In order to illustrate the impact of increasing percentages of older adults in a society, coupled with a decrease in the percentage of younger individuals, it will be helpful to discuss what gerontologists call the **old age dependency ratio**. Basically, the old age dependency ratio (Butler, 1983) is the proportion of individuals in a society over age 65 in relation to individuals aged 18 to 64 years. The basic assumption of this ratio is that the individuals 18 to 64 years of age are providing the goods, services, and resources supporting the old population (65+ years) as well as those under 18 years of age. The relationship between the number of individuals under 18 and over 65 years of age to those 18 to 64 years of age is referred to as the overall dependency ratio. Since we are dealing with adulthood and aging, our discussion will concentrate on the old age dependency ratio and its implications.

Data (Ward, 1984, p.22) indicate that in the United States the old age dependency ratio was .17 in 1980, projected to be .20 in the year 2000, .26 in the year 2020, and .32 in the year 2030. The following example and Table 2.7 should help clarify the concept of old age dependency ratio.

In order to understand these ratios and their implications for adult development, let us use the data presented in Table 2.7. Since 1930 the number of individuals over age 65 per 100 individuals aged 18 to 64 has been increasing. This means that since 1930 the number of older individuals who are supported in terms of contributions to various pension systems by those still considered in the work force (18–64 years) has been increasing. The more this number (ratio) increases, the more individuals who are still working must

TABLE 2.7

NUMBER OF INDIVIDUALS 65 YEARS+ PER 100 INDIVIDUALS AGED 18–64 FOR SELECTED YEARS

Year	Number of Individuals 65 Years + Per 100 Individuals Aged 18–64
1930	9.1
1950	13.4
1970	17.7
1980	18.6
1990 (estimated)	20.0
2020 (estimated)	26.0
2040 (estimated)	30.6

Source: R.N. Butler. (1983). A generation at risk. *Across the Board,* July/August, 37–45.

contribute to the pension system. For example, in 1930, approximately 9 older adults were supported by 100 individuals still in the work force; in 1980 the number of older individuals supported by 100 workers had increased to approximately 18; by the year 2040 it is estimated that there will be 30 older adults supported by 100 workers. With successive cohorts, the amount each individual worker will have to contribute to support older adults will increase.

This example illustrates that as a society has more and more older adults who are dependent upon younger generations for support, goods, and services, and as the number of individuals in the young generation decreases, a greater proportion of the resources must be taken from the young to support the old. What are the implications of these figures?

Economic System   Perhaps the most noticeable area of impact of increased life expectancy and a subsequent increase in the percentage of older adults in a population is that of economics (Habib, 1985). Specifically, who will pay for the support and maintenance of the older adults in our society? In the United States and many other industrialized nations, the majority of older adults receive economic support from the government, such as social security and/or private pensions or retirement funds (Habib, 1985).

The benefits given to the older individual come from financial contributions to retirement funds by the individuals still working. As the percentage of older adults increases, and the number of younger contributors to the system remains constant or decreases, more and more of the younger individuals' pay will have to be taken to maintain solvency of the benefit system. Often, this leads to frustration and anger on the part of the young, who resent the loss of this additional money, which they feel they need to support themselves and their families. Frequently this is due to the fact that members of the younger generation overlook the fact that someday they will retire, or not be working, and others will be supporting them. This may also be due to negative attitudes of the young toward the old (see Chapter 9).

Recently, there has been some concern about the survival of the American Social Security system. This system has been approaching depletion in the last few years, and it is doubtful if the situation will improve in the future, given life-expectancy projections.

Therefore, in the economic realm, the most significant implication of increased life expectancy is determining how older adults will be supported—who will pay the bills. That is, will those working continue to support those who are not, or will government take funds from other areas, such as education or defense, to maintain older adults? This question will prove challenging for future generations (Habib, 1985; Hudson & Strate, 1985).

Political and Legal System   In a democracy such as the United States, the majority rules. As the percentage of older adults increase, especially in states with high concentrations of older adults, they will be able to form political action groups to elect candidates sensitive to their issues and needs (Hudson & Strate, 1985).

These political action groups, for example the Gray Panthers, and the representatives they elect could potentially pass or change legislation to include mandatory retirement (recently raised in 1977 to the age of 70; see Robinson, Coberly, & Paul, 1985), as well as to restructure allocation of all resources, an issue which affects everyone (Robinson et al., 1985). Therefore, as the percentage of older adults increases in a society, the greater potential political power these adults can exert on the entire society (Hudson & Strate, 1985). Such power may also have a long-term benefit to many older persons who would otherwise exercise little control over their environments. Political decisions will need to be made requiring the allocations of funds to support the training of personnel who might otherwise be forcibly retired or unemployed.

Educational System   Increased life expectancy can also have an effect on the educational system and institutions of a society. As more individuals retire and live to advanced old age, a number of those individuals will want to return to high school or college to either complete a degree or for enrichment purposes (see Chapter 7). In fact, as the number of available traditional college-age students (17–22 years of age) decreases, colleges and universities are attempting to recruit nontraditional students for their programs and are showing a new interest in adult education, which we will discuss further in Chapter 7.

A major question revolves around whether our educational institutions will be prepared for these nontraditional students (older learners). That is, will colleges and universities offer extended weekend and evening course offerings, provide easy access to facilities for individuals who may have decreased physical capabilities, and provide activities for these students?

Health Care Systems and Institutions   Health is central to our ability to care for ourselves and to our psychological well-being. The second area of greatest impact of increased life expectancy is on health care systems and institutions (Fairchild & Burton, 1982; Rice, 1981; Tobin, 1975). That is, there will be more older adults alive that will need nursing, medical, and dental services, ranging from annual routine examinations to long-term hospitalization. More than ever, these services will require coordination and integration. Relative to the current lack of emphasis on geriatric medicine (U.S. Congress, House of Representatives Select Committee on Aging, 1978), there will be an ever-increasing need for medical/dental professionals trained in the treatment and care of older patients (Shanas & Maddox, 1985). A greater *range* of care, as well as facilities capable of dealing with greater numbers of older persons with more debilitating illnesses (nursing homes, hospices), might be needed (Cantor & Little, 1985).

Further, this need for training and education for nursing, medical, and dental professionals will also affect educational institutions. In order to train and educate the nurses, physicians, and dentists of the future, professional schools will need to incorporate classroom material, topics, and curriculum offerings relevant to older adults into the curriculum (see Chapter 7 on learning).

The increase of older adults in the population will also create a greater demand for hospital beds and services (Fairchild & Burton, 1982). As previously discussed, most older adults die of diseases that are chronic and do not have a known cure at the present time. Therefore, since medical science has not discovered cures for these diseases, afflicted individuals will still need to be hospitalized on a long-term basis. Short-stay beds are also likely to be in greater demand to support hospices and families caring for older persons. The increase in older adults with chronic diseases decreases the number of beds available for younger individuals and older ones with acute diseases or disorders. This may result in a need to build more hospitals and nursing facilities or to develop procedures for the treatment and care of older individuals in their homes. Sussman (1985) argues that such health care systems must supplement, not replace, the family's caregiving role. Perhaps this may lessen the guilt many families experience in having to institutionalize an older family member, but the stress of caring for and living with an impaired elder may have a serious impact on family life (see Chapters 8 and 9).

Another implication in this area that is also related to the economic system is the high cost of health care, which continues to increase. The major portion of the health care cost is paid by the government and private insurance companies (Rich & Baum, 1984). As the number of older adults increases, many of whom will have chronic disorders, the greater the strain put on these systems to fund the cost of medical care will be. The end result may be either a decrease in coverage (which expenses a medical insurance plan will pay) or an increase in fees or premiums paid into the system by policyholders. That is, you may pay more in annual premiums, and your overall extent of coverage may decrease.

Overall, the increase in life expectancy may have a significant impact on our medical systems and institutions. This impact will be manifested in a greater demand for professionals trained in the disorders of aging, a need for more hospital beds, and a strain on those systems that traditionally fund the cost of medical care.

Housing and Transportation Increased life expectancy (particularly for women; see Fairchild & Burton, 1982) will likely increase the need for adequate housing units and transportation systems for older adults. Access to transportation, for example, has a direct effect on isolation and therefore impacts on the well-being of older persons (see Chapter 13). This need for additional housing and transportation will ultimately become an economic issue in terms of allocation of available resources, leading to debates about the age-appropriateness of criteria for services of all types (Neugarten, 1976, 1982). For instance, will the funding for additional housing units for the elderly be at the expense of other needed services, such as educational grants to support continued learning, or child-care services to free parents who want to pursue new careers?

Attitudes Toward Aged Persons/Intergenerational Relationships Perhaps most importantly, such changes may effect a shift in our attitudes toward older adults (see Chapter 9), either leading to a more realistic, caring stance toward them (based on more viable role models of aging) or to more conflict and hostility, under the assumption that the old are a necessary burden on the young (see Binstock, 1983).

As the number of older persons increases relative to the number of young, children will likely have more (and different types of) contact with their grandparents, who may be healthier for a larger proportion of their lives. They may be more highly educated, or more politically involved, and consequently expect and exert more control over their own lives and perhaps participate more actively in their children's and grandchildren's lives, despite being physically separated by great distances.

SUMMARY

In this chapter, the biological (cellular) aspects of the aging process were discussed. These include the various *biological* and *physical* changes that are associated with each specific segment of the adult life cycle. The effects on *behavior* and *well-being* of these changes for the individual were also elaborated; these seem to be most apparent in middle and later adulthood.

A number of biological and physiological theories of a *genetic, nongenetic* and *physiological* nature that attempt to explain the aging process were presented. Due to the complexity of the aging process, no one specific theory can adequately explain all aspects, and thus these theories remain as educated guesses or speculations about aging. While *neuronal loss* with age is characteristic of the brain, such losses vary within (by cortical area) and between persons. Moreover, recent evidence suggests some *plasticity* in brain function well into later adulthood.

The historical, current, and future trends in life expectancy in the United States and other nations were presented. Research suggests that specific *intrinsic or primary* and *extrinsic or secondary* factors appear to be related to longevity in humans.

Intrinsic factors are those that are generally considered fixed or determined, since they are inherited from our parents or are related to biological/physiological processes. These factors are *genetic inheritance, gender* and *race,* and *health condition.* Extrinsic factors are assumed to *modify* the limits projected for life expectancy. Their effects on longevity could be either positive or negative. Examples of extrinsic factors include *nutrition* and *diet, climate* and *physical environment, exercise* and *activity,* and *personality* and *stress avoidance.*

Finally, the implications of increased life expectancy upon society were discussed. Increased longevity will likely have effects upon the economic, political, legal, educational, and health care systems of our society, as well as on our attitudes toward older adults.

Menopause	Cross-over effect
Empty nest	Poverty level (index)
Time perspective	Type A/Type B individuals
Existential questioning	General adaptation syndrome
Midlife crisis	Elder abuse
Biological theories (genetic, nongenetic) of aging	Wisdom factor
	Terminal drop
Physiological theories (single organ systems, physiological control mechanisms) of aging	Old age dependency ratio
	Neuron
	Senile plaques
Longevity	Neurofibrillary tangles
Life expectancy	Lipofuscin
Intrinsic/primary factors	Brain plasticity
Extrinsic/secondary factors	Neurotransmitter substances

- Why is it important to study research methods? Is there a relationship between how we gather our facts and what these facts are?
- What is the distinction between developmental and nondevelopmental research?
- What similarities and differences exist between experimental and correlational approaches to research? What are the advantages and disadvantages of each?
- What is internal and external validity? Why is this distinction important?
- What are the purposes, advantages, and disadvantages of cross-sectional, longitudinal, and time lag designs?
- How do Schaie's time sequential, cohort sequential, and cross sequential methods propose to solve the problems of each of the more basic designs?
- What is Baltes's bifactorial model? How does it differ from Schaie's trifactorial approach? How do the two complement one another?
- What are the major ethical concerns to keep in mind when conducting developmental and nondevelopmental research?

CHAPTER · 3

RESEARCH METHODS IN ADULT DEVELOPMENT AND AGING

■

Nearly all of what you will read in this text regarding early adulthood, middle adulthood, and old age is based on some kind of research methodology. Consequently, being able to understand the methods by which the facts of adult development are gathered will put you in a more favorable position to judge their relevance to you or their more general truth or falsity. The more confidence you have in the method by which facts about adulthood are gathered, the more useful those facts will be to you in dealing with adults of all ages.

Consider the two following situations:

A 65-year-old man comes in to apply for a part-time cashier's job in a department store. After a short interview and an arithmetic skills exam, he is told that he is too old for the position and that others who are younger are better qualified because they scored higher on the exam. The personnel manager suggests, "Our young people are just better qualified, but when you get old, this is often what happens. Try not to feel too bad. I'm sure that even the younger applicants for our position won't be as sharp as they once were when they reach your age. They'll probably perform about as well as you did on the skills test."

What assumptions about younger and older applicants' arithmetic skills might the personnel manager be making on the basis of the test data? He may be concluding that just because the man is older and has been outscored by a younger person, this younger person's skills will probably deteriorate when that individual reaches age 65, too. As we shall see, there are *many* reasons to account for our 65-year-old's poorer arithmetic performance other than his age. Moreover, those younger persons may or may not lose their arithmetic ability when they age, and our older applicant may be more competent than when *he* was young! Thus, our personnel manager's ageist comparisons between younger and older job applicants (i.e., influenced by his method of gathering his facts) probably influenced his *conclusions* about who was better qualified. In this case, then, faulty conclusions about the older applicant's skills rest upon a method of gathering data that is itself flawed. This serves as an excellent example of the job discrimination older persons often face.

A young mother is awakened by her child's crying in the middle of the night. She goes into his room and instinctively puts her hand on his forehead to check for fever. He feels "hot," so she gets the thermometer and puts it under the squirming child's arm. After several minutes she returns, removes the thermometer, and after reading only 99 degrees, calls her doctor. The first question asked of her is *"How* did you take his temperature?" After she describes her method, her physician advises her to retake her child's temperature, this time by putting the thermometer under the child's tongue. After watching her child carefully as she retakes his temperature, she now discovers the reading to be 102 degrees. She redials her physician, who, upon hearing the news, advises her to bring her son in for an examination.

While these examples have little to do with one another, they both serve a useful purpose in illustrating the relationship between our *methods* of acquiring knowledge (comparing younger and older job applicants, and whether the child's temperature was obtained via the "under the arm" or "under the tongue" method), and the *significance* of that knowledge (Is the older applicant less competent because he is aged 65? Did the child have a fever or not?). While it is easy to see the potentially harmful consequences of having an inaccurate picture of a young child's body temperature or an individual adult's job skills, information about an adult's memory, learning capacities, or response to psychotherapy all hinge on *how* the data dealing with these questions are gathered. Likewise, broader questions regarding the course of development as it relates to these and other issues are equally influenced by basic decisions made about *how* such questions are to be answered; that is, are young adults more intelligent than older adults? Who is a better candidate for psychological treatment? Do different aspects of one's personality change as one ages?

In this chapter we will explore a variety of approaches to gathering the facts about adulthood and aging. In general, we will discuss research methods, keeping in mind the distinction between *nondevelopmental* and *developmental* research.

DEVELOPMENTAL VERSUS NONDEVELOPMENTAL RESEARCH

Nondevelopmental research seeks to examine relationships between factors or variables the investigator is seeking to understand that might apply to all adults, *regardless* of age. Such research is often, but not always, conducted with the intention of establishing a *causal* relationship between one factor (or set of factors) and another factor (or set of factors). **Developmental research**, on the other hand, seeks to determine if any relationship exists between *chronological age* (or, more accurately, the processes that account for aging) and some other factor of interest.

In many cases, both developmental and nondevelopmental research complement one another. For example, the nondevelopmental researcher might be interested in whether there is a relationship between similarity of spouses (e.g., interests, abilities, backgrounds) and marital satisfaction. That is, are persons who see themselves as similar to one another more happily married? What is the role that similarity (versus other factors) plays in determining a married couple's satisfaction with their relationship? The investigator might feel such knowledge is important in that if one knows that similarity between spouses is not the most important factor in determining happy marriages, one can better provide counseling to prospective newlyweds or to persons experiencing marital difficulties.

The developmental researcher, on the other hand, might define this problem differently. That is, for newlywed couples who are similar to one another versus those who are not, who is more happily married 10 or 15 years later? When compared with couples who have been married for many years, is similarity an "essential" ingredient in the relationship of newlyweds?

In other words, the developmentalist is interested in exploring the contribution that couple similarity plays in the "aging" of a relationship. The nondevelopmentalist, however, is more concerned with the relative importance that this factor has in determining marital happiness among couples regardless of length of marriage. While the couples who participate in such a research project may be young or old, their ages are considered to be irrelevant or extraneous to the problem the nondevelopmental investigator is examining. Quite often, nondevelopmental research is done as a basis for work that may be developmental in nature.

EXPERIMENTAL VERSUS CORRELATIONAL RESEARCH

Another basic distinction we wish to draw at this point is that between *experimental* (manipulative) and *correlational* (descriptive) research.

Experimental Approaches to Research

Experimental research seeks to establish *causal* relationships between a factor or factors that is (are) *manipulated* by the researcher, termed the *independent variable(s)* (IV) (McGuigan, 1983; Rosenthal & Rosnow, 1984). This independent variable derives its name from the fact that persons can be *independently* assigned to conditions (e.g., treatments or training programs) thought by the researcher to be causally related to some result that the investigator is seeking to produce (e.g., enhanced skills, more positive attitudes). This intended result(s) is(are) termed the *dependent variable(s)* (DV)—so termed because the result is *dependent upon* the effects of the treatment.

For example, if we wish to determine whether the type of instruction older students receive affects their attitudes toward learning, we might **randomly assign** students as they register to one section (instructor-present taught) or to another (instructor-absent [television] taught). If extraneous factors, such as differences among our older students in motivation, previous education, intelligence, personality factors, socioeconomic status, or marital status, are thought also to influence attitudes toward learning, randomly assigning students might distribute these effects equally across class sections. In this case, type of instruction functions as our independent variable, and changes (before and after instruction) in attitudes toward learning represent our dependent variable. In order to compare our classes validly, we must further ensure that they are as comparable as possible in other aspects (e.g., size of the class, content of the material to be learned, seating arrangement, number of class meetings, length of classes, time of day, sex or age of instructor) that could also conceivably affect the students' attitudes toward their class experience. We must also ensure that all participants are treated equally during the course of their classroom experience (e.g., being tested on course content at equal points in the semester, adequate lighting/temperature conditions throughout the class).

Ultimately, the conclusion should be reached that *only* the manipulation of the independent variable accounts for the differences between our groups' attitudes toward learning. If our efforts to do so were not successful, or we were unaware of the influence of an extraneous variable, its effects would be potentially **confounded** with (inseparable from) those associated with the independent variable. In most cases of experimental research, where we have specified a hypothesis (e.g., that instructor-led classes will produce more positive attitudes), we would term the persons receiving the manipulation or treatment members of the **experimental** group, while those not receiving the treatment of interest (in our case, the automated instruction class) would be termed a **control** or *comparison* group. Typically, experimental research is most consistent with the mechanistic world view (see Chapter 1), in that the manipulatable, immediate, objectively measurable antecedents (causal factors) of a phenomenon (developmental or nondevelopmental in scope) are the focus of study.

Correlational Approaches to Research

Correlations describe a *relationship* or an *association* between at least two factors. **Correlational** research is often, but not always conducted by those favoring an organismic approach to adult development and aging (see Chapter 1). The emphasis of the organismic approach is upon *correlationships* between underlying structural (organizational) factors (assumed to exist within the individual) and observable behaviors.

Correlational research seeks to establish whether or not a factor *covaries* with or *correlates* to another factor. That is, are changes in one factor accompanied by systematic changes in another? To the extent that this occurs, the variables (e.g., personality traits, assertiveness, intelligence, or other factors such as age) are said to be *correlated* (see Figure 3.1). While **correlation** is a

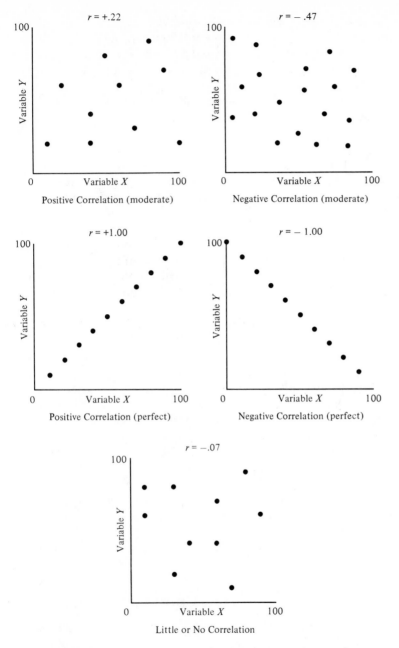

Figure 3.1   The nature of correlation: examples of varying degrees of
correlation between variables.

necessary condition for **causation** (two factors must at least be correlated in
order to be causal), it is not a *sufficient* one.

For example, while more assertiveness may be accompanied by more
intelligence (see Chapter 6) or by increased chronological age, it does not

follow that more intelligence or increased age *causes* one to act more assertively (or vice versa). In fact, it may be that intelligent people recognize that assertive behavior is sometimes adaptive and sometimes not (intelligence is causal). Characteristics of assertive individuals (e.g., good interpersonal skills or the ability to analyze situations) may also account for their higher intelligence (assertiveness is causal). Intelligence and assertiveness might also be correlated because they both stem from a common third factor (e.g., a sense of curiosity fostered by one's parents about one's surroundings). Intelligent, assertive individuals may share common behaviors (and therefore they are highly correlated) because of their inquisitive nature. In this case a third factor (learning history or present environment) accounts for the relationship between two factors (assertiveness and intelligence) that are *correlated but not causally related* to one another.

What about the apparent causal relationship between age and assertiveness? Individuals who are older may be more assertive because their experience has taught them that they must take the initiative in order to survive (age-related experience is causal). Alternatively, the trait of assertiveness could be an adaptive characteristic (learned early in life) that permits one to live longer (assertiveness is causal).

Regarding age and intelligence, intelligent individuals may live longer because they are more knowledgeable about avoiding stressful situations. It could also be that intelligence and age would appear to be causally related because those who were less intelligent have since died (e.g., they are careless). Intelligent people may live longer because they are more adaptive (intelligence is causal) or the accumulation of experience and knowledge associated with age may cause individuals to behave more intelligently (age-related factors are causal). A "third" variable in this case explaining the age-intelligence relationship might be level of education. Highly educated persons not only live longer and tend to experience less intellectual decline (see Jarvik, Blum, & Varma, 1972; Jarvik & Falek, 1963), but also may seek further education to keep themselves mentally stimulated and involved (see K.W. Schaie & Willis, 1978). Some individuals live longer than others and/or are more or less intelligent or assertive for a number of reasons. Thus, as we have seen in each of the above situations, one should be very cautious about assuming that correlation equals causation.

Applications of Experimental and Correlational Research

Before moving on, let us make several important points regarding experimental and correlational research.

Whether an experimental or correlational research approach is taken is often dictated by the nature of the problem that the investigator is researching.

Studies of naturally occurring phenomena (e.g., aging, retirement, marriage, parenthood, death) deal with issues whose effects must be *inferred* (we cannot directly observe them but can conclude via the weight of the evidence that they are present). Where participants are selected according to the criterion of whether they have experienced a given event or not, such research is, by definition, correlational. People cannot be randomly assigned to a "retired" versus a "nonretired" group, just as the experimenter cannot arbitrarily say, "For the purposes of this research, you will be sixty years old and you will be twenty years old." A correlational-naturalistic (observing behavior in its natural surroundings) approach to some research topics is then, by definition, required as the variable of interest (e.g., age; see Birren & Renner, 1977; Wohlwill, 1970a) is not manipulatable by the researcher. For example, if we were interested in studying the effects on morale of being relocated from one's home to a nursing home, randomly assigning participants to "groups" would not only be unfeasible but also unethical. How could one person be denied nursing-home care and another receive such care? Who would decide? Who would be responsible for any negative effects that those denied such care might suffer? On this basis, it is somewhat unfair and, in fact, inaccurate to conclude that experimental research is "better" than correlational research.

Experimental research can, however, if carried out carefully, lead to relatively unambiguous conclusions regarding a causal relationship between our independent and dependent variables. If such conclusions can be made, our experimental study is more likely to be **internally valid**.

Unfortunately, while experimental methods permit more control over extraneous (confounded) factors, they sometimes lack **external validity**. If a study is externally valid, findings are **generalizable**; they can be *generalized* to other samples or measures of either our independent or dependent variables. It is precisely because the conditions under which the data are collected are often well specified, yet narrow in scope (i.e., IV-DV relationships, selection of a sample, control over extraneous influences) that they often cannot be generalized to other sets of treatments, measures of such effects, samples of participants, or experimenters. In other words, they lack external validity. Moreover, the phenomenon that one is interested in studying under highly controlled conditions may itself be changed as a function of our studying it! In the real world, events rarely are caused by a single underlying factor (IV), and there are always extraneous influences that confound the study of the problem we are attempting to view "in isolation." To the extent that our research (purpose, sample of participants, selection of IV/DV) mimics problems people confront in everyday life outside the laboratory, it is said to have **ecological validity** (Hultsch & Hickey, 1978; K.W. Schaie, 1978; Scheidt, 1980; Weisz, 1978).

A partial solution to the external validity issue is to simply replicate our research, though it must be stressed that replication does not guarantee generalizability of our findings. Frequently, however, replications are not seen as being as interesting or as exciting as first-time exploratory projects.

If our findings are specific to a given sample of participants, or particular to a given intervention, then they are going to be of limited use to *both* the basic researcher (as a stimulus for further work) and the practitioner (as a potential solution to an everyday problem). To the extent that our findings are reproducible, we can be more confident of the meaningfulness of our findings.

It is for reasons of both internal and external validity that the researcher must be especially careful and precise in:

1. formulating a problem and an hypothesis,
2. defining the population from which a sample of participants will be selected,
3. assigning participants to clearly defined conditions/treatment groups,
4. selecting and measuring the dependent variables,
5. collecting data,
6. analyzing and reporting the results of this data collection,
7. drawing conclusions based on the analysis of these data regarding the extent to which the hypothesis is supported, and
8. making inferences based on one's study of that phenomenon.

All of these requirements are characteristics of the *scientific method* (McGuigan, 1983; Rosenthal & Rosnow, 1984).

Concerns regarding the above aspects of doing research are equally important in both experimental and correlational research, which can be either nondevelopmental or developmental in scope. If one selects participants according to their chronological age, the study must in the strictest sense be considered correlational, given that we cannot randomly assign participants to levels of age. That is, we must correlate age and the variable we are interested in studying—we cannot arbitrarily designate some persons to be older or younger than they really are.

Frequently, as in the case of developmental/nondevelopmental research, experimental and correlational approaches can be combined to better our understanding of a phenomenon. For example, we may discover under everyday conditions that being fatigued causes some adults to perform more poorly. Subsequently, in a controlled situation, we may confirm this relationship by manipulating fatigue (making a task shorter or longer) and observing its effects on performance.

We now turn to specific types of research strategies that are particular to developmental research—cross-sectional, longitudinal, and time lag designs.

DEVELOPMENTAL RESEARCH METHODS: CROSS-SECTIONAL, LONGITUDINAL, AND TIME LAG DESIGNS

As we noted above in our distinction between developmental and nondevelopmental research, the developmentalist is primarily interested in the relationship between chronological age and some other factor(s). For the purposes of our discussion, the assessment of age effects in developmental research is assumed to be the central interest of the developmental investigator.

Traditionally, the measurement of age effects on behavior has been accomplished via the use of **cross-sectional** or **longitudinal** designs (see Achenbach, 1978; P.B. Baltes, Reese, & Nesselroade, 1977; Botwinick, 1984; Friedrich, 1972; and K.W. Schaie, 1977). As does experimental and correlational research, each approach to measuring developmental change has its own unique purposes, advantages, and drawbacks. Each suffers from certain problems associated with both internal (is age causally related to the dependent variable of interest?) and external (are our findings generalizable?) validity.

It is best to consider both cross-sectional and longitudinal designs as *descriptive.* That is, the data they yield may or may not indicate that chronological age causally relates to whatever we are studying (e.g., intelligence, reaction time). However, while we can derive an **age function** (a picture of how age and our variable of interest are related) based upon findings from each design, they can only describe the fact that intelligence or reaction time vary with chronological age. *Why* they vary is quite another matter! (Recall our example at this chapter's outset dealing with younger and older job applicants.) With these points in mind, let us discuss these "classical" developmental designs.

Cross-sectional Designs

Cross-sectional designs compare individuals who vary in age at one point in time, for example, 20-year-olds, 40-year-olds, 60-year-olds in 1985. Persons are *selected* to form a *cross section* of the age continuum. Obviously, we could select our participants so that they would vary along some other factor (e.g., socioeconomic class, sex, or race). The **samples** of individuals (comprising each age range) are said to be gathered **independently** of one another (e.g., 20-year-olds are sampled independently of 40-year-olds).

In conducting cross-sectional research, one must assume that the samples are relatively **homogeneous**. That is, all the persons in our 20-year-old group should be similar regarding age. If this assumption could not be reasonably met, it would be unwise to compare our samples. Even if age were reliably felt to be responsible for differences in the variables of interest, under these circumstances, this fact would be difficult to establish. Furthermore, if age correlates with other factors that *also* affect our variables of interest, cross-sectional comparison will also be hampered. These "other factors" (e.g., socioeconomic status, health, level of education) make it difficult to describe our samples accurately (Would we have a cross section of samples based on age or education?). This issue also affects the basis upon which comparisons are made: is age or education (or both) responsible for the differences in the factor of interest (intelligence)? Because we cannot "assign" participants to levels of age, it is quite possible that these other factors would be *confounded* (intercorrelated and thus inseparable) with age. In an experimental sense, had random assignment to ages been possible, a reasonable assumption would be that the effects of these other confounding variables would be equally distributed across groups. While younger samples are more **homogeneous** (the individuals are more similar to one another), older samples are likely to be more **heterogeneous** (Bornstein & Smircina, 1982; Krauss, 1980; Maddox & Douglass, 1974), making overall comparisons difficult.

Assuming age-homogeneous groups that are heterogeneous regarding other factors that are *not* correlated with age, we could assume that the results of our cross-sectional study would yield valid conclusions regarding *average* **interindividual age differences** in the dependent variable (that factor dependent upon presumed variation in the age of our samples). Moreover, if we could assume perfect age homogeneity within samples (e.g., every person were 20 or 40 years old), we could just as easily select at random a 20-year-old and a 40-year-old and find that the differences between these two individuals would parallel the differences between our groups as a whole. The term *average* is used to indicate that each individual's score within each group can validly be represented as an average, assuming relatively homogeneous groups.

Cross-sectional designs are, however, time of measurement specific— our sample comparisons are specific to a given point in time. The real object of our interest, **intraindividual age change**, cannot be studied cross-sectionally in that the participants have not changed—they all have been measured only once! Moreover, we are looking at averages, not individuals.

The cross-sectional researcher who is unaware of the age difference/ age change issue when examining the difference between 20-year-olds and 40-year-olds is assuming that if the test were repeated on the same subjects twenty years later, the 20-year-olds would then resemble the 40-year-olds in the original cross-sectional study! Because each person in a cross-sectional study is only measured once, whether these 20-year-olds (20 years later) would resemble the 40-year olds cannot be determined.

In a practical sense, cross-sectional research can be quite useful, however. It is relatively cheap and efficient—a great deal of data can be gathered on a "one-shot" basis. We can also establish *normative* trends, that is, judgments about an individual's standing relative to his age peers, using cross-sectional methods.

PROBLEMS WITH CROSS-SECTIONAL DESIGNS

From a developmental standpoint, the internal validity of the cross-sectional study is difficult to establish. There are several rival explanations for the effects of age (maturation) on our dependent variable. That is, if we wish to infer that age is related to sample differences in our dependent variable, we may have difficulty in doing so. Work by P.B. Baltes (1968) and K.W. Schaie (1967, 1970, 1973) suggests that the following are potentially *confounded* with chronological age in a cross-sectional design: **cohort effects, selective sampling, selective survival**, and **terminal change**.

Cohort Effects   While problems in the definition and interpretation of cohort effects have been raised (Rosow, 1978), *cohort* is usually defined in terms of *year of birth* (or in terms of a range of years). Individuals from a particular cohort or generation share a common set of experiences that separate them from others preceding or following them in historical time. Thus, persons

Persons unique to a given birth cohort grow up with sets of experiences particular to their year of birth. Those who precede or follow them in historical time are likely to have different sets of experiences.

who have experienced such events as the Great Depression or World War II (i.e., persons born between 1920–1940) would differ from those who have seen astronauts land on the moon or benefited from the polio vaccine (i.e., persons born between 1940–1970). Each cohort grows up with different attitudes, experiences, skills, and values. Cohorts can also be defined in terms of specific psychosocial events such as marriage, parenthood, divorce, or retirement in that those who have married, had children, been divorced, or retired would each share a common set of experiences (see Botwinick, 1984).

P.B. Baltes (1968) illustrates the potential age-cohort confound in cross-sectional findings for intelligence where different cohorts are tested at different points in their individual life spans. On a within-cohort (average intraindividual) basis, Figure 3.2 illustrates that intellectual growth clearly accompanies the aging process, assuming that cohorts begin with differing levels of knowledge. As Figure 3.2 illustrates, the cross-sectional comparison yields a curve that *appears to* present a picture of decline with age, however. Awareness of the substantial cohort effects in intelligence (because cohorts differ in their level of education) (see Chapter 6) and personality (see Chapter 10) bear out the misleading age effects that cross-sectional research may portray, leading to potentially faulty conclusions about intraindividual change across the adult life span.

Selective Sampling In cross-sectional studies, age may also be confounded with *selective* (nonrandom) *sampling* (see P.B. Baltes et al., 1977; Friedrich, 1972; Salthouse, 1982), where those who are the most able, most available, most highly educated or in the best health tend to volunteer, producing positively biased samples. This sampling bias may cause one to *underestimate* reliable age

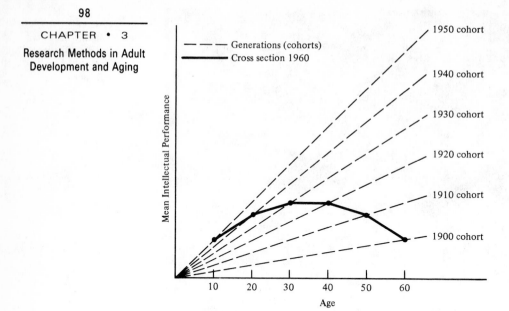

Figure 3.2 Age-cohort simulation: illustration of age-cohort confounds in cross-sectional research and of cohort differences in intellectual functioning. *Source:* P.B. Baltes. (1968). Cross-sectional and longitudinal sequences in the study of age and generation effects. *Human Development, 11,* 152. Reprinted by permission of S. Karger AG, Basel.

effects. Even if one "randomly" selects potential participants, they cannot be forced to participate on a random basis. Thus, in many cases, what appears to be an aging effect may really be a sampling effect based on volunteer samples that are not representative of the pool of potential participants.

Selective Survival Age effects may also be confounded with *selective survival,* referring to the tendency for those who live longer to differ from those with less longevity. This survival effect also causes cross-sectional studies to underestimate age effects. Those who are initially in better health, more highly educated, married, or employed in low-stress occupations may all live longer and consequently no longer be representative of their *original* cohort, that is, those who died earlier (see P.B. Baltes, 1968; P.B. Baltes et al., 1977; K.F. Riegel, R.M. Riegel, & Meyer, 1967). For example, a sample of 60-year-olds may no longer be representative of its original cohort; it is a *positively biased* sample.

Terminal Change *Terminal change* (drop) may also be confounded with age effects in cross-sectional studies (Kleemeier, 1962; K.F. Riegel & R.M. Riegel, 1972; Siegler, 1975). Terminal change refers to the fact that with increased closeness to death, individuals show declines in their functioning—their standing relative to others may be lower, or they may decline to a greater extent than others (Botwinick, West, & Storandt, 1978). Depending upon how many of our older participants are in this "terminal phase," terminal change effects will either depress or elevate group means in older samples, leading to potentially faulty conclusions about the relationship of our dependent variable to chronological age (see Chapter 2 on terminal drop).

In a cross-sectional study, the above factors (cohort effects, selective sampling, selective survival, and terminal change) are all potentially confounded with chronological age differences. Because they are inseparable, the researcher cannot draw clear, unambiguous conclusions regarding the basis for the apparent age effects one's cross-sectional design portrays. Not only do these confounds affect the internal validity of cross-sectional research, they also affect its external validity. That is, we do not know to what extent these age (cohort) effects can be *generalized* to other times of measurement (remember our cross-sectional study is time of measurement specific). If there are alternative explanations for the effects of age in our data (e.g., cohort effects), our results subject to these influences may not be replicable. Unfortunately, the cross-sectional researcher would never be able to answer such a question without replicating his study at a different historical point in time (i.e., doing the study again 10 years later). Assuming similar ages (i.e., 20, 40, 60 years of age), this new cross-sectional study would necessarily involve different cohorts (see Figure 3.3).

Longitudinal Designs

As opposed to cross-sectional designs, longitudinal research measures *average intraindividual age changes* (P.B. Baltes, 1968; P.B. Baltes et al., 1977). Longitudinal studies are restricted to a particular cohort, and each person is assessed more than once. Longitudinal studies utilize *dependent* sampling, where data for participants at the second (repeated) sampling are *dependent upon* those data gathered at the first testing. For example, individuals, all born in 1900, are first tested at age 20 in 1920, again at age 40 in 1940, and again at age 60 in 1960. In that different individuals may age at differing rates, the longitudinal researcher is primarily interested in exploring the basis for the resulting interindividual differences that can exist at any point in time. The researcher is not interested in between-group variability (as in the cross-sectional design), but

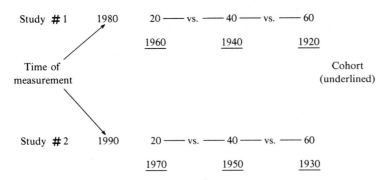

Figure 3.3   Replication of a cross-sectional study at another time of measurement.

in *within-group* (cohort) *variability*. If we are interested in studying the cohort as a whole, our longitudinal study might permit us to estimate *average intrain-dividual variability* with age. Consequently, the longitudinal study allows us to study aging both on a group and on an individual level, by examining differential rates of change for a factor or factors between persons within a given cohort. Differential changes across time in a given factor or changes in patterns of relationships among factors (e.g., health and ability at age 20 versus age 40) within persons (P.B. Baltes, 1968; P.B. Baltes et al., 1977) can also be studied longitudinally. Because individuals are repeatedly interviewed, they obviously have the opportunity to undergo change that is perhaps in some manner related to the aging process.

Despite its potential for assessing developmental change, the longitudinal method is considerably more expensive (involving multiple observations of each person), and the investigator may face practical difficulties in the storage of data, record keeping, or changing characteristics of the measuring instruments (e.g., reliability, validity). If for some reason (lack of interest, death), there is a change in researchers, this becomes a source of error in itself, especially where the investigators collect their own data.

PROBLEMS WITH LONGITUDINAL DESIGNS

Time of Measurement   The major internal validity problem for the longitudinal researcher is the potential *confounding* of *age changes* and **time of measurement**. A time of measurement effect (K.W. Schaie, 1965, 1970) is one that affects all persons, regardless of age or cohort. For example, in general, persons interviewed in 1950 might be more anxious or score more highly on a scale of intelligence than those interviewed in 1960.

While cohort effects have an impact that is more long-term and specific to individuals born in a given year who share a common set of experiences, time of measurement effects are of relatively short duration and generalize across persons regardless of age. For example, one might ask whether longitudinal changes between ages 20 and 40 are determined by maturational (aging) changes in personality or whether they reflect specific happenings particular to most people who are alive in 1920 versus 1940 (e.g., post-WWI optimism versus pre-WWII anxiety or ethnocentrism). Given this potential confounding of age and time of measurement, the longitudinal researcher cannot draw clear-cut conclusions regarding the role that maturational change plays in determining age changes in, for example, political views, personality structure, or intelligence. It is worth noting that if one is studying aspects of development that are culturally influenced (e.g., the impact of economic changes) however, time of measurement specific events may influence individuals in very different ways. For example, an economic depression may affect older workers differently from younger workers, or established businessmen differently from "upstarts" (see Elder, 1979).

While selective sampling, selective survival, and terminal change can be confounded with age in both cross-sectional and longitudinal research, **selective dropout**, **practice effects**, and **regression to the mean** are internal validity problems particular to the longitudinal design.

Selective Dropout refers to the tendency for participants to nonrandomly withdraw from a study for a variety of reasons (lack of interest, poor performance, lack of time, illness, unavailability). If the reasons for such dropout are correlated with age effects in our dependent variable, then selective dropout is said to be intertwined (confounded) with aging effects in our longitudinal data. Siegler and Botwinick (1979), for example, found that with repeated testings over a 20-year span of time, the less-able subjects tended to drop out, yielding data suggesting little age-related decline in intelligence, based upon this rather elite sample of older persons.

Practice Effects (P.B. Baltes, 1968; Botwinick, 1984; Cerella & Lowe, 1984) associated with increased test sophistication, item familiarity, or lessened anxiety can also confound age changes measured longitudinally. In most cases, these practice effects lead to more favorable estimates of age changes. Practice effects can be dealt with by creating "alternate forms" of the same measure, one of which is administered to each person at each occasion.

Practice effects can be studied (assessed) by comparing the scores of a sample of persons who have been tested once with those who have been repeatedly tested (dependent samples) (Labouvie, Bartsch, Nesselroade, & P.B. Baltes, 1974; K.W. Schaie, Labouvie, & Barrett, 1973; K.W. Schaie, Labouvie, & Buech, 1973). If differences do occur, the repeated measurements data can be "corrected" for this difference (Labouvie et al., 1974).

By utilizing "fresh participants" who are not "testwise," independent sampling also helps to deal more completely with practice and attrition issues inherent in longitudinal research. It is worth noting (see Botwinick, 1977, 1984; Schaie & Hertzog, 1983; Schaie, Labouvie, & Buech, 1973) that there is some controversy regarding whether longitudinal samples gathered independently do in fact differ from traditional longitudinally gathered samples, so the correction discussed above may not be necessary.

Regression to the Mean (P.B. Baltes, Nesselroade, Schaie, & Labouvie, 1972; Campbell & Stanley, 1963; Nesselroade, Seigler, & P.B. Baltes, 1980) is a potential confound in longitudinal studies, especially where participants are selected along the extremes of some continuum (e.g., high versus low intelligence, conservative versus liberal), or where selective sampling/selective survival effects have produced positively biased samples. Those at these extremes are said to be more likely to "regress" (statistically) toward a less extreme position at occasion two (relative to occasion one). That is, those who initially score very high (high intelligence, more liberalism) become less so. In a sense their scores cannot go much higher because they are so already—there is no "room" for them to improve further. Alternatively, those who have initially scored the lowest (lower intelligence, more conservative) appear to get brighter (or more liberal) when this change is viewed relative to where they began. They could not score much more poorly; their improvement was simply the only direction they could change. Regression to the mean may mask genuine aging trends—change may appear to occur when none has really come about. Those at the extremes simply "regressed" to a less extreme value at occasion two relative to occasion one.

As with the cross-sectional design, these internal validity concerns (factors confounded with age change) also affect the external validity (generalizability) of the longitudinal study. If these confounding factors are substantial in their impact, it is less likely that our longitudinal findings will generalize to other cohorts—recall that our longitudinal sample is cohort specific.

Replicating our longitudinal study with a different cohort (measured at the same age) will require a new data collection effort at a different historical point in time. If the culture has changed in any significant way, it is unlikely that the two longitudinal studies would agree (see Figure 3.4). Because the longitudinal study is cohort specific, our researcher cannot determine whether the results will generalize to other cohorts or not. Despite these problems, longitudinal studies remain very valuable due to their ability to measure average intraindividual age change.

Time Lag Designs

In contrast to cross-sectional and longitudinal designs, whose focus is the assessment of age-related differences and changes, the purpose of the **time lag** design is to assess some aspect of *cultural change* (P.B. Baltes, 1968; P.B. Baltes et al., 1977; Friedrich, 1972; K.W. Schaie, 1965, 1970). Chronological age effects, by intent, are *not* the focus of the time lag design. The researcher may be acting on a hunch or previous research suggesting age to be unimportant (relative to other factors) in accounting for differences in the scores of different individuals of varying ages (cross-sectional) or within individuals as those persons get older (longitudinal). Time lag studies are a valuable source of information to the extent that cultural changes, and not age-related factors, are responsible for our political attitudes, behaviors in various roles, or feelings about social issues.

Time lag designs may actually involve at least two separate data collec-

Longitudinal Study #1	Occasion 1 ⟶ (1920)	Occasion 2 ⟶ (1940)	Occasion 3 (1960)
Cohort 1900	Age 20	Age 40	Age 60
Longitudinal Study #2	Occasion 1 ⟶ (1960)	Occasion 2 ⟶ (1980)	Occasion 3 (2000)
Cohort 1940	Age 20	Age 40	Age 60

Figure 3.4   Replication of a longitudinal study with a different cohort.

tion efforts, or they may be accomplished archivally, utilizing existing data—for example, high school records or voting patterns. Time lag (*lagged* or *delayed* across historical time) research equates at least two samples in terms of age—for example, 20-year-olds in 1960 (1940 cohort) versus 20-year-olds in 1980 (1960 cohort). Thus, a time lag design may enable one to know whether being a young adult is a similar experience for those born in 1940 and those born in 1960. If we find the two groups (independent samples—one cannot be 20 years old both in 1960 and in 1980!) to be equivalent in some way, we can infer that the aging process may be responsible for this lack of a difference (recall our samples are of equivalent ages). If our time-lagged results suggest that our samples are different, however, then we may infer that this difference is either due to differences between the samples in times of measurement (1960 versus 1980) or cohort membership (1940 versus 1960 cohort). Because we cannot separate the effects of each (both indicative of sociohistorical change), the internal validity of the time lag study (given differences between our samples) suffers. Cohort membership and time of measurement are confounded.

From an external validity point of view, the time lag study is restricted to a given set of ages for all of our participants (e.g., 20- or 40-year-olds) and a given set of cohorts and times of measurement. What would happen if we were to compare two samples of 40-year-olds (e.g., 1990 [1950 cohort] vs. 2010 [1970 cohort]), or replicate our study at different times of measurement utilizing individuals of a similar age (e.g., 20-year-olds in 1990 vs. 20-year-olds in 2010)? To the extent that individuals (regardless of age) are differentially affected by what is happening in 1960 versus 1980, we would *not* expect our time lag study to be replicated with individuals from different cohorts assessed at different historical points in time (see Figure 3.5). Time lag samples are, of course, also subject to the effects of selective sampling, selective survival, and terminal change, making the inference of an age effect in a time

Time lag #1   Occasion 1
                 (1960)
               20-year-olds
               (1940 cohort)   Occasion 2
                                  (1980)
                                20-year-olds
                                (1960 cohort)

Time lag #2   Occasion 3
                 (1990)
               20-year-olds
               (1970 cohort)   Occasion 4
                                  (2010)
                                20-year-olds
                                (1990 cohort)

Figure 3.5 Replication of a time-lag design utilizing different cohorts measured at different times of measurement.

lag study especially meaningful. That is, despite these confounds, our time lagged comparison suggests that cultural changes are relatively small, allowing us to infer that age may be important.

Summary: Cross-sectional, Longitudinal, and Time Lag Designs

Based upon our discussion of each design, we can reach several conclusions regarding the ability of each to measure developmental change (see P.B. Baltes, 1968; K.W. Schaie, 1965):

1. Cross-sectional, longitudinal, and time lag designs cannot provide unambiguous conclusions regarding age effects or cultural effects respectively, due to the numerous potential confounding influences affecting each design's internal and external validity.

2. Even if this were not true, we would be making *descriptive,* not explanatory (causal), statements. We cannot randomly assign individuals to levels of age, cohort, or time of measurement.

3. Without controls for the effects of numerous potential confounding factors, these designs cannot provide accurate estimates of intraindividual age change (or sociocultural change).

4. In focusing on a single variable (e.g., age) neither cross-sectional nor longitudinal designs are able to describe adequately the possible *interaction* between factors, for example, age and cohort, age and time of measurement, time of measurement and cohort (P.B. Baltes, 1968; Friedrich, 1972; K.W. Schaie, 1965).

Table 3.1 summarizes each of these basic designs from both an internal and external validity point of view.

SEQUENTIAL DESIGNS

Schaie's Trifactorial Approach

In an attempt to deal with these internal and external validity concerns, K.W. Schaie (1965, 1970) proposed a more complicated set of approaches, each derived from the three basic designs we have discussed rather thoroughly. Collectively, these designs are termed *sequential designs* (see also Chapter 6 on intelligence and Chapter 10 on personality). That is, they involve *sequences* of cross-sectional, longitudinal, or time lag studies. We term Schaie's approach a **trifactorial** one, where *three* factors—age, cohort, and time of measurement—are the dimensions of interest. These dimensions are not independent of one another (participants cannot be independently assigned to levels of each) although Schaie (1965, 1970) feels that they are conceptually meaningful. According to Schaie, these three factors can both describe and explain developmental change.

Schaie's trifactorial model specifies three sequential designs. Each involves replications (sequences) of the basic designs (cross-sectional, longitu-

TABLE 3.1

BASIC DEVELOPMENTAL DESIGNS

	Cross-sectional	Longitudinal	Time Lag
Type of change/difference measured	Average interindividual differences	Intraindividual change or average intraindividual change	Cultural change
Uncontrolled factors (internal validity)	*1. Generation differences confounded with age differences 2. Selective survival 3. Selective sampling 4. Terminal change	*1. Time of measurement confounded with age changes 2. Practice effects 3. Selective dropout 4. Selective survival 5. Selective sampling 6. Terminal change 7. Regression effects	Time of measurement confounded with generation difference (age held constant)
Uncontrolled factors (external validity)	Generation generalizability (are differences between ages stable at times of measure?)	Generalizability at other generations (may be generation specific)	Generalizable at different times of measurement or different generations?
1. Sequential extension 2. Purpose 3. Factors confounded	1. Time sequential 2. Separates age effects from time of measurement 3. Cohort is confounded	1. Cohort sequential 2. Separates cohort and age effects 3. Time of measurement confounded	1. Cross sequential 2. Separates cohort and time of measurement effects 3. Age is confounded

*Major internal validity problem.

Age ⟶ Maturation effects

Cohort ⟶ Generation (genetic, cohort specific) effects

Time of measurement ⟶ Environmental treatment effects

Source: Adapted from D. Friedrich. (1972). *A primer for developmental methodology.* pp. 35–38 Burgess Publishing Co., and from P.B. Baltes. (1968). Cross sectional and longitudinal sequences in the study of age and generation effects. *Human Development, 11,* 145–171.

dinal, time lag). Given that chronological age may not be the only explanation for developmental changes persons experience, results from cross-sectional (often presenting a picture of decline) and longitudinal (often portraying stability or growth) may not yield similar findings (see P.B. Baltes, 1968; P.B. Baltes et al., 1977; K.W. Schaie, 1965, 1970). Thus, more complex designs are necessary to understand fully the course of developmental change. These designs are illustrated in Figure 3.6.

Time Sequential Designs   **Time sequential** studies replicate a cross-sectional study at a new *time of measurement,* allowing for independent (unconfounded) estimates of age (independent samples) and time of measurement effects. Time sequential studies *assume* that cohort effects are minimal. Thus, while age and cohort are confounded, this confounding would not be deemed to be serious.

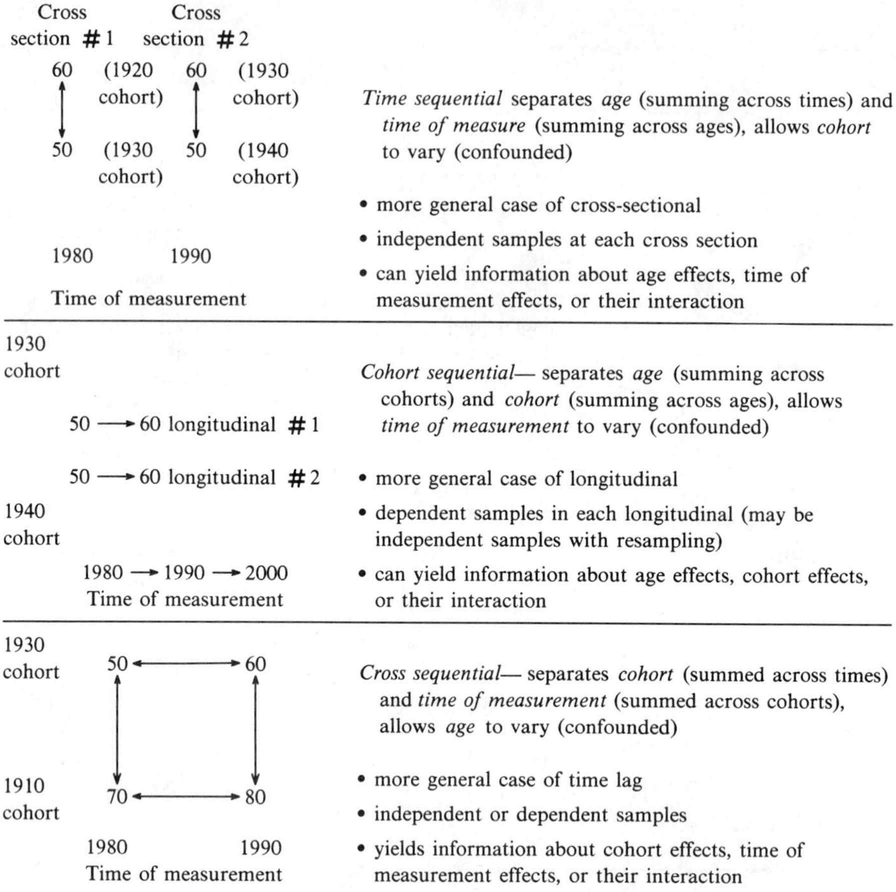

Cross   Cross
section #1   section #2

60   (1920   60   (1930
        cohort)   cohort)

50   (1930   50   (1940
        cohort)   cohort)

1980   1990

Time of measurement

Time sequential separates *age* (summing across times) and *time of measure* (summing across ages), allows *cohort* to vary (confounded)

- more general case of cross-sectional
- independent samples at each cross section
- can yield information about age effects, time of measurement effects, or their interaction

---

1930
cohort

50 —→ 60 longitudinal #1

50 —→ 60 longitudinal #2

1940
cohort

1980 —→ 1990 —→ 2000
Time of measurement

Cohort sequential— separates *age* (summing across cohorts) and *cohort* (summing across ages), allows *time of measurement* to vary (confounded)

- more general case of longitudinal
- dependent samples in each longitudinal (may be independent samples with resampling)
- can yield information about age effects, cohort effects, or their interaction

---

1930
cohort   50 ◄————► 60

1910
cohort   70 ◄————► 80

1980   1990
Time of measurement

Cross sequential— separates *cohort* (summed across times) and *time of measurement* (summed across cohorts), allows *age* to vary (confounded)

- more general case of time lag
- independent or dependent samples
- yields information about cohort effects, time of measurement effects, or their interaction

Figure 3.6 Schaie's sequential designs: time sequential, cohort sequential, cross sequential. *Source:* See K.W. Schaie. (1965). A general model for the study of developmental problems. *Psychological Bulletin, 64,* 92–107.

Cohort Sequential Designs   **Cohort sequential** studies replicate a longitudinal study utilizing a different cohort. In this case, however, time of measurement is deemed irrelevant. Cohort sequential studies allow us to *independently* estimate age (using independent or dependent samples) and cohort effects.

Cross Sequential Designs   **Cross sequential** designs are a more general case of the time lag method. Cross sequential studies allow age to be confounded (irrelevant), and make possible *independent* estimates of cohort and time of measurement effects.

In general, each design rests upon a distinct set of assumptions about which component is irrelevant or confounded (based upon the investigator's knowledge or upon empirical research). In addition, each design, being a more general case of the more basic designs (e.g., cross-sectional), tries to deal with internal validity issues by assuming one of the three components (age, cohort, time) to be irrelevant, therefore allowing for unbiased estimates of the remaining two. External validity issues are dealt with in each case by replicating (see Figures 3.3, 3.4, 3.5, and above discussion) each basic design, therefore allowing for the generalizability of findings. Note in Figure 3.6 that each sequential design must involve a minimum of one replication (at least two data collection efforts) of the basic design from which it is derived.

In more basic terms, each design asks a somewhat different question and, everything else being equal, is more appropriate for some topics than others. Table 3.2 presents the basic questions and likely situations in which each sequential strategy might be employed (see Friedrich, 1972; K.W. Schaie, 1965, 1970). Of course, it would be unlikely that one would naively conduct a certain sequential study simply based upon a "hunch" about which component to allow to vary (consider irrelevant), so in most cases, previous research would most likely dictate one's choice of designs. Despite the importance of cohort effects in adulthood and aging research, it does not necessarily follow that they will be more important than age effects in all instances (see Kausler, 1982).

Using Sequential Designs in Developmental Research

More likely, however, the researcher would establish which factor(s) were most important in the data, using a "grand design" allowing for all possible

TABLE 3.2

SCHAIE'S SEQUENTIAL DESIGNS

	Basic Question	Likely Topics/Situations
Time sequential	What happens to people of *different ages over time,* regardless of cohort membership?	Generalizability over *time,* for the study of psychological attributes (e.g., personality, learning, intelligence, memory—these are unlikely to be cohort specific).
Cohort sequential	What happens to individuals of *different cohorts as they age,* regardless of *when* they are measured? Estimates age effects, but less efficiently than does the time sequential method.	Generalizability over *cohorts,* for the study of physical attributes or for use in animal research (where time of measurement specific influences are thought to be minimal).
Cross sequential	What happens *regardless of age,* to persons of *different cohorts* at *different historical times?*	Generalizability across *cultural units* (cohort effects over time). Not likely to apply to the very young or the very old (due to maturational influences). Applies to most areas regarding adults.

Source: Adapted from D. Friedrich. (1972). *A primer for developmental methodology,* pp. 35–38. Burgess Publishing Co., and from K. W. Schaie. (1965) A general model for the study of developmental problems. *Psychological Bulletin, 64,* 92–107. American Psychological Association.

comparisons; for example, in finding age effects via time sequential comparisons (multiple cross-sectional designs), one could verify this by using cohort sequential comparisons (using multiple longitudinal designs and hope for few cohort effects), or cross sequential comparisons (and hope for evidence supporting age effects).

Schaie (1965) suggests that decisions such as the above (e.g., how important is age?) can be made by relying on cross sequential and time sequential analyses. Botwinick (1984) and P.T. Costa and McCrae (1982), however, advocate a more conservative approach for making decisions about the importance of age, cohort, or time effects involving the "weight of the evidence," based upon multiple comparisons. Obviously, some basic problems remain even with these more complex designs; for example, selective sampling, selective survival/dropout, terminal change. Moreover, they are necessarily expensive and involved, requiring great resources to carry out. While many (e.g., Adam, 1978; Botwinick & Arenberg, 1976; Botwinick & Siegler, 1980; Kausler, 1982) have criticized Schaie's approach on both conceptual and methodological grounds, our goal, however, is to convey a basic understanding of Schaie's approach and its potential for yielding important data about adult development and aging. Recently, Schaie (1986) has revised his approach somewhat to define more clearly the trifactorial model.

Baltes's Bifactorial Approach

P.B. Baltes (1968) objected to Schaie's three-factor (age, cohort, time of measurement) approach on several bases. Initially, he felt that a two-factor model was simpler; one needs to study only *age* and *cohort*, for developmental purposes. While any two of Schaie's three factors might be studied in order to more fully measure developmental change, Baltes felt that time of measurement was the least meaningful, in that the passage of time per se does not cause developmental change, but instead time-related processes are responsible (see P. B. Baltes, 1968; Birren & Renner, 1977; Wohlwill, 1970a). Second, Baltes felt that time of measurement was redundant in that if one had information about age (e.g., 60) and cohort (e.g., 1920), time of measurement (1980) would necessarily follow (it is not new information). Time of measurement could therefore be derived from age and cohort.

Baltes thus rejected Schaie's cross sequential and time sequential methods, due to Schaie's treatment of time of measurement as an important cause of developmental change, in favor of a cohort sequential approach. Schaie's use of three components, according to Baltes, was unnecessary, and in fact the three are always confounded. Third, Baltes also argued that even if age, cohort, and time of measurement were independent factors, questions would still remain regarding their *causal* role in development.

For Baltes, *age* and *cohort* were thus the most important dimensions to be studied; he treated them descriptively. For Schaie, on the other hand, age, cohort, and time were not just descriptive, but also explanatory.

Regarding the estimates of aging effects, Baltes advocated the use of **cross-sectional sequences** (using independent samples) and **longitudinal sequences** (using dependent samples). Figure 3.7 illustrates the bifactorial

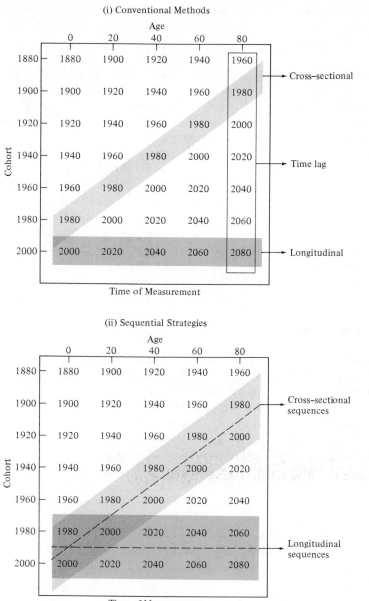

Figure 3.7 Baltes' bifactorial model. (i) Illustration of simple cross-sectional, longitudinal, and time lag designs. (ii) Illustration of cross-sectional and longitudinal sequences. *Source:* Adapted from P. B. Baltes, H. Reese, & J. Nesselroade. (1977). *Life-span developmental psychology: Introduction to research methods* (p. 134). Belmont, CA: Wadsworth Publishing Co. Copyright © 1977 by Wadsworth Publishing Company, Inc. Reprinted by permission of Brooks/Cole Publishing Company, Pacific Grove, California 93950.

approach using each design, both of which separate age and cohort effects. As Figure 3.7 illustrates, cross-sectional sequences (measuring *average* intraindividual age change) represent independent samples of all cohorts at all ages of interest. Thus, we have at least two cross-sectional studies (one conducted in 1980 and taken again in 2000), each covering the age range of birth to 80, involving cohorts 1900 to 2000. Looking at it another way, we get two independent aging samples from four different cohorts (1980, 1960, 1940, 1920), with an independent observation of the cohort 2000 at birth (in the year 2000) and an additional single observation of the 1900 cohort in 1980 (at age 80). *Longitudinal sequences* (measuring intraindividual age change) involve people who are members of at least two cohorts (e.g., 1980, 2000) of which each is repeatedly measured every 20 years (from 1980 through 2080) at the same age points (birth, 20, 40, 60, and 80 years of age). In either case, our main variables of interest are *age* and *cohort.* We also have the advantage of comparing results from independent *and* dependent samples taken from the same cohort at comparable ages. For example, we might measure cohort 1980 at birth and cohort 1980 at age 20 (different people), versus measuring cohort 1980 at birth and at age 20 (same people), to evaluate dropout and/or retest effects.

Which Designs Seem To Be Used Most Often?

Hoyer, Raskind, and Abrahams (1984) reviewed recent aging research and noted a continuing problem in accurately describing one's sample(s) and the methods by which they were recruited. While the cross-sectional method continues to be the most popular, it seems to ignore the importance played by cohort effects, according to Hoyer et al. (1984). Longitudinal studies, while more frequent than before, nevertheless were found to be still comparatively rare. Arenberg (1982) has cautioned those who conduct research in aging to be especially careful in carrying out sequential designs in order that they fairly assess age effects apart from cohort and/or time of measurement effects (Botwinick & Siegler, 1980). Arenberg also suggests that researchers should be sensitive to sample biases created by selective attrition/selective survival effects.

These cautions suggest that despite the sophistication of our methods for gathering data about adults, we still need to be careful to design studies that are well executed to help us separate myth from fact regarding adulthood.

ETHICS AND RESEARCH IN ADULTHOOD

Regardless of one's area of interest or methods used, the rights of those persons from whom we gather our data should be given the highest priority, especially where our methods might induce anxiety or otherwise put the participant "at risk" for physical or psychological harm. These concerns apply to research subjects regardless of age, but are especially relevant when children or elderly persons are being studied (American Psychological Association, 1982; Lawton, 1980a; Strain & Chappell, 1982; Yordi, Chu, Ross, &

Wong, 1982). Minimizing unnecessary "risks" can be accomplished by obtaining *informed consent* from all participants. Informed consent implies that all persons, prior to the project's outset, *fully* understand the purpose of the research and their participation in it in terms they can understand. All questions must be answered and all who participate must understand that in no way will the individual be asked to give up anything (e.g., information, services being received) that might be seen as contingent on participation in the study. Should they consider withdrawing from the project, participants *must* understand that such withdrawal in no way penalizes them, particularly if the research is done within a health care setting (e.g., a nursing home). All data taken must be *confidential,* and thus an individual participant's identity should not be shared with anyone not connected with the project. In many cases when the researcher is studying highly sensitive or personal aspects of behavior (e.g., sexuality), confidentiality is a central concern to the participant. Naive researchers may also need to be especially sensitive to the importance of confidentiality by being careful to avoid casual references to individual participants in their work.

The researcher also has a special ethical obligation to protect the welfare of those who may not be competent to judge whether they should become involved or not and thus unable to give informed consent. Moreover, where a treatment is offered to an experimental group of participants, those in the control or comparison group should also be able to benefit from such treatment or intervention. In addition, feedback regarding the project should be provided, so as to lessen a person's concerns about poor performance or to reduce misconceptions about the overall purpose of the research. Despite the emphasis on the "how" of conducting research in this chapter, such work (no matter how well designed) must be carried out with openness and honesty regarding the ethics of its purposes and methods.

SUMMARY

Regardless of our purpose in doing so, *how* we gather our facts has an important bearing on *what* those facts are. In understanding research methods, distinctions between *developmental* (where age is of interest) and *nondevelopmental* approaches are important. Likewise, *correlational* (where co-relations between variables are of importance) and *experimental* (where *causal* inferences between *independent* and *dependent* variables can be made) have different purposes. While correlational and experimental research studies are frequently conducted with different purposes in mind, they are often coordinated in a larger, more organized effort.

While *chronological age* is often assumed to cause developmental change, it cannot be manipulated and is, therefore, more accurately seen in terms of being *dependent upon* other underlying sets of processes.

Cross-sectional studies measure *average interindividual age differences,* whereas *longitudinal studies* measure *average intraindividual age changes. Time lag* studies assess *cultural change.* Each design should be considered as *descrip-*

tive, as participants cannot be randomly assigned to levels of age, cohort, and time of measurement. Each of these designs has its own set of *internal* and *external validity* issues, which have been in part addressed by the development of sequential methodology.

Time sequential, cohort sequential, and *cross sequential* designs are extensions (replications) of the cross-sectional, longitudinal, and time lag methods respectively. In each case, by assuming one of the *confounding factors* affecting the internal validity of each basic design to be irrelevant, each sequential design addresses internal validity concerns. In the case of each sequential design, external validity is dealt with by replication of one of the three basic designs.

As an alternative to these three sequential designs manipulating *age, cohort,* and *time of measurement (trifactorial)* by K.W. Schaie, P.B. Baltes has proposed a *bifactorial* model (cohort and age) that eliminates time of measurement as a causal factor in measuring developmental change. *Cross-sectional sequences* (using *independent samples*) and *longitudinal sequences* (using *dependent samples*) are proposed as *data collection strategies* within Baltes's bifactorial scheme.

Regardless of how sophisticated we become in research design, our *ethical* obligation to those who participate in our studies must never be overlooked, particularly as it bears on obtaining *informed consent* from those who may not be competent to give such consent. In addition, we should carefully preserve the *confidentiality* of information we gather from each participant and protect volunteers from undue physical or psychological harm.

KEY TERMS AND CONCEPTS

Developmental versus nondevelopmental research	Longitudinal
	Time lag
Experimental versus correlational research	Homogeneous versus heterogeneous samples
Correlation versus causation	Confounding
Random assignment	Interindividual age differences
Generalizability	Intraindividual age changes
Independent versus dependent variables	Age function
	Independent versus dependent samples
Experimental versus control group	Cohort/generation effects
Internal validity	Time of measurement effects
External validity	Selective sampling
Ecological validity	Selective survival
Cross-sectional	Terminal change

Practice effects   Cross sequential

Selective dropout   Bifactorial model

Regression to the mean   Cross-sectional sequences

Cohort sequential   Longitudinal sequences

Trifactorial model   Informed consent

Time sequential   Confidentiality

- What is sensation, and how do sensory processes change during the life cycle?
- What is perception, and how do perceptual processes change during the life cycle?
- How will our behaviors and activities change as a result of changes in sensation and perception with aging?
- What are the major structural changes in the visual system that accompany aging? How do these changes affect visual abilities?
- How do the structures of the auditory system change with age, and what implications do these changes have for behavior and activity?
- What happens to our ability to taste and smell substances as we age?
- What are some of the known changes in touch sensitivity and the ability to detect vibrations, tolerate extreme temperatures, maintain balance, and detect pain as we age?
- What do researchers hope to learn by investigating age differences on sensory information processing tasks? What are the implications of some of these age differences?
- What are the life-span trends for performance on perceptual information processing tasks? What are some of the implications of these age differences?
- Does attentional ability decrease with age? What are some of the implications of this?

CHAPTER ■ 4

SENSORY AND

PERCEPTUAL

PROCESSES

■

INTRODUCTION

The focus of this chapter is life-span trends in **sensation** (which we will define as the *reception* of physical stimulation and the translation of this stimulation into neural impulses) and **perception** (defined as the *interpretation* of sensory stimulation). For instance, imagine yourself walking across campus and off at a distance you see an individual approaching you. Upon closer examination of the features of this approaching person, you realize it is one of your friends. From this common example, we can see the distinction between sensation (the reception of a shape or form by the visual system) and perception (the interpretation of this stimulation as a friend). In fact, sensation and perception are closely intertwined in real life. For example, the clarity with which you hear a sound (sensation) influences your interpretation (perception) of that sound (is that Dad's voice on the phone?).

Both of these topics have been widely studied in individuals at all points along the life cycle, for a number of reasons. First, our ability to successfully cope and interact with our environment is in large part due to our ability to detect, interpret, and respond appropriately to sensory information (Kline & Schieber, 1985). Simply think of the amount of contact you would have with the environment, and others in it, if you were unable to hear, see, and taste. Second, with regard to perception, researchers have repeatedly demonstrated the relationship between a number of perceptual processes and many other behaviors and traits, such as driving accidents, personality, and learning style (see Chapters 7 and 10). For both of these

115

reasons, it is important to know what effect changes in these processes have upon our behavior and performance with increasing age.

The importance of studying age changes in sensation and perception, as well as the other abilities we will discuss in other chapters (e.g., memory, learning, intelligence, and perceptual-motor reaction time) can be further underscored by embedding them in an **information processing approach** to aging.

INFORMATION PROCESSING APPROACH (IP) TO AGING

Information processing models have become very popular in psychology, human development, and education. By viewing the individual in information processing terms, one can easily understand both individual differences in performance and the implications of age changes in the various abilities we will discuss on the individual's level of interaction with the environment. While there are many information processing models (IP), they all attempt to explain human behavior and performance in machinelike terms, such as those used in discussing computers. The person, like a computer, receives certain inputs or data from the environment. These inputs are processed by various systems or processes in the computer that result in various outputs (behaviors, performance in specific situations). An example of such an information processing (IP) model is illustrated in Figure 4.1, which is based on the work of Panek, G. V. Barrett, Sterns, and Alexander (1977). This model presents a framework within which to structure our discussion regarding the implications of age changes in sensation and perception as well as in various other abilities.

This approach suggests that once a person has received stimulation from the environment, this stimulation (information) must pass through four distinct information processing stages before a response in the form of observable behavior occurs. A breakdown in functioning at any of these stages can affect this relationship between stimuli (input) and responses (output).

Let us briefly discuss each of the functions and processes of each of

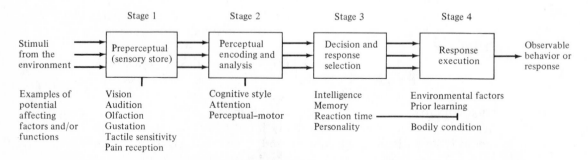

Figure 4.1   Four stages of information processing. *Source:* P.E. Panek, G.V. Barrett, H.L. Sterns, & R.A. Alexander. (1977). A review of age changes in perceptual information processing ability with regard to driving. *Experimental Aging Research, 3,* 388. Copyright © EAR, Inc., 1988.

the stages in Figure 4.1. Stimuli from the environment can be viewed as all the factors and events that repeatedly impinge on the individual daily. These include sounds, sights, sense impressions, feelings, conversations, questions; in short, all our daily experiences. As diagrammed in Figure 4.1, the person's first contacts with environmental stimulation come at the first stage of information processing (IP) called the *preperceptual stage* or sensory store. The basic function of this stage is to receive and register sensory information and experience, that is, to notify the person that this store or filter has been stimulated. We commonly term the type of information processing going on in this stage *sensation.* Examples of functions relevant to this stage of IP are vision, audition (hearing), olfaction (smell), gustation (taste), tactile sensitivity (touch), and pain sensitivity. As one can imagine, if the receptors for these processes are not functioning adequately, the individual's quantity and quality of information received from the environment will be quite limited. Further, if we have limited or faulty input at this stage of IP, the other stages will have less, or perhaps incorrect, information with which to work and process.

The second stage of IP is labeled *perceptual encoding and analysis.* The basic functions of this stage are to encode, interpret, and classify the information passed to it by the preperceptual stage; that is, to analyze the information received by the senses. Psychologists often label the type of processing going on at this stage *perception.* Examples of factors operating at this stage of IP are cognitive (perceptual) style, selective attention, short-term (primary and secondary [see Chapter 7]) memory, and perceptual-motor reaction time.

Again, if limited or incorrect information was received by stage one and passed on to stage two, the quality and quantity of the information interpreted and classified is severely impaired. This may result in an incorrect interpretation of this information that can lead to further inaccuracies at later stages of processing.

Information is then passed on to the third component of IP system, which is termed *decision and response selection.* The primary function of this stage is to make some form of decision about the information received from the preceding two stages and, in turn, decide upon the appropriate response or course of action. Many abilities, traits, and experiences of the individual come into play at this stage. Examples include intelligence, memory, and personality. Simplistically, after information has arrived at this stage, numerous factors can affect the informational input as well as the resultant output. As before, if incorrect input has reached this stage, the probability of making a correct decision and responding appropriately is severely impaired or reduced.

After information has been received and processed by the other stages, a specific response is executed, which is the final stage of information processing. This stage is usually reflected in some type of behavior or course of action: answering a question, fighting, fleeing, turning left in a car, and so forth. The type of response executed can be viewed as a result of both the information processed at preceding stages as well as factors such as past experiences, situational factors, and physical/health condition.

Using an information processing approach can enable one to understand more easily the implications of age changes in sensory abilities. For example, sensory loss can have a serious impact on the older individual's ability to make sense of the environment, leading to maladaptive behavior or faulty decision making. Further, this approach highlights the difficulties in specifically explaining age changes or differences in abilities due to the complexity of factors affecting our interaction with the environment. We can select almost any topic discussed in this text and potentially explain variability in performance both between and within age-groups in terms of how the individual's information processing system is functioning.

Our goal in this chapter is to make you aware of the changes that our sensory and perceptual processes undergo through adulthood to old age and the implications of these changes.

SENSATION

When psychologists speak of sensation, they are simply referring to sensory experience at the receptor level, such as the experience of pain, taste, or temperature. That is, some form of stimulation has been registered by the **sensory receptors**.

Each of the primary senses responds to particular stimuli and is associated with a specific type of receptor. These are presented in Table 4.1.

In most instances, when researchers discuss the suspected change in these senses from early adulthood to old age, they often make reference to

TABLE 4.1

CLASSIFICATION OF SENSORY SYSTEMS IN TERMS OF THE TYPES OF STIMULI TO WHICH THEY RESPOND

Stimulus	Sense	Receptors
Electromagnetic energy	Vision	Rods and cones in retina
Mechanical energy		
Sound waves	Audition	Hair cells in the basilar membrane, inner ear
Displacement of skin pressure	Skin senses	Various types in skin and tissues
Movement of joints	Kinesthetic body sense	Nerve endings in tendons, muscles, and joints
Gravity, acceleration	Vestibular body sense	Hair cells in semicircular canals of ear
Thermal	Skin senses	Various types in skin and tissues
Chemical substances		
Dissolved in saliva	Taste	Taste buds on the tongue
Molecules in air	Olfaction (smell)	Cells in upper nasal cavity

Source: R.E. Smith, I.G. Sarason, & B.R. Sarason. (1982). *Psychology: The frontiers of behavior* (2d ed.) (p. 132). New York: Harper & Row.

what is called the **absolute threshold**. An absolute threshold is the minimum level of stimulus energy/intensity required for the individual to detect the stimulation. Examples of absolute thresholds for the various senses are presented in Table 4.2. Related to absolute threshold is the concept of **difference threshold**, which we shall define as the degree to which a stimulus (sound, light) must be louder or brighter to be perceived as such.

Most research reported in this section has utilized cross-sectional designs, and in light of the methodological problems inherent in such designs, as highlighted in Chapter 3, caution is urged in overgeneralizing these age-differences data to reflect age changes. Similarly, it should be stressed that there are vast *individual differences* within and between groups of young and old individuals on many of the abilities and/or variables discussed in this chapter (Hoyer, 1974).

SENSORY PROCESSES: VISION

Of all our sensory processes, we probably obtain the most information about our world through the visual system. Therefore, as we discuss life-span trends in the visual system, think of the implications each of these functions might have upon your ability to interpret what you see, as well as your everyday behavior. For instance, what effect would decreased vision have upon your reading, driving, or interacting with others? While the extent of visual impairment does vary across persons, it is quite likely that you will eventually encounter some form of visual impairment sufficient to require treatment or influence your daily activities (Kline & Schieber, 1985). Moreover, loss of vision has been the second-most (next to cancer) feared consequence of aging (R. T. Verrillo & V. Verrillo, 1985).

The major age differences in visual functioning are the result of two types of changes in the structure of the eye (Fozard, Wolf, Bell, McFarland, & Podolsky, 1977; McFarland, 1968). The first type are those related to *transmissiveness* (allowing light to pass through) and *accommodative power* (adjust-

TABLE 4.2

APPROXIMATE ABSOLUTE THRESHOLDS FOR SELECTED SENSES

Sense Modality	Absolute Threshold
Vision	Candle flame seen at 30 miles on a clear, dark night
Hearing	Tick of a watch under quiet conditions at 20 feet
Taste	1 teaspoon of sugar in 2 gallons of water
Smell	1 drop of perfume diffused into the entire volume of a large apartment
Touch	Wing of a fly or bee falling on your cheek from a distance of 1 centimeter

Source: R.E. Smith, I.G. Sarason, & B.R. Sarason. (1982). *Psychology: The frontiers of behavior* (2d ed.) (p. 144). New York: Harper & Row.

A significant number of older adults experience
visual problems, which can be prevented or
treated by timely eye examinations.

ment or focus) that begin to be manifest between the ages of 35 and 45. These
include such functions as distance vision, sensitivity to glare, binocular depth
perception, and color sensitivity.

The second type of change concerns changes in the *retina* and the
nervous system that usually occur between 55 to 65 years of age (Panek, G.
V. Barrett, Sterns, & Alexander, 1977). These affect the metabolism of the
retina and are reflected in such changes as the size of the visual field, sensitivity to low quantities of light, and sensitivity to flicker.

In the next several pages, a number of the major changes that occur
in the visual system with age will be highlighted.

Structural Changes in the Visual System

With normal aging, a number of visual structures undergo change. In most
instances, peak functioning occurs during late adolescence or early adulthood,
maintains a fairly constant level through adulthood, then begins to decline
during the late fifties and early sixties. These changes have many implications
for both the quality and quantity of visual information available to the
individual. To facilitate our discussion, an illustration of the structure of the
eye is presented in Figure 4.2, and the functions of a number of these structures are presented in Table 4.3.

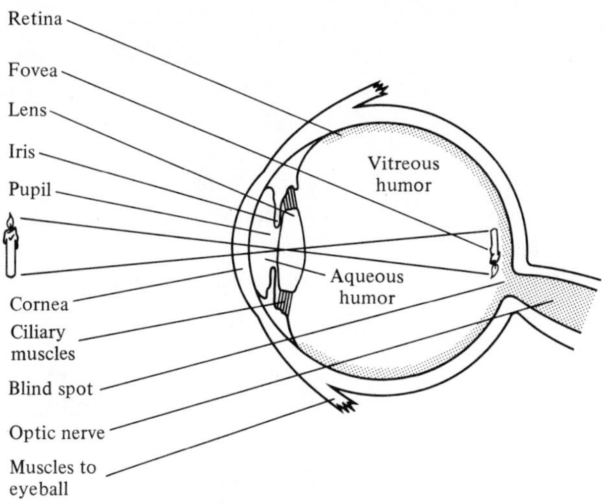

Figure 4.2   Cross section of the eye. *Source:* R.E. Smith, I.G. Sarason, & B.R. Sarason. (1982). *Psychology: The frontiers of behavior* (2d ed.) (p. 133). New York: Harper & Row. Reprinted by permission.

Research (Kline & Schieber, 1985; R. T. Verrillo & V. Verrillo, 1985) indicates that beginning in early adulthood many of the eye structures begin to change, causing some loss of efficiency and effectiveness in functioning. But these decrements are gradual, so individuals often do not notice the changes until their fifties or sixties. As we noted before, there are vast individual differences in the magnitude of these changes. You may or may not experience such changes as rapidly as someone else.

Some of these changes include (1) the lens of the eye gets thicker and yellows, which results in less light being projected onto the retina; (2) the

TABLE 4.3

SELECTED STRUCTURES OF THE EYE AND THEIR FUNCTIONS

Structures	Functions
Cornea	Protection Light refraction
Aqueous humor	Provides nutrients to lens Transportation of metabolic waste products from anterior and posterior chambers
Iris	Eye color
Ciliary muscles	Adjustment of lens
Pupil	Controls amount of light entering
Lens	Focusing on objects
Retina	Visual receptors

ciliary muscle gets weaker, which affects the focusing capability of the lens; and (3) the iris loses pigmentation, resulting in a lack of luster in eye color. These changes are considered normal aging processes, and they result in a decrease in both the quality and quantity of visual information obtained by the individual from the environment.

In addition, there are a number of visual disorders associated with the structures of the eye that can occur at any age and that significantly affect vision; these are presented in Table 4.4. As indicated in Table 4.4, some of these disorders are the result of normal aging processes, while others are caused by pathological disease processes or physical injury. For example, diabetes is a major cause of blindness for individuals at all age levels.

These changes in the structures of the eye lead to changes in a number of visual abilities that are used every day to interact with the environment and others in it. As these various visual abilities are discussed, think of how your current behavior would change if you began to experience these changes.

TABLE 4.4

SELECTED VISUAL DISORDERS

Affected Structure	Disorder	Description	Implication	Treatment
Cornea	Arcus senilis	A gray, opaque ring forms around the cornea. It is the result of normal aging processes and is noticeable by age 50.	Decreased peripheral vision	None
Aqueous humor	Glaucoma	Excessive fluid buildup within the aqueous humor resulting in excessively high pressure in the eye. Can occur at any age.	May lead to blindness as a result of retinal or optic nerve damage	Early detection. Once structural damage has occurred, it cannot be corrected
Retina	Detached retina	Retina separates from optic nerve as a result of a physical trauma (e.g., head injury). Can occur at any age.	Blurred vision or blindness	Surgery
Pupil	Senile miosis	Decrease in the size of the pupil	Less light enters the eye, which results in decreased vision, especially with dim light.	None
Lens	Cataracts	Opacity (clouding) of the lens. May occur at any age, but usually associated with advanced old age.	Blurred or decreased vision	Surgery

Changes in Visual Abilities with Aging

ABSOLUTE THRESHOLD

The quality and quantity of the visual information extracted from the environment is largely determined by the amount of illumination falling upon the retina. Absolute threshold is the minimum overall amount or quantity of ambient illumination required for the detection of this environmental stimulation; that is, for the person to report that the stimulation is visible. Basically, how bright an object must be in order to be seen would define the absolute threshold for vision.

Research consistently reports that older individuals require a greater intensity of light (higher illumination) than younger individuals to detect the visibility of a stimulus (McFarland, 1968; R. T. Verrillo & V. Verrillo, 1985). Perhaps the greatest implication of this increase in illumination required for vision has to do with the mobility of older persons during periods of darkness. Generally speaking, as we get older we require higher levels of illumination to perform most visual activities, such as reading. Moreover, since many older adults do not see well in the dark, they are often afraid to go anywhere at night. This in turn may affect their self-perceptions and limit their activity and interaction with others. Due to difficulty in seeing at night, many older adults may become homebound in the evening. Difference thresholds also increase with age (Kausler, 1982), making it more difficult to separate various brightnesses of light (e.g., a 60–watt vs. a 75–watt bulb). This inability to discriminate may result in lower levels of ambient light, interfering with one's reading.

ACCOMMODATION

Accommodation is the process whereby the eye adjusts itself to attain maximal image resolution (clarity). The accommodation process involves an adjustment of the ciliary muscle, which effects a change in the refractive power of the lens by altering its focal length. The overall outcome of this process is the eye's ability to alternatively focus near and far and to discriminate detail.

Research indicates that with increasing age there is a decrease in the ability of the eye to focus on objects at varying distances (Panek, Barrett, Sterns, & Alexander, 1977). The most common manifestation of this process with age is the progressive decline in the eye's ability to focus on near objects. This is termed **presbyopia** and results mainly from a loss of elasticity in the lens. This is why many individuals in late middle age start to require glasses for the purpose of reading or for working with objects that are close to them (prescriptions, instructions in fine print).

Further, with increased age, the time required for refocusing, or changing focus from near to far, increases. One major implication of the increased time required for accommodation is with regard to one's driving skills. While driving on a highway, drivers must constantly and alternately focus on the instrument panel and monitor the vehicles immediately in front of them (near), then refocus on exit signs and autos in the distance (far), and then refocus on objects that are near again. Since a longer time is often required to refocus with advancing age, many older drivers may accidently miss important signs, since they cannot quickly focus (Panek & Rearden, 1987). They may consequently compensate for this increased time to accommodate by driving more slowly.

ACUITY

Visual acuity refers to the eye's ability to resolve detail and is most often equated with accuracy of distance vision compared with that of the "hypothetical normal person." Anyone who has taken an eye examination is probably familiar with how visual acuity is measured by means of an eye chart called the Snellen chart, which is a standardized series of letters, numbers, or symbols that must be read from a distance of 20 feet. Each line of the chart is of a different size that corresponds to the standard distance at which the letters on that line can be distinguished by a person of normal vision. For example, the individual with normal vision can read a designated size of letter on the Snellen chart at a distance of 20 feet, which is called 20/20 vision. A person who can distinguish at only 20 feet a letter that a person of normal vision could distinguish at 100 feet is said to have a visual acuity of 20/100.

Studies of visual acuity across the life span report a definite developmental trend, where visual acuity tends to be relatively poor in young children, improves in young adulthood, and follows a slight decline from the mid-twenties to the fifties. Beyond this point, the rate of decline is accelerated (Colavita, 1978; Panek, Barrett, Sterns, & Alexander, 1977). Research on visual acuity across the life span suggests the *average* acuity of individuals over age 65 is 20/70. (This decrease in visual acuity can easily be simulated by putting on a pair of clear glasses that have a piece of wax paper placed over the lenses.)

There are many manifestations of this decreased visual acuity with advanced age, such as greater difficulty in reading, watching television, reading instructions on medicine bottles, and reading a newspaper.

COLOR VISION

Color vision refers to the faculty by which colors are perceived and distinguished. The registration and detection of color is due to light-sensitive cells in the retina of the eye called *cones.* In addition to being involved with color vision, cones are employed primarily in daylight vision and are concentrated in the center of the retina in an area called the *fovea.*

What limited research is available on color vision suggests that with increased age, there is an increased difficulty in discriminating among blues, blue-greens, and the violets (the low to middle range of the visible light spectrum), with much better success in discriminating among the reds, oranges, and yellows (the upper middle to high range of the visible light spectrum). The consequences of distortions in color vision are minor compared with those of other visual functions.

ADAPTATION

Adaptation is defined as the change in sensitivity of the eye as a function of change in illumination. There are two types of adaptation: *dark adaptation,* improvement in sensitivity to light in a dark environment, and *light adaptation,* increased sensitivity to light in a light environment. The best example of how these processes operate would be a situation where you enter a dark movie theater and then leave to go outside during daylight.

When you enter the dark theater from the light outside, your pupils will automatically expand in order to increase the amount of light entering your eyes—this process takes about 30 seconds. The reverse happens when you leave the theater; that is, your pupils will automatically contract to cut down the amount of light entering your eyes—this process requires a shorter time than does dark adaptation.

Research appears to indicate that the time required for both adaptation processes increases with age (Kline & Schieber, 1985). The primary implication of this change is that as we age it will take longer for us to adapt to extreme changes in illumination, which will make us more susceptible to environmental hazards during the first few minutes of being in a differently illuminated environment. For example, coming out of the theater into bright sunlight may blur your vision to the point that you stumble off the curb. If one is older, there might also be a greater tendency to experience "snow blindness."

GLARE SENSITIVITY

Relatively bright light that results in unpleasantness or discomfort and/or that interferes with optimum vision is termed **glare**. Glare is produced when light rays are diffused via a change in the composition of the vitreous humor (see Figure 4.2). The most vivid examples of this process occur during night driving when drivers in the other lane shine their high beams at your car or when you are reading printed material on glossy paper.

Research indicates the effects of glare on visual performance to be greater with increasing age, with an increasing deterioration of performance from age 40 on (Burg, 1967). However, there are no differences in glare sensitivity between males and females at any point across the life span. With regard to driving, the longer vision is affected by glare the less information from the environment can be detected and the greater the potential for an accident (one's attention to the road is disrupted).

PERIPHERAL FIELD

Visual field is defined as the extent of physical space visible to an eye in a given position—that whole area you see given that your head is in a fixed position.

The **peripheral field** is the outer area of your overall visual field. Research has documented that the peripheral field shrinks several degrees per decade after age 45 (Kline & Schieber, 1985). Therefore, with increasing age the ability to view and observe information in the peripheral areas of the visual field decreases substantially. For example, the overall visual field for a young adult is typically 170 degrees; by age 50, it has decreased to approximately 140 degrees (Kline & Schieber, 1985; Panek, Barrett, Sterns, & Alexander, 1977) and continues to decrease with advancing age. It is as though one has blinders on.

VISUAL SEARCH BEHAVIOR

Visual search behavior pertains to how an individual searches, scans, or processes a visual scene. Basically, looking around the environment for important cues and information involves visual search. Laboratory studies are consistent in showing that the visual search behavior of individuals becomes less efficient, less systematic, and more incomplete as a function of age (Kline & Schieber, 1985). The ability to perform visual search tasks decreases dramatically after age 30. This visual information processing ability has many important implications for everyday functioning; the implications of this change will be discussed in our section on selective attention.

Effects of Visual Changes

The numerous age changes we have discussed in the preceding pages concerning the structure and function of the visual system have significant implications with regard to everyday interaction with the environment, especially for older adults. One can readily comprehend the difficulty experienced by persons who have these visual problems in performing simple, routine tasks we all take for granted, such as watching television, driving a car, reading a book, reading can labels in stores, and so forth. As Whitbourne (1985) notes, when less light is available to be processed, images become more blurred. Deficits in color vision may make it difficult to match colors (blue and black socks!) and lessen the appreciation of paintings (one may cease to visit a museum). Details on dials (as on a stove or a radio) may be difficult to pick out, as may subtle facial features (Kausler, 1982). For persons whose vision has always been good, such effects may be particularly distressing— they may cook or watch TV or listen to their favorite music less, or be more fearful in social situations due to their inability to process new facial features or remember old ones (Whitbourne, 1985).

It should be stressed that often persons do not truly comprehend or notice the extent of the changes in their visual ability, since these decrements occur gradually over the life span. Because they are so gradual that individuals do not notice them they may not seek professional help to correct these deficits. Tragically, some older persons who *do* realize their visual abilities have declined may not seek professional help because they feel these changes are just signs of getting old; that is, their vision is supposed to get worse. They may also believe that because they signal aging, these deficits cannot be corrected.

For some of us, there will be numerous changes in our visual ability that will have a pronounced effect upon our behavior and activities. Further, as we begin to realize these changes are occurring, our self-confidence may decrease due to the fact that we are unable to do all the things we used to quite as well. Because we cannot see them, we may falsely interpret these changes as signs of aging, when such changes *can* often be corrected or prevented via routine eye examinations.

INTERVENTION TECHNIQUES

The older individual experiencing visual impairments can be helped in many ways (Shore, 1976). For example, many books and newspapers are now printed with large print, and "talking books" are available. Also, large numbers on rooms, clocks, and elevator doors can facilitate the functioning of visually impaired older adults. Color coding of rooms, floors, or levels can be helpful. Simply increasing levels of ambient light (turning up the lights) *without* creating glare can remedy things a great deal. If individuals' dark adaptation ability is impaired with age, illuminating halls or stairways may help persons avoid falls. The use of flat paints (versus enamels) may help to reduce glare.

AUDITION

We rely upon **audition**, or our hearing sense, to obtain information about our environment. Alarm clocks wake us. The phone rings. If our audition is impaired, we may oversleep or miss an important call. If for no other than these obvious reasons, it is important that we discuss changes in auditory functioning that are part of aging. These changes in our ability to hear are a function of both normal aging processes and external forces, such as exposure to high levels of noise.

The ability to hear decreases quite dramatically across the life span, to the point that by old age most individuals have some form of hearing disorder (Olsho, Harkins, & Lenhardt, 1985). Age changes in hearing ability are often characterized as progressive, irreversible, and detrimental to successful adaptation and interaction in the later years (Olsho et al., 1985). In a sample of normal older adults, using the standard criteria for the definition of hearing impairment, 46 percent were hearing impaired (P.D. Thomas, Hunt, Garry, Hood, J.M. Goodwin, & J.S. Goodwin, 1983).

The most common auditory disorder of older adults is **presbycusis**. Presbycusis is characterized by a progressive bilateral (both ears) loss of hearing for tones of high frequency due to degenerative physiological changes in the auditory system as a function of age. It has been estimated that 13 percent or more of older adults show signs of presbycusis, which suggests the need for expanding existing audiological services for the aged.

Since it is quite likely that we will experience some form of hearing loss as we age, it is important that we have some understanding of such losses and their effects on our behavior.

The human auditory system consists primarily of two subsystems that interact: the structural system (outer ear, inner ear), and the neural pathways (auditory nuclei, fiber tracts). Figure 4.3 illustrates the structures of the auditory system.

Outer, Middle, and Inner Ear

With aging, there are a number of changes in the structures of the **outer, middle, and inner ear** that have potential implications for receiving auditory information. The pinna (structure in the outer ear) becomes hard, inflexible, and may change in size and shape (Olsho et al., 1985). There may be an increase in wax buildup. The functional significance of these changes, if any, has not been investigated.

The two primary structures of the middle ear are the *eustachian tube* and the *ossicular chain.* Often elderly persons have an accumulation of fluid in the middle ear due to an obstruction in the eustachian tube. The cause of this blockage is usually a cold, and hearing difficulties will be present as long as the tube remains closed. With regard to the ossicular chain, research indicates that there are arthritic changes in the middle ear joints with aging (Whitbourne, 1985). Also, as age increases, arthritic changes become more severe. However, these changes do not appear to impair sound transmission through the middle ear.

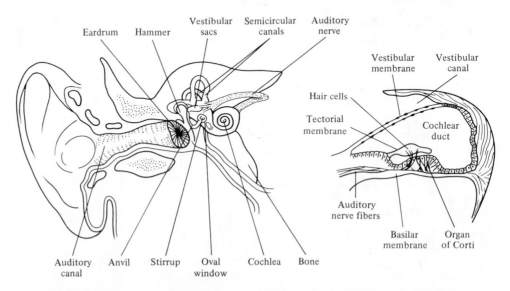

Figure 4.3 A cross section of the ear showing the structures that transmit sound waves from the auditory canal to the cochlea. There they stimulate hair cells in the organ of corti. The resulting nerve impulses reach the brain via the auditory nerve. The semicircular and vestibular sacs of the inner ear contain sense organs for equilibrium. *Source:* R.E. Smith, I.G. Sarason, & B.R. Sarason. (1982). *Psychology: The frontiers of behavior* (2d ed.) (p. 140). New York: Harper & Row. Reprinted by permission.

Schuknecht and Igaraski (1964) suggest there are four general types of disorders observed as a function of age in the structures of the inner ear: (1) atrophy and degeneration of hair cells in the basal coil of the cochlea, called *sensory presbycusis,* (2) loss of auditory neurons, called *neural presbycusis,* (3) atrophy of the stria vascularis in the scala media with corresponding deficiencies in the bioelectric and biochemical properties of the endolymphatic fluids, called *metabolic presbycusis,* and (4) atrophic changes in the structures associated with vibrations of the cochlear partition, called *mechanical presbycusis.*

Each of these types of disorders shows a characteristic hearing pattern. For example, sensory presbycusis produces a high-frequency hearing loss that does not involve the speech frequencies. Neural presbycusis affects speech discrimination without an accompanying loss in pure tone thresholds. With metabolic presbycusis, there is a nearly uniform threshold loss for all frequencies with loudness recruitment. Finally, mechanical presbycusis produces increasing hearing loss values from low to high frequencies.

Age Changes in Basic Hearing Functions

ABSOLUTE THRESHOLD

There is a loss of auditory acuity, the ability to hear certain frequencies or ranges (especially high frequencies), that occurs as part of the normal aging process. It has been estimated that 70 percent of all individuals over age 50 have some type of hearing loss (Anderson, Porrata, Lore, Alexander, & Mercer, 1969; Olsho et al., 1985).

The rate of sensitivity loss depends on several factors, including (1) the population of individuals studied, (2) the history of exposure to noise, and (3) the population's homogeneity with respect to hereditary and environmental factors (Bergman, 1971a, 1971b). For example, cross-cultural studies indicate less decrement in hearing sensitivity for the higher frequencies with normal aging in nonindustrialized populations, due to lack of exposure to high noise levels (see P. B. Baltes et al., 1977).

When discussing the absolute threshold for hearing in older adults and others with hearing disorders, one must keep in mind the importance of the ambient noise level of the environment. That is, the higher the ambient noise level, the greater difficulty the hearing impaired individual will have in hearing what you are saying. Thus, speaking more loudly and clearly, especially in noisy situations (a party), or seeking quiet areas is very important.

PITCH DISCRIMINATION

The ability to detect small changes in the pitch of sounds is not only important for musical listeners and performers but also is a significant factor in the perception of speech. Since presbycusis involves high-pitched tone hearing loss, **pitch discrimination** is poorest for those consonants that have higher frequency components in their acoustic patterns (Corso, 1977). Older adults may be unable to discriminate between phonetically similar words, and thus, they may have problems in following normal conversation, especially in noisy environments. Though these observed difficulties in speech discrimination by older adults are well documented (Olsho et al., 1985; Whitbourne, 1985), the locus or cause of this difficulty is still in question.

HEARING LOSS AND EXPOSURE TO NOISE

A significant relationship exists between excessive noise exposure and permanent hearing loss at all age levels (Corso, 1977; Kryter, 1970). The greatest impetus for this research comes from industrial settings. The basic question for investigation is whether the hearing losses due to noise exposure and age are additive or interactive. That is, is hearing loss due to constant and repeated amounts of excessive noise (additive) or due to the combination or contribution of many factors (interactive), each of which contributes to the eventual hearing loss? Overall, this research suggests that the effects of age and noise exposure are independent and nonadditive. This implies that hearing loss can be attributed to external noise factors alone, or age factors alone, and in most instances the effects of external noise are more pronounced than those of normal aging. In fact, Corso (1977) refers to the damaging effects of repeated noise exposure upon hearing in adults and the middle-aged as **premature presbycusis**. For this reason, many industries require workers to wear protective ear plugs.

Relationship Between Speech and Hearing

As one would expect, any serious impairment of hearing will probably produce a concomitant problem in speech communication. That is, hearing disorders may lead to speech disorders, which will eventually lead to decreases in normal verbal and social interaction. For example, due to the fact that people may have to speak quite loudly for you to hear, they may not want to interact with you at a social gathering because they may feel embarrassed talking loudly. You may avoid conversations with others, causing you to feel less confident and more isolated. Therefore, hearing disorders can affect the social and psychological adjustment of persons regardless of age, especially during later adulthood (Whitbourne, 1985).

Hearing plays such an important part in our communication with others that decrements with advancing age cause older adults to suffer considerable social and emotional disturbances as a result of this progressive hearing loss (Campanelli, 1968). Research suggests the magnitude of adjustment problems experienced by individuals with hearing disorders is directly related to the severity of the hearing disorder and the time of its inception (at what age it began). That is, the later it begins in life, and the greater the severity, the greater the adjustment problems individuals experience (Corso, 1977). The probable consequences in this case are: (1) not being able to hear adequately leads to a lowered self-concept, and (2) not being able to hear adequately often leads to feelings of paranoia—"are those people talking about me?" (Eisdorfer & Stotsky, 1977; Whitbourne, 1985).

The hearing-impaired aged individual is often pictured as withdrawn, insecure, depressed, confused, and isolated (P.D. Thomas et al., 1983). A research study that dramatizes this point is that of Eisdorfer (1960), who administered a projective personality test, the Rorschach (see Chapter 10), to 48 community-living older adults (60 years +) who were divided into six groups on the basis of three visual and two auditory levels of functioning.

Results indicated no significant difference on selected scoring categories of the Rorschach between older adults with normal vision and those with vision that was impaired but was functioning normally through the use of corrective lenses, nor were there significant differences between those with impaired vision and those without such an impairment. However, there were significant differences on selected personality scores between older adults with normal hearing and those with impaired hearing. Additionally, the test performance of individuals with both vision and hearing impairments was not significantly different from that of those individuals with hearing disabilities alone. Eisdorfer (1960) concludes that aged individuals react to hearing loss by withdrawal and by increased rigidity of personality.

These studies imply that the effects of hearing disability, especially with aging, are more dramatic for normal social and personality functioning than are the effects of visual impairment.

INTERVENTION TECHNIQUES

The effects of hearing impairment upon social interaction can be simulated by putting cotton in the ears and then attempting to hold a conversation with others. Many things can be done to help older adults with hearing impairments. Shore (1976) suggests numerous methods for improving the communication skills of such older adults. For example, face the individual directly and speak slowly and distinctly. This will allow the person to lip-read. Also, facial expressions and arm and hand movements help communicate information. Finally, it may be helpful to carry a paper and pencil for communication purposes.

Language and Voice Impairments

There are four major classifications of speech disorders: (1) *articulation;* excessive repetition of phonemes or sound substitutions; (2) *stuttering;* (3) *voice;* the processes of phonation and resonation are altered with deviations in pitch, loudness, and vocal quality; and (4) *symbolization;* the individual is unable to associate meaning with language symbols in a normal manner (aphasia) (Bergman, 1980; Obler & Albert, 1985).

These disorders are found in individuals of all ages and may arise from a number of causes such as vascular insufficiency, neoplasms, trauma, stroke, and progressive degenerative illnesses, as well as extensive vascular lesions or disease in the brain. Their incidence, especially that of aphasia, increases with advanced age as a result of strokes and cardiovascular conditions (Obler & Albert, 1985).

It should be noted that the altered communication processes of older adults are not restricted to language and hearing impairments but may also involve the acoustic characteristics of the voice. Specifically, the frequency range becomes smaller, vocal intensity is decreased, and voice quality is impoverished, depending upon the kind and extent of organic changes that have occurred in the larynx (Benjamin, 1981, 1982).

Rehabilitation of Hearing, Speech, and Language Disorders

With regard to hearing disorders, therapeutic approaches run the continuum from hearing aids and medical-surgical procedures to rehabilitative therapy programs, depending upon the nature and extent of the hearing disorder as well as the age of the individual (Olsho et al. 1985). Two rehabilitation programs that are widely used with older adults whose level of hearing impairments are not classified as severe are **speechreading** (lipreading) and **auditory training**. Both of these procedures are based on the integration of both visual and auditory information by the client. Speechreading is a skill that enables a person to understand language by carefully observing the speaker's lips move. The technique is widely practiced by older adults as a compensatory adjustment to help cope with the effects of hearing loss. Auditory training involves the client attending to certain key sounds, words, and so forth in the conversation while at the same time watching the speaker's lips move.

Interestingly, though hearing rehabilitation procedures can be effective with older adults, they tend to be underutilized for three reasons. First, though most older adults with speech and hearing problems believe they need professional assistance, many feel that they have neither the time, money, or motivation to attend rehabilitation programs. Some older adults may not have the money to pay for luxury items, such as aural rehabilitation, when they do not have enough money to pay for more basic necessities. Second, some of the staff of such programs may regard older adults that do attend as being so dependent and incapable of managing themselves that they alienate the individuals they hope to treat by talking down to older adults in the same manner they would to young children. Finally, older adults are often targeted as easy prey by unscrupulous individuals who attempt to portray themselves as insurance agents, investment counselors, or health professionals. Therefore, older adults often regard such individuals who are offering services with distrust. While these are certainly major concerns in older adults' use of these services, we should be cautious about overgeneralizing them to all service providers or to all aged persons.

Effects of Auditory Changes

Though it makes good common sense to believe that hearing deficits have severe effects upon individuals (see above), these effects are not clear-cut. The exact ramifications of these decrements depend upon a number of factors, such as the seriousness of the problem, its locus, age of onset, and support from others, to name but a few. We might also distinguish a measured hearing loss (via an audiometer) and a conversational hearing loss that is obvious to the individual or others. For example, if hearing loss is progressive and mild, the individual may adapt to the problem and may not experience or exhibit any major change in personality, self-concept, emotional stability, adjustment, and so forth.

This point was amply illustrated by P. D. Thomas et al. (1983), who investigated the relationship between untreated hearing deficits, emotional state, cognitive functioning, and social interaction in otherwise healthy older adults. These researchers could not find any negative effects of uncorrected hearing impairment upon the person's emotional status, memory, or social interaction. It does sometimes happen, however, that severe hearing loss is associated with paranoia (see Chapter 13).

On the other hand, Granick, Kleban, and Weiss (1976) and Ohta, Carlin, and Harmon (1981) have reported a significant association between hearing loss and intellectual functioning in older adults. Additionally, the association between hearing loss and intelligence appears to be greater for verbal intellectual measures than for nonverbal intellectual measures (Granick et al., 1976).

It is important to point out that the difference in results between these two studies vividly illustrates many of the factors discussed in Chapter 3 on research methods. For example, the differences between these studies may be partially attributed to sampling differences, as well as differences in the dependent measures utilized. This contradiction highlights the need for additional research regarding the extent and effects of hearing disorders on the well-being and functioning of individuals at all points along the life cycle.

TASTE AND SMELL

Interestingly, though we are exposed to numerous tastes and smells every day, we know comparatively little about what exactly happens to these abilities as we age. Results of studies regarding age differences can vary as a function of the method employed (to assess taste or smell) as well as the substance investigated. Therefore, many of the facts presented in this section will lack consistent research support. Though our taste (gustatory system) and smell (olfactory system) sensitivities function interactively (together), for presentation purposes we will discuss them separately. For example, when you have a cold and your nose is stuffed up, you are often unable to taste your food.

Taste

Humans are able to detect four basic taste qualities: sweet, salty, bitter, and sour. Figure 4.4 illustrates a taste bud and the location of the taste buds on the tongue for each taste quality. While research has attempted to determine what happens to our ability to detect these taste qualities as we age, the literature regarding the effect of aging upon taste sensitivity presents a paradox. This paradox is the apparent discrepancy between objective assessments of older adults' ability to taste in the laboratory and the subjective report of older adults regarding their inability to taste food in everyday situations. Laboratory studies in this area have involved various psychophysical procedures to determine the so-called concentration threshold necessary for an observer to identify a certain taste quality. For example, what concentration level of sucrose is required to make a solution taste sweet to the participant? The keener the sensitivity, the lower the concentration threshold. The usual research paradigm involves the use of vials of colorless, odorless liquids in which the experimenter varies the concentration of the test "taste stimulus" to determine if there is a significant difference between age-groups in percent of concentration required to report a taste, for instance, salty. Applied research is basically nonexistent due to the vast number of potential confounds that would have an effect upon the results. These include food preferences, cultural factors, and personality, to name a few.

On the basis of available laboratory research (Corso, 1971; Engen, 1977), it appears that sensitivity for all four taste qualities remains fairly constant and unimpaired until the late fifties, followed by a sharp decline in all four qualities (Whitbourne, 1985). But older adults report they can still taste and differentiate between all four qualities in experimental laboratory situations. Still, there is a paradox here. Let's suppose on the way home this group of older adults, who were just in the laboratory study, stop at a restaurant to eat. It would not be uncommon for them to state that the food was tasteless, did not contain enough salt, or was too salty. Interestingly, these very same individuals in the laboratory would not have reported diminished taste. *Why* there is an apparent discrepancy between food in the labora-

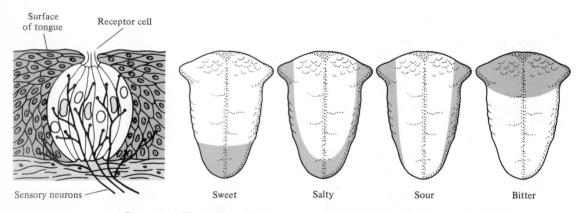

Figure 4.4   The receptors for taste are specialized cells located in taste buds in the tongue. The taste buds are grouped in different areas of the tongue according to the taste sensation to which they respond. The center of the tongue is relatively insensitive to taste qualities. *Source:* R.E. Smith, I.G. Sarason, & B.R. Sarason. (1982). *Psychology: The frontiers of behavior* (2d ed.) (p. 141). New York: Harper & Row. Reprinted by permission.

tory and in the real world will be discussed in the section on psychosocial influences on taste sensitivity.

For the most part, research in the area has *assumed* there has to be a diminution of taste, or an increase in taste disorders, with advancing age, though the experimental findings are equivocal. These assumed age changes in taste sensitivity are usually attributed to structural changes in the taste receptor system, gender of the individual, smoking, and psychosocial factors, which will be discussed below.

Structural Changes in the Gustatory System (Taste)

There are specific neuroanatomical and physiological changes in the basic structures of the gustatory system with age. El-Baradi and Bourne (1951) report a gradual diminution in the number of taste buds with increasing age. It appears that the taste buds become fully developed around the age of pubescence and remain relatively unchanged until signs of atrophy begin to appear in the mid-forties. W. Harris (1952) estimated that as many as two-thirds of the papillae atrophy in old age.

Additional age changes include the loss of elasticity in the mouth and lips, a decrease in the flow of saliva, and a fissuring of the tongue. Though these changes in the gustatory system would appear to have devastating effects upon the ability of older adults to taste, they do not seriously affect taste sensitivity until relatively late in life, if at all.

Gender Differences and Smoking

Though it has been suggested that older adult females are more sensitive to taste than males (Corso, 1971, 1977), this literature is sparse and controversial. Thus, there is currently no definitive research evidence indicating the existence of gender differences in taste sensitivity among older adults.

Also, on a commonsense level, while it would appear that smoking would affect taste sensitivity, the literature on this issue is equivocal and controversial. Therefore, as is the case with regard to gender differences, no one definitively knows whether smoking affects taste sensitivity in adulthood.

Psychosocial Factors

In the extreme, decreased taste sensitivity could result in malnutrition (Whitbourne, 1985). However, due to the discrepancy between findings in the laboratory and the real world, it is now assumed that food complaints and taste aberrations on the part of elderly persons are in part the result of psychosocial influences. That is, the high incidence of food complaints among the aged is not based on sensory impairment but is related to such factors as problems in personal adjustment, attitudes toward self, or feelings of abandonment. They may also be influenced by inflammation or disease.

This explanation appears to make sense, since eating is such a social event in our culture. Isn't it more fun to eat with others rather than alone? Eating is often a time of social interaction, and the companionship may be more important than the meal itself. Therefore, when one is alone, the joy and pleasure of eating may be gone. Even if one likes to cook, it may make little sense to prepare a meal if one must eat alone.

Overall, we still know very little regarding suspected age changes in taste sensitivity. The available information is not definitive, and many studies are dated. As aptly stated by Dye and Koziatek (1981), though many studies report a decline in taste acuity with advanced age, the age at which the decline is observed, as well as the manifestation of any age differences in taste acuity between young and old individuals, varies noticeably between studies. Therefore, on the basis of what we know, we cannot make generalizations and recommendations that may be of practical use for such things as diagnosing sensory deficits or planning diets. Clearly, the possibility for such deficits must be recognized as a first step in designing any nutritional program for the aged. However, psychosocial influences (e.g., isolation) may undermine even the best efforts in this respect.

Olfaction (Smell)

Although there is a substantial amount of research on olfaction per se, very little of it concerns changes across the life span. Research evidence that does exist, moreover, sheds little light on the manner in which olfaction changes, if at all, with age. Further, it is difficult to separate the effects of the interaction between olfactory and gustatory sensitivity.

Since the primary olfactory receptors are the neurons on the olfactory bulb, most research investigations of potential age changes have concentrated on studying the olfactory bulb and tract. Liss and Gomez (1958) found in postmortem examinations of individuals aged 70 years and above that changes in the olfactory bulb and tract are similar to those that occur in the central nervous system with age (see Chapter 2). That is, there is a generalized atrophy with a moderate loss of neuronal elements. Interestingly, the severity of the degeneration was not correlated with age. In fact, Liss and Gomez (1958) reported that one individual over 100 years of age had only a mild loss of neurons. This finding suggests that damage to the olfactory bulb and tract and therefore changes in sensitivity to smell are more likely attributable to environmental factors, such as occupational odors, airborne toxic agents, and smoking, rather than age per se. If individuals who are isolated do experience deficits, they may, for example, not pick up on body odors that may offend others, further contributing to their isolation. There is some evidence suggesting that using one's olfactory abilities tends to preserve them (Engen, 1982).

A considerable amount of research still needs to be performed in this area before age effects on olfaction are definitively established (Engen, 1977; Whitbourne, 1985). Again, as in the case of taste, we should be especially cautious in making generalizations and recommendations that may be of practical use.

AGE CHANGES IN TOUCH, VIBRATION, TEMPERATURE, KINESTHESIS, AND PAIN SENSITIVITY

Our sensitivities to touch, vibration, temperature, kinesthesis, and pain are collectively referred to as **somesthesis**, since they arise from normal and intensive stimulations of the skin and viscera (Kenshalo, 1977). Age changes in somesthetic sensitivity can best be understood when described in terms of the changes in the anatomical and physiological characteristics of the aging skin, muscles, joints, viscera, and the nervous system. Additionally, it is important to keep in mind that research reports of age changes or age differences in these senses vary significantly as a function of the method and procedure used and by the part of the body for which the sensitivity was determined. For example, the sensitivity of the feet to all stimuli starts to decrease at an earlier age than that of the forearm (Kenshalo, 1977).

Touch (Tactile Sensitivity)

Though we rely upon our sense of touch every day, data are noticeably absent in the area of tactile sensitivity and the effects of age. In addition, the absolute threshold for touch varies with the part of the body stimulated. As before, the absolute threshold is considered the level of stimulation required for persons to first report they feel the stimulation. On the basis of what sparse information exists, it appears that touch sensitivity remains relatively unchanged from early childhood through about age 50 to 55, with a rise in the absolute threshold thereafter. This is usually attributed to a loss of touch receptors, but this explanation is still considered tentative (Whitbourne, 1985).

Vibratory Sensitivity

Age changes in sensitivity to vibration have been of greater interest than touch in both clinical and laboratory investigations because these changes have been found to be of diagnostic value in assessing disorders of the nervous system (Kenshalo, 1977).

In general, research indicates that for older adults vibratory sensitivity differs with regard to the part of the body stimulated. For example, in older adults, vibratory sensitivity is better for the wrists, elbows, and shoulders than for the ankles, shins, and knees (Corso, 1971). It appears the lower extremities are more affected by age than the upper extremities.

Several hypotheses have been advanced to account for the observed age and body part decrements in vibratory sensitivity: (1) inadequate blood supply to the spinal cord, which produces damage to the nerve tracts; (2) a decline in the number of myelinated fibers in the spinal roots; (3) dietary factors, such as thiamine deficiency; and (4) diminished blood flow in the peripheral structures of the body (Corso, 1971).

In conclusion, clinical and experimental findings clearly indicate that vibratory sensitivity declines with age, but the thresholds are very dependent upon the specific part of the body that is stimulated. Additionally, the cause of this decrease as well as the potential implications of such changes are still to be determined.

Temperature Sensitivity

The American Society of Heating, Refrigeration, and Air-Conditioning Engineers handbook, which sets the standard conditions for attaining comfort in heated and air-conditioned spaces, reports the preferred temperature for persons over 40 years is about 0.5 degrees higher than that desired by younger persons. Interestingly, however, older adults have similar temperature preferences relative to middle-aged adults.

Although thermal comfort criteria may not change dramatically with advancing age, the ability of the elderly temperature-regulating system to cope with extreme environmental temperatures, both hot and cold, appears to be impaired. Apparently, older adults and very young children may not accurately detect how hot or cold it actually is and thus suffer physical/medical complications, such as hypothermia, heatstroke, and frostbite, more readily than older children and adults.

Kinesthesis

One of the important and distressing problems of older adults is their susceptibility to falls and the complications, sometimes fatal, that occur as a consequence (Ochs, Newberry, Lenhardt, & Harkins, 1985). It is conceivable that decreased or failed input from the kinesthetic receptors may be a contributing factor. Though this sensory system is so important for everyday interaction and mobility of younger and older adults, the specific sensory receptors that are responsible for the kinesthetic sense are still a matter of debate.

Discussion of our kinesthetic sense usually centers on two forms of movement, active and passive. *Passive movement* describes a situation where the individual is stationary but is in a vehicle or apparatus that is moving, such as an airplane. *Active movement* pertains to actual movement of the body or body parts, such as walking. Report of movement varies as a function of the method used as well as the part of the body stimulated.

With regard to passive movement, research fails to indicate a progressive deterioration in perception of movement for the great toe with increasing age, while deterioration has been found for several joints, the knees, and the hips (Ochs et al., 1985). Concerning active movement, judgments of tension of differing degrees of muscle or tendon strain produced by discrimination of weights are relatively unaffected by age.

Kenshalo (1977) states that additional studies in this area to compare active and passive joint rotation, discriminations, and weight discriminations in the young and old are sorely needed. The implications of these changes will be discussed in the section on home accidents.

INTERVENTION TECHNIQUES

We can facilitate the mobility of older adults by providing environmental aids such as handrails in corridors and benches for resting (Shore, 1976). Further, many older adults use the backs of couches, chairs, tables, or other furniture in the process of navigating from one area to another.

Pain

Age changes in pain sensitivity are the most well researched of all changes in the skin senses, yet general age trends are still unclear (Harkins, Price, & Martelli, 1986). It should be kept in mind that reports of pain thresholds vary strikingly between individuals, between experimenters, between experimental conditions, and between parts of the body in the same individual. Additionally, the experience and report of pain is more than just a sensory phenomenon; it involves cognitive, motivational, personality, and cultural factors.

Individuals can be classified as hyposensitive (less), normally sensitive, and hypersensitive (more) in terms of their reactions to painful stimuli. Research suggests that with increasing age, most individuals become more hyposensitive (less) to pain (Whitbourne, 1985). That is, clinical and experimental research evidence suggests older people do not feel pain as intensely as do younger individuals. Schludermann and Zubek (1962) investigated pain sensitivity in five areas of the body (forehand, forearm, upper arm, thigh, and leg) across the life span. Results indicated overall pain sensitivity remains relatively constant until one's fifties, after which it shows a sharp decline. The decline after 60 years was highly significant. With regard to specific parts of the body, pain sensitivity with increased age showed a greater decline for the forehand, upper arm, and forearm than for the thigh and leg.

The decrease in pain sensitivity in older adults may be due to certain degenerative changes that occur in the receptors and the peripheral nervous system with increased age. These include: (1) a decrease in the number of Meissner's corpuscles and other receptor end organs in the skin, (2) a decline in the number of myelinated fibers in the peripheral nervous system, (3) changes in the elasticity of the skin, and (4) changes in blood flow and/or characteristics of the circulatory system. Additionally, amounts of exposure to environmental elements could produce changes in the thickness and elasticity of the skin, which would lessen the effectiveness of the impinging stimulus to elicit pain (Corso, 1971). Recently, J. G. Arena, Hightower, and Chong (1988) have successfully used relaxation therapy to treat tension headaches in elderly persons. This approach may hold much potential in the treatment of other types of pain in the aged.

EFFECTS OF SENSORY DECLINE UPON ENVIRONMENTAL INTERACTION

Now that we have presented and discussed some of the major age differences or age changes in our sensory processes, we shall discuss the potential impact of these changes upon our interacting with or adapting to our environment. Again, we stress caution; individual differences in such changes are substantial. Examples of how decrements in sensory abilities with increasing age can affect our interacting effectively with the environment are presented in Table 4.5. These examples should not be considered exhaustive; you may be able to suggest others.

Our discussion will be structured around experiments that have been performed to investigate potential age differences or age changes in sensation upon the individual's level of interaction and coping with the environment. These experimental tasks are usually referred to as **sensory information processing tasks**. In most instances, performance on these experimental tasks does not decline (if at all) until later adulthood. Therefore, the majority of studies (see Botwinick, 1984 for a review) will compare performance between young and old participants and for the most part will not include middle-aged adults, since there would not likely be a significant difference between young adults and middle-aged individuals.

Further, at first glance these laboratory tasks may appear somewhat "dry" and evoke the questions: Why is this information important? What implication does this have for me? Though the tasks themselves may not be important, they serve as a focal point of study, or well-understood methods of determining if there are potential age decrements in sensation (sensory registration of stimuli). Realizing that this is very important should help you to understand the real-life implications of such research. For example, let's suppose when you visit with your grandmother and you ask her questions about her childhood, she fails to respond to your questions or answers with some statement completely unrelated to your question. After a number of such experiences, you may begin to feel your grandmother's memory is beginning to deteriorate. But can this inability to recall events from your grandmother's past be attributed only to her deteriorating memory? Perhaps your grandmother failed to hear your questions. That is, the auditory stimulation failed to register in her sensory system or registered but was not transmitted through the sensory system (see Table 4.5).

If this were the case, you could recommend that your grandmother get a hearing aid that would allow her to register and pass on this sensory stimulation; or you might talk more loudly but not raise the pitch of your voice in doing so. Therefore, the major importance of the laboratory tasks is that they serve as a method of accurately determining the condition and efficiency of our sensory system. Ultimately (as in this case), such findings can be used to enhance our communication with others.

Since there are numerous experimental procedures used to investigate sensory information processing, one research procedure (paradigm) will be selected and briefly discussed for each sensory modality in order to give you

TABLE 4.5

EXAMPLES OF THE EFFECTS OF SENSORY DECLINE WITH AGE UPON INTERACTING WITH THE ENVIRONMENT

Sensory System	Structural/Anatomical Changes	Functional/Ability Changes	Possible Behavioral Implication
Gustatory	Decreased taste buds (papillae)	Inability to correctly determine taste qualities?	Loss of appetite? Distorted taste? Decreased socialization
Olfactory	Degeneration of neurons on olfactory bulb	Inability to correctly detect and determine various odors?	Loss of appetite? Distorted odors? Inability to detect the presence of potentially harmful odors?
Somesthesis (touch, vibration, temperature, kinesthesis, pain)	Decreased number of sensory receptors for each somesthetic sense	Inability to correctly detect stimulation from the environment	Exposure to potentially dangerous temperature levels Susceptibility to falls Inability to discriminate among clothing materials
Visual	Deposits forming on lens Atrophy of ciliary muscles	Decreased ability in accommodation Decreased visual activity Decreased visual field	Difficulty in reading Difficulty in mobility Difficulty in driving Difficulty in writing letters Difficulty in watching television Decreased activity
Auditory	Wax buildup Accumulation of fluid in middle ear Degeneration of hair cells in the basal coil of cochlea Loss of auditory neurons	Increased absolute threshold Difficulty in pitch discrimination Hearing loss	Inability to hear on the telephone Inability to hear during normal conversation Difficulty in hearing questions on intelligence test Difficulty in interpersonal communication

an example of the research in the area. It might be helpful to refer periodically to Table 4.5 or to our previous example as you learn about these tasks to realize again that such research does have real-life implications for all adults. What does each task tell us about sensory processes?

SENSORY INFORMATION PROCESSING TASKS

Critical Flicker Fusion (CFF)

A classic and frequently used measure of visual sensory information processing is critical flicker fusion (CFF). Basically, CFF experiments involve presenting a flashing light to the participant; the frequency and deviation of the flashes are very well controlled by the experimenter. Research (see Botwinick, 1984; Kline & Schieber, 1985) has shown that if the flashes follow one another in very rapid order, they will appear to fuse for the individual and therefore be perceived as a steady light.

One of the most replicated findings (see above) in the field of aging is that the fusing point comes sooner for older people than it does for younger people. That is, it takes a higher rate of on-off flickering for young individuals to perceive a steady or constant light than it does for the old. Since this finding is so extensively replicated, its cause has been of great interest.

With regard to cause, common sense suggests that CFF threshold may be related to peripheral factors such as thickening of the lenses of the eye, but central factors (decision making, sense of cautiousness) must also be implicated. One central explanation is referred to as **stimulus persistence theory** (Botwinick, 1984). This theory is based on the assumption that stimulus traces persist longer in the nervous systems of older people than younger ones. That is, a stimulus must be cleared through the nervous system before another can be registered and processed. Since the first stimulus persists longer in the nervous systems of older adults, they (older adults) do not register the second stimulus. Since they do not register it, they cannot remember or respond to it.

Stimulus persistence theory is still considered tentative, because though it explains the results of CFF experiments quite well, it does not explain the results of studies that have used other sensory information processing procedures, for example, figural aftereffects or spiral aftereffects (Botwinick, 1984; Kline & Schieber, 1985) (see Table 4.6).

Of all the sensory modalities, the most widely researched, in terms of information processing ability, has been vision. Examples of other research procedures that have been used to investigate age differences in visual sensory information processing are presented in Table 4.6 (see Botwinick, 1984).

Click Fusion

Click fusion is the auditory analogue of CFF. Basically, two sound clicks are presented in rapid order to both ears of the participant. The individual's task is to determine whether these sound like two discrete clicks or a fused click.

TABLE 4.6

VISUAL INFORMATION PROCESSING PROCEDURES

Experimental Procedure		General Findings
Figural aftereffects	Individual stares at figure (stimulus) for a specified period of time, then this figure is removed from view. Dependent measure is time subject reports seeing the afterimage of the figure after it has been removed.	No age differences usually observed.
Spiral aftereffects	A spiral is drawn on a disk, beginning at the center and spiraling out to the edge, and is rotated by a motor at a high speed. The individual fixates on the rotating spiral for a specified time, at which point the motor is turned off. The dependent measure is the time the spiraling image remains, as reported by the individual, after the actual spiraling stops.	Age differences, if any, are a function of the length of the stimulus exposure period.
Color afterimage	Individual is instructed to focus on a patch of color presented on a neutral background. After a specific length of time, the person is instructed to take eyes off color patch and focus on a neutral background. When this is done, the person sees an image of color that is close to the exact color complement of the color on which the subject originally focused (e.g., focusing on green results in a red afterimage). Dependent measure is the duration of the afterimage.	Age differences. Afterimages persist longer among the old than the young. Support for stimulus persistence theory.

Research findings suggest fusion of the two clicks comes about more readily for the old than the young, which is often taken as support for stimulus persistence theory (Weiss, 1959).

Fusion of Discrete Shocks

In this research paradigm, the individual receives mild electrical shocks to some part of the body such as the hand or fingers. Again, the separate shocks are presented in rapid succession, and the task of the participant is to determine if he or she is receiving one continuous (fused) shock or a series of successive, discrete shocks.

An example of this type of research is the study of Axelrod, Thompson, and Cohen (1968), who stimulated the fingers of participants' hands with mild shocks. Participants were informed that sometimes the shocks would be applied simultaneously and sometimes successively, and their task was to judge whether the stimuli were presented together or separately. Results were in line with the stimulus persistence model—older adults fused the successive presentations more readily than the young.

Judging Weights

One method used to test the effect of age on kinesthetic acuity is discrimination of lifted weights. This is exemplified by the study of Landahl and Birren (1959).

Briefly, Landahl and Birren (1959) had a group of young (18 to 32 years) and old (58 to 85 years) make a number of comparisons of weights, using a number of experimental procedures. They reported the young participants to be only slightly more accurate than the old in judging the heavier of two weights. Additionally, the old were as accurate as the young when the weight differences were small.

We have discussed some of the major changes in our sensory receptors that accompany aging for most of us. We have observed general decrements in ability/capacity after middle age for the senses of vision and audition that are subject to individual differences. On the other hand, documented decrements in taste, smell, touch, vibration, temperature, kinesthesis, and pain tend to be speculated and assumed, rather than experimentally confirmed.

These changes in sensation, both confirmed and speculated, have definite effects upon the aging individual's ability to interact, cope, and adapt to the environment. They definitely contribute to the perceptual and ultimately to the behavioral deficits some persons experience (recall our discussion of the information processing model at the beginning of this chapter). When they exist, decrements at the sensory level result in the individual not being able to register, or pick up, many of the important stimuli and cues that are needed to cope and interact with the environment and others in it. That is, if individuals fail to hear, see, or touch aspects of the environment (or others in this environment), they cannot react appropriately to the information (stimulation). This may lead to misunderstanding or isolation from others, accidents, burns, falls, or other tragic consequences. For example, let's look at the effects of sensory decline upon something most of us do every day—drive a car. Think of how different this would be if you were unable to distinguish between a red or green light, unable to detect other autos approaching you from the side, or unable to hear other cars honk their horns (or the difference between the sound of car horns, the horns of bicycles or trucks, or train whistles). Also, how can individuals carry on normal social interaction with others if they are unable to comprehend others' speech due to faulty hearing?

Further, there are many other implications of decreased sensory abilities, ranging from the changes in the design of educational materials (such as size of print, more contrast) and the redesign of long-term care facilities (such as color coding of buttons on elevators) to changes in the labeling on cans and medicine bottles. For example, oversize printing (lettering) on medicine bottles and brightly colored signs may compensate for sensory decrements of middle-aged and older adults and facilitate more adaptive (normal) functioning. For example, medicines will be more likely to be taken in appropriate doses by the older person; older individuals are less likely to feel disoriented or get lost in unfamiliar surroundings.

As will be discussed in Chapter 5, there is often a slowdown in speeded performance with age, and one possible explanation is that the slowdown can be attributed to decrements in our sensory receptors. That is, since older adults cannot hear, see, or feel as well as they used to, they slow down to compensate for their real or imagined decrease in sensory abilities. For example, it is not uncommon to see older drivers slow down to give themselves more time to react.

In the next section, our discussion will focus on age changes and age differences in *perception*—the process by which we *interpret* information received by our senses from the environment. Perceptual processes are influenced by many factors such as gender, education level, culture, experience, personality, and age, to name but a few. Further, many of the perceptual processes discussed are theoretical constructs, or ideas, that do not have any physical reality. This means they cannot be observed directly as would a pain receptor, or a structure in the eye. Our goal will be to highlight the research in the area and discuss its implications for everyday functioning.

PERCEPTUAL INFORMATION PROCESSING TASKS

Geometrical (Visual) Illusions

Numerous studies have investigated susceptibility to geometric illusions across the life span, for example, the Muller-Lyer illusion and Titchner circles (see Figure 4.5). Investigation of perceptual phenomena, such as geometric illusions, gives credence to our distinction between sensation and perception. That is, our sense receptors receive specific stimulation in terms of line segments, circles, and so forth, and our perceptual processes organize and interpret this stimulation. Our interpretation and organization of these perceptions of environmental input depend upon numerous factors such as the accuracy/reliability of the sensory input (sensation), central factors (intelligence, memory, changes in the central nervous system), and psychological/environmental factors (motivation, education level, life experience, and gender).

With regard to the Muller-Lyer illusion, research has consistently reported age differences in susceptibility over the course of the life span (Eisner & K. W. Schaie, 1971; Wapner, Werner, & Comalli, 1960). This research indicates that there is a decrease in susceptibility from age 6 to 12 and, after a rise at 15 to 19, susceptibility remains fairly constant until about age 40, beyond which there is an increase in susceptibility with advancing age (Comalli, 1970). Similar life span trends have been found with the Necker cube illusion (Holt & Matson, 1976).

In contrast to the Muller-Lyer illusion, the life-span differences in susceptibility to the Titchner circles illusion indicate illusory effects increase with increasing age (approximately 6–12 years), remain fairly consistent during late adolescence and adulthood (16–39 years), followed by a decrease in susceptibility in old age (50 years +) (Comalli, 1970).

Researchers have been interested in explaining *why* these life-span trends in susceptibility occur, and why the life-span trends vary as a function of the type of illusion investigated. There are a number of theoretical explanations for both of these questions, such as stimulus persistence (Atkeson, 1978); cohort specific effects (Eisner & Schaie, 1971), and intelligence (Holt & Matson, 1974; Pollack, 1966). However, the idea with the greatest empirical support is referred to as the **orthogenetic principle** (Wapner et al., 1960; Werner, 1948).

According to the orthogenetic principle, perception of shapes, forms, objects, and stimuli follows a specific and predictable life-span trend. This principle states that early in life children perceive the world in a diffuse or global manner; that is, they view and respond to the whole stimulus pattern, without much attention to detail (parts of the stimulus pattern). As the children get older, they learn to integrate the parts of the stimulus pattern with the whole stimulus pattern simultaneously, in relation to each other. These points are illustrated in Figure 4.6.

What do you see in the figure? Do you see a bird or chicken (whole), or do you see individual fruits (part), in Form *A?* In Form *B,* do you see a clown's face (whole), or do you see a telephone, lampshade, etc. (part)? If you saw both aspects to each form, you saw the specific parts of the forms, as well as the overall form, which you integrated into your response.

Since the Muller-Lyer illusion involves the assimilation of part-whole relationships, the decrease in susceptibility from adolescence to middle age reflects a decrease in **global perception**, or the greater ability in integrating the parts with the whole of a stimulus configuration. The increase in suscepti-

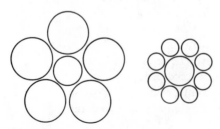

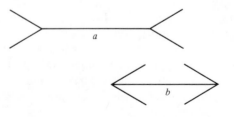

Which inner circle is larger? Check and see.   Which line, *a* or *b*, is longer? Compare them with a ruler.

Figure 4.5 Examples of the Titchner circles and Muller-Lyer illusions. *Source:* R.E. Smith, I.G. Sarason & B.R. Sarason. (1982). *Psychology: The frontiers of behavior* (2d ed.) (p. 154). New York: Harper & Row. Reprinted by permission.

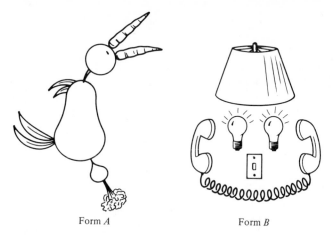

Form *A*   Form *B*

Figure 4.6 Part-whole perception. *Sources:* D. Elkind, R.R.
Koegler, & E. Go. (1964). Studies in perceptual development: II.
Part-whole perception. *Child Development, 35,* 81–90; and H.W.
Reese & L.P. Lippsitt. (1970). *Experimental Child Psychology* (Figure
11.3, p. 366). New York: Academic Press. Used with permission.
Copyright © The Society for Research in Child Development,
Inc.

bility to the illusion from late middle age to old age may reflect a regression
back to global perception (recall that this regression with age is characteristic
of the organismic model of development). This global perceptual mode makes
children and older adults more susceptible to illusions, which are based on
the assimilation of part-whole relationships such as with the Muller-Lyer
illusion. Since a greater ability to contrast parts with the whole increases your
susceptibility to illusions such as the Titchner circles, susceptibility is greatest
in age-groups that are simultaneously integrating parts with the whole
(young and middle-aged adults) and least in age-groups that are employing
a holist mode of perception (children and older adults). It is, however, possible that older adults are processing the illusion *differently*—perhaps they see
it as more complex and therefore process it as if it were perceptually simple.

The study of illusions and other perceptual phenomena are important
because they tell us how persons are interpreting their environment and to
what cues in their environment they are attending. Though there are many
examples of how inaccurate perception of environmental cues can lead to
incorrect or inappropriate behavior and performance, the most vivid example
is in the area of accident behavior. For example, a driver fails to perceive a
child darting out into the road (part) between a number of parked cars
(whole) to retrieve a ball. The major value of the laboratory investigations of
illusions and other perceptual phenomena is to determine why and how the
perceptual processes we use every day to interact effectively with the environment change with age.

We can also see susceptibility to illusions as a special case of *depth
perception.* That is, an illusion works because it deprives us of information
about an object's depth—we may use the relative size of two objects or
persons as a cue for deciding which is closer. What was a three-dimensional

problem has been transformed into a two-dimensional one. Some of the age-related decline (most evident between the ages of 40 and 50; see B. Bell, Wolf, & Bernolz, 1972) in standard depth perception task performance appears to be a function of increased glare or lessened amounts of light reaching the retina (Kausler, 1982). In that depth (relative distance) is a cue we use in everyday life to estimate how far objects are from us (cars, people) or to make judgments regarding how steep hills are or how far down a step is, the potential of impaired depth perception to affect our physical safety is obvious.

Perceptual/Cognitive Style

The construct of perceptual or *cognitive style* has been developed to explain individual differences in perception (Kogan, 1973; Witkin, Lewis, Hertzman, Machover, Meissner, & Wapner, 1954). One aspect of cognitive style is the **field dependence/independence** dimension (Witkin et al., 1954), which can be described as bipolar cognitive styles that are accompanied by discrete patterns of behavior (Witkin & Goodenough, 1977). Persons who are field dependent make judgments that are heavily influenced by the surrounding, immediate environment, while field-independent persons' judgments are not influenced by the immediate environment. Research suggests a relationship between field dependence/independence and a number of dimensions of personal functioning such as personality, behavior, and task performance (Long, 1974; Panek, 1982b; Panek, G.V. Barrett, Alexander, & Sterns, 1979; Witkin & Goodenough, 1977).

An individual's placement along the field dependence/independence dimension is usually based on performance on: (1) the Embedded Figures test, which requires the location of an element embedded in a geometrically complex figure; (2) the Rod-and-Frame test, which requires accurate adjustment of a luminous rod to the true vertical when it is suspended within a tilted frame; or (3) the Body Adjustment test, which requires the individual to adjust his or her body to the true vertical following rotation of the chamber in which the person is sitting in a nonupright position (Kausler, 1982; Kogan, 1973). Good performance on one or more of these measures indicates field independence while poor performance indicates field dependence.

Extensive cross-sectional data on the field dependence/independence dimension across the life span have been reported (Comalli, 1970; Eisner, 1972; Panek, G.V. Barrett, Sterns, & Alexander, 1978; Schwartz & Karp, 1967). Results generally show a curvilinear trend with age, indicating progressive and regressive changes with age over the life span. That is, a shift from field dependence to independence during adolescence, continuity during adulthood, and a shift again to field dependence during old age.

Though consistent age differences in perceptual style are reported in the literature, the explanation for these observed differences is still a matter of experimental investigation (Kausler, 1982; Panek, Barrett, Sterns, & Alexander, 1978). Since perceptual style has been shown to be related to many behaviors and traits across the life span, this shift toward field dependence with aging has numerous implications with regard to one's interaction with the environment. One implication of the shift toward field dependence with age has to do with driving behavior (Panek, Barrett, Sterns, & Alexander, 1977). Perceptual style has been found to be highly related to emergency behavior in a controlled driving simulation (Barrett & Thorton, 1978; G.V. Barrett, Thornton, & Cabe, 1969), and actual accident involvement (Mihal & G.V. Barrett, 1976) in adults.

Further, the age-related changes in perceptual style appear to mirror the curve for automotive accident involvement. That is, the shift or change in perceptual style approximates the accident curve, with younger drivers exhibiting more accident involvement, a drop in accident rate after age 25, followed by an increase in rate after age 65. Support for this assumption has been obtained by G.V. Barrett, Mihal, Panek, Sterns, and Alexander (1977).

In conclusion, perceptual style has received a great deal of research attention in the adulthood and aging literature. The major implications of this research have to do with the numerous documented relationships between an individual's perceptual style and performance on a variety of everyday and laboratory behaviors at all points along the life span (Long, 1974).

Selective Attention

Selective attention is an integral component of perception and human information processing (Panek & Rush, 1981). Attention plays an important role in almost all areas of our daily functioning, such as reading this book or taking notes in class. The age-related changes in the ability to maintain attention have been well documented (Giambra & Quilter, 1988; Hoyer & Plude, 1980).

Although there has been extensive investigation of attention from both theoretical and life-span perspectives, attention is not a unitary concept, and there are numerous research procedures all attempting to measure attention (Kahneman, 1973; Kausler, 1970; Panek & Rush, 1981). The most encompassing definition of selective attention was that proposed by Plude, Kaye, Hoyer, Post, Saynisch, and Hahn (1983), who defined *selective attention* as the control of information processing so that a particular source of information is processed more fully than any other simultaneous sources of information. That is, though we are constantly exposed to numerous sources of information at the same time, we are able to attend selectively to specific information (that to which we wish to attend). A good example of this process is attempting to read this text in one's room while our roommates are simultaneously carrying on a conversation and listening to the stereo. We have all probably experienced how difficult this can be. Since the literature is quite extensive, our discussion will concentrate on studies of attention that attempt to generalize their results to applied problems. Studies of attention focus on either auditory or visual selective attention.

Auditory Selective Attention   One widely used measure of auditory selective attention is a *dichotic listening task.* In a dichotic listening task, the individual is presented with simultaneous but different stimuli (numbers or letters) or messages in each ear, usually at a high rate of speed. The individual is required to repeat or recall some particular stimulus or stimuli designated by the experimenter as the target, such as all the odd numbers. This ability to selectively attend to one message in the presence of other competing messages is an information processing task that is widely investigated in the laboratory (Hoyer & Plude, 1980; Panek, Barrett, Sterns, & Alexander, 1977). These tasks are also referred to as *divided attention* or *controlled attention* tasks. Dichotic listening is a fine example of a fast-paced situation that causes special problems for many older persons, since successful performance requires simultaneous attention to two alternatives (Broadbent & Heron, 1962; Welford, 1951).

With regard to age differences, Panek and Rush (1981) demonstrated that the ability to maintain and reorient attention significantly decreases with age. Further, within all age-groups, reorientation of attention was more difficult than the maintenance of attention. The difference in performance between these two components of selective attention (maintenance, reorientation) are magnified with increasing age. These results suggest that increased age involves definite and significant decrements on tasks that require maintenance as well as reorientation of attention. But there are important individual differences; not all older adults perform poorly. It must be pointed out that more research studies in this area have employed cross-sectional designs. It is certainly possible that the age differences reported are influenced by cohort differences or due to sampling effects; however, many (Kausler, 1982) do feel that cross-sectional research is appropriate, given the unlikelihood of cohort effects.

It is important to note that on divided attention tasks the performance of both young and old individuals declines as the tasks increase in difficulty. But the decline is generally greater and more rapid for older adults (Wright, 1981). When the attentional demands of the task decrease, the performance of older adults increases (Madden, 1982; Lorsbach & Simpson, 1988).

Visual Selective Attention   With regard to visual selective attention, the most common measure is the Stroop test (Stroop, 1935), which measures the individual's capacity to maintain a course of action in the face of intrusion by other stimuli. The task is composed of three cards. The "A" card consists of 100 color words (RED, BLUE, and GREEN) printed in black ink and arranged in random order. On this card the participant has to read the words aloud as quickly as possible. Card "B" consists of 100 randomly arranged rectangular color patches (of red, blue, and green). The task is to correctly *name the colors* as quickly as possible. Card "C" presents, in random order, 100 color words (RED, BLUE, and GREEN) printed in an ink whose actual color is different from the color designated by the word (the word *blue* might be printed in red ink). Because reading is an overlearned, automatic (W. Schneider & Shiffrin, 1977) process, inhibiting the response blue might be very difficult (Kausler, 1982).

In terms of age differences, the literature (Comalli, 1970; Comalli, Krus, & Wapner, 1965; Comalli, Wapner, & Werner, 1962; Eisner, 1972) indicates only marginal life-span differences in the response time for naming the ink color of color patches (color-naming response). However, older adults are significantly slower than young adults in a color-naming response when the color is *inconsistent* with the color word stimulus, which is called the *age-Stroop interference effect* (Burke & Light, 1981).

In general, life-span investigations of the Stroop interference effect report a significant curvilinear trend across age-groups beginning with a large Stroop effect for young adults and then increasing again for older adults (Comalli et al., 1962; Panek, Rush, & Slade, 1984). There are numerous explanations for why age differences occur on the Stroop test. For example, Burke & Light (1981) and Kausler (1970) suggest encoding and retrieval processes (see Chapter 7) appear to be crucial to an explanation of difficulties exhibited by older adults on a perceptual task such as the Stroop. That is, older adults have extreme difficulty in encoding the cognitive-semantic information (color/word) and then retrieving the correct response because of the incongruence between the color/word. Young adults have more efficient encoding and retrieval processes and therefore perform the task faster. Support for this view was found by Panek et al. (1984).

Visual selective attention is also investigated by procedures referred to as *stimulus masking* or *stimulus enhancement*. In a masking study, the individual is presented, usually for an extremely short duration, a stimulus that is called the first test, or *target stimulus,* followed by the presentation of a second stimulus called the *masking stimulus*. This is called *backward masking* when the first stimulus obscures the second (Hoyer & Plude, 1980). In an "enhancement study," the second stimulus is integrated with the first (both stimuli have overlapping presentation times).

According to stimulus persistence theory, older adults should experience the effects of the first stimulus for a longer time than younger individuals. That is, if the trace of the first stimulus takes longer to clear through the nervous system, then the second stimulus will, depending upon its nature, either mask or enhance the first stimulus (see Botwinick, 1978, 1984).

Research using the masking paradigm has generally supported stimulus persistence theory (Kline & Szafran, 1975; Kline & Birren, 1975). Additionally, Till (1978) and Walsh (1976) have obtained similar results but explain the young-old differences in terms of speed of perceptual processing rather than stimulus persistence. That is, it takes longer for older adults, compared to younger adults, to encode, retrieve, and process the stimulus information. Salthouse (1980) suggests that performance decrements in these situations reflect the lessened *efficiency* of the older person's nervous system to separate relevant and irrelevant aspects of perceptual stimuli—that is, older persons require greater time intervals between stimuli and more stimulus exposure time to process perceptual cues accurately.

An alternative to the stimulus persistence model emphasizing a qualitative difference with age in perceptual functioning has been proposed by Kline and Scheiber (1981, 1985) based on the assumption that different types of visual stimuli are processed by different neural channels in the visual system. **Sustained visual channels** detect *stable high spatial frequency* stimuli (slow-moving objects, e.g., fine print) with little contrast and respond more slowly yet more persistently over a longer span of time. **Transient** neural channels, on the other hand, respond to *low spatial frequency* (coarse) stimuli that are *moving* (flickering or motion) and respond more quickly and for shorter periods of time. Research reviewed by Kline and Scheiber (1985) suggests that older adults relative to younger ones tend to process less efficiently (1) high spatial frequency (finely detailed) objects that are stationary versus low spatial frequency ones, and (2) low spatial frequency stimuli (coarsely detailed) that are moving. According to Kline and Scheiber (1985), older persons tend to experience a loss in the effectiveness of transient visual channels and rely more heavily on sustained channels, leading to greater stimulus persistence. Where information is presented sequentially, older persons need a greater time interval between the first and second letter or number to process them accurately, consistent with their reliance on sustained channel functioning.

Overall, research clearly indicates that with aging there is a significant decrease in the speed and efficiency of both audition and visual selective attention ability, often found among persons in their forties and fifties. At the present time, there is no adequate single theory of age-related changes in attention (Madden, 1984).

Implications Though we must use visual and auditory selective attention each day in order to deal effectively with our environment, the implications of decreases in these abilities are just beginning to be studied. Available studies demonstrate the relationship between individual differences in selective attention ability and such real-life situations as aircraft flight proficiency and accident involvement (G.V. Barrett et al., 1977; Gopher & Kahneman, 1971; Kahneman, Ben-Ishai, & Lotan, 1973; Mihal & G.V. Barrett, 1976; Panek, Barrett, Sterns, & Alexander, 1978).

The findings indicating substantial individual differences *within* age-groups in performance in terms of selective attention ability may hold promise as a measure of functional age. Though recent court litigation (G.V. Barrett & Jorgensen, 1986) has upheld age cutoffs for certain occupations, many individuals (Senator Claude Pepper, who is himself in his eighties) continue to express disfavor with chronological age as a criterion for retirement, preferring instead an alternative criterion of functional age for retirement decisions. Since selective attention tasks measure abilities that exhibit individual differences within and between age-groups, selective attention may be an effective measure of functional age (Mihal & G. V. Barrett, 1976).

Vigilance

Vigilance is the ability to maintain attention to a task for a sustained period (Panek, Barrett, Sterns, & Alexander, 1977). This ability is very important for successful performance on tasks such as driving, assembly line work, and other activities where the individual must maintain attention for a fairly long period of time (e.g., monitoring a screen for hours as air-traffic controllers or computer programmers must). For example, Thackray and Touchstone (1981) found age differences (favoring young adults) in performance on simulated tasks for air-traffic controllers. Older adults were less accurate at detecting

Air-traffic controllers are required to maintain vigilance for long periods of time; this skill appears to decline with age, though there are individual differences in vigilance throughout adulthood.

targets, responded more slowly, and made more false-alarm responses (falsely identifying a target as such) than did young adults. Middle-aged adults were intermediate in their performance, relative to the young and the old. Vigilance is usually studied with monitoring or inspection tasks such as monitoring a pointer on a clocklike devise.

Regarding age difference in vigilance (monitoring) performance, results vary as a function of a number of factors such as type of task, sensory modality investigated, length of time the individuals must remain vigilant, and the speed of performance required. Additionally, there are significant individual differences in performance within age-groups.

Griew and Davies (1962) conducted a series of three experiments of auditory vigilance with young and old individuals. Basically, the task was to listen to a tape recording of a series of digits at the rate of one per second for 40 minutes. In experiment one, the task was to record the occurrence of any three consecutive odd digits by writing them down on paper. Experiment two required participants to check the spoken digits on a list and strike out those at variance with the list. Experiment three required the individuals to press a key whenever they heard three consecutive odd digits. Results indicated that the only task on which there were significant age differences in performance was experiment one. These results suggested to Griew and Davies that any observed age decrement in vigilance performance was not attributable to vigilance ability per se, but to memory processes, such as remembering what digits to write down (see Giambra & Quilter, 1988).

In terms of duration, Surwillo (1964) found performance of older adults did not show a decrement in performance on a visual monitoring task until after about 45 minutes of sustained performance. Concerning speed and modality, Thompson, Opton, and Cohen (1963) presented old and young individuals with an odd-even vigilance task in both the auditory and visual modalities. No significant differences in performance were found at the slower rates of presentation (intervals of four and two seconds between stimuli), but the elderly individuals demonstrated a marked decrement at the fastest speed (one-second intervals between stimuli).

The only longitudinal investigation of age changes in vigilance performance is that of Quilter, Giambra, and Benson (1983) who investigated 18-year changes in performance of individuals who participated in previous investigations of vigilance (Surwillo & Quilter, 1964, 1965). Quilter et al. (1983) reported that at about 70 there was a noticeable reduction in vigilance performance. In addition to observing age differences and age changes, there were individual differences within age-groups. Results indicated the largest performance decrement for the older adults was found in the auditory task (modality). Giambra and Quilter (1988) found that when vigilance tasks minimize memory, age effects are minimal. However, these investigators did find that when long-term vigilance is required to monitor a stimulus, detection, accuracy, and speed of response generally decline with age. Thompson et al. (1963) attribute the observed age deficits to speed of perceptual motor performance. Kausler (1982) suggests that vigilance is most impaired when the task is presented at a fast rate, is lengthy, or when the individual must hold the information in memory to be vigilant. Interestingly, when the task involves **pattern recognition** (a certain kind of blip on the screen means small plane, another type of blip means airliner), older persons seem to be at a greater disadvantage when two stimuli are semantically dissimilar (they *mean* different things) versus when they are perceptually dissimilar (they *look* different) (Kausler, 1982).

To the extent that two bits of information (blips, patterns of speech, faces) are of varying similarity, how do older persons fare? Research involving the detection of audio **signals** that are or are not embedded in a background of **noise** (static) (as one might encounter in tuning a radio or listening to a garbled telephone conversation) (Kausler, 1982) helps us understand whether performance differences (accuracy of correct identification of a signal versus a signal + noise) are a function of sensory loss or some perceptual process (decision making).

In most cases, researchers have found older persons to make few mistakes but also to make fewer correct identifications than young adults in such situations where the signal-to-noise ratio is nearly equal or where the signal is only slightly louder than the noise, because they tend to be more *cautious* or *conservative* (see Kausler, 1982).

Many of the differences in sensory functioning (vision, audition) we discussed earlier may *in part* be a function of older persons' reluctance to report seeing or hearing a stimulus until they were absolutely certain that it was present. We must therefore consider the person's "private threshold" in interpreting research dealing with the perception of pain (symptoms of illness) or judgments of the heaviness of weights; in short, anytime one makes a *decision* about either physical or environmental stimulation (Is one head of lettuce heavier than another? Is one grapefruit bigger than the other?) such **response biases** may be involved. Those who market products of all types (particularly if they are targeting a product to a younger or older audience) will most likely take such decision-making processes into account if they are to be successful (see Chapter 5 for a further discussion of decision-making processes in adulthood). As our information processing model illustrates and these examples reinforce, the processes of sensation and perception are closely related to one another.

Implications   You may be wondering what relevance these laboratory studies, as well as the construct of vigilance, have for your own life. Again, the two best examples of the relevance of this work concern driving and industrial performance. While driving, a person must constantly maintain vigilance (looking at the white center lines on a road at night for long periods of time) and monitor the environment in order to avoid accidents. The successful assembly line worker must constantly monitor the line in spite of fatigue or monotony. Interestingly, only a few studies have attempted to make this link between laboratory monitoring and real-world performance for older adults as well as young adults. In fact, older adults may be more vigilant than young individuals in real-life tasks. For example, Murrell and Griew (1965) believe that experience gained over months or years of work on the job may compensate for a decrease in overall capacity with age; therefore, no decrement in performance would be observed. The older worker, realizing his or her capacity may not be as good as it used to be, compensates for this decreased capacity by being more vigilant. In this sense, this person may be a *better* employee—make fewer mistakes and do better quality work.

The role of experience and speed of performance on a simulated industrial vigilance task was investigated by Panek, Barrett, Alexander, & Sterns (1979). These researchers attempted to answer two major questions: (1) do older workers prefer to work at a significantly slower pace than younger workers, controlling for experience, and (2) are there significant differences in the performance of older and younger workers in accuracy of performance when controlling for experience? Results of the study indicated there were no significant differences between younger and older workers in accuracy of performance, but there were significant differences in pace (speed) at which older and younger workers preferred to work on the task. Basically, younger workers preferred to work at a significantly faster rate than older workers.

In conclusion, vigilance plays an integral part in our everyday interactions with the environment. Though this perceptual process is important, there have been few definitive studies in the area and little attempt to relate this process to applied situations. As we have become more aware of the importance of vigilance in the performance of those in such professions as air-traffic controllers (see Thackray & Touchstone, 1981), research in this area will most likely increase.

SUMMARY

In this chapter, we discussed age differences in *sensation* and *perception*. The relationship between these processes can be understood in terms of an *information processing model* of aging. The numerous changes with age in vision, hearing, taste, smell, and the somesthetic senses were described and their implications for our everyday functioning were discussed. Though a fairly large number of visual and auditory functions decrease with age, there are substantial individual differences in the degree to which persons experience deficits in visual and auditory functioning. In contrast, definitive findings in terms of the effects of the aging processes on the other senses (taste, smell, touch) is less clear. A number of diverse sensory information processing tasks such as *critical flicker fusion* or *judging weights* can be used to measure sensory functioning across the life span.

Further, in this chapter we detailed and described life-span trends on a number of perceptual processes. Based upon data gathered using visual illusions, information about a number of important perceptual processes such as *cognitive style*, and *part-whole perception* was presented. As a general rule, in cases where adults must *divide* their *attention* in complex situations, their performance suffers. These changes have been explained in terms of Werner's *orthogenetic principle*.

In cases where information is *processed sequentially*, both the speed and efficiency of such processing seems to be affected by the aging process. These age-related differences have been explained in terms of *stimulus persistence* and *transient versus sustained channel* theories. Research investigating *vigilance* has suggested that while the ability to maintain sustained attention appears to decline with age, numerous decision-making biases exist in older persons; these biases clearly affect the reporting of sensory impressions, illustrating the interrelatedness of *sensation* and *perception*. Where deficits in sensory or perceptual functioning exist, they have a number of implications for everyday functioning.

KEY TERMS AND CONCEPTS

Information processing approach
   to aging

Sensation

Perception

Sensory receptors

Absolute threshold

Difference threshold

Presbyopia

Accommodation

Visual acuity

Color vision

Adaptation (dark, light)

Glare sensitivity
Peripheral field
Visual search behavior
Audition
Presbycusis
Outer, middle, inner ear
Pitch discrimination
Premature presbycusis
Speechreading
Auditory training
Somesthesis
Sensory information
  processing tasks
Stimulus persistence theory

Sustained and transient visual
  channels
Perceptual information processing
  tasks
Orthogenetic principle
Global perception
Field dependence/independence
Selective attention
Vigilance
Pattern recognition
Signal
Noise
Response bias

- Why is it important to study psychomotor reaction time in a life-span framework?
- Is there a general slowdown in behavior with advancing age? What implication does this slowdown have for the aging individual?
- What factors affect whether age differences are observed on a psychomotor reaction time task?
- What explanations have been postulated to explain the slowdown in behavior with age?
- Can training or practice improve the performance of older adults on perceptual-motor reaction time tasks?
- Do individuals become more cautious in their behavior and decision making with increasing age?
- Do individuals become rigid with advancing age?
- What are the general attitudes of business and industry with regard to the older worker?
- What does the Age Discrimination in Employment Act (ADEA) prohibit?
- Are the myths held by business and industry regarding the older worker accurate? What seem to be the bases for such attitudes?

CHAPTER ▪ 5

PSYCHOMOTOR

PERFORMANCE

▪

INTRODUCTION

One of the best-documented observed changes with increasing age is a slow-down in performance and behavior (Birren, Woods, & Williams, 1980). From age 40 onward, accuracy appears to be stressed at the expense of speed in performing a psychomotor task (Welford, 1977). This is often referred to as the **speed versus accuracy trade-off** (concentrating on performing correctly rather than quickly). This theme is quite pervasive in the adulthood and aging literature and has been observed in numerous laboratory and real-life task performance situations. These include tasks of memory, intelligence, and reaction time, as well as measures of industrial performance, driving, and decision making (Birren et al., 1980; Panek, G.V. Barrett, Sterns, & Alexander, 1977; Salthouse, 1985; J.A. Stern, Oster, & Newport, 1980).

Due to the extensiveness of the work in this area and the goals of this text, we shall concentrate on the applied aspects of the suspected slowdown in behavior and performance rather than presenting an exhaustive review of this literature. Our primary goals are to discuss: (1) the effects of aging upon psychomotor performance, (2) what explanations have been offered to explain these age changes, and (3) the implications of these changes. Changes that persons experience in their psychomotor skills influence many aspects of their lives, for example, everyday decision making, one's driving behavior, the likelihood of having an accident, and job performance.

It should be stressed that our discussion will concentrate on overall normative trends across the life span, since there are vast individual differences in performance within all age-groups. As we have stressed previously, such differences are an important component of psychomotor performance in adulthood. Additionally, the magnitude of the resultant age differences in performance, as well as the appearance of any age differences, is often a function of the type of task used (J.A. Stern et al., 1980).

PERCEPTUAL-MOTOR REACTION TIME

Studies of reaction time are concerned with the speed of the individual's response to some external or internal stimulus or event. The study of reaction time performance in adulthood and aging is of great importance due to the fact that many situations in our everyday work and life involve reacting to stimuli quickly and accurately, such as driving a car, working on a machine in industry, typing, and the avoidance of everyday hazardous events (such as burning oneself with hot water while cooking).

Researchers currently describe reaction time tasks as **perceptual-motor reaction time** tasks since successful performance involves substantially more than just a simple motor response. Successful performance often involves other factors such as perception, sensation, attention, short-term memory, intelligence, decision making, and personality as well as motor behavior. Further, as noted by Welford (1977), in a reaction time task the individual must (1) *perceive* that an event has occurred, (2) *decide* what to do about it, and (3) carry out the decided-upon *action.* Thus, observed poor performance on a perceptual-motor reaction time task can often be attributed to one or more of these other factors, rather than to just speed of motor performance. Consequently, our previous discussion of sensation and perception should be a valuable asset to your understanding the material in this chapter dealing with psychomotor performance and its everyday implications.

In the most basic and simplistic sense there are three types of perceptual-motor reaction time tasks: simple, choice, and complex. Each of these types of tasks differs in its level of difficulty.

Simple Perceptual-Motor Reaction Time

Simple perceptual-motor reaction time is considered the least difficult of the above tasks. The distinguishing characteristic of a simple reaction time task is that there is only *one* possible stimulus that is to be associated with only *one* response. An example of this type of task would be having a person seated in a chair at a table on which there is a light bulb and a key. The individual is told "to press the key as soon as the light comes on." The person's reaction time is the length of time elapsed between the onset of the light and the key being pressed. With a little more sophistication, we would be able to derive two components from our reaction time task: (1) **decision/premotor time**, and (2) **motor time**. For instance, we could have the participant rest a finger on another key, which was also connected to electrical recording devices, while waiting to respond to the light stimulus. The time lapsed between the onset of the light stimulus and the removal of the finger from the resting key would be considered *decision time,* while the time between removing the finger

Many jobs require skilled psychomotor performance. A careful assessment of both
the job and the adult's psychomotor skills is essential for both the employee and
the employer.

from the resting key to the completion of the appropriate response would be
motor time, or *movement time.*

Research has reported consistent age differences in overall simple reaction time, as well as for each of these individual components (Botwinick &
Storandt, 1972, 1974b; Panek, Barrett, Sterns, & Alexander, 1977, 1978; Welford, 1977). Interestingly, when one separates the overall reaction time into
decision/premotor time and motor time, the most noticeable difference between young and old participants is in the decision time aspect. That is, it
takes older adults a longer time to initiate the response, compared to those
who are younger.

Choice Reaction Time

Choice reaction time is a somewhat less difficult reaction time task. While
there are many variations in terms of procedure, the distinguishing characteristic of a choice reaction time task is that while there is only one response that

is paired with only one stimulus, there is more than one stimulus-response pair. Let's go back to our simple reaction time task, but this time introduce two lights, red and green, and two response keys, which are marked 1 and 2. The individual's task is to press the number 1 key when the red light comes on, and the number 2 key when the green light comes on. An everyday example of a choice reaction time task is typing (Salthouse, 1984). Research investigating performance at various points across the life span on such tasks usually indicates slowing (or increased reaction time) with increased age (Rabbitt, 1965). The magnitude of such differences increases with the number of distracting stimuli, response/stimulus complexity, and cognitive (memory, attention) demands (Welford, 1977). For example, a typewriter with few keys on it will be for most typists, especially older ones, easier to type quickly on than one with more keys. Older typists may however, compensate for such complexity by being more efficient regarding hand movements (Salthouse, 1984).

Complex Reaction Time

The most difficult level of reaction time tasks measures complex reaction time. A good example of a complex reaction time task is driving an automobile. In driving and other complex reaction time tasks, the stimuli are infinite, as well as responses being quite diverse in number. For example, as we drove our cars to class, we probably encountered many critical situations (stimuli), to which we had to react quickly and accurately to avoid an accident. One of the most important things to keep in mind about complex reaction time tasks is the *diversity* of possible responses. In our driving to class example, let's

While driving performance is a complex psychomotor skill, many older adults still retain their driving skills and have little difficulty in driving safely.

imagine as you were driving down a street a car pulled out of a driveway about 25 yards in front of you. To this one stimulus, you had the choice of many responses—to step on the brakes, honk the horn and continue to drive, quickly turn left, or quickly turn right. As one can infer, in complex reaction time situations, many factors are involved in performance—perceiving the stimulus, deciding on what to do, and then doing it. (You may want to review the information processing model of sensation and perception in Chapter 4.)

Overall, there appear to be significant age differences on each of these types of perceptual-motor reaction time tasks (Welford, 1977). That is, a general performance slowdown or decrement with aging occurs. It is important to note that the magnitude of the age differences appears to increase with the complexity of the perceptual-motor reaction time task in a linear manner (Cerella, Poon, & Williams, 1980). Thus, older persons are at a greater disadvantage in more demanding or complex situations. Though there are age differences on all three types of levels of perceptual-motor reaction time tasks, the magnitude of these differences is greater for choice versus simple tasks, and greater still for complex versus choice tasks.

Since a slowdown in performance with aging has been documented in many situations, researchers have attempted to determine (1) what causal factor or factors are involved, and (2) whether this slowdown can be remediated (Birren, Woods, & Williams, 1980).

THEORETICAL EXPLANATIONS FOR THE PSYCHOMOTOR SLOWDOWN

The primary cause of the slowdown in behavior and performance with age is still not known. While there are a number of explanations, some of which have more empirical support than others, all are limited to some extent in explaining this behavioral slowdown. Moreover, in many cases these theoretical notions explain the slowdown in performance on a specific laboratory task quite well but cannot explain performance on other tasks adequately.

Each theory or hypothesis can be characterized as either a *peripheral* or *central* explanation (Botwinick, 1984). These distinctions will become more evident as we discuss examples of theories derived from each perspective.

Peripheral Explanations

Peripheral explanations view the loss of speed due to decrements in the sense organs and/or peripheral nervous system (Botwinick, 1984). In order to understand and appreciate these theories more fully, you might review the information discussed in Chapter 4 on sensation and perception. Peripheral explanations see the slowdown as due to factors such as sensory discrimination, loss of muscle contraction, and change in the length of neuromuscular pathways and speed of the pure movement or motor response (Botwinick, 1984). In effect, these theories assume the slowdown in behavior is the result of factors such as the inability to hear or see a stimulus, or solely due to decreases in speed of motor movement. Subsequently, if old and young individuals were equated on such factors, such as hearing ability, no age differences should be observed.

In a sequence of studies, Botwinick and his associates (Botwinick, 1971, 1972; Botwinick & Storandt, 1972) tested the belief that behavioral slowing on reaction time tasks was due primarily to age differences in sensory ability. For example, when a stimulus tone is presented in a laboratory reaction time task, older individuals, due to decreased hearing ability, should not hear the tone as well as young individuals and therefore should respond more slowly. However, Botwinick (1972) found that even when the stimulus tone was presented at an intensity level well above the individual's absolute threshold required for registration of the stimulus 100 percent of the time, older adults were still found to be slower in reaction time than young adults.

Weiss (1965) and Botwinick and Thompson (1966) separated reaction time of young and old participants into a *premotor* component (detecting a stimulus, identification, and decision regarding a response—a central process) and a *motor* component (literal time to move one's finger, for example—a peripheral process), and found that though older adults were significantly slower on both components, the most dramatic difference was on the premotor component. This demonstrates that the contribution of the pure motor aspect of age differences in reaction time is important but relatively small compared to the contribution of central processes. On the basis of extensive research, peripheral explanations of the behavioral slowing with age have been discarded (Botwinick, 1984; Cerella et al., 1980; Welford, 1977).

Central Explanations

Central explanations are now used in determining the major cause of the slowdown in behavior with aging (Salthouse, 1985; Welford, 1977). At the present time we do not have a definitive theory that explains the slowdown in behavior with aging that is appropriate in all situations or research paradigms. These approaches tend to explain one type of slowed response quite well but have not been tested and/or are inappropriate with other situations. Therefore, each explanation should be considered tentative.

All central explanations view the slowdown in behavior/performance with age as being due to some higher level *internal* process. These explanations stress factors such as delay in neural transmission, difficulty in establishing a psychological (expectation) set (preparation time), declines in psychophysiological function, neural interference, cautiousness, difficulty in decision making, and task complexity (see Botwinick, 1984, for a review).

NEURAL NOISE

One of the first central theories that was presented to explain response slowing with age was the **neural noise** hypothesis (Welford, 1965). As stimulus information passes from the receptors to the brain and/or from one part of the brain to another, this information can be disrupted by neural noise. Neural noise is thought to be produced by either random background neural activity or by irregularities in the action of the cells transmitting the signals, which according to Welford may be related to several factors: (1) a reduction in the number of functional cells, (2) an increase in random neural activity, (3) longer aftereffects of neural activity, and (4) the level of activation or arousal. A good example of neural noise would be seen in watching what happens to a television picture as a number of other electrical appliances cause interference with the picture.

NEUROPHYSIOLOGICAL EXPLANATIONS

There are many variants of the neural noise explanation, all of which identify the locus of the slowdown as some aspect of neurophysiological functioning. For example, several researchers have attempted to link certain psychophysiological processes, such as the alpha wave pattern of the electroencephalogram (EEG) to declines in reaction time performance (Surwillo, 1968; L.W. Thompson & Botwinick, 1968; Marsh & L.W. Thompson, 1977). The basic assumption is that these neurophysiological measures are accurate indicators of the integrity or condition of the central nervous system, and any abnormality in transmission would affect all aspects of behavior and performance, including reaction time. The relationship between neurophysiological functioning and reaction time performance holds promise, but the research must still be considered equivocal (see also Botwinick, 1984, for a discussion).

EXPECTANCY/SET THEORY

Expectancy or **set theory** views the slowdown in responding with age to be the result of older individuals' inability or difficulty in preparing their response to the stimulus (Birren, 1964). This explanation has received extensive support by Brinley (1965), who studied cognitive tasks requiring speeded performance. Though the set hypothesis makes good common sense, it is not readily applicable to many applied situations where stimuli are not presented in a predictable, paced manner. For example, in driving, we very rarely have time to prepare to look for a stimulus and then respond. In reality, we are most often confronted with an unexpected situation to which we must act immediately to avoid an accident.

Rabbitt (1965) conducted several reaction time studies with individuals from 17 to 82 years of age. Results led Rabbitt to suggest that the age differences in performance could be attributed to older adults having difficulty in ignoring *irrelevant* or *redundant* information. This explanation appears quite plausible based on the known decrements in selective attention ability with age that we previously discussed in Chapter 4.

COMPLEXITY EXPLANATION

The **complexity explanation** (Cerella et al., 1980) of the psychomotor slowdown with increasing age is based on the fact that as a task becomes more complex, the magnitude of the age decrement in performance increases. Complexity is defined in terms of such factors as increased cognitive demands, increased numbers of stimuli, and increased response attention. A study that illustrates this concept is one by Panek, Barrett, Sterns, and Alexander (1978).

These researchers administered two perceptual-motor reaction time tasks (as well as a number of other tasks) that differed as a function of the level of complexity to 175 community-living female volunteers, ranging in age from 17 to 72 years. Participants were placed into one of seven groups on the basis of their chronological age and were each administered both simple choice reaction time and complex reaction time tasks. For each task participants were seated in a simulated driver's seat with standard controls. The stimuli for the simple choice reaction time task consisted of four different signals—a green left-turn arrow, a red braking disk, a green right-turn arrow, and a yellow disk for a horn blow response. In the complex reaction time task, the stimulus consisted of a photograph of an actual driving scene in which was embedded a signal or sign indicating that the participant should respond in the same way as in the simple choice reaction time task. For example, one photo contained a stop sign, in which case the correct response was to depress the brake pedal.

Results for both simple choice and complex reaction time indicated significant age differences in performance. These results are presented in Figure 5.1.

Figure 5.1 illustrates two important points regarding life-span trends in psychomotor performance. First, regardless of the task there is basically a linear decrease (a slowdown) in performance. Second, as the complexity of the task increases (as Rabbitt, 1965 and Cerella et al. 1980 suggest), the magnitude of the age differences increases. This fact can easily be determined by comparing the average differences in performance, both between age-groups within tasks and for each age-group between tasks.

INFORMATION OVERLOAD

Szafran (1965, 1968), working with a group of older pilots, found that there was only a decrement in performance in stress situations—what he called **information overload**. According to this assumption, as the amount of stim-

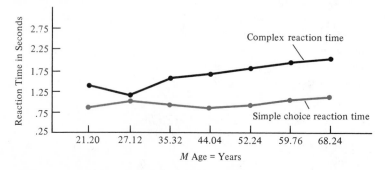

Figure 5.1 Life-span trends for simple choice and complex reaction time.

uli or events to be processed and the responses to be carried out increase, the performance of older adults decreases. Therefore, if only one stimulus response pairing is used, the psychomotor slowdown with age is not as drastic as if there were more. As the stimulus information from the environment increases, the individual's information processing systems may become overloaded, and they will not be able to perform quickly and correctly.

PERCEPTUAL NOISE

B.J. Layton (1975) suggests that age decrements in performance on many tasks, including perceptual-motor reaction time, are due to the presence of irrelevant or interfering stimuli. This assumption, which is based on an age decrement in ability to suppress irrelevant stimuli, is called **perceptual noise theory**.

Evaluation

Since the literature on psychomotor slowing with age is so extensive, we hope our brief presentation gives you a flavor for the types of research and controversies in the area. Before we conclude this section, it is important to leave with a basic summary of the literature regarding life-span trends in psychomotor reaction time performance:

1. The decrement in perceptual-motor reaction time with increasing age is centrally mediated (Cerella et al., 1980) and begins to manifest itself during middle age, usually around age 45 (Birren, 1969; Panek, Barrett, Sterns, & Alexander, 1977; Surwillo, 1968). Thus, deficits in the sensory receptors alone cannot account for these decrements (Botwinick, 1972; Botwinick & Storandt, 1972). Overall, the specific locus or cause of the slowdown in performance is still unknown, though researchers are now suggesting the slowdown appears to be a general rather than specific factor (Salthouse & Somberg, 1982a, 1982b).

2. Set has an effect on performance on perceptual-motor reaction time tasks, especially for older adults (Brinley, 1965; Rabbitt, 1965). Set refers to a level of preparedness, such as "get ready, get set, go," prior to responding. Therefore, the more prepared older adults are to respond, the better they are likely to perform.

3. Changes in the central nervous system with age (Birren, 1965, 1969; Wang & Busse, 1969; Woodruff, 1972) have been related to lower reaction times (Botwinick & Storandt, 1974a, 1974b; Surwillo, 1968) and have been used in the prediction of survival (Muller, Grad, & Engelsman, 1975).

4. There are vast interindividual differences within all age-groups on perceptual-motor reaction time tasks (Maddox & Douglass, 1974) and between genders (Murrell, 1970).

5. Decrements in performance are most likely to be evidenced among older adults under stressful situations (Szafran, 1968) or when the stimuli are presented at a rapid rate (Kemp, 1973).

6. Practice can improve perceptual-motor reaction time performance in older adults (Murrell, 1970; Sterns, Barrett, Alexander, Greenawalt, Gianetta, & Panek, 1975, 1976; Sterns, Barrett, and Alexander, 1980).

7. Perceptual-motor reaction time performance is related to many real-life situations and tasks, such as driving (G.V. Barrett, Mihal, Panek, Sterns, & Alexander, 1977), industrial performance (Panek, G.V. Barrett, Alexander, & Sterns, 1979), and typing (Salthouse, 1984).

8. The age-related decline in performance is closely related to the attentional and memory demands of the task (Madden, 1983).

9. Older adults may need considerable task warm-up before they begin to approach their actual level of competency (Raskind, Hoyer, & Rebok, 1983).

EFFECTS OF TRAINING ON PSYCHOMOTOR PERFORMANCE

Only recently did training studies become popular in adulthood and aging, due in most part to the belief that decrements in performance in most human abilities associated with aging could not be corrected, remediated, or improved (see Chapters 1, 2, and 6).

Murrell (1970) found that while age differences in speed of performance can be largely eliminated by practice, the number of practice trials required for improvement is often quite large. For example, Murrell found young participants started to show improvement immediately, while many older adults did not show improvement until after 300 practice trials.

Sterns and Sanders (1979) and Sterns and his associates (Sterns et al., 1975, 1976, 1980; Sterns, Barrett, Alexander, Panek, Avolio, & Forbringer, 1977) have demonstrated the effectiveness of training with older adults on perceptual-motor reaction time tasks. They also found that this improved performance could be maintained over a six-month period.

Studies in applied settings such as business and industry report that on jobs where speed is a necessary performance component, older workers are able to partially mask the slowdown in behavior by taking advantage of improved skills and knowledge gained through experience (Schwab & Heneman, 1977).

The effects of the psychomotor slowdown with age are often avoided by job change and promotion. That is, as individuals gain experience and seniority, they are often transferred or promoted to positions where speed is not a primary prerequisite of successful performance. Therefore, the aging worker is taken off a physical/psychomotor task prior to the time where a slowdown in responding would be a serious detriment to successful performance. This issue will be addressed further in our sections on industrial gerontology.

It should be emphasized that at the present time we know very little about the potential for permanently remediating the psychomotor slowdown with age. We hope this issue will be resolved in the future due to the significance of speeded performance in our everyday functioning.

In the next few sections, we shall discuss topics that are often viewed as causally related to the behavioral slowdown with aging. These topics are cautiousness, decision making, and rigidity.

CAUTIOUSNESS/DECISION MAKING

Cautiousness and conservatism in behavior and **decision making** have often been hypothesized as manifestations of psychological and biological aging. This increased cautiousness in behavior and decision making is often considered an overall behavioral and/or personality characteristic of the aging individual (Kausler, 1982). That is, it is thought to affect all areas of behavior and performance.

Support for this hypothesis comes from many real-world situations and laboratory tasks in which older participants' performance is marked by more errors of omission (omitting an answer) than errors of commission (giving an incorrect answer) (Basowitz & Korchin, 1957; Korchin & Basowitz, 1956; Okun, 1976; Okun, Siegler, & George, 1978). Moreover, cautiousness may be reflected in requiring more time and information prior to responding (Botwinick, Robbin, & Brinley, 1959; C.W. Eriksen, Hamlin, & Breitmeyer, 1970; Silverman, 1963; Taylor, 1972) and having difficulty in performance under conditions of uncertainty (Botwinick, 1966; Coyne, 1981; Danziger & Salthouse, 1978).

However, as reported by Panek (1982c) and Okun (1976), support for the cautiousness hypothesis varies as a function of the measure of cautiousness used as well as the task itself. Additionally, as is the case with many phenomena in adulthood and aging, what we have are numerous descriptions of situations where the performance of the individual appears to demonstrate cautiousness, but this conclusion is not definitive. Though the literature indicates a general slowdown in decision making or increased cautiousness with normal aging, exactly what factor(s) are responsible has not yet been identified. In the next several pages, we plan to highlight examples of the types of research on which the cautiousness hypothesis is based, briefly present some theoretical explanations for cautiousness, and discuss the real-world implications of the cautiousness hypothesis.

Omission Errors

Research that apparently supports the hypothesis of increased cautiousness with age comes from laboratory studies investigating paired-associate learning (Eisdorfer, Axelrod, & Wilkie, 1963), short-term retention (Kirchner, 1958), and auditory selective attention (Panek, Barrett, Sterns, & Alexander, 1978), in which **errors of omission** were more common than **errors of commission**, called the *omission error effect.*

For example, Basowitz and Korchin (1957) compared the performance of two age-groups on two tests of perceptual closure from the Gestalt completion test and found that older adults demonstrated excessive cautiousness as evidenced by a significant omission error effect between the age-groups. In a word recognition study, Silverman (1963) obtained evidence for a general reluctance to guess in older participants. Matching participants for ability to recognize rapidly presented words under a forced response condition, Silverman found that older adults gave fewer responses relative to their actual perceptual ability and took longer than younger individuals to identify forms even when they were matched on visual acuity.

On the other hand, some research has reported that cautiousness does not appear to be an appropriate explanation for age difference on a vigilance task (Tune, 1966) or an auditory selective attention task (Panek & McGown, 1981).

Overall, it does appear as though older adults make more errors of omission than younger adults on a variety of tasks. But we do not know if this is due to a decrement in performance ability, to increased cautiousness, or to other factors. For example, Szafran (1965, 1970) reported the speed and accuracy of decision-making performance of older pilots appeared to be highly dependent upon the individual's cardiovascular-pulmonary status rather than chronological age. Surwillo (1964) has suggested that the decision-making performance of older adults may be dependent upon the individual's electroencephalogram alpha wave frequency (see Botwinick, 1984).

Ambiguous Stimuli

Another line of research in which results are often attributed to the cautiousness hypothesis involves the perception of ambiguous stimuli. Korchin and Basowitz (1956) had young and old individuals judge whether each of 13 successively presented drawings were of a cat or a dog. The series started with a clear picture of a cat, then through small modifications became a dog. These researchers found the decision times for the older group to be significantly slower in shifting to the dog response.

Botwinick et al. (1959) presented 74 males between 19 and 81 years of age with Boring's ambiguous figures of "my wife" and "my mother-in-law." Results indicated older adults were less able to reorganize the initial precept with which they began.

These studies (see Botwinick, 1984 for a review) suggest older adults prefer more concrete information from a situation before they commit themselves to a response. This finding is interpreted as a sign of being more cautious. But again, it is difficult to determine if these age differences in performance are due to cautiousness or some other factor.

Uncertainty

Another situation in which older adults are characterized as cautious is where the participants are uncertain about the stimuli to which they are responding. Studies of uncertainty use stimuli quite similar to those described in studies using ambiguous figures. For example, young and old participants may be shown a picture of a cat under three levels of uncertainty: *high,* where just a series of lines or dots are present, *moderate,* where there is some degree of structure to the stimuli, and *low,* where the stimulus definitely looks like a cat. Research suggests that older adults have especially poor performance, compared to young participants, when uncertainty is introduced into the experimental situation (Panek, Barrett, Sterns, & Alexander, 1977).

A number of investigators challenge the validity of the cautiousness hypothesis in explaining the age decrement in task performance and suggest the observed decrement can be attributed to other processes (Danziger, 1980; Danziger & Salthouse, 1978; Coyne, 1981; Rees & Botwinick, 1971).

Incomplete Figures

Perhaps the most definitive study of the cautiousness hypothesis was that of Danziger and Salthouse (1978). In a series of well-designed studies, Danziger and Salthouse tested four hypotheses that are often used to explain the apparent cautiousness on the part of older adults on perceptual tasks, such as incomplete figures. Hypothesis one suggests older adults have a *higher criterion* (threshold) for reporting stimulation or emitting a response. That is, older adults have a greater reluctance to venture a response that may be incorrect and therefore require the incoming information to exceed a higher criterion (compared to young adults) before they are willing to produce a response.

The second hypothesis is *unfamiliarity.* This hypothesis assumes older adults are less accurate at identifying incomplete figures simply because they are less familiar than young adults with the complete version of the figures.

A third possible explanation is that older adults extract *less useful information* from the stimulus display than younger individuals. Older individuals are less accurate at judging the information value of the stimulus components, thereby attending to unimportant and irrelevant aspects of the stimulus rather than the most important information.

Finally, the poorer performance of adults could be due to a less effective perceptual inference process (Danziger & Salthouse, 1978). This hypothesis suggests older adults do not utilize incomplete information as effectively as young adults do.

Results of the experiments led Danziger and Salthouse to conclude that the fourth hypothesis was correct. That is, older adults perform more poorly than young adults because they are unable to utilize stimulus information as effectively as younger adults in making perceptual inferences. These findings are important because they eliminate peripheral processes as the locus of the "cautiouslike" behavior of older adults and identify the locus as a central or cognitive process.

Overall, the literature (see Botwinick, 1984, for a review) indicates that as we age, we appear to exhibit increased cautiousness in behavior. However, there is still controversy over whether these differences in performance are due to cautiousness per se or are the result of other factors (Danziger & Salthouse, 1978; Davies, 1968). Other explanations for cautious behavior on the part of older adults include decreased receptor sensitivity (Weale, 1965), slower perceptual encoding time (Kline & Szafran, 1975), perceptual noise (Layton, 1975), compensation of real or imagined decrements in information processing capacities (Rabbitt, 1968), and personality (Panek, 1982c).

Regardless of whether cautiousness per se increases with age, or which theory explains the phenomenon correctly, this increase in cautiousnesslike behavior has many applied implications. These include explaining the psychomotor slowdown with age, driving behavior, and industrial performance. For example, Taylor (1972) found older business managers (compared to young) tended to acquire more information, took longer to reach a decision, and were less confident of the decision they eventually reached. Welford (1977) believes the trend in road accidents is in the same direction as the research on age differences in cautiousness in decision making. That is, accidents typically sustained by older drivers seem to be due to slowness and a tendency toward confusion, while accidents of young drivers are due to various kinds of recklessness.

RIGIDITY

Just as it has been assumed that as we age we become more cautious in decision making, it has also been assumed that we become more rigid or less flexible in our behavior, attitudes, habits, and personality. Moreover, it is often assumed that as we get older we will find it difficult to shift from one activity or behavior to another. We may tend to perseverate rather than act, or we may adhere rigidly to a routine. All these characteristics, plus others, were thought at one time to be typical of middle-aged and especially older adults. This belief is called the **rigidity hypothesis** (see Botwinick, 1978).

In other words, as we age it was believed we became exceedingly inflexible in all aspects of our behavior, interaction with the environment, and life-style. In fact, rigidity was once considered an intrinsic consequence of the aging process. As we shall see, this view of rigidity is oversimplistic and no longer considered appropriate by researchers (K.W. Schaie & Parham, 1960, 1975). The concept of rigidity is still of great interest in the field of adulthood and aging because in order to function effectively with our environment, we must constantly change, adapt, and be flexible to new situations, events, and demands from the environment and other people. We cannot persist in behavior patterns that are not adaptive or appropriate. Therefore, if individuals do become more rigid with advancing age, research can help isolate and identify the antecedents or causes of rigidity. Then, training and remediation procedures can be implemented to modify these apparent decrements.

Problems with the Rigidity Hypothesis

While the concept of rigidity has enjoyed great attention and speculation, it is somewhat controversial for a number of reasons (Panek, Stoner, & Beystehner, 1983). First, there has been great difficulty in defining it theoretically and specifically. For example, is rigidity a unidimensional or multidimensional factor? Second, there has been great difficulty in obtaining reliable and valid measures of rigidity. In fact, research in the area generally *infers* rigidity from performance on the experimental task (dependent measure) under investigation. Additionally, in many cases, the researchers have not designed their study to test the rigidity hypothesis; it has just been a convenient explanation for the observed results. Third, there is still controversy regarding whether rigidity is a separate behavioral characteristic or is dependent upon other processes such as sensory ability, intellectual level, and personality. Finally, whether we find increased rigidity with age is often a function of the type of research design employed (cross-sectional, longitudinal).

A good example of a laboratory study that explored the rigidity hypothesis is that of H. Kay (1951). The laboratory task consisted of an apparatus on which there were ten lights and ten response keys, one key for each light. Kay found that the older participants tended to repeat their same learning errors. That is, they failed to modify their incorrect responses. Therefore, the older participants in Kay's study were described as more rigid than the younger participants.

Another good illustration of the rigidity hypothesis is a study by Heglin (1956). Basically, Heglin investigated problem-solving ability in three age-groups—14 to 19 years, 20 to 49 years, and 50 to 58 years. Participants were compared on a series of progressively more difficult problem tasks; each task involving similar and/or repetitious operations on the part of the participant. Heglin arranged the tasks so a fairly easy technique (solution) would be quite effective and efficient in solving the early problems but not the later ones. In fact, it (the easy solution) became increasingly more inefficient as the problems advanced and eventually could not be used to solve the problem.

Results indicated the oldest age-group tended to stick with the original solution, even when it was no longer adequate or effective for solving the problem. Though the two other (younger) age-groups exhibited similar rigidity-type behavior, they did so to a lesser extent and did switch to another method of solution when the first technique was no longer adequate. Based upon studies of this type, the rigidity hypothesis received its impetus.

It is interesting to note that while studies of the rigidity hypothesis have not been unanimous in their interpretation that older adults are more rigid than young adults (see below), this myth still persists. For example, many of the studies we discussed earlier regarding cautiousness and aging might easily be interpreted as supporting the notion of rigidity. Yet, while cautiousness can be quite adaptive (it may give us more time in which to make a decision), rigidity is often seen in negative terms; to be rigid is to be unwilling or inflexible. Indeed, the research we discussed in the preceding section suggests that cautious behavior may reflect an inability to utilize incomplete information accurately (Danziger & Salthouse, 1978). Perhaps we are quick to accept the notion of rigidity because it is consistent with the negative expectations we often have regarding older adults. Moreover, what passes for rigidity may simply reflect cohort-specific experiences. For example, having grown up in a politically conservative time may exert a long-term influence on attitudes or risk-taking behavior that might falsely be interpreted as rigid. Thus, if rigidity as a construct does exist, we do not know if it is a personality construct or a behavioral construct.

In order to understand the limitations of the rigidity hypothesis better, it may be helpful to describe some real-world situations where the label of rigidity is often applied to behavior. Let's suppose your grandmother, who is 72 years of age, lives at home with your family. She is a healthy, intelligent, and active woman. Your grandmother has lived with your family for the past four years, when she decided to move after the death of your grandfather. Every Saturday, your grandmother drives to the mall, a drive of nine miles through suburban and city streets that takes about 30 minutes. But suppose two years ago, another road was built that would allow someone to drive from your home to the mall in 10 minutes. This road does not have any stoplights and allows for high-speed driving. In fact, an entrance ramp is two blocks from your house, and there is an exit at the mall. Though you constantly point out to your grandmother that there is a shorter and faster route to the mall, she continues to persist in driving the old route. Therefore, under these circumstances, you might say your grandmother is rigid.

But is this behavior rigidity? What other possible reasons could cause her to drive on the old route? Other reasons for this behavior could be her dislike of driving on expressways, her enjoyment in driving by a house with a pretty flower garden in the front yard and looking at the flowers, the mall exit off the expressway not having a traffic light, making it extremely difficult and dangerous to get from the exit to the mall entrance, and so forth. As this example demonstrates, there are many alternatives to rigidity in explaining the behavior of older adults.

Three Types of Rigidity

From a theoretical perspective, the most definitive research in the area has been done by K.W. Schaie and associates (K.W. Schaie, 1958; K.W. Schaie, 1962; K.W. Schaie & Parham, 1960, 1975). Briefly Schaie and associates have suggested behavioral rigidity is a multidimensional factor consisting of three independent components labeled **motor-cognitive rigidity**, **personality-perceptual rigidity**, and **psychomotor speed rigidity**. Motor-cognitive rigidity refers to an individual's relative ability to shift from one activity to another. Personality-perceptual rigidity indicates the individual's relative ability to adjust to new surroundings and change in cognitive and environmental patterns. Psychomotor speed rigidity indicates the individual's relative rate of emission of familiar cognitive responses.

These factors are independent and manifest different life-span trends. Research using cross-sectional designs has repeatedly demonstrated that individuals apparently do become more rigid with increasing age on all rigidity factors (K.W. Schaie & Parham, 1960, 1975). However, the greatest increase in rigidity is seen with motor-cognitive rigidity, and the least is observed in personality-perceptual rigidity. Similar but less strong age differences/age changes are observed with various sequential designs (K. W. Schaie & Labouvie-Vief, 1974; K. W. Schaie, Labouvie, & Buech, 1973) (see Chap. 3).

It should again be noted that the concept of rigidity increasing with age is not universally accepted, and it is thought to be moderated by intelligence, education, and gender as well as age (Brinley, 1965). An example of the moderator effects of these factors can be observed in a study by Panek, Stoner, and Beystehner (1983). These researchers administered a test of behavioral rigidity and a test of intelligence to young and old individuals. They found that when intelligence and education level were statistically controlled among the age-groups, there were significant age effects for only motor-cognitive rigidity. But, contrary to predictions, the young participants were significantly *more* rigid than the old participants, which does not support the rigidity hypothesis. Recall that we noted above that all studies do not support the rigidity hypothesis.

Overall, the topic of rigidity across the life-span is quite controversial and open to debate. What we may have is a phenomenon in search of an explanation. That is, many sources clearly indicate that rigiditylike behavior increases with age. We do not know if this is due to rigidity per se, a decrease in cognitive/intellectual skills, increased cautiousness, a psychomotor slowdown, or compensation for decrements in ability (Botwinick, 1978).

Finally, individuals who appear to be rigid in one situation may not be rigid in another. This was nicely illustrated in a study by Ohta (1981). Ohta designed a study to investigate response selection tendencies of older adults in two spatial problem-solving situations: (1) a hypothetical life situation, and (2) an actual problem-solving situation conducted in a real physical environment. Results indicated that in the hypothetical situation there was a marked tendency for elderly persons, as opposed to young individuals, to choose to avoid an alternative course of action no matter what the probability of success (an indication of rigidity). But in the real-life situation, there were no age differences in selection of approaches to solve the problem. That is, neither young nor old participants appeared to be rigid. These findings illustrate the complexity in investigating concepts such as rigidity and cautiousness, and demonstrate that behavior in one type of situation may not be related to behavior in others.

In the final two sections, we shall discuss topics that are related to the applied aspects of the psychomotor slowdown with age. These topics are accident involvement and industrial gerontology.

ACCIDENT INVOLVEMENT

Perhaps the best illustration of the relevance of the material discussed in this and the preceding chapter to adulthood and aging is found in the literature on accident involvement and that dealing with the older worker (industrial gerontology). By studying these topics, we can clearly observe the effects of decrements in sensory/perceptual processes, faulty decision making, and psychomotor slowing (see Chapter 1) on accident behavior.

Accidents can be considered **nonnormative influences** (P. B. Baltes, Cornelius, & Nesselroade, 1978; P. B. Baltes, Reese, & Lipsitt, 1980). That is, they do not happen to most individuals as a function of natural maturational processes. Further, the study of accidents demonstrates the dynamic and interactive relationship between the individual and the constantly changing demands of the environment, as we pointed out in Chapter 1.

General Life-Span Trends in Accident Involvement

If we analyzed accidents along the life span, we would observe that children, compared to all other age-groups, have the highest injury rates. But older adults have the highest death rates from accidents and the highest dysfunction and disability rates from automotive accidents, falls, fires, and burns. Further, older adults have relatively low accident frequency rates compared to other age-groups but have extremely high disability and fatality rates compared to other age-groups (Sterns, Barrett, & Alexander, 1985).

How important is the study of accidents across the life span? Upon looking at the statistics, one would easily come to the conclusion that it is very important. Specifically, for ages 1 to 44, a person is more likely to die from an accident than from any other cause. In fact, among individuals of all ages, accidents are the fourth leading cause of death (Statistical Abstract of the United States, U.S. Bureau of the Census, 1986).

In order to get a better picture of accidents along the life span, it is necessary to discuss nonfatal and fatal accidents separately.

Nonfatal Injuries   With regard to nonfatal injuries, Baker and Deitz (1979), Hogue (1980, 1982a, 1982b), and Sterns et al. (1985) reported that for children 5 years of age and under, falls are the largest cause. For adolescents and young adults (15–24 years), contact sports and motor vehicles cause the most injuries. Regarding adults (25–64 years) and older adults (65–74 years), accidents are usually job related, involve motor vehicles, or occur at home. It should be noted that these results are general findings, and there are differences on the basis of gender, race, and socioeconomic level.

Fatal Injuries   For fatal injuries, Baker and Deitz (1979), Hogue (1980, 1982a, 1982b), and Sterns et al. (1985) report that for children the major fatal injuries occur through motor vehicle accidents, drowning, and fires. For adolescents and young adults, the major fatal injuries are from firearms and drowning. The major cause of fatal injuries for adults (26–64 years) are motor vehicle and/or job related accidents. Finally, for older adults, motor vehicles, falls, fire, and burns cause the greatest number of fatalities.

On the basis of these data, we are able to reach some conclusions. First, motor vehicle accidents are a significant cause of accidental death at all points across the life span. Second, during adulthood and old age, most accidental deaths occur on the job and/or involve motor vehicles. Third, in old age, the majority of accidental deaths occur from falls and motor vehicles. Finally, older adults have extremely high fatality rates from accidents, compared to other age-groups, due to poorer recovery and greater susceptibility to complications.

In conclusion, during adulthood we are more likely to be involved in a nonfatal or fatal accident at work or while driving. In old age, the accident is more likely to be fatal than nonfatal and most likely will occur while driving or at home.

Since the majority of nonfatal and fatal accidents involve motor vehicles or occur at home or at work, it is of some importance to discuss them separately.

Motor Vehicle Accidents

There are currently about 146 million licensed drivers in the United States. Though studies of motor vehicle accident involvement and causation cannot be considered conclusive, they do suggest that individuals have different types of motor vehicle accidents, or accidents that are the result of different causes, at different points during their lives.

First, if we view absolute frequency of accidents (the overall number), we would find that adolescents and young adults (under age 20) have the highest frequency of motor vehicle accidents. There is a gradual decrease in the absolute frequency of accidents after this point with increasing age. But if one takes into account the number of miles driven, often referred to as the **exposure factor**, both young and older drivers have extremely high accident rates.

This fact clearly illustrates the extremely high potential for accident involvement of older adults. It should also be stressed that, in most cases, older adults do not do much driving. In fact, many older adults drive only when absolutely necessary, such as to go to the doctor, to go grocery shopping, and so forth.

Secondly, motor vehicle accidents are related to a number of factors/ abilities and involve the same skills at all age levels. G.V. Barrett, Alexander, and Forbes (1977) proposed a **perceptual information processing model** of driving behavior. G.V. Barrett, Alexander, and Forbes (1977) suggested the abilities of perceptual-style, selective attention, and perceptual-motor reaction time were related to driving performance. It is interesting to note that these same abilities exhibit life-span changes as well as individual differences with age-groups. This model has received empirical support for young and adult commercial drivers (Mihal & G.V. Barrett, 1976), and young, adult, and old commercial drivers (G.V. Barrett, Mihal, et al., 1977).

An example of how many of the abilities we have previously discussed are thought to affect driving is presented in Figure 5.2. As Figure 5.2 indicates, many factors are related to successful driving performance.

Finally, research suggests at different points along the life span the types of accidents individuals are involved in are different and are often the result of different causes, though the abilities and skills required for driving remain the same. For example, McFarland, Tune, and Welford (1964) found drivers under 25 years of age were most often involved in accidents caused by speeding, driving on the wrong side of the road, and faulty equipment, while drivers 65 years old and older were involved because of failure to give right of way, improper turning, ignoring stop signs, and improper starting. Planek and Fowler (1971) reported that older adults were prone to making inattentive responses and were involved in errors of omission, such as failure to read traffic lights and running red lights and/or stop signs.

Avolio and Panek (1983) found that though younger and older drivers experienced different types of accidents, there was a common factor linking these different types. That is, in both age-groups, accidents were due to improper decision making and failure to selectively attend to important driving cues, such as stop signs (see also Panek & Rearden, 1987).

Panek, Wagner, G.V. Barrett, and Alexander (1978) found that different personality characteristics appeared to be related to accidents as a function of age. That is, for young drivers (17–48 years), a characteristic/trait that could be labeled impulsivity was related to accidents, but this factor was not related to accidents in the old group. For older drivers (49–72 years), the characteristic of directiveness (exerting one's will on others) was related to accidents.

Overall, there is still much information to be gathered regarding motor vehicle accidents across the life span. It is important to remember that research indicates many factors we have discussed previously have been shown to be related to accident involvement at all points along the life span.

Home Accidents

Accidents in the home, such as falls and burns, are most common among the young (children) and the old. This is due to the fact that both of these groups of individuals are likely to be less competent in the areas of hearing, vision, motor skills, and mobility.

Home accidents account for approximately one-fifth of all accidental deaths and one-third of all disability injuries (Planek, 1982; Sterns et al., 1985). However, it is difficult to get an accurate estimate of nonfatal home accidents because they often go unreported and/or untreated.

According to Sterns et al. (1985), older adults (65 years +) have the highest frequency of home accidents. With increasing age, the death rate

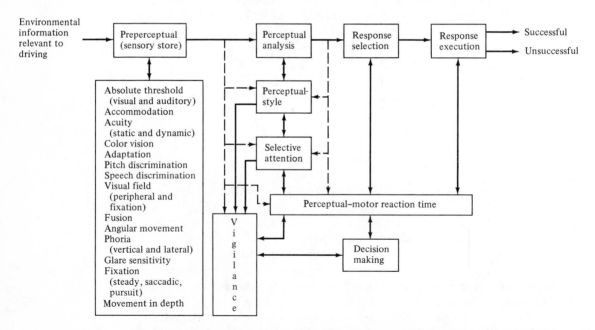

Figure 5.2 Overall interaction among vision, hearing, selective attention, perceptual style, perceptual-motor reaction time, decision making, vigilance, environmental information and driver decision making. *Source:* P.E. Panek, G.V. Barrett, H.L. Sterns, & R.A. Alexander. (1977). A review of age changes in perceptual information processing ability with regard to driving. *Experimental Aging Research, 3* (Figure 5; p. 434). Copyright © EAR, Inc., 1988.

increases for falls, fires, and burns. In fact, for individuals 65 years and above, falls are the leading cause of home fatalities. It is quite easy to understand why older adults are susceptible to falls due to the decrements in abilities that we have discussed previously (hearing, vision, balance).

Industrial Accidents

The literature indicates there is a specific, yet complex, relationship between age and frequency of accidents in the workplace (Sterns et al., 1985). Older workers (age 45 years +) are injured much less frequently than younger workers (less than 25 years of age) and about as often as adult workers (age 25 to 44 years). It should be stressed, however, that this is a generalization, and there are known differences in terms of the type of job, industry, and numerous other factors.

For example, for blue-collar employees, older workers have the lowest incidence of permanently disabling injuries, while at other occupational classifications, they have the highest (or close to the highest) incidence of these type of injuries. Overall, older workers tend to have the lowest incidence of temporary (minor) injuries, but tend to lose more work time per injury than younger workers.

Perhaps the most definitive study in the area of life-span trends in industrial accidents was that of Root (1981), which was based on data from over a million worker compensation records in 30 states. This represented approximately 40 percent of the American wage and salary work force.

Root found that occupational injuries occurred at a lower rate for older workers than for younger workers. Basically, the highest work injury rates for almost all types of industries were for workers 20 to 24 years of age, and the lowest were for workers 65 years and older.

There are several plausible hypotheses to explain this trend. One is that with increasing age and seniority, individuals tend to be promoted to supervisory or other positions within the organization. Thus, they are less likely to be in a position with high risk of injury. Another possible explanation is selective survival or job tenure. Each year the least-able members of the work force, for a given position, either leave on their own or are fired from the position. Therefore, the oldest workers at any given position (job) may be the best qualified. Finally, experience with the job may be a factor. That is, with added experience in working on a job, the worker gains experience in how to avoid accidents and how to perform the job more efficiently.

Though the research is not conclusive, it is strongly suggestive of the importance of the experience factor. In fact, the second major conclusion one can draw from Root's (1981) data is that experience on the job is significantly related to accidents. Specifically, a significant number of injuries occur during the first year of the individual's employment on the position, regardless of age.

Overall, research indicates that older workers appear to be less likely to be injured on the job, but their accidents will lose them more work time or are more likely to be fatal or lead to permanent disability.

Our discussion of accidents will indicate the seriousness of the problem. We are currently in the descriptive stage of research on accident involvement, and we need substantially more investigation concerning the types and causes of accidents. Additionally, there is a tremendous need for the development of training strategies to help reduce all types of accident involvement.

Finally, various abilities, such as selective attention, vision, and perceptual-motor reaction time, which are known to manifest life-span changes as well as individual differences, are related to accident involvement (Sterns et al., 1985) and job performance (Stagner, 1985) (see Figure 5.2).

In the next section we shall discuss another topic that stresses the importance of life-span changes in psychomotor abilities: industrial gerontology. Given the common assumption of the older worker as less efficient, slower, or more accident-prone (Stagner, 1985), discussing industrial gerontology not only helps illustrate the real-world implications of psychomotor performance but also helps us put those changes into a larger context of the work world.

For example, Stagner (1985) suggests that such biases have pressured employees to accept early retirement based on a presumed decline in competence and job performance. Indeed, it is an overemphasis on normative trends and an underconcern for mediating factors and individual differences that has contributed to such biases.

INDUSTRIAL GERONTOLOGY

We are currently experiencing what is called the **"graying" of the American work force**. Due to economic factors, increased longevity, and federal legislation, more individuals are remaining in the work force for a longer time (Work in America Institute, 1980). For these reasons business and industry is beginning to consider the needs and abilities of the older worker as important (D.R. Johnson & J.T. Johnson, 1982; Meier & Kerr, 1976; Rhodes, 1983).

The study of the older worker is referred to as *industrial gerontology* and is basically a new field in which we are just beginning to acquire information (Sheppard & Rix, 1977; Stagner, 1985). Therefore, many of the factors we will discuss should be considered tentative. Our goal will be to make you aware of attitudes of business and industry toward the older worker, to summarize the literature regarding the abilities of older workers, and to present some suggestions for dealing with older workers. We will discuss retirement in a future chapter.

Who is the older worker? According to the Work in America Institute (1980), the United States Bureau of Labor Statistics considers anyone, regardless of occupation, aged 55 years or above to be an **older worker**; those between the ages of 25 to 54 years are described as **prime age** (Sheppard & Rix, 1977). The term *older worker* is often applied at age *40* (Barnes-Farrell, 1983). It should be noted that this designation is an overall one and would vary substantially as a function of specific occupation. For instance, 35 years of age may be considered old for a professional athlete, but relatively young for a brain surgeon.

In many job situations, performance remains unaffected by age. The older employee has many skills that can be relied upon and communicated to younger, less experienced employees.

Discrimination Against Older Workers

Business and industry, as well as many younger workers, have many negative attitudes and stereotyped images of older workers (Sheppard and Rix, 1977; Stagner, 1985). Older workers are often characterized as (1) being less productive than younger workers, (2) being slow doers, slow thinkers, and adjusting to change more slowly, compared to younger workers, (3) lacking physical strength and endurance, (4) being set in their ways and more stubborn, (5) being difficult to train and slow to learn, (6) lacking drive and imagination, (7) having less education, and (8) having learned to get by with less effort. Research indicates individuals tend to "age-type" occupations, and this age classification is strongly influenced by the job level (Barnes-Farrell, 1983). Occupations that require a high degree of training and experience for successful performance are generally associated with being older (dentist, college professor, physician).

AGEISM IN EMPLOYMENT

Before we discuss the literature regarding the truth of these assumptions, let us note that research indicates that implicit and explicit **"ageism" in employment** occurs for both sexes in all types of jobs (Rosen & Jerdee, 1976; Sheppard, 1976), though it is against the law. Ageism was coined by Butler (1969) to refer to the process of systematic stereotyping of and discrimination against people because they are old, just as racism and sexism accomplish this regarding skin color and gender. In this light, Avolio and Barrett (1987) found evidence for ageism in a simulated interview even when it was made explicit that the young and old job applicants were *equally* qualified.

Barrow and Smith (1983) report the unemployment rate for adult males 55 to 64 years of age is higher than for those aged 25 to 54 years; this trend has been common for the past 20 years. Further, once out of work, older workers are likely to remain unemployed much longer than younger workers at all occupational levels for both sexes and all races. Sheppard (1976) studied laid-off professional men, engineers and scientists, and found age to be the most significant variable related to their status. Wachtel (1966) studied 2000 hard-core unemployed individuals in Detroit and found age to be the major reason for their unemployment. Further, when reemployed, they often found jobs at lower pay, that required less skill, and at lower occupational levels (Barnes-Farrell, 1983). An example of such ageism is seen in Figure 5.3.

Why do older workers tend to be laid off or unemployed earlier than younger workers? The answer to this question is quite complex, but there are several major reasons. First, due to the fact that they have seniority, they tend to remain in declining industries and occupations until the jobs finally disappear as a result of economic and technological change (D.R. Johnson & J.T. Johnson, 1982). A good example is the U.S. automotive industry, which suffered dramatically during the late 1970s. At this time there were many layoffs and plant closings. When these plants reopened, many of the assembly line positions no longer existed, these functions having been replaced by industrial robots. Second, older workers tend to have lower levels of formal education and therefore are excluded from entrance into positions and occupations with higher and specified educational requirements. Third, they have less mobility (D.R. Johnson & J.T. Johnson, 1982) due to increased responsibilities and obligations compared to younger workers. Finally, they have inferior job-seeking attitudes and skills, compared to younger workers, due to the fact that they may not have interviewed for a job in 10 or 15 years (D.R. Johnson & J.T. Johnson, 1982). Also, research indicates many current personnel selection tests and interview procedures may be unfairly discriminating against older job applicants (Arvey & Mussio, 1973; Salvendy, 1974; Stagner, 1985). For example, selection tests may not have norms for older workers, or may measure abilities that undergo decline with age but have nothing to do with actual job performance (Stagner, 1985).

HERMAN

"I'm sorry, Wilson. After 16 years of
loyal service, you're being replaced
by this microchip."

Figure 5.3 *Source:* HERMAN by Jim Unger, *Charleston Times-Courier*
(1983, August 20). HERMAN © 1983 Universal Press Syndicate.

Discrimination against workers as a function of age may even begin
at age *30* in some occupations. For instance, in a widely publicized incident
that occurred in 1983, a young woman (age 38) brought a lawsuit against a
television station at which she was the coanchor of the news. She was apparently demoted because some viewers considered her "too old."

AGE DISCRIMINATION IN EMPLOYMENT ACT (ADEA)

The problem of age discrimination was so severe in the past that federal laws
had to be enacted to prohibit it. The legislation was titled the **Age Discrimination in Employment Act (ADEA)**, originally passed in 1967 but amended
in 1974 and 1978 to provide more comprehensive coverage. Basically, this
legislation protects workers between the ages of 40 to 70 years. Specifically,
the law prohibits: (1) failing to hire someone between 40 and 70 years because
of age, (2) discharging a person because of age, (3) discriminating on pay or

benefits because of age, (4) because of age, limiting or classifying an individual to that individual's disadvantage, (5) instructing an employment agency not to refer a person to a job, or to only certain kinds of jobs, because of age, and (6) placing any advertisement that shows preference based on age or specifies an age bracket. However, this legislation is not universal; that is, it does not cover all employees in all occupational settings. Exempt from this legislation are the federal government, employers of less than 20 persons, and jobs where age is a **bona fide occupational qualification (BFOQ)**. Overall, though age discrimination is against the law, it still exists today.

Research on the Older Worker

Perhaps the most in-depth reviews of the literature regarding the older worker have been accomplished by Meier and Kerr (1976), Rhodes (1983), and Stagner (1985). The following is a summary of conclusions drawn on the basis of the work of these reviews with regard to specific issues involving the older worker.

JOB SATISFACTION

Concerning job satisfaction, the literature indicates a positive and linear relationship between age and overall satisfaction until at least 60 (Rhodes, 1983). That is, as age increases, the individual's overall satisfaction with the job increases. Interestingly, this relationship holds for both blue-collar and white-collar jobs, as well as for males and females.

JOB PERFORMANCE

The crucial issue in industrial gerontology concerns the potential relationship between age and actual job performance. Specifically, does performance decrease as a function of age? Though this is the most important issue, it is difficult to assess, and findings often vary as a function of a number of factors, such as type of occupation studied and performance criteria employed. For example, in occupations where physical capacity is extensively required for job performance (manual laborer), older workers may show performance decrements due to the known changes or declines in physical functioning. While in other occupations, where these abilities are not highly related to successful performance (college professor), little age decrements in performance are observed (Sheppard & Rix, 1977). Though physical strength may decrease with age, most jobs today have physical demands well below the capabilities of most normal aging workers (Meier & Kerr, 1976).

PSYCHOMOTOR SPEED AND JOB PERFORMANCE

As we noted above, research is somewhat supportive of an age decrement in job performance that is, in jobs where speed is a major component of successful job performance (Panek et al., 1979). In reality, the age-performance relationship has been quite difficult to study in real-life situations for a number of reasons. First, with advancing age and job tenure, individuals tend to be promoted to more supervisory positions. Therefore, it is difficult to compare speed of performance of young and old workers on the same job. Second, when older workers are still employed in positions where speed is important, they are often able to compensate effectively for their decrease in speed through experience with the job—they know all the shortcuts and efficient methods (D.R. Johnson & J.T. Johnson, 1982). For these reasons, we often generalize from the laboratory studies of psychomotor reaction time that we have reviewed in this chapter and from job simulations. In conclusion, due to the multitude of potential confounds and difficulty in obtaining reliable and valid criteria for job performance, we still know very little that is conclusive regarding the actual relationship between age and job performance. Further, in many industries and occupations, there may be very little or no age-related decline in productivity (Sonnefeld, 1978).

Finally, though there are documented age-related changes in physical capacity, certain aspects of cognitive functioning, hearing, vision, and psychomotor speed, the literature is not definitely clear in how these changes or decrements affect actual job performance (Barnes-Farrell, 1983).

As we noted above, overgeneralizations about the relationship between age, specific abilities/skills, and job performance simply strengthen the bias against older employees, who in some cases are as young as 30.

JOB TURNOVER AND ABSENTEEISM

There is a negative relationship between age and job turnover. That is, as age increases, individuals are less likely to leave their current position (Rhodes, 1983).

Research indicates the age–absence from the job relationship is partially a function of type of absence (avoidable, unavoidable) and gender of the employee. Avoidable absences are those that cause the employee to be absent without permission and prior approval, such as just not showing up for work. Unavoidable absences are those that are due to sickness or accidents.

Regarding avoidable absence, the literature has generally found an inverse relationship with age for males, and no clear-cut pattern for females (Rhodes, 1983). For males, as age increases, avoidable absence decreases. For females, the relationship does not change as a function of age. It is unclear why there are sex differences in the age–avoidable absence relationship. One potential explanation centers on the assumption that working females still serve as the primary caretakers of the house and family. Therefore, when a child in the family is ill or needs to go to the doctor, it is often the mother who takes care of the child and therefore misses work.

In terms of unavoidable absences, the relationship with age for males is significant and complex, while for females it is nonsignificant. That is, for males, higher unavoidable absences occur for younger and older workers, while the fewest unavoidable absences occur for middle-aged workers. A partial explanation for this trend is based on the material we discussed previously regarding accidents. Specifically, younger and older workers tend to have the most time lost due to accidents. For females, the pattern is not significantly related to age and is similar to that for avoidable absence, which Rhodes (1983) believes is consistent with the family responsibility explanation of high female absence.

VALUES, NEEDS, AND JOB PREFERENCES

Research clearly demonstrates there are significant relationships between an employee's values, needs, and job preferences and a number of important factors such as job satisfaction and work behavior in numerous settings and occupational levels. Therefore, it is important for management to know if the employees' needs, values, and job preferences change as a function of age.

Regarding the value of work, though findings are somewhat mixed, they do tend to support the assumption that older workers have a stronger belief in the "Protestant work ethic" than do younger workers (Aldag & Brief, 1977; D.R. Johnson & J.T. Johnson, 1982).

In terms of needs and job preferences, research appears to indicate that age is consistently and positively related to factors such as job satisfaction, satisfaction with work itself, job involvement, internal work motivation, and organizational commitment. Further, research suggests that the worker's needs and preferences change as a function of age. With increasing age, workers tend to have higher needs for security and affiliation and fewer needs for opportunities for self-actualization and growth (Rhodes, 1983).

Concerning the motivational aspects of pay, research indicates older workers value financial rewards of work more than younger workers (D.R. Johnson & J.T. Johnson, 1982). Additionally, both male and female older workers are motivated by more than monetary compensation; older workers of both sexes often report that they continue to work (1) in order to remain active and engaged, (2) in order to enhance meaningful life experiences, and (3) in order to socialize (D.R. Johnson & J.T. Johnson, 1982).

Regarding the job itself, younger workers often respond very unfavorably to jobs they see as lacking significance or meaning; older workers do not. Additionally, older workers do not like jobs with a high degree of complexity.

JOB TRAINING

Due to the fact that we live in a highly technological, rapidly changing world both on and off the job, training and retraining are important issues regarding workers of all ages. Interestingly, though research indicates older adults are capable of learning and acquiring new skills (see Chapter 7), industry for the most part has held to the belief that older adults cannot learn or be retrained—"you cannot teach an old dog new tricks." Parnes and Meyer (1972) found skill obsolescence to be a major factor involved in the voluntary withdrawal of middle-aged men from the work force. There is a noticeable absence of training studies with the older worker. What studies do exist *do not* support the myth that older workers cannot acquire new skills (Meier & Kerr, 1976).

D.R. Johnson and J.T. Johnson (1982) present some excellent suggestions to facilitate learning and training of older workers. The effects of training and retraining of older workers will become a rapidly increasing area of interest as the "graying" of the American work force continues.

CAPABILITIES OF THE OLDER WORKER: CONCLUSION

The myths regarding the older worker, for the most part, are not valid. In fact, as D.R. Johnson and J.T. Johnson (1982), Rhodes (1983), and Meier and Kerr (1976) suggest, research indicates that older workers have the work attitudes and behaviors that are valued by business and industry. They have experience, loyalty to the company, and value the work ethic. Moreover, they are reliable, have good work habits, less absenteeism and turnover, and satisfactory job performance. Therefore, it would appear to make more sense for industry to actively attempt to keep and obtain older workers, rather than directly or indirectly avoid them.

One approach to end discrimination in employment has been to derive measures of **functional age (industrial)** (see Chapter 1). McFarland (1973) reports that during the labor shortages of young men during World War II, it became necessary to reemploy large numbers of retired older workers in industry. This served as the major emphasis behind investigations of the capabilities of older workers.

McFarland and others have suggested that research at that time and since has indicated that instead of judging workers by their chronological age, it is of more value to judge them "functionally," that is, in terms of what they can do. The concept of functional age has led to attempts to derive measures of functional ability required for each job and to place individuals, regardless of age, in jobs which are the best match with their abilities (Meier & Kerr, 1976).

Though this approach is commendable and makes good sense, research has not been overly supportive of the functional age approach in industry. As many (Avolio, G.V. Barrett, & Sterns, 1984; P.T. Costa and McCrae, 1980) point out, there are many difficulties with the functional age literature. Since the topic is very complex and extensive, these criticisms will only be highlighted.

These reviews suggest that the major difficulty with approaches to functional age measures that have been used is that the abilities investigated, such as vision, hearing, physical strength, intelligence, and memory, presuppose declines or decrements with age. They overlook individual differences in ability at all age levels, which we have repeatedly pointed out in this text as important sources of variability in performance and behavior. Further, approaches to functional age have attempted to derive an overall global measure of a person's functional age or ability. This does not take into account different performance levels on different abilities at all points along the life cycle (see Chapter 6 on intelligence). As Maddox and Douglass (1974) point out, individuals tend to maintain their ranks with regard to their peers on many abilities throughout adulthood and old age. For these and other reasons, Avolio and Panek (1981) indicated that in most cases the courts and legal system have upheld chronological age as a valid criterion for retirement decision, due to the difficulties with the functional age approach.

In conclusion, though previous investigations of functional age in industry have led to a blind alley, researchers in this area have suggested various alternative strategies that have the potential to be more fruitful.

SUMMARY

In this chapter we have discussed life-span trends in psychomotor performance and concluded that one of the most noticeable changes with age is a slowdown in speed and performance. Four types of reaction time tasks were discussed, with performance decrements appearing most reliably in *complex reaction time tasks.* Numerous explanations have been proposed for declines in psychomotor performance ranging from deficits in *sensory receptors* to *task complexity.* There are substantial *individual differences* in psychomotor performance. Researchers suspect the moderator of the slowdown to be *central,* rather than *peripheral* in nature.

Two commonly held assumptions regarding psychomotor performance of older adults are prevalent: (1) increased cautiousness in decision making (manifest in errors of omission) and behaviors with advancing age; and (2) increased *rigidity* (a multidimensional concept) of behavior with increasing age. These constructs are difficult to define and appear to be influenced by numerous factors that argue against their being intrinsically related to the aging process.

The constructs of *psychomotor reaction time, cautiousness,* and *rigidity* have all been linked to life-span research regarding both *accident involvement* and *industrial gerontology.* Life-span trends in *automobile, home,* and *industrial accidents* were discussed, as were the capabilities of older workers. Numerous *biases* regarding older workers abound, most of which lack consistent support or are weakly related to *job performance.*

KEY TERMS AND CONCEPTS

Speed versus accuracy trade-off	Cautiousness
Perceptual-motor reaction time	Decision making
Decision/premotor time	Errors of omission versus errors
Motor time	of commission
Peripheral explanations	Perceptual inference
Central explanations	Rigidity hypothesis
Neural noise	Motor-cognitive rigidity
Expectancy/set theory	Personality-perceptual rigidity
Complexity explanation	Psychomotor speed rigidity
Information overload	Nonnormative influences
Perceptual noise theory	(life events)

Perceptual information processing
   model
Exposure factor
"Graying" of the American
   work force
Age Discrimination in Employment
   Act (ADEA)

Older worker
Prime age
"Ageism" in employment
Bona fide occupational
   qualification (BFOQ)
Functional age (industrial)

- What is intelligence, and why is an understanding of intelligence important in everyday life?
- What are the major approaches to understanding and measuring intelligence?
- What approaches to intelligence are most useful in understanding its development in adulthood?
- Does intelligence decline as we age?
- What factors influence intelligence in adulthood?
- How can intelligence be optimized in adulthood?

CHAPTER 6

COGNITIVE PROCESSES I: INTELLIGENCE

▪

WHAT IS INTELLIGENCE?

This chapter discusses the construct (underlying quality) of intelligence and its development over the adult life span. How and why intelligence grows and changes with age has been the subject of much research and debate over the last 30 years, not only involving those in the field of adult development and aging, but also those in the areas of psychology and education (see Jensen, 1969; Matarazzo, 1972).

We will organize our discussion of intelligence and its development during adulthood around several issues: (1) what intelligence is and why an understanding of it is important to us, (2) major ideas and approaches to intelligence and their relevance to adult development and aging, and (3) whether intelligence declines with increasing age.

Intelligence: Its Relevance to Our Daily Lives

As many of us are aware, a number of important decisions about our lives made by us and others are either explicitly or implicitly based on an estimate of how "intelligent" we are. For example, whether we enter into school, our suitability for a given curriculum (college preparatory versus vocational), whether we are hired for or are promoted to a new job, and whether we should be forced to retire or be institutionalized (see K.W. Schaie & Willis, 1978) in some way are influenced by our own or others' judgments about our intellectual skills.

Regardless of whether we understand intelligence and intelligent behavior in terms of an IQ score, a grade point average, performance on the job, or in terms of specific abilities, most of us are attempting to understand our own (or another's) capability, or underlying competence, when we use the term **intelligence**. Moreover, our ideas about whether intelligence declines with age or not affect not only our estimates of our competence at present but also influence decisions we make about our lives (our occupational goals) that will in turn influence future plans we make for ourselves. Thus, the answer to the often-heard question, "What do you want to do when you graduate?" for many of us involves an evaluation of our general ability, or perhaps more pointedly, an evaluation of our ability in a specific area of expertise (should you go on to medical school?). To say that someone is "bright" or "dull," whether we are referring to the young child in elementary school, the budding executive, or the older person returning to college, can have important emotional or vocational consequences for that individual.

Intelligence is a value-laden term, perhaps one that we are quick to fall back on but nevertheless have difficulty in defining. It means different things to different individuals, depending upon (1) their background and training, and (2) the everyday behaviors they are attempting to understand or predict. For many reasons, then, intelligence is a concept that demands clear definition throughout the adult life span. With these thoughts in mind, let us more formally discuss definitions of intelligence, with an emphasis upon its change and malleability over the adult years.

Defining Intelligence: A Brief History

Historically, ideas about intelligence have evolved from being very philosophical in nature to being more empirical and objective. This shift tends to be associated with Binet's (1905) development of the concept of **mental age**, reflecting an individual's performance on a variety of intellectual tasks relative to those of a given age level (Matarazzo, 1972). The mental age concept arose out of the need to classify children based on levels of mental retardation in the Parisian school system. Soon thereafter, it was utilized to study intellectual capacity. For a variety of reasons, the use of mental age in defining intelligence began to lose its appeal. The primary reason for this was that the **IQ** (mental age [MA] divided by chronological age [CA]) lost its value because the relationship between mental age and chronological age was not constant at all age levels.

Even at this point in history, biases about whether intelligence would increase with age or not influenced arguments about whether to retain the mental age concept in determining IQ. Matarazzo (1972) notes that regarding the use of MA/CA method with adults, "This brings us to the second result that may be expected from a study of the growth curve, namely the ultimate arrest of mental growth. . . . The successive increments by which test scores increase with advancing chronological age not only diminish progressively, but ultimately vanish altogether" (pp. 99–100).

This assumption of decline, thought to be valid in the early twentieth century, led to a shift away from a mental age based concept of IQ to a manner of calculating IQs based on deviations from the mean. These **devia-**

tion intelligence quotients were more straightforward, allowing us to compare individuals regardless of age in *standard score units.* As Botwinick (1973) has noted, an **age credit** was given to the older persons to allow for the comparison of these standard scores, using data collected from subjects 20 to 34 years old. On the other hand, an **age debit** was used to compute the IQs of individuals who were younger. The resulting scores were set to be equivalent to an "average" IQ of 100, using this method of correction. Here we see that bias about whether persons can maintain and/or increase their intelligence as they age has literally been "built into" the calculation of IQs, derived from the Wechsler Adult Intelligence Scale (WAIS) (see Table 6.1), perhaps the most commonly used test of "intelligence" among psychologists and educators today.

What Do Intelligence Scores Mean?

It is important that we note that IQ is simply *one* index by which to represent that quantity or quality we call intelligence. That an IQ of 100 indicates "average" intelligence is an arbitrary decision or value judgment (see Mata-

TABLE 6.1

WAIS-R SUBTESTS

Scale	Sample Items
Verbal Tests	
General information	1. How many wings does a bird have? 2. How many nickels make a dime? 3. What is steam made of? 4. Who wrote "Tom Sawyer"?
General comprehension	1. What should you do if you see someone forget his book when he leaves a restaurant? 2. Why is copper often used in electrical wires?
Arithmetic	1. Sam had three pieces of candy and Joe gave him four more. How many pieces of candy did Sam have altogether? 2. Three women divide eighteen golf balls equally among themselves. How many golf balls did each person receive?
Similarities	1. In what way are a lion and a tiger alike? 2. In what way are a circle and a triangle alike?
Vocabulary	This test consists simply of asking, "What is a _____?" or "What does _____ mean?" The words cover a wide range of difficulty.
Performance Tests	

In addition to verbal tasks of the kinds illustrated above, there are a number of performance tasks involving the use of blocks, cut-out figures, paper and pencil puzzles, etc.

razzo, 1972); the figure could just as easily be 150 or 60! Moreover, whether these numbers necessarily indicate anything about an individual's innate ability or not is certainly arguable. The particular items that appear on any intelligence test are themselves quite arbitrary—a function of the test constructor's own beliefs about what exactly intelligence is.

We need to take into account a number of very diverse factors in both defining and measuring intelligence, as well as in interpreting an intelligence test score, whether the person tested is 15 or 75 years old. For example, the individual's health, work or living environment, family background, interests, motives, personality, or skills in other areas (memory) all influence performance on any test of intelligence. Despite these cautions about the use of IQ scores as a predictor of behavior or as an index of underlying competence, we must point out that intelligence tests can serve as a useful standard against which to measure what individuals know about their culture. Because intelligence tests are closely related to academic abilities and school achievement (Anastasi, 1982; Cronbach, 1984), they may be able to predict academic difficulties, later occupational involvement, or vocational success. Moreover, they are currently used in many diverse situations (primary and secondary schools, industry, civil service, the armed forces, mental hospitals, private clinics) for a variety of purposes (personnel selection and evaluation, diagnosis and treatment, vocational counseling) with much success. Perhaps it is most important to point out that one should rely upon intelligence test data sensibly and without bias for both practical and basic research use. How such data are interpreted ultimately dictates their utility. In this sense, how individuals *use* their intelligence can reveal a great deal about their personalities and relationships with others in a variety of contexts. We will raise this issue again later in this chapter.

As opposed to testable intelligence, we might be more interested in an individual's **functional ability** (Matarazzo, 1972). Scoring high on an intelligence test may be a necessary but not sufficient condition for functional ability—for example, in making decisions, coping with one's environment, continuing to be open to new experiences, profiting from previous learning, or communicating effectively with others. Ultimately, what we are seeking to predict is *intelligent behavior,* which in some way we believe to be a reflection of an underlying set of abilities or skills that intelligence tests measure.

One should always keep in mind that IQ is at best an index of *relative* brightness, reflected in intelligent behaviors that one displays in either solving test items or in functioning on an everyday basis. You might more easily understand this point if you reflect on your grade point average. For any number of reasons, that number will also be somewhat arbitrary—relative to the particular courses you have taken, your energy level, state of health, whether you were motivated to do well during a particular semester, your family or work responsibilities, and whether your course load itself was a heavy one or not. Someone with an undergraduate GPA of 3.8 who has few responsibilities, whose academic load is light and composed of beginning-level courses, might not be seen as doing as well as someone whose GPA was 3.0 but who worked full-time, was raising a family, and whose course load was a comparably heavy one, composed of more difficult upper-level courses. In this case, who is the better student? We might also ask whether grades give us reliable information about who will ultimately be the most successful in real life or who will even be the better graduate student. Likewise, a 4.0 on a 6-point scale means something different than does a 3.5 on a 4-point scale.

Like GPA, IQ must always be seen within a much larger arena of personal, cultural, community, and familial factors in order to be understood and used in a practical manner. Scoring high in certain scales of the WAIS-R such as vocabulary, comprehension, or information (see Table 6.1) may reflect one's educational background or simply be a function of an avid interest in reading and acquiring diverse facts. Being intelligent in this sense may predict success in fields such as Library Science or English but do little in explaining why an individual would have difficulty in following directions or in reassembling a lawn mower engine!

Only when we thoroughly understand what intelligence is (and is not), as well as why it changes with age, are we in a position to help individuals (young children, adults, or elderly persons) use their abilities to the fullest. At this point, we feel it prudent to review some major current ideas about intelligence in order to perhaps introduce some order amid the confusion about just what intelligence is.

INTELLIGENCE—THE PSYCHOMETRIC APPROACH

Historically, ideas about intelligence have been heavily influenced by research derived from the **psychometric tradition**. The psychometric approach to intelligence focuses on the assessment of an individual's testable intelligence via the use of distinct scales to measure such. This approach assumes that scores obtained from these scales reflect real qualities (abilities) that exist within the person. What has emerged from this tradition is a concern for issues regarding how intelligence is organized *structurally*—is there one general ability under which all types of performance can be subsumed, or is intelligence more complex—say, 2 factors, or 7, or 100?

From a very practical point of view, the answer to this question will influence one's ideas about the development of intelligence or its assessment. For example, does the manner in which intelligence is organized develop in an orderly, systematic fashion? How many different measures must one choose in order to assess an individual's intellect adequately? Should similar scales be used to assess individuals of varying ages and backgrounds?

Factor Analysis and the Psychometric Approach

These conceptions of intelligence have been fathered by those who rely on a statistical technique known as **factor analysis** to provide an empirical guide to how many underlying factors explain relationships among a number of scales measuring various abilities and skills. For example, if we were to administer 20 ability measures to each of 100 individuals, factor analysis would enable us to identify any common ability or set of abilities accounting for performance in this battery of 20 scales. Depending upon what specific scales were used (as well as how they were administered) and the nature of our sample (whether it was a very diverse one or not), several common factors or just one could be derived from the factor analysis. Factor analysis, however, cannot provide us with a guide as to what scales to select in the first place—perhaps we would have developed guidelines for this, based upon a particular theory or our experience in everyday life. Additionally, the "factors" identified by factor analysis are merely statistical abstractions. When we label factors, for example, as "verbal" or "performance," we are making a value judgment based on the nature of those scales comprising that "factor" (those with high factor loadings).

Thus, depending upon a number of other variables (our choice of scales, method of administration, nature of the persons comprising our sample), we can arrive at somewhat different conclusions about whether intelligence (in this case actually test performance) is explained by a single factor or by many factors. Thus, there are probably many equally plausible answers to this question regarding the structure of abilities. Table 6.2 illustrates a factor analysis solution of relationships between the subtests of the WAIS and a verbal comprehension factor across age (Cohen, 1957). In this case, some of the tests "load" on (are highly correlated with) this primary factor of verbal comprehension that accounts for a portion of the performance on the subtests of the WAIS in a sample of approximately 850 adults (aged 18 to 75 and over) (Cohen, 1957). Table 6.2 indicates that for most adults, Information, Comprehension, Similarities, and Vocabulary define this Verbal Comprehension factor.

TABLE 6.2

FACTOR STRUCTURE OF WAIS VERBAL COMPREHENSION ACROSS AGE

Subtest	Age			
	18–19	25–34	45–54	60–75+
Information	30*	21*	36*	29*
Comprehension	33*	45**	27*	39*
Arithmetic	09	01	06	04
Similarities	23*	20*	32*	42**
Digit span	−10	−05	−06	00
Vocabulary	24*	48**	37*	37*
Digit symbol	08	04	01	06
Picture completion	07	03	04	07
Block design	−03	−01	00	00
Picture arrangement	14	06	00	30*
Object assembly	−08	00	00	−01

*Loadings between .20 and .39

**Loadings of .40 and higher

Source: Adapted from J. Cohen. (1957). The factorial structure of the WAIS between early adulthood and old age. *Journal of Consulting Psychology, 21* (284).

Early Theories of Intelligence: Stern and Spearman

Ideas about how intelligence is organized range from Stern's (1914) *unifactor* notion and Spearman's (1904) two-factor theory to, in the extreme, Guilford's (1967) *structure of intellect* (SI) model, which specifies 120 different factors.

As we noted earlier, ideas about how many "intelligences" really exist have been varied. One of the earliest is Stern's (1914) unifactor theory, which suggests that individuals differ in terms of the degree to which they possess *general intelligence.* By this we mean that their performance on many different types of tests (vocabulary, arithmetic, object assembly, block design) can be explained in terms of a *single* underlying ability common to *all* scales. To the extent that we could validly combine scores from such diverse tests and represent them collectively via an overall index of some sort (IQ), this theory implies that a single ability could explain performance in all of these measures. As we shall soon see, this issue has generated much discussion in the adult development and aging literature.

A somewhat more complex idea about the composition of intelligence is that of Spearman (1904), who suggested that intelligence was best explained by referring to two factors, "g" and "s" (see Figure 6.1). It is Spearman with whom "g" or a general intelligence factor has historically been associated. In addition to "g," test-specific ("s") abilities also were thought to contribute to intelligence. One's specially developed (or especially deficient) skills in, for example, block design or information would also determine performance on these measures in addition to general ability. Subsequently, Cyril Burt (1909), a British psychologist, modified Spearman's ideas to propose what he termed a *hierarchical* model of intelligence (Vernon, 1950), which specified four factors, differing in terms of their generality. The general intelligence factor is the broadest of these, in addition to two group factors (termed verbal-educational and spatial-mechanical) that are more specific, followed by specific (task) factors, and finally, chance factors.

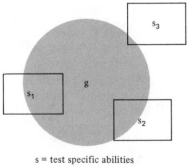

s = test specific abilities
g = general ability

Figure 6.1 Spearman's two-factor theory of intelligence. *Source:* Adapted from A. Anastasi. (1982). *Psychological testing* (5th ed.) (p. 365). New York: Macmillan. Reprinted with permission of Macmillan Publishing Company from *Psychological Testing* by Anne Anastasi. © 1982 by Anne Anastasi.

Guilford's 120-Factor Theory

On the other end of the continuum, we find the approach of Guilford (1967), termed the **structure of intellect** (SI) model of intelligence. Guilford separates abilities into three major types: (1) *operations,* referring to the basic psychological processes involved in ability formation (memory, cognition [awareness, knowing]), and (2) *contents,* referring to the nature of the material dealt with (numbers, letters or words, behaviors). The third general class of abilities within the SI model is *products,* referring to the consequence of the interaction among *operations* acting upon *content.* For example, a class of objects or relationships between ideas might be considered as products. In that the above three classes of abilities are seen by Guilford as independent of one another, the resulting model theoretically allows for 120 factors (Guilford, 1967). Consequently, Guilford would not see a general intelligence factor underlying all of these 120 abilities. In addition to its complexity, which in itself makes it impractical, research (E. Brody & N. Brody, 1976; Butcher, 1968; Resnick, 1976) does not support the actual existence of all 120 abilities, nor is the hypothesized independence between such factors supported.

While Guilford's theory of intelligence has generated a great deal of research, the structure of intellect model has for the most part yet to be integrated into adult developmental research on intelligence. The major exception to this has been studies of "divergent thinking" (being able to think in many ways, generating novel uses for common objects) in the young versus the old. Studies by Albaugh and Birren (1977) and by Albaugh, Parham, Cole, and Birren (1982) have found less divergent thinking with age in cross-sectional comparisons of younger and older adults. This difference in divergent thinking has been likened to drops in cognitive flexibility (creativity), which are more than likely produced by everyday environments that stifle intellectual curiosity, rather than by biological decline.

We now turn to two somewhat less complex theories that have, historically, been more closely identified with adult developmental research in intellectual functioning. These theories are Thurstone's primary mental abilities (PMA) approach, and the Horn-Cattell theory of crystallized (Gc) and fluid (Gf) abilities.

Thurstone's Primary Mental Abilities Theory

While Spearman considered "g" of primary importance, with secondary factors of lesser magnitude, Thurstone's ideas emphasized the opposite. His theory of **primary** (group) **mental abilities** (PMA) specified several factors: spatial ability, perceptual speed, numerical ability, verbal relations, words, memory, and induction (see Figure 6.2). These abilities are correlated with one another to a degree. Thus, some estimate of one's general intelligence could be obtained by noting performance on scales measuring each PMA factor.

Primary mental abilities have served as the measurement framework within which K. W. Schaie has conducted perhaps the most extensive studies of adult intellectual development to date (see K.W. Schaie, 1979). Before

A. Verbal Meaning (V)

This is the ability to understand ideas expressed in words. It is used in activities where information is obtained by reading or listening to words. The task requires verbal recognition via a multiple–choice format. In the following example the subject must select that alternative which is the best analog of the capitalized stimulus word:

BIG   A. ILL   B. LARGE   C. DOWN   D. SOUR

The test contains 50 items in increasing order of difficulty with a time limit of 4 min.

B. Space (S)

Measured here is the ability to think about objects in two or three dimensions. It may be described as the ability to imagine how an object of figure would look when it is rotated, to visualize objects in two or three dimensions, and to see the relations of an arrangement of objects in space. The more recent technical definition of this ability is *spatial orientation.* Space is measured by 20 test items, with a time limit of 5 min. In the example given below every lettered figure that is the same as the stimulus figure, even though it is rotated, is to be marked. Figures that are mirror images of the first figure are not to be marked.

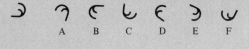

C. Reasoning (R)

The ability, which in current factor taxonomies is often more specifically identified as *inductive reasoning,* involves the solution of logical problems—to foresee and plan. The Thurstones (1949) propose that persons with good reasoning ability can solve problems, foresee consequences, analyze a situation on the basis of past experience, and make and carry out plans according to recognized facts. Reasoning is measured by such items as the following:

a b x c d x e f x g h x   h i j k x y

The letters in the row form a series based on a rule. The problem is to discover the rule and mark the letter which should come next in the series. In this case the rule is that the normal alphabetic progression is interrupted with an x after every second letter. The solutions therefore would be the letter i. There are 30 test items with a time limit of 6 min.

D. Number (N)

This is the ability to work with figures and to handle simple quantitative problems rapidly and accurately. It is measured by test with items of the following kind:

$$\begin{array}{r} 17 \\ 84 \\ 29 \\ \hline 140 \end{array}$$

The sum of each column of figures is given. However, some of the solutions given are right and others are wrong. Sixty test items are given with a time limit of 6 min.

E. Word Fluency (W)

This ability is concerned with verbal recall involved in writing and talking easily. It differs from verbal meaning further in that it concerns the speed and ease with which words are used, rather than the degree of understanding of verbal concepts. The measurement task requires the subject to write as many words as possible beginning with the letter S during a 5-min. period.

Figure 6.2   Thurstone's Primary Mental Ability (PMA). *Source:* Reprinted by permission of the publisher from *SRA Primary Mental Abilities, Ages 11-17, Form AM* by L. L. Thurstone & T. G. Thurstone. Chicago, IL: Science Research Associates, Inc. Copyright 1948 by Science Research Associates, Inc.

turning to Schaie's work and the more general issue of intelligence in adulthood and old age, let us examine the Horn-Cattell theory of crystallized (Gc) and fluid (Gf) abilities.

Crystallized (Gc) and Fluid (Gf) Abilities

While R. B. Cattell presented his ideas about the existence of Gf/Gc in the early 1940s, it was not until 1965 that Cattell's doctoral student, John Horn, more or less popularized the theory based upon research with a wide range of adults whose ages spanned from the twenties to the sixties. In contrast to previous ideas about the structure of intelligence, the distinction between crystallized (Gc) and fluid (Gf) abilities is especially suited to adult development in that both intelligences (seen as two general types of ability) are defined in such a way that predictions about developmental change are possible.

Fluid ability is defined in terms of the "processing of perceiving relationships, educing correlates, maintaining span of immediate awareness in reasoning, abstracting, concept formation, and problem solving" (Horn, 1978, p. 220). It can be measured using unspeeded as well as speeded tasks involving figural, symbolic, or semantic content. What is perhaps most distinctive about fluid ability is that it can be measured in tasks in which relatively little advantage comes from intensive or extended education and acculturation (Horn, 1978). Gf is a function of what Horn (1982) terms "causal" learning experiences.

Crystallized ability is similarly defined, but "the content of the tasks that best characterize Gc indicates relatively advanced education and acculturation either in the fundaments (contents) of the problem or in the operations that must be performed on the fundaments" (Horn, 1978, pp. 221–222). Crystallized skills come about as a function of more organized, systematic, acculturated learning (Horn, 1982).

Thus, Gf is largely situational in character, whereas Gc is a function of the accumulation of formal/informal experience and skill over time. Due to different sets of underlying causal factors (decreased neurophysiological functioning with age for Gf; cumulative intensive acculturation/education for Gc), Gf increases and then declines over the life span, whereas Gc generally increases and/or remains stable over most of the adult years (Horn & Cattell, 1966, 1967; Horn, 1970, 1978) (see Figure 6.3). As the terms suggest, Gf is *fluid,* or fluctuates with the demand made on the individual in novel situations. On the other hand, Gc *crystallizes* or takes on a definite form or character with experience—early learned skills are the basis for and facilitate both the acquisition and maintenance of those acquired later on in life. In some cases, where the problem or situation demands that the individual manufacture a novel response to it, Gf will come into play, whereas when previously learned skills are required, Gc will be called upon. Horn (1970, 1978) suggests, however, that this distinction is in some cases not as clear-cut as it would appear, as when the task could require the exercise of either general ability.

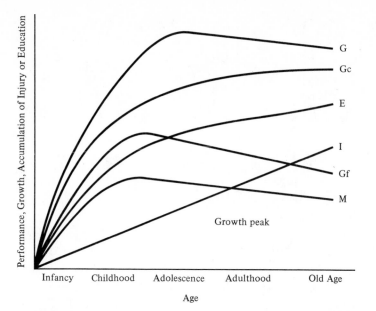

Figure 6.3 Gf-Gc curves across age. Development of fluid intelligence (Gf) and crystallized intelligence (Gc) in relation to maturational growth and decline of neural structures (M), accumulation of injury to neural structures (I), accumulation of educational exposures (E), and overall ability (G). *Source:* Adapted from J. Horn. (1970). Organization of data on life-span development of human abilities. In L. Goulet & P.B. Baltes (Eds.), *Life-span developmental psychology: Research and theory* (p. 465). New York: Academic Press. Reprinted by permission of the author.

Gc is best measured via measures of vocabulary skill, general information, or remote associations (e.g., with what word can plain, Tarzan, and Dick be associated? In this case, the answer is *Jane*—as in "plain Jane," "Tarzan and Jane," or "Dick and Jane"). Gf is best measured via a matrices task or an induction task (see Figure 6.4).

One might also choose measures to tap both kinds of intelligence. For example, in verbal analogies, the *content* or *meaning* of the words could be emphasized (edema is to medicine as homicide is to law) to assess Gc and to a lesser extent Gf. In the opposite case (emphasizing the *relationship* between the words whose meaning is well-known), Gf might be more important (happy is to sad as dark is to light).

Whether the Thurstone or the Horn-Cattell system is more valid than others we have discussed is arguable (E. Brody & N. Brody, 1976) and most likely depends upon what one is seeking to *predict* using any theory of intelligence (vocational success, school achievement, everyday intelligent behaviors, competence in later life).

Because considerable variation can be observed both within and across individuals in the level of Gf and Gc functioning, we must be cautious in interpreting the curves of growth and decline for Gc and Gf (Figure 6.2) in adulthood too rigidly. For example, some individuals may make more effort

Induction (Letter Series)

In these questions, write the letter that comes next in a series of letters.

Example:

A B C D E F G   ____ NA

The next letter in this series is H. Try another example.

Example:

A B B C C C D D D D E E E   ____ NA

This time the next letter is E. You can see that A occurs once, B twice, C three times, D four times, and so E should occur five times. But there are only four E's listed. Therefore, the next letter in the series should be E.
   Here are some examples with the right answer given. Study these examples to make sure you understand this kind of question.

Example:

G F E D C B A Z   _Y_ NA

In this series the alphabet is written backwards. When the series comes to A, it goes to the end of the alphabet to the letter Z, and continues on backwards, so Y is next in the series.

Example:

R S R T R U R V R   _W_ NA

Here the letters in the series S   T   U   V are separated by an R. The last letter to appear is one of these R's, so the next letter is W.

Figural Relations (Matrices)

Find the picture on the right that should be in the empty square on the left. Write the letter that corresponds with the correct answer in the space to the far right next to the problem number.

Example:

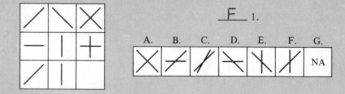

The correct answer —F.—has been written in the answer space. Make sure you understand why this is the correct answer. Here is another example for you to try:

Example:

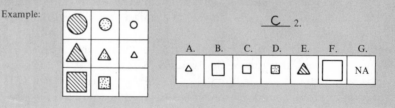

Figure 6.4   Induction (letter series). Measures of Gf-typical induction and figural relations items. *Source:* Adapted from J. Horn (1975). Gf-Gc Sampler. University of Denver Mimeo. Reprinted by permission of the author.

to sharpen their skills than do others (Horn, 1978). Moreover, some individuals are more prone to fatigue, anxiety, or attentional lapses than are others (Horn, 1978; Kennelly, Hayslip, & Richardson, 1985). These factors may either raise or lower the performance on a measure of Gc or Gf for a given individual.

Recently, there has been considerable debate regarding (1) the inevitability of losses with age in fluid ability, and (2) whether such losses in Gf are primarily neurophysiological in nature and are thus not amenable to training or intervention (see P.B. Baltes & Schaie, 1976; P.B. Baltes & Willis, 1982; Donaldson, 1981; Horn & Donaldson, 1976). Box 6.1 details a major effort at Pennsylvania State University by Paul Baltes and Sherry Willis to improve the fluid ability skills of older persons.

As Butcher (1968) has noted, much of the confusion about how many factors define intelligence has been caused by the comparison of factors that exist at different levels in the hierarchy of abilities. As we noted above, this, in turn, is largely due to the initial selection of both tests and people in one's sample. For this reason, all models trying to establish what *the* structure of intelligence is are to some extent arbitrary, and it is especially important that some criterion be developed to allow us to evaluate these models. For our purposes, this criterion is whether a theory allows us to better understand the

BOX 6.1

CAN INTELLIGENCE BE LEARNED?

Paul Baltes and Sherry Willis of Pennsylvania State University believe that it can! On the assumption that *declines* with age in intelligence are *not irreversible* and that intellectual functioning in old age is characterized by a great deal of *plasticity,* these investigators have developed a cognitive-educational training program to help older adults enhance their intellectual skills, termed project *ADEPT* (Adult Development and Enrichment Project). Specifically, they focused upon the skills required to solve items measuring *fluid intelligence* (Gf). By comparing those elderly who received such training with those who received no training or with those who simply practiced (without the benefit of any training), they concluded that older persons can in fact enhance their intellectual skills. They based their conclusions about the efficacy of their training program upon evidence they gathered suggesting (1) a *hierarchical pattern of transfer* and (2) *maintenance of training effects over time.* This hierarchical pattern of transfer (where tests measuring fluid ability [near transfer task] should be affected by training to the *greatest* extent, and those measuring *crystallized ability* [Gc] should be *least* affected) was attained. For those who had sim-

ply been allowed to practice with the items measuring Gf, *no* hierarchical pattern of transfer to Gf versus Gc was found. Moreover, the *magnitude* of training effects was greater for training program participants than for those who served as members of the control group (where no training, but only practice, was provided); these effects were maintained at a point one month after training and to a somewhat lesser extent at six months.

These findings vividly demonstrate that aging need not be characterized by loss and decline, and that if given the opportunity, older adults can indeed continue to grow intellectually. Such a view should give both the old and the young the message that our ideas about older persons being "over the hill" intellectually are clearly without basis in fact. To perpetuate this myth of intellectual decline does both the young and the old a terrible disservice.

Source: P.B. Baltes & S.L. Willis. (1982). Plasticity and enhancement of intellectual functioning in old age: Penn State's Adult Development and Enrichment Project (ADEPT). In F.I.M. Craik & S. Trehub (Eds.), *Aging and cognitive processes* (pp. 353–389). New York: Plenum.

existing facts dealing with intellectual aging. We are assuming, then, that one's intellect is acquired, maintained, and, in some cases, lost in a developmental context.

HOW MANY INTELLIGENCES?—EVERYDAY IMPLICATIONS

We conclude our discussion of the psychometric tradition with the caution that because they rest upon different assumptions, use different scales and methods for data collection, and because of sampling differences, studies based on different theories about how intelligence is best structured are difficult to compare (see Reese & Overton, 1970). Clearly, however, the evidence overwhelmingly indicates that general intelligence is not adequate to explain performance on the myriad of tests and scales investigators have devised to assess that elusive quality we call intelligence. Instead, intelligence is complex, and thus it should not surprise us if different aspects of intelligence change in different ways (and for different reasons in one person versus another) as we get older (see Chapter 1).

The *particular form* (e.g., structure) that intelligence takes is a question that investigators obviously do not agree on, and we must note (with some confidence) that this question of structural change with age in intelligence has yet to be answered unequivocally (see P.B. Baltes, Reese, & Lipsitt, 1980; Cunningham, Clayton, & Overton, 1975; Garrett, 1946; Hayslip & Sterns, 1979; Horn, 1978; Reinert, 1970). Clearly, there are differences of opinion regarding this question that have yet to be resolved.

This question of structure has very definite implications for the assessment of intelligence across the life span. For example, in a group of children, we might only require one scale (with items all measuring, say, general ability) to adequately assess intelligence for the purpose of predicting class performance. On the other hand, in a sample of adults, for the purpose of predicting performance in a complex job situation, we might require measures of five different abilities. Thus, it would *not* be appropriate to compare the scores obtained from each group of persons (see Chapter 3 for a discussion of cross-sectional research).

For our purposes, how intelligence is organized deserves serious consideration because of its implications for the *assessment* of intelligence in adulthood. If intelligence is composed of more than one general ability, it challenges the wisdom of comparing persons of different ages in terms of some overall index of intelligence (IQ). If, as in the above example, we were trying to predict *different types* of intellectual performance, we might, by design, not want to use the same ability measures in each case. Recently, Howard Gardner (1983) has proposed a theory of multiple intelligences that is decidedly practical in that it specifies many domains of intelligence that seem to relate to the everyday world and/or to occupational success. For example, linguistic, musical, bodily-kinesthetic, logical-mathematical intelligence all exist (see Gardner, 1983 for a thorough discussion). It remains to be seen whether this newer view will come to be accepted as a viable approach to intelligence, particularly as it relates to our knowledge of adult development and aging.

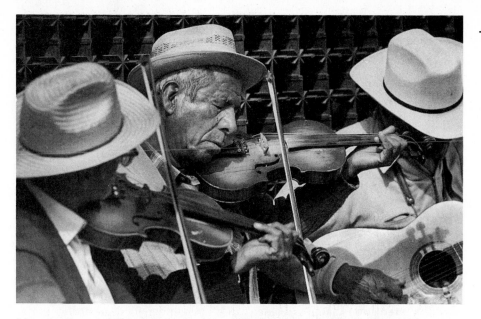

Many intellectual abilities may be domain-specific (e.g., musical ability). Often, with sufficient use, one's intellectual skills can be maintained well into late adulthood.

Another, perhaps more practical, implication of the fact that multiple intelligences reflect a more accurate picture is that one need not see oneself as more or less intelligent (relative to others) in an overall sense. Rather, it is more accurate to say that some individuals are brighter than others with regard to certain classes of abilities but not other classes. For example, the highly educated older individual may have excellent verbal skills or command a wealth of information but do poorly in visualizing relationships between objects in space (a critical skill in assembling or disassembling an engine), or have difficulty in understanding and recalling directions.

Thus, in a sense, we see that the very complexity of intelligence supports the notion that we all can develop our skills in some areas to perhaps compensate for deficiencies in other areas. One can observe this frequently among many older adults who maintain and even make an effort to improve their vocabulary skills while shying away from tasks or situations in which they cannot use their past experience to their advantage—these situations are often seen as too difficult, personally irrelevant, or simply requiring too much effort (Hayslip, 1989). Thus, these adults develop those skills that are already intact, while neglecting those skills that they do not see as critical or where everyday life experience does not demand their use.

INTELLIGENCE—THE INFORMATION PROCESSING APPROACH

In contrast to the psychometric approach to intelligence, a newer approach, termed the *cognitive* **information processing** perspective, has enabled researchers to understand intelligence more completely (see Resnick, 1976;

Sternberg, 1985; Sternberg & Detterman, 1979). Up to the present, the intelligence and aging literature (see below) has been dominated by the psychometric approach, mainly due to the ease with which large batteries of scales can be administered relatively quickly to large numbers of people varying in age. In light of this fact, it is important to understand the general thrust of this newly emerging area in intelligence research.

By more clearly specifying the "representations, processes, and strategies" (Sternberg, 1985) individuals use in solving items that measure intelligence, we can better understand and thus facilitate intellectual development among adults of all ages. Research in this area is very diverse, focusing on specific tasks or types of items commonly found in most intelligence tests, for example, spatial relations, analogies, or block design (see Carroll, 1979; Keating, 1982; Sternberg, 1979). Those who support this approach to understanding intelligence argue that while factor analysis has allowed us to understand that intelligence is complex, a more promising approach would be to focus upon *component processes* (e.g., encoding, storage, retrieval, rule formation, pattern analysis) that are themselves a function of the interaction between *task* variables and *person* variables. It is principally through the study of this complex interaction that intelligence can best be understood, according to the cognitive information processing theorists. Typically, this is accomplished through a *task* analysis, whereby performance on an intelligence test item(s) is broken down into more basic units (processes) that can be studied thoroughly.

Information processing researchers (Keating, 1982) have distinguished between a "bottom-up" and a "top-down" approach to accomplishing this task. Briefly, a bottom-up approach studies intelligence in terms of the more basic qualities of the person, seeing that person as an information processing system (e.g., short-term memory efficiency or retrieval from long-term memory), without reference to intelligence per se (see Chapters 4 and 7). A top-down approach, on the other hand, assumes that the intelligence test item is itself a complex task and proceeds to break this task down into more basic skills essential to its solution. For example, performance on a measure of fluid intelligence (inductive reasoning, matrices or analogies) can be broken down into its basic components, involving *content* and *process* (Pellegrino & Glaser, 1979) (see Figure 6.5). This component (top-down) approach to intelligence has been used as a basis for enhancing performance on measures of Gf in the aged by P.B. Baltes and Willis (1982) with a great deal of success (see Box 6.1). In this sense, the top-down approach represents a kind of "marriage" between the psychometric and information processing approaches. While factor analysis has defined fluid ability as an important dimension of intellectual development that also varies across age, the identification of those basic processes critical to the solution of tasks measuring Gf has been accomplished by the componential researcher. Crucial to the information processing approach is the selection of tasks, for example, reading, arithmetic analogies, that relate to the everyday world (Keating, 1982) (refer to our discussion of ecological validity in Chapter 3). Ideally, then, by using such a strategy, we may discover *and* foster component skills that individuals of *all* ages may use on an everyday basis. This approach to intelligence, particularly if combined

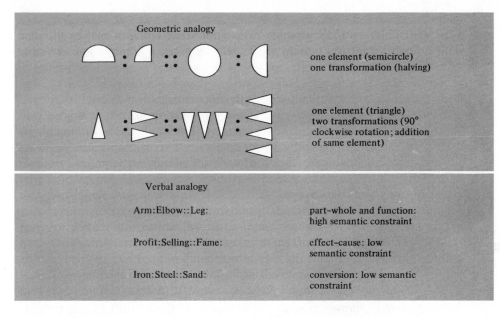

Figure 6.5 Pellegrino and Glaser's (1979) top-down information processing approach to the understanding of Gf performance. Examples of the different items used to assess fluid ability. Item descriptions are in terms of the relational *content* or features that must be *processed* and held in memory. *Source:* Cognitive correlates and components in the analysis of individual differences. In R. J. Sternberg & D. Detterman. (1979). *Human intelligence: Perspectives on its theory and measurement* (p. 76). Norwood, N.J.: Ablex. Reprinted by permission of Ablex Publishing Corp.

with the psychometric view, may be very fruitful in many ways and ultimately shape the intelligence tests of the future (see Horn, 1979; Resnick, 1979; Sternberg, 1979 for discussions of intelligence testing in the year 2000).

PSYCHOMETRIC INTELLIGENCE IN ADULTHOOD AND OLD AGE

We now turn to a central topic of this chapter—whether intelligence declines with age. We have discussed what intelligence is and how it has been defined under the assumption that understanding intelligence can lead to a better understanding of its development over the course of adulthood. On the basis of our discussion, we concluded that the idea of intelligence as a single underlying ability can probably be rejected. In contrast to, yet complementing, this tradition, the information processing approach has chosen to understand more completely *how* intelligence is exercised through the study of the underlying *processes* individuals utilize in demonstrating their competence in situations requiring intelligent behavior.

Early cross-sectional studies (Doppelt & Wallace, 1955) found overall WAIS performance with increased age (relative to the reference group of those 20 to 34 years old as a standard) to peak between ages 20 to 34 and to decline slowly with age until about age 60, with more severe declines afterward. Longitudinal studies typically display an increase in overall perform-ance with age (K.W. Schaie & Labouvie-Vief, 1974).

While a number of studies using the WAIS (see Botwinick, 1977, 1978) have found a "classic aging pattern" (declines in performance scores, relative stability in verbal scores), we can more profitably understand intellectual aging by focusing on more specific abilities. K.W. Schaie's work using pri-mary mental abilities and Horn's research using the crystallized-fluid ability distinction are two outstanding examples of such an approach.

Schaie's PMA Research

As we noted above, developmental research on intelligence has, to this point, been dominated by the psychometric tradition. K. W. Schaie's work on intel-ligence and aging best exemplifies the work done in this area. Schaie (1979), in a comprehensive account of his research program, describes a series of cross-sectional and longitudinal studies that began in 1956.

Initially, a cross-sectional comparison of over 500 adults ranging in age from 20 to 70 years of age (spanning seven different cohorts) was carried out. In 1963, a *new* cross-sectional sample was drawn, and, *in addition,* a 7-year longitudinal follow-up of those subjects tested in 1956 using a battery of scales based on Thurstone's primary mental abilities theory of intelligence was carried out (you may want to refresh your memory of Thurstone's theory [above] and of sequential designs [see Chapter 3]). In 1970, a *new* random sampling of subjects was taken and successive follow-ups of subjects origi-nally interviewed in 1956 and 1963 were conducted. Additionally, new ran-dom samples from those originally tested in 1956 and 1963 were also drawn. In 1977 (see K.W. Schaie & Hertzog, 1983), this process was essentially repeated, so that Schaie now had independent samples from *each of seven cohorts* at 1956, 1963, 1970, and 1977, and longitudinal follow-ups (dependent sam-ples) involving subjects of seven *age* ranges who had been originally inter-viewed at each of four *measurement points* (1956, 1963, 1970, 1977).

In relying on data collected in this fashion, Schaie was able to examine the relative impact of age, cohort membership, and time of measurement on different aspects of intelligence in adulthood. Additionally, these analyses permitted an assessment of mortality effects (see Chapter 3) on intelligence in adulthood.

Schaie's results yield a picture of intelligence in adulthood and old age that is somewhat complex but nevertheless consistent with the multidimen-sional, multidirectional nature of development, as we discussed in Chapter 1. In view of the complexity of Schaie's work, we will focus on only the most relevant findings bearing on the question of intelligence and age.

Data from the first cross-sectional study conducted in 1956 suggested that different types of abilities demonstrated *diverse age-related* peaks of func-tioning (see Figure 6.6), where PMA reasoning peaked most early (chronolog-ically), versus space, verbal fluency, word fluency and number, which all peaked later. Moreover (see Figure 6.6), for abilities where better performance was observed (relative to other skills) in the young, this pattern did not parallel that found in those who were older (e.g., 46+ years old).

The 1963 data collection yielded evidence for a *time of measurement* effect, where those in 1963 at comparable ages were superior (except for word fluency) to those in 1956. In this case, Schaie utilized data from *two* cross-sectional studies; subjects of the same age are compared at two occasions—a *time sequential* analysis. Moreover, longitudinal (1956–1963) findings suggested (again, except for word fluency) that age-related changes in intelligence were minimal until subjects reached their sixties.

Recall from Chapter 3 that *cross sequential* analysis pits longitudinal (*within* cohort) time of measurement changes (where age and time of measurement are confounded) against cohort differences (where age and cohort are confounded), involving comparisons of *different* cohorts at *similar* times of measurement. Schaie's cross sequential data suggested that *cohort* differences were *more* important in explaining the cross-sectional or longitudinal age effects found for many abilities than was chronological age. These cross sequential analyses, however, also implied that in early adulthood *and* in very late adulthood, age effects on abilities within cohorts might also be substantial. Schaie's 1956 to 1963 analyses illustrated the marked time of measurement, between cohort and within cohort aging effects (applying to the youngest and oldest cohorts especially) on aspects of intelligence (PMA) in adulthood (see K.W. Schaie, 1979; K.W. Schaie & Strother, 1968a, 1968b).

Additional cross sequential and time sequential analyses (see Chapter 3) of these data suggested positive cohort effects (more favorable performance with successively younger cohort membership) for verbal meaning, space, reasoning, and number. For word fluency, both age and time of measurement effects were found.

The 1970 follow-up analyses clearly suggested what Schaie's earlier data had pointed to: what had initially appeared as a decrement associated with age was, upon examination, attributable to cohort differences. Furthermore, as revealed by a cohort sequential analysis of the data, the extent to

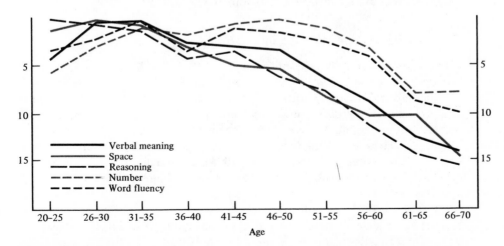

Figure 6.6 PMA curves across age: mean decrement in the primary mental abilities from mean peak levels in standard scores. *Source:* Adapted from K.W. Schaie. (1958). Rigidity-flexibility and intelligence: A cross-sectional study of the adult life span from 20–70. *Psychological Monographs, 72,* No. 9 (Whole No. 462), 15.

which age decrements were found varied with (1) the type of ability examined *and* (2) cohort membership.

Cross-sectional and longitudinal replications of seven-year (1956 vs. 1963; 1963 vs. 1970) follow-up analyses (both done earlier) to a large extent yielded similar findings (see above discussion of Schaie's initial cross-sectional and longitudinal findings): clearly the extent of age decrement in abilities varied with cohort membership. Moreover, for most abilities, decline was only apparent relatively *late* in life (age 67).

The third cross-sectional (1970) study, again permitting a time sequential analysis, yielded substantial time of measurement effects (1956 vs. 1963 vs. 1970) at equal ages, with advantages to those tested in 1970 for all PMA factors, except word fluency. When the data were rearranged by cohort (see Schaie, 1979), dramatic cohort specific patterns, again varying by PMA ability, emerged. Cohort sequential analysis of these data (see Chapter 3) permitting Schaie to measure age *changes* over seven-year intervals from 25 to 81 years and cohort *differences* for cohorts 1889 to 1938 again clearly indicated that cohort membership was more important in explaining these data than was age.

It is important to realize that the evidence for age, cohort, or time of measurement effects were found for *both* the independent *and* dependent samples, data making them even more impressive. Schaie's analyses (P.B. Baltes, K.W. Schaie, & Nardi, 1971; K.W. Schaie, Labouvie & T. Barrett, 1973) had also indicated that, in general, dropouts had tended to initially score more poorly than those who did not drop out (retestees). Thus, longitudinal findings (varying in part by cohort) suggesting minimal declines with age may have been presenting an unduly positive picture of intellectual change with age.

A similar cohort sequential analysis (K.W. Schaie & Hertzog, 1983) again yielded cohort effects, utilizing the 1977 sampling. Schaie and Hertzog (1983) also found clear declines for most PMA factors after age 60, but with some minimal evidence for decline somewhat earlier.

WHAT CAN WE LEARN FROM SCHAIE'S RESEARCH?

What is perhaps most important to learn from Schaie's 21-year study of adult intelligences is that the notion of irreversible, biologically based decline with age in abilities is clearly unfounded. In most cases, depending upon the interaction of the sociocultural environment (whether it is stimulating or supportive) and aging, the age decrement in intelligence may be reduced or intensified. Thus, according to Schaie, there is no such thing as universal, true decline (P.B. Baltes & K.W. Schaie, 1976). Moreover, the nature of this interaction between historical change and aging seems to vary with cohort membership—a complex picture indeed!

Thus, with intervention in mind, Schaie's data indicates that declines in ability are largely restricted to those 70 or over. Most importantly, they paint an optimistic picture for those who are educators and for those young, middle-aged, or elderly persons who believe that declines in their mental abilities are inevitable or beyond remediation.

Schaie (1983), however, recommends caution regarding the everyday significance of a "statistically significant" drop in performance. For example, does recalling two fewer digits, solving arithmetic problems three seconds more slowly, or defining correctly five fewer vocabulary items imply that one's abilities in these areas have declined to the point where they will interfere with an individual's daily life? Perhaps not, especially if the individual has aids available (having calendars or hand calculators to aid in recall, making lists of things to be done or remembered, note-taking, or consulting dictionaries or libraries). These "aids" can thus enable the individual to compensate for "losses" in ability.

Despite the wealth of information that has been gathered about intellectual aging, we must use our common sense in interpreting any data suggesting growth and/or decline as they apply to specific individuals. What remains, of course, is the further study of those factors and methods of remediation to prevent or reverse the apparent loss of mental capacities with increased age. To a certain extent, such efforts have begun (refer to our discussion of the Baltes-Willis ADEPT program for enhancing intellectual performance among the aged). Schaie and Willis (1986), using a training program similar to Baltes's ADEPT approach (see Box 6.1) have been able to reverse documented 14-year declines in several PMA abilities (reasoning and space) among older persons. These training procedures, moreover, actually *enhanced* the skills of those persons whose skills had remained stable over the previous 14 months.

SCHAIE'S PMA RESEARCH: SUMMARY

Schaie (1979, pp. 104–105) summarizes the primary implications of his research regarding the decline of intelligence in adulthood:

1. Reliable decrement cannot be found for all abilities for all persons. Decline is not likely at all until very late in life.

2. Decline is most evident for abilities where speed of response and peripheral nervous system (external to the brain and spinal cord, involving the sensory organs or muscles) are involved.

3. Declines will be evident for most abilities for individuals *of any age* who have severe cardiovascular disease and for those in their fifties and sixties who live in deprived environments (see Hertzog, K.W. Schaie, & Gribbin, 1978).

4. Data on intelligence and aging obtained from *in*dependent samples will *over*estimate loss for abilities where losses in fact occur (given that these persons do not have the benefit of practice). Dependent (repeated-measurement) samples data will accurately estimate age changes for those in better health and in more stimulating environments, while *under*estimating loss for those in worse health and/or living in more impoverished situations.

5. Cohort effects account for more of the variance in intelligence with age than do ontogenetic (age-related, maturational), biologically based factors, with age effects assuming more importance only late in life.

6. Individual differences in what skills decline, as well as in the extent of such decline, are substantial. Many older people, dependent upon their health, their educational background, whether they are isolated from others or not, and whether they have maintained those skills developed earlier, sustain and even improve their skills, while others decline much earlier in life.

While Schaie's research program has provided us with the most extensive knowledge base about intelligence and age, it is by no means the only program devoted to this task—a great deal of equally valuable information has been collected by others (see Botwinick, 1977, for a detailed review).

Crystallized (Gc) and Fluid (Gf) Intelligence and Aging

As we noted earlier, the Cattell-Horn crystallized-fluid intelligence theory has also generated much interest and research about the intelligence-aging relationship. The distinction between fluid (Gf) and crystallized (Gc) intelligence (Horn, 1978, 1982) (see also our discussion on pp. 200–203) reinforces the complex picture of intelligence and aging we have painted thus far. In this case, too, the diverse curves of stability/growth and decline for Gc and Gf, respectively, suggest intelligence to be both multidirectional and multidimensional in nature. Thus, it would be inappropriate to compare older and younger adults in terms of IQ, when those scales contributing to this IQ are partially crystallized and partially fluid in nature. As we noted earlier, each ability is, to a large extent, a function of different underlying factors that dictate differential paths of developmental change for each class of ability (Horn, 1978, 1982). Figure 6.7 illustrates these different paths of development, versus that which one would expect using a global index of intelligence (Horn, 1970). Of course, this global test fails to separate crystallized and fluid intelligences.

In recent years, Horn has expanded the notion of Gf and Gc (refer to our discussion of Gf/Gc above regarding theories of intelligence) to include other components and in so doing has broadened the empirical and conceptual base of the Gf/Gc theory. To accomplish this, Gf and Gc have been interrelated with other measures of personality traits (carefulness), sensory/perceptual-motor slowing, short-term memory, and attention (Horn, 1978, 1982) to more fully explain those *processes* that contribute to intellectual functioning and thus more completely explain *why* Gf and Gc exhibit differential paths of growth and decline over the life span. This approach is hierarchical. Thus, these general factors are organized by *levels* (from sensory, the most basic, to thinking, the most general).

Horn (1982) is quick to point out that apparently simple distinctions such as learned/unlearned, or verbal/performance are in fact complex and thus are *not* equivalent to the Gc-Gf distinction. "Thus neither the distinction between Gc and Gf nor the distinction between the two IQ dimensions of the WAIS is well characterized as a contrast between verbal and performance abilities" (Horn, 1982, p. 850).

Horn (1982) further defines Gf and Gc in terms of the *kinds* of learning experiences that underly each. Gc is determined by purposeful, *"acculturational" learning* provided by societal institutions, such as the home environ-

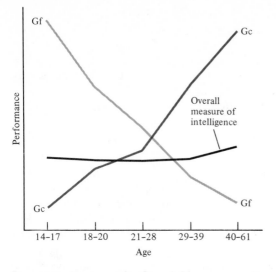

Figure 6.7   Age curves for Gc and Gf versus overall intelligence. *Source:* J. Horn. (1970). Organization of data on life-span development of human abilities. In L. Goulet and P. Baltes (Eds.), *Life-span developmental psychology: Research and theory* (p. 463). New York: Academic Press. Reprinted by permission of the author.

ment or the school (and by implication, the work environment). Gf is, on the other hand, determined by idosyncratic, largely self-determined *casual learning* influences. Both Gc and Gf are, to a certain extent, a function of neurological factors (e.g., numbers of active brain cells, the effects of stroke damage), though evidence for the differential, age-related relationship between neurological damage and Gf versus Gc is indirect and somewhat sketchy (see Horn, 1982, 1985).

Physiological influences are but one set of antecedent (causal) factors that Horn (1970, 1978, 1982) sees as critical to the development and maintenance of intelligence in adulthood. Other influences involve selective learning, family size/composition, values of parents/peers, one's own attitude toward one's development, or labeling by others (e.g., being labeled "disadvantaged" or "old"). Consequently, in adulthood, a *number* of factors contribute to the growth and/or decline of Gc and Gf abilities, both within and between persons, some of which are traceable to earlier experiences and some of which are concurrent in nature (in the present environment).

Piagetian Abilities and Aging

In contrast to psychometric intelligence, it is only recently that Piaget's notions of intellectual development have been applied to adult development and aging (F. Hooper, J. Hooper, & Colbert, 1984). Piaget and Inhelder (1969) have suggested that intellectual development progresses through a series of discrete biologically based stages from infancy through adolescence. While a discussion of Piaget's theory is beyond our scope, what distinguishes later childhood and early adolescence (ages 7 and older) from infancy and early childhood is *operational thought.* Operational thought is characterized by the ability to use symbols (words) to solve problems and perform various mental activities, versus *preoperational thought,* which requires that the child physically act out things in solving problems (see Piaget & Inhelder, 1969).

Preoperational children are influenced by what their senses tell them. For example, when asked, they will say after comparing two rows of equal numbers of blocks (one of which is longer than the other), that the longer row (where there are bigger spaces between the blocks) has more blocks. Older children, however, whose thinking is *operational,* realize that regardless of how the blocks appear, each row has an equal number of blocks in it. They can *manipulate* or *transform* the space between the blocks *mentally* in making a judgment; they have the ability to *conserve* on a number. Their thinking is less *egocentric,* in that they can make judgments and solve problems more independently of what their senses tell them. While children in the *concrete operational* stage can solve problems logically, as in the above example, and manipulate symbols to represent ideas, they are limited to the here and now. *Formal operational* thinking, characteristic of adolescents, is more abstract. Such individuals can logically reason and solve *hypothetical* problems—those that they have not necessarily had direct experience with.

Under the *assumption* that older persons *regress* back to an earlier level of development, many early researchers in this area have investigated performance on Piagetian tasks of intelligence among the aged. The implication is that older persons regress from formal operations back to a concrete operational or in some cases a preoperational level of thinking. Whether such regression occurs at all is difficult to ascertain in that nearly all studies (see Papalia & Bielby, 1974) are cross-sectional in nature. Moreover, whether regression, even if it accompanies the aging process, occurs for the same reasons that are responsible for cognitive growth in childhood and adolescence (e.g., biological change) is dubious. These studies clearly reveal age differences in Piagetian task performance—older persons are less able to successfully solve conservation tasks (space, volume, number, mass). That is, as in the above example, they fail to *conserve* on number—the number of blocks in each row is thought to vary with the length of the row; older persons cannot make the necessary mental transformations in order to solve the problem. Their thinking is more egocentric because they draw conclusions on the basis of what their senses tell them rather than on the basis of their understanding of concepts and relationships (i.e., that four blocks are *still* four blocks regardless of how they are arranged).

Hornblum and Overton (1976), however, suggest that older persons may see Piagetian tasks (e.g., arrangements of blocks) as childish or irrelevant to them personally. Moreover, Kausler (1982) notes that deficits in Piagetian task performance are rarely found in healthy, educated elderly persons, and that errors on these tasks are also common among younger persons. Thus, rather than interpret these findings as evidence for a *qualitative* shift (regression) in intellectual functioning with age, we might see them as *quantitative* in nature, as artifacts of noncognitive factors.

Rybash, Hoyer, and Roodin (1986) have suggested that Piaget's formal operational stage of cognitive development is of limited use to the adult developmental theorist and research. According to these authors, formal operational thinking is characterized by (1) a rational, logical, deductive approach to problem solving and understanding the world. Formal operational thinkers must therefore ignore the context in which the problem to be solved is embedded. Other limitations they note are (2) an overemphasis on abstract thinking, ignoring the importance of affect (emotion) in making everyday decisions of a social or interpersonal nature that are potentially influenced by many real-life concerns. They may be ambiguous and ill-defined. Rybash et al. (1986) note that "real-life problems, in contrast, are 'open' to the extent that there are no clear boundaries of a problem and the context within which it occurs" (p. 32). They provide, as an example, the problem confronting a woman who is deciding whether to have a child. Postformal operational thinking would not see this decision as a purely abstract, logical one. Instead, it is influenced by a number of factors, for example, her self-concept, demands on her time via her career, her socioeconomic status, whether she has the support of her husband and her relationship with him, whether she has other children, as well as her health. How she defines this problem (as well as its solution) depends on the particular factors that influence her decision and how these factors influence and are influenced by her decision to have or not to have a child. In other words, postformal operational thought is *dialectical* in nature (see Chapter 1). Formal and postformal operational thinking are qualitatively different. Arlin (1975, 1984) has termed postformal thinking as *problem finding* (discovering a new question to be answered) rather than as problem solving (thinking that is logical, leading to a well-defined answer).

Postformal reasoning is *relative;* that is, knowledge is *temporary* rather than absolute. For example, we often solve a problem only to realize that there are new things to learn and new questions to ask; for example, we enter into the adult work world with a specified set of skills that we think will enable us to be successful only to find that our success brings new challenges and problems. Our work world is different from what it once was because of our success.

Recently, many adult developmental researchers (Arlin, 1984; G. Cohen, 1979; Commons, Richards, & Armon, 1984; Kramer, 1983; Labouvie-Vief, 1982; Labouvie-Vief, Adams, Hakim-Larson, & Hayden, 1983; Sinnott, 1984) have explored age differences in the extent to which older versus younger adults engage in formal or postformal thinking. Labouvie-Vief et al. (1983), for example, presented a story to children and adults of varying ages of a woman who threatened to leave her husband if he came home drunk again. Each person was asked what the woman might do if he indeed did come home drunk again. With increased age, persons were *less* likely to give answers that ignored different situations (contexts), ruling out other interpretations of the problem. G. Cohen (1979) presented college students and older adults with a short passage involving an older man (a grandfather) and woman (a mother) engaged in different activities (e.g., cooking in the kitchen versus reading in the living [sitting] room). Traffic is outside and disturbing to those in the front of the house (the living room). Each person was asked who was most disturbed by the traffic. College students invariably said "the grandfather," a product of logical, deductive (formal) thought. Older adults, on the other hand, were more likely to offer other interpretations based upon other possibilities (see Labouvie-Vief, 1985); for example, the grandfather may have been deaf, the traffic may not have been constant, the grandfather might move to a different part of the house to read. It is possible to infer some breakdown in the logical thinking processes of the older adults from these data. However, as Labouvie-Vief (1985) notes, "Is it not possible that the adults in this study perceived *different* logical relationships from the ones of interest to the experimenter rather than none at all?" (p. 525). In contrast to thinking that is regressive (see above), Labouvie-Vief (1985) argues for an important *qualitative* difference in the thinking processes of older adults that is characteristic of the problem finding (Arlin, 1984) stage of postformal operational cognitive development. On this basis of their review, however, Rybash et al. (1986) suggest that postformal thought represents a different *style* of thinking, rather than reflecting a new stage of cognitive growth. While research in postformal operations with adults is somewhat sparse (see Labouvie-Vief, 1985; Rybash et al., 1986), it represents a new, exciting approach to intelligence in adulthood that has emerged as an alternative to the psychometric or information processing approaches. Such research may lead to a merging of these positions, increasing the ecological validity of our work in intellectual aging by allowing us to understand more fully the thinking processes (intelligent behaviors) adults use to cope with everyday problems.

DOES INTELLIGENCE DECLINE WITH AGE?

What shall we make of the data we have presented relating to declines in intelligence with increased age, for example, Schaie's work as well as Horn's? As you might imagine, a simple "yes-no" answer to the question, "Is this correct?" or "Is that the better theory?" is nearly impossible. In fact, debates between Schaie and Horn (see Botwinick, 1977; Horn & Donaldson, 1976, 1977; P.B. Baltes & K.W. Schaie, 1976; K.W. Schaie & P.B. Baltes, 1977) have raged over the validity of Schaie's analyses. They have focused on the issue of whether the decline in intelligence is a "myth" or not (referring to beliefs that supported universal irreversible decline) (see P.B. Baltes & K.W. Schaie, 1976; K.W. Schaie & P.B. Baltes, 1977). These debates about whether intelligence declines with age are indicative of the difficulty in accepting one approach over another.

In light of our goal of understanding intellectual aging, we might tentatively say that while some might argue with Schaie's choice of Thurstone's PMA framework (see K.W. Schaie, 1979), the wealth of data that he has gathered has proven invaluable in getting "the big picture" about intelligence and age. On the other hand, while the Horn-Cattell notions of Gf and Gc are, by definition, developmental and a great deal more complex than the

PMA approach (incorporating other processes; see Horn, 1982), they lack the broad empirical base that Schaie's approach has. Nearly all of Horn's research to date has either been cross-sectional, or age irrelevant (descriptions of single samples of age-homogeneous persons). At the risk of oversimplifying the issue, in much of Schaie's work (see Schaie, 1970, 1979), there are, however, some parallels regarding developmental (age-related) change/cohort specific effects on PMA factors that are similar to what one might expect from Gf-Gc theory.

EXPLAINING THE DATA: SCHAIE'S STAGE THEORY ABOUT INTELLIGENCE AND AGING

On the basis of his research, Schaie (1977–1978, 1979) has advanced a **stage theory** of adult intellectual development, which he claims is experientially (environmentally) grounded, versus such theories as Piaget's, whose ideas about intellectual development in childhood and adolescence are biologically based (see our discussion on pp. 213–216). According to Figure 6.8, in childhood and adolescence, intellectual development is best seen in terms of *acquisition* (where skills and abilities are being formed). During young adulthood, in the stage of *achieving,* these skills are directed to the creative application to and solution of real-life problems. *If* these skills are used in this fashion, growth will continue. In middle age, next follows the *responsible* stage, where such skills are applied to the management of "increasingly complex environmental demands" (p. 109) varying with individual and historical change. Such demands may stem from career choice and advancement or the balancing of multiple roles (e.g., parent, worker, spouse). Similarly, many middle-aged individuals are establishing an orientation to future goals (retirement planning, planning for one's children's future), and may be coping with technological changes in their jobs that they were not originally trained for (new

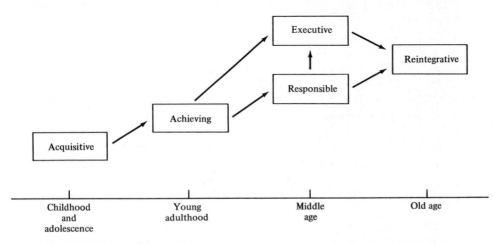

Figure 6.8   Schaie's stage theory of intelligence. *Source:* K.W. Schaie. (1977–1978). Toward a stage theory of adult cognitive development. *International Journal of Aging and Human Development, 8,* 133. © 1977, Baywood Publishing Co., Inc.

computer languages and systems). Coinciding with the responsible stage, Schaie suggests an *executive* stage, which more specifically targets the use of skills to deal with "systems transcending the nuclear family or self-confined job responsibility" (p. 109). In this sense, Schaie notes the executive stage to apply more so to individuals of higher social status (regarding educational level and occupation) who often make higher level decisions affecting others. The last stage, termed *reintegrative,* is a highly personal, pragmatic one, which in many respects bears little resemblance to the previous stages, where issues such as job-related achievement, occupational responsibilities, or active raising of one's family were important. Instead, one's intellect may be *applied* to the solution of more *ecologically relevant* (K.W. Schaie, 1978; Scheidt & K.W. Schaie, 1978) intellectual tasks; such skills require "the organism to restrict attention to those aspects of the environment which continue to be meaningful and adaptive, while ignoring those formal aspects which have lost interest and relevance" (K.W. Schaie, 1979, pp. 109–110). As Schaie and Geiwitz (1982) have observed, this last stage is characterized by "intellectual integrity," which implies a reintegration of all that has been acquired and experienced up to that point in life.

This point of view, emphasizing stages of intellect, contrasts with those ideas about intelligence that stress its study at a *processes* level or define it solely in terms of tasks that are specific to certain arenas, for example, achievement-oriented or educational in nature.

INTELLIGENCE AND EVERYDAY LIFE

Schaie's ideas about late adulthood (reintegrative stage of intellectual development) are indeed intriguing. It remains to be seen whether the approaches to intelligence and its assessment that psychologists and educators have devoted nearly 70 years of effort to can further our understanding of the "intelligence of everyday life." An important step in this direction has been provided by Scheidt and Schaie (1978) and by Willis (1982). Scheidt and Schaie (1978) actually developed a taxonomy (system for classification) of situations that reflected everyday intelligent behaviors. They did this by having older adults actually list those situations they felt critical to their intellectual competence. While this represents a first step in the process of understanding the intelligence of everyday life, it may prove valuable in future research with older persons. Architects, for example, might design environments for the specific purpose of improving various aspects of an older person's intellectual functioning believed to be related to the everyday skills older persons actually need for survival and continued growth. Table 6.3 illustrates those situations defining various ecologically relevant aspects of everyday intelligence for older adults in Scheidt and Schaie's study.

Willis (1982) found that among older adults, measures of fluid intelligence, and to a lesser extent, crystallized ability, correlated highly with performance on a variety of everyday tasks that we are confronted with daily, for example, reading maps, understanding labels, filling out forms, and un-

TABLE 6.3

SCHEIDT AND SCHAIE'S ECOLOGICALLY VALID INDICATORS OF INTELLIGENCE

Situational Attributes	Social	Nonsocial
High Activity		
Common-supportive	Arguing with person about important point Being visited by son or daughter and their children	Gardening in yard, planting seeds, weeding Doing weekly shopping in crowded supermarket
Common-depriving	Pressured by salesperson to buy merchandise Quarreling with relative	Climbing several steps to building entrance Cleaning apartment or household
Uncommon-supportive	Having sexual intercourse Traveling around city looking for new residence	Preparing large meal for friends Exercising for a few moments each day
Uncommon-depriving	Waiting at end of long line for tickets to entertainment Returning faulty or defective merchandise to store	Moving into new and unfamiliar residence Driving auto during rush-hour traffic
Low Activity		
Common-supportive	Seeking aid/advice from friend or family member Offering money to son or daughter who needs it	Browsing through family photo album Making plans for future
Common-depriving	Hearing from friend that he/she is considering suicide Hearing that close friend has recently died	Eating meal alone in own home Worrying about ability to pay a debt
Uncommon-supportive	Entering darkened nightclub to take dinner Attending art exhibit	Recording day's events in diary Wading in waist-high water in ocean
Uncommon-depriving	Opening door to stranger selling product or soliciting opinion While talking with someone, feeling you have unintentionally hurt feelings	Slipping on slick part of floor and falling Discovering you locked keys in car while shopping

Source: R. Scheidt & K. W. Schaie. (1978). A taxonomy of situations for an elderly population: Generating situational criteria. *Journal of Gerontology, 33,* 851.

derstanding charts and schedules. Cornelius, Caspi, and Harnum (1983), however, found that among older adults, indicators of Gf and Gc (both general intelligence factors) were positively related to a *general* measure of coping and negatively related to a *general* measure of defensiveness. However, these relationships were less strong when *situational* measures of coping were used. In this fashion, the Scheidt and Schaie (1978), Willis (1982), and Cornelius et al. (1983) research studies provide a starting point for understanding those abilities common to a variety of everyday intellectual situations (i.e., their adaptive value) and thus can enable us to design training programs more precisely in order to enhance adults' use of these basic everyday skills.

ALTERNATIVE THEORIES ABOUT INTELLIGENCE AND AGING: BALTES'S AND DENNY'S CONTRIBUTIONS

More recently, P.B. Baltes, Dittmann-Kohli, and Dixon (1984) have proposed a theory of life-span intellectual development that does not rely on the notion of stages. P.B. Baltes et al. (1984) instead suggest a *dual process* concept of intellectual development, emphasizing a distinction between the **mechanics** (basic cognitive skills such as speeded performance of Gf), and the **pragmatics** (reflecting more organized systems of knowledge, e.g., social intelligence, wisdom, Gc) of intelligence. The mechanics of intelligence are more structural and involve basic skills such as logic, information processing, and problem solving. The pragmatic aspect of intelligence is more applied or adaptive and thus reflects intelligent behavior in a specific context or situation. What characterizes the early years (infancy, childhood, adolescence) is the development of mechanics, while "intellectual pragmatics appear to be the centerpiece of intelligence during adulthood and old age" (P.B. Baltes et al., 1984, p. 64). During adulthood, intellectual mechanics "involve adjusting to losses in related functions with aging," while pragmatics "undergo further changes during these periods due to developmental changes in goals and contexts" (P.B. Baltes et al., 1984, p. 64).

Within normal limits, P.B. Baltes et al. (1984) suggest that while mechanics form the basis for pragmatics during adulthood, the mechanics of intelligence could be trained or improved (see P.B. Baltes & Willis, 1982) if necessary. According to P.B. Baltes et al. (1984), future research would involve "testing the limits" of older persons' pragmatic/mechanistic aspects of intelligence. Thus, intervention research with older persons (see Box 6.1) might improve the mechanics of intelligence and therefore indirectly affect its pragmatics. Even under the best conditions, however, regarding mechanics, younger persons will outperform older persons, while the opposite is true for the pragmatics of intelligence.

Baltes et al. (1984) see intelligence in adulthood as enabling the individual to *cope* with a variety of age-graded, history-graded, and nonnormative events (see Chapter 1). Intelligence thus helps all individuals to *selectively optimize* (enhance) their continued growth, or to compensate for biological/ social losses by narrowing their frame of reference, so to speak. They may apply their pragmatic abilities to problems that affect them personally. All of this is accomplished within the context of each individual's own life history and current life situation. Intelligence in adulthood, then, helps different individuals in different ways to master life's problems and age successfully, consistent with each person's interests, interpersonal/financial resources, educational background, health, and current environment. In contrast to Schaie's approach emphasizing structural change (i.e., stages), P.B. Baltes et al. (1984) advocate a more functional (adaptive) approach to intelligence in adulthood.

The "dual process" approach of Baltes can be compared to Denny's (1982) distinction between **unexercised** ability and *optimally* **exercised** (improved via use or training) ability. In contrast to Baltes, Denny maintains that both unexercised and optimally exercised abilities will decline with increased age during adulthood (see Figure 6.9). Furthermore, due to biological and environmental factors (poor health, isolation from others), the differences between the levels of unexercised and optimally exercised abilities will be least for a given person during childhood and old age versus during adolescence and adulthood. It is important to see that Denny's distinction is a quantitative one (unexercised/optimally exercised ability), while Baltes's is a qualitative one (mechanics vs. pragmatics of intelligence).

GETTING AN ACCURATE PICTURE: INFLUENCES ON INTELLIGENCE TEST PERFORMANCE

In interpreting any test finding, or more generally data on intelligence and age, we need to be aware of the fact that other factors contribute to the measured performance on our test(s) of intelligence (recall our discussion at this chapter's outset). We *assume* that whatever index or score we obtain from an individual accurately reflects that quality or qualities we term intelligence, but does it? What Botwinick (1970a) and Furry and P.B. Baltes (1973) have

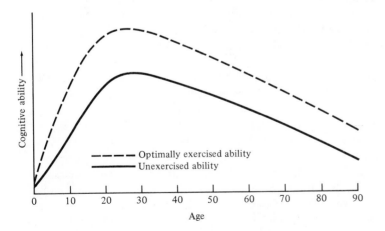

Figure 6.9 Denney's curves for unexercised and exercised abilities. Developmental functions of unexercised and optimally exercised cognitive abilities. *Source:* Nancy Wadsworth Denney, "Aging and Cognitive changes," in *Handbook of developmental psychology,* B. Wolman, ed., © 1982, p. 819. Reprinted by permission of Prentice-Hall, Inc., Englewood Cliffs, New Jersey.

termed *noncognitive* factors or *ability-extraneous* factors can cover up or cloud the accurate assessment of an individual's skills and create a falsely negative picture of intellectual deficits, with sometimes disastrous consequences for the individual (recall our opening discussion). We will discuss the influence of noncognitive factors on learning in adulthood in Chapter 7.

Interestingly, M. Lachman and Jelalian (1984), using tests of Gc and Gf, have found older and younger adults to attribute good performance to their own ability but poor performance to task difficulty. In other words, successes were internalized and failures were externalized. Moreover, despite the fact that others may have attributed their success to luck and their failure to a lack of ability, older persons were nevertheless accurate in estimating their own strengths and weaknesses, consistent with the attributions they made for good or poor performance. Perhaps this "style of attribution" can be traced to a lifetime of self-assessment (one comes to know what one is or is not good at). It can also be that this attributional style is an ego defensive response to the message from others that one *necessarily* becomes less able with age. Thus, the older person takes credit for personal strengths and attributes weakness to the difficulty of the task, *rather than* to lessened ability. Much of this tendency to externalize failure may be due to the relative difficulty/unfamiliarity of many tasks (e.g., Gf) put to older persons (Cornelius, 1984).

Using Intelligence Findings Intelligently with Adults

Regardless of our theory, for *interpretative* purposes, we must take into account the effects of such factors as the clarity of the test materials, whether the individual understands the nature of the task or not, whether the individual is fatigued or anxious, whether the task demands a speeded response or not, and perhaps most importantly, the individual's overall attitude toward the testing. Is the testing important or meaningful to the individual? What does the individual think (or fear) will become of the data? How will the person react to success or failure?

Recent research dealing with older adults (Botwinick, 1977; Cornelius, 1984; Denny, 1982; Storandt, 1977) has tended to place less emphasis on the importance of noncognitive factors such as response speed *per se* (the use of time limits when examining an individual) or fatigue (Cunningham et al., 1978; Furry & P.B. Baltes, 1973; Hayslip & Sterns, 1979; Furry & K.W. Schaie, 1979) than was the case earlier (see P.B. Baltes & Labouvie, 1973). In practice, however, it is wise to assume that these factors influence performance to a certain extent for adults of all ages, particularly those who lack formal education or have poorer self-images or poorer health. Such persons may not have confidence in or recent practice with their existing skills. Perhaps these persons are also the most failure prone and therefore will be more likely not to take credit for successes that they *do* experience during testing. Consequently, establishing rapport, clearly explaining the purpose of the testing as well as what is to be done with the data obtained, and conducting the testing at a pace that the individual sets are very important. It is also imperative that one clearly explain (rereading if necessary) the instructions preceding a task (and perhaps include practice items) and reduce the individual's anxiety about failure (Hayslip, 1989; Labouvie-Vief & Gonda, 1976; Kooken & Hayslip, 1984), utilizing a setting that is quiet and adequately lighted. Rewarding the individual for attempting to solve every item (Birkhill & Schaie, 1975) can be very helpful.

Doing such things will make it more likely that the obtained test scores *accurately* reflect the individual's underlying skills and abilities (intelligence) and thus not simply reflect the individual's level of competence *specific* to the test situation (Schaie & Geiwitz, 1982). If older persons attribute success to their own abilities and efforts (see our discussion on page 222), it makes sense to create a testing situation that makes such success likely.

While the level of an individual's performance may decline with age, its *quality* may not (Botwinick, West, & Storandt, 1978). Rewarding individuals for responding more quickly (Denny, 1982; Hoyer, Labouvie, & P.B. Baltes, 1973) and using cohort appropriate (age-fair) materials (the older Wechsler-Bellevue memory scale versus the newer WAIS-R digit span) (Popkin, K.W. Schaie, & Krauss, 1983) can also ensure that performance reflects the individual's underlying ability.

Many (Botwinick, 1977) feel, however, that if it is *performance* one is interested in, then the above influences on such performance (fatigue) may be of interest in themselves. For example, if one has a job that is by nature physically or mentally fatiguing (accounting), then one's susceptibility to fatigue might be of interest.

In interpreting the evidence we have discussed regarding intelligence and age, factors such as cohort differences in education (K.W. Schaie, 1983) and individual differences in level of education (in that those most highly educated and/or most able decline the least) (see Botwinick, 1977) make it difficult to assign a causal role to the aging process. Moreover, such factors as selective survival (where the most able are likely to live the longest, positively biasing both cross-sectional and longitudinal estimates and terminal drop [see Chapter 3]) and the lack of recent use of one's once-intact skills all "muddy the waters," so to speak, regarding whether intelligence declines or not with age. Considering these factors, we certainly might question whether low test scores necessarily imply lessened ability, *even* among younger adults. Interpreting scores in light of existing norms may create further problems, given the tremendous variability among adults and cohort differences in the level of performance for many abilities (K.W. Schaie, 1979; K.W. Schaie & J.P. Schaie, 1977). An individual's intelligence test scores are thus better utilized *ipsatively* (on a within-person basis, by creating a profile of high and low abilities) to examine that person's strengths and weaknesses relative to one another. Rather than complicate matters by comparing this person to someone else, using test scores in this way enables us to understand that individual more completely.

Certainly, you are not at your "best" when you take an exam after you have stayed up all night. Moreover, if you are anxious, or do not understand what is asked of you, your test performance will most likely suffer. This should perhaps make it easier to understand the difficulties involved in accurately assessing intelligence among adults.

Just as you would want to be treated "fairly" in situations (where your course grade is on the line), you should approach the measurement and assessment of intelligence in adulthood with similar fairness and accuracy where the implications of such decisions about who is intelligent and who is not are no less far-reaching. Where inferences about one's intelligence are being made, getting accurate data and using that data wisely are equally important to young adults and older adults.

SUMMARY

Regardless of our age, our own (or others') assessments of how intelligent we are is likely to be important to us. While intelligence can be defined in numerous ways, one's definition of intelligence hinges on personal bias about intelligence and the behaviors one is attempting to predict or understand via the use of the term.

Based upon early biases about whether IQ continues to increase or not with age, a mental age based concept of intelligence was abandoned in favor of one where individuals could be compared to others of their own age. While this remains the most popular method of measuring intelligence, it reflects a bias against older adults in the IQs so derived.

The *psychometric* approach treats intelligence as a *structural* concept—it is composed of various well-defined abilities that relate to one another in various ways. These abilities can be identified by a technique known as *factor analysis.* A number of theories about how intelligence is structured have been proposed, ranging from a simple *1-factor* approach to a complex *120-factor theory.* The Cattell and Horn 2-factor theory of *crystallized* and *fluid* intelligences and the Thurstone 7-factor *primary mental abilities* (PMA) approach have most influenced research on intelligence in adulthood. The *information processing* approach to intelligence specifies the underlying processes individuals use when they behave intelligently.

Intelligence does *and* does not decline with increased age, depending upon how one chooses to define and measure it. Research by K.W. Schaie and by John Horn has confirmed the complex nature of intelligence in adulthood. Its growth and development depend upon both the influence of the immediate environment *(time of measurement)* and cultural differences between *cohorts* of individuals born at different points in historical time.

In light of research on intelligence and age, it is important to distinguish between *cognitive* (ability-sensitive) and *noncognitive* (ability-extraneous) influences on intelligence. Noncognitive influences often cover up what might otherwise appear to be adequate intellectual functioning, particularly among elderly persons. When allowances for these influences are made, one can more accurately assess an individual's true abilities.

KEY TERMS AND CONCEPTS

Intelligence

IQ

Mental age

Deviation IQ

Age credit

Age debit

Structure of intellect

Factor analysis

Crystallized ability

Intellectual plasticity

Information processing

Primary mental abilities

Wechsler Adult Intelligence
Scale (WAIS)

Noncognitive influences

Functional ability

Psychometric tradition

Structure of intellect

Spearman's two-factor theory

Fluid ability

Postformal thinking

Schaie's stage theory of adult
intelligence

Mechanics versus pragmatics
of intelligence

Exercised versus unexercised
abilities

- Why is the study of learning and memory in adulthood important?
- In what ways are learning and memory similar? How are they different from one another?
- Define interference. What is its relationship to learning and memory?
- Why is the context in which learning and memory occur important in adulthood?
- What is the difference between rote and mediated learning?
- What is the difference between a structural approach and a process-oriented approach to understanding memory?
- What is a levels of processing approach to memory? How does it help us to understand memory and aging?
- What is the distinction between cognitive and noncognitive influences on learning and memory in adulthood? What are some examples of noncognitive factors affecting performance?
- What is task pacing? How does it affect learning and memory in younger versus older adults?
- What is ecologically valid learning? What are some examples of ecologically valid learning tasks that have been used with older adults?

CHAPTER • 7

COGNITIVE

PROCESSES II:

LEARNING AND

MEMORY

■

INTRODUCTION

Learning and memory during the adult phases of the life cycle have been areas of great interest in the last decade (see Arenberg & Robertson-Tchabo, 1977; Kausler, 1982; Labouvie-Vief & Schell, 1982; Poon, 1985). Moreover, understanding how adults learn has many implications for the individual's well-being, regardless of age (Ansello & Hayslip, 1979; Birren & Woodruff, 1973b; Hayslip & Kennelly, 1985; K.W. Schaie & Willis, 1978; Sterns & Mitchell, 1979). Indeed, continued growth and change is one of the hallmarks of human development, as we pointed out in Chapter 1.

In an era when universities face the prospect of declines in the numbers of traditional (18–22 years of age) college-age students (see Box 7.1), it becomes imperative that the basic processes of learning and memory as well as whether one's learning and memory skills vary with age be clearly understood. Moreover, educators face the challenge of designing appropriate learning environments that provide these **nontraditional** older students who want to upgrade their existing skills or acquire new skills with the best possible means to do so (see Lumsden, 1985). Ideally, learning environments or training programs in adult education should reflect the interests, strengths and weaknesses, background, and goals of the individual adult learner. For these reasons and others, understanding how adults learn and whether this ability declines with age is important.

For instance, making decisions about adults of *all* ages regarding entrance into college, promotions, mandatory retirement, institutionalization, job performance and/or retraining, or the ability to benefit from counseling requires that we be able to assess each person's skills in one manner or another. In each of the above situations, inferences about the adult's abilities or potential are being made (see Chapter 6).

Literally *all* the topics we deal with in this text are related to our capacity to learn, remember, and solve problems (e.g., intelligence, personality, interpersonal relationships, parenthood, or retirement). Experiences about nearly endless topics are accumulated and processed by each of us. If we could not do this, we would never have been able to learn from the

BOX 7.1

DEFYING TRADITION: OLDER STUDENTS ATTEND COLLEGE

A Census Bureau report released [recently] says that during the 1970s the college population became older and increasingly female.

The report, "School Enrollment—Social and Economic Characteristics of Students," surveyed school enrollments for 1980 and 1981.

The shifts in education it reflects are posing new and difficult choices for policymakers. For example, at a time when officials are debating the proper focus of college-student-aid programs, the survey found that 52 percent of college students are now 22 or older, defying the traditional notion that a college student is a young person who is still able to rely on parents for support.

Students aged 18 and 19 represented 25 percent of the total number of college students, according to the report, down from 31.6 percent in 1970.

Meanwhile, the proportion of students aged 25 to 29 increased from 11.4 percent in 1970 to 14.2 percent in 1981. The proportion of students aged 30 to 34 nearly doubled between 1970 and 1981, jumping from 5 percent to 9.9 percent.

Education Secretary William Bennett, defending his controversial proposals to cut college-student aid, has argued that families could make up much of the difference by belt tightening and better financial planning.

More recently, Emily Feistritzer of the National Center for Education Information, sparked an emotional debate in the education community when she wrote in a column for *The Washington Post* last month that older students have been hogging student aid intended for the 18 to 22 year olds.

"We are now seeing younger, poorer seekers of higher education competing with older, richer ones

Age breakdown of college students

Student age	1981	1970
14–17 years old	1.9	3.2
18–19 years old	25.1	31.6
20–21 years old	20.9	22.6
22–24 years old	16.4	16.5
25–29 years old	14.2	11.4
30–34 years old	9.9	5.0
Over 35 years old	11.5	9.5

for long-term, low-interest federal loans as the newcomers take advantage of a program that was not created for their benefit," she wrote. Her column sparked some angry responses from older students who contended that they are not in a better position to pay the high cost of a college education.

According to the Census report, much of the growth in the older student population can be attributed to women. Women students in the older age-groups more than doubled their numbers between 1970 and 1981.

"You just can't look at higher education in the same old way," said Allan Ostar, president of the American Association of State Colleges and Universities. He said the shifting student population is changing the way professors teach, since older students who work tend to be more demanding and prefer evening classes.

Source: *Dallas Times Herald* (November 1985).

experiences as children that enabled us to become parents. Nor could we learn from our school experiences, which make it possible for us to make decisions about our careers. Indeed, all that has happened to us throughout our adult lives would cease to have meaning if we did not learn or could not remember (Kausler, 1982).

229

Learning and Memory Deficits: A Consequence of the Aging Process?

LEARNING AND MEMORY DEFICITS: A CONSEQUENCE OF THE AGING PROCESS?

Despite the potential of continued learning to guide our development throughout our adult lives, the major issues and concerns regarding learning and memory have been usually limited to childhood or old age. For example, we might want to know at what age humans begin to learn, or whether they cease learning when they reach a certain age. Answers to such questions might, for example, influence decisions we make about whether to retire or not, or whether to institutionalize an elder.

While psychosocial issues (parenthood, divorce, work, sexuality, and marriage) are often linked to young adulthood or middle age, many feel that it is only when we discuss late adulthood that the topics of learning and memory should be considered crucial. There are several problems with this reasoning. First, it segregates the study of learning and memory in adulthood from the study of aging. Second, it reflects a continuing bias or myth that implicitly suggests that older adults *cannot* continue growing cognitively. A moment's thought reveals the folly in such reasoning. Indeed, *all* of us suffer from memory lapses or have difficulty in learning from our experiences from time to time. Yet memory loss or learning difficulties are rarely concerns of most adults until they sense that it may be "appropriate" for them to be experiencing such problems. Though they may be transient, such difficulties convince many that "they must be getting old." To further make our point, not many college students today would give a second thought to forgetfulness, whether it be on an exam or in an everyday social situation (e.g., forgetting a phone number, someone's name, or an address). Nor would they necessarily be concerned about their difficulty in mastering new material— they might instead feel that the material was too difficult or that they had not studied enough. Yet for older adults in the classroom or in everyday life, such difficulties might be seen as a sign of impending "senility"—a cause for alarm, anxiety, or depression. This "senility" myth leads some to feel less self-confident; it may cause them to lose their self-respect. Other people may indeed expect less of them because they are forgetful. A vicious cycle has thus been established. Further problems with learning or memory create more worry, and such worry contributes to more difficulties in concentration, thereby interfering further with one's learning and memory skills. Thus, learning difficulties or memory loss with increased age become a "self-fulfilling prophecy" for some. For this reason alone, it is important to separate fact from myth. Does age bring with it such losses? Are they reversible? Under what conditions and for what types of individuals do we observe such losses?

It is with these questions in mind that we now turn to the topic of memory
and learning in adulthood. Before doing so, let us briefly discuss exactly what
we mean by learning and memory. After our review of memory and learning
in adulthood, we will discuss factors that get in the way of your efforts to
learn or recall information, whether it be what you had for lunch yesterday
or the name of your first household pet.

LEARNING AND MEMORY: DEFINITION AND MEASUREMENT IN ADULTHOOD LEARNING

Learning is usually understood in terms of the acquisition of *stimulus-response
(S-R) associations* (Kausler, 1982). In other words, all learning is associative. The
stimuli (S) eliciting or evoking a response (R) may lie in your environment
(a sound causes you to turn your head) or be produced by you yourself (a
sensation of pain in your leg causes you to walk more slowly). Kausler (1982)
suggests that these stimuli firstly evoke an internal, inferred (S-R) connection
to them. This connection may be a particular thought or image (the sound I
heard means class is over). This internal S-R connection, in turn, leads to or
mediates the observable, external response (R) (putting one's notes away and
leaving the classroom). In either case, a threshold (a certain loudness of sound
or a critical level of pain) must be reached in order for you to respond
appropriately (Kausler, 1982).

Learning has also been defined as a systematic change in behavior
"that occurs in some specified situation" (W. Estes, 1975, p. 9). It usually
implies some effort or intention on the part of the learner. **Memory**, on the
other hand, has been defined as a more abstract process, also dependent upon
experience, but not necessarily tied to a specific situation, as is learning (W.
Estes, 1975; Kausler, 1982)

Craik (1977) suggests that how learning and memory are defined depends on one's point of view. From an *S-R associative* point of view (the one
we have just discussed), learning involves the *acquisition* over time of S-R units
(i.e., a stimulus-response pair that has presented for a fixed number of trials)
where forgetting is defined as the *breakdown* (loss) of these associations (usually assessed somewhat later; hence the use of such terms as *short-term* or
long-term memory). In contrast, an *information processing approach* deals with one's
memory for information to be learned that is presented only once, and the
individual's memory for such information is understood in terms of factors
affecting the **registration, encoding, storage** and **retrieval** (all types of cognitive processes) of this material.

In research on learning in adulthood, two basic *types* of learning have
attracted the most attention: **rote learning**, where an association is acquired
repetitively (by simply going over and over the material) and **mediated learning**, where the learner utilizes a visual or verbal mediator that has been
acquired in the past (e.g., 30 days hath September, April, June, and November . . .). This mediator links the stimulus and response elements of the
association together (using this rhyme to recall that February only has 28

days). The more active rehearsal or the more efficient use of a mediator by the individual, the more effective learning and memory should be. While more rote learning or better mediated learning usually makes for more efficient performance in younger adults (see Schmeck, 1983), this does not necessarily hold when explaining how older adults learn and recall information, as we shall see.

We can also distinguish between memory for general rules or basic meaning, termed **generic** or **semantic** memory, and memory for specific events, termed **episodic** memory (Craik, 1977; Kausler, 1982). One's memory for specific events or general rules may be enhanced via learning the material either rotely or via the use of mediators, depending on a number of factors, which we will discuss below.

Measuring learning in adulthood usually involves creating a situation (a paired associates or serial learning task) where such associations can be acquired, while memory for these tasks is assessed somewhat later (by asking the individual to recall those associations acquired during learning). Typical learning situations or tasks that allow us to measure and understand both learning and memory are illustrated in Table 7.1.

Distinguishing Between Learning and Memory

Though we have treated learning and memory as separate, in reality they are related to one another. Because both learning and memory cannot be observed directly, they must be *inferred* from performance (a test score). They are often difficult to separate logically, though. When one's ability to learn a list of words is assessed, it is often only through the *recall* of that list that conclusions about how many words one has learned are reached. One cannot recall information that has not been learned to some extent. As Botwinick (1978, p. 261) states, "If a man does not learn well, he has little to recall . . . If his memory is poor, there is no sign of his having learned much." Thus, in practice, the distinction between these two processes is often difficult to make. For example, in studying for a test, you acquire information by reading, organizing, and reviewing. If your test is in two days, you must be able to store or hold that information for a time until you retrieve it when you actually take your exam. Thus, we infer your learning and memory for the test material on the basis of your test score.

MEMORY—STORES AND PROCESSES

Memory in adulthood can be understood via an emphasis on memory *structures* and the use of associated memory *processes,* as illustrated in Table 7.2 (p. 233). This manner of studying memory implies that there are distinct *structures* or "hypothetical entities" defining memory. Typically, differences between sensory, primary, secondary, and tertiary memory stores are expressed in terms of the *time* elapsing from exposure to recall of information.

While such terms as short-term or long-term memory as well as work-

TABLE 7.1

EXAMPLES OF PAIRED ASSOCIATES AND SERIAL LEARNING TASKS

Paired Associates Task

Trial 1		Trial 2	
Stimulus	Response	Stimulus	Response
ocean	water	ocean	_____
dream	sleep	dream	_____
eagle	bird	eagle	_____
hand	foot	hand	_____
blue	sky	blue	_____
woman	man	woman	_____
dark	light	dark	_____
stomach	food	stomach	_____
dog	cat	dog	_____
bow	arrow	bow	_____

Serial Learning Task

Trial 1

Stimuli are presented in a fixed serial order (e.g., ocean, dream,
eagle, hand, blue, woman, dark, stomach, dog, bow).

Trial 2

Each stimulus is presented, whereupon the individual responds
with the stimulus that should follow. Feedback is given; the
presentation of each stimulus should serve to elicit the next item
in the list.
E.g., ocean *(response)*,
  dream *(response)*,
  eagle *(response)*, etc.

Note: The S-R pairs in the Paired Associates Task are first presented together on Trial 1, followed
by a second trial in which each stimulus is presented singly, to which the individual responds
with the correct associate. The second trial might also be presented where the correct S-R pair
follows the person's response.

ing memory are often used (see Craik, 1977; Fozard, 1980), we will adopt for
the present those used by Poon (1985), namely the **sensory**, **primary**, **second-ary**, and **tertiary** memory stores.

Briefly, each memory store serves a different function within our mul-
tistore memory system (see Table 7.2). *Sensory memory* is preattentive or
precategorical—what exists is in the form of unprocessed image. As Craik
(1977) notes, the notion of capacity is somewhat difficult to apply when

TABLE 7.2

233

Memory—Stores and
Processes

MEMORY STRUCTURES AS SEEN FROM AN INFORMATION PROCESSING POINT OF VIEW AND EVIDENCE FOR AGE DEFICITS IN EACH

Memory Structure	Major Characteristics	Age Deficit
Sensory store (iconic-visual information, echoic-auditory information)	Preattentive, very short duration of memory trace (e.g., ½ second).	yes/no
Primary memory short-term store (measured via serial recall of a span of letters, digits, or words)	Temporarily (e.g., up to a minute) stores and organizes information—information is processed in terms of its physical qualities (e.g., loudness, form, location, brightness). Limited capacity, relatively short duration. Memory trace decays unless further processed.	yes/no
Secondary memory (measured via learning/retention of lists of words)	Relatively short duration. Stores newly learned information. Involved when primary memory capacity is exceeded.	yes
Tertiary memory (long-term store)	Permanent duration, very large capacity. Highly organized episodically (regarding time and place) or semantically (regarding personal meaningfulness) recall of overlearned information.	yes/no

Source: Adapted from J. Fozard. (1980). A time for remembering. In L. Poon (Ed.), *Aging in the 1980's: Psychological Issues* (pp. 273–290). Washington, D.C.: American Psychological Association.

discussing sensory memory. Instead, items in sensory memory are said to decay very rapidly (within ⅓ to 1 second). *Primary memory* contains items that are within one's conscious awareness. Our access to this information is limited; it decays if it is not processed further. As Poon (1985) states, while its capacity is small, primary memory "plays an important role in the control and assimilation of information" (p. 431). It serves more as a "temporary holding and organizing *process* than as a structured memory *store*" (Craik, 1977, p. 387). When the older adult's attention/attentional resources are divided, age deficits are more apparent (Craik, 1977).

When material to be remembered exceeds primary memory, it enters the *secondary memory* store, whose capacity is less limited (5–7 items). This is most likely what the layman refers to via the use of the term *short-term memory*. Age differences (favoring young adults) are commonly found in measures of secondary memory (immediate or delayed recall of longer spans of digits, paired-associates, designs) (Poon, 1985), though more highly educated, brighter older adults may maintain more efficient memory systems.

While short-term storage in part encompasses both primary and secondary memory, tertiary memory, whose storehouse is limitless and permanent, refers to recall of remote events or extended recall for recent events. Researchers studying remote or tertiary memory typically use questionnaires to gather their data. Using this approach, there is minimal evidence for a decrement with age in tertiary memory (Poon, 1985).

Given the recent attention to memory processes, it is perhaps better to consider the sensory-primary-secondary-tertiary memory distinction as a continuum, rather than as distinct memory stores (Craik, 1977). We might also be interested in how adults *use* various memory processes to deal with material that has been encoded (learned) and stored for varying amounts of time in each of these memory stores. Figure 7.1 (modified from Craik, 1977, p. 386) illustrates how each of these stores can be linked together via memory processes.

Rather than rely solely on memory structures, a newer, more widely accepted approach to memory (Craik, 1977; Poon, 1985) emphasizes processes that account for *how* material is transferred from one memory store to another. These processes, referred to as *registration, encoding, storage,* and *retrieval,* (see Figure 7.1) build upon and interact with one another. *Registration* refers to whether the material is literally heard or seen (its size or loudness exceeds one's sensory threshold). In other words, if you did not hear what someone said or you were not listening or paying attention, we might say that the words spoken did not enter your sensory store—they were not *registered* (see Chapters 4 and 5). Thus, whether information is "registered" or not is an obvious prerequisite for your processing that information in some way so that it can be learned and recalled later. If, for example, an older adult suffers from sensory loss (e.g., poor eyesight), it is unlikely that what has been presented visually will be adequately registered. *Encoding* refers to the process of *giving meaning* to incoming information after it has been registered and has entered the sensory store. Creating a visual or verbal mediator (a rhyme or an image) to help you learn and recall a list of words involves encoding. Encoding

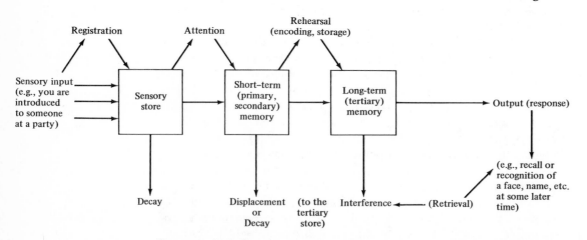

Figure 7.1 Links between memory stores via memory processes. *Source:* Modified from F. Craik. (1977). Age differences in human memory. In J. E. Birren and K. W. Schaie (Eds.), *Handbook of the psychology of aging* (p. 386). New York: Van Nostrand Reinhold. Used with permission of the publisher.

information requires that we attend to and rehearse (actively process) information that has been registered. The ease with which material "stays in" the system is determined by the *efficiency* of the learner's encoding system. *Storage* implies that information, having been encoded in some form, is then *organized* via some overall scheme (in terms of a hierarchic general-to-specific pattern). On the basis of current research, older adults often encode and store information differently from the way younger adults do (they are less likely to spontaneously organize or to use mediators, and they store information less efficiently). A good way of expressing the relationship between encoding and storage is to say that encoding involves *establishing* a memory *trace,* whereas in storage, this trace is *maintained* (rehearsed) until it must be retrieved (Kausler, 1982). *Retrieval* is, quite simply, the "getting out" of the information that presumably has been registered, encoded, and stored. If you are anxious, that anxiety may make it difficult for you to retrieve what you have in storage. (Hence the tip-of-the-tongue phenomenon we have all experienced.) If you cannot recall a name or a date on an exam, we would say that something has **interfered** with either your learning (acquisition [encoding] and storage) or your recall (retrieval) of that information.

UNDERSTANDING LEARNING AND MEMORY IN ADULTHOOD

Interference and Transfer

Obviously, we do not recall everything that we have learned. Moreover, our learning for some things is more permanent than for others. How can we explain this? It is commonly assumed that older persons are more *interference prone* (Goulet, 1972) than are younger persons. Moreover, as observations of many older persons will confirm, the wealth of information that they have acquired can be helpful or hurtful in their learning of and memory for new or old information.

Interference is thought to occur by either *unlearning* and **competition at recall** (Hulse, Egeth, & Deese, 1980; Kausler, 1982). **Unlearning** occurs when this new association interferes with the maintenance of an old association. Thus, the old association loses some of its strength and may be partially or entirely forgotten. For example, learning a new address at college may actually interfere with the recall of your original home address. *Competition at recall* occurs when old associations, perhaps not completely unlearned, interfere with the learning of new associations, leading to our forgetting of newly learned information. For example, learning someone's married name is often difficult if you have known that person by her maiden name all of your life. Table 7.3 illustrates how interference between old and new associations is created via unlearning and competition at recall using remembering names and adjusting to streetlights as examples. If, for example, Miss Jones and Mrs. Smith are *similar* in some way (or perceived to be so), the potential for **negative transfer** (interference) exists. *Negative transfer* occurs when the learn-

TABLE 7.3

EXAMPLES OF UNLEARNING AND COMPETITION AT RECALL IN EVERYDAY LIFE

	Situation 1	Situation 2	Result
Example 1:	$S_1 - R_1$ Person A—Miss Jones	$S_2 - R_2$ Person B—Mrs. Smith	Failure to recall: Miss Jones *(unlearning)* Mrs. Smith *(competition at recall)*
Example 2:	Red light = "stop" (at *top* of streetlight, town #1)	Red light = "stop" (at *bottom* of streetlight, town #2)	If, when you return to town #2, the light changes from yellow to red (at bottom) and you accelerate ("go")—*competition at recall.* If, when you return to town #1, the light changes from yellow to red (at top) and you accelerate ("go")—*unlearning.*

ing of Miss Jones's name or Mrs. Smith's is *interfered with* because of their similarity to one another. To use another example, playing racketball and playing tennis involve similar movements, but playing racketball a great deal usually detracts from one's tennis game (there is negative transfer from racketball to tennis). Learning to ride a tricycle helps in later riding a bicycle, as many of you recall from your childhood. In this case, similarity between activities or types of information creates **positive transfer**.

In working with both younger and older adults, we quite simply want to minimize conditions that make interference (and thus negative transfer) more likely and capitalize on situations that allow for positive transfer from previous learning tasks and situations.

LEARNING, MEMORY AND AGING

Having reviewed the major concepts associated with learning and memory, what conclusions can we reach regarding differences among adults in these processes? What factors contribute to differences with age in learning and memory? How might such differences be understood?

Current research suggests that the ability to learn and remember with age is highly dependent upon a number of factors. Most of this research has concentrated on *verbal learning* performance, using either a **paired-associates** (where pairs of words to be associated are presented together for a certain number of trials) and/or a **serial learning** task (where a string of numbers,

The development of good study habits enhances both learning and memory for
adults of all ages.

words, or letters is presented several times for later recall) to measure learning
and memory (see also Table 7.1). While these tasks per se are relatively
unimportant, they do provide us with examples of the individual adult
learner's behaviors in highly structured learning situations.

While there are little clear age differences/age changes favoring young
adults regarding both sensory and primary memory (Arenberg & Robertson-
Tchabo, 1977; Botwinick, 1984; Craik, 1977; Fozard, 1980; Perlmutter, 1983;
Poon, 1985), age deficits in secondary memory (see Table 7.2) are commonly
found. Moreover, what little information that does exist argues against age
effects in both *iconic* (visual) and *echoic* (auditory) *sensory* memory (Kausler,
1982; Poon, 1985). Indeed, it is difficult to demonstrate that sensory memory

even exists for elderly adults who may be experiencing serious sensory or attentional deficits. Recent evidence by Walsh and Prasse (1980) has suggested that the *rate* at which information can be processed while in sensory memory is *slower* for older versus younger adults. This slowing might be explained in terms of older persons' relative difficulty in *shifting attention* rather than due to a sensory memory deficit per se (Fozard, 1980; Kausler, 1982).

By far the greatest amount of life-span research on learning and memory has focused on *primary* and *secondary memory* (see Table 7.2). Both primary and secondary memory may reflect our ability to recall information that is only seconds or minutes old, though tertiary memory may be involved with even newly acquired information (Craik, 1977). As a general rule, if this information is not actively rehearsed, it will be forgotten. The limits of primary memory seem to be between two and four distinct bits of information (e.g., digits or words) (Craik, 1977). Some researchers (Botwinick & Storandt, 1974b; Hayslip & Kennelly, 1982) have obtained slight age decrements in digit span performance (where digits of varying span lengths [2–7 digits] are read to the individual, and the individual repeats this span either in the same or reversed order). Hayslip and Kennelly (1982), moreover, found larger age decrement for digits backwards (which require more processing and storage effort) than for digits forward. However, the bulk of the evidence to date suggests that primary memory is relatively stable across adulthood (Craik, 1977; Fozard, 1980; Poon, 1985). When the limits of primary memory are exceeded, secondary memory becomes active. In order to keep this information "on tap," so to speak, it must be *actively* rehearsed, processed, or organized in some way. With enough rehearsal, information enters the *tertiary* (long-term) store, which, as we noted above, is nearly limitless and holds information permanently. Arenberg and Robertson-Tchabo (1977) report 6-year longitudinal age deficits in secondary memory across a number of age ranges (30 through 80 years of age) in a highly select sample of men. Such deficits appear to be linked to a more basic problem in encoding and retrieving information (Poon, 1985). When original rates of learning are controlled for, what were formerly believed to be storage deficits with age (borne out of interference, making retrieval more difficult) are nearly absent (Poon, 1985).

It is particularly important that we understand the basis for these findings (age declines in secondary memory) so that efforts to minimize such losses can be developed—it is secondary memory losses to which most of us respond with some concern—"I must be getting old because my memory is poorer than it used to be" is an often-heard remark, frequently indicating not only modest (at the least!) concern about such failures but also a belief in their irreversibility.

While age differences in *tertiary* memory do exist, they tend to favor older adults (Perlmutter & Mitchell, 1982). Deficits with age in tertiary memory are difficult to demonstrate, however, given the confounding of the age of the individual and the age (datedness) of that which is to be recalled (Botwinick, 1984). When we ask someone to recall an event, name, etc. from long ago, we may be assessing *many* things. For example, people who know more, because they are older or are more experienced and educated, may actually appear to show *poorer* long-term memory because what they have stored is more complex and extensive. They place a greater burden on their encoding, storage, and retrieval skills. It may appear that persons who have less material to search through are more likely to appear to have better memories! However, older persons with a greater storehouse of information may be able to recall accurately a *greater percentage* of what they know. Because we do not know exactly what they knew at the time the memory was *originally* encoded and stored, it is difficult to know who has the better long-term memory, younger persons whose "store" is less extensive or older persons who have accumulated more knowledge. If older adults can recall more information removed from the present, it may be because they can efficiently encode and store (rehearse) information that is more personally meaningful to them. When we control (by using items that are equally salient) for rehearsal effects (stemming from the use of items that are differentially personally meaningful) or for the datedness of the information to be recalled (see J.L. Lachman & R. Lachman, 1980), age differences in tertiary memory are nearly absent (Botwinick, 1984; Craik, 1977; Poon, 1985). Where age deficits in long-term memory do exist, they seem to be understood best in terms of the older person's problems in retrieving old information (Botwinick, 1984).

Finding out exactly where (at a point in the system) a person's memory problems are can be accomplished, however, via the use of certain experimental procedures. For example, if the information to be remembered is presented in a **recognition** format (e.g., as in a multiple-choice test) versus a **recall** format (simply asking individuals to recall what they can, as in an essay exam) deficits in *recall performance only* allow us to infer *retrieval* as the locus of the problem. Recognition tests provide learners with definitive support cues with which to direct their retrieval efforts. If a person were to have a memory deficit in both recall *and* recognition situations, this would suggest not only retrieval but also encoding and storage problems. Typically, recognition formats portray fewer age differences than do recall tasks (Poon, 1985), highlighting retrieval as a critical skill that is essential to both secondary and tertiary memory (Craik, 1977; Poon, 1985).

As we learned in Chapter 3, cohort differences are often confounded with age differences in cross-sectional research. A study by Storandt, Grant, and Gordon (1978) clearly suggests that older people remember *more* accurately items pertaining to them personally when they were young. Thus, they have better memories for "old" information, whereas younger adults have better recall of "younger" information! Thus, cohort effects in tertiary memory do seem to exist.

Perlmutter, Metzger, Miller, and Nezworski (1980) asked younger and older adults to make "recency judgments" (judgments about when something occurred historically) for events occurring in each of three time periods between 1862 and 1977. These authors found no age differences in the number of correct dates or correct recency judgments. They did, however, find evidence for an encoding/retrieval deficit with age, where older persons remembered fewer recent events and events in their youth than did younger adults. These authors attribute educational differences between their research subjects and those of Storandt et al. (1978a), and the influence of the media focusing on current events as explanations for their age deficits. While memory for general historical facts may not be impaired, their results indicate that recall for more detailed, episodic, historical information is affected by cohort differences.

Contextual Influences on Learning and Memory Among Adults

Even if one makes an arbitrary distinction between learning and memory, *both* are affected by the *context* or learning environment in which the adult learner functions. Moreover, because we also see this individual as acting upon the environment (see Chapter 1), we can best understand the learning and memory skills of both younger and older adults in *relative* terms. That is, whether one is a superior learner or has a good memory is relative to (1) the *nature of the information* to be learned, (2) the *needs, abilities,* and *motives* of the individual, and (3) the requirements of the *situation* in which one uses learning and memory skills (see Willis, 1985).

Thus, those methods of intervention that we might use to help someone improve learning and memory skills must be flexible—different approaches will work best for some (e.g., organizing material to be learned), while for others, these same methods will fail miserably! Both of these consequences (success or failure of our intervention) must also be understood in light of (1) *what* we are asking someone to learn, (2) that person's own *needs, abilities,* and *skills,* and (3) the *environment* in which the person learns. Our discussion here reflects the *information processing* approach regarding the development and improvement of an adult's learning/memory that we introduced in Chapter 1.

Goulet (1972) has pointed out that the learning-memory distinction is more difficult to make for older adults than for younger adults. Older persons typically need more practice or familiarity with the task used to adequately assess learning and subsequent recall. Thus, for the older adult learner, it is especially important to create an environment that maximizes learning and memory. In understanding learning and memory deficits among adult learners, it would be advantageous (1) to identify the nature of the memory store involved (i.e., *what kinds* of information [old or new] present the most difficulty) and (2) to identify what processes need to be strengthened (*how* was the information processed?).

Willis (1985) has advocated studying the adult learner in terms of efforts to enhance performance. The factors Willis suggests as important in this process are:

1. *The learner's characteristics—factual knowledge,* existing skills versus one's self-assessment or *metaknowledge* of one's abilities, and susceptibility to factors that may interfere with the learning process (e.g., anxiety, fatigue)

2. *Activities/behaviors the individual is expected to engage in*—asking more effective questions, using mediational aids, more effective rehearsal, utilizing techniques to reduce anxiety

3. *Nature of the training/intervention program* regarding *content* (the use of materials that are meaningful, concrete, organizable, clearly read and understood) or *process* (rewarding participants for responding to all items, reducing anxiety, providing feedback, practice with learning materials)

4. *The specific goals/behaviors the learner is expected to acquire*—whether the program is narrowly focused or not in terms of skills to be learned and whether the program's goals are personally meaningful to the learner

Using this fourfold approach (see Figure 7.2), we can come to a fuller understanding of those factors that do and do not facilitate learning throughout adulthood.

Before specifically discussing learning, memory, and aging, we briefly mention a somewhat different approach, emphasizing *levels* of processing (Craik & Lockhart, 1972; Craik, 1977) as a means by which to understand learning and memory. Craik separates **shallow processing**, where only an item's *sensory features* are stored (e.g., the image of a boat) from **deep processing**, where boat is processed and stored *semantically*—in terms of its *meaning* (what does *boat* mean?). While shallowly processed information is more susceptible to interference via a variety of factors (anxiety, fatigue), more deeply

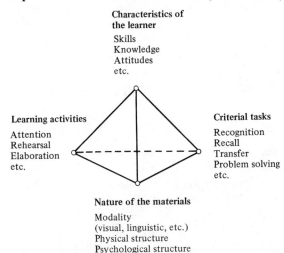

Figure 7.2   Willis's (1985) four-dimensional approach to educational intervention in adulthood: The learner in context. *Source:* Adapted from Jenkins (1979) and Smith (1980). In J. E. Birren & K. W. Schaie (Eds.), *Handbook of the psychology of aging* (2d edition) (p. 835). New York: Van Nostrand Reinhold. Used with permission of the publisher.

processed items are more permanent and less likely to be forgotten. It is commonly assumed (see Craik, 1977) that older adults process information *less* deeply than do younger persons.

PACING AND LEARNING/MEMORY

While deficits in learning and secondary memory (using the paired associates task) have been found when material to be learned is presented at both fast and slow rates of presentation (Arenberg & Robertson-Tchabo, 1977), when various aspects (e.g., the amount of time given to originally learn an item or to search one's memory for a correct response) of the task are **paced** (referring to restricting the time per item or the time between items), age deficits in secondary memory are increased. For example, a paced task would require that one learn and recall material at a fixed rate of presentation (e.g., one item per minute), while proceeding through each item at one's own speed would be learning in an unpaced situation. Older persons make the most errors in learning (recall the fewest correct words) when they are not given sufficient time to *respond.* When the time interval is short in order to *learn* a stimulus-response pair (termed the inspection interval), the memory of older adults is somewhat impaired, but to a lesser degree. Clearly, however, varying the **anticipation interval** (governing the time available to search and retrieve a correct response) seems to be more important in lessening age differences in learning and memory than does varying the **inspection interval**. The inspection interval reflects the time needed to register, correctly associate, and rehearse a particular stimulus-response pair (Arenberg, 1965; Canestrari, 1963; Monge & Hultsch, 1971). Moreover, giving more *overall* time for the task (Kinsbourne & Berryhill, 1972) clearly aids the adult learner in that more time can be taken to register, encode, search, and retrieve an appropriate response.

MEDIATED LEARNING

In addition to pacing, much research has also suggested that a number of factors affecting the effective use of *encoding* determine secondary memory deficits among adults. For example, encouraging and training adults in the use of *verbal* (a verbal association involving the words to be learned) or *visual* (a mental picture involving the words to be linked) *mediators* seems to help matters greatly (Canestrari, 1968; Hulicka & Grossman, 1967; Rowe & Schnore, 1971). Robertson-Tchabo, Hausman, and Arenberg (1976) had great success with the *method of loci,* where the learner was asked to imagine a walk through his home, picking out several stopping points during the journey. The learning/memory of words was greatly helped by instructions to associate each of these familiar loci with each word.

Likewise, specific instructions to *organize* the material (Denny, 1974; Hultsch, 1974, 1975) have been shown to enhance learning/memory. Hultsch (1969, 1971, 1975) has effectively used the alphabet as an aid in the organization of a to-be-learned list of words (e.g., words beginning with *a* might be learned and recalled first, followed by words beginning with *b,* and so on). Schmidt, Murphy, and Sanders (1981) likewise found that specific instructions to organize items by category aided in their recall.

It is especially important to create a "positive environment for learning" by being supportive (Ross, 1968), thus making it more likely that the learner can use any number of learning aids, termed **mnemonic devices**, using visual or verbal mediators or organization by category. It is important to realize that those strategies that you utilize and that might work well for you may not work so well for persons who are older or who can generate their own learning aids (Treat & Reese, 1976; Treat, Poon, & Fozard, 1981). In some cases, those individuals may be incapable of generating their own "helpers" (termed a basic *mediational deficiency*) or may simply not wish to use mediators of their own or those that you might provide them (termed a *production deficiency*). Additionally, it may be helpful to reward the individual for making any effort, even if it is wrong (an error of commission). Research by Leech and Witte (1971) has shown that rewarding the learner (particularly the older adult) for making errors of *commission* (responding incorrectly), as well as correct responses, improves performance. Lessening such errors makes persons better able to take advantage of those mediational aids provided (see Botwinick, 1984).

By being supportive and rewarding any response (right or wrong), the chances for the individual's becoming *inappropriately aroused* (thus interfering with learning or memory) or *anxious* are reduced (see Botwinick, 1984; Eisdorfer, 1968; Furchgott & Busemeyer, 1976; Kooken & Hayslip, 1984; Wine, 1971). For example, you have at some time probably been so "psyched-up" for an exam that this extra energy or emotion actually interfered with your performance. In these situations, perhaps you did not listen carefully to the instructions or failed to read each question carefully. Should you manage to be more relaxed yet still alert, your performance would likely improve. If the task were amenable to the use of a variety of learning aids (mediators, organization), the extra effort that would otherwise be required to deal with your anxiety could be used to deal with the requirements of the task!

The debilitating effects of the inappropriate use of your attention (see Arenberg & Robertson-Tchabo, 1977; Craik, 1977; Craik & Simon, 1980; Hasher & Zacks, 1979; Hartley, Harker, & Walsh, 1980) are also observed in adults when the task itself requires a great deal of *attention.* As we mentioned in our discussion of sensation and perception (Chapter 4), when older persons must *divide their attention* when they are anxious or when they are confronted with a complex task (or a simple task requiring a complex response), their attentional resources are further compromised by having to devote effort to *how* their attention is used (see Perlmutter, 1983; Plude & Hoyer, 1981; Hoyer & Plude, 1980). This leaves them few resources with which to deal with the task itself and to respond appropriately.

A common example of such a situation might involve driving at night on a strange highway. Dealing with your fears about whether you might be lost causes you to miss road signs or perhaps actually causes you to drive *faster* when you should be driving *slower* so that you can read these signs. In this sense, encouraging adults to process information in a more *systematic, orderly* manner would be most helpful (by stopping, trying to relax, getting out the map, or getting out of the car to get one's "bearings"). To the extent that the task *is* affected by the use of attentional processes (see Chapter 4) or is itself a complex task (Wright, 1981), the adult learner will have even further difficulty with the task (Botwinick, 1984). For example, learning to program a computer or running a program at a terminal are complex tasks that demand a great deal of concentration and attention. Many of you have probably had some difficulty with computers because of your "computer phobia"; these fears make a hard task even harder! Once you are able to conquer this fear, working with computers becomes easier.

NONCOGNITIVE INFLUENCES ON LEARNING IN ADULTHOOD

We have raised the question, "How can we best develop the adult's learning/ memory skills?" earlier in this chapter. One approach may be to utilize a variety of **cognitive** interventions affecting the basic processes of learning and memory. We might also choose to focus upon the **noncognitive**, performance-related, or ability-extraneous (Botwinick, 1967) aspects of learning and memory in adulthood. Hayslip and Kennelly (1985) suggest that a variety of noncognitive factors interact with the learning situation and the learner's personality and skills to create an overly negative picture of the adult's continued ability to learn with increased age. Saying that an older person's potential for learning is impaired implies that there is a high correspondence between some *outward* sign of this learning (poor performance on a task) and those *cognitive* abilities or skills that one must infer to exist *inside* the individual. If other factors "cover up" or mask the expression of this underlying ability, they are termed *noncognitive*—they affect the *expression* of these qualities we are really interested in knowing about. For example, your fears about getting lost at night or about failing an exam might actually make it more difficult for you to find your way or to do well on the exam. A number of factors that would be considered noncognitive have already been discussed above: overarousal, willingness to use learning/memory aids, not wanting to guess and be potentially wrong, anxiety about failure, sensory or attentional deficits (see Granick, Kleban, & Weiss, 1976), task pacing, and cautiousness. Among these, we would especially note the importance of minimizing sensory deficits where they exist (see Chapter 4 on sensation), thus enhancing your registration of the material that you must learn and recall. Arenberg (1976), Taub (1975), and Dixon, Simon, Nowak, and Hultsch (1982) have all demonstrated that for material that is personally meaningful and that can be reviewed, visual presentation may be most helpful. On the other hand, for more complex and less familiar material, auditory augmentation of visually presented material may be helpful (e.g., speaking as one is presenting slides). Other noncognitive variables affecting learning/memory are health status (e.g., cardiovascular disorders) (see Abrahams, 1976; Hertzog, K.W. Schaie, &

Gribbin, 1978), perceived relevance of the learning and/or memory task (Calhoun & Gounard, 1979; Hulicka, 1967; Hultsch, Hickey, Rakowski, & Fatula, 1975), and fatigue (Cunningham, Sepkowski, & Opel, 1978; Furry & P.B. Baltes, 1973; Furry & K.W. Schaie, 1979; Hayslip & Sterns, 1979).

Hayslip and Kennelly (1985) point out that when the adult learner must divide attention in complex learning situations, or when *depression* is present (Gribbin & K.W. Schaie, 1978; Kennelly, Hayslip, & Richardson, 1985; Zarit, 1980), becoming fatigued makes the learning and or retention of new material particularly difficult.

As we noted above, depression is often associated with memory deficits among adults (Breslau & Haug, 1983; Salzman & Shader, 1979), particularly when the material to be remembered places demands upon one's use of attentional resources. Persons who show symptoms of depression also tend to evidence more memory complaints (O'Hara, Hinnicks, Kohout, Wallace, & Lemke, 1986). Thus, if depression (see Chapter 13) is suspected, a separate evaluation is in order and, if necessary, treatment is recommended, *prior to* making any efforts at new learning.

Hayslip and Kennelly (1985, pp. 21–22) conclude that when a number of allowances for the influence of noncognitive factors on performance are made, accurate conclusions about older persons' learning and memory capacities can be reached. These factors are listed in Box 7.2.

These recommendations and the research we discussed above on learning/memory emphasize the potential of cognitive interventions in help-

BOX 7.2

SUGGESTIONS FOR IMPROVING THE ADULT LEARNER'S LEARNING AND MEMORY PERFORMANCE

1. using *meaningful*/familiar materials emphasizing prior experience
2. *self-pacing* learning, or providing more overall learning time
3. a sensitivity to the effects of *poor health* and *less* formal *education* on performance
4. compensation for *sensory-perceptual deficits* in the presentation and design of learning materials
5. *sensory enhancement* (e.g., auditory augmentation of material presented visually)
6. providing *practice* with novel materials and/or testing formats
7. minimizing *fatigue*
8. avoiding the creation of an environment that would provoke excessively high levels of *anxiety*
9. using age(cohort)-appropriate *instructions*
10. employing *distributed* (frequent breaks) rather

than *massed* practice, lessening interference and distraction (see Schonfield, 1974)
11. providing and encouraging the use of *organizational cues and mnemonic aids* where possible
12. focusing on *concrete* rather than *abstract* concepts
13. *minimizing interference* by overlearning material
14. *minimizing attentional demands,* especially where the material is unfamiliar, difficult, or complex
15. recognizing and allowing for *individual differences* among adults in learning and memory
16. recognizing the importance of *depression* and its effects on learning and memory

Source: From B. Hayslip & K. Kennelly. (1985). Cognitive and non-cognitive factors affecting learning among older adults. In B. Lumsden (Ed.), *The older adult as learner* (pp. 73–98). Washington, D.C.: Hemisphere Publishing.

ing adults of all ages increase their learning and memory skills. Goulet (1972) and Poon (1985), among others, have noted the importance of the adult's learning the to-be-remembered material to the greatest extent *before* an assessment of memory is made.

Thus, from an intervention standpoint (Willis, 1985), we might improve an adult's learning and memory skills by altering either:

1. the *material* (task) to be learned (by making it more meaningful, or easily seen or heard);

2. the *learner* (by a skills-training program, altering one's *expectations* of success/failure and *motivations* for improvement, or by minimizing noncognitive factors such as anxiety or fatigue); or

3. the *context* in which learning occurs (using instructions that are easily comprehended, task pacing).

Langer, Rodin, Beck, Weinman, and Spitzer (1979), in working with institutionalized elderly, found that by simply providing either interpersonal or practical *rewards* for attending to and recalling recent events in the everyday environment, real improvements in short-term memory could be achieved. Beck (1982) found that when nursing-home residents were provided with incentives for remembering aspects of their daily lives, they not only increased their memory performance but also were rated as more socially involved by the staff.

Much of the research investigating age-related differences in learning and memory has been cross-sectional (Perlmutter, 1983). With a few exceptions (Arenberg & Robertson-Tchabo, 1977), this evidence must be viewed cautiously, to the extent that it simply *describes* the performance of individuals of varying ages who have been presented with various learning and memory tasks. These performance differences varying by age may be confounded by *cohort differences* in learning histories and thus do not tell us about intraindividual age *changes* in learning and/or memory processes (refer to Chapter 3 for a detailed discussion of cross-sectional and longitudinal research methods). A great deal of research, however, has investigated numerous factors that either lessen or magnify these age differences and thus allow us some room for understanding those factors that determine the course of cognitive growth across the adult life span.

Poon (1985) suggests that intervention studies demonstrating the positive benefits of many of the above learning aids on learning and memory performance among older persons reveal (1) great individual and situational differences in the benefits of mnemonic training and (2) short-term but not long-term benefits. Older persons often choose not to use such memory aids, unless reminded to do so (Poon, 1985; Schaffer & Poon, 1982). Attending to the older learner's reasons for using or not using such techniques needs to be our prime focus. "How can such techniques be helpful? How can I benefit from them?" are questions that must be answered up front. It is interesting to note that Cavanaugh, Grady, and Perlmutter (1983) and Schaffer and Poon (1982) have found that "internal" learning and memory aids such as imagery or organization are rarely used by both younger and older adults in everyday situations (see discussion below of "ecologically valid" learning). Instead, they use "external" techniques such as lists, notes, or a string tied to the finger (see Poon, 1985).

ECOLOGICALLY VALID LEARNING

We introduced the concept of *ecological validity* in Chapter 6, referring to the degree to which a task or a procedure to measure learning/memory accurately reflects those tasks that the adult learner actually confronts in *everyday life.* While much work that we have discussed in this chapter has involved arbitrarily chosen lists of words or numbers, more recently investigators have become concerned with the adult's learning of and memory for **ecologically valid** materials. What is ecologically valid regarding the everyday learning/ memory demands of adults of varying ages is itself a question yet to be fully answered (Hartley, Harker, & Walsh, 1980). Clearly, however, there is a recent concern for ecologically valid (relating to the everyday context) learning and memory in adulthood.

Relative to research with paired associates tasks, relatively little research to date has been conducted with ecologically valid learning tasks. We will briefly touch on two areas in this newly emerging field: learning of or memory for *text materials,* and *metamemory.*

Memory for Text and Aging

Botwinick (1984), Hartley, Harker, and Walsh (1980) and Hultsch and Dixon (1984) reach different conclusions regarding *memory for text* (sentences, prose paragraphs). This is not unusual in a newly emerging area of research. While Botwinick concludes that age differences in the learning/memory of real-life *discourse* (text material) favor the young, he indicates that the lower levels of *comprehension* in the aged account for memory deficits with meaningful material—a conclusion that again illustrates the relationship between learning and memory that we discussed earlier.

Hartley et al. (1980) point out that these age differences are highly dependent upon *how* comprehension and memory for such materials is assessed (e.g., whether the materials to be learned and recalled are visually or orally presented). Thus, just as in the paired associates learning task, performance in such real-life tasks is also determined by that task's characteristics (is it cohesive or organized?). Hultsch and Dixon (1984) also conclude that while age differences in "text processing" sometimes occur, performance is influenced by a number of factors.

Hultsch and Dixon (1984) argue that text comprehension is an active, constructive process, where the learner processes each sentence selectively, piecing it together with existing knowledge to generate a new interpretation about what a sentence means. Hultsch and Dixon (1984) see the processing of text materials as reflecting a variety of logical operations the learner goes through in constructing the meaning of text, based on a hierarchical organization of arguments (propositions) linked together by verbs. In the learner's mind, arguments may or may not be connected in the text, depending on their relationship to one another. Out of this organization that the learner constructs, a sentence's meaning can be understood and sentences can be linked together and summarized to glean an overall meaning of something that one has read.

Hultsch and Dixon (1984) discuss a number of factors that affect the ability to efficiently process and recall text. Depending upon whether or not the learner is given instructions to process deeply (at the level of meaning) a list of words that precedes the text material, recall of text is enhanced among young adults but interfered with among older persons. Moreover, whether (1) a recall or recognition format is used, (2) recall is immediate or delayed, (3) presentation is oral or visual, and (4) whether one is examining recall for details or for main ideas, all affect the magnitude of age differences in performance. Depending upon their breadth of prior knowledge, level of education, and verbal ability, older *and* younger adults may or may not show adequate memory performance for text material. For those with little prior knowledge of the topic, who are poorly educated, and who have the least verbal ability, performance is poorest. Hartley (1986) found that the effectiveness of reading ability rather than age determined memory for text. Thus, we see that as with traditional verbal learning materials, age differences in the processing of more ecologically valid tasks are also dependent upon a number of factors. Consequently, we must ask the question, "Under what circumstances do age differences in memory for text exist?"

Metamemory

Metamemory refers to "how much we know about what we know" (J.L. Lachman, R. Lachman, & Thronesbery, 1979). The study of metamemory is important because confidence in one's own abilities influences the amount of preparation for or effort put into dealing with everyday tasks. For example, whether one makes a grocery list out or not before leaving for the store depends on a personal estimate of memory skills. A common observation is that many individuals, because they (realistically or not) underestimate their learning or memory skills, rely heavily on calendars, datebooks, or diaries to keep track of appointments or meetings. While we might be tempted to conclude that older persons, realizing that their encoding and/or retrieval skills were failing, would utilize these aids to a greater extent than would younger persons, needing a datebook may be a function of having *more* to organize or remember. On the other hand, *not* using such devices may be due to the fact that one's secretary or administrative assistant does so!

The literature regarding age differences in metamemory is mixed. For example, many (J.L. Lachman & R. Lachman, 1980; Perlmutter, 1978; Rabinowitz et al., 1982) have found that older persons are as accurate in predicting what they can and cannot remember as are younger adults, regardless of whether old or new information is being dealt with. A study by Murphy, Sanders, Gariesheski, and Schmitt (1981), however, suggests that older persons tend to overestimate the extent of what they can remember compared with younger adults. Zelinski, Gilewski, and Thompson (1980), on the other hand, found older adults to be more accurate in estimating their performance than were the young, while Bruce, Coyne, and Botwinick (1982) found age differences in metamemory favoring the young. Moreover, while some researchers have found little relationship between older persons' subjective estimates of their memory skills and objective performance (Poon & Schaffer, 1982; Zarit, Cole, & Guider, 1981), others have found that older persons' predictions about their performance and such performance were related (Poon & Schaffer, 1982). Poon (1985) suggests that the key to resolving these inconsistent findings lies in accurately measuring metamemory.

Despite the mixed character of the evidence, this newly emerging area of research can perhaps provide a more accurate base for training programs for the adult learner. It may be that such programs can be more effective if they are targeted at the particular older learner whose metamemorial skills are poor—perhaps this person has poor self-esteem (Breyspraak & George, 1979). If such persons are depressed (Zarit, 1980), they may not have used existing skills for some time (recall our discussion of Denny's unexercised abilities in Chapter 6), or have become isolated from feedback about the intactness of their skills. Poon (1985) suggests that reminding older learners to use memory strategies that have been learned and proven effective in the past, promoting a greater awareness of one's metamemorial skills, and clearly specifying goals may be viable strategies through which to enhance the memory performance of older persons on laboratory tasks and in everyday situations.

Many of these factors contributing to differences among individuals in metamemory and memory performance might be considered *noncognitive*. In light of the correlation between predictions of memory and performance (see above), improving individuals' *estimates* of their own abilities by reducing anxiety or altering self-perceptions (see Meichenbaum, 1977) might be an effective way of increasing a willingness to become involved in new learning or renovate old skills (Hayslip, 1989) with a subsequent improvement in performance.

Hultsch and Dixon's (1983) research on aspects of metamemory in text recall performance among young and old adults suggested that while a "knowledge" aspect of one's memory skills (awareness of memory aids) related to performance in the young, achievement, motivation, and anxiety aspects predicted performance in older persons. These results reinforce a concern for noncognitive factors as influences on the learning and memory performance of older persons and suggest that we should be interested in adult learners' sense of **self-efficacy** (Bandura, 1977) regarding whether they *should* continue to grow intellectually. As we noted at this chapter's outset, such a point of view may literally be critical to the well-being of many adults, particularly if they value their own competence; perhaps they fear its loss with increased age.

Both formal and informal opportunities for continued learning are important to
many older persons.

EDUCATION AND THE ADULT LEARNER

D. Peterson (1985) sees education as one very powerful means by which to
"normalize" the roles older persons play in our society, as well as an activity
that can preserve the adult's sense of personal dignity and facilitate personal
growth and actualization (Sterns & Mitchell, 1979). Their approach to continued education is self-expressive rather than instrumental (leading to a
clearly defined goal) (Hiemstra, 1976). While research examining the impact
of formal educational interventions with adult learners is rare (Davenport,
1986; Peterson & Eden, 1981), a review by Willis (1985) suggests older persons to be quite capable of acquiring a variety of cognitive skills.

Hiemstra (1985) has reviewed the literature on self-directed learning
(learning that is self-initiated and tied to one's personal experiences—learn-

ing for learning's sake) among adults. Using several criteria, Hiemstra (1985) suggests such learning activities to have positive effects on the degree of involvement in learning, self-esteem, responsibility for self-involvement, and self-fulfillment. This predisposition toward learning (for meaning [internal] versus achievement [external] related reasons) has been termed *learning style* (Schmeck, 1983). Even older adults' learning is affected by learning style. Davenport (1986) suggests that the personal and educational benefits of *Elderhostel* (see Box 7.3) for older participants varies with sex and various learning styles but not age. Kaye, Stuen, and Monk (1985) found factors such as age, sex, previous teaching experience, level of formal education, and both race and ethnicity all to play a role in determining older persons' acquisition of leadership skills in an older adult-teacher training program. Moreover, while these skills were retained on a short-term basis, participants did not always maintain their skill level six months later.

By altering any or all of the above cognitive and noncognitive factors, we can not only encourage the adult learner, who could be as young as age 25 (Hiemstra, 1985), in the pursuit of educational goals but also, and perhaps more basically, reinforce the perception that one's mind can still work quite well! Willis (1985) notes a study by Flanagan and Russ-Eft (1976) who found that among project TALENT volunteers, those in their mid-*thirties* were *least* satisfied with their status regarding the use of their mind "through learning, attending school, improving your understanding, or acquiring additional knowledge." These individuals had been followed up 15 years after having first participated in the project as high school students. Given the generally negative views about changes in one's abilities with age (Ansello & Hayslip, 1979; P.B. Baltes & Labouvie, 1973; L. Harris, 1975; K.W. Schaie & Willis, 1978) held by some persons, it seems as if these individuals might be even more prone to negative self-expectations about their "intellectual life" as they age.

As many (Ansello & Hayslip, 1979; Birren & Woodruff, 1973b) point out, altering expectations about continued learning throughout adulthood can provide an important influence on adults of all ages. (Should they learn new skills? Can they continue to feel productive and worthwhile?) Moreover, interventions that are based upon individual differences in abilities, interests, and both educational and personal goals are critical to enhancing learning skills. Wanting to learn new skills may be influenced by changes in one's career plans or may simply reflect a desire to acquire new knowledge for its own sake (see Daniel, Templin, & Shearon, 1977; Hiemstra, 1985; M. Romaniuk & J. Romaniuk, 1982).

Reflecting this broader perspective toward lifelong learning and education, Willis (1985) has suggested five possible goals that the adult learner might achieve, either through formal educational or through more informal (noncredit, self-directed) educational activities (see Box 7.3). These goals view the goals of education as:

1. aiding the individual in understanding changes in body and behavior that reflect basic biological processes of aging;

2. helping the adult learner to understand and cope with technological/cultural change (becoming computer literate);

3. making possible the development of skills to help overcome the obsolescence created by rapid cultural change (skills that help in maintaining an independent life-style—e.g., comprehending or remembering schedules or forms);

4. helping in the pursuit of second (or third!) careers; and

BOX 7.3

ELDERHOSTEL: CONTINUED OPPORTUNITIES FOR GROWTH IN LATE ADULTHOOD

Using the youth hostels in Europe as a model, *Elderhostel* provides older persons with both intellectual stimulation and physical challenges. Developed by Martin Knowlton in 1975, *Elderhostel* began with five institutions of higher education offering programs to 200 *Elderhostelers.* The growth of the program has since been quite dramatic; in 1983, over 700 schools in the United States and Canada and 67,000 elderly learners participated in *Elderhostel.* Moreover, *Elderhostel* programs are offered in Great Britain, Denmark, Finland, Norway, Sweden, France, Germany, and Holland. They are based "in the belief that retirement does not mean withdrawal, that one's later years are an opportunity to enjoy new challenges" (*Elderhostel* brochure, 1984).

Elderhostel offers a wide variety of liberal arts and science courses at low cost that "explore various aspects of human experience." Students usually enroll for one or two weeks' duration for one to three courses and participate in a variety of extracurricular activities at each campus. There are no exams and no required homework assignments, though instructors often make suggestions for outside reading. Each course assumes no previous knowledge of the subject, so that elders regardless of background can enroll. Participants, living in college dorms and eating with other students, young and old, often travel from campus to campus or combine *Elderhostel* with family visits or vacations.

The following is a smattering of the offerings to *Elderhostel* students. *Elderhostel*'s aim is to provide those interested in continued learning with high quality education that is both rich in content, personally relevant, and fun!

Meet the Southwest
Historical approach to ranching, mining, railroads, and lumbering through on-site visits supplemented by lectures, slides and optional Narrow Gauge Rail trip. Relive the years that the Southwest was "tamed."

Bites, Bytes, the Computer, and You
An introduction to the development and use of microcomputers in the home, classroom and industry. Hands-on experience with word processing, spread sheet, and database software packages. Located in a new computer facility.

Backstage at the Theatre
Class includes involvement with a summer theatre production, including a backstage visit during rehearsals, meeting the actors, learning about sets, costumes, etc., as well as attendance at a performance.

Holistic Health Workshop
Introduction to the holistic health concept, including wellness, prevention and self-responsibility. Intervention for stress-management with relaxation techniques, nutritional support, as well as identification of health and lifestyle behaviors.

Drawing—From the Inside Out
How many times have you said, "I can't draw a straight line!"? Using a step-by-step approach, you will learn how to look at an image and coordinate the use of eyes and hands to interpret your unique vision as a permanent creation.

Comedy, Wit & Humor
Psychology of humor and wit in contemporary America. What makes us laugh? Why? What humor reveals about ourselves, others. Its various forms of expression—political, social, economic are examined through anecdotes, stand-up comics, etc.

Source: *Elderhostel Catalog,* Summer 1988, *Vol.10,* No. 2.

5. facilitating the formation of skills that are personally relevant, rather than occupationally relevant, after retirement (gaining information to find satisfying leisure activities or volunteer roles).

Thus, education can serve many ends for different adult learners at different points in their lives. Moreover, it is important that such efforts begin *early* in adulthood (Ansello & Hayslip, 1979; Willis, 1985), making it more likely that individuals will see their learning and memory skills positively. Such views about one's learning skills not only reflect what existing skills might be used for but also indicate one's potential for developing *new* skills (see Birren & Woodruff, 1973b) for both personal growth and career-oriented reasons (Sterns & Mitchell, 1979). For many adults, there is seemingly no reason to develop their cognitive skills, because these efforts are seen as being doomed to failure, based on expectations of decreased ability with increasing age and a youth-oriented "production mentality" (Ansello & Hayslip, 1979). This mind-set also suggests that one's skills, interests, and abilities *must* lead to the attainment of a well-defined goal (a college diploma, a new or better job, preparation for a future life role [parenthood, retiree]). This shift was dramatically illustrated in a recent poll of college-age students taken by *Newsweek,* showing that greater numbers of students are attending college solely to get better jobs or make more money.

This very orientation may prevent many adults from pursuing their formal education (in terms of both access to such opportunities and the educational process) (Ansello & Hayslip, 1979), or simply hinder the desire for new learning. In encouraging the adult learner to continue to "be alive" mentally, and thus enhance his learning and memory skills, we must not only focus upon cognitive and noncognitive means by which to achieve this (Hayslip & Kennelly, 1985) but also be aware that we must change our attitudes about the underlying reasons for doing so. We can distinguish "instrumental" (goal-oriented) interventions from "expressive" (non-goal-oriented, individually centered) ones in this regard (Danish, 1980; Hiemstra, 1976). Consequently, the *ends* as well as the *means* for enhancing cognitive abilities in both young adulthood and old age need to be given equal consideration.

Robertson-Tchabo (1980, p. 516) has suggested that "the answer to the question, 'Why should old dogs learn new tricks?' is the *same* as that for younger dogs—because they want and need to learn new behaviors." We would add that before our "dog" (old *or* young) has learned his new "tricks," we must closely examine both our own and the "dog's" purpose in wanting to do so. Just as the susceptibility to the variety of cognitive and noncognitive influences on learning and memory will vary with the individual and with the context, so too will the goals of such training or interventions designed to facilitate these skills.

The question of how best to enhance the potential for continued cognitive growth in adulthood, which we initially raised in this chapter, needs to be accompanied by the question, "To what end are these newly acquired skills to be put?" If at all possible, these goals, and the means by which we reach them, should be relevant to the adult's individual abilities, personality, interests, and life situation.

SUMMARY

In this chapter we discussed *learning* and *memory,* which are both *inferred* processes. They are inferred because we cannot observe them directly. Further, they are of great importance and have many implications regarding how all of us develop and learn during the adult phase of the life cycle. We pointed out that learning and memory are separate but interrelated processes, since one cannot remember what has not been learned. Learning in its most basic sense involves the *making* of *stimulus-response (S-R) associations.* Memory (or forgetting) refers to the *breakdown* of these associations. Unlearning and competition at recall are forms of interference that cause this breakdown.

Research in learning and memory during all phases of the adult life cycle has focused upon the distinction between *rote learning* and *mediated learning.* In addition, we can separate a *structural* (sensory, primary, secondary, tertiary memory stores) and a *process* (registration, encoding, storage, retrieval) approach to memory. Deficits with aging occur at the *encoding* and *retrieval* stage of memory processing and in the *secondary* memory stores. Findings for *primary* and *tertiary* memory in some cases are unclear (not definitive) but generally suggest a lack of age effects in performance.

Such deficits, where they exist, can be lessened in learners of all ages. Learning and memory performance can be improved by a number of *cognitive* and *noncognitive* interventions such as using mediators or reducing anxiety. Recently, attention has been directed to the study of learning and memory in *ecologically valid contexts.* The context in which learning occurs has been recognized as an important factor in the design and implementation of adult education and lifelong learning programs that serve a number of diverse needs for the adult learner. We must place equal emphasis on the *ends* as well as the *means* by which to improve the cognitive skills of individuals during all phases of the life cycle.

KEY TERMS AND CONCEPTS

Adult education

Nontraditional student

Learning

Memory

Acquisition

Retrieval

Deep versus shallow processing

Recognition versus recall tasks

Inspection versus anticipation
  intervals

Negative/positive transfer

Paired associates task

Serial learning task

Stimulus-response (S-R)
  associations

Cognitive/noncognitive
  influences

Rote versus mediated
  learning

Ecologically valid learning

Memory for text

Secondary memory

Tertiary memory

Registration

Encoding

Storage

Generic (or semantic) memory

Episodic memory

Interference

Unlearning

Competition at recall

Task pacing

Self-efficacy

Mnemonic devices

Sensory memory

Primary memory

Metamemory

- What role do interpersonal relationships play at all stages of the life cycle? What is a convoy? What functions does it serve?
- What are "interest-related" and "deep" friendships? How do these differ as a function of the individual's age and sex?
- What is filial responsibility, and how does it vary as a function of age, racial/ethnic group, and culture? How is it different from filial maturity?
- What are the major types of interpersonal relationships that are considered marriages, and how are they similar and different?
- Why are individuals attracted to one another? What theories have attempted to explain this attraction?
- Do individuals' ratings of marital satisfaction change throughout the life cycle? What are some of the problems with measuring marital satisfaction?
- What are some of the problems that result in becoming a widow/widower? What factors seem to influence responses to widowhood?
- Why is it difficult to obtain accurate information regarding sexual behavior? How do these problems relate to myths about sexuality and aging?
- What causes spouse abuse and elder abuse? How can this abuse be prevented?
- What are the life-span trends for sexual "interest" and "activity"? What extrinsic and intrinsic factors are related to sexual "interest" and "activity" across the life cycle?

CHAPTER • 8

INTERPERSONAL

RELATIONSHIPS

AND SEXUALITY

■

INTRODUCTION

Life-span trends in interpersonal relationships and sexual behavior are the primary focus of this chapter. Friendships, marriage, sexuality, divorce, and widowhood all play vital roles in determining the quality of our lives throughout adulthood and most directly relate to the **interpersonal** sphere of development (see Chapter 1). It may seem self-evident to most of us, but our relationships to others are critical to our morale, or life satisfaction, and our self-concept, as well as to the maintenance of our physical health (Cobb, 1976).

Kahn and Antonucci (1980) have used the terms *convoy* or *personal network* to represent the interpersonal system of support that we all utilize to help us cope with change. These authors suggest that this convoy serves as a psychological *buffer* to help support us in times of stress—when we are faced with changes in our lives brought on by such factors as marriage, parenthood, illness, retirement, and death. The convoy is especially important in this way when such changes are unforeseen or unwanted. The function of the convoy in adulthood is parallel to that of the infant's sense of **attachment** to its parents. This convoy, however, differs from person to person and changes throughout the life cycle, providing different types and levels of support at different times and in different situations. Kahn and Antonucci (1980) argue that as infants become less and less attached to mother or father (who are both working) as a function of being virtually raised in day care, and less attached to grandparents (who are more likely to be living separately from them), those infants' future needs for support over the life span will change.

Just as "securely attached" children have a firmer base from which to explore their world (Ainsworth, 1973; Ainsworth & Bell, 1972), adults with well-defined convoys of support, who are attached to others at a more intimate level, can also cope with change more effectively (Lerner & Ryff, 1978). Figure 8.1 illustrates a hypothetical convoy (Kahn & Antonucci, 1980).

The concept of the convoy can help us to understand how different types of relationships can fulfill our needs to be wanted and loved, confirm decisions we make, or help us in times of need (Kahn & Antonucci, 1980). As Figure 8.1 illustrates, a typical convoy includes supportive relationships with others that are intimate and stable as well as those that are more instrumental and changing. These include friendships, professional or work rela-

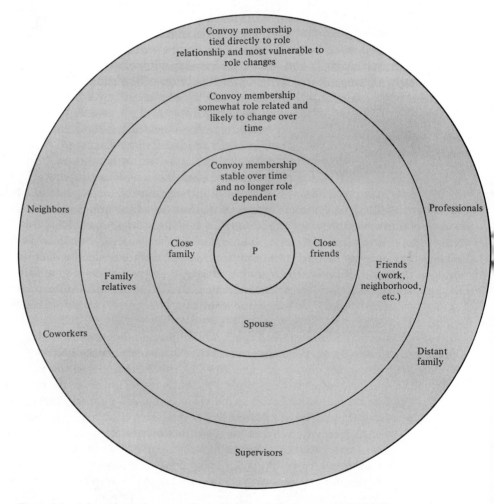

Figure 8.1 A hypothetical convoy. *Source:* R. Kahn & T. Antonucci. (1980). Convoys over the life course: attachment, roles and social support. In P. B. Baltes and O. G. Brim, Jr. (Eds.), *Life-span development and behavior* (Vol. 3, p. 273). Orlando, FL: Academic Press. Reprinted by permission of Academic Press and Robert L. Kahn.

The family is an important component of our personal convoy in adulthood.

tionships, and close family members (parents, grandparents, children, spouse). This relatively new concept of the convoy allows us to consider many different types of relationships that are supportive at various times of our lives and in varying situations. It is the more stable types of relationships that define the convoy (e.g., friendships, close family, and spouse) that we discuss in this chapter. As noted above, aspects of this convoy do change over the life course. In such cases, we are breaking and remaking relationships with others who help define our convoy.

INTERPERSONAL RELATIONSHIPS

As our above discussion implies, regardless of age, people are constantly developing and ending relationships with others in their personal convoys, such as friends, coworkers, and marriage partners. The first year of life is thought to be critical to the foundation of an individual's basic sense of *trust* in others (Bowlby, 1969; Erikson, 1963). Specifically, trust develops on the basis of individuals' experiences with their primary caretakers (mother, father, grandparent, relative) during the first year of life. According to theorists such as Erikson, these experiences serve as the foundation upon which other social and interpersonal relationships are built (O. G. Brim & Ryff, 1978). If we have formed positive relationships with our primary caretakers in the past, we will more likely be able to form meaningful intimate relationships with others in the future. On the other hand, if this first interpersonal relationship has been destructive, we may have difficulty in forming and maintaining interpersonal relationships throughout life. Our convoy becomes ill-defined and unstable; it may not fulfill its supportive function well.

Friendships

WHAT'S A FRIEND?

Friends can be important sources of support and affection; they can give our lives meaning and help us get perspective on things. Friends build a sense of kinship between people, based upon common needs and interests and most of all, a shared trust (R. R. Bell, 1981). To understand this, reflect on a friendship that is important to you. What were you doing when you first met that person? What changes in your life have you been able to share with that person over the years? If you were hurt or experienced a tragedy in your life (for example, the death of someone you loved), would you want that person to be with you? L. Wheeler, Reis, and Nezlek (1983) and Williams and Solano (1983) have found that among college students, feelings of loneliness are primarily determined by whether persons thought they had both *intimate* and *meaningful* friendships with others (Berkowitz, 1986; Penrod, 1986). Larson, Mannell, and Zuzanek (1986) found that among retired adults, friendships were an even greater source of satisfaction than were family members.

While there is some disagreement about what factor is most important in how people choose their friends (based on perceived similarity versus proximity), clearly both of these factors are important (J. L. Freedman, Sears, & Carlsmith, 1981). Moreover, qualities such as honesty, understanding, kindness, and sympathy emerge as clearly important in choosing friends (J. L. Freedman et al., 1981). Self-disclosure (Jourard, 1961) is an important component in the formation and maintenance of friendship.

Papalia and Olds (1982) and R. R. Bell (1981) suggest that before the age of six, friendships are based on more superficial aspects of a relationship, (e.g., similarity in age, gender, activities, physical proximity). After this point, with increasing experience, children are more likely to define friendship in terms of *reciprocity* (give and take) stemming from the ability to consider another person's feelings/perspective on things. Leitner (1977) suggests that reciprocity is an important element in friendship even among children as young as 4½ years (although the children may not be aware of the reciprocity per se in their relationships). For example, children who approach others with a friendly smile and in a noncoercive way are more likely to get a positive response (Papalia & Olds, 1982) from them.

Stevens-Long (1984) suggests that friendships among children in middle childhood (aged nine or older) and among adults are defined in terms of *mutuality,* that is, self-disclosure, commitment, agreement as to norms bearing on how the friendship is to exist. Friendships can therefore have an important socializing influence on us (Dickens & Perlman, 1981) and thus help to strengthen one's personal convoy.

While proximity and similarity may be important components of friendship among the young, C. I. Cohen and Rajkowski (1982) did not find similarity in age or gender to be an important factor in elderly persons' definitions of friendship. "Subjective importance," exclusive of age, gender, physical proximity, or frequency of contact principally separated "friends" from "nonfriends" in these authors' sample of elderly persons living in SRO (single-room occupancy) hotels. Indeed, long-term emotional ties with individuals who did *not* live in the hotel most often defined friends for these individuals. Rather than thinking of the best-adjusted persons as having a great number of friends, we would emphasize the importance of maintaining a few close friendships to help stabilize our convoy of support throughout one's life as reflecting good adjustment.

Studying the role and meaning of friendships at any point in the life cycle reveals that numerous factors may affect friendship patterns (Usui, 1984). These may include such factors as age, gender, race, marital status, ethnicity, religion, occupation, and educational level. Aizenberg and Treas (1985) note that the death of one's spouse often changes friendship patterns that were developed during marriage, though Lopata (1973) suggests that age peers can fulfill an important supportive role in adjusting to widowhood. Gubrium (1973) indicates that upper and middle socioeconomic class elderly have more lasting friendships than do working-class elderly persons. Perhaps this is so because they hold better paying, more stable jobs.

Friendships vary in level. We can distinguish between what are called interest-related and deep friendships.

Interest-Related Versus Deep Friendships **Interest-related friendships** are based on some similar life-style or interests (such as plants, pets, hobbies, softball, and bridge) between the individuals in the relationship (Bensman & Lilienfeld, 1979). **Deep friendships** are those in which there is an intimacy between the individuals beyond interests, that is, based on a feeling of personal closeness to the other individual.

Interest-related friendships are usually formed on the basis of current transient interests and physical proximity, are quite casual, and are easily broken when one moves to another neighborhood, geographic region, changes jobs, or changes interests (see Figure 8.1).

Individuals usually have three or four interest-related friends (casual acquaintances), such as coworkers and neighbors. This group of friends is constantly changing as individuals change jobs, move, or change interests and activities. During later adulthood, the overall number of interest-related friendships may decrease due to death, lack of mobility, or health problems.

On the other hand, once deep friendships are formed, they tend to be some-what permanent. They seem to be impervious to the effects of time, distance, and interests and are usually only broken by the death of one of the individuals. Persons tend to have one or two deep (close) friends throughout life.

There appear to be gender differences in friendship patterns. Males tend to have greater numbers of friends, overall, but they are less *close.* In fact, for older males, intimacy with friends appears to have little influence on psychological well-being (Keith, Hill, Goudy, & Powers, 1984).

The importance of distinguishing between deep and interest-related friendships was highlighted by K. A. Roberts and Scott (1986), who studied the importance of *equity* in older persons' satisfaction with friendship. Equity in a relationship refers to one's perception that the costs of giving something to the friendship are at least equal to the rewards. Roberto and Scott (1986) found that older persons who felt they were part of an inequitable relation-ship were less satisfied with that friendship. In cases where these relation-ships involved best friends, satisfaction was high regardless of their equity. However, in contrast to the study by Keith et al. (1984), men were involved in more equitable friendships than were women and were more intimate and self-disclosing than were women. Women were more diverse in the friend-ships they had, had friendships that were both intimate and instrumental, reported being more intensely involved, and were more *concerned* about equity (having invested more in the relationship). Men's friendships were activity oriented yet seemed to fulfill an intimacy function. This study suggests an important qualitative difference between men's and women's friendships—intimacy needs may be defined and fulfilled in different ways for older men and women. Thus, this component of the personal convoy may differ greatly for men and women. Females tend to have fewer friends overall, but those they have tend to be of the deeper variety. We know very little about opposite-sex friendships, due to the fact that such relationships are often not viewed as friendships per se by others but as dating, with sexual overtones. Society tends to discourage opposite-sex friendships among married in-dividuals because these relationships are potentially sexual. When opposite-sex friendships are formed, however, males tend to be more likely to report having opposite-sex friendships than do females (Usui, 1984).

Sibling Relationships

One type of friendship pattern that is beginning to generate interest is sibling relationships. The interaction pattern among siblings tends to be maintained into adulthood and old age. That is, siblings who had a close relationship during childhood tend to be close during adulthood and vice versa (Cicirelli, 1980; Mosatche, Brady, & Noberini, 1983). This conclusion is, however, tempered by whether sibling closeness is defined in terms of frequency of contact versus feelings of affection and closeness.

The literature (using feelings of closeness as a dependent variable) suggests that regardless of age, sister-sister pairs are closer than either brother-brother or mixed-sex pairs (B. N. Adams, 1968). Additionally, though proximity is important in terms of visits or actual contact with adult siblings, siblings tend to maintain some form of regular contact throughout the adult years. As with other types (deep) of friends, siblings can provide considerable interpersonal support for individuals in times of crisis. Cicirelli (1980) maintains that sibling rivalry, thought to dissipate with age, may occur in some situations (inheritance) and not in others (illness).

Intergenerational Relationships

Intergenerational relationships are interactions between individuals of different cohorts or generations (Troll & Bengston, 1982). In a majority of situations, intergenerational relationships occur within the context of the larger *family* or **kinship network** (aunts, uncles, cousins) but typically involve grandparents, parents, and children. Parent-child relationships tend to be strongest (Troll & Bengston, 1982). Helping patterns between child, parent, and grandparent within a family are referred to as *lineage generational* in nature (Dunham & Bengston, 1986). While we know a great deal about parent-child contacts over the life span, information about grandparent-grandchildren contacts is generally absent. In this light, most of our contact with older adults and/or subsequent attitudes toward them are in part accounted for via our limited personal interactions primarily with our grandparents, or secondarily with other elderly relatives. Older family members may, however, also be an important source of socialization (see Chapter 9).

Demographic shifts have tended to make us more aware of the importance of intergenerational contact. For example, Troll, Miller, and Atchley (1979) suggest that increased longevity makes four-generation (and even five-generation) families more likely, while declines in the birthrate limit the numbers of persons within generations. Moreover, couples seem to be delaying both marriage and childbirth (though children tend to be spaced more closely). All of these factors increase the likelihood of greater chronological age differences between grandchildren and grandparents. Moreover, children and grandparents are likely to interact differently when children are little and grandparents are in good health and vigorous versus when grandchildren are adolescents and grandparents are frail (Troll & Bengston, 1982).

Intergenerational contacts can serve many functions for each participant. Among other things, older members transmit political and religious information about expected gender roles and sexual behaviors as well as values about work and achievement. Perhaps most importantly among these are values concerning life-style and the importance of family (a family "theme") as a source of support and identity.

However, there are many individual as well as cultural differences in intergenerational relationships, since family values and patterns clearly vary as a function of a number of factors, such as ethnicity (Sussman, 1985) or race (D. M. Schneider and Smith, 1973). Troll and Bengston (1982) note more similarity between parents and children in political and religious views relative to other issues. Friends may also mediate transmission of certain values (e.g., drug use) from one generation to the next.

Within the family kinship network, individuals usually give assistance to and interact and visit with the older members of the family (Shanas, 1979;

Troll & Bengston, 1982). Bankoff (1983) notes the positive supportive role that older parents can play in helping a daughter adjust to widowhood. Interestingly, while such support can and does occur, it has limits. As reported by Clark and Anderson (1967), good relationships between family members of different cohorts often depend upon the independence and autonomy of the individuals. That is, relationships between different generations tend to be better when they do not live within the same household and each feels independent and autonomous (Sussman, 1985). Children and adults enjoy visiting with their older relatives and vice versa, but they prefer to do it on a voluntary and mutual basis.

Brody, Johnson, and Fulcomer (1984) found that while adult women were quite willing to adjust their family schedules and to help with the costs of health care, they would not agree to adjust work schedules or share households to help an elderly parent. For both children and parents, receiving emotional support or help in money management was more acceptable than was supplementing income.

When children are just beginning their lives as adults, help of a psychological and economic nature flows from parents to child (B. N. Adams, 1968). One aspect of intergenerational relationships within families when children are middle aged and parents are elderly that has been of some interest to researchers pertains to what is called **filial responsibility** (Brody, 1979). Filial responsibility refers to the perceived obligation (frequently determined by law, custom, or personal preference) with regard to the various types of services and social support that children should provide for their older parents (Hanson, Sauer, & Seelback, 1983). Ideally, however, there are "no strings attached"—such help is offered freely, and parents feel they can "count on" their children without being a burden on them. This is termed **filial maturity** (Blenkner, 1965)—we see our parents as *real people* who need our help.

The obligations adult children feel toward the care and support of their aged parents can be very revealing, however, regarding the quality of such behavior. Sussman (1985) and Troll et al. (1979) suggest that *intimate* (based on love, commitment, and caring) support is more enduring and satisfying than is *instrumental* (obligatory, born out of guilt or criticism) aid, highlighting the difference between filial maturity and filial responsibility as a basis for intergenerational exchanges.

It is widely held that there are cultural, ethnic, and racial norms regarding these obligations or expectations. In cultural/ethnic/racial groups that are traditionally viewed as **extended**, such as black families, there might be a greater importance placed upon filial responsibility than in groups that are not traditionally viewed as extended (Hanson et al., 1983). The black extended family serves as a mechanism for meeting the physical, emotional, and economic needs of the individual (its members) at all age levels (J. J. Jackson, 1970; Stack, 1974; Sussman, 1985). Many (J. J. Jackson, 1985; Markides, 1983b; Sussman, 1985) feel that ethnicity and race have a very powerful influence on intergenerational relationships. Contrary to what one would expect on the basis of older minority groups being the most disadvantaged (referred to as the "double jeopardy" hypothesis; see J. J. Jackson, 1985) support contact with family and friends was no less for Mexican American and black aged than for Anglo elderly (Dowd & Bengston, 1978). While there is some disagreement regarding the presumed supportiveness (in light of urbanization and modernization) of minority families toward their aged (Maldonado, 1975), Markides's (1983b) review suggests that Mexican American and black families tend to provide more contact and support in the care of an aged family member than do Anglo families. Such support, moreover, may preclude institutionalization for those elderly who are unable to care for themselves. As Markides (1983b) notes, however, data is extremely scarce, and increased contact with one's family may not be positive for some elderly persons.

Sussman (1985) echoes the centrally supportive role that minorities play in caring for an elderly family member in light of that person's often impoverished financial resources, lessened access to health care/social services, and poor health. Over and above these factors is the culturally rich tradition of relying on one another among black and Hispanic families that encompasses the elderly person in many roles, for example, teacher, advisor, conveyor of values and tradition, role model, and caretaker (Sussman, 1985). In view of the diversity among older minorities, one must be especially cautious about overgeneralizing about kinship networks among ethnic and/ or minority aged. Each subcultural group responds differently to available social services, holds different values regarding their relationships with the majority (i.e., Anglos), and interacts differently with service providers who might otherwise aid the family in caring for an elderly family member.

The hypothesis that filial responsibility would be greater in racial/ ethnic groups that are traditionally considered extended than in those groups that are not was tested by Hanson et al. (1983). These researchers investigated the racial (black, white) and cohort (adult, middle-age, old) variations in filial responsibility. In contrast to assertions by Sussman (1985), their results indicated that for all age-groups and races, filial responsibility was not considered very important. These findings were interpreted as indicating a strong desire for independence and autonomy on the part of both middle-aged children and their aged parents. Also, contrary to expectation, whites had a higher belief in the importance of filial responsibility than did blacks during adulthood and middle age. In old age, however, the differences between the races were smaller. In general, Hanson et al. (1983) suggest the most important finding was that the younger the individual, the more likely he or she would support the importance of filial responsibility. Thus, based on the Hanson et al. (1983) study, the quality and quantity of intergenerational relationships appears to rest more on individual differences and a family's particular economic or physical (home, distance from elders) situation rather than general factors such as ethnicity or race.

It is important to observe that even among families that are financially well-off, some may be more helpful in certain situations than in others. While older persons turn to their adult children or another close relative (when the couple have no children) in the case of serious illness or death (Shanas, 1962), middle-aged parents who are dealing with the stresses of raising adolescents (Rossi, 1980) may find it necessary to provide support or take primary responsibility for an aging parent as well, due to failing health or widowhood (Aizenberg & Treas, 1985). In such cases, parent-child conflicts may reemerge, and the parent, lacking decision-making power as an older person, may have to assume a passive-dependent role. While this pathological role reversal may occur in some families, its importance has probably been overstated (Aizenberg & Treas, 1985; Brody, 1979). Such cases most likely only emerge when past conflicts have not been resolved and when the adult child feels that pressure or obligation (instrumental support) is the primary reason for caring for a frail parent.

Adding to the stressfulness of the situation are the physical, psychological, and financial pressures of caring for an ill parent (see Chapters 12 and 13). Such pressures affect both adult parents and their children. In intimate relationships, fears about becoming dependent or a burden *can* be talked through and settled. Intergenerational relationships will reemerge as an issue when we discuss grandparenting and cross-cultural perspectives on attitudes toward aging. In Chapter 13 we will also discuss the unique difficulties adult caregivers face in caring for an elderly parent with Alzheimer's disease.

MARRIAGE

Why Marry?

Most of us, sometime during our adult lives, will marry. In fact, the chances are well over nine in ten that we will do so (Glick, 1977). Perhaps during our high school years we begin to define those qualities and characteristics that our "ideal" marriage partner should have. In the process of dating, we come not only to define more closely what marriage means to us, but also to redefine more clearly who that person will be that we hope to spend the rest of our life with. For some, however, this special person never seems to appear. For others, it is only after a "false start" or two that they come to know what it is that truly makes them happy in a marital relationship.

People get married for a variety of reasons. For many of us, it is a response to the **social clock** (Neugarten, 1973), in that we learn, implicitly or explicitly, that one "should" get married in one's early twenties. Going much beyond this (for women, their mid to late twenties; for men, their early thirties) may evoke criticism, doubt, and, at the very least, a stream of questions from one's peers or relatives. One's own anxiety about one's "marriage-ability" is also likely to increase, though the growing tendency is for couples to marry somewhat later (Aizenberg & Treas, 1985; Troll et al., 1979).

People also marry for security, or to compensate for perceived social and/or personal inadequacies. They may wish to get away from their parents, to enhance their position in business, or to settle down (you might marry someone with "common sense" or who has a "cool head"). Still others put off marriage until they have reached a certain valued goal or attained some stability in their lives. One might delay marriage until graduation, discharge from the service, landing that "first job," or until one's income reaches a certain level. Of course, many do marry for love, but it is often difficult to separate the "chicken from the egg." Looking back on one's marriage "after the fact" makes it difficult to know for sure what led to what! Did you marry because you were in love, or did love grow out of your relationship?

Developmentally, we can see that the choice to marry can grow out of what Erikson (1963) terms a person's *intimacy* needs. B. Newman and P. Newman (1979) define intimacy as "the ability to experience an open, supportive, tender relationship with another person, without fear of losing one's identity in the process of growing close. . . . Intimacy implies the ability for mutual empathy and mutual regulation of needs. One must be able to give pleasure within the intimate context" (pp. 371–372). Thus, if you do not have a sense of "who you are"—of what your values are, of what is most important to you—a sense of self-competence, and a set of personal goals, the process of meeting these intimacy needs will likely be threatening to you. To put it another way, you cannot give of yourself within a relationship if that which you have to give is poorly defined or loosely held together. It is this ability to share oneself with another that perhaps is the central component in the establishment of intimacy. You may be uncertain that part of you will not be lost in the process or may feel that in making compromises with another (which ultimately are necessary in any relationship) you are having to *give up* something that is crucial or necessary to your well-being or makeup. Consequently, you will either not get married at all, delay marriage, or experience a great deal of conflict within the marriage.

Above all, perhaps, marriage presupposes a sense of "I know who I am," and successful, happy (but not necessarily long-lived) marriages are characterized by the willingness *and* the ability to compromise, to be flexible, to accept failure and inadequacy in oneself as well as in someone else. Not only, then, does intimacy depend upon a well-established sense of personal *identity,* it also is rooted in having established a sense of *trust* in *others*—that they can be depended upon to meet your needs as well. Successful marriages are also characterized by a sense of *mutuality*—being able to satisfy your own needs, in part, through the meeting of someone else's needs (K.W. Schaie & Geiwitz, 1982). In this sense, each individual gives of herself or himself to the couple. Thus, each person's needs are met when the *couple's* (as a dyad or unit) are met.

Just as many persons make the decision to marry for a number of reasons, they may choose not to divorce due to a variety of factors that have little to do with the breakdown of mutuality. They may continue to stay married "for the sake of the children," for economic or business reasons, or because to divorce would evoke social disapproval from friends or relatives (J.B. Kelly, 1982). Ultimately, the decision to dissolve the marriage legally may result from a perceived lessening of the impact that the above factors have on each member of the dyad. Pressures stemming from living together may lessen by being separated. Emotionally speaking, however, the couple may have divorced at some point much earlier, when each determined that the costs of maintaining the relationship had become more important than the *couple's* needs. What is important here is that a distinction has been made between the individual and the couple, to the extent that they are now seen as working at cross-purposes with one another. In a truly intimate (mutual) relationship, the needs of the individual would be redefined in terms of those of the couple as a unit. Some individuals who never marry or whose marriages are unhappy never seem to reach this level of "mutuality." Their ideas about what marriage *should* be like are rooted in myth—they search but never find the ideal mate. Others lead lives never characterized by mutuality with anyone, be it parents, siblings, or friends.

As we learned in our discussion of the convoy, marital relationships are a core component in this support network. Though there are a number of types of marriages as well as great controversy regarding the status of traditional marriage in society today, marriage is still considered important by adolescents and adults of both genders.

Before we discuss types of marriages and life-span trends regarding marriage and divorce, it is important to examine briefly what brings individuals together. This behavior is widely studied by social psychologists and sociologists and is often generically referred to as *interpersonal attraction*. There are many theories of attraction, and the literature is quite extensive, so an in-depth discussion is beyond the scope of this text. Our goal here is to briefly discuss and highlight the factors that appear to be related to the selection of a marriage partner.

Why Individuals Are Attracted to Each Other

There are a number of factors that tend to facilitate interpersonal relationships and attraction to the point where the individuals involved develop close relationships that often result in marriage. These factors are familiarity and proximity, satisfaction of personal needs, similarity, reinforcement, and parental models.

Familiarity and Proximity In order for people to meet and become familiar with each other, they must have some form of regular contact or association (Festinger, Schachter, & Back, 1950; Zajonc, 1968). This includes such situations as attending the same class, working in the same office, and living in the same apartment building. Through the greater frequency of such contacts, individuals have more opportunities to develop and nurture interpersonal relationships. Subsequently, these relationships may develop to the stage of marriage.

Personal Needs Another important factor related to the development of interpersonal relationships is the satisfaction of our personal needs. We are attracted to individuals who satisfy our needs and desires. These include the need for love, emotional support, and the desire for financial status and attractive physical appearance. Social psychologists have found that physical attractiveness, as defined by cultural stereotypes, plays an important part in the choice of friends and potential mates. That is, people like to associate with attractive people. This effect appears stronger for males compared to females (Sigall & Landy, 1973). Individuals with needs for strong emotional support tend to be attracted to individuals who will meet these needs; individuals who seek wealth are attracted to individuals with a great deal of financial resources.

An alternative view suggests that individuals are attracted to those who complement their needs. This is referred to as **complementarity**, the notion that opposites attract. This view assumes we are attracted to individuals who have specific traits, attitudes, and characteristics that are different from our own, thereby satisfying our need to possess those traits. For instance, someone who is shy and introverted may seek individuals that are outgoing and extroverted. Though this view appears to make good common sense, research has not been generally supportive of it. For example, Bentler and Newcomb (1978) examined happiness in married couples and found that happiness was linked to similarity, not complementarity.

Similarity We tend to be attracted to individuals to whom we are **similar**— similar in terms of socioeconomic level, race, religious beliefs, and education level. For example, in a study with students, C.T. Hill and Stull (1981) found that women and, to a lesser extent, men preferred roommates who possessed similar values. Therefore, we are likely to develop relationships with individuals to whom we are similar on a number of factors.

Reinforcement Individuals tend to be attracted to individuals who reinforce and support their own opinions, values, and ideas, or who share similar interests, such as hobbies and activities. Essentially, when individuals share the same attitudes, ideas, or activities, they provide mutual support for each other. According to this exchange theory point of view (Ahammer, 1973; Murstein, 1982), the rewards and cost regarding the relationship are likely to balance out; each person is likely to perceive the relationship as an equitable one.

Parental Models It is sometimes suggested that we are attracted to individuals who possess the traits of our opposite-sex parent. This is called parental-image theory and is basically psychoanalytic in nature (Murstein, 1982). According to this theory, males are oedipally attracted to females who possess the traits of their mothers; females are attracted to males who have the traits of their fathers.

It should be stressed that the study of interpersonal attraction in terms of why people marry is still in the exploratory stage. These factors have been shown to be *related* to why people marry, but they cannot be considered causal. Thus, it is doubtful whether any one of these factors alone can account for why people marry. Further, though these factors help explain how individuals are attracted to each other, they do not explain the individual's choice of a particular marriage partner from a group of potential mates who may be similar on a number of these factors. Finally, the actual selection of a marriage partner is highly subjective and based upon many personal and individual preferences that we often refer to as "love."

A viable alternative to the ideas of similarity and complementarity is what is termed **filter theory** (Udry, 1974). This suggests that in selecting a mate people do so via the use of a hierarchical set of "filters." Simply put, the person who passes through each of these filters is the person whom you will marry. These filters, in order of importance, are:

1. *Propinquity:* you select persons who are closest to you in a geographic sense—these are the ones who are most likely, by virtue of frequency of contact, to be marriageable; long-distance romances are more difficult!

2. Potential candidates enter the *attractiveness* filter (looks, build, age).

3. The *social background* filter operates next; this means that you are most likely to marry persons who are similar to you in socioeconomic status, religion, occupation, or race. Thus, persons from similar backgrounds are likely to have similar values and goals.

4. The *consensus* filter acts further to eliminate persons who do not share similar attitudes toward specific topics (e.g., abortion, sex, women's roles, money).

5. The *complementarity* filter next acts to select persons who, despite sharing specific attitudes and values, "fill us out" or make us complete. For example, a socially adept woman marries a shy, introverted man.

6. Lastly, a *readiness* filter excludes persons who are "off time," maritally speaking. Thus persons who want to marry early or postpone marriage are likely to have a more difficult time finding someone who meets this last criterion.

Thus, while similarity and complementarity are important, they are only one of many factors, according to filter theory, that make for good mates.

Murstein (1982) proposes a *stage theory of mate selection,* whereby couples go through a series of stages by which they come to know one another well enough to make a decision regarding the other individual's marriageability. The first stage of this process is the *stimulus stage,* where observable characteristics such as physical attractiveness or knowledge of profession or occupation dominate. If each person's stimulus attributes are equal, the couple moves on to the *values comparison stage,* where evaluations of mutual interests, attitudes, personal beliefs, and needs are made via gathering of verbal information. If such evaluations are positive by each person's own criteria, the courtship reaches the *role stage,* the couple make clear their feelings about each other, and expectations about the relationship, individual self-concepts, and perceptions of the other person are confirmed. Thus, an evaluation of one's own and the other's ability to function in the role of married person is made in this last stage. As couples progress through these stages of courtship, the importance of the stimulus and value-comparison dimensions lessen relative to marital-role expectations.

Life-Span Trends in Love

Just as it is difficult to explain causally why people are attracted to each other, it is also difficult to describe the precise function of love that is characteristic of this relationship. While love may bring individuals together, it also develops out of a commitment to one another. Further, research suggests that the meaning of love and the factors related to why people love each other vary with age. This point was illustrated by Reedy, Birren, and K.W. Schaie (1982). Reedy et al. (1982) investigated the relative importance of six factors or components of love (emotional security, respect, communication, help and play behaviors, sexual intimacy, loyalty) for young adults, middle-aged individuals, and older adults. The study demonstrated two important facts regarding the components of love across the life span. First, the rank order (position) in terms of these six components were identical for each age-group. This ranking, from highest to lowest, was as follows: emotional security, respect, communication, help and play behaviors, sexual intimacy, and loyalty. Second, though the rank of the six factors was the same in each age-group, the rated importance of these factors was different for different age-groups. Emotional security was considered the most important factor/component for each age-group but increased in importance during old age. Respect, the second-most important factor, decreased with increasing age. The component of communication decreased in importance with increased age, while help and play behaviors remained fairly constant across the life cycle. The importance of sexual intimacy, which ranked fifth for all age-groups, was highest during middle age and decreased substantially during old age. Finally, though loyalty was ranked the lowest for all age-groups, its rated importance increased across the life cycle.

This study suggests that while the factors that contribute to a loving relationship are similarly ranked at all points along the adult life span the importance of these factors does vary by age.

Marital Satisfaction

Most of us assume that happily married couples are in love. We have many times made reference to successful or "happy" marriages. What does it mean to be "happily" married? Unfortunately, this is a difficult question to answer clearly. Simply asking couples whether they are "happy" or not may or may not tell us anything. Much depends upon the reasons the persons married in the first place (e.g., emotional versus financial security). An examination of the literature on marital satisfaction in adulthood (Alpert & Richardson, 1980) reveals a great deal of confusion about how marital satisfaction is best defined. For some, the extent to which the partner carries out expected duties (meets the other partner's expectations regarding child care, being steadily employed) would define a good marriage. For others, sharing common interests or activities suffices. For still others, "mutuality" may be uppermost in their definition of what being happily married is all about. Perhaps the most realistic approach to this problem is to accept the fact that just as people "compartmentalize" their lives, so do they separate aspects of their marital relationship (some of which are satisfactory, some of which are not); different areas (sexual versus emotional satisfaction, being able to grow as a person, being a good breadwinner versus being a good parent) are likely to be more important to some persons than are others.

Simply asking people "how satisfied" they are with their marriages (Rollins & Feldman, 1970) reveals that "happiness" within the marriage peaks when the couple is newly married and again after the children have finally left home. During the years when the children are being raised, satisfaction is lowest, suggesting that the demands of having offspring to care for are seen as detracting from marital quality. This does not mean, however, that during this period these couples were necessarily unhappy—they were simply *less* satisfied (in a global way) than before or after child rearing. It stands to reason that, dependent upon a number of factors (refer to our discussion of parenthood below), children will affect marital happiness in *different* ways for *different* couples. We might note that for some persons, being happily married and being married to someone who is seen as a good parent are perhaps indistinguishable. It might be difficult for these individuals to separate or compartmentalize various aspects of their relationship when they think about their own marriage. Moreover, what of couples who have never had children? You might also consider the role that sexuality per se plays in marital satisfaction. Is it crucial? Perhaps, to an elderly couple, sexuality might be redefined to include simply embracing or holding hands, or being happily married might be simply seen in terms of having a pleasant "companion" (versus the decision to be alone, or to divorce, which may be socially unacceptable). We will discuss sexuality in adulthood later in this chapter.

Recent evidence of the complexity of marital satisfaction in adulthood has been provided by Otero-Sabogal, Hayslip, & Sabogal (1987). These investigators found that such factors as marital strain, parental strain, social support from others, parental competence, and family life cycle stage all contributed to couples' marital quality. Moreover, different sets of factors defined marital satisfaction for men versus women.

How do we form our ideas about marriage? Certainly the culture has an influence (popular writings, movies, the media); so do the experiences of our own parents. We may be socialized (see Chapter 9) to believe that those who are happy personally (being self-confident, having high self-esteem, being well adjusted) are the most satisfied maritally, that persons whose parents were happily married are also likely to be so, that persons who are overinvolved in their work are necessarily less happily married, or that to be happily married, one must be sexually fulfilled via one's partner (or alternatively, be able to express oneself sexually with anyone—spouse or otherwise). While research (Doherty & Jacobson, 1982) supports some of these notions (good adjustment makes for happy marriages, having high self-esteem promotes marital bliss, coming from homes where the marital relationship is sound also contributes to marital satisfaction), it does not speak to all them. Much of what we believe is actually infused with our own values about many issues. For instance, our feelings about work, the importance we place on possessions versus people, the role that we feel prior experience plays in governing our lives are all important. Being happily married is thus *relative* to a number of factors, and thus it is difficult to say in an *absolute* sense what characterizes satisfying marriages.

At this point, you might ask yourself some questions: (1) Which of the above factors in mate selection is most important to me? Least important? (2) What does being happily married mean to me? To my parents? To my grandparents?

Types of Marriages

Just as it is difficult to specify exactly why people choose to marry, it is also not easy to contrive a definition or description of the marital relationship that is all-encompassing. For instance, what type of relationship *you* consider a marriage depends upon a number of factors, such as your personal views, religious orientation, sexual preference, and value system. There are basically seven types of relationships between individuals that are generally considered marriages. These types are traditional, companionship, colleague, open, group, homosexual partnership, and childless marriages.

The **traditional marriage** is based on a relationship between a husband (male) and wife (female). In the classic traditional marriage, the husband is considered the head of the family; he supports the family and is the major decision maker. On the other hand, the wife's role is well-defined and usually limited to child care and household matters (Duberman, 1974). Though this type of marriage is still common, its relative frequency is decreasing for a number of reasons. One of the major reasons is the increase in the number of women working outside of the home. As reported by Haygh (1984), in 1984 approximately 60 percent of married women were engaged in full-time employment (see also Knox, 1980).

A **companionship marriage** includes a husband and a wife but no differentiation between male and female roles is made (Duberman, 1974). Each partner can take on the rights, obligations, and duties of the other. For example, each month the individuals may change duties and responsibilities, such as housework, cooking, and child care. This type of marriage is growing in popularity among individuals with high levels of education as well as among middle-class and upper middle class couples.

Colleague marriages are quite similar to companionship marriages, except in the colleague marriage, the partners recognize role and responsibility differences (Duberman, 1974). Each partner assumes responsibility and authority for specific duties and tasks within the family, and these are generally stable, rather than constantly changing. For example, both partners assume responsibility for earning income to support the family, but the wife is responsible for deciding how the money is spent and the husband for yard work and housecleaning. This type of marriage relationship takes into account individual differences in abilities, interests, and preferences. Again, this type of marriage is popular among highly educated, middle-class and upper middle class couples.

The **open marriage** is based on a legally sanctioned union between a husband and a wife (according to the law they are legally married), but it differs from the three types of marriages previously discussed regarding fidelity. In the traditional, companionship, and colleague marriage, it is generally assumed that each partner will have intimate and/or sexual relations exclusively with the other marriage partner. Partners in an open marriage relationship feel that it is perfectly acceptable for each to have intimate and/or sexual relations with other partners. It is difficult to determine the relative frequency and popularity of this type of marriage due to the fact that society in general does not view such behavior in a favorable light.

A **group marriage** is one in which a number of couples are legally married in a traditional manner (a husband to a wife), but these individuals share living arrangements, duties, responsibilities, and sexual partners. Again, it is difficult to obtain a fairly accurate picture of the frequency and popularity of this type of marriage relationship due to society's views, but such arrangements were more common in communal situations in the 1960s and early 1970s.

A **homosexual partnership** is a situation where two gay individuals make a personal commitment to each other to live together as married partners. Each partner shares or takes individual responsibility for specific roles and duties within the relationship. At the present time there is comparatively little data regarding these relationships (see Corby & Solnick, 1980). However, as societal attitudes toward gay individuals have changed, more and more information will likely become available, particularly relating to older gay life-styles. It is quite possible that fear of AIDS (Acquired Immune Deficiency Syndrome) will ultimately make such marriages more enduring among homosexual men, though it is becoming quite clear that heterosexuals can also acquire AIDS.

Corby and Solnick (1980) suggest that we know more about the impact of aging on the individual who is predominantly homosexual than about the frequency of homosexual behavior per se among older persons. Aging can be particularly difficult for older male homosexuals, who may be labeled as "old" as early as age 30. Rather than supporting a perception of all older gays as lonely and isolated, Corby and Solnick's (1980) review suggests that older gays may actually be insulated from the stresses of aging, having learned much earlier in life to cope with loneliness because of their homosexuality. Older gays may also feel less pressure to assume a traditional male role than do older heterosexual men (Francher & Henkin, 1973). This more positive attitude toward the older gay man may be in part a consequence of our increased acceptance of homosexuality. As Corby and Solnick point out, however, our knowledge about older lesbians is virtually absent. For those older gays who face discrimination, loneliness, or isolation, self-help groups are available in some cities.

The **childless marriage** is becoming more common for a number of reasons, such as personal concerns with overpopulation, time commitments, economic costs of children, and career demands. Research indicates that compared to couples with children, childless couples enjoy more marital communication, maintain a more egalitarian power structure, and report higher marital satisfaction and adjustment (Lupri & Frideres, 1981). However, this finding should not be interpreted to mean that couples who have children are necessarily unhappy.

When professionals discuss interpersonal relationships along the life span, they usually differentiate three major groups: the married, the single (widows/widowers, divorced, never married), and those living in institutions or nursing homes. These are often viewed as *life-styles,* and a separate discussion of each is important to understanding interpersonal relationships along the life span.

LIFE-STYLES DURING ADULTHOOD

The Married

Though marriage is still quite popular, statistics reflect two noticeable phenomena regarding marriage at the current time. First, figures from the United States Bureau of the Census (1981) indicate that there has been a noticeable shift in the age of first marriages of males and females from 1890 to recent times, a trend presented in Table 8.1. As this table indicates, for females the median age at the time of first marriage in 1890 was 22.0 years, 20.3 years in 1950, and 22.3 years in 1981, indicating that from the beginning to the middle of this century, the median age of first marriage gradually decreased, and that since that time it has been gradually increasing. The same general trend is observed for males. For males, in 1890 the median age of first marriage was 26.1 years, in 1950 it was 22.8 years, and in 1981 24.8 years.

These data suggest that (1) males generally tend to be older than females at the time of their first marriage, and (2) people are currently marrying later in life than they have previously during this century. We shall discuss some reasons for these trends throughout the remaining sections of this chapter.

TABLE 8.1

MEDIAN AGE OF MALES AND FEMALES AT TIME OF FIRST MARRIAGE IN THE UNITED STATES FOR SELECTED YEARS

Year	Males	Females
1890	26.1	22.0
1900	25.9	21.9
1940	24.3	21.5
1950	22.8	20.3
1960	22.8	20.3
1970	23.2	20.8
1978	24.2	21.8
1981	24.8	22.3

Source: U.S. Bureau of the Census. (1981). *Current Population Reports* (Series P–20, No. 365). Washington, D.C.: U.S. Government Printing Office.

Our discussion of marital satisfaction notwithstanding, what do we know about marital happiness in adulthood? Many researchers have reported that there is a curvilinear relationship between marital satisfaction and one's stage in the life cycle (Lupri & Frideres, 1981; Rollins & Cannon, 1974), and that gender differences exist in marital satisfaction, males being more satisfied than females with marriage (Rhyne, 1981).

For example, Lupri and Frideres (1981), in interviews with 464 Canadian couples, found that marital satisfaction declines steadily from the beginning of marriage until the children are gone from home. An increase in satisfaction occurs as couples go from postparental years toward the retirement stage.

This finding suggests that in contrast to the rather common belief that children increase marital satisfaction, the presence of children has just the opposite effect. In a series of studies, Glenn and McLanahan (1981, 1982) categorized couples by educational level, religion, race, gender, employment status, and age, and found that child rearing had a negative impact on marital enjoyment for all subgroups. Further, regarding an older sample (age 50 and above) whose children were grown and not living at home, there were no general positive effects of having children on the happiness of their parents. Similarly, Lupri and Frideres (1981) found that a higher proportion of childless couples reported higher marital satisfaction than couples with children.

Perhaps the most extensive study of marital satisfaction throughout the life cycle was conducted by Rhyne (1981), based on a sample of 2190 Canadian couples. Rhyne investigated the quality of marital satisfaction in terms of factors such as friendship, sexual fulfillment, and so forth and aspects of the marital experience such as love, interest, help at home, and so forth. Presence of children, age of the eldest child, and number of children at home were the criteria used to determine the stage in the family life cycle (Hill, 1965). These were: Stage 1, *Preparental* (married people who did not have children); Stage 2, *Preschool* (couples where the eldest child was under 6 years of age); Stage 3, *Youngsters* (couples where the eldest child was between 6 and 12 years); Stage 4, *Teenagers* (couples where the eldest child was between 13 and 19 years); Stage 5, *Grown children at home* (couples where children were grown and still at home); Stage 6, *Launching* (cases where some, but not all, of the children had left home); and Stage 7, *Postparental* (all children had left home).

Regarding the quality of marital satisfaction, results indicated a U-shaped function (highs in the early and later stages, lows in the middle stages). Basically, people's evaluations of overall marital quality were lower during the child rearing stages of the family life cycle and highest at the point when all the children had left home. In terms of gender differences, males generally evaluated their marriages higher than did women. Specifically, in Stages 1 and 2, females were more satisfied than men, and in all other stages, men were more satisfied than women. Also females exhibited greater variability in their ratings in all stages. Again, in interpreting these findings, our discussion of what couples actually mean when they report on their marital happiness should be kept in mind.

Rhyne's results also indicated that men and women assess their marriages in different ways. No gender differences were found in terms of meeting sexual needs, but there were significant differences in all other aspects of the marital experience; women were less satisfied than men. Further, the magnitude of the gender differences were the greatest with the "spouse's help at home" and "spouse's time with children" factors.

Just as marital satisfaction changes during the life cycle, research also suggests that marital satisfaction changes throughout the life period of later adulthood. For example, Gilford (1984) investigated two dimensions of marital satisfaction, "positive interaction" (desirable aspects of relating to one another) and "negative sentiment" (negative feelings about the relationship), among three age-groups of older married couples, 55 to 62 years of age, 63 to 69 years of age, and 70 to 90 years of age. Gilford found that higher levels of the positive interaction factor were found for the middle group (63 to 69 years) of older adults, and least for the youngest group (55 to 62 years). Regarding the negative sentiment factor, the lowest scores was also manifested by the middle group (63 to 69 years) and the highest for the oldest age-group (70 to 90 years).

Gilford's study demonstrates that marital happiness apparently increases during the earlier stages of old age and declines over the latest stage. Though a number of factors could contribute to this observed relationship, Gilford suggests these results may be due to what can be called a "honeymoon stage" stemming from recent retirement. That is, individuals in this group are still in relatively good health, have more leisure time available to them to spend time together, and now do the things they have always wanted to do, such as travel, visit relatives, and spend time together. Thus, they report higher marital happiness due to the influence of this honeymoon effect.

While we may speak in terms of overall satisfaction, or aspects of satisfaction, it is important to note that within marriage, the relationship between the spouses is actually quite dynamic and changing. Ahammer (1973) suggests that this is due to changes in the balance of power within the relationship. R. Hill (1965), however, views marriage as a sequence of progressive stages along the life cycle. Recall that Rhyne (1981) used this framework to investigate marital satisfaction in adulthood.

STAGES OF A MARRIAGE

Stage 1 (Establishment)   This is a newly married couple who are childless and are learning to "live with each other." Each partner is learning about the likes and dislikes of the other as well as the other's strengths and weaknesses.

Stage 2 (New Parents)   This stage corresponds to the time between the birth of the first child and the point when that child reaches 3 years of age. During this stage, the relationship between the spouses changes to incorporate the child into the family unit.

Stage 3 (Preschool Family)   According to Hill, this is the time when the oldest child is between 3 and 6 years of age.

Stage 4 (School-Age Family)   This stage corresponds to that time when the oldest child is between 6 and 12 years of age. During stages 2 through 4, many additional strains are placed on the marital relationship. These strains are the result of children placing demands on the parents' free time, economic resources, and housing accommodations. Also, the level of interaction between the spouses is affected. Further, the presence of children may affect parental employment patterns.

Stage 5 (Family with Adolescent)   During this stage, the oldest child is between 13 and 19 years of age. Given the turbulent period of adolescence, there is great potential for strain on the marital relationship.

Stage 6 (Family with Young Adult)   This corresponds to the time when the oldest child is 20 years of age until the time the first child leaves home.

Stage 7 (Family As Launching Center)   This is the period of repeated departures of all children from the home.

Stage 8 (Postparental Family)   According to Hill, this stage begins after all children have left home and ends with retirement. This is the time that parents may experience the "empty nest" syndrome and its associated consequences.

Stage 9 (Aging Family)   This is the time during which both spouses have retired and have extensive leisure/free time.

Another popular conception of the family life cycle has been offered by Duvall (1971) and is illustrated in Table 8.2.

Featherman (1983) and R. Hill and Mattessich (1979) have argued that the concept of the family life cycle may not be useful. Just as chronological age has proved to be an inadequate means of predicting individual development, age-graded events (such as the birth of one's first child, empty nest, retirement) are not sufficient to understand family development. Instead, demographic and cultural changes may change the timing and thus the meaning that such events have for the family. An approach that sees the family as a dynamic changing *system* composed of individuals who are themselves changing has emerged (Featherman, 1983; Herr & Weakland, 1979; G.R. Weeks & Wright, 1985). As families change because of rising divorce rates, to be replaced by stepfamilies, singles, or widow(ers), the static, predictable nature of the family life cycle will change. Families, like individuals, are constantly evolving, and many feel that more dynamic reciprocal (where each family member influences and is influenced by the others) approaches to family development make more sense (Lerner & Spanier, 1978). From this perspective, each family is unique.

Though stage theories of marriage, such as Hill's or Duvall's, should be considered as descriptive, they can function as starting points for studying the dynamic and changing aspects of the marital relationship quite effectively. Given the dynamic nature of marriages, it is not surprising that the quality and subsequent satisfaction with the marital relationship varies with age.

TABLE 8.2

THE STAGES OF THE FAMILY LIFE CYCLE

Family Life Cycle Stage	Emotional Process of Transition: Key Principles	Second Order Changes in Family Status Required to Proceed Developmentally
1. Between families: The unattached young adult	Accepting parent-offspring separation	a. Differentiation of self in relation to family of origin b. Development of intimate peer relationships c. Establishment of self in work
2. The joining of families through marriage: The newly married couple	Commitment to new system	a. Formation of marital system b. Realignment of relationships with extended families and friends, including spouse
3. The family with young children	Accepting new members into the system	a. Adjusting marital system to make space for child(ren) b. Taking on parenting roles c. Realignment of relationships with extended family to include parenting and grandparenting roles
4. The family with adolescents	Increasing flexibility of family boundaries to include children's independence	a. Shifting of parent-child relationships to permit adolescent to move in and out of system b. Refocus on midlife marital and career issues c. Beginning shift toward concerns for older generation
5. Launching children and moving on	Accepting a multitude of exits from and entries into the family system	a. Renegotiation of marital system as a dyad b. Development of adult-to-adult relationship between grown children and their parents c. Realignment of relationships to include in-laws and grandchildren d. Dealing with disabilities and death of parents (grandparents)
6. The family in later life	Accepting the shifting of generational roles	a. Maintaining own and/or couple functioning and interests in face of physiological decline; exploration of new familial and social role opinions b. Support for a more central role for middle generation c. Making room in the system for the older generation without overfunctioning for them d. Dealing with loss of spouse, siblings, and other peers and preparation for own death. Life review and integration

Source: E. Duvall. (1971). *Family Development.* Philadelphia: Lippincott.

Despite the conceptual and methodological difficulties we have discussed in measuring marital happiness across the life span, a number of factors do appear to contribute to a good marital relationship (Stinett, Walters, & Kaye, 1984). Good marital relationships reflect a mutual respect for one another, a commitment to and a responsibility for meeting each other's needs, and a concern for one another's happiness and welfare. Persons who are happily married report strong emotional support and understanding from one another—each feels that his or her good and bad qualities are accepted by the other spouse.

VIOLENCE WITHIN THE FAMILY

On the other end of the spectrum of the happily married couple are family situations that are termed "conflict-habituated" marriages (Stevens-Long, 1984). In these situations, open fighting of a verbal and a physical nature characterizes the relationship. Within such a context, abuse is often common. When punishment (physical or otherwise) is carried to extremes, "battered" or "abused" children result. The very young and often helpless child is frequently the victim of such treatment. He or she may be premature, sickly, or simply not wanted. Unfortunately for such children, this abuse has many negative and long-lasting effects. If these children do not die, or are not maimed, paralyzed, or malnourished, they may themselves be more physically aggressive with other children or avoid them all together. Having learned that they are not worthy of love by another, they lose trust in their ability to receive love as well as to give it. They may also be expressing anger over treatment by someone who is supposed to love and care for *them* (see C. George & Maim, 1979; Papalia & Olds, 1982). Often, they themselves grow up to become abusing parents. Not knowing how to give or receive love, they place inordinate demands on their children to provide that emotional closeness that they themselves lacked as children. When these unrealistic expectations are not fulfilled, they strike out at their children. Abusing parents also tend to be poor, to come from large families, to feel negatively about themselves; they consequently deal with the stresses and demands that child rearing brings with it less adequately (Cater & Easton, 1980).

Not only have children been victims of both physical and psychological abuse, adult parents and the elderly are likely to be targets. Women more often than not tend to be the objects of such violence in both cases (Wetzel & Ross, 1983). "Battered women" are often overpowered by their husbands, who are in many cases also the primary earners in the family (Rosewater, 1985; Wetzel & Ross, 1983). Such women tend to be more passive and submissive, have low self-esteem, accept traditional female and male roles, and feel that they have few basic rights as human beings (see Box 8.1, p. 282). In many cases, these characteristics are *intensified* by the violence within the home (Rosewater, 1985). Such a woman is frequently prone to deny the serious nature of her situation and paradoxically clings to the relationship, often out of fear, isolation from others, or guilt. The "batterers" (men) are often insecure, violent persons who have learned that physical and psycho-

Timely intervention and counseling are important in dealing with abuse within the family.

logical abuse is a form of control; they often drink excessively and tend to come from violent families. They are unpredictable yet preoccupied with controlling their wives. Obviously, not only do women suffer, but children are often emotional victims, too, caught in a situation they do not understand but yet feel responsible for. Counseling (see Wetzel & Ross, 1983) focuses not only upon correcting the violence per se (usually involving the woman's leaving her husband) but also on dealing with the battered woman's feelings of repressed anger and guilt as well as her sense of self-esteem and control over her life. Perhaps most importantly, counseling must also focus on the offending husband after he and his wife have been physically separated. In some cases, marital counseling for the couple is an option.

Older persons are not immune to physical and psychological abuse, known as **elder abuse** (often referred to as "granny bashing"). Though interest in this area of family violence is high, our knowledge about the extent of the problem and more importantly *why* older persons are abused is minimal. Because of the responsibility adult children feel toward caring for their parents, both are often thrust into situations that create tension for both the older parent and the adult child. The fact that people are now living out more of their life spans makes caring for an elderly relative who is chronically ill more likely. Lacking other alternatives, many families feel compelled to care for an aging parent at home; in some cases they may also be caring for their own children or, at the least, sending them to college. In many instances, the abuse may be cyclical; some elderly abused their children and may be as a consequence more tolerant of the treatment they receive from their adult children (T. Hickey & Douglass, 1981). Physical or psychological abuse often results from stress and frustration, stemming from the daily demands on one's

BOX 8.1

FACTS AND FIGURES ON SPOUSE ABUSE

Profiles of men who batter their wives:
1. extreme, irrational jealousy of partner
2. control and isolation of partner
3. Jekyll and Hyde personalities
4. explosive temper
5. a history of legal difficulties
6. a lifelong pattern of blaming others for one's problems
7. verbal as well as physical abuse
8. a history of family violence (being abused as children)
9. more violence while partner is pregnant or soon after birth
10. denial of his own violent behavior

Profiles of women who are battered:
1. accepts traditional male and female roles
2. is passive and placating: easily dominated
3. accepts male dominance and the myth of male superiority
4. equates dominance with masculinity
5. feels she has no basic human rights—often not even the right not to be hit
6. accepts guilt even where there has been no wrongdoing
7. accepts partner's reality
8. feels that she must help her mate
9. acts as a buffer between her partner and the rest of the world
10. has strong needs to be needed
11. underestimates or downplays the dangerousness of her situation
12. has unshakable faith that things will improve or feels that there is absolutely nothing she can do about her situation
13. bases feelings of self-worth on her ability to "catch" and hold a man
14. suffers low self-esteem
15. doubts her own sanity

Source: L. Wetzel & M. A. Ross. (1983). Psychological and social ramifications of battering: Observations leading to counseling methodology of victims of domestic violence. *Personnel and Guidance Journal, 61,* 423–427.

physical, psychological, and financial resources of having to care for an aging parent (see Box 8.2). Not having a "safety valve," feeling guilty about *not* caring for a parent, and a history of violence within one's own past are critical factors in the abuse of elderly persons, who themselves are often physically (being in poor health) and psychologically (being dependent upon others or otherwise living alone) vulnerable (J.J. Costa, 1984; Hickey & Douglass, 1981; Pedrick-Cornell & Gelles, 1982). Given older persons' tendency to deny being abused, any evidence of neglect or deliberate physical/psychological abuse should be followed up with referral to a social worker and/or other professional who can pursue matters further. Intervention consists of not only providing the family with a respite from care but also may involve family counseling to deal with pathological patterns of handling stress and frustration.

The Divorced

Unfortunately, all marriages, however happy, come to an end. The breaking of the marital bond can occur in only two ways: through divorce and through death. Therefore, a topic related to marital satisfaction and the *second*-most noticeable trend in marriage statistics today pertains to divorce. As reported by Leete (1979) and Furstenburg (1982), during the past 10 to 15 years the divorce rate has risen substantially, and if it continues its current trend, it is

BOX 8.2

ELDER ABUSE: AN UNRECOGNIZED FORM OF FAMILY VIOLENCE

Forms of elder abuse:
1. physical abuse—evidence of bodily harm (hitting, slapping, burns, sexual abuse, being tied up or locked up)
2. psychological abuse—use of threats of violence to cause emotional distress, fear, or mental disturbances (e.g., being insulted, degraded, having one's dignity taken away)
3. neglect—willful lack of care resulting in injury or violation of the person's individual rights
4. financial exploitation—theft, conversion of the elder's money or property, often accompanied by threats, violence, or deception (e.g., cashing social security checks, spending savings, falsely collecting on insurance claims)

Profile of the elder who is abused:
1. female
2. aged 75 or older
3. physically or mentally impaired
4. physically, emotionally, or financially dependent

The typical abuser:
1. close relative (son, daughter) or a "primary caregiver"
2. lives with the victim
3. usually under stress, often financially poor
4. frequent abuse of alcohol or drugs
5. often sees the elder as the source of the problem

estimated that 40 percent of all current marriages will end in divorce. Divorce rates (see Figure 8.2) have increased still more (approaching 50 percent) over the last 5 years (U.S. Bureau of the Census, Statistical Abstract of the United States, 1986). The increase in divorce has been stimulated by a number of factors. These include the belief that divorce is a reasonable alternative to an

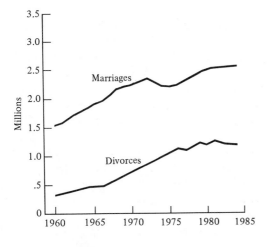

Note: Rate for marriages and divorces is per 1000 unmarried women, 15 years old and over.

Figure 8.2 Marriages and divorces: 1960 to 1984.
Source: U.S. Bureau of the Census. (1986). Statistical abstract of the United States. Washington, D.C.: U.S. Government Printing Office.

unhappy marriage, the removal of the social stigma attached to divorce, and legislation making divorce easier, to name a few.

K. W. Schaie and Geiwitz (1982) have suggested that increasing equality between men and women is both a cause for and an effect of this trend. For example, when men more or less "owned" their wives (who were often financially dependent upon their husbands) and marriage and parenthood were literally obligations or responsibilities that a man was expected to take on as he reached adult status, divorce was then looked down on as a "shirking" of his responsibility/duty to care for his dependents. When women attained more education, total dependence upon men was unnecessary, as in the past.

FACTORS RELATED TO DIVORCE

Just as people marry for a variety of reasons, so too do they divorce. We noted above that some couples *fail* to divorce due to social pressure, for the sake of their children, or for religious, professional, or business reasons. In some cases, the commitment to one another has long since deteriorated; these marriages have been termed "devitalized" (Stevens-Long, 1984), though the couple remains married. Some couples agree to "separate," giving them the freedom to pursue other relationships and yet retain the legal advantages (such as tax breaks) associated with being married or having children. For these couples, psychologically speaking, the intimacy that they once shared is gone; legally, however, they are quite married.

Those who do decide to dissolve their relationship formally through divorce (or informally through separation) may do so for many reasons. They may have simply found someone else whom they love more (although they may still love their first partner), or they may be overwhelmed and frustrated by their attempts to manage two careers, particularly if they are separated by great distances. In some cases, divorce may come as a complete surprise, leaving one of the partners with a deep sense of failure and rejection (J. B. Kelly, 1982). While "absence makes the heart grow fonder" in some cases, extended absences, due to job responsibilities, can split some couples up in spite of their genuine affection for one another. Ultimately, however, one must weigh the "costs" (psychological, social, financial) of staying together against those of being a single, independent person.

While children are the first intrusion into the intimacy created by the husband and wife, they can promote a sense of the "family," providing many satisfactions in spite of a personally unfulfilling relationship with one's spouse. Divorce in spite of the children, despite its advantages for those who are unhappy in failing relationships, creates a new set of difficulties for the newly separated person (B. L. Bloom, Hodges, & Caldwell, 1983). Moreover, divorces per se are expensive, particularly for women (B. L. Bloom et al., 1983). One may need to find a new place to live, learn to manage on a day-to-day basis, arrange for child care, possibly find a new job (B. L. Bloom et al., 1983), and at the same time deal with feelings of guilt, sorrow, and anger over the perceived failure and/or loss of a primary relationship (J. B.

Kelly, 1982). One may feel one has to be "both parents" now. Arrangements for custody, alimony, and visiting privileges must be made (Warshak & Santrock, 1983), all of which create both practical and deeper, more substantive difficulties to be overcome. While one may look forward to "being in circulation" again, one may find that dating and courting skills have rusted, so to speak. There may literally not be time to see others socially or to become intimately involved with another person. One's children may object to increased work loads or to the intrusion of a "new" mother or father into their lives. A new circle of friends may need to be established as the divorced person is now considered a "threat" or a "rival," in competition with a former married friend for his or her spouse.

In many respects, the norms for those who are divorced are ill-defined in our culture, leading to a kind of identity crisis. In fact, divorce has been treated as a nonnormative life event that is stressful (P. B. Baltes et al., 1980; Bloom et al., 1983). In light of the unforeseen problems many divorced persons face, it is not surprising that they might later question whether getting divorced was a wise choice or not. Many experience contradictory emotions that are difficult to resolve or are torn between what their children expect of them versus expectations they sense from family and friends. Many, overwhelmed by these pressures and lacking help and support from others who are judgmental or who suddenly have difficulty relating to them because they are now divorced, become chronically depressed, suffer physical or work difficulties (K. W. Schaie & Geiwitz, 1982), or have difficulty in forming new relationships with others, further isolating them from the support they may need. Women report more anxiety and conflict prior to separation, while men experience more "practical" problems during the year following their divorce (Hetherington, M. Cox, & R. Cox, 1982; Stevens-Long, 1984; Stinnett & Walters, 1977). B. L. Bloom et al. (1983) feel that women do tend to fare better within the first eight months after divorce than do men. In any event, the primary effect in both men and women is in terms of dealing with the loss of a relationship, feelings of failure, and loneliness (J. B. Kelly, 1982). While many divorced individuals do report feelings of enhanced growth and self-esteem and ultimately remarry and enjoy satisfying relationships, the immediate aftereffects of the divorce itself, as well as the experiences leading up to and actually including the divorce process, are very stressful for both individuals, children (if there are any), family, and friends. B. L. Bloom et al. (1983) note that support from others in the workplace can lessen the stressfulness of the divorce and its aftermath.

Though divorce is more socially acceptable (Furstenburg, 1982), it results from many factors, and research has indicated there are a number of social and demographic variables related to divorce. These factors were illuminated in a study by Glenn and Supancic (1984), who analyzed data from seven U.S. national surveys conducted from the 1970s to 1980 to investigate the relationship of ten social and demographic variables to divorce. Glenn and Supancic's results indicated three variables were strongly related to divorce: race, age of first marriage, and frequency of attendance of religious services.

Race   One of the most consistently reported factors related to divorce is race. Blacks are more likely to divorce and/or separate than whites (Glenn & Supancic, 1984). Further, blacks are more likely than whites to separate and not to divorce soon thereafter (Cherlin, 1981; Norton & Glick, 1979).

Age at First Marriage   The younger the age at the time of the first marriage (particularly where the woman is pregnant), the higher the probability of divorce (J. B. Kelly, 1982). As Glenn and Supancic (1984) report, the rate of divorce for persons who marry very young (before age 20) is substantially higher than for those who marry after age 20.

Frequency of Attendance of Religious Services   The frequency of attendance of religious services is negatively correlated with divorce rates. That is, the more frequently a person attends religious services, the lower the divorce rate. Glenn and Supancic (1984) feel this relationship may reflect religiosity and/or a high propensity for social participation, both of which may have favorable effects on a marriage.

In terms of religious preference, persons who expressed "no religion" had the highest divorce rates, followed by Protestants, Catholics, then Jews. Also, contrary to what one might expect, the more conservative Protestant denominations (Nazarene, Pentecostal, Baptist) exhibited relatively high divorce rates in spite of their strong disapproval of divorce (Glenn & Supancic, 1984; Thornton, 1978). Overall, religiosity appears to be an important deterrent to divorce and separation.

THE IMPACT OF DIVORCE ON CHILDREN

Children, regardless of age, suffer from the breakup of their parents' marriage (Hetherington et al., 1982; Warshak & Santrock, 1983). While some older children may understand why things happened the way they did, they may also be likely to identify closely with each parent and experience much of the pain and confusion that their mother and father do; they may even attempt to fill the parent role (Papalia & Olds, 1982). Younger children may, if not told, assume that the breakup was somehow their fault or may fear losing the remaining parent. They may become particularly guarded about the quality and quantity of time they have with each parent at a time when the adults are least able to sit down and talk to them and them alone. Children who actively witness conflict between their parents, who are not told the reasons behind the divorce or that the divorce is final, or who are forced to "take sides" are particularly prone to a variety of difficulties: depression, physical/school difficulties, sleep disturbances, anxiety, difficulties in controlling aggressive and sexual behavior, and guilt. What seems to be important in restoring a sense of stability to these children's lives is clear, honest communication and unqualified support and love from *both* parents. As Papalia and Olds (1982) note, children of divorce are usually better off in a stable one-parent home than in a conflict-ridden, unhappy two-parent one. With appropriate support from their parents and school personnel, most children are able to reestablish balance in their lives within a year or two after the divorce (Hetherington, 1979). While their own later self-esteem and marriages may be affected by the experience of divorce, research has yet to be conducted bearing on the long-term effects of divorce in children's *adult* lives (J. B. Kelly, 1982).

DIVORCE LATER IN LIFE

It is interesting to note that there are increasing numbers of middle-aged and older adults divorcing (Hayghe, 1984; Knox, 1980). Divorce at any age level has numerous economic, social, emotional, and psychological effects upon individuals, but research is beginning to suggest that women have extremely severe problems when they become divorced in middle adulthood or later in life. There are a number of reasons why divorce has a significant effect upon these older women. First, they may find themselves without their former husband's pension income, and due to their age and lack of occupational skills and/or experience, they are often unemployable, which causes a severe financial strain. Second, there is severe stress associated with a loss of support caused by loss of friendship networks. Third, there is a decrease in self-esteem stemming from these factors (J. B. Kelly, 1982; Knox, 1980).

We still do not know why the divorce rate among older adults is increasing, but it has been suggested that the trend is partially due to couples remaining together for the sake of the children; when the children finally leave home, there is no longer a reason for the couple to stay together (Glenn & Supancic, 1984). Due to the fact that the husband and wife now see more of each other because they have retired, they may become aware of how unhappy they are with their relationship and subsequently divorce. We need to gather further information regarding the causes and effects of divorce beyond young adulthood. Many researchers view the increased rate of divorce among middle-aged and older adults with alarm, while others feel it is a transitory phenomenon that is just characteristic of current middle-aged and older cohorts. That is, these individuals were in the periods of childhood, adolescence, and adulthood when divorce had many negative connotations associated with it. Therefore, the couples remained together unhappily for many years rather than experience the social stigma of divorce. But when current young cohorts who have been reared in a society that views divorce in a positive or acceptable manner reach middle age and old age, they will not have to divorce, because they will have already terminated unhappy marital relationships many years before. This question will need to be answered in the future.

The Remarried

Most divorced individuals remarry, usually within three years of being divorced (Glenn & Weaver, 1977, 1978; Furstenburg, 1982). Statistics suggest that while approximately 75 percent of divorced women and 80 percent of divorced men remarry (U.S. Bureau of the Census, 1986), the likelihood of remarriage after divorce decreases with increasing age. Further, research indicates the majority of remarried individuals of both sexes tend to view their second marriage as being somewhat better on a number of dimensions (Furstenburg, 1982). In light of our earlier discussion regarding the difficulty of measuring marital satisfaction, this conclusion regarding the quality of second marriages may be premature.

Hetherington, M. Cox, and R. Cox (1982) report that remarriages that involve children often present difficulties. Though individuals often describe their second marriages as happier than their first, statistics do indicate that the divorce rate for remarried individuals is somewhat higher than for first marriages (Glenn & Weaver, 1977, 1978). In fact, Kompara (1980) suggests that the group of remarrieds who have the most difficult adjustment problems are those in which both husband and wife have children from previous marriages living within the household.

Cohabitation

Prior to discussing singles, we must discuss a life-style that fits somewhere between married and single, that of living together or *cohabitation*. Cohabitation is often either a precursor to or substitute for marriage (Crooks & Bauer, 1980). There are many factors related to the significant increase in couples living together in recent years. Some of these include a questioning of traditional mores and values by younger generations, increased availability and more effective methods of birth control, and a matter of personal preference.

Among older adults, cohabitation is also increasing in popularity. For this age-group, the primary purposes of cohabitation are companionship/ emotional support, economic purposes, or necessity, such as sharing the costs of housing, utilities, and food.

Overall, marriage, cohabitation, or some type of companionable relationship are important areas of study in adulthood and aging because they have been found to be related to life expectancy (Timiras, 1972; Wantz & Gay, 1981) as well as to psychological well-being and adjustment. They, of course, help to define the convoy (Kahn & Antonucci, 1980). The exact reasons for the positive relationship between marriage, cohabitation, and companionship and increased life expectancy are not known, but it is thought that they serve the important function of emotional and psychological support necessary in dealing with the stresses of life (Doherty & Jacobson, 1982).

Singles

Singles are those individuals who have never been married, are widowed, or are divorced. Statistics indicate that of those individuals currently viewed as singles in the United States, approximately 58 percent have never been married, 27 percent are widowed, and 15 percent are divorced. Single adults are considered the "heads" of about one household in five. It is estimated that by 1990, they will control one household in four, because individuals are now divorcing more often, getting married later, and waiting longer to remarry. During the period of young adulthood, about 85 percent of single parents are females.

As will be discussed in Chapter 9, parenting is a difficult task. It becomes more difficult and complex when there is only one parent available to provide all the activities normally required of two. Some facts regarding single parents are provided in Box 8.3.

Individuals who never marry may feel that their primary obligation is to care for aging and/or ailing parents. Older "never married" individuals, however, may be better adjusted than widows of the same age, never having had to cope with the death of a spouse. This may also be due to the fact they have experienced living alone, being independent, and doing things for themselves for a longer time. Further, they do not experience the dramatic change in life-style that can occur as the result of losing a spouse, since, in our couples-oriented society, they have developed friendship networks independently of a marriage partner. These individuals see nothing wrong with the single life-style, value their independence and freedom, and have developed interests in solitary activities, such as reading and going to movies.

A number of reports suggest that approximately 81 percent of all individuals over age 65 live alone, due to any number of reasons, such as the death of a spouse (Ward, 1984). Living alone may contribute to medical and physiological difficulties. A good example of living alone potentially contributing to medical or health problems is in the area of diet/nutrition. For instance, eating is a highly social event in many societies, including ours. Dating, parties, and social gatherings often center on eating. Since we are accustomed to eating with others, eating alone may lead to, or be associated with, feelings of loneliness and isolation. Further, often individuals who are

BOX 8.3

SINGLE PARENTS

United States government statistics continue to point out that the divorce rate is increasing. Therefore, the percent of single parents is also increasing. Clingempeel and Reppucci (1982) report that current estimates indicate approximately 40 percent of families are headed by one parent. Of these families, 85 percent are headed by females and 15 percent by males.

Though society has generally frowned on single fathers, the number of single men heading families has increased by 127 percent since 1970 (Meredith, 1985). As research indicates, courts still favor the mother in terms of "physical" custody of the child. This is based on the assumption that the mother plays the most critical role in the nurturing, caregiving, and development of the child. When fathers are awarded physical custody of the child, they often must learn child rearing skills, since in most cases child rearing has been the primary responsibility of the mother.

What research is available suggests that, with experience, single fathers are quite successful and effective in child rearing. Students interested in getting additional information regarding single-parenting, the effects of divorce on children, and related topics are encouraged to read Clingempeel and Reppucci (1982) and Meredith (1985).

alone do not have the desire or interest to cook a full and nourishing meal, and therefore their diet may consist primarily of snacks and junk food.

WIDOWHOOD

During later adulthood, the largest group of single older adults are those who are widowed. Statistics indicate that by age 65, three in five women will be widows; by age 75, four out of five will be (Statistical Abstract of the United States, U.S. Bureau of the Census, 1986). Men do not usually become widowers until after age 85, if at all. A number of facts regarding widowed persons is presented in Box 8.4.

The single most catastrophic event people experience is the death of their spouse (Holmes & Rahe, 1967). While most of us equate widowhood with old age, the fact is that death does not pick and choose in this way. Younger marriages are often broken by death, also with potentially disastrous consequences for the survivors. Being a widow(er) is difficult in many respects. A young widow's husband is more likely to have died suddenly; she may be left emotionally defenseless. If she has children, she may have to continue caring for them and at the same time try to come to grips with the void in her life. This can be difficult for a young widow, despite the fact that she herself may be in good health and may have been left life-insurance benefits. On the other hand, an older widow may be in poorer health and may be living on a fixed income, but she may have had the opportunity to "prepare," emotionally speaking, for her husband's death (V. Marshall, 1980). At the same time, older women in particular, while not likely to be caring for children, probably have grown up in an era where they were not likely to have developed employable skills (beyond child care) so that they are at a real disadvantage in getting a job as a means of coping with the economic stresses of widowhood.

BOX 8.4

PROFILE OF WIDOWHOOD/WIDOWERHOOD

1. Current statistics indicate that there are approximately 9.3 million widowed older adults in the United States.

2. In 1984 half of all older women were widows.

3. Approximately 84 percent of all widowed persons are women.

4. Approximately 33 percent of all widows live with one of their children. The majority live alone or with others (e.g., friends).

5. Though many widowed individuals could potentially live with one of their children, the majority prefer their privacy and independence to living with their children.

6. Widows are more likely to live with a daughter than a son.

7. Widowers are less likely to live with children than widows.

Sources: American Association of Retired Persons (AARP). (1985). *A profile of older Americans: 1985.* Washington, D.C.: AARP; H. Lopata. (1979). *Women as widows: Support systems.* New York: Elsevier; and E. Shanas, P. Townsend, D. Wedderburn, H. Friis, P. Milhoj, & J. Stehourver. (1968). *Old people in three industrial societies.* New York: Atherton Press.

All widows, regardless of age, are likely to experience problems adjusting to the loss of a spouse (Sanders, 1980–1981; Troll et al., 1979). The same could be said for widowers, in that being alone may pose a number of problems. For example, such problems may relate to caring for and feeding oneself, learning to relate to someone else on an intimate, trusting basis, and dealing with child care responsibilities or health problems (though research is very scanty in this respect) (Troll et al., 1979). On the other hand, there is (particularly for older men) a greater selection from which to choose an eligible mate. One's own ideas about the sanctity of marriage and the quality of that marriage are also factors that determine how one adjusts to widow(er)-hood (Carey, 1979–1980). Emotional reactions to widowhood are complex (denial, anger, relief, guilt), and widowhood can, under some conditions, predispose one to a variety of psychological/physical problems, ranging from depression to serious illness or death (Rowland, 1977; R. Schulz, 1978). Thus, we can probably assume that persons who are widowed are vulnerable in many ways and that they need active support, not only immediately after the death but also for many months afterward. In almost all cases, the grief that accompanies the death of one's mate is very personal and complex and may require a great deal of time and help to be resolved (see Chapter 12). For some, it is never resolved.

Becoming a widow/widower seems to cause many psychological, sociological, economic, and potentially physiological and medical problems (Gallagher, Breckenridge, L. W. Thompson, & Peterson, 1983). For example, L. W. Thompson, Breckenridge, Gallagher, and Peterson (1984) investigated multiple indices of self-perceived physical health for 212 older widows and widowers (ranging in age from 55 to 83 years) two months following the loss of their spouse and compared them to a control group. Results indicated the widow/widowers reported significantly more recently developed or worsened illnesses, greater use of medications, and poorer general health ratings. Interestingly, these differences were independent of sex and socioeconomic level. Further, at any age, widow/widowerhood can bring about a number of changes ranging from a lack of sexual fulfillment to loss of social interaction and support (Lopata, 1979; Shanas, Townsend, Wedderburn, Friis, Milhoj, & Stehourver, 1968).

Gender Differences   As we suggested in Chapters 1 and 2, there is a fairly high predominance of widows compared to widowers in old age for two primary reasons. First, there is a difference in terms of life expectancy between males and females in favor of females (see Chapter 2). Second, men tend to marry women younger than themselves. Therefore, due to genetic predisposition and social customs, females are likely to outlive their husbands. Research suggests that females tend to manifest greater stress at losing a spouse in old age than males, due to the loss of status, friendship networks, and financial support that are usually derived from the husband (Gallagher et al., 1983), though for men the loss of spouse may be more unexpected. Since more and more women are now entering the work force, it will be interesting to see in future cohorts if males exhibit increased stress upon losing their spouse because of the financial support and other benefits derived from the wife's occupation.

Being widowed is so common, especially during late middle age and old age, that society has even ascribed a variety of "roles" to widows (Lopata, 1975) (see below). What roles women play seem, however, to depend upon their former relationships with (or dependence upon) their husbands (Lopata, 1975). For some women, the role of the widow is to work to keep the family together and keep the husband's memory alive; further, they are not supposed to be interested in other men. For other women whose lives have evolved more independently of their husbands', role changes are less drastic, though these women are still lonely and grieve for their husbands (Lopata, 1975). When the immediate support is withdrawn soon after their husbands' deaths, many women experience difficulty in adjustment, in that clear role expectations do not exist (Lopata, 1975). Just as women adjust to the deaths of their husbands in varying ways, the long-term consequences for widows seem to vary. Lopata (1975) found several postwidowhood life-styles, or **types of widows**, in her study of widows living in Chicago:

1. *liberated women*—have worked through death and moved on; are leading complex, well-rounded lives

2. *"merry widows"*—life-styles filled with dating, fun, and entertainment

3. *working women*—career oriented, involved in work, *or* women who are poorly trained and who take most any job available

4. *"widow's widows"*—living alone, valuing independence, preferring the company of other widows

5. *traditional widows*—living with children, highly involved in their children and grandchildren

6. *grieving women*—willingly isolated widows who cannot work through their husbands' deaths, *or* women who are isolated due to a lack of interpersonal or job skills but nevertheless wish to become more involved

Comparatively speaking we still know very little regarding widowers, due to the lack of their significant numbers (V. Marshall, 1980).

Remarriage—Widows/Widowers As previously discussed in our section on divorce, the majority of individuals who get divorced during adulthood do remarry. Interestingly, remarriage after widowhood is less likely to occur than following divorce, though the tendency to remarry following the death of a spouse tends to be highly related to the age and gender of the widowed individual (Ward, 1984). With increasing age, the tendency to remarry following the death of a spouse decreases. The probability of remarriage following the death of a spouse is high for individuals in their twenties, thirties, and forties, but declines significantly thereafter. Most individuals remarry out of a desire for companionship and affection.

With regard to gender, research indicates widowers are more likely than widows to remarry, especially with advancing age. For instance, though less than 20 percent of males over age 65 remarry, less than 5 percent of females over age 55 remarry (L. George, 1980).

There are numerous reasons and explanations for why more widowers than widows remarry. First, given the gender differences in life expectancy in favor of females, there are simply fewer available males with advancing age. Also, with advancing age, females tend to be in better health than males of similar age. Therefore, the widow may not want to experience the same emotional hurt of losing another spouse to a health-related problem. Finally, males are usually unprepared or inexperienced in the skills required to live alone, such as cooking, cleaning, and grocery shopping (V. Marshall, 1980). When individuals do marry following the death of a spouse, especially after age 50, they tend to marry someone they have known for a long period of time and do so for companionship and affection (see Chapter 12).

SEXUAL BEHAVIOR OVER THE LIFE SPAN

A crucial component of interpersonal relationships, especially those that are intimate, is sexuality. Perhaps no other aspect of interpersonal relationships has been viewed with such a taboo attitude in our society in the past as that of sexual behavior. Society's attitudes are, however, generally becoming more liberal. This change is due to several factors: increased cohabitation; larger percentages of young adults, both males and females, experiencing or approving of premarital sex; sex outside of marriage becoming more common; and increased tolerance of alternative life-styles and sexual relations such as homosexuality. Though society's attitudes toward sexual behavior have apparently become more liberal, there is still great difficulty in obtaining factual data regarding any point of the life cycle. Despite this general trend toward more liberal views regarding sex, it is important to point out, however, that the AIDS epidemic may have reversed this trend somewhat. Some individuals do, nevertheless, maintain an open attitude toward sexuality.

Problems with Obtaining Accurate Information

Broadly speaking, human sexuality has been defined as "the individual's capacity for pleasure from intimate physical contact" (Laws, 1980, p. 249). There are two major reasons why it is difficult to obtain reliable information regarding sexual behavior at any point along the life span, despite the fact that sexuality is an important, normal characteristic attribute of human beings (Laws, 1980). The first pertains to societal and personal values. That is, the majority of Americans feel sexual behavior is a matter of personal concern and no business of others, including researchers (Laws, 1980). This bias may be further compounded when we talk about sexual behavior among older adults, since these individuals were raised in a time in which there was a conservative attitude toward sexual behavior. In addition, the types of individuals who often participate in research studies and interviews regarding sexual behavior are not representative of the general population. For example, they may be involved in sex therapy, have sexual problems, or have extremely liberal views on sexual behavior.

The second difficulty has to do with how information or data on sexual behavior is obtained. There are three major methods of acquiring data regarding sexual behavior. These are (1) surveys and questionnaires; (2) observation (e.g., taking physiological recordings during sexual activity in the laboratory); and (3) experimental manipulation (measuring sexual excitation physiologically in the laboratory while showing sexually stimulating material). All three of these methods are potentially confounded. These confounds range from an individual's tendency to distort information on questionnaires to the artificiality of the laboratory situation and stimuli used in experimental research.

Keeping all these difficulties in mind, we will begin our discussion of life-span trends in sexual behavior. We will concentrate primarily on middle age and old age, since a detailed, in-depth presentation of the sexual anatomy, physiological aspects of sex, and sexual behavior during childhood and adolescence are likely to be covered in other courses. Our primary goal will be to highlight the literature regarding sexual behavior during middle and late adulthood and to discuss the potential implications of the changes in sexual behavior that occur during the later phases of life.

Life-Span Trends in Sexual Behavior

There is a basic lack of detailed information regarding sexual behavior during middle and old age. Therefore, our discussion will be in general terms. As our above discussion implies, it will often be based on studies with small sample sizes, consisting of individuals who may not be truly representative of the population. Further, there is significant individual variability in sexual behavior at all age levels.

In order to discuss sexual behavior adequately, we must distinguish between the impact of *extrinsic factors,* such as personal beliefs and attitudes toward sex, and *intrinsic factors,* such as physical health and physiological condition on sexual activity. All these factors interact in a complex manner to determine our sexual activity and interest at any age.

It is also important to distinguish between sexual interest and actual sexual activity. Sexual interest is primarily a psychological factor and pertains to the individual's interest in engaging in sexual behavior. Sexual activity pertains to one's actually engaging in sexual behavior. Life-span trends for each are graphically indicated in Figure 8.3, based on collections of experimental studies and reports (Comfort, 1980; Cameron, 1970a; Ludeman, 1981; Pfeiffer, Verwoerdt, & Wang, 1968; Masters & Johnson, 1966, 1970). It should be stressed that the trends reported in Figure 8.3 should be seen only as generalizations, since they are based on studies with many potential confounds (see discussion on page 295). Further, there are vast individual differ-

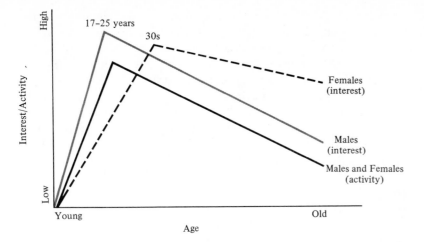

Figure 8.3   Suspected life-span trends in sexual interest and activity for males
and females.

ences within all age-groups in terms of both sexual interest and sexual activity, as discussed earlier.

A number of facts are indicated in Figure 8.3. *First,* at all points along the life span there is a discrepancy between interest in sexual behavior and actual sexual activity; interest and desire are always higher than activity. *Second,* there are gender differences in both age of "peak" sexual interest and life-span trend in sexual interest. Specifically, for males, sexual interest peaks in early adulthood (ages 17–25 years, approximately) and then gradually declines with advancing age. For females, the peak in interest is not reached until the thirties (approximately) and then declines in a more gradual manner. We shall discuss the reasons for this later in this chapter. *Third,* during the entire life span, the activity level of males and females is almost identical. This is due primarily to the fact that in young adulthood individuals tend to couple (pair) and engage in sexual activity only with their spouse or a limited number of partners.

In the next section we shall discuss a number of extrinsic and intrinsic factors that affect sexual interest and activity across the life span. We should note here that as we move along the age continuum, our data base becomes more sketchy and controversial, due to the fact that most older adults were not reared in a time when there was open discussion of sexual matters, so they do not readily give information or participate in studies pertaining to sex. Some researchers (L. E. Thomas, 1982) do not see anything positive coming from research of this type. In fact, L. E. Thomas (1982) considers such research potentially harmful to older adults and the interpretation of research findings subject to contamination by young and middle-aged values. For example, one may conclude that older adults will lose self-esteem, based on finding that their level of sexual activity is less frequent relative to that of younger persons. According to Thomas, this reflects a young bias that at least average levels of sexual activity are important to the well-being of older persons.

It should be noted that attitudes toward sex have changed substantially with successive cohorts during this century. For instance, Zelnick and Kantner (1981) surveyed young, unmarried white women regarding the age at which they experienced premarital sex. In 1971 they found that by age 18, 40 percent reported they had engaged in premarital sexual intercourse. In 1976, the figure was 51 percent, and in 1979, it was 57 percent. This study illustrates that attitudes toward sexual behavior are becoming more liberal. Moreover, attitudes toward diverse forms of sexual behavior seem to recognize such variability (Broderick, 1982). However, anxiety over AIDS, which appears to be transmitted both homosexually and heterosexually, may mitigate such a shift.

MYTHS REGARDING SEXUAL BEHAVIOR DURING OLD AGE

There are many myths regarding sexual behavior during old age that are held even by the old themselves (Salamon & Charytan, 1984). According to J. Rubin (1976), the two major myths are (1) sexual behavior is not typical for older adults (not normal or average), and (2) if sexual behavior does persist into old age, it is silly, wrong, or sinful.

It is perhaps the lack of separation among sexual interest, attitude, and behavior that predisposes many to assume that **menopause**, referring to the cessation of menstruation (fertility), accompanied by lessened estrogen production, atrophy of the breasts and genital tissues, and shrinking of the uterus, implies less sexuality. While symptoms such as hot flashes or night sweats are experienced by most women, the extent to which one's ideas about growing older are linked to menopause and the degree of one's overinvolvement with one's children accounts for the negative psychological impact of menopause on women (Newman, 1982). For women whose identity does not solely rest with their bearing and mothering children, menopause can allow them to get involved in new tasks (returning to school, community work). This negative perception of menopause and the generally negative sexual connotation given to older persons contributes to stereotypically negative attitudes toward sexuality in later adulthood, an attitude that seems to be directed at women in particular (Laws, 1980).

General Factors Related to Sexual Behavior

There are numerous major **extrinsic factors** and two **intrinsic factors** that affect sexual behavior (both interest and activity) for both males and females during the life cycle (Crooks & Bauer, 1980).

EXTRINSIC FACTORS

One factor that affects an individual's sexual behavior is that person's *personal attitude* toward sex. Some individuals enjoy engaging in sexual activity more than others, have more liberal views than others, and so forth. Second, the *beliefs* and *attitudes* of our ethnic, cultural, and/or social group affect our sexual behavior. For example, research (Crooks & Bauer, 1980) indicates that individuals from middle and upper socioeconomic classes tend to have a more open or liberal attitude toward sex. A third factor is *educational level,* where individuals with more education are more sophisticated and liberal regarding sexual behavior. Fourth, there is a significant relationship between sexual activity and *marriage.* That is, married individuals are more likely to engage in sexual activity due to the availability of a partner. Another factor related to sexual behavior is the *quality* of the marital or interpersonal relationship. The closer and warmer the relationship, the greater the potential for sexual activity. Persons' personal *religious* beliefs affect their sexual behavior. Often religious beliefs set standards and expectations regarding sexual behavior, such as only engaging in sexual behavior to have children. It should also be observed that there is a general *consistency* in sexual behavior. Individuals tend to maintain a particular pattern of sexual behavior throughout the life cycle, in terms of type and frequency of sexual behavior, though the level of such activity will vary with the above factors.

All these factors potentially influence our sexual activity and interest, regardless of age (Broderick, 1982). These factors are considered extrinsic since they result from influences external to the individual—that is, social and environmental influences (divorce, remarriage, illness, widowhood). We will next discuss general intrinsic factors, which are those related to the medical and/or physical condition of the body.

INTRINSIC FACTORS

The primary intrinsic factors that affect sexual behavior for both males and females are health, mental status, and physical condition.

AGE CHANGES IN BODILY FUNCTIONING RELATED TO SEXUAL BEHAVIOR

Research has documented a number of specific biological-physiological changes in the body structures and organ systems that are part of the normal aging processes and are related to sexual behavior (Ludeman, 1981). It is important to note that these changes have a more significant effect upon one's interest and desire to have, rather than one's ability to engage in, sexual behavior. We will discuss the changes for males and females separately.

Males There are a number of normal age-related changes in male biological-physiological functioning that have a potential effect upon sexual behavior. Based on interviews and laboratory observation of men ranging in age from 50 to 90 years, Masters and Johnson (1966, 1970) found a number of biological-physiological changes with age. Some of these were: the time required for erection increased with advancing age, the penis did not get as hard or extend its maximum length, the amount of preejaculatory fluid decreased; though ejaculatory control increased, the force of ejaculation and volume of seminal fluids decreased; orgasm was briefer; and the refractory period increased with age. These biological-physiological changes may affect both sexual interest and activity.

Females Based upon similar sources of data as for men, Masters and Johnson (1966, 1970) studied women ranging in age from 40 to 80 years, documenting a number of biological-physiological changes that could affect sexual behavior with aging. For example, the production of vaginal lubricant was delayed, the vaginal barrel constricted in size, and the vaginal walls became thinner. These changes often resulted in pain during intercourse. Finally, orgasm was of a shorter duration.

The above data indicate that there are a number of biological-physiological changes that normally occur with age and that may potentially affect our sexual behavior (Ludeman, 1981; Masters & Johnson, 1966, 1970). These changes appear to have a more pronounced effect upon psychosocial influences related to sexual behavior than upon actual sexual behavior per se (see Box 8.5). There is no evidence that any of these changes in themselves produce any actual limitations that would affect an older person's ability to engage in normal sexual activity. Thus, it is not one's physical condition itself that reduces activity but one's *belief* about the physical disability that is the causal factor.

In the next section we shall discuss studies that have investigated general attitudes toward sexual behavior by older adults, as well as reports of sexual interest and activity by older adults.

BOX 8.5

WOMEN HEART ATTACK VICTIMS FEAR RESUMING SEXUAL ACTIVITY

Women recovering from a heart attack fear resuming sexual activity could bring pain, another heart attack, or even death, researchers said Thursday in a medical journal.

An estimated 300,000 women survive a heart attack each year.

"Most studies on sexual activity after myocardial infarction (heart attack) have considered only male patients," Dr. Chris Papadopoulos of the University of Maryland in Baltimore said.

"Information about the sexual function and activity of women who have experienced myocardial infarction is notably absent," he said in the American Medical Association's Archives of Internal Medicine.

Papadopoulos, a cardiologist, and colleagues in-

terviewed 130 women, ages 38 to 65, who suffered their first heart attack between 1976 and 1979.

"Sexual concerns soon developed in 30 percent of those sexually active before the myocardial infarction," the researchers said.

"Fear of resumption of sexual activity was expressed by 51 percent of the patients and 44 percent of the husbands. Sexual activity was not resumed by 27 percent, was unchanged by 27 percent, and was decreased by 44 percent."

Symptoms during intercourse—chest pain, palpitations, sweating, shortness of breath, and fatigue—were reported by 57 percent of the patients, the researchers said.

Source: *Charleston Times-Courier*. (1983, August 19).

Research Regarding Sexual Interest and Activity in Older Adults

Though it is quite normal for older adults to engage in sexual behavior until advanced old age, that is, in the eighties and nineties, society in general believes that the elderly *do not, should not,* or *cannot* engage in sexual behavior. For example, Cameron (1970) examined beliefs about sexuality with three age-groups, young (18–25 years), middle age (40–55 years), and old (65–79 years). Results indicated that in all age-groups, even the oldest, the old were viewed as being below average on a number of dimensions regarding sexual behavior: desire for sexual behavior, skill in performing, capacity for sexual behavior, frequency of attempts at sexual behavior, social opportunities for sexual behavior, and frequency of sexual activity. Findings such as these indicate there is a discrepancy between the biological-physiological capabilities of older adults to engage in sexual behavior and their *own* attitudes as well as those of others toward older adults engaging in sexual behavior.

Longitudinal research investigations of sexual interest and activity find that sexual interest remains fairly constant throughout most of life and does not begin to decline until after age 75 (Pfeiffer et al., 1968). In terms of activity, Comfort (1980) reported that 47 percent of all individuals between 60 and 71 years of age, and 15 percent of individuals over age 78, engaged in regular and frequent intercourse. On the other hand, some studies have found sexual activity begins to decline in the sixties (see Ludeman, 1981).

Apparently, as age increases, the discrepancy between interest and activity widens for women (see Figure 8.3). In fact, male interest and female activity also seem to be parallel. In a survey of older unmarried women (65 years+), though these women reported little or no activity, about 25 percent still expressed interest (Wantz & Gay, 1981). The decrease in activity can be attributed to a number of social-environmental factors, such as a loss of interest in sex by the male, loss of spouse, and institutionalization.

Longitudinal studies indicate sexual intercourse persists into advanced old age (Ludeman, 1981); if sexual intercourse ceases in old age, it is due primarily to the male. That is, it is the male who makes the decision not to engage in intercourse. The data in Figure 8.3 bear out the relationship between male disinterest and declines in sexual activity in later adulthood.

Factors Related to Decreased Sexual Activity over the Life Span for Males and Females

We have previously discussed general factors that are related to sexual behavior across the life span. In this section, we shall discuss specific factors that researchers have found to be related to decreased sexual activity for males and females with increasing age.

As we have seen in Figure 8.3, after reaching its peak in early adulthood (mid-twenties), there is a steady decrease in sexual activity for males and females. Interestingly, though the trend for males and females is approximately identical, the causal factors are somewhat different for each sex.

For males, research suggests a number of causal factors are involved (Masters & Johnson, 1966, 1970). These include monotony and boredom, preoccupation with career or other activities, mental or physical fatigue, physical health, and fear of failure. It is difficult to rank or determine which is the most significant factor or reason for losses in sexual activity.

Regarding females, research is much more definitive (Masters & Johnson, 1966, 1970). The research clearly indicates that the primary cause of a decline in sexual activity for females with increasing age is the lack of a male partner. That is, her partner is either dead or unable or unwilling to perform. Additionally, there may simply be no available male partners. Other factors include physical and/or health limitations and social-psychological factors, such as attitudes or beliefs toward sexual behavior. For instance, many women may feel they are unable to function sexually after menopause (Comfort, 1980). Overall, however, the major limiting factor is the lack of a male partner. It should be noted that this research is somewhat dated and that studies of current and future cohorts of older adults may yield different results. For instance, future cohorts of females may report boredom and preoccupation with their job as limiting factors in sexual behavior.

Alternative Sexual Life-Styles

Given the facts that (1) the peak of sexual interest varies between males and females, that (2) females live longer than males, and that (3) the cessation of sexual activity is due primarily to the male, some researchers are now challenging traditional views about masturbation and homosexuality and the traditional custom of males marrying younger women.

For instance, Lipinski (1979) reports that many researchers believe the Western tradition of the male being older than the female in a relationship works against the chances of the couple's remaining sexually active. That is, since females live longer than males and reach their sexual peak later than males, it would seem more appropriate if the female were older than the male in a relationship. Though this appears to make common sense, Lipinski points out the negative attitudes of society toward relationships of this type.

Society is beginning to view masturbation as a socially appropriate sexual outlet for older females. Studies indicate that approximately 50 percent of older adult females masturbate due primarily to the lack of a male partner for sexual activity (Ludeman, 1981).

Wall and Kaltreider (1977) interviewed 100 females ranging in age from 19 to 75 years (*M* age = 31 years) regarding bisexuality and homosexuality. These individuals were selected at random from a group of gynecological outpatients. The findings of this study demonstrate the changing attitudes of society toward bisexuality and homosexuality. First, though 63 percent regarded themselves as purely heterosexual, about one-third of the overall sample reported they had seriously considered bisexuality and felt bisexuality was an acceptable alternative for others. Also, approximately 23 percent reported incidental homosexual feelings. Though this study has a number of limitations, it does highlight that individuals are becoming more accepting of these alternative sexual life-styles, though again it remains to be seen what impact AIDS will have on such attitudes.

Sexual Dysfunction

Sexual difficulties and impairments in normal sexual functioning are termed *sexual dysfunction,* and it is estimated that at least half of all married couples at some time may be affected by some form of sexual dysfunction (J. L. McCary & S. P. McCary, 1982). Most sexual dysfunctions are due to psychosocial factors, such as fear of failure, guilt, and low self-esteem (Hyde, 1982; H. S. Kaplan, 1974, 1975; Masters & Johnson, 1970; Masters, Johnson, & Kolodny, 1982; J. L. McCary & S. P. McCary, 1982); some examples of these sexual dysfunctions are presented in Table 8.3. In cases where couples are experiencing sexual dysfunction, psychological interventions can be very helpful, regardless of age (Broderick, 1982; Zarit, 1980).

There is still the need to accumulate additional reliable data regarding sexual behavior that is both normal and dysfunctional at all points along the life span. Such information is required by counselors, nurses, physicians, social workers, and other mental-health professions in order to deal more effectively with individuals who are experiencing sexual problems both within and outside the context of marriage. Students interested in learning more about sexual behavior in older adults are encouraged to read Ludeman (1981) and Wantz and Gay (1981). Further, Salamon and Charytan (1984) and

TABLE 8.3

EXAMPLES OF SEXUAL DYSFUNCTIONS IN MALES AND FEMALES

Dysfunction	Definition	Estimated Prevalence
Males		
Erectile dysfunction	When intercourse is unsuccessful 25% of the time or more, due to an inability to have or to maintain an erection	50%
Premature ejaculation	Absence of voluntary control of ejaculation	50%
Retarded ejaculation	Inability to ejaculate into the woman's vagina, though the person may be able to ejaculate through other means of stimulation (e.g., masturbation)	unknown
Females		
Orgasmic dysfunction	Inability to have an orgasm	10–20%
Vaginismus	Severe involuntary contractions of the muscles surrounding the vaginal entrance that makes intercourse too painful	unknown, but thought to be rare

Source: Hyde (1982); Kaplan (1974, 1975); Masters & Johnson (1970); Masters, Johnson & Kolodny (1982).

Zarit (1980) discuss programs designed to deal with medical, emotional, and social problems related to sexuality in the aged.

SUMMARY

The two major topics discussed in this chapter were *interpersonal relationships* and *sexual behavior.* A variety of relationships, such as *sibling relationships, friendships, intergenerational ties,* and *marital bonds* help to define the *convoy,* an emotional support system that contributes to feelings of well-being in adulthood. Distinctions were made between *interest-related* and *deep* friendships, which seem to vary with both age and gender. Though most individuals do eventually marry, individuals obviously get married for a variety of reasons. In many respects *similarity* and *complementarity* seem to be related to why individuals are attracted to each other. Alternatively, we might view marital attraction in terms of *filter theory* and as a series of *stages* through which the couple learn more about one another along several dimensions. While marital satisfaction seems to vary with the presence of children, the *family life cycle* approach to family development has been criticized in favor of one emphasizing the *dynamics of family interactions.*

The *divorce* rate in the United States has been increasing among all age-groups. Divorce can have a variety of short-term and long-term effects on the individual. Persons respond differently to both *divorce* and *widowhood,* consistent with the influence of numerous factors.

Life-span trends differ in *sexual interest* and *activity* for both males and females, as does the peak of sexual interest. However, there are significant differences between interest and activity at all points along the life span. Specific factors that relate to decreased sexual activity for both males and females with increasing age were discussed. For females, the primary factor that seems to result in decreased sexual activity is a *lack of available male partners;* for males, the factors are less clear. We still do not have an extensive and reliable data base regarding sexual behavior in adults, especially from middle age to older adulthood. This research area is still considered somewhat taboo and contributes to why we lack definitive information.

KEY TERMS AND CONCEPTS

Interpersonal relationships	Social clock
Interest-related friendships	Traditional marriage
Deep friendships	Companionship marriage
Kinship network	Colleague marriage
Filial responsibility	Open marriage
Filial maturity	Group marriage
Extended family	Homosexual partnership

Childless marriage

Menopause

Extrinsic factors related to sexual
behavior

Intrinsic factors related to sexual
behavior

Convoy

Attachment

Filter theory of mate selection

Stage theory of mate selection

Complementarity

Similarity

Types of widows

Elder abuse

Spouse abuse

- What is socialization, and why is it viewed as a lifelong process?
- What are roles, and how are they developed at different stages along the life cycle?
- How are gender roles developed and maintained along the life cycle?
- What are some of the major contributions of the individual's "family" toward development and socialization along the life cycle?
- What are some of the major advantages and disadvantages of parenthood?
- How does having children affect individuals, their life-style, and their behavior?
- What are some of the major types of "grandparenting" styles common today? What is it about grandparenthood that is meaningful and fulfilling?
- Are attitudes toward aging negative in the United States today? Are attitudes toward aging in the United States today similar to or different from those of other cultures/countries? How can these negative attitudes be changed?
- What is "ageism"? How does it develop, and how is it maintained?
- What are the "universals" and "variations" of aging?

CHAPTER 9

ROLES IN ADULTHOOD, SOCIALIZATION, AND ATTITUDES

▪

INTRODUCTION

This chapter will focus on the process of *socialization* during the adult and later phases of the life cycle and attitudes toward the aging process in the United States and other countries. In order to adequately understand socialization in a life-span perspective, we must consider a number of diverse topics, such as roles, role transition, gender stereotyping, families, parenting, and grandparenting. Each of these factors plays an important part in the socialization process. In that we are often poorly (and negatively) socialized for changes that we will experience in adulthood (Albrecht & Gift, 1975), parents and grandparents become especially important as socializing agents or role models. It is also important to realize that socialization as a process is *dynamic;* throughout the life span, we are constantly *undergoing* socialization or *anticipating* socialization (Albrecht & Gift, 1975; Emmerich, 1973).

Just as the socialization process impacts upon individuals of all ages, attitudes toward aging significantly affect the developing person. The attitudes we personally have toward the aging process, as well as those of society, will have significant effect upon our behavior, self-concept, and identity. They, to a certain extent, affect the extent to which we internalize age-graded expectations about our behavior and thus influence the process of socialization. Later in this chapter we shall discuss attitudes toward aging in the United States from a historical perspective in order to understand more fully current attitudes toward aging. Further, attitudes toward aging in the United States will be compared with those of other countries in order to clarify cultural similarities or differences in such attitudes. This discussion can lead to further understanding about how your own attitudes toward the aging process are developed and might be modified. To the extent that the process of socialization is beneficial to us as individuals, we can utilize the social convoy (see Chapter 8) as a means of support to help cope with change.

PROCESS OF SOCIALIZATION

Socialization is the process that molds each of us into a member of a particular society or subculture as we acquire the roles appropriate to our age, gender, social class, or ethnic group (Neugarten & Datan, 1973). Through socialization we gain the knowledge, skills, attitudes, values, traits, and behaviors to function in the roles we currently occupy, or will occupy in the future. Society socializes young individuals, who then internalize these expectations (Emmerich, 1973). The knowledge, skills, and traits acquired during the process of socialization vary substantially as a function of such factors as ethnicity, race, culture, and socioeconomic level. Throughout our discussion of socialization, we will constantly refer to the term **roles**. Roles are the behaviors, traits, and characteristics expected by others of individuals who occupy a specific social position in society, such as parent, child, teacher, lawyer, and student (Emmerich, 1973; Hagestad & Neugarten, 1985; Rosow, 1985; Sears, Freedman, & Peplau, 1986). Individuals are assumed by others to know what is expected of them in their roles, and roles are influenced by society's norms, values, and attitudes. These norms are *relative* to expectations varying with who is to occupy them. That is, members of a given society have specific expectations of what individuals in each role are able, and unable, to do. Society tends to impose sanctions in terms of rewards or penalties when an individual does not comply with social definitions and expectations of appropriate role behavior (Hagestad & Neugarten, 1985), and those who fail to fulfill these expectations may be labeled as deviant or abnormal. The costs of violating such expectations may be high. Imagine the reactions of the local community if the mayor were openly to have an extramarital affair or refuse to pay property taxes! As society changes, the roles ascribed to persons on various bases also change (Rosow, 1985).

Theories of socialization vary in terms of the mechanism(s) by which society/societal representatives perform their function. On the one hand, some approaches emphasize environmental influences as socializing agents, whereas others attribute this process to characteristics lying within the person (Emmerich, 1973). Social learning theory (Mischel, 1970), for example, tends to view socialization as "the process by which the individual's behaviors are selectively drawn to situational (role) definitions through mechanisms of social learning and performance" (Emmerich, 1973, p. 126). Alternatively, theories such as Kohlberg's cognitive developmental approach (Kohlberg, 1973) stress the importance of one's cognitive level as a shaper of individual definitions and responses to social situations. Psychodynamic (Freudian) and trait (Cattell) approaches emphasize enduring qualities such as the ego, super-ego, and traits (such as sociability) as structures that permit persons to respond to cultural-societal influences.

Life-Span Trends in Socialization

Perhaps the most in-depth attempt to describe the socialization process throughout the life span has been proposed by O. G. Brim (1966). Though socialization is a lifelong process, Brim suggests that the process of adult socialization is distinctly different from that of childhood. This is due to the fact that different demands are placed on the individual by the environment/society and other individuals at different points of the life cycle. Further, the *contents* or goals of the socialization process, such as what attitudes and behaviors are learned, are also different during adulthood.

According to Brim, the major factor that contributes to socialization involves the individual learning the "role of other." In other words, socialization involves the person learning to anticipate the *other* individual's response to *one's own* behavior, then reflecting upon this behavior, and judging it as either good or bad.

During childhood, socialization agents tend to have an emotional and/or personal tie to the individual, such as a parent, while during adulthood socialization agents tend to be more objective and impersonal, such as one's boss or employer. Therefore, during childhood, these socialization agents are concerned with the child acquiring rules or values regulating behavior, such as not stealing, working hard, and being responsible. On the other hand, during adulthood, socialization agents are concerned with the adult acquiring specific role behaviors, such as how to be a college professor, banker, minister, or teacher (O.G. Brim, 1966). Lerner and Spanier (1978) and Zeits and Prince (1982) argue for a bilateral, *bidirectional* approach to socialization between children and parents (and perhaps grandparents as well). Each member of this socializing dyad wields a host of personal and historical-cultural influences that have a dialectical, *dynamic* effect on individuals and on the family as a whole. Children, for example, may influence not only their parents' tastes in music, TV, or clothes but also political opinions and values. Even within a family life cycle approach (see Chapter 8 and our discussion of parenthood in this chapter), the birth and development of the child have a number of pervasive influences on the parents' life-style, relationships with one another, sexual behavior, and orientation toward other family members in the extended family network. Parents and grandparents, of course, are important socializers of their children with regard to sexuality, values, peer relations, aggressive and/or moral behavior, career orientation, and self-concept. This bidirectional, dynamic process continues through life (Hess & Waring, 1978). In adulthood, for example, socialization continues to involve value orientations and role expectations (parenthood, marriage, retirement). These commonalities not only reinforce affectionate bonds formed early in life and solidify relationships across family lineage lines (see Chapter 8 for a discus-

Parents are important agents of socialization and may serve as role models for gender-specific behaviors. In so doing, their own views on parenting are likely to change.

sion of intergenerational relationships), but they may also promote the emotional and physical well-being of all involved (Hess & Waring, 1978).

Adult socialization agents are usually not interested in the *individual* per se but the individual's behavior. Therefore, adult socialization agents tend to be far less tolerant of deviations from behaviors departing from well-defined roles.

Old age is often considered a *roleless* period of life (Rosow, 1985). Very few roles with **status**, with the exception of senior citizen, retiree, and grandparent, are available to older adults in our society (Rosow, 1985). Since our roles contribute substantially to our identity and self-esteem (Sears et al., 1986), the unavailability of viable roles can have potentially negative effects upon the picture one has of oneself, resulting in a loss of self-esteem. According to the disengagement theory (Cumming & Henry, 1961), there is a tendency to separate from those social roles that have been the basis of our identity during adulthood, a separation that can be beneficial and is a mutual process between society and the older individual. Activity theory, on the other hand, socializes individuals to remain active (Maddox, 1965).

To understand socialization during adulthood and aging, we must discuss *roles* in greater depth. Adults are expected to acquire and perform behaviors associated with many roles simultaneously, for example, teacher, parent, husband, male. Our discussion will focus on two significant roles usually associated with adulthood. These pertain to the family and gender.

ROLES

The entire life cycle can be viewed as a succession of roles (Neugarten & Datan, 1973). We are constantly acquiring, modifying, and changing roles. Adult roles affect our life-style, friendship patterns, adjustment, socialization, identity, and self-concept (Cottrell, 1962). For these reasons, adequate functioning in our roles is critical to the maintenance of positive feelings toward ourselves. Since roles are dynamic, in order to understand current adult roles, we must look at past, present, and future role learning.

In most instances roles are age-graded (see Figure 9.1). That is, certain roles and behaviors are usually acquired, and expected, as a function of age (Atchley, 1975; Rosow, 1985). For example, exercising one's right to vote, obtaining a driver's license, getting married, and purchasing alcoholic beverages are but a few of the age-related privileges associated with chronological age changes in our culture.

Expectancies for age-appropriate behavior are incorporated into a system of explicit and implicit norms for behavior within all cultures (Nardi, 1973). Therefore, age serves as a normative criterion with regard to both role entry and exit as well as influencing the types of socialization agents (parents, grandparents) with whom we have contacts. Rosow (1985) separates roles in terms of their characteristics; each type of role assumes a varying degree of importance across the life span. Each can assume positive or negative status. **Institutional role types** assume a given status for persons who have definite roles (e.g., social class, sex, race, age); **tenuous role types** reflect persons in definite social positions (status) who do not have well-defined functions or roles (aged persons, younger divorced women, the unemployed). **Informal role types** assume no institutional status but have definite roles attached to them (for example the family scapegoat, heroes, blackmailers, homosexuals); **nonrole types** have neither status nor definite roles. These role types vary in terms of their importance over the life span (see Figure 9.2). For our purposes it is important to note in Figure 9.2 that among older adults, relative to younger persons, Rosow sees institutional role types as decreasing in relative importance while tenuous role types increase in relative importance. This generally negative trend has important implications for the socialization of, and attitudes toward, older persons—with increased age, important, well-defined roles are lost and replaced with less well defined ones. Whether this

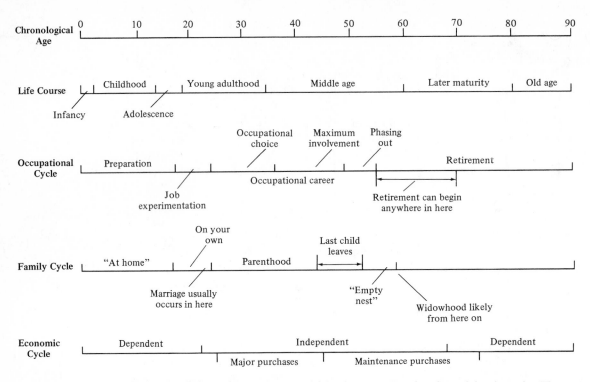

Figure 9.1   Relationships among age, life cycle, occupational cycle, and family cycle. (These relationships fluctuate widely for specific individuals and for various social categories such as ethnic groups or social classes.) *Source:* R. Atchley. (1975). The life course, age grading, and age-linked demands for decision making. In N. Datan & L. Ginsburg (Eds.), *Life-span developmental psychology: normative life crises* (p. 264). New York: Academic Press. Reprinted by permission of Academic Press.

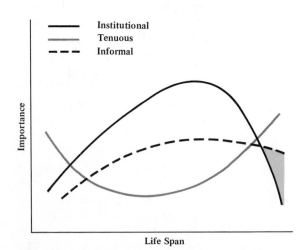

Figure 9.2   Relative importance of role types in the life span. *Source:* I. Rosow. (1985). Status and role change through the life cycle. In R. Binstock & E. Shanas (Eds.), *Handbook of aging and the social sciences* (p. 80). New York: Van Nostrand Reinhold. Used with permission of the publisher.

negative attitude toward aging is a consequence of anticipatory socialization into later adulthood as a "roleless" time of life or the result of being thrust into a tenuous role is uncertain.

Role Transition and Role Change

As we progress along the life span, we are constantly **shifting roles** (L. George, 1980) and reacting to such role changes. Role shifts may occur in two ways: **role transition**, such as from mother to grandmother; or **role change**, such as from student to professor. As these examples indicate, a role transition is simply the process of evolving from one form of a specific role to another *form* of that same role. A role change involves the complete shifting from one *type* of role to another. The degree of difficulty associated with role shifts is influenced by (1) their normative significance, (2) their personal significance, (3) their effect on established patterns of behavior, and (4) the extent to which the individual has been socialized for the role shift (L. George, 1980). For this reason, the shift from father to grandfather will be substantially less difficult than from husband to widower.

With aging, there are two basic types of role change (Cottrell, 1962). The first involves the giving up of social relationships and roles typical of adulthood, such as relinquishing the role of worker, mother, or company vice-president. The second involves the acceptance of retirement and social relationships typical of the later years and their accompanying roles. This process resembles the change in role types with age as described above (Rosow, 1985). If older adults are to maintain positive feelings about themselves, new social roles must be adopted to replace those that have been lost. This is accomplished by becoming involved in new activities that can provide new roles, for instance, changing from the role of mother to grandmother, or bank president to president of the senior volunteers organization.

Gender Roles

One of the most significant roles we acquire during the life span is our **gender role**. Our gender role affects our role within the family (e.g., husband-wife), and may often affect our occupational selection (as indicated in Box 9.1).

Gender roles can be defined as those behavior patterns that are considered appropriate and specific to each gender. They are formed (acquired) early in life and maintained until death. Because the expected traits and behaviors associated with males and females are highly related to factors such as culture, ethnic group, socioeconomic level, and occupation, our discussion of gender roles will be in general terms.

There are a number of explanations of how gender roles are formed. One explanation with substantial research support suggests gender roles are acquired (learned) by the child identifying with the same-sex parent (or model) and incorporating that person's traits, attitudes, and behaviors as part of this role (Hall & Lindzey, 1985; Sears et al., 1986). These acquired traits and behaviors are subsequently reinforced by society, institutions, and other individuals—"You're just like your father!" As these behaviors and traits

BOX 9.1

GIRLS SHY AWAY FROM COMPUTERS: DISADVANTAGE IN HIGH-TECH JOB MARKET

Three new studies show girls shy away from computers, which will put them at a disadvantage in the high-technology dominated job market, two Stanford University psychologists said Monday.

Drs. Irene Miura and Robert Hess told the American Psychological Association convention that by 1995 there will be an estimated 48 million computers in the United States and that 9 of 10 women will be employed outside the home.

"Competence in mathematics and technology is an important prerequisite for a wide variety of occupations, not only those in computer science," they said. "As in careers in mathematics and the natural sciences, careers in business and the social sciences are now requiring a strong background in math and computers because of the increasing reliance on statistics and computer technology in those fields."

In the first study of 87 middle and upper income students in grades five through eight, the 13 percent who reported owning home microcomputers were all boys, Hess said.

"This was unexpected in a population evenly divided between boys and girls who had had equal exposure to computer activities at school," he said.

One year later, the original group was polled again, with 13 boys and 6 girls reporting having a home computer.

The second survey, of 23 summer camps and classes around the country offering training in computer use, showed an enrollment of three boys for every girl.

When the total enrollment of 5,533 was analyzed, girls accounted for 27 percent of students in the beginning and intermediate classes, 14 percent in advanced programming courses and only 5 percent in high-level programs.

The fact that the number of girls decreased in proportion to the increase in the cost—from as low as $25 for a two-week day session to more than $1,500 for a four-week stay—"may reflect the general inclination of parents to encourage computer literacy more aggressively for their sons, perhaps looking ahead to their futures in a technical career," the researchers said.

Source: Charleston Times-Courier. (1983, August 30). Reprinted by permission.

---

continue to be reinforced, they may be internalized (Kohlberg, 1966), and thus they become stronger and eventually become part of the individual's identity and self-concept. Interpersonally, *beliefs* about roles or behaviors particular to each gender are termed *gender stereotypes* (Sears et al., 1986).

PERCEPTIONS OF GENDER ROLES

The literature is quite extensive regarding how society as a whole tends to support perceptions of behaviors associated with traditional gender roles for males and females. For instance, males are generally described as aggressive, domineering, active, and independent, while females are generally described as passive, supportive, dependent, and submissive (Sears et al., 1986). These traditional gender role expectancies are often facilitated and reinforced early in life and subsequently maintained throughout life by friends, parents, teachers, and other socialization agents (Sex Equity in Education Bulletin, 1983). In a sense, from the cradle females are prepared for the roles of wife and mother, while males are prepared for the roles of husband, father, and provider. Even during the early years of life, gender role identifications and expectancies are apparent. Research indicates that children as young as 2 or

3 years of age have already absorbed many of society's stereotypes about what behaviors are expected of each gender. Further, these stereotypes are maintained throughout the child's educational experience by teachers reinforcing certain behaviors and punishing others, as well as suggestions for courses to take in high school. For example, males are encouraged to take science and mathematics, while females may be encouraged to take child-care courses (Sex Equity in Education Bulletin, 1983).

In the past 10 to 15 years, there has been great pressure for a change in the traditional gender roles associated with males and females, a shift toward **androgyny** (Bem, 1981), in which individuals integrate the characteristics, traits, and behaviors of both genders. This androgynous approach is supported by the fact that gender differences in such abilities as verbal, mathematical, or spatial skills and behaviors such as conformity, aggression, or persuadability are small (Sears et al., 1986). Moreover, there is a greater amount of situational variability in behavior that cuts across gender (Emmerich, 1973).

The impetus to modify the traditional stereotypical view of gender roles apparently stems from an interaction of three factors: changing societal attitudes, economic factors, and changing child rearing practices.

Society's attitudes toward women have changed substantially due to the feminist movement, greater awareness and consciousness, and government regulation (EEOC and Affirmative Action). As more women enter the work force for economic, personal, and self-actualization reasons, attitudes and stereotypes as well as behaviors begin to change. Finally, for a number of personal and economic reasons, more males are actively involved in child

Current sex-role stereotypes regarding roles and behaviors are breaking down, with a trend toward androgyny.

rearing than ever before, due to the prevalence of dual-career families (F. P. Rice, 1979). Therefore, these factors should have a significant effect on how gender roles are viewed by society today and in the future.

But, one may ask, are attitudes toward traditional gender roles really changing? The answer to this question depends upon a number of factors, such as the perceiver's age, religious orientation, socioeconomic level, and educational level.

For example, Gibb and Bailey (1983) investigated attitudes toward the Equal Rights Amendment (ERA) in males and females ranging in age from 15 to 76 years. They found women to have significantly more favorable attitudes toward the ERA than did men. For females, there was a significant negative relationship between age and attitude to the ERA; older women were less positive toward the ERA. One possible explanation for the reason many middle-aged and older women still subscribe to the traditional ideas about males and females is that they lacked role models, such as female physicians and female lawyers, during their childhood and adolescent years. Given the current trend of females now entering "nontraditional" female fields (Sears et al., 1986), future cohorts of middle-aged and older females may no longer manifest these traditional roles ascribed to females due to the availability of more diverse role models. Panek, Rush, and Greenawalt (1977) investigated gender role stereotyping of a number of occupations by male and female college students; their results are presented in Table 9.1. As indicated in this table, of the investigated occupations, eight were significantly perceived as male occupations (lawyer, city planner, police officer, letter carrier, truck driver, banker, baker, office manager), six as female occupations (elementary school teacher, dietitian, social worker, typist, librarian, nurse), and nine were considered neutral (art historian, linguist, psychologist, cook, clerk, high school teacher, historian, computer operator, and speech therapist). Interestingly, both male and female raters agreed on all gender associations, except for "cook." Since gender stereotyping of occupations was found in a college population (a group one might consider to be progressive in their attitudes),

TABLE 9.1

SEX ASSOCIATION OF SELECTED OCCUPATIONS BY MALE AND FEMALE RATERS

Male Field	Female Field	Neutral Field
Lawyer	Elementary school teacher	Art historian
City planner	Dietician	Linguist
Police officer	Social worker	Psychologist
Letter carrier	Typist	Cook
Truck driver	Librarian	Clerk
Banker	Nurse	High school teacher
Baker	Speech therapist	Historian
Office manager		Computer operator
Medical doctor		

Source: Reprinted with permission of the publisher from P.E. Panek, M.C. Rush, & J.P. Greenawalt. (1977). Current sex stereotypes of 25 occupations. *Psychological Reports, 40,* pp. 212–214.

it appears that there is still a great deal of progress to be made in changing attitudes toward women in certain occupations. As more females enter what were traditionally considered male fields and more males enter what were traditionally considered female fields, future cohorts of males and females will have great exposure to divergent role models (see Emmerich, 1973), and these may subsequently change their attitudes. Further, it is important to note that gender role stereotypes not only affect females but also affect males in terms of what is expected of them in society. Therefore, a male entering a traditionally female gender-typed occupation, such as that of secretary, may often experience similar negative attitudes and barriers to successful performance as would a female entering a traditionally male gender-typed occupation, such as police officer.

Overall, though there are noticeable changes, such as women entering nontraditional fields such as law, medicine, and managerial-level positions (Rytina & Bianchi, 1984), traditional gender role stereotypes unfortunately still exist today.

As the birthrate declines and more women continue to enter the work force, there may be major shifts in views toward the "traditional" woman's role. When women decide to return to the work force during adulthood or middle age because of divorce, widowhood, necessity, or for self-actualization, they often lack the necessary job skills, education, and experience to obtain high-paying jobs (Lopata, 1975). Further, returning to work may even have a negative effect on the marital relationship (F.P. Rice, 1979).

Overall, gender roles are acquired and continuously modified throughout our life. These gender roles become part of our identity and self-concept and tend to be maintained throughout the life span; that is, we tend to maintain and enhance our self-concept with behavior that is consistent with our gender role.

An equally important set of roles is related to the family. These include those of husband, wife, father, mother, grandmother, and grandfather. As part of the socialization process and through the acquisition of expectations about our gender role, we may implicitly and/or explicitly be expected to attain these roles.

Roles Within the Family

Families are generally the primary socialization agents and social groups for individuals at all stages of the life span (Emmerich, 1973). Therefore, knowing what roles individuals play within the family, how they are acquired, and how they change is very important. Expectations about roles within the family do change with age (Riley, Johnson, & Foner, 1972) and individuals may be playing many family roles at once (father, son, brother) (Nock, 1982).

Though there are many types of families (see Table 9.2), our discussion will center on what is called the **nuclear family**, that is, a husband, wife, and children. Recently, there have been questions raised regarding the relevance of the "traditional" nuclear family in society. It is often assumed that due to changing values in American society, urbanization, and high mobility, the concept of the nuclear family is outdated and not relevant. Interestingly,

TABLE 9.2

TYPES OF FAMILIES

Type	Characteristic
Traditional nuclear family	Husband, wife, children
Dyadic nuclear family	Husband, wife (no children)
Single-parent family	One parent and children. Result of death, divorce, abandonment
Three-generation family	Three generations in a single household
Middle-aged/old-age couple	Husband, wife (children have all departed from the home)
Homosexual couple	May have child or children from previous heterosexual relationship
Communal family	Two or more nuclear families sharing living quarters, duties, child rearing, etc.
Sibling family	Unmarried siblings living together

research *does not* support the assumption that the family is considered irrelevant in American society. Studies (Doherty & Jacobson, 1982) suggest that: (1) there is still a high degree of family involvement among individuals of all age levels, (2) the family is still considered important to a majority of Americans (Lowenthal, Thurnher, Chiroboga, & Assoc., 1975), and (3) families will continue to be viewed as important in the future (Nock, 1982). As a consequence, we attribute a great deal of importance to the caring and socializing roles fathers, mothers, and children play (Biller, 1982; Field & Windmeyer, 1982; Lamb, 1981; Lerner & Spanier, 1978).

All cultures and societies have some form of "family." According to the United States Department of Labor, Bureau of Labor Statistics (1983), there were approximately 61.8 million families in the United States in 1983. The primary functions of families in all cultures and societies are to provide care and socialization for the young and serve as a network of support and identity for individuals within the family/clan unit. Further, the study of families is quite difficult due to the fact that the family types presented in Table 9.2 do not function in a vacuum (Nock, 1982); that is, each of these types is often related to a similar or different type within a more extended family unit.

TRADITIONAL NUCLEAR FAMILY

The traditional family consisting of a husband, wife, and children is still extremely popular and valued in the United States (see Chapter 8). However, there are a number of ways the current nuclear family differs from nuclear families of previous cohorts. As discussed in Chapter 8, one characteristic of nuclear families that has been changing is family size; it is gradually decreasing, due to families having fewer children. The average number of births for married women decreased steadily from 7 in 1880 to 2.3 in 1940, which was followed by an increase known as the **baby boom period** (1940s–1957) when the average was 3.8; this has since declined to about 2.1 (Statistical Abstract of the United States, U.S. Bureau of the Census, 1986). This decrease in family size has led to many social, economic, and personal changes.

The second major change in families has been with regard to the number of parents who are employed outside the home. Historically, the majority of nuclear families in the United States had one wage earner, the father, while the mother remained at home. This arrangement is changing; in fact, current statistics indicate that 51 percent of nuclear families in the United States have two wage earners (United States Department of Labor, Bureau of Labor Statistics, 1983). As these figures suggest, more women are leaving home to pursue careers or attain higher education. This is due to the economic pressures of inflation, the influence of the women's movement, and the psychological need to develop one's self-identity (M.J. Davidson & Cooper, 1986).

Furthermore, when a woman enters the work force, there is often a redefinition of roles within the family unit. For instance, a husband may now have to take on more duties with regard to child rearing. This may lead to potential conflicts, stress, and conflicts over roles, activities, and decision making within the family unit (Marcus & Hayslip, 1987).

Families in which both the husband and wife are employed in full-time jobs outside the home are referred to as dual-career couples (see Box 9.2). A study that illustrates the potential for stress within dual-career couples is that of M.E. Rawlins, L.D. Rawlins, and Rearden (1985). Specifically, these researchers investigated stresses and coping strategies of dual-career couples affiliated with a university and found that the women reported more stress about parenting and family-career conflict while the men were more concerned if their wives earned more money. In terms of coping, women were found to be more accommodating by being willing to change locations, compromise domestic standards, and prioritize responsibilities. Given the increasing number of dual-career couples and the potential for stress and conflict in these relationships, they are likely to be the focus of considerable research in the future. While many women work solely for economic reasons, as Box 9.2 indicates, there are many advantages as well as difficulties of a psychological nature that dual-career couples face. Marcus and Hayslip (1987) found that even among higher socioeconomic women who worked part-time to enhance their self-images and gain a sense of personal achievement, a substantial amount of *role strain* (having little time to fulfill the role of wife/mother *or* worker) and *role overload* (having multiple demands via having to balance both family and career) was present. The supportiveness of the husbands in this case was no less important than for women who worked full-time. Women who were either highly committed to parenting and not highly committed to career (or vice versa) experienced the greatest degree of difficulty versus those who were either very committed or not committed at all to their dual-career life-styles. Interestingly, while voluntary childlessness is more common, given the pressure to have children that many feel, *not* being able to conceive (infertility) can be a source of stress to many young dual-career couples (R. Matthews & A. Matthews, 1986).

American society is still family oriented (Lowenthal et al., 1975). That is, people of all ages see the family as being important to them. The family provides the primary orientation for the individual's activities and serves as the primary socialization agent for individuals at all points along the life cycle. The basic family unit serves to provide care and support for its members in addition to being the central source of self-concept, life-style, value system, and identity for members at all age levels.

SPECIFIC ROLES WITHIN THE FAMILY

For each individual within the family, there are specific roles and expected behaviors at all stages of the life cycle. These roles, however, do not exist in a vacuum and are responsive to societal changes as well as to changes in intrafamily dynamics (Lerner & Spanier, 1978). These roles are also age-graded (Nock, 1982) but nevertheless consistent in a basic familial sense. For example, during early adulthood, the father, in a traditional gender role sense, works to earn money for the family (fulfills the role of provider) (Biller, 1982). At the same time, during early adulthood, the mother, in a traditional gender

BOX 9.2

DUAL-CAREER MARRIAGES—DO THEY WORK?

Characteristics of career women:
1. less likely to marry
2. typically pursue a career *after* marriage
3. tend to have small families
4. longer than average (greater than 5 years) between marriage and the birth of the first child
5. first child is born when the woman is in her late twenties or early thirties
6. higher socioeconomic class backgrounds
7. more likely to be only or eldest child
8. tension with father—career orientation is defense against insecurity of childhood experiences in the family

Characteristics of husbands:
1. take their wives' work seriously
2. want wives "to be happy" or "to be the kind of person she wants to be"
3. are clear in their behaviors reflecting their support
4. tend to be mature, secure, and well-adjusted individuals

Benefits of dual-career marriages:
1. financial stability
2. opportunities for self-expression, creativity, achievement, and recognition

3. greater independence and resourcefulness among children; well-defined role models enhance their identity

Difficulties found in dual-career marriages:
1. discrimination against women who work full-time and part-time
2. fatigue and stress; role strain and role overload
3. greater likelihood of moving with two careers
4. difficulty in finding satisfying employment for both husband and wife when family moves
5. more time away from family if both parents' jobs require traveling
6. frequently necessary to commute
7. problems in getting maternity leave
8. periods when children are unsupervised ("latch-key" children)
9. making satisfactory day-care arrangements
10. diminished time for family outings or visits to family
11. identity and competitiveness problems between husband and wife

Sources: F. P. Rice. (1979). *Marriage and parenthood.* Boston: Allyn & Bacon; and S. Marcus & B. Hayslip. (1987, April). *Effects of maternal employment and family life cycle stage on the psychological well-being of women.* Paper presented at the Annual Convention of the Society for Research in Child Development, Baltimore, MD.

role sense, provides care and nurturance for other members of the family (Field & Widmayer, 1982). As these individuals enter middle age, they now start to plan for their children's continuation of the family unit by not only assisting in their careers and educational planning but also providing maintenance, support, and care for older and younger members of the family. Finally, in later adulthood, the parents may continue to assist in the care and maintenance of the younger members of the family unit (Nock, 1982). Therefore, as we age, our roles and expectations within the family unit change (Biller, 1982; Field & Widmayer, 1982), but a common theme that ties them together is the maintenance of the family unit.

In the next section we shall discuss another of the major roles within the family, the role of parent. Though parenthood and the roles associated with it are crucial for child development, and society has definite expectations of parental behavior, individuals often become parents without any formal training in how to parent. In a sense, you learn how to parent while on the job.

Parenthood

Many of the important roles persons play in adulthood are in some form related to the role of parent. As we noted above, immediate family (parents) are an important part of the convoy of social support for many, and parents serve as important socializing agents with regard to roles within the family, as well as roles that are both age and gender related.

PARENTING: JOYS AND ORDEALS

What does it mean to be a parent? Who affects whom—does the parent primarily affect the child, or does the child have an impact upon the parent(s)? The answers to these questions are complex, but we can say that there is a *mutuality* in parenting—parenting must be understood in terms of the bond between parent *and* child. That is, being a parent is likely to mean different things to parent and child dependent upon a variety of factors: (1) where the children are developmentally, what is important to them; (2) whether they are male or female; and (3) when the child is born—in reference to what is most likely going on in the lives of the parents at that point (whether they are working or not) (Marcus & Hayslip, 1987).

Thus, parenting, whether it is rewarding or not, needs to be seen from the point of view of *both* the child *and* the adult (Lerner & Spanier, 1978). While the child cannot possibly be directly affected by decisions the parents make before conception, most of us have our own ideas about what parents do, and what is expected of us as fathers or mothers, long *before* we marry and have children of our own. Regarding the parental role, then, we all go through a process of anticipatory socialization (Ahammer, 1973). We learn these roles (as defined by society) early in childhood (for example, that mothers care for children or work; that fathers provide for the family) by observing our own parents and through the reinforcement of these roles by others (through teachers, television, books, etc.). These parental roles may be further strengthened (or diminished) prior to or after marriage. Thus, parenthood, as a complex of role-related behaviors and expectations, begins long before childbirth and continues throughout life. One might continue to fulfill the parental role for an adult child who asks for advice or seeks support (emotional or financial) long after that person has left home, married, and has an established family of his or her own (Alpert and Richardson, 1980). While parenthood is often viewed as being necessary for feelings of fulfillment and self-esteem, many individuals tend to underestimate the amount of work, time, and economic cost involved in parenthood (*Changing Times,* 1983). Despite the fact that most of us will marry and have children, there is little *actual* preparation for being a parent.

While one might be skeptical about the family life cycle (see Chapter 8) as *the* means by which to understand family functioning (Featherman, 1983; R. N. Rapoport & Strelitz, 1977), parental roles and behaviors do in part vary with the demands of children of different ages. You might see parenthood progressing through five descriptive stages (based upon the age of the oldest child): (1) before becoming parents, (2) childbirth and postpartum, (3) early and middle years of parenting, (4) parenting with adolescent children, and (5) parenting with adult children.

WHY COUPLES HAVE CHILDREN

Couples decide to have children for a variety of reasons: they may do so in the belief that their own relationship might be further strengthened, or they may simply be responding to what others (parents, peers, in-laws) expect of them ("When are you going to have children?") (Williamson, 1966). They may alternatively see a child as a way of mending a not-so-satisfying marital relationship or see children as extensions of themselves that will live on beyond their own death (termed *generativity;* Erikson, 1963). Sometimes parenthood is couched in socioeconomic terms (as a tax deduction), or the child may be perceived as someone who can care for its parents when they are old. If persons put off having children (barring an inability to conceive), it is often for a variety of reasons: not being able to afford a child or conflicts over children versus one's career.

Access to birth control has certainly given us a great deal of choice over whether and when we have children, but there are risks, too, associated with the use of birth control—for example, the increased risk of having deformed or handicapped children. Also, there is an increased risk of having an infant with heart defects or a malformed infant if oral contraceptives are taken *after* conception. In addition, there is a heightened chance of birth defects when oral contraceptives are taken *and* the pregnant woman smokes more than one pack of cigarettes a day (Braken, Holford, White, & Kelsey, 1980; Papalia & Olds, 1982). Such women also face an increased probability of illness and risk not being able to fully enjoy and participate in their children's lives.

In deciding whether to have children or not, one needs to be aware of both the advantages and the drawbacks of such a choice. Having as *realistic* a picture as possible regarding what having and raising children are all about is crucial. Alpert and Richardson (1980) have stated that based on current research, "people in this society have little idea of what is entailed when they make the decision to be a parent" (p. 444). In addition to lack of information leading to ignorance, idealization, or romanticized ideas of parenthood (Stevens-Long, 1984), what often makes the decision to have children a difficult one is the pressure that we feel to be creative, to develop our "selves," to be productive and successful in our work. In this light, Alpert and Richardson (1980) and Marcus and Hayslip (1987) note that persons' perceptions of their roles as parents are most positive when work and parenting are seen as *complementing* one another. Another factor is simply that once the child is born, he cannot be "sent back"! (This is most poignantly seen when children are not planned—"accidents".) By virtue of your child's birth, you *are* a parent; he or she is *your* child. Lastly, our culture does not endorse, nor have experts agreed upon, an *ideal* way of raising a child. How a child is disciplined, whether parents are "open" or not (related to family discussions and responsibilities), whether they are affectionate toward and interested in their children as individuals, certainly all have a bearing on the child's development and obviously also affect each adult's perception of self as a good or a poor parent (Sarafino & Armstrong, 1986).

There is, however, no guarantee that decisions one makes regarding the raising of one's children will be the "right" ones. In many respects, there are a variety of people and experiences that shape children's lives (school, peers, mass media) that parents cannot control. Once children "leave the nest," obviously, they will encounter a great deal that will change them further as human beings. Yet many feel that as parents, they are solely responsible for how their children "turn out"—regarding the values they have, whether they are happily married or successful, or whether they themselves are happy as individuals. Feeling as if one is to blame for one's children's failures and disappointments has created much unhappiness for many a parent and may cause many couples to put off having children, based on the experiences of peers or their experiences with their own parents.

Currently, more couples are opting not to have children for a number of reasons: their needs for the intimacy of a dyadic relationship would be interrupted, career goals would be threatened, or their life-style would be altered. This is a particularly difficult decision when we realize that we live in a culture that defines marriage partly in terms of our ability to *parent*. Not to have children is to be perhaps accused of being selfish. Not to have children is a risk of sorts in that one will never experience the joys of being a parent or a grandparent; there are no easy solutions to this problem. It is one that must be made by the couple, and they should be prepared for the uncertainty that comes with the making of any decision—"What would have happened had I chosen differently?" Ultimately, this choice to have children must reflect their preferences for (or the extent to which they can adequately perform) the parent role, their religious and moral values regarding birth control, the value they place on children, and their own feelings about what impact children will have upon their relationship.

Children can meet many of our basic needs to love and be loved. Erikson (1963) expresses this in terms of *generativity*—being the caretaker/ protector of someone whom we have created—guiding and supporting that person throughout life. The intimacy that we seek with someone else within the context of marriage can also find expression in having children. The love we feel toward a spouse is by extension given without reservation, with "no strings attached," to our children. Being needed by someone who is both fragile, vulnerable, and dependent upon us can be very rewarding.

Despite the many advantages to parenting, there is ample reason to believe that regardless of preparation, most couples experience having a child as a "crisis" of sorts. As Lamb (1976) has pointed out, interest in childbirth as a *psychological* experience is very recent. Leifer (1977) has found that, irrespective of their attitude toward childbearing or their own body image, women tend to see pregnancy as an anxiety-filled period in their lives; that is, they are concerned about the sexual implications of the changes in their bodies and they report a variety of negative emotional (depression) and physical symptoms, particularly during the last trimester of pregnancy. Women who see their pregnancy as a chance for personal growth "rather than a symbol of security or status" (Stevens-Long, 1984) seem to report more positive feelings.

Overall, research suggests that a woman's feelings about her as-yet-unborn child, her husband, herself, and her own mother *do* change with time, and that the quality of the pregnancy and perhaps most importantly the quality of the woman's relationship with her husband *best* predict her adjustment to pregnancy and parenthood (Alpert & Richardson, 1980).

Pregnancy and childbirth also have very definite effects on men as well. They may represent the first *intrusion* into a man's relationship with his wife or alternatively be viewed as an *extension* of that relationship. He may reevaluate his relationship with his own father and can similarly experience bouts of anxiety or depression as the pregnancy progresses and after the birth itself (Biller, 1982).

The experience of childbirth itself is closely linked to whether the child is a welcome event or not and seems to be tied to each individual's preferences regarding the degree of active participation in the birth experience, either via "natural" childbirth (without the use of drugs) or by the father's being present in the delivery room to offer support to his wife or to assist in the delivery (see Sarafino & Armstrong, 1986). In terms of the child's health, the avoidance of painkilling drugs during childbirth makes for healthier babies (i.e., faster weight gains, more attentiveness, and greater initial gains in such skills as sitting, standing, or moving around) (Brackbill & Broman, 1979). Just after childbirth, the chief problems women tend to report center on feeling depressed, isolated, or bored with child care. Men seem to have more difficulty with learning to relate to *both* wife and child or in dealing with a loss of attention from their wives.

Hartup and Lempers (1973) have discussed the mutual, dyadic relationship between mother and infant (e.g., reinforcement of adult talking by infant vocalizations; the effects of mother gazing at child and vice versa; mutual touching by mother and child). They note that what seems to be critical in understanding these parent-child interactions is each person's *expectancy* about the behavior of the other. When our expectations about our children's behaviors are reinforced (and theirs about our behavior as well), the basis for a stable, mutually satisfying parent-child relationship is formed. When these expectations are not met, communication breaks down; dissatisfaction, hostility, or abuse (see Chapter 8) may result.

PARENTS AND CHILDREN

The early and middle years of parenting (infancy to adolescence) are often (but not always) characterized by a great deal of strain brought on by the routinized life of housewifery, the intense, constant demands of the children on the parents, and financial/occupational stress. Further still are these pressures on single parents, who must both care for and support a family. Alpert and Richardson (1980) point out that regardless of their individual preferences, the presence of children do force men and women into traditional sex-typed roles. It may be particularly in cases where parents initially see children in terms of personal growth or have children out of choice that the subsequent limitations that children place upon them account for reports of lower marital happiness during the years children are at home (R.A. Lewis & Spanier, 1979). While changing the family configuration, children also force the parents to redefine their life-styles—they make new friends, spend their time literally *doing* different things (e.g., housework, attending school-related functions, outings, etc.), and spend less time with each other.

Parenting with adolescents is sometimes seen in terms of a power struggle between child and parent related to a number of issues—personal values, sexuality, discipline, performance in school. While these differences are not quite as great as generally believed (Bengston & Troll, 1978), it is clear that just as parents may fulfill the function of interpreting and representing the world to their young children, the adolescent may serve as a representative of the culture, thereby influencing his parents (e.g., in such areas as politics, religion, sex roles, personal tastes in dress, and work-achievement orientation) (Lerner & Spanier, 1978). Thus, the "generation gap" may not be so great as we previously believed!

It must also be noted (Blenkner, 1965) that the parents of adolescents are often the children of aging parents. They are faced with the dual responsibility of caring for their children and their own parents. They thus may be in the process of coming to terms with their own aging as well as the aging and eventual death of their parents. The "postparental" years (where the children have left home and are on their own) is in many respects a misnomer. While children may not be living at home, they may continue to visit regularly and ask for support or advice on a variety of matters (e.g., child care, marital problems, financial planning, job changes), many of which pertain to the continuing role as parent that they see their parents as playing. However, many middle-aged individuals are quite willing to give up their parent role and resent playing it involuntarily.

THE EMPTY NEST

Some parents do become depressed when children leave home ("the **empty nest**") because it signals the end to their roles as such (see the discussion in

Chapter 2 on existential questioning) and may lead to divorce if they have not really communicated for years about what is most important to them. Most, however, do not react this way to the empty nest. They in fact may welcome this time as an opportunity to renew their relationship, pursue new interests, travel, or simply relax, knowing that they have raised and "launched" their children successfully (Nock, 1982). With regard to depression at the children's leaving, what seems to be crucial at this point is whether each person has *principally* defined himself or herself in terms of the role of mother or father. If this is so, when the children leave, they are left with nothing to "hang onto." Both parents, in the process, have not taken the time to keep in touch with each other; they may discover that they now have, after years of role-playing, little in common to share with one another (Nock, 1982).

On an individual basis, there are, however, many advantages to the empty nest. For a woman, this period may bring a particular sense of relief if the burden of child care has fallen upon her; she also is not likely to need to worry about becoming pregnant. For a man, the financial pressures brought on by children are lessened considerably; he may be free to explore new interests or even a second career with little economic risk to his family.

Research does indicate that there is a considerable amount of parent-child interaction (visiting, communication, helping) during this time that may be mutually satisfying (see Chapter 8 on intergenerational relationships).

Thus, it would certainly be inaccurate to characterize older parents as necessarily ill and dependent on their adult children (Troll et al., 1979). Most want to live close to but not with their adult children. Most can expect good health well into their seventies (see K.W. Schaie & Geiwitz, 1982). Moreover, as we discussed in Chapter 8 regarding filial maturity versus filial responsibility, rather than a "role reversal" when an adult child cares for a "childlike" elderly parent, the most satisfying relationships are nonobligatory, where children are seen as "dependable."

EFFECTS OF PARENTHOOD

There are six major types of effects or changes resulting from becoming a parent (Harper, 1975).

Economic Effects   Parenthood involves many predictable and unpredictable costs. These include providing such essentials as health care, food, clothes, activities, housing, toys, and transportation. For instance, it is estimated that it will cost a family $226,000 to raise and educate a son born in 1980 to age 22, with girls being about 10 percent more expensive to raise (*Changing Times,* 1983). For these reasons, individuals must often re-rank priorities for how money is spent, for example, paying for braces for the children's teeth as opposed to spending the money on a vacation.

Mobility Effects   Another effect children have upon parents is in the area of mobility. Parents cannot, on an impulse, pack up the car and go for a weekend trip. Trips must be planned in advance and must take into account the children and their needs. These may include such things as cribs, heated pools, game rooms, and so forth.

Social Activity Effects   Parenthood often results in a decreased social activity level. For instance, prior to going out, parents must arrange for baby-sitters or other forms of child care. Due to unpredictable events, such as the child being hurt or becoming sick, it is difficult for parents to maintain an active and routine activity schedule, for example, bowling every Tuesday evening or golf on Sunday. Also, having children may influence friendship patterns. Parents of young children generally plan activities with other couples who have children of the same age, as opposed to interest-oriented friends who do not have children.

Career/Education Effects   Having children also affects the parents' careers and educational opportunities. Parents may have to postpone educational opportunities and certain careers because of the demands of parenting. Parenthood results in less flexibility in job changes, career attainment, and career shifts. That is, individuals who are parents tend to be more cautious about changing jobs because they have to think of more than just their own individual goals.

Family Relations Effects   Family relations and interactions are also significantly affected by parenthood. Children result in parents having less time to spend with each other and with each child alone. Further, children disrupt the parents' pattern of sexual activity. Additionally, children change the interdynamics of the family significantly.

Time Effects   Finally, parenthood involves a substantial amount of time. The time required to feed, bathe, dress and take the child to activities decreases the amount of time available for the parents to be with each other and pursue their own activities.

There are many joys in parenthood, but there are also a great many costs of which all prospective parents must be aware (Williamson, 1966). Parenthood is one of the most crucial and expected developmental tasks of young adulthood and should be considered seriously.

As we noted above, parents have many roles within the family unit, and these roles are dynamic and shift as children and parents age. The basic shift is from one of caretaker to one of advisor and confidant. In addition to their primary roles as caretakers, parents may fill other roles associated with the fact that they are parents. Many a parent has been a nurse, teacher, police officer, judge, lawyer, taxi driver, cook, housekeeper, athlete, art critic, and servant from time to time! The relative time the adult spends in some of these associated roles varies as a function of the number of children as well as their ages.

Is there a best time to have children? The answer depends upon a number of factors. Biologically for females, the best time is between 21 and 35 years of age. But factors such as the couple's emotional stability, financial situation, and whether there is time available to care for children, are also important. In light of our discussion to this point, it should be clear that both

husband and wife should want to have children and that the marital relationship should be free of major conflicts.

We now turn to what most of us see parenting (and grandparenting,
for some) as being all about: *how* we raise our children (or grandchildren).

CHILD-REARING PRACTICES

Qualitatively, a number of child-related characteristics seem to affect how
children are raised. The outcome of decisions about child rearing that parents
make that *are influenced by* the child in turn *have a bearing upon* the child's
adjustment (Lerner & Spanier, 1978).

Parents respond differently to children based on their sex, health, birth
order, and temperament (Ahammer, 1973; Papalia & Olds, 1982). Parents may
vocalize more with their female children in the belief that boys are supposed
to be more action-oriented and assertive. They may handle their child differently (e.g., playing more roughly with a boy). They may reinforce dependent
behavior in girls that they would not tolerate in boys. Rightly or wrongly,
our culture tends to reinforce the existence of sex-typed expectations of
behavior that parents utilize and that children use in dealing with one another
as well as in making judgments about themselves in many areas (attractiveness, social acceptability, competence).

Another factor that determines how parents interact with their children is the children's bids for attention (help, approval). Thus, when children
act dependently, they may be reinforced for doing so. On the other hand,
independent and/or stubborn behavior may also be rewarded when it is
exhibited by children.

Children who are overly active, difficult to control, or are not prone
to want to be physically close also are likely to influence the warmth and
affection they receive, whether and how they are disciplined, as well as how
much they are praised, talked to, touched, or ignored by their parents. The
extent to which children seek affection and want to be close to and talk with
their parents determines the likelihood that they will identify with those
adults as role models (see Papalia & Olds, 1982; Sarafino & Armstrong, 1986).
As infants, those who like to be held and cuddled will, most likely, be held
more often than those who do not. Children who are chronically fearful or
are in poor health are likely to be protected more, to have less demands made
upon them, or be punished less (or less severely) than others. Children who
do not respond to punishment are likely to be punished the most severely.

Parents may also deal with firstborns differently than later-borns.
They may be more protective, more affectionate, or more lenient than otherwise. Alternatively, they may punish more freely, or socialize along sex-
typed expectations to a greater degree than with their later-born children.
Obviously, the effect of birth order on parents' behavior toward their children will vary with the nature of the pregnancy, whether the child was
"timed" appropriately (consistent with the family's career goals or financial
resources), and the sex of the firstborn (see Sarafino & Armstrong, 1986).

Styles of Child Rearing Parents' styles of relating to their children, in part influenced by their behavior, also have a definite impact on those same children's personality development and adjustment. Baumrind (1971) has defined three **styles of child rearing**: *authoritarian, permissive,* and *authoritative.* Authoritarian parents are very controlling and usually have "set" standards for behavior, deviations from which are punished severely. This kind of style, lacking in warmth, spontaneity, and closeness, tends to produce children who are withdrawn, fearful, distrusting of themselves and of others, and unhappy.

Permissive (laissez-faire) parents make few demands on their children. They exercise little control, punish infrequently, and relate to their children almost as peers. These children tend to lack judgment and social skills, are impulsive and immature, and are without a sense of control over themselves. They seem to lack the ability to make decisions and express great anxiety over making choices.

Authoritative parents are in many respects like their permissive and authoritarian peers. They exercise control and punish when necessary but nevertheless see their children as *individuals,* and attempt to treat them as such. Most importantly, they are *consistent* in their behavior toward their children, in meting out punishment, making decisions, acting in a rational manner, and being loving and affectionate. They realize that they as parents can make decisions about family matters *with* their children, not just *for* them, but that they as parents are still the standard-bearers. This style of parenting tends to create children who are more self-reliant and self-confident, happier, and have more self-control (Baumrind, 1971).

While parents tend to be classified as behaving toward their children predominantly via one of these three "styles," their behavior will, nevertheless, vary with the situation (Sarafino & Armstrong, 1986). Even a permissive parent, when the child's behavior demands it (the child is about to hit another child, or stick his finger in an electrical wall socket) will *behave* in an apparently authoritarian manner, exercising firm control, and forcefully punishing the child, if he or she feels it is necessary. Human behavior *is,* to a certain extent, situationally influenced (Mischel, 1970)—the greatest, most rational parents have their own limits as well!

What differentiates these parents from others is, perhaps, their *intentions* or *expectations* about themselves and their own children. Simply punishing a child can be very different in terms of its effects on that child. For example, punishment without explanation is very different from making clear the distinction between how you feel about the child and how you are going to deal with the child's behavior. Punishments used concurrently with rewards (love, affection, praise), and punishments that are timely and in proportion to the misdeed (rational) are likely to be the most effective (see Siefert & Hoffnung, 1987).

The primary role transition relating to parenthood during middle adulthood is from parent to grandparent. Grandparents, too, can serve as important socializing agents. In the next section, we shall discuss grandparenting in the United States.

Grandparents can be important agents of socialization; having a viable influence on their grandchildren's lives is very meaningful for many middle-aged and elderly adults.

Grandparenting

Being a grandparent is often considered by society to be a developmental task of middle or late adulthood. For many, having a grandchild may be considered a symbol or marker of middle age or even of "getting old." Individuals who are overly concerned with being considered young may react with anxiety when others know they are old enough to be grandparents.

Interestingly, though most of us have experienced a relationship of some sort with our grandparents, the literature on grandparenting is not extensive. It does suggest, however, that there are many *styles* or types of *grandparenting* that are affected by a number of individual, environmental, and socioeconomic factors.

Because couples who have children have recently done so earlier (Troll et al., 1979) and because life expectancy has increased, the chances of one's becoming a grandparent in one's forties or fifties is much more likely. What does being a grandparent mean? Is it satisfying?

Obviously, given the above, the popular image of the grandparent as a kindly, elderly person in a rocking chair is often inaccurate—grandparents are more likely to be men and women who are much younger, who are employed, or who even have adult children still at home! This same individual may also be caring for a mother or father who is quite old. While the frequency of contact between grandparents and their grandchildren is fairly regular (often daily), it is rare for grandparents, parents (adult children), and grandchildren to live under the same roof (Troll et al., 1979).

Perhaps the most detailed analyses of grandparenting styles in the

United States has been the work of Neugarten and Weinstein (1964), who suggest there are five distinctive types of grandparenting styles. These styles are termed *formal, fun-seeker, surrogate-parent, reservoir of family wisdom,* and *distant figure.*

Formal Style The formal style can be described as our mythological and traditional grandparenting role or style. This style includes grandparents who are highly interested in their grandchildren; they provide special treats and presents for the children, and they often baby-sit. Though these grandparents often take care of their grandchildren, they are not viewed as primary or surrogate caretakers of the grandchildren. Formal grandparents engage in activities with the grandchildren and often have authority and control over the children in the absence of the parents.

Fun-Seeker Style The fun-seeker style is very informal, compared to the formal style. These individuals are involved in playful, free relationships with their grandchildren and do not exert any control or authority over them. Grandparents exercising this style do not usually perform any caretaker behaviors and look upon being with their grandchildren as a leisure activity.

Surrogate-Parent Style Regarding the surrogate-parent style, these grandparents are often the primary caretakers of the children. This style is quite common today due to the increasing number of single-parent families and families where both parents work outside the home.

Reservoir of Family Wisdom Style The reservoir of family wisdom style is characterized by grandparents who provide special skills, resources, and knowledge to younger members of the family structure. A good example of this type is found in families that own and operate a business. That is, though your parents manage the tire store opened by your grandparents, your parents do not make any major business decisions without at least consulting your grandparents.

Distant-Figure Style The final style, distant figure, was considered nontraditional and relatively rare when Neugarten and Weinstein proposed their styles in 1964. But due to society becoming increasingly mobile, as well as more older adults moving to the "sun belt," it is becoming more common. In this style, contacts are infrequent, usually on holidays, and they are perceived as benevolent but remote in terms of physical contact and distance.

Research regarding these styles of grandparenting, as well as grandparenting in general, is limited. What research does exist suggests *grandmothers* are most usually associated with the grandparent role. Also, the most common styles found in the United States today are the formal, fun-seekers, and distant figure, while the reservoir of family wisdom is the rarest and usually associated with the grandfather.

GRANDPARENTING—ITS MEANING IN ADULTHOOD

What do grandparents value about their role? Obviously, one does not become a grandparent by choice! Being a *valued* grandparent is not automatic, however; it must be earned. Whether grandparenting is satisfying or not seems to be dependent principally upon the relationship with one's adult children. If that relationship is positive and lacks conflict, then the grandparent role is likely to be more fulfilling to all involved (Troll et al., 1979), although approximately a third express conflicts over a number of issues— their responsibility in raising the grandchildren, relations with their adult children, and their feelings about *being* a grandparent.

Grandparenthood means different things to different people. Depending upon how one perceives this role, it may be satisfying or not.

V. Wood and Robertson (1976) classified grandparents into four types, based on the perceived *meaning* of grandparenthood:

1. *apportional*—deriving satisfaction from one's own personal experiences *and* social norms (providing a role)

2. *remote*—not deriving any meaning from either personal experience or social expectations

3. *symbolic*—seeing grandparenthood as rewarding in terms of social norms

4. *individualized*—where satisfaction is found primarily through one's own personal experiences

In general, apportioned and individualized grandparents spent more time with their grandchildren. These persons were also older and had *more* grandchildren, on the average. Wood and Robertson found, however, that having grandchildren did not substitute for having friends of one's own age in terms of personal satisfaction.

This question was also studied in some detail by Robertson (1977), who studied grandmothers. Robertson's research resulted in a number of important findings. First, the largest percentage of grandmothers surveyed described themselves as being the "remote figure" style, and they enjoyed having that form of relationship with their grandchildren. Additionally, most grandmothers enjoyed the role for a number of reasons, such as it made them feel younger; they felt they were assisting in carrying on the family line; they got satisfaction from providing "things" for the grandchildren that they could not provide for their own children. Moreover, they achieved satisfaction and enjoyment from helping their grandchildren achieve more than their parents or grandparents were able to.

Not only are there many types of grandparenting styles, individual differences exist in attitudes toward grandparenting. In fact, as research suggests, our conception of the "old-fashioned grandparent," that is, one who is intimately and actively involved with the grandchildren and their supervision and care, is in a majority of cases a thing of the past. For instance, Lopata (1973) studied the attitudes of grandmothers who were widows toward their grandchildren. Lopata reported that many of these grandmothers often resented the time demands placed upon them for baby-sitting and other service/care activities involving their grandchildren. For the most part, these women felt they had busy lives of their own, and these activities often interfered with their own plans.

There are often gender differences in attitudes toward grandparenting. E. Kahana and B. Kahana (1970) found maternal grandmothers and paternal grandfathers tended to manifest closeness and warmth toward their grandchildren, while maternal grandfathers and paternal grandmothers appeared to manifest the most negative attitudes toward grandchildren. J.L. Thomas (1986) found grandmothers to be more satisfied with their role than grandfathers. This was perhaps due to their relative familiarity with intimate family relationships, having been principally responsible for raising children. Men who expressed more satisfaction were older, had active relationships with their young grandchildren, and were happy with their involvement in the task of child rearing. Thomas (1986) suggests that exposure to such grandfathers may have an impact on grandchildren's tendency to define themselves androgynously (see also Kivnick, 1985).

On the basis of what we know (largely limited to grandmothers), grandparenthood *can* be satisfying to those persons who value the role, have the opportunity to interact with grandchildren, and whose relationships with their adult children are positive. As Troll (1980) has noted, the real value that grandparenthood has for many middle-aged and elderly persons is that it reinforces the sense of family. Wilcoxon (1987) terms such persons "significant grandparents." That is, the grandparents can derive a great deal of satisfaction in knowing that the "family theme" is being carried on by the grandchildren, even if their contacts with their adult children and their children's children are minimal.

Grandparents can influence *and* are influenced by their grandchildren. Thus, as with parenthood, we see the bidirectional nature of socialization. An older family member can communicate values, instruct, make history "real," and support his or her grandchildren regarding issues related to work and education. In Hagestad's (1978) research, satisfying grandparent-grandchild relations were also characterized by decisions to avoid discussing certain topics—sexuality, religion, or political issues—to minimize conflict and enrich the relationship. Simply being older does not guarantee that one will derive a great deal of personal satisfaction from having grandchildren. As with many things in life, the role must be worked at, shaped, and strived for if it is to have any meaning for *both* grandchild and grandparent.

While grandparenthood can be very rewarding, recently, grandparents (many of whom have actually been recruited to reassume child rearing roles by their adult children) have been thrust into the arena of divorce (S.H. Matthews & Sprey, 1984). In many cases, they may not be permitted to visit the grandchild they have been caring for upon the divorce of their adult child. Complicating the situation is the fact that (in spite of the grandparents' critical supportive role), in times of family crisis and positive intergenerational influence, their legal visitation rights are often ambiguous or unenforceable, cutting them off from an important source of emotional nourishment—an ongoing warm relationship with a grandchild (K.B. Wilson & DeShane, 1982).

From a life-span oriented point of view incorporating developmental tasks, for those who find the role of grandparent satisfying, it can be considered a natural transition or evolution of the role of parent during middle and/or old age.

In the next section, we shall discuss attitudes toward the aging process in the United States and other cultures. The attitudes we have toward aging as well as those of our society/culture in general are related to specific actual or expected roles at different points along the life cycle (Rosow, 1985). Often, how well we meet these role expectations will determine our attitude toward ourselves and the attitudes of others toward us and our behavior.

ATTITUDES TOWARD AGING

Currently, nearly 12 percent of our population is aged 65 and older (Statistical Abstract of the United States, U.S. Bureau of the Census, 1986). Consequently, the false beliefs and misperceptions surrounding older persons affect the lives of a significant proportion of citizens in this country. So potentially destructive are the negative attitudes we hold toward the elderly that Robert Butler (1975) has defined **ageism** as "a process of systematic stereotyping of and discrimination against people because they are old, just as racism and sexism accomplish this with skin color and gender. Old people are categorized as senile, rigid in thought and manner, old-fashioned in morality and skill. . . . Ageism allows the younger generations to see older people as different from themselves; thus they subtly cease to identify with their elders as human beings" (R. Butler, 1975, pp. 11–12). This disdain for the aged is manifested, as Butler notes, in stereotypes, jokes, overt avoidance, hostility, and discrimination in housing and employment, among other things. It may even result in poorer quality care for those who are institutionalized (R. Butler, 1975; P.M. Keith, 1977; J. Levin & W.C. Levin, 1980). Such an attitude may perhaps be manufactured through selective exposure to, or "indirect experience" (Ansello, 1977) with elderly persons (e.g., one's elderly parents or grandparents, casual acquaintances, those living in nursing homes or in retirement communities).

This selective exposure to the elderly is then combined with the primarily negative image of the older person maintained by books and literature (see Ansello, 1977; Bishop & Krause, 1984) and the media, though this has been questioned by Holtzman and Akiyana (1985) and Pasuth and Cook (1985). Such experiences may cause both the young *and* the old to see older persons in unrealistically negative terms—dependent, sick, lonely, incapable of change (J. Levin & W.C. Levin, 1980), or forgetful (Cameron, 1970a, 1970b, 1973; L.A. Powell & Williamson, 1985; K.H. Rubin & Brown, 1975; Tuckman & Lorge, 1952a, 1952b). Within all cultures there are expectancies for age-appropriate behavior that are incorporated into an explicit and implicit system of norms for behavior and activity (Nardi, 1973). Often, age serves as the primary normative criterion with regard to both entry into a particular role and exit from that role, as well as a guide for age-appropriate behavior. For example, to be a teacher (a role), you must be at least 21 years of age; when you reach 65 or 70 years of age, it is expected that you will retire (exit from the role of teacher). During this entire period, society has held certain expectancies of you and how you should behave while in this role.

Research indicates that at every age level there are different expectancies regarding all aspects of our behavior, even our "personalities." These expectancies are held by most individuals at different age levels along the life span. This point was demonstrated quite well by Nardi (1971), who investigated perceived age differences in personality of three distinct age-groups, adolescent (average age 15), adults (average age 40), and elderly persons (average age 65).

Nardi systematically varied the age of a stimulus person (target) to examine the effects of perceived age on subsequent age-related perceptions of adolescents, adults, and older adults. Participants (whose actual ages corresponded to the target) made judgments regarding the personalities/characteristics of individuals (targets) at different age levels (15 years, 40 years, 65 years). Nardi found that all participants shared similar perceptions of each target age. Results indicated the targets representing adolescence, adulthood, and old age were perceived differently by all age-groups (raters), and each age-group felt the target age-groups (adolescence, middle age, old age) had specific personality characteristics. That is, each age-group felt there were specific personality characteristics associated with each of the three target ages, and these characteristics were similar in all rater age-groups.

Though the literature strongly suggests that society has negative attitudes toward aging (Butler, 1969; J. Levin & W.C. Levin, 1980), the empirical evidence is not completely supportive, because a number of research investigations have failed to obtain evidence of negative attitudes toward older adults (Kogan, 1979; Lutsky, 1980). It is worth noting that not only do all studies not support such negative attitudes toward the aged (Austin, 1985; Green, 1981; McTavish, 1971), but also that Schonfield (1982) feels that the belief that Americans hold negative attitudes toward the aged is itself a myth, unsupported by research. Such shifts may be due to the increasing "graying" of our population or increased political power among elderly. Binstock (1983), however, suggests that formerly negative biases have simply been replaced with equally inaccurate positive and negative stereotypes (most elderly are well-off, older persons are a drain on our financial resources, older persons are politically self-interested) based on generalizations about them that ignore subcultural and individual variations.

From the point of view of the elderly person, what realistically represents being "old" may often involve living up to others' expectations about aging in order to survive. In the process of living up to such views, significant self-derogation may occur (Ward, 1977). Such self-perceptions are expressed in a poem written by an elderly woman:

Old Age Is Hell

The body gets stiff, you get cramps in your legs.
Corns on your feet as big as hen's eggs.
Gas in your stomach, elimination is poor
Take Ex-Lax at night, but then you're not sure.
You soak in the tub, or the body will smell,

It's just like I said, "Old age is hell."
The teeth start decaying, eyesight is poor,
Hair falling out all over the floor,
Sex life is short, it's a thing of the past,
Don't kid yourself, friends, even that doesn't last.
Can't go to parties, don't dance anymore,
Just putting it mildly, you're a hell of a bore.
Liquor is out, can't take a chance,
Bladder is weak, might pee in your pants.
Nothing is planned for, nothing to expect.
Just the mailman bringing your security check.
Now be sure your affairs are in order, and your
Will is made right, or on the way to your grave
There'll be a hell of a fight.
So if in the new year, you feel fairly well,
Thank God you're alive, cause "Old age is hell."

Reprinted by permission of the *Journal of Gerontology, 32,* 227–232, 1977.

Older persons may come to subjectively define themselves as "old" as they experience events that indicate they are now an "elderly" person (e.g., retirement, changes in physical appearance, loss of spouse, low income, social security, becoming institutionalized). At some point, one is then forced to accept the fact that one is old, which subsequently affects one's attitudes toward oneself and others and thus one's behavior in a variety of contexts. Acquiring such a self-view reinforces the negative stereotypes about old age and aging held by others (see Brubaker & Powers, 1976).

This process of self-definition resulting in a negative view of the self has been challenged by Brubaker and Powers (1976), who propose an alternative model that emphasizes both the positive and negative aspects of the stereotype of "old." Which aspect of this stereotype is incorporated into the older person's self-definition is a function of (1) whether the person subjectively defines himself or herself as "old," (2) objective indicators of old age, and (3) previous self-concept. The refreshing advantage of this model is that it does not predict that all elders will necessarily adopt a negative stereotype of old age. In fact, Brubaker and Powers point out that many researchers have found that the "signs" of aging in our society (e.g., retirement) are not always viewed as negative by the old and the young (Cameron, 1972; Ivester & King, 1977).

Recent evidence for variability in the stereotypes held by younger persons has been provided by Schmidt and Boland (1986). They found that the term *older adult* serves as a superordinate category (gray hair, wrinkles, false teeth, retired, poor eyesight) within which different stereotypes that are both positive (John Wayne conservative, perfect grandparent, sage) and negative (bag lady, recluse, vulnerable, shrew, severely impaired) exist. Different older persons evoke different reactions. Institutionalized, ethnic, and dependent aged are most likely to hold and be the object of negative attitudes toward older persons (Schmidt & Boland, 1986). On the other hand, independent, highly educated, and high occupation elderly are the objects of at least ambivalent, if not positive, stereotypes of aging.

From the point of view of those who have not yet reached later adulthood (arbitrarily defined as age 65), it would seem that on the whole, those elderly about whom the more salient attitudes toward aging are formed would be the dependent, institutionalized elderly persons who may be the victims of a fire or burglary or the recipients of a new therapeutic program. The highly educated, independent, healthy older person is implicitly portrayed as the exception to the rule and thus more likely to be viewed more positively, albeit unrealistically. One consequence of such experience is to view them (the aged) as a "problem" that must be dealt with. The aged person may be treated as a necessary burden, an unfortunate by-product of medical advances, social change, and industrialization (Atchley, 1984; Bengston, Dowd, Smith, & Inkeles, 1975). To devalue the aged in this way (even if the concept only applies to certain older persons) is to deny that we are aging and will someday too become elderly and may be a way of handling what we fear most: losing our youthfulness, good health, a circle of friends, or facing the inevitability of our deaths and ultimately accepting responsibility for our own lives (see Chapters 10 and 12). Too often older persons are mentioned in the same breath with the mentally ill, the handicapped, and the dying. While part of society's treatment of and attitudes toward its aged may be a function of a resentment of some elderly who may exploit their position, intergenerational conflict (see Datan, Green, & Reese, 1986) may stem from the strain of financial support of the very young and the very old by the middle-aged (Binstock, 1983; Butler, 1975). To the extent that stereotypes and myths of aging are adopted by the young and the old, the experience of aging becomes a self-fulfilling prophecy for the young.

Common Myths and Stereotypes of Old Age and Aging

Probably the most important point to be made about myths of growing older is that such views simply have no realistic basis and have often been proven false by research conducted by social scientists who study the aging process.

Stereotypes are perceptions that are factually incorrect, produced by illogical reasoning, and rigid (Lippmann, 1922). Brubaker and Powers (1976) note that stereotypes, due to lack of contact or selective exposure, help others to minimize ambiguity and bolster self-esteem. Because they are generalizations with the purpose of exemplifying groups rather than individuals (Ansello, 1977; Rosow, 1974), they may attribute characteristics to the old that do not exist in reality and often are at odds with what elderly themselves perceive. Because the older population is more heterogeneous than homogeneous (Maddox & Douglass, 1974), beliefs about all older people or the "typical" aged person from the outset have little basis in fact (Binstock, 1983; Schmidt & Boland, 1986; Schonfield, 1982). Experience does not make people more similar, it differentiates them. Thus, out of the fact that different individuals, each with unique experiential histories, cope with life events in discrepant ways (see Chapter 10), we can conclude that (1) older people are more diversified than are younger people, and (2) no two persons age in the same manner (see Chapter 1). Furthermore, within the individual, different bodily systems (skeletal, cardiovascular, renal) age at different rates (see Chapter 2).

Another false belief that many hold is that the term *aging* should be reserved for persons who reach a particular chronological age (65), who assume certain roles (those of widow, retiree, nursing home resident, social security recipient), or who display many of the physical and behavioral characteristics generally held as common to most or all older persons. All persons age, regardless of what they choose to call the psychobiological changes that accompany the passage of time (Birren & Renner, 1977). Whether one chooses to call the first 60 or so years of life "growth," "development," and/or "maturity," the fact remains that although *aging* is a term many reserve for the latter 15 to 20 years of our probable life span, organisms (people) do change in a variety of ways (both positive and negative) that are age-related. To treat aging as a natural process, on the same plane with other changes that covary with, but are not caused by, age (see P.B. Baltes & Goulet, 1970; Wohlwill, 1970a), reflects a point of view discussed above that suggests we treat later adulthood as an integrated portion of the life span. A 79-year-old woman expressed her feelings about the unfortunate results of being labeled "old"—itself a function of our fascination with chronological age as a basis for the way we relate to others, and what we expect from them.

Reflections on Old Age: "I Have Lived My Life"

I live in a beautiful retirement home, in a good neighborhood. We are surrounded by many trees, green grass, gardens. The building itself is a beautiful one—a lovely, big dining room, lounges, roof deck. Every apartment has a Pullman kitchen, a fine bath, walk-in closet, wall-to-wall carpet, floor-to-ceiling windows.

It accommodates over 200 people—and there is a long waiting list. It is for medium-income people. It is not a Nursing Home—no doctor or nurse on duty. It is a Retirement Home.

Why am I not the happiest person in the world? The answer is AGE.

I should be dead, or should die soon. I have lived my life—one full of happiness, sorrow, tragedy; long and interesting work as a secretary; two husbands, one child, three grandchildren, two great-grandchildren. I have very good health for my age.

But I don't enjoy being old and being surrounded by old people.

I love animals, have had pets since I was 5 years old—until living here, where we cannot have them. I could be happy if I had a cat or dog of my very own.

I can no longer afford the apartments I had (always with a pet) since 1942. (I didn't stop working until I was nearly 70.)

I read, write, listen to news on the radio. I don't have, or want, a television. I get indoor and outdoor exercise. I have cat, dog, and bird friends in the neighborhood.

So, the answer is "age." A lifelong friend, a Baltimorean as I am (I came to Washington in 1918 to work as a paid secretary for the Red Cross) who is now dead, once wrote me, "Age—it's for the birds!"

I agree.

Washington Star (1977, August 22)

Many of the false beliefs surrounding the elderly are simply not supported by statistics regarding the demographic characteristics of the aged. For example, all old persons do not live in institutions—only 5 percent do so (see Butler & Lewis, 1982; American Association of Retired Persons, 1985). Most older persons (over 65 years old) do not live alone—only 30 percent live alone or with nonrelatives (American Association of Retired Persons, 1985). All old people are not sick. In fact, while many do suffer from chronic diseases, these illnesses are not necessarily incapacitating. Consequently, many older persons do lead worthwhile, happy, satisfying lives, despite a greater probability of experiencing chronic illness than the young (Butler & Lewis, 1981). Not all older people are senile. Senility, as Butler and Lewis (1982) and Zarit (1980) point out, is a legal-medical term often misapplied and ultimately leading to the diagnosis of being untreatable (see Chapters 13 and 14). Where chronic brain damage or arteriosclerosis has produced an organic condition that is irreversible (see Chapter 13), there can be overlays of depression, anxiety, and psychosomatic disorders that *are* responsive to medical and psychotherapeutic interventions (Butler & Lewis, 1982; Zarit, 1980). In addition to this illusion of senility, Butler and Lewis note several other myths of aging lacking in substance: the "tranquility myth" that sees old age as a period of serenity, where the person is permitted to enjoy his past accomplishments. Given society's devaluation of many aged, a greater need for medical care combined with decreasing earning power to meet such costs, inadequate public transportation, losses in status, discrimination, and interpersonal loss associated with the increased probability of death of spouse and friends, it seems ludicrous to view the older person as tranquil or serene. Clayton (1975) suggests that most older people in today's society are more likely to have a feeling of "despair" (Erikson, 1959)—regret over their lives, unhappiness, and a feeling of time "running out." While a sense of integrity—a feeling of adequacy, self-satisfaction, and wholeness—is possible, perhaps achieved through a process of life review (Butler, 1963), Clayton nevertheless feels that older persons have incompletely resolved or compromised their way through previous psychosocial crises. This, according to Clayton, leads to feelings of despair rather than ego integrity in later adulthood.

Butler and Lewis (1982) note two other pervasive myths about the aged: those of unproductivity and resistance to change. The notion of unproductivity reflects a belief that older people are no longer able to produce on the job or do not wish to remain active and creative. Many elderly do in fact remain employed (almost 3 million—30 percent of the aged) and continue to work beyond retirement age when their health permits it (see Chapters 5 and 11). Health may in fact improve after retirement, permitting (if adequate finances are available) the older person to pursue work-substitute, leisure, or work-related interests after formal retirement age (see Chapter 11). While Neugarten (1977) notes an increasing tendency with age to maintain an inward orientation (interiority) toward life (see Chapter 10), the person who disengages (withdraws) from social role contacts and responsibilities may not necessarily be unhappy. Disengagement (Cumming & Henry, 1961) may prove to be very adaptive and lead to a high level of life satisfaction (see

Chapter 10). Individuals rarely disengage from all roles to the same degree (Streib & Schneider, 1971), and psychological disengagement may not coincide with disengagement from social roles. Furthermore, an individual's response to the aging process occurs in a social context, as we pointed out at this text's outset.

Relating to the myth of unproductivity (see Chapters 5 on the older worker and Chapter 11 on retirement) can be added the stereotype of the older adult as incapable of learning (see Chapter 7). A prime reason for such attitudes is the nature of developmental research until approximately ten years ago. Briefly, such research (see Chapter 3), comparing elderly persons with younger individuals at one point in time (a cross-sectional design), presents a misleading picture of decline with age on most types of tests designed to measure intelligence, problem solving, learning, and memory. Although each group compared obviously differs in chronological age, individuals within each group differ among themselves, and more importantly, the groups as a whole differ on a number of factors that are *independent* of chronological age (e.g., level of education, health status, culturally relevant social changes, differential life experiences). Given that a certain loss in function with age may be realistic for some but not all persons (certain aspects of memory, reaction time, perceptual-motor skills, visual and auditory capability), researchers who study the elderly have found that in many cases such declines have been overestimated. We have restated and expanded on each of these points in many chapters throughout this text.

In general, then, the assumption of universal, *irreversible decline* in capability with increased age has been questioned. A viewpoint (termed the **decrement with compensation model**) that accepts losses in function, which can be compensated for by using intervention strategies (e.g., prosthetics) that are either physical (hearing aids) or psychological (adopting more efficient means of approaching tasks to be learned or problems to be solved) in nature, has instead surfaced (K.W. Schaie & Gribbin, 1975; Woodruff & Walsh, 1975).

Researchers who study the aging process are thus coming to terms with this myth of universal cognitive decline (termed **irreversible decrement model**), and a more optimistic view of what older people can and cannot do, emphasizing that some functional losses with age can be reversed, clearly is taking its place. It is with this model in mind that we have stressed the applied, everyday implications of the facts of adult development wherever possible throughout this text.

Other myths persist—that of the sexually uninterested and incapable aged person. Ludeman (1981) dispels this stereotype in noting that older people do retain both interest and ability for sexual relations (see Chapter 8). A last misperception of the elderly is that of resistance to change, or rigidity (see Chapter 5). Butler and Lewis (1982) suggest that rigidity may be a function of long-established personality traits or socioeconomic pressures rather than anything inherent in the aging process. Moreover, rigidity may be adaptive for some persons in helping them structure their lives, making events more predictable. As we saw in Chapter 5, whether rigidity is more characteristic of older people versus those who are younger is a complex question, not simply answered, and related to a variety of cultural or experiential factors that are potentially independent of age (see Botwinick, 1984). If, for example, one assumes that age and rigidity are related, this might lower expectations about an older person's capacity to learn a new job (see Chapters 5 and 11) or change via counseling or therapy (see Chapter 14).

The fact that stereotypes are generalizations and thus inaccurate descriptions of the nature of the aging process is also buttressed by extensive evidence suggesting that the manner in which the elderly are perceived by others versus their self-perceptions are frequently at odds. Many variables seem to mediate this discrepancy (see above discussion of Nardi's work on perceptions of elderly persons): perceiver age, whether one is describing oneself or someone else (that is, an "average" person), gender, social class, level of education, professional ideology, extent of contact with elderly persons, personality characteristics of the perceiver, and the manner in which such attitudes toward elderly persons are assessed (Ahammer & P.B. Baltes, 1972; Kilty & Feld, 1976; McTavish, 1971; Nardi, 1971, 1973). While a few studies indicate that the aged hold relatively low self-opinions (see Chapter 10), many studies report discrepancies between the perceptions of older people and those of the young, with elderly persons reporting more positive feelings about themselves than those attributed to them by younger persons.

In this light, it is interesting that Weisz (1983) and E. Langer (1982) suggest older persons to underestimate their skills (1) simply by being labeled as *old* (connoting inferiority), (2) by being denied the opportunity to engage in a task formerly engaged in that is now being performed by someone else (as in the case of the retiree), and (3) by allowing others to help them (implying that they cannot help themselves). Indeed, when provided with no other information than an individual's age, R. Reno (1979), Banziger and Drevenstedt (1982), and Gekoski and Knox (1983) all found persons more likely to attribute the poor performance of a 65-year-old (versus someone younger, e.g., 35) to a lack of ability or task difficulty. M.E. Lachman and McArthur (1986) found that older persons' lack of ability was more likely to be attributed (by the young and the old) to poor performance in social, physical, or cognitive situations, while the opposite was true for good performance. When older persons' attributions (explanations) for such performance were examined, however, it was found that they were more likely to take credit for good performance and deny responsibility for poor performance, suggesting that they may have used such explanations to cope with feelings of inferiority or expected poor performance.

The most convincing data regarding the disparity between older persons' perceptions of aging and those of younger persons has been reported by the National Council on Aging through a Harris public opinion survey (1975) entitled "The Myth and Reality of Aging in America." This study involved polling over 4000 people of all ages to ascertain their perceptions of aging. Significant discrepancies between general public opinion of the elderly (over 65) and those public who were actually 65 and over were found on such variables as "brightness and alertness," being "physically and sexually active," being "open-minded and adaptable," and being "very good at getting things done."

The message the older public is delivering here is that our mental capabilities have not deteriorated and we have additional wisdom from our life's experiences to boot. While the public at large may vastly underestimate the effectiveness, the open-mindedness, and the alertness of most people over 65, the older public themselves have as much confidence in their own abilities as do the young and a whole lot more confidence in themselves than the public has in them (Harris & Assoc., 1975, p. 55).

Significantly greater proportions of the public versus the aged felt that people over 65 spent "a lot of time" doing such things as just sitting and thinking, sleeping, "just doing nothing," and watching television. Unhappily, those over 65 saw themselves as less physically and sexually active than did those under 65, indicating that to some extent they had internalized some of the myths of aging we have discussed above.

The authors of "The Myth and Reality of Aging in America" (Harris & Assoc., 1975) underscore the impact of the many stereotypes of the aged upon the young and the old:

Until the public at large, and especially the young, see most older people in the same way that they see themselves as individuals, the opportunities for older people to pitch in and help solve society's problems will remain as limited as young people's current respect for the elderly. . . . In asserting in large numbers that older people get too little respect from the young these days, the younger public may well be revealing a real sense of guilt over treatment of older people today (p. 68).

If such a modification in attitudes toward the elderly is in fact occurring, it may make later adulthood a more truly satisfying time of life for many, characterized by feelings of personal worth and adequacy. Old age would be a period of life filled with promise, rather than one to deny and devalue. As Binstock (1983) suggests, it may be more fruitful to focus on *age relations,* rather than on older persons per se, thus reinforcing the interconnectedness between younger and older persons. As we pointed out in Chapter 1, to the extent that your expectations about a number of characteristics or skills (reaction time, depression, learning, memory, intelligence) are linked to your knowledge or estimate of your own (or another's age), such perceptions affect what kinds of information about such characteristics you take seriously or dismiss.

A theory that attempts to explain the basis of interpersonal relationships, called **exchange theory**, has been adapted to help explain negative attitudes toward aging (E. Kahana & Midlarsky, 1982). According to exchange theory, individuals attempt to maximize rewards and reduce costs in interpersonal relationships. All relationships are viewed on a "debits and credits" basis. Since older adults may have few credits, such as money, material possessions, and physical attractiveness, and a large number of debits, such as poor health, they are not valued by others. This lack of value contributes to the negative images of aging.

If aging is apparently viewed so negatively in the United States at the present time, it may be worth considering whether this has always been the situation. This question was addressed by Fischer (1977), who traced the attitudes toward older adults in America from colonial to modern times.

Attitudes Toward Aging in the United States: Historical Perspective

According to Fischer (1977), during the colonial period in America there were very few older adults. It was estimated that about 2 percent of the population was over 60 years of age. Since achieving old age was so rare, due to a lack of medical care and sanitation, the presence of many diseases, and the hazards of frontier life, reaching old age was taken as a sign of being one of the "elect." That is, God had elected or chosen such persons to live for a long time because they had lived a good life and were being rewarded for it. Since they were favored by God, others respected them. Thus, elders occupied places of honor, prestige, and leadership in society and business. In a sense, older adults were considered models to be emulated, in terms of behaviors and activities, if one hoped to achieve old age. At this time, then, America exhibited the **cult of the aged**. It was acceptable and positive to be old. In fact, fashions were designed to highlight old age, such as loose-fitting clothes and white-haired wigs.

A good example from American history that illustrates this respect for elders can be found in the life of Benjamin Franklin. When younger individuals argued about revolution and writing the Declaration of Independence and other documents, they always sought Benjamin Franklin's advice before reaching a final decision. At this time, Benjamin Franklin was in his late sixties. Also, Franklin was chosen as the first ambassador to a foreign country. This highlights the type of respect, power, and authority designated to older adults during the colonial period.

It should be stressed that this positive attitude toward older adults during the colonial period was due to more than just religious factors. For instance, a major motivating force for respecting one's elders and doing their bidding could be due to economic factors. Since elders held title to the land, property, and business, younger individuals attempted to protect their economic survival by favoring those individuals who could guarantee it. In order to understand this explanation, you have to envision America at this time. During this period most of the population was huddled in isolated little villages and cities along the Eastern and Southern coasts. Most of the interior of the continent was not as yet settled by European immigrants, travel was slow and hazardous, communication was difficult, and families were quite large. Since individuals were not geographically or economically mobile, their future was tied to the family and their business or property. They were, in a sense, in competition with siblings for parents' farmland or business. In order to guarantee their share of this property or business, they had to do their parents' bidding.

After the American Revolution, the status of the elderly began to deteriorate for a number of reasons. First, society became more mobile. There was westward expansion, the result being a backup of large families and individuals moving away from the family unit to seek their own independence and destiny. Second, there was industrialization. Individuals no longer had to base their economic future on the family land, property, or business; they could work in someone's mill and earn their own money, independently of the family. Finally, society began to value functional roles, activity, and productivity rather than wisdom and experience. Since younger individuals had greater physical stamina and could work harder and longer than older adults, the young had a greater value than the old, according to society.

Though there are other possible factors responsible for the decline in positive attitudes toward older adults, we have discussed those considered by most to be the major factors involved. For these reasons and others, American society continually moved toward a young/youth-oriented culture. This culminated in the 1960s and was described as the **cult of the young**. That is, youth was good, positive, highly valued, and something to emulate. Therefore, individuals had to attempt to hide their age and look young in order to enjoy life and status and be viewed positively by society and others. This was evidenced by the vast number of products that were introduced into the market to either hide old age or restore youth, such as hair colorings to remove the gray, antiaging skin creams, and moisturizers. In a sense, old was bad/negative—something to hide or cover up.

Research now suggests that the cult of the young has peaked, and we are now moving toward the **cult of the adult**. That is, one can still be over 30 and enjoy life. This may be due to the fact that between 1980 and 1990 (projected) the fastest-growing age-group in the United States are individuals between 35 and 49 years of age (Robey, 1984) (see Chapter 1). Media programming, commercials, advertisements, and industries are beginning to take note of this fact. For example, companies such as the Ford Motor Company have established "mature advisory" boards to address "adult" consumers and their needs.

Since our society has traditionally valued youth and the traits associated with youth, those traits usually associated with later life are devalued. How do older adults view old age? Do they see it in negative terms, as do younger individuals?

These questions were addressed by W. C. Thomas, Jr. (1981). Thomas found that people between 18 and 64 years old do not view old people (65 years+) in a favorable light. Further, older adults do not view younger people in a favorable light either, but they (older adults) view themselves quite favorably. While these findings reinforce the separateness with which the young and old view one another, they also underscore the discrepancy between older adults' views of themselves and perceptions of them by the young.

Aging in Various American Subcultures

American society does not consist of a homogeneous group of individuals in terms of race, religion, ethnicity, and cultural heritage. By the year 2050, a fifth of all aged persons will be nonwhite (G. C. Myers, 1985). In fact,

American society is quite heterogeneous; that is, it is a collection of many different races, religions, ethnic groups, and cultural heritages. This is particularly important in that it reinforces the inaccuracies of many of the myths and stereotypes we discussed earlier. Not only are aged persons heterogeneous, but there are also variations among aged individuals by subculture. In this section we shall briefly discuss and highlight information regarding aging in a number of subcultures (minority groups) within the overall American culture: blacks, Hispanics, Asian/Pacific Americans, and native Americans.

J. Keith (1985), in a discussion of the social position of the old, stresses the importance of ethnicity. According to Keith, a recognition of ethnicity is itself a form of diversity among aged persons. Each ethnic group has its own history of traditions that affect behaviors and values. Older persons "manipulate" these traditions in a way that not only helps them cope with societal change via their relationships with younger generations but also guarantees continued status and prestige within the family. In Boston, for example, traditional kinship patterns determine who cares for the aged person (e.g., the child who lives nearest the aged person) among Irish and Chinese persons (Ikels, 1982). Among Japanese Americans, sensitivity to others' feelings is the value reinforced by the culture to facilitate intergenerational ties (Kiefer, 1974).

In some cases, however, ethnicity can work against the realities of coping on an everyday basis. Depending upon who (son or daughter) is caring for the elder, that aged person may or may not be seen as continuing to be independent. This may run counter to the elder's perception of himself or herself as independent, making that person's needs for social services more pressing. The elder's position within the family also hinges on the acceptance of ethnic traditions by the young, influencing whether the aged person can use his or her status to elicit care or rely on established ritual (e.g., by joining an ethnic club) to maintain "ethnic distinctiveness" (Cuellar, 1978; J. Keith, 1985). This social group can be an important means of informal support to the elder; such groups exist in San Francisco, Los Angeles (J. Keith, 1985), and in many other large urban cities such as Cleveland, New York, and Dallas.

THE BLACK AGED

Blacks are the largest minority group in the United States, and therefore constitute the largest group of minority aged. In fact, the black aged population has grown substantially during the last decade (Gelfand, 1982) and is growing at a greater rate than is the white aged population (American Association of Retired Persons, 1987). They are in **double jeopardy** (see Dowd & Bengston, 1978; J.J. Jackson, 1985)—they are both black and elderly and thus suffer due to prejudices against blacks *and* elderly persons. Research clearly indicates that aged blacks are in a significantly worse economic situation than whites (J.J. Jackson, 1985) and that income over the last decade has risen less for aged blacks than for older whites (Chen, 1985). The primary reason for this is that blacks have tended to have the lowest paying jobs, and since social security benefits are tied to earnings, in old age they receive less benefits. Another significant difference between black and white aged is with regard to health. Research indicates that older blacks have poorer subjectively rated health and more chronic disorders than whites. This is due to many reasons: having less money to pay for health care, living in poor, substandard housing, or the limited availability of medical care (J.J. Jackson, 1985), though as Jackson notes, studies are not always consistent in their support of the double jeopardy hypothesis. Using objective measures of health status, Ferraro (1987) did not find differences between white and black aged, suggesting that age "levels" health differences between blacks and whites. Black elderly also tend to be significantly more religious than white elderly (M. Jackson & Wood, 1976).

Interestingly, Dancy (1977) points out that black elderly persons share many of the same problems as do the white aged. That is, both black and white elderly report the major problems they face are low income, poor health condition/care, crime, poor nutrition, inadequate transportation, and substandard housing (see Ferarro, 1987). On the other hand, blacks generally provide more support and care for their aged family members than do white Anglo families (J.J. Jackson, 1985) (see Chapter 8 on intergenerational support).

J.J. Jackson's (1985) review of the literature suggests that double jeopardy may not be as important a concept as it once was in understanding ethnic or subcultural variations in the aging experience. Instead, other factors in addition to race may be necessary to study ethnicity and aging, given that blacks, for example, are extremely heterogeneous (J.J. Jackson, 1985). While blacks are often believed to provide more support to their aged than do whites, this may not be so much a function of the economics of race and aging (double jeopardy) as of the cultural heritage inherent in the extended family network characteristic of blacks and Hispanics. For both blacks and Hispanics, a rich cultural tradition stressing the extended family network as a unit, rather than as separate individuals, bonds people together. Consequently, they may be distrustful of service providers (Markides, 1983b) and in fact may withhold information regarding service needs. Additionally, the family kinship network may compensate for the failure of service providers to adequately meet their needs. Sussman (1985) argues that service providers may be more helpful if they complement the functions of the extended family in caring for their aged rather than recommend institutionalization of the elderly family member. Antonucci's (1985) review of social support and ethnicity suggests that most ethnic groups provide more familial support to their aged and consequently hold more positive attitudes toward aging than do whites. However, it may be that more support given to minority aged is a consequence of these aged persons being in greater need than are elderly whites, rather than due to their ethnicity (Antonucci, 1985). Thus, ethnic differences in caregiving are less obvious when one accounts for factors that predict need for social services—income and social class. Nevertheless, ethnicity as a cultural factor influencing family relationships and coping needs to be given serious consideration (Markides, 1983b).

THE HISPANIC AGED

The term *Hispanic* is used to refer collectively to a very diverse group of individuals, such as Puerto Ricans, Cubans, and Mexicans. Hispanics are the second largest minority group in the United States. Though Hispanics share the same language, Spanish, they have vastly different traditions and cultural heritages. Maldonado & Applewhite-Lozano (1986) report that 1980 census figures indicated over 14 million persons in the United States were of Hispanic origin (this figure did not include illegal aliens). These same figures indicated approximately 60 percent of Hispanics were of Mexican heritage, 14 percent of Puerto Rican heritage, and 6 percent of Cuban heritage.

The following are a number of facts regarding this group of older Americans (see Maldonado & Applewhite-Lozano, 1986) regarding Hispanic elderly: (1) over 25 percent live below the current poverty level; (2) they receive inadequate health care; (3) they have the second highest illiteracy rate among racial/ethnic groups (only native Americans have a higher rate); and (4) they generally work at the lowest occupational and pay levels. Hispanic elderly tend to stay in the work force longer than the white elderly because they may not receive social security or social services for a number of reasons, such as having entered the country illegally. In part for this reason, many Hispanic elderly have suffered racial discrimination and have encountered many barriers to cultural assimilation.

On the other hand, as is true with black aged, Hispanic families typically are quite supportive of elderly persons who are in need of care (Markides, 1983b). In fact, Cantor and Little (1985) suggest that Hispanics are more supportive in this regard than are other minorities, when one considers the influence of social class, health, and income.

Markides notes that with the continued immigration of some minorities of impoverished rural backgrounds (Hispanics), there will be difficulties in adjusting to urban, modernized American life with accompanying poor health and reduced income. Markides (1983b) also suggests that increased occupational mobility may create changes in kinship relations among Hispanics in the Southwest (and perhaps among blacks as well). If pressures via socialization of the dominant culture become strong enough, many (Cantor, 1979; Maldonado, 1979) feel that ethnic differences in family-helping patterns may disappear entirely. Obviously, only by carefully observing ethnic identification (J. J. Jackson, 1985) in the future can we answer this intriguing question.

THE ASIAN/PACIFIC AMERICAN AGED

According to Liu and Yu (1985), individuals identified as Asian/Pacific American are the fastest-growing minority group in the United States today. Between 1965 and 1975 alone, there was a fourfold increase in the number of Asian/Pacific Islander elderly (American Association of Retired Persons, 1987). This designation comprises a large number (approximately 30) of diverse groups, such as Chinese, Japanese, Filipino, and Vietnamese. For this reason, it is difficult to discuss Asian/Pacific Americans as a whole, since there are often vast differences in culture, language, and religion of the individuals who are placed in this category. Asian/Pacific aged share in common the experience of racial hatred, language barriers, and discriminatory legislation in the United States. For example, many were forcibly placed in settlement areas during World War II, despite the fact that they served in the armed forces. It is estimated that there are approximately 2 million Asian/Pacific elderly in the United States and that the number is growing. Liu and Yu (1985) suggest that the number of individuals in this category is growing because of (1) increased immigration, (2) increased birthrate, and (3) inclusion of new groups into the category.

Conflict between generations in terms of values and ideas may be quite pronounced in the Asian-American communities. For example, in traditional Asian culture, the eldest son assumed responsibility for his aging parents (filial piety). In the United States, many Asian-American young are moving away from these values, which causes great conflict between the generations.

Unlike the white majority and other ethnic minority populations, there are more elderly Asian/Pacific Islander men than women. Further, of all minority elderly, Asian/Pacific Islanders have the greatest proportion of high school graduates (American Association of Retired Persons, 1987).

THE NATIVE AMERICAN AGED

The native American population, both old and young, has been almost completely neglected by researchers, social services agencies, and the government (Blakely, 1979). Native Americans have had a long and tragic history of discrimination, persecution, and destruction in the United States.

As was the situation with the other ethnic/racial groups we have discussed, one must not view all native Americans as being homogenous. In fact, they are an extremely diverse group with different languages and traditions. Many tribal groups do not associate with others and have been enemies for hundreds of years. Additionally, most native Americans have values and beliefs that are vastly different from white american culture.

Though the percent of native American elderly is small, they may constitute the most disadvantaged of all groups of older adults when compared with whites and other minority groups on a number of factors. In fact, nearly a third of native Americans live below the poverty level (American Association of Retired Persons, 1987). Since a significant number of native Americans were unemployed as young adults, they do not have jobs from which to retire and collect a pension.

The life expectancy for native Americans is substantially less than for white Americans. According to Gelfand (1982), the life expectancy for native Americans is approximately 63 years, and only about 6 percent live to be 65 years or older.

Among the native American older population, approximately 47 percent have completed less than five years of schooling, and three-fourths of the housing on reservations is considered to be substandard.

Regarding health status, Benedict (1972) reports that native American elderly are more susceptible to many chronic diseases than elderly whites. The major health problems of elderly native Americans are tuberculosis, diabetes, liver and kidney disease, high blood pressure, pneumonia, and malnutrition (American Association of Retired Persons, 1987). Given the fact that native Americans have generally faced a lifetime of lessened income, inadequate housing, poor medical care, and nutrition (Markides, 1983b), it is not surprising that they are in poor health during late adulthood. On the other hand, Ferraro (1987) found little evidence that elderly blacks had poorer health than older whites relative to blacks' and whites' health in general. Ferraro's (1987) findings are therefore contrary to what the double jeopardy hypothesis would predict (Dowd & Bengston, 1978). Overall, however, these facts point out the difficulties faced by native Americans, both young and old, at the present time. According to the American Association of Retired Persons (1987), the status of minority elderly is not likely to improve in the immediate future. This is due to the fact that factors that affect health conditions will not vary much among the minority population now approaching retirement age. The outlook for younger minority group individuals is somewhat better due to increased opportunities for education and employment. Therefore, the next generation of minority elderly may enjoy a higher quality of life than their predecessors.

Attitudes Toward Aging in Other Cultures

At this point, it may be interesting to consider the question of how similar to or different from our own attitudes toward older adults are those of other cultures. The attitudes and behaviors toward older adults in a cross-cultural perspective were investigated in detail by Cowgill and Holmes (1972). Their work regarding the universals and variations in aging help us address the issue of how older adults are viewed in other cultures. Societies and cultures throughout the world exhibit vast differences and similarities in terms of their treatment of and attitudes toward aging individuals (Palmore, 1980). In general, the culture's values significantly affect the status of the aged as well as that of other individuals within that culture. Some cultures have attitudes toward the aging individual that lead to happy, contented, and meaningful later years, while other cultures have attitudes that lead to feelings of worthlessness and abandonment on the part of older adults.

CROSS-CULTURAL AGING: UNIVERSALS AND VARIATIONS

The many similarities and differences regarding aging among various ethnic and racial groups within the United States are reflected in similarities and differences between aging in the United States and aging in other cultures. Those factors pertaining to the aged that are similar across cultures are referred to as **universals of aging**, while differences are referred to as **variations in aging**.

Universals of Aging   Cowgill and Holmes (1972) identified eight factors that are assumed to be present in all societies regarding the aged. The universals of aging are as follows:

1. *The aged always constitute a minority within the total population.* Additionally, the age at which one is considered "old" or "aged" varies from culture to culture. This age is usually related to the average or expected longevity for a member of the society. For example, in a culture where very few individuals reach 40 years of age, 20 may be considered "aged," while in another where a longevity of 80 years of age can be expected, 70 may be considered the marker. But regardless of the particular age (marker) or cultures, the aged do not represent a large percentage of the population.

2. *In an older population, females outnumber males.* This is most common in industrialized societies where females repeatedly outlive males.

3. *Widows comprise a high proportion of an older population.* As previously reported in our discussion of life expectancy (see Chapter 2), with increasing age the ratio of females to males expands in most cultures. Given the tendency of women to marry men who are older than they are, most women may spend the last 10 to 15 years of their lives as widows.

4. *In all societies, people that are classified as old are treated differently because they are so classified.* All societies have specific folkways or role expectations that govern interactions with those who are defined as old. These may be positive, negative, or neutral.

5. *There is a widespread tendency for people defined as old to shift to more sedentary, advisory, or supervisory roles involving less physical exertion and more concern with group maintenance than with economic production.* Examples here relate to shifting from the "worker" to "retiree" roles in industrial societies and shifting from a "warrior" to a "headman" in nonindustrial societies.

6. *In all societies, some old persons continue to act as political, judicial, and civic leaders.* For example, in our industrialized society, older adults are justices on the U.S. Supreme Court, and in nonindustrialized societies, they are old sages. Cowgill and Holmes (1972) believe that in nonindustrialized societies, older adults are vital to the maintenance and survival of the society because they possess information about social customs, habits, history, and ritual. Therefore, since the aged have this vital information, they are highly esteemed. On the other hand, in industrial societies, rapid technological and social change make much traditional information obsolete. Thus, information held by older adults is not highly valued.

7. *In all societies, social mores prescribe some mutual responsibility between old people and their children.* That is, in all cultures the young and the old know what behaviors toward each and by each are expected, such as care of the old by the young or abandonment by the young. Further, we have discussed the concept of "filial responsibility" in Chapter 8.

8. *All societies value life and seek to prolong it, even in old age.* This universal is quite self-explanatory.

Variations in Aging   Variations among cultures in terms of the aging experience are more common than universals; for example, Cowgill and Holmes

(1972) have identified 22 such variations, though a detailed discussion of this topic is too extensive to be presented here. The three most significant differences between cultures are:

1. *Modernized societies have older populations.* This is to be expected due to better medical care, sanitation, and diet.

2. *The status of older adults is higher in preindustrial societies, in which older people constitute a low proportion of the total population and the rate of social change is slower.* This factor is similar to our discussion of the high status of some aged in the universals of aging.

3. *The individualistic value of Western (industrialized) societies reduces the economic security of older people, and responsibility for providing economic security has shifted to the state.* In general, the family as a system of economic support is not available to older adults in industrial societies because extended families are not common. Moreover, the values of individual achievement are more compatible with the needs of an industrial economy. This leaves the older adult vulnerable to the pressures of the economic system. Therefore, the state has to step in to provide older adults with basic material necessities. An exception to this trend within our culture is the supportive role that the extended family plays in the care of its aged among blacks and Hispanics.

Generally, however, the status of older adults in modernized, industrialized, technological societies tends to be low. Along with low status, there are negative attitudes. On the other hand, in nonindustrialized societies, older adults serve necessary and functional roles and activities. Thus, their status is high and attitudes toward them are positive.

These observations resulted in the development of *modernization theory* (Cowgill, 1974; Cowgill & Holmes, 1972). This theory views the status of the elderly within any society as influenced by four factors associated with modernization: health technology, economic technology, urbanization, and education. These four factors interact to lower the status of the aged in a modernized society.

Test of Modernization Theory   A good test of the Cowgill and Holmes hypothesis regarding the lowered status of older adults in modernized societies is the study of attitudes toward older adults in Japan. Prior to World War II, Japan was a tradition-oriented, agrarian society, struggling to become industrialized. After World War II, the entire Japanese society was transformed into an industrialized society, along with the introduction of many new societal values and ideas from the West.

Most Westerners have always held to a romantic view of the status accorded the elderly in Asian countries such as China and Japan. This romantic view suggests that older persons in pre-World War II Japan were held in high regard, honor, and respect. But whether this idealized view is accurate often depends upon the source of the information. For example, Buck (1966) and Palmore (1975a, 1975b) present support for the idealized view, while O'Brien and Lind (1976) present a more pessimistic view. Plath (1973) presents both a positive and negative perspective.

Overall, the actual evidence indicates reality is not consistent with the idealized stereotypes of old age in Japan, either pre- or post-World War II. For instance, though the value of filial piety toward elders may have been stressed to some extent in pre-World War II Japan, the value system of the time also stressed that when elders became burdensome to the family, they had the obligation to the rest of the family to "leave this world."

But since World War II and increased modernization, the status and attitudes toward older adults in Japan have become more pessimistic and negative. This is due in part to the modern stressing of youth, work roles, functional ability, and so forth. This rapid change in societal values has had a significant impact on all age-groups in Japan and has led to an increasing incidence of mental-health problems and suicide.

Therefore, when one views Japan, there is definite support for the modernization theory. Maeda (1983) summarizes the situation in present-day Japan quite well. Maeda suggests the family is, and will continue to be, the most important source of support for the elderly in Japan but will decline in the future due to increased numbers of frail and impaired elderly as well as increased industrialization and urbanization—modernization.

It is important to note, however, that not all nonindustrialized societies provide a more positive and supportive environment for older adults than that observed in industrial societies, nor does social change per se automatically reduce the quality of life for older adults in that society (Harlan, 1968; Sokolovsky, 1985). Harlan (1968), for instance, disagrees with the hypothesis that every preindustrial society gives the aged high status and believes that not all of the current problems of the aged are consequences of urban industrialization.

A Caution Regarding Attitudes Toward Aging

In terms of our society, currently the answer to whether there are negative attitudes toward older adults depends quite heavily on the situation or source of the material. In a sense, the study of attitudes toward older adults is quite enigmatic because of contradictory research and literature. Though a majority of the research (see Butler, 1969; Hayslip, 1984) and reports from applied settings, such as business and industry (Harris & Assoc., 1981), present numerous reports of negative attitudes, bias, and myths toward aging, some studies have not observed negative attitudes toward older adults (Kogan, 1979; Lutsky, 1980; Schonfield, 1982). For example, Drevenstedt (1981) did not observe any age bias in the evaluation of a newspaper article (supposedly written by an old or adult writer) by young adult evaluators. Panek (1982a) found that college students did not believe many of the myths regarding older adults (which have negative connotations), and Panek and Merluzzi (1983) found that counselor trainees did not exhibit any bias against older clients. On the other hand, Turkoski (1984) found the existence of negativism toward older adults among nurses.

Perhaps a resolution of the question is based on the known difference between what individuals do and what they say. That is, in situations where individuals are asked to openly state negative attitudes toward older adults (as in a questionnaire), they either see through the situation or do not want to appear prejudiced toward older adults and therefore do not exhibit any bias. But these same individuals who did not exhibit bias on the questionnaire may directly or indirectly react negatively toward older adults in terms of their actual behavior. Support for this assumption was found by Panek (1984), who had students in an adulthood and aging class write the three terms that came into their mind when they heard the word *old* or *aged*. Results indicated that most adjectives reported were negative. Interestingly, these same students were part of the sample reported by Panek (1982a) who did not believe many of the negative myths toward older adults.

In conclusion, the study of attitudes toward older adults in the United States generally suggests that these attitudes are somewhat negative, but the research is not totally consistent in this regard (see above discussion of age stereotyping). If negative attitudes do exist, they are often based on a combination of factors such as misinformation, myths, and presentation by the media (Ansello, 1977; Butler, 1969; Hayslip, 1984).

Changing Attitudes Toward Elderly Persons

Given that such discrepancies in the perception of the aged exist, what efforts can be made to change the view that the young have of the old and of the experience of being old? While some researchers (Auerbach & Levinson, 1977; Drake, 1957) report no positive change in perception of the elderly as a function of increased contact, many others have found that the young come to see the aged in a more positive light and report less generational conflict with increased exposure to older persons, both in general and within the context of a personalized family unit (Bengston, 1970; Stinnett & Montgomery, 1968; Nardi, 1973; Tuckman & Lorge, 1958; Weinberger & Millham, 1975). Ansello (1977) notes a study by Seefeldt, Jontz, Galper, and Serock (1977), who found that less than one-fourth of their sample of 3 to 11-year-old children knew any older persons outside the family. For those children who had more contact, it was limited to no more than two visits per year.

Birren and Woodruff (1973a), in a discussion of the enhancement of life-span human potential through education, make several recommendations that, if taken seriously, could have a significant long-term impact on altering the predominantly negative view that the young (and in many cases, also the old) have of the elderly. Such efforts at intervention include (1) training teachers in life-span development to effect a shift in attitudes early in life, (2) age integration of classes and training in life-span development at the elementary, high school, and undergraduate levels, (3) designing courses around interest groups instead of age-groups, and (4) encouraging the development of affective experiences and motivation (e.g., through small-groups discussion) rather than simply cognitive skills in the classroom. T. Hickey (1974) and Shore (1976) discuss the utility of simulating sensory loss with age in improving attitudes about the aged.

Those who adopt an intervention-oriented approach in making overt efforts toward altering perceptions of the aged have experienced success in doing so. For example, Labouvie-Vief and P. B. Baltes (1976) have demonstrated the usefulness of training programs designed to reduce misperceptions of the aged by adolescent girls. T. Hickey, Rakowski, Hultsch, and Fatula (1976) found significant positive changes in attitudes toward the elderly in a sample of over 300 female geriatric center/social service employees as a function of a short-term in-service training program. Such success, as the authors note, lays the groundwork for more comprehensive intervention strategies to include effecting behavioral as well as attitude changes toward older persons.

SUMMARY

In this chapter the process of *socialization* across the life span was discussed, with specific reference to crucial roles based upon gender or related to the familial or occupational status that have important implications for life-span development. Socialization was found to be a *dynamic,* lifelong process that is *bidirectional.* Further, it was observed that throughout the life cycle individuals are constantly acquiring and changing roles via the process of *role transition* and *role change.* Persons are socialized along a number of dimensions, with *gender* and *age* being two of the most important. Roles within the family such as *parent* and *grandparent* are also important socializing forces. While parents and children influence one another, the joys and ordeals of parenting vary in part with age-related demands of children. Though they have little actual preparation, persons obviously have children for a variety of reasons that are social, economic, and psychological in nature. Parenting, as is socialization, is a dynamic process of interacting with one's children and redefining one's role and often continues well into one's sixties or seventies.

Grandparenting is not limited to older adults and is characterized by very diverse *styles (formal, fun-seeker, surrogate parent, reservoir of family wisdom, distant).* Grandparent *means* different things to each person, and satisfaction with grandparenting varies with one's *style* and by *sex.*

Attitudes toward the aging process and the aged in the United States do seem to vary when examined from an historical perspective. During the *Colonial period,* the aged were viewed positively due to religious and economic reasons. However, from the time of the American Revolution, society, for a number of reasons, gradually began to value traits associated with youth, a trend that apparently reached its high point in the 1960s. Currently, many theorists who emphasize the *universals* of aging suggest that society values traits associated with young adulthood, such as strength, good looks, and vitality.

Though it is generally assumed that older adults are at present viewed negatively in the United States, as expressed in *ageism* and *myths/stereotypes,* research evidence does not consistently document negative attitudes toward aging. Variations in aging exist on both a *cross-cultural* level and on a *culture-specific* level.

KEY TERMS AND CONCEPTS

Socialization	Variations in aging
Roles	Status
Shifting roles	Institutional role types
Role transition	Informal role types
Role change	Tenuous role types
Gender roles	Exchange theory
Androgyny	Empty nest
Nuclear family	Decrement with compensation model
Baby boom period	(of aging)
Ageism	Irreversible decrement model
Cult of the aged	(of aging)
Cult of the young	Styles of child rearing
Cult of the adult	Styles of grandparenting
Universals of aging	Double jeopardy

- What approaches have been used to define and study personality? How might these approaches be characterized? Is one better than another?
- Does personality change with the aging process? What factors govern whether the answer to this question is yes or no?
- What do the views of Buhler, Erikson, Jung, Levinson, and Gould have to say regarding change and consistency in adult personality?
- What does Freudian theory have to say about adult personality development? In what ways are Gould's transformations similar to the Freudian approach?
- What is meant by the life structure? In what manner is it changed throughout adulthood? What are its limitations?
- What are psychosocial crises? How are they similar to and different from psychosexual stages? What objections have been raised regarding psychosocial crises as a way of understanding adult personality change?
- Are adult developmental stages descriptive or prescriptive? What are the advantages and disadvantages of each point of view? What does dialectical theory say about this issue?
- What are the Oakland-Berkeley studies and the Kansas City studies? What do they say about the question of personality and its effects on aging? What do the findings of Maas and Kuypers suggest regarding the role of personality in adjustment to aging?
- What are psychological "traits"? What do data using psychological tests measuring these traits suggest regarding the stability of personality with age?

PERSONALITY

■

DEFINING AND STUDYING PERSONALITY IN ADULTHOOD

For some of us, when we use the term **personality**, we are literally referring to the *behaviors* or *observable responses* to everyday situations that an individual demonstrates. On the other hand, we may choose to focus on that person's underlying qualities or traits. For example, depending upon our own bias about personality, understanding a person's behaviors exhibited in some situations and not others (e.g., a person is quiet in class and quite talkative at a party) may not present a problem for us; we might assume that such behavior *should* vary with each situation. On the other hand, if we assume that these behaviors should reflect the individual's "real" personality they may be either ignored ("He just wasn't himself, he was probably tired, he's really a very outgoing, social person") or may be seen as out of character and a cause of concern ("maybe he's depressed about something . . . I'll try and talk with him tomorrow").

When we make statements about someone's behavior being out of character, we *may* be saying that this behavior does not "fit" the situation (e.g., "He overreacted to criticism"). We might also assume that there is some underlying set of qualities of the individual that explains individual's behavior in most situations (the person is just oversensitive). Thus, our interpretation of our own or another's behavior often rests on very different beliefs (or theories) about personality and its relationship to behavior.

The approach to personality emphasizing consistency of behavior is in direct contrast to that emphasizing variations in one's behavior that are determined by the situation. Thus, according to one perspective, our individual's behavior can vary from day to day, or from situation to situation. This variation does not trouble us because we see these situations as requiring certain behaviors and not requiring others. Thus, an individual can be quiet when necessary (as in class while the professor is lecturing) and quite social when the situation permits it (as at a party). In fact, according to this view, if one's behavior (personality) is stable across time, it is because the situations have not changed (P.B. Baltes & Nesselroade, 1973; H. Moss & Sussman, 1980).

The other approach assumes an underlying set of qualities or traits that give meaning to the individual's behavior in most situations. This underlying constancy accounts for stability in personality across time (P.J. Costa & McCrae, 1980). At this point it may be instructive to ask "Who is more correct in his views about personality—the individual who assumes an underlying set of qualities or characteristics, or the individual who emphasizes the situation?" As we shall soon see, *each* point of view adds something to our knowledge about personality development in adulthood.

This contrast in views about personality (see Atchley, 1982; P.J. Costa & McCrae, 1980; Hall & Lindzey, 1985; Lawton, 1983; Mortimer, Finch, & Kumka, 1982; Neugarten, 1977; Thomae, 1980) has implications for the researcher and the practitioner alike. For example, the quality and quantity of our helping interventions with adults of all ages (see Chapter 14) are affected by ideas about how their personalities function. Likewise, larger issues regarding the prediction of behavior and concerns about the stability of adult personality hinge upon a basic view about how personality is organized as well as what factors are responsible for change. Indeed, our ability to make

Depending on one's views about personality, behavior in one situation (e.g., in the classroom) may or may not be seen as out of character for the individual.

sense of our own behavior as well as that of others hinges upon some understanding of our own and others' personalities.

Most of us probably live our lives with some hypotheses as to why we behave the way we do—what motivates us. Furthermore, most of us would like to believe that our behavior is consistent. When it is not, we attempt to understand why. Thus, whether we are discussing "normal" personality development or deviations from this norm (schizophrenia, depression, paranoia—see Chapter 13), understanding the above two points of view is important.

In fact, there are many who feel disagreements about how to best understand and measure personality in adulthood have hindered the development of therapeutic interventions for elderly adults (R. Kastenbaum, 1978b) and in general created a "crisis" of sorts for those in the field of research in adult personality development (P.J. Costa & McCrae, 1980; Neugarten, 1977).

Each of the approaches (and the specific theories that are derived from them) that we will discuss makes somewhat different assumptions about the importance of internal, unobservable processes versus external, observable behaviors. Each point of view, however, is necessarily going to be limited in some respects. Each theorist is limited to studying personality *as he or she has defined it;* no approach can be all things to all people. Furthermore (see Chapter 1), because each point of view does begin with differing assumptions about what personality is, what is to be studied, and how it is to be studied, one should resist the temptation to say that approach *A* is "better" than approach *B.* Rather, differing approaches are more or less *useful* (see Hall & Lindzey, 1985) in making predictions about that which one has decided to study (adjustment to life events, psychopathology, stability or change in adulthood). Ultimately, you should make your own choice about whether you will agree with a given approach or perhaps you will pick and choose from several in defining personality.

Personality, like intelligence (see Chapter 6), can be defined in many ways. Each point of view will make different assumptions about how to best measure personality and thus will draw different conclusions about personality stability and change in adulthood, or about how best to deal with specific life events (retirement, parenthood, divorce, death) across the life span.

Rather than think solely in terms of the extremes contrasted at this chapter's outset, views about how personality is best defined are better understood as ranging along a *continuum,* where those who emphasize internal processes (traits) are on one extreme, and those who emphasize observable behaviors that the individual emits in response to the immediate environment are located on the other end of this continuum.

On one end of the continuum is the perspective emphasizing underlying qualities or characteristics in personality that generalize across situations. While a *psychoanalytic* point of view, emphasizing unobservable constructs such as ego, id, or superego, has been used to understand the workings of personality (Hall & Lindzey, 1985), many feel that it has little relevance beyond adolescence in explaining adult personality development (see Bengston, Reedy & Gordon, 1985; Neugarten, 1977; Noam, Higgins-O'Connell, &

Goethals, 1982). The major exceptions to this are in the writings of Erik Erikson and Roger Gould, whose work we shall discuss later in this chapter. The psychoanalytic approach lies on the one extreme of this internal-external continuum of personality, where one's behavior is explained in terms of the underlying personality dynamics among the ego, id, and superego. Another point of view emphasizing internal processes is termed a *trait-centered* approach (P.J. Costa & McCrae, 1980; Thomae, 1980); that is, behavior reflects the existence of traits, which we all possess in varying degrees. At a different point along our continuum lies the *cognitive view* (Ryff, 1984; Thomae, 1980), which emphasizes the *perception* of oneself in studying personality. According to the cognitive view, whether personality change occurs depends upon whether the individual *perceives* or recognizes this change. Further along our continuum lies the perspective stressing external, observable responses to either internal or external sets of factors. It is referred to as the **social learning theory** approach (Bandura, 1977; Mischel, 1981) to personality. According to this view, individuals *construct* a set of internal standards to govern their own behavior in the absence of external guides. It is through the observation of others who are valued, competent *models,* whose behaviors are seen as important to imitate (their behavior is internalized) that personality development takes place. Individuals reinforce themselves for desirable behavior that they have learned in this manner or acquired vicariously by observing others and develop a sense of *self-efficacy* (Bandura, 1977).

Mischel's (1981) views are similar to Bandura's but stress the interaction between an individual's expectations (constructs), ideas about how the world works (G.A. Kelly, 1955), and the environment. Individuals do not randomly react to the environment, according to Mischel. Instead, they select aspects of the environment to relate to in accordance with their skills, interests, biases, strengths, and weaknesses. Individuals who maintain a stable self-concept are able to cope better with experiences that do not agree with this established sense of self. In other words, they *selectively* avoid situations that do not agree with their established personality. Those whose personalities are not consistent or are negative are not as effective in coping with their environment (Atchley, 1982).

According to this view, as people age, they incorporate experiences that reinforce their acquired "expectancies." Those who are in poor health or who have unstable, negative views of themselves have more difficulty in coping with many of the negatives (loss of self-esteem due to divorce, the "empty nest," middle age "crisis," relocation to a nursing home, retirement, menopause, death of loved ones) that sometimes accompany the aging process (Atchley, 1982).

On the other extreme of our continuum is Skinner (1974), who sees personality in purely external terms. No internal, unobservable traits, qualities, or ideas about oneself are necessary in order to understand the person. For Skinner, personality dynamics and personality development are best understood in terms of behaviors that *operate* upon or *change* the environment; these behaviors are termed *operants.* Operants enable the individual to *successfully* cope with the environment; that is, they produce situations that are pleasurable or allow the individual to escape negative situations. Thus, these

TABLE 10.1

REPRESENTATIVE APPROACHES TO DEFINING PERSONALITY IN ADULTHOOD

Psychoanalytic Approaches	Trait Approaches	Cognitive Approaches	Social-Learning Theory Approach	Functional-Behavioral Theory Approach
Freud, Gould, Erikson	Allport, Cattell, Costa, and McCrae	Thomae, Ryff	Mischel, Bandura	Skinner

| Internal (unobservables) | | Continuum of emphasis | | External (observables) |

behaviors increase in frequency and in strength; they are *reinforced* by the changes in the environment (termed reinforcing stimuli) that they produce. Those behaviors that are not adaptive drop out (they are *extinguished*), due to the fact that a pleasurable result has not come about or the individual's behavior has introduced something negative into the environment. Emotions, motives, or traits only function as labels to conveniently link behaviors (dependent variables) that are *functionally related* to identifiable environmental or situational antecedents (independent variables). Skinner (1983), for example, has discussed the self-application of operant principles to the management of thinking/intellectual behaviors in later adulthood.

Thus, as illustrated in Table 10.1, we can see ideas about personality as organized along a continuum. On one end lie those emphasizing *internal* processes (psychoanalytic, trait approaches). Distinct from this view are those incorporating *cognitive processes* as mediating factors determining the individual's adaptation to the environment (social learning theory). On the other extreme are those whose emphasis is entirely on *external, observable behaviors* (Skinner's operant behavioral approach).

APPROACHES TO PERSONALITY AND DEVELOPMENT

We have said that the multitude of approaches to personality are by definition difficult to compare. Maddi (1976, 1980), however, has attempted to reconcile those points of view emphasizing the *commonalities* among people (trait, psychoanalytic approaches) versus those emphasizing *differences* among individuals (functional-behavioral theory). Maddi has put forth a broader approach that makes possible the study of all aspects of behavior—those that generalize across individuals and those that do not. In terms of our initial example, we can determine under what conditions an individual's behavior is or is not "out of character." Maddi distinguishes between those pervasive, inherent "characteristics or tendencies" that give individuals direction (their personalities) and behaviors that are learned and vary with the situation. The internal forces that give people direction are referred to as the **core** of personality; behaviors that vary with the situation are termed the **periphery** of personality. Maddi's definition of personality reflects this dual emphasis on universal qualities and situation-specific behaviors in understanding what personality is and how it develops (changes) over the course of time.

As Figure 10.1 illustrates, Maddi's core-periphery concept of personality would encompass each of the more specific approaches we discussed earlier. In this sense, it is superior to discussing in depth each specific theory of personality. For a more extensive discussion of each of these theories, see Corsini (1977), Hall and Lindzey (1985), Maddi (1980), Monte (1977), or Rychlak (1973). As can be seen in Figure 10.1, the *core statement* provides the framework within which core characteristics interact with the external environment to produce the peripheral aspects of the individual. Most important for our purposes in studying adult personality development, the link between the core and the periphery is accomplished via *development*.

The solid developmental line linking core and periphery in Figure 10.1 represents an *ideal* set of developmental influences that most directly express core tendency and peripheral characteristics. The dashed lines represent *less than ideal* developmental experiences producing less adequate personality types and more specific associated peripheral characteristics (traits).

Regardless of our approach, however, we assume that it is one's personality that makes one's behavior *consistent* or *lawful*. That is, each approach to personality is governed by sets of assumptions or laws that make one's behavior *understandable* or *predictable*. Moreover, most personality theorists are concerned with the *whole* individual as he or she copes with, or adjusts to, the environment.

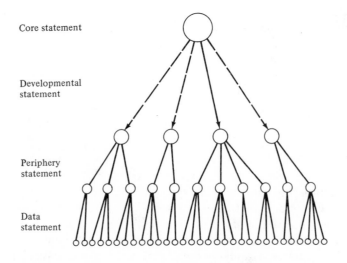

Core statement

Developmental statement

Periphery statement

Data statement

Core tendency: Overall direction of living
Core characteristics: Common structural entities (e.g., goals, ideals, instincts)
Interaction of core tendency and characteristics with outside world (parents, others, society)
Statement on the nature of *society*
Typology: The life–styles or general orientations that can occur through learning (e.g., anal character)
Concrete peripheral characteristic: The smallest learned units of personality that are organized into types (e.g., stubbornness, cleanliness)
Thoughts, feelings, and actions that have regularity in an individual and distinguish him from others

Figure 10.1 Maddi's core and periphery of personality. *Source:* S. Maddi. (1980). *Personality theories: a comparative analysis* (p. 16). Homewood, Illinois: Dorsey Press. Reprinted by permission of Dorsey Press Publishers, Richard D. Irwin, Inc.

STABILITY AND CHANGE IN ADULT PERSONALITY: MAJOR THEORETICAL VIEWPOINTS

As we noted earlier in this chapter, stability versus change with age in personality has a number of basic and applied implications. For example, we may find it necessary to rethink adult personality as distinct from that in childhood or to reconsider the design of interventions (see Emery & Lesher, 1982) directed to helping adults of all ages solve problems in their daily lives. These problems might be quite different, ranging from coping with marital difficulties to dealing with retirement and death.

Neugarten (1977) suggests that two questions come to mind when examining the personality-age interaction: does aging affect personality (do people change with increased age), and does personality affect aging (does one's personality influence adaptation to the aging process)? These two questions will guide our discussion of personality in adulthood and aging. As Neugarten suggests, even a commonsense approach to both questions demands an answer of a qualified yes to each—people do change in *some* ways as they age, and different persons do cope with aging in different ways. Thus, on the basis of research dealing with both questions (see P.J. Costa & McCrae, 1980; Neugarten, 1977; Thomae, 1980), the answer is *yes and no.* The answer(s) to each question are a function of (1) one's *theoretical biases,* (2) the particular *design* (see Chapter 3) utilized to gather facts about personality, (3) the *level* of personality that is studied, and (4) how one *assesses* personality. Depending upon these factors, or interactions among them, personality is at once stable and yet changing across adulthood. This should perhaps confirm your own self-assessment. In some ways, you are much like you were years ago. In other ways, however, you have changed.

Theories of Adult Personality Change

Just as definitions of personality differ, various theorists have expressed their own ideas about how personality develops through the life span.

BUHLER'S BIOGRAPHICAL APPROACH

Among the earliest notions of personality development in adulthood is that of Charlotte Buhler (1953, 1961, 1962, 1982) who studied development *biographically*—by using life histories. On the basis of these life histories, she identified two categories of life events: those that were **biographical** (experiential) (thought to increase through most of adulthood) and those that were **biological** (increasing and subsequently declining after age 50). Buhler (1962) integrated these sets of life events and the notions of **life tendencies**, each of which provided organization and direction to persons' behavior, serving to develop the *core self* to the fullest. Each life tendency assumed a special importance at distinct periods during the life span (see Table 10.2). Buhler's ideas, while they were not based on empirical data, gave structure to later work and underscored the developmental study of the *whole person* (Havighurst, 1973).

As Hall and Lindzey (1978, 1985) note, Buhler's ideas are less focused on describing development in terms of distinct developmental stages and more oriented toward understanding the ongoing, adaptive *processes* of psychological growth. They thus might predict important *qualitative changes* in

TABLE 10.2

BUHLER'S BIOGRAPHICAL APPROACH TO PERSONALITY

Age Period	Basic Tendency				
	Need-Satisfaction	Adaptive Self-Limitation	Creative Expansion	Establishment of Inner Order	Self-Fulfillment
0–1.5 yr.	Trust and love, evolvement and discovery of self-sameness				
1.5–4 yr.		Obedience and super-ego ideal versus independence			
4–8 yr.			Autonomous, value-setting, ego-ideals aspect of task		
8–12 yr.				Attempts to objective self-evaluation in social roles	
12–18 yr.	Sex needs and problem of sexual identity			Review and preview of self-development (autobiographical)	Fulfillment of and detachment from childhood
18–25 (30) yr.		Tentative self-determination to role in society			
25 (30)–45 (50) yr.			Self-realization in occupation, marriage, and own family		
45 (50)–65 (70) yr.				Critical self-assessment	
65 (70)–80 (85) yr.					Self-fulfillment
80 (85)–death	Regression to predominant need-satisfaction				

Source: R. Havighurst. (1973). History of developmental psychology: Socialization and personality development through the life span. In P.B. Baltes & K.W. Schaie (Eds.). *Life-span developmental psychology: Personality and socialization* (p. 8). New York: Academic Press.

adult personality as the influences of diverse life tendencies become more pervasive. All of these changes, of course, need to be seen in terms of their role in the development of the whole person.

ERIKSON'S PSYCHOSOCIAL APPROACH

Erik Erikson (1959, 1963) sees personality development (specifically *ego* development) in terms of eight psychosocial crises. Erikson feels that each psychosocial crisis can be resolved positively or negatively. The ego is that aspect of the personality that must mediate the instinctual demands of the *id* and the restrictions of the *superego* to cope with reality (Hall & Lindzey, 1978). According to Valliant (1977), as one ages, the ego becomes more mature and more clearly differentiated from the id and the superego, permitting one to cope with the demands of the outside world in a more decisive, rational manner. Additionally, as one ages, the ego is said to resort to more sophisticated, effective defense mechanisms (e.g., sublimation, intellectualization) to deal with anxiety brought on by a loss of control over one's instincts (residing in the id) or with anxiety related to the superego's restrictions on pleasurable experiences that are deemed immoral.

As an attempt to understand ego development, Erikson's psychosocial crisis theory is an *age-graded* approach to ego development closely aligned with **developmental tasks** particular to various life periods (see Chapters 1 and 2). While Freud preferred to speak of possible *fixation* at a given psychosexual stage, Erikson suggests that individuals deal with each crisis in a cumulative manner. Difficulties in resolving earlier **psychosocial crises** can seriously interfere with but do not completely prevent adults from attempting to resolve later crises. Furthermore, each crisis, regardless of its resolution, comes to help redefine later crises. These crises are said to be *epigenetic;* they arise out of a **maturational ground plan** and eventually come together to form the *whole individual.* This ground plan is preordained, or biologically determined.

Individuals vary in terms of their timing of each crisis in chronological terms, and, as we noted above, crises are never "left behind." Thus, the *trust-mistrust* crisis, which is especially relevant to issues regarding one's faith in being cared for in a timely way (characteristic of the trust-mistrust crisis of infancy), may reemerge in adulthood when decisions about educational or career goals, values regarding one's ideals, and relationships with the opposite sex are being crystallized. All of these require the ability to project oneself into the future. To be able to come to grips with these issues literally requires *trust in one's own skills* and abilities, and more importantly a *sense of trust in time itself*—the trust that with effort one's goals will be realized (being successful in one's work, becoming a parent and subsequently raising children). Clearly then, while one is not "dependent upon" another as infants are upon their mothers, issues regarding "trust in time" do reemerge later on.

Likewise, the crisis central to young adulthood, *intimacy versus isolation,* requires the individual to be able to merge with another to form a relationship that is built upon mutual trust and love. The young adult develops a sense of *inter*dependence (K.W. Schaie & Geiwitz, 1982) that characterizes this relationship with another. The ability to enter into a relationship with another individual that is mutual, reciprocal, or intimate is a function of the individual's previous efforts in establishing a stable sense of *ego identity* (vs. identity confusion) in adolescence. If one's identity is poorly formed or not formed at all, the crisis of *intimacy* will be perceived as too threatening. This inability to commit oneself to another (in a sense merge one's identity with that of another) (see Hall & Lindzey, 1978, 1985) is termed *isolation*.

Characteristic of middle age is the crisis of *generativity* versus *stagnation*, where individuals are redefining their lives in terms of "time left to live" versus "time since birth." To be generative literally means *to generate*—to produce things or people that symbolize one's continued existence after this life. Knowing that death is a reality (see Jaques, 1980) implores one to accept one's own mortality and to make preparations for future generations. Generativity may be expressed by being productive in one's work (in writing or teaching), personal creativity (finding a novel solution to a problem, painting a unique picture), or most directly in having children, caring for them, and raising them to be adults (Erikson, 1959, 1963). Thus, in the selection of a career, the decision to marry (as well as whom to marry; see Chapters 2 and 8), and in relationships with one's children, choices that may have been made earlier in life predispose one toward generativity (see Erikson, 1963). Obviously, a change in identity will accompany this process as well. Intimacy will likewise be *redefined* to include relationships with one's children or perhaps a few trusted friends. On the other hand, *stagnation* implies a withdrawal into oneself. Those who are stagnated may become self-indulgent, bitter, and isolated from others. They may not feel needed—a feeling that that which they have to give is not worth giving.

Integrity versus *despair* characterizes old age. In a word, integrity implies a sense of *completeness*, of having come full circle. The person who has integrity has, through the process of *introspection* (looking inward and examining what one finds), been able to integrate a lifetime full of successes and failures to reach a point where he or she has a "sense of the life cycle." Despairing individuals fear death as a premature end to a life (good or bad) that they have not been able to take personal responsibility for. The person who has a sense of integrity accepts death as the inevitable end of having lived. As Erikson notes, "Only in him who in some way has taken care of things and people and has adapted himself to the triumphs and disappointments adherent to being, the originator of others or the generator of products and ideas—only in him may gradually ripen the fruit of these seven stages. I know no better word for it than ego integrity. . . . Each individual, to become a mature adult, must develop to a sufficient degree all of the ego qualities, so that a wise Indian, a true gentleman, and a mature peasant share and recognize in one another the final stage of integrity" (1963, pp. 268–269). In paralleling the trust of infancy and integrity, Erikson writes, "And it seems possible to paraphrase the relation of adult integrity and infantile trust by saying the healthy children will not fear life if their elders have integrity enough not to fear death" (1963, p. 269). Butler's (1963) concepts of the **life review** and **reminiscence** (M. Romaniuk, 1981; M. Romaniuk & J. Romaniuk, 1981) are similar processes allowing one to reach ego integrity.

Despite the popular influence of Erikson's work in adult development, it has not gone uncriticized. Ego integrity (as with other concepts defining psychosocial crises) is difficult to define (Neugarten, 1977), though recent attempts to measure these concepts (i.e., intimacy, generativity, integrity, wisdom) have been made (Clayton & Birren, 1980; Walaskay, Whitbourne, & Nehrke, 1983–84) with some success. Clayton (1975) argues, moreover, that rather than accept complete resolution of crises as the norm, it is more realistic to see individuals as "compromising" their way through previous crises. This does not, however, permit them to reach Erikson's last stage, as Erikson defined it. Peck (1968) felt Erikson's stages (particularly the latter two) were entirely too global and really reflected new solutions to previous crises; too much emphasis was placed on adjustment during the first 20 years of life, to the detriment of one's adult years.

LEVINSON'S LIFE STRUCTURE

D. Levinson (1978) conducted an intensive study of 40 men aged 35 to 45 to investigate the process by which these men created a **life structure**, defined as a coherent relationship between one's own goals and various life arenas (e.g., career, family, marriage, social roles), "the basic pattern or design of a person's life at a given time" (D. Levinson, 1978). Levinson found, on the basis of detailed interviews and psychological test data, that this life structure evolves through a sequence of distinct periods. Moreover, this changing life structure serves as the framework within which each person's own individual life cycle can be understood. It shapes and is shaped by decisions that each individual makes at varying times in adulthood.

Levinson suggests that this life structure is three-dimensional—it includes (1) the individual's "*sociocultural* world as it impinges upon him"—a multitude of social contexts (e.g., occupational structure, social class, ethnicity, family); (2) the individual's *self,* to the extent that certain aspects of this self are expressed or inhibited (e.g., wishes, conflicts, anxieties and ways of fulfilling/controlling them, skills and abilities, feelings); and (3) the manner in which the individual *participates in the external world.* More specifically, we are referring to how we define and use the variety of roles that we may wish or be required to play in the world (spouse, parent, citizen, lover, worker, boss, friend). Levinson is clear in saying that his concept of life structure is not equivalent to ego development and/or occupational developmental stages but instead refers to a more general, diverse structure in which each of these dimensions change as they relate to one another.

Several cautions are noted regarding Levinson's work; for instance, since his subjects were aged 35 to 45, information they provided about the years bracketing this age range would be considered retrospective (young adulthood) and prospective (later adulthood). Levinson (1978) admits that his initial interest was to study what he intuitively thought to be a crucial period in adult development (ages 40–50). Later on in his research, fully realizing that his sample was, despite being studied intensively, small and limited to men, he chose to make a more general statement about the nature of adult development. (See Figure 10.2 for an illustration of the following stages.)

The *early adult transition* (approximate ages 17–22) links adolescence and early adulthood. During this period, one reevaluates the preadult world and one's role in it. One's relationships with people and institutions principally involving parents, siblings, extended family members, friends, or teachers are either terminated or altered such that the adolescent (preadult) life structure is left behind, so that an initial step in the adult world can be made, a kind of "testing of the waters." One becomes less psychologically dependent upon parental support and authority and more autonomous and independent, though Levinson notes that this process is never fully complete. He, instead, chooses to speak in terms of *degrees* of separation/attachment during various life periods.

Entering the adult world (ages 22–28) functions to allow the individual to create a *provisional* life structure that provides a link to adult society. The young person is entering a *novice phase,* where important dimensions of what may become a more permanent fixture of the life structure are shaped (e.g., occupational choice, marriage and family, peer relationships, values, lifestyle). Levinson (1978) suggests that in this novice phase, the individual must leave alternatives open and thus not prematurely commit to a given course. At the same time, the person must create a "stable life structure" and make some decisions indicating responsible behavior. Thus, these first decisions must be made, but they should be ones that allow for future change and flexibility.

These decisions are made within the context of one's *Dream.* Levinson interpreted the Dream as "a vague sense of the self-in-adult-world" (p. 91). It may be occupational or parental in nature (e.g., being president of one's

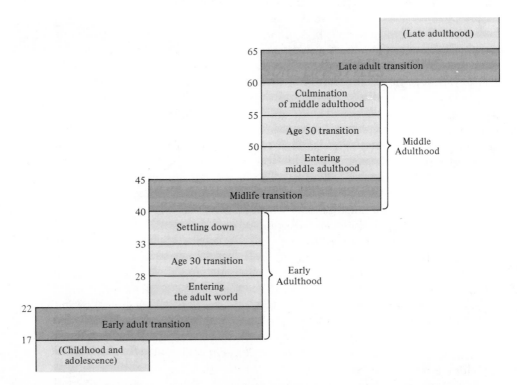

Figure 10.2 Levinson's changes in the life structure. *Source:* D. Levinson. (1978). *The seasons of a man's life* (p. 57). New York: Knopf. Reprinted by permission of Alfred A. Knopf, Inc. and by permission of the author.

own company, being a loving parent, or simply being good at one's trade). The novice's task is to define more precisely this Dream and realistically live it out. The individual must overcome setbacks and disappointments and learn, as well, to accept and profit from successes so that the "thread" of this Dream is not lost in the process of moving up the ladder or revising the life structure.

The age 30 transition (ages 28–33) "provides an opportunity to work on the flaws and limitations of the first life structure and to create the basis for a more satisfactory structure with which to complete the era of young adulthood" (Levinson, 1978, p. 58). For most of the men he studied, Levinson found this transition to be a traumatic one, in that the changes were often ill-advised (out of step with the individual's wishes or abilities), or based on a poorly formed initial life structure. For some (whom Levinson found to be a minority), this transition was a smooth one. The age 30 transition implies a shift away from tentative choices regarding family and career to ones that will be more permanent and almost irreversible. This transition leads to the *settling down* period, where the man invests himself in those components of his initial life structure that were somewhat tentative earlier. These major components are the "nuts and bolts" of a framework that allows him to "establish a niche" for himself and to "make it" (succeed at whatever is most important), where his progress can be monitored by himself as well as others (authority figures) along a "timetable" of sorts. He begins to map out a path for success in his work or with respect to his roles as husband or father. This settling down period has a strong sense of his commitment to a personal, familial, and occupational future to it that implies "I am a responsible adult now," as opposed to the "I'm just beginning to find out what is important to me/what my opinions are" stage characteristic of the first life structure. At the end of this period (ages 36–40), according to Levinson, the individual is "Becoming One's Own Man" (BOOM) and begins to ascend the "ladder" to become a respected authority.

It is at this point persons may assume the role of **mentor** for someone younger than he who is just beginning work on his own life structure, the elder male having terminated his relationship with his own mentor. Mentors can fulfill (some with more success than others) a *formal,* more *external* role, in that they serve a guiding, teaching function in helping the novice define his *Dream.* (Recall that it is the dimension of the Dream that defines the planning done in the novice phase.) Alternatively, the mentor can also fill a more *informal, internal* advisory role that is *emotionally supportive,* much like that of a parent. Some men and women are more adept at some aspects of the mentor role than others; individual insecurity or unfulfilled needs for success can cause them to manipulate those they supervise. Like active parenting, the mentor role will be shed (willingly or not) as that young adult reaches the "settling down" (BOOM) period and the point where he or she will serve as someone else's mentor. We know little that is substantive about the mentor role; it can, however, be a very enriching experience, much as parenting can help one gain a sense of perspective about life and about one's own occupational and personal goals. On the other hand, it can be painful and disruptive (a role in which the *mentor* is the one who is manipulated) depending on the quality of the mentor-underlying relationship. Levinson rarely found men over 40 who still maintained an active mentor relationship with someone their senior.

The midlife transition (ages 40–45) represents a shift from an acquisition orientation regarding the life structure to a more evaluative one. This is a period of soul-searching, questioning, and assessment regarding the extent to which all that has been accomplished within the life structure has any real meaning or not. It typifies what is popularly referred to as a midlife crisis. For some, it is a rather gradual, relatively painless change; for others, it is full of uncertainties and often has an "either/or" quality to it—either one starts anew or perceives that one has failed in some way to define what is important (literally one's *self*) meaningfully. Levinson notes that for these individuals, several years may be needed "to form a new path or to modify an old one" (p. 60).

Having resolved (more or less satisfactorily) issues regarding whether those people and things to which one has committed oneself are really satisfying, Levinson finds the individual next *entering middle adulthood,* wherein choices must again be made regarding a new life structure. In some cases, these choices are defined by *marker events*—divorce, illness, a shift in occupations, or the death of someone close. In other cases, changes are less obvious, but nonetheless significant—subtle shifts in enthusiasm for one's work, changes in the quality of one's marriage. As before, the resulting life structure varies in terms of its ability to truly satisfy the individual, to the extent that it is connected to the self—it may or may not intrinsically be happy or fulfilling. The quality of this newly revised life structure more or less sets the tone for the remainder of the fourth decade. Levinson tentatively proposes an *age 50 transition* (ages 50–55), which basically represents an opportunity to further solidify and/or change the life structure established during middle adulthood. For some, this may be *experienced* as the midlife transition, as in cases where individuals have done little in altering the life structure or have not been very successful in doing so. It is important to note that for Levinson, "It is not possible to get through middle adulthood without having at least a moderate crisis in either the midlife transition or the age 50 transition" (1978, p. 62). The period from 55 to 60 is seen as a relatively stable one, analogous to the settling down stage, where the life structure is solidified, followed by a *late adult transition* (ages 60–65), which terminates middle adulthood and prepares one for older adulthood. Of course, since Levinson did not interview men in their fifties and sixties, his views on later middle age and old age are highly speculative, culture-bound, and obviously heavily influenced by his own biases. Moreover, it remains to be seen whether Levinson's observations are equally true of women. Based on biographical research, Roberts and Newton (1987) found some similarity in women's timing of the above stages. However, women worked on these tasks differently and achieved different outcomes. According to Roberts and Newton, women had more complex Dreams, and had more difficulty in fulfilling these Dreams.

GOULD'S TRANSFORMATIONS

Roger Gould (1980a, 1980b) points out that chronological age is a weak predictor (see Wohlwill, 1970a) of who may or may not be working through a given stage or task. He instead recommends studying people who are faced with a *common problem*—loss of the parenting role due to the empty nest, or retirement, *regardless* of their ages. He also emphasizes a shift in time perspective that defines the adult life cycle, from the seeming infinity of time that is available to us when we leave high school to a more limited but plentiful sense of time that eventuates in our winning "the prize" (similar to Levinson's Dream). This sense of time becomes more constricted in our late twenties, when we begin to realize that there is not enough time to test out all the choices that have opened up. In our late thirties or early forties and thereafter, time becomes precious as we become more aware of and confront our own mortality and begin to question whether our "prize" was worth it, or if it even exists. Briefly put, this prize is freedom from restrictions by the persons who have formed us (our parents). In order to travel this bumpy road to its end, we must free ourselves of the **illusion of absolute safety**. This process involves **transformations**, whereby we give up the security of the past to form our own ideas, a necessarily troublesome task, according to Gould. (Note that while Levinson suggests that one begins adulthood with a life structure that is absent, Gould feels that the structure (illusion) that we have created for ourselves must be given up in order for growth to occur.) For Gould, adult development consists of alterations in or challenges to this illusion of absolute safety, which is based upon four major false assumptions spanning the age range from 18 to 35 (Gould, 1980b, p. 66):

1. I will always belong to my parents and believe in their version of reality (late teens, early twenties).
2. Doing it my own way with willpower and perseverance will bring results, but when I am frustrated, confused, tired, or unable, they will step in and show me the way (the twenties).
3. Life is simple, not complicated. There are no significant unknown inner forces within me; there are no multiple coexisting, contradicting realities present in my life (late twenties, early thirties).
4. There is no evil or death in the world; the demonic has been expelled (mid-thirties to 50).

Through such experiences as leaving home to go to college or to work (1. above), the necessity to make decisions about work, family, marriage (2. above), experiencing early successes in (and conflicts among) these dimensions (3. above), persons in their late thirties begin to rid themselves of the illusion of absolute safety. It is at this point that we begin to confront the ultimate loss of power of our parents that comes with advanced age. We also, especially if our parents are very ill or have died, (4. above), may confront our own eventual deaths, and our time orientation shifts to the more limited future that lies before us. We question where we are going and decide that wherever we should go, we'd better "get on with it" before time runs out.

By about age 50, we are forced to see our lives in terms of "I own myself," with its own sense of the potential for success and failure, rather than "I am theirs" (parents). Ultimately, we give up trying to control the world and thus do not experience feelings of safety stemming from this sense of ultimate control. After 50, Gould says, one may come to accept what one *is*—good or bad, successful or not—growing out of the giving up of childhood illusions of control. Gould's ideas are, of course, perhaps the most representative extension of Freud's psychoanalytic theory, itself not a very fruitful one for the study of adult personality development (Havighurst, 1973). It is, therefore, childhood centered, with growth or maturity more or less boiling down to a complete resolution of the separation anxiety in childhood that we feel when we are first forced to "stand on our own" psychologically. It is in direct contrast to the view of adulthood espoused by the life-span developmental theorists (see Chapter 1) such as P.B. Baltes, who see adulthood as influenced by *many* factors—those rooted in childhood are but *one* set of influences.

Gould's ideas are in many respects similar to those of Levinson, as well as to those of Havighurst (see Chapter 1) and Erikson, in breaking down the adult life span into different sets of issues or tasks that are age related. Both Gould and Levinson explore changes in how people deal with culturally relevant shifts in the self (career, marriage, family) brought about by and causing changes in the *life structure* (Levinson) and by *transformations in the illusion of absolute safety* (Gould). Havighurst and Levinson advocate positions suggesting *qualitative changes* in adult personality. Gould's position, however, supports a *stability* of personality point of view stemming from transformations in the self that are extensions of childhood separation anxiety.

ADULT DEVELOPMENTAL STAGES IN PERSONALITY—DESCRIPTIVE OR PRESCRIPTIVE?

One should always keep in mind (see Birren & Renner, 1977; Lerner, 1986) that any approach to personality development emphasizing developmental stages (Erikson, Havighurst, Buhler, Levinson, Gould) is more properly thought of as a *descriptive* framework within which to view individual development rather than as *prescriptive* in nature.

The desire to "predict" the crises of adult life, presumably so that one can inoculate oneself against (prepare for) them, perhaps accounts for the popularity of Gail Sheehy's (1976) *Passages.* In fact, depending upon one's definition of "crisis," one could easily argue that crises are, by definition, not predictable. They are instead individual-specific—*nonnormative* (see Chapter 1). On the other hand, we may feel that any adjustment to changing capabilities or expectations constitutes a crisis of sorts, in that demands on one's adaptive skills or changes in one's identity may be required (see Atchley, 1982; Eisdorfer & Wilkie, 1979a, 1979b; Lowenthal & Chiriboga, 1973).

J. Layton and Siegler (1978) suggest that crises may or may not accompany the aging process (i.e., the midlife crisis) in that individuals seek to maintain a *consistent* sense of identities (physical, occupational, familial, interpersonal). Challenges to our sense of **self-efficacy** (Bandura, 1977) (a sense of competence, control or mastery) are brought about by "marker events" (birthdays, occupational changes, marriages, births of children, divorces, retirement, having one's picture taken). Such events cause us to compare ourselves at present with ourselves in the past. We then can project into the future some ideal that we have set for ourselves. Depending upon the nature of the event or change *and* the adaptiveness of our efforts to cope with that event, a "crisis" may be experienced. For example, while some people shrug off routine physical exams, others (even if they pass with flying colors!) are alerted to the possibility that in the future something *may* go wrong with their bodies—they may turn a harmless comment about their weight into a compulsive diet or exercise regimen. Instead of alleviating their fears, the physical exam magnifies them!

Likewise, while parenthood or marriage (normative life events) in one's twenties may be expected or even prepared for (via anticipatory socialization in the roles of parent or spouse), some individuals obviously cope with the changes these roles bring about more positively than do others. Some individuals also deal with parenthood in their forties (more nonnormative in nature) more adaptively than do others (see Danish, Smyer, & Nowak, 1980; Hultsch & Plemons, 1979; Reese & Smyer, 1983).

Thus, whether psychosocial stages and developmental tasks are prescriptive and/or inherently stressful or not is a function of a complex set of internal processes and external events (some of which are age-graded and some of which are not). Personality change may or may not accompany experiences that some, but not all, people have as they age.

References to developmental stages are really attempts to expain the behavior of individuals at a given point in their lives that are exhibited *most* of the time—their "modal" behaviors (Lerner, 1986). As we noted in Chapter 1, there are wide individual differences between individuals who are at a given "stage" of development. These persons may actually display behavior that is characteristic of more than one stage. Thus, the transition from one stage to another is a *gradual* process, not an all-or-none affair (see Chapter 1).

Taken too literally, "stages" become "shoulds" rather than "maybes." Furthermore, one should keep in mind that they are intended to be normative (they should apply to most individuals at given points in their lives). There are substantial differences among individuals as to *when* such crises or stages are experienced and *how* they are experienced. We suggest that they are best seen as "hurdles to be overcome" or as one in a series of *many* choice points or decisions to be made *throughout* adulthood. Consequently, they may or may not meaningfully apply to you.

Although stage theory approaches have provided a viable *descriptive* framework for understanding adult personality development, they need to be evaluated in terms of their *potential* for understanding *intra*individual change or stability. This potential is limited by (1) individual differences in the timing and meaning of each stage, (2) the impact of the cultural context on the response to a given psychosocial crisis/developmental task, and (3) the interaction between persons and their environment that affect (and are affected by) such individuals' efforts to cope with changes in areas such as marriage, family, career, and self.

Riegel's Dialectics of Adjustment to Developmental Stages

Resolving a crisis is often seen as a hurdle of sorts to be overcome. Between each "hurdle" one might assume that "all is well," so to speak. Klaus Riegel (1975, 1976) suggests that the *process* of resolving crises can be quite beneficial.

In fact, Riegel suggests that the periods of stability that come between these crises are the exception rather than the rule. Though Riegel would not be considered a personality theorist, his ideas about coping with change can help us put the developmental stage theories in perspective.

To suggest that there is a fixed sequence to the problems one encounters in adulthood, each yielding an outcome (integrity or despair), is to miss the point entirely, according to Riegel (see also Lieberman, 1975; Lowenthal & Chiriboga, 1973; Schlossberg, 1976 for process approaches to coping with change). In fact, the cultural-historical context in which we live influences whether or not a crisis is experienced at all (see Riegel, 1977b). According to Riegel, if society is "in sync" with individual life events, no crisis will be experienced by a given individual. For example, while childbirth at age 20 normally would not be seen as a crisis, it could be considered as such, depending upon the culture's prohibitions about birth control, day care, abortion, equal job opportunities, or single parenthood. In such cases, having a child could present a major problem for a young woman. Similarly, depending upon a man's options in retirement (access to part-time work, viable volunteer roles), leaving the work force may or may not precipitate an "identity crisis" of sorts.

In each case (parenthood, retirement), we may learn more about personality from the *process* (Thomae, 1980) of coming to terms with the contradictions created by a society that is "out of synch" with the age-graded life events that most of us experience, according to Riegel. It is because "crises" create the necessity for either positive or negative outcomes (stemming from *processes* of problem solving and decision making that are more or less adaptive) that Riegel chooses to look to development in this way. He has used the term **dialectical operations** (an extension of Piagetian formal operations) to define the individual's continual *efforts at coping* with life events such as parenthood at age 40 or early retirement. Dialectical operations (Riegel, 1973) involve the cognitive ability to deal with, recognize, and work through contradiction and crisis. Riegel suggests that it is through the study of the dialectics of development, *not* through the study of age-graded sets of developmental tasks or psychosocial crises, that we can learn about *how* people change.

Regardless of whether one speaks in terms of psychosocial crises or developmental tasks, these choice points or stages need to be seen as attempts to describe and give structure to adult personality development. In most cases (see Buss, 1979; Riegel, 1975, 1977b), while they are attempts to describe *individual* development, they are, by definition, specific to a given culture or subculture. So, as the culture changes (either through the efforts of ourselves or others) (Mortimer et al., 1982), the nature of the developmental task or psychosocial crisis requiring one's adaptation to cultural expectations will also change. In a dialectical sense, we must assume that at least *one* of the consequences of the individual's efforts to cope with the environment is that the *environment* will also change to a certain extent, and that this change will have repercussions for the individual who is "embedded" in the continuous "person-environment dialectic." In some cases this change works against the individual. The individual-environment dialectic becomes even more out of sync, and a crisis might be precipitated.

According to Riegel, nothing, so to speak, is ever finished—we are always in the process of coming to grips with change. Some of these efforts are simply more effective than others. Thus, we should distinguish between the *processes* or *efforts* individuals bring to bear in coping with change and the *consequences, outcomes,* or *products* of these efforts (see Danish, 1981).

Thomae (1980), who espouses a cognitive approach to personality and aging, also defines personality in terms of underlying "biological, social, and perceptual processes" (Thomae, 1980 p. 303). An emphasis on the role of personality in helping us cope with change is consistent with this process-oriented approach to personality and reinforces a dialectical approach to coping in adulthood.

Cognitive Personality Theory

As we noted at this chapter's outset, in contrast to a trait approach is a process-cognitive approach to personality. From this point of view, personality is one of *many* factors that *mediate* one's response to such life events or role changes such as job entrance, parenting, intergenerational (adolescent) conflict, job skill obsolescence during middle age, the empty nest, institutionalization, widowhood, poor health, or impending death (Thomae, 1980).

Thomae (1980), in fact, refuses to provide a list of more or less adaptive personality characteristics (traits) or personality types, due to the complexity of the process approach to personality. In other words, certain traits or characteristic **personality "types"** may or may not be adaptive in a certain situation for a given individual (or cohort) at a particular point in that person's life. Thomae (1980) suggests that "patterns of successful aging" are best understood in terms of a complex interaction of a number of subsystems (e.g., heredity, changes in health, economic factors, changes in intellectual and personality functioning, self-concept, values, adaptive skills).

A process approach to personality is consistent with Riegel's dialectics in that the underlying, ongoing dynamic between the individual and the culture (and changes in the culture) is emphasized as crucial to understanding *how* people change with time. Many of these cultural changes are programmed into our lives, a consequence of the constraints on our behavior and attitudes that may have positive or negative effects for us (Atchley, 1975).

Personality processes play an important role in helping us adapt to such changes, either by assisting us in evaluating (assessing its degree of threat or change) and modifying our response to the situation or task to be coped with (Hultsch & Plemons, 1979; Lieberman, 1975; Thomae, 1980), or by enabling us to utilize our resources (e.g., financial, physical, psychological, interpersonal) to deal with change. It is variation in these personality processes that accounts for how some individuals deal with numerous normative and nonnormative events (Brim & Ryff, 1980) in their lives. Differences between persons (interindividual variability) in coping skills that are consistent within persons define the construct of **genotypic continuity** (where persons with certain clusters of traits change in characteristic ways) (N. Livson, 1973). Thomae (1976, 1980) notes that persons also vary in the degree to which they are consistent across time, depending upon the situation (event), one's perception of the event as requiring change, and one's available resources. These factors create intra-individual variability across time.

Hultsch and Plemons (1979) and Lieberman (1975) emphasize that personality factors such as **self-concept**, self-efficacy, or a tendency to avoid or deny threat *mediate* whether persons evaluate or appraise an event as threatening or not. Personality also mediates whether or not that event is perceived as a personally meaningful one (Lazarus & Delongis, 1983). This emphasis on stress and coping processes also highlights one's beliefs about personal control over events in one's life (Langer, 1983). Moreover, persons' personal commitments to a set of values and ideals (Lazarus & Delongis, 1983) emerge as sources of variability in how they assess and respond to change over the life span. Lazarus and Delongis (1983), for example, suggest that with increased age, individuals may withdraw energy (disengage) from commitments they have made earlier in their lives because of poor health (they can no longer do work that has been very important to them) or nonreward (they are passed over for a promotion, demoted, or forcibly retired, even though their work may be of high quality). In these situations, disengagement (see below) is adaptive—it allows the individual to cope with stress.

Such control beliefs are the central focus of what Seligman (1975) has termed **learned helplessness**, where individuals cease to see a causal relationship between their behaviors and important events or consequences in their lives. Seligman's model has been reformulated by Abramson, Seligman, and Teasdale (1978) to include the individual's tendency to attribute (interpret) such noncontingent patterns of behavior-consequences in particular ways. For example, individuals who are most easily made helpless may attribute failure (nonreward) to internal, stable causes (their own lack of ability) and success to external, unstable ones (luck). We shall have more to say about learned helplessness later on in this chapter.

Cutrona, Russell, and Rose (1986) have found that while reliable, nurturant social support by others predicted physical health (over a six-month period), such support in concert with the extent of stressful life events experienced by older persons predicted mental health. These results reinforce the complexity of the problem in understanding adaptation to aging via the process approach to personality in contrast to the trait approach (P.J. Costa and McCrae's NEO model) discussed below, which stresses generalizability of traits (and their adaptive meaning) across situations and persons.

By its very nature, the process approach is complex and, therefore, most consistent with the multidetermined, pluralistic life-span approach (P.B. Baltes, 1973) to adult development and aging that we discussed in Chapter 1.

PERSONALITY AND ITS EFFECTS ON AGING—COPING WITH CHANGE

Activity and Disengagement

We stated above that one's theoretical orientation in part determines whether personality in adulthood is stable or not. There has also emerged a separate body of literature dealing with the relationship between aging and adjustment. In this case, we might ask, how might one best adjust to the aging process? As we discussed earlier, according to Thomae's cognitive theory, personality mediates the relationship between aging and coping strategies to life events, some of which are age related. As we shall also see, different types of persons tend to utilize different styles of adaptation to the aging process. This coping with change issue can best be understood in light of the differences between **activity theory** (Havighurst & Albrecht, 1953; Maddox, 1964) and **disengagement theory** (Cumming & Henry, 1961; Cumming, 1963). Simply put, activity theory suggests a *positive* relationship between activity (involvement in social roles, interpersonal relationships, solitary activities, formal commitments) and **life satisfaction** or morale (see D.L. Adams, 1969; Lawton, 1975; Havighurst, Neugarten, & Tobin, 1963; Lemon, Bengston, & Peterson, 1972; Maddox, 1965). The older person maintains or substitutes for when necessary (via poor health or retirement) those activities and relationships carried over from earlier times. Disengagement theory, on the other hand, suggests the opposite—not only is decreased involvement beneficial, but the process of disengagement is a *mutual* one. That is, society and the individual withdraw from one another, with benefits to both. The individual gains in that unwanted commitments (through changes in one's value system

Activity theory suggests that older adults who remain both mentally and physically active cope more adequately with the aging process.

or ill health) can be given up, and the person is permitted to disengage from others and become more self-absorbed. Society gains in that younger, more productive individuals can replace those who are older. Cumming (1975) has modified and clarified disengagement somewhat, claiming that disengagement does not necessarily imply passivity, loneliness, or isolation from others; nor was the theory ever intended to predict morale or life satisfaction. Hochschild (1975) notes that disengagement may be cohort-specific. While withdrawing from an ageist society in the 1950s may have been adaptive, this may not be the case in our more enlightened culture, where attitudes toward the aged are more positive (Atchley, 1987).

In actuality, both approaches (activity, disengagement) involve *value judgments* about how to age optimally (Havighurst, Neugarten, & Tobin, 1963), in the sense that each may also refer to a *legitimate* process by which *some* individuals come to terms with a multitude of changes that may accompany aging. Viewed in this way, they can be seen as "options" that may or may not be exercised. Moreover, regarding disengagement, it is important to distinguish between *psychological* (being emotionally vested in the outside world) and *social* (being formally committed to social roles and activities) disengagement. Disengagement may be involuntary (via relocation or poor health) or voluntary (in avoiding a stressful situation). Likewise, involuntary levels of high activity (having to work for economic reasons or despite poor health) can be very maladaptive.

A great deal of controversy and subsequent research has been generated by these two approaches (see Botwinick, 1984; Neugarten, 1973, 1977; Thomae, 1980, for discussions of evidence bearing on each).

Consistent with the cognitive approach to personality, a number of factors have been found to *mediate* the relationship between the aging process, activity, and life satisfaction (e.g., health status, the presence of a "confidant," and expected or desired levels of activity and socioeconomic status) (Larson, 1978; Maddox & Eisdorfer, 1962; Maddox, 1965). Those who are in better health, who can share life's intimacies with someone else, who are more highly educated and of higher socioeconomic status maintain higher levels of both interpersonal and noninterpersonal activity (Maddox, 1965) that is fulfilling to them personally. In fact, Neugarten (1977) points out that to the extent that individuals differ on these factors, evidence for personality change may not show up. Homogeneous cross-sectional (and longitudinal) samples (see Chapter 3) are thus more likely to demonstrate change across time in adaptation (see also Moss & Sussman, 1980).

Interestingly, in his study of the Terman gifted men 50 years later, Sears (1977) found that stability in personality was the rule. However, the degree to which early personality factors (life satisfaction, work satisfaction and persistence, family life satisfaction, success in marriage) predicted these same variables later diminished with time. Though these men were all quite successful in their work, they nevertheless placed greater importance on their family life than on their work. In fact, their personal qualities as younger men did a better job of predicting work satisfaction than current family-life satisfaction. S. Folkman, Lazarus, Pinley, and Novacek (1987) found *both* age-graded and contextual (situational) variations in coping patterns in adulthood. We see in these cases that the **stability versus change** issue is one of degree. Regarding personality and coping, much depends on the sample of persons one is studying and what one is trying to predict.

Personality Types and Adjustment to Aging

BERKELEY-OAKLAND LONGITUDINAL STUDIES

In the early 1970s, Norma Haan and Jack Block (J. Block, 1971; Haan, 1972) reported on longitudinal data dealing with personality and adjustment among persons living in the Oakland and Berkeley, California areas. These longitudinal research efforts are known as the Oakland Growth and the Berkeley Guidance Studies from adolescence through early middle adulthood. At this point, the children of the original 142 parents in these studies were about 30 years old. To measure personality, these investigations used **Q-sort** methodology (J. Block, 1962). Briefly, in a Q-sort, individuals sort statements along a continuum of "least like me" to "most like me" to gain a picture of those persons' self-perceptions of qualities or characteristics in terms of their relative applicability within each individual. Haan (1972) found separate clusters of adjustment types for men and women in their thirties, based on these Q-sort data. For men, Haan found five types of adjustment patterns:

1. ego-resilient—integrated, balanced personalities
2. belated adjusters—these men grew more self-confident and socially competent with age
3. vulnerable overcontrollers—these persons were very defended and attempted to control events to achieve stability
4. anomic extroverts—anxious about aging and tended to deny these feelings
5. unsettled undercontrollers—disorganized individuals

For women, these adjustment types were:

1. cognitive coping—very skilled and intellectually competent
2. hyperfeminine repressive—very passive women, unable to express their needs to others
3. dominating narcissists—very self-involved women who dominated others
4. vulnerable undercontrollers
5. lonely-dependent—isolated women

Again, for the most part, there was a great deal of longitudinal stability (genotypic continuity; see above) in these patterns of adjustment.

While the change/stability issue in personality is a central focus of this chapter, stability can be defined in many ways. N. Livson (1973) separates *genotypic continuity* (where persons with certain clusters of traits change in different but predictable ways) from **phenotypic persistence** (stability in specific traits over time). While many longitudinal studies focused on specific traits do show consistency over time (Douglas & Arenberg, 1978—Baltimore longitudinal study), a series of studies by F. Livson and her colleagues stemming from the Berkeley-Oakland studies (N. Livson, 1973; F. Livson, 1981; N. Livson & Peskin, 1981; Peskin & F. Livson, 1981) do show much evidence for genotypic continuity. For example, while traits such as responsibility predicted psychological health at age 40 for men, they did not at age 50, while a somewhat opposite pattern was observed for women.

F. Livson (1981) separated women into *traditional* and *independent* types. While traditionals seemed to maintain a satisfaction with life and with other close relationships over a ten-year period (ages 40–50), independents moved from a less satisfied pattern in this respect to a more satisfied one. Livson suggests that with the advent of the adult children's leaving home, independents were able to fulfill their needs for achievement. Patterns for men (F. Livson, 1981) were similar in that men who improved in their adaptation to life became closer to and more intimate with others. On the other hand, men who conformed to the controlled, rational, realistic, culturally bound image of men were more stable in their happiness. The above studies by Haan (1972) and F. Livson (1981) are consistent with this genotypic pattern of stability with age.

Strong evidence for genotypic continuity also comes from a 40-year follow-up of men and women (original surviving parents) in the Berkeley studies conducted by Mussen, Honzik, and Eichorn (1982). For women, a "buoyant, responsive attitude toward life," and for men, "emotional and physical health" at age 30 predicted high life satisfaction at age 70. Interestingly, for men, their wives' emotional stability at age 30 was an even stronger predictor of these men's life satisfaction at age 70.

Most recently, Haan, Millsap, and Hartka (1986) followed up a selected subsample of persons from the Berkeley-Oakland longitudinal studies. Objectively defined aspects of these persons' Q-sorts (self-descriptions) were compared in early to late childhood (ages 5–10) versus early to late adulthood (50 years later). These dimensions of personality were (1) self-confident/victimized, (2) assertive/submissive, (3) cognitive commitment (achievement oriented and innovative), (4) outgoing/aloof, (5) dependability, and (6) warm/hostile. These investigators found evidence for both consistent, orderly development of a comparatively short-term nature *and* for complex, highly unstable, non-age-related change in personality. This apparent contradiction was resolved by understanding personality in terms of both enduring qualities (that change in a predictable way across age, varying by level) and situationally relevant aspects (varying with the situation and the individual). (Recall our initial discussion of personality.)

In general, personality change in the above dimensions in the Haan et al. (1986) study reflected childhood as a period of systematic development and stability, whereas personality changes in adulthood were more dynamic and experiential in nature. Thus, personality changes were equally likely in adulthood, in contrast to an emphasis on changes in childhood espoused by those in the psychoanalytic tradition. Sex differences in experiences and situational differences requiring problem-solving skills, and characteristics such as outgoingness and dependability outweighed consistent, predictable life-span trends in personality.

Haan et al. (1986) interpret the dimensions of cognitive commitment, dependability, and outgoing/aloof as more developmental (enduring change over time), while the characteristics of self-confident/victimized, warm/hostile, and assertive/submissive were experiential or situational in nature. Haan et al. (1986) suggest that personality development across the life span is highly adaptive in nature, subject to influences varying by age period and by individual/situational factors.

Based on the above longitudinal data, we can conclude that perhaps the most important mediator of styles of adaptation to aging is *personality type* (Filsinger & Sauer, 1978; Havighurst et al., 1963; Havighurst, Neugarten, & Tobin, 1968; Mass & Kuypers, 1974; Neugarten, 1977). This view suggests that individuals form characteristic "styles" of coping that are *maintained* across time. However, some styles of adapting are accompanied by higher levels of life satisfaction or morale than are others (D. L. Adams, 1969; Havighurst, Neugarten, & Tobin, 1963; Lawton, 1975). Moreover, these personality types cover the continuum from activity to disengagement, though they are somewhat different for men versus women (Guttman, 1975, 1977; Maas & Kuypers, 1974; Neugarten, Crotty, & Tobin, 1964; Reichard, F. Livson, & Peterson, 1962). Neugarten (1973) summarizes these personality types, based upon what have become known as the *Kansas City Studies*.

KANSAS CITY STUDIES

The Kansas City studies were a series of cross-sectional and longitudinal studies of nearly 1000 people (cross-sectional age comparisons of 700 individuals aged 40–70; six-year longitudinal studies of 300 individuals aged 50–90). The investigators used measures of personality tapping the inner world of the individual. These approaches to studying personality are termed **projective techniques**, in that individuals project their own wishes and needs upon a neutral stimulus (e.g., an ambiguous picture, an inkblot, or an incomplete sentence).

Figure 10.3 illustrates common examples of projective items, where the individual may tell the investigator what a hand might be doing or what an inkblot might remind that individual of. The individual may also complete a neutral sentence by filling in personal thoughts and feelings.

In addition to information about the inner world of the individual, information was gathered about each person's judgments about the extent of individual involvement in a variety of daily activities and performance in various roles (worker, parent, spouse). Ratings of life satisfaction were also taken.

From these data, the investigators were able to ascertain how "ego-involved" persons were in their roles and as well as their feelings about current levels of role activity. These investigations yielded four clusters of personality types, broken down into eight specific patterns of adaptation, each varying along a high, medium, or low continuum of role activity and yielding varying levels of life satisfaction. These personality types and their respective subtypes were as follows (see Neugarten & Hagestad, 1976; Neugarten, Havighurst, & Tobin, 1968):

1. *Integrated*—well-functioning, complex people who are psychologically intact and competent—high in life satisfaction
   a. *Reorganizers*—maintaining high levels of activity, their lives have been successfully reorganized after retirement.
   b. *Focused*—showing moderate levels of activity, but their involvement is selective.
   c. *Disengaged*—well-integrated, life-satisfied individuals who are not active—their disengagement is voluntary and preferred.
2. *Armored or defended*—very achievement-oriented, hard-driving individuals who experience anxiety about aging that must be controlled by defenses—they maintain control over, rather than are open to, their own desires and inner needs and are less highly (moderately) life satisfied.
   a. *Holding on*—aging is seen as a threat; these individuals hold on to their past—their high levels of activity defend them against their fears of growing old.
   b. *Constricted*—these people defend against aging by withdrawing

Gerontological Apperception Test stimuli

Figure 10.3.   Projective test stimuli. Hand test from E. E. Wagner. (1962). Copyright 1969 by Western Psychological Services. Reprinted from *The Hand Test, Revised 1983* by permission of the publisher, Western Psychological Services, 12031 Wilshire Boulevard, Los Angeles, California 90025. Holtzman Inkblot Technique (HIT). Copyright 1958, 1972 by The Psychological Corporation. San Antonio, TX: The Psychological Corporation. Reproduced by permission. All rights reserved. Gerontological apperception test (GAT) from G. Wolk and S. Wolk. (1971). New York: Behavioral Publications. Reprinted with permission.

from others and become preoccupied with losses and deficits—this constriction permits them to maintain a sameness in their lives to ward off the inevitable losses of aging.

3. *Passive-dependent*—less highly life satisfied individuals, for whom a source of happiness in life is letting others care for and make decisions about them
   a. *Succorance-seeking*—very dependent upon others—individuals who may be both moderately active and life satisfied, but whose physical/emotional needs are met by leaning on someone else
   b. *Apathetic*—markedly passive, not very active, medium life satisfaction—most likely always have been passive and apathetic, and aging simply reinforces this pattern of meeting their needs.
4. *Unintegrated*—physically and emotionally incapacitated, low levels of life satisfaction
   a. *Disorganized*—grossly psychologically dysfunctional, not active, but maintaining themselves in the community

Wagner's Hand Test card

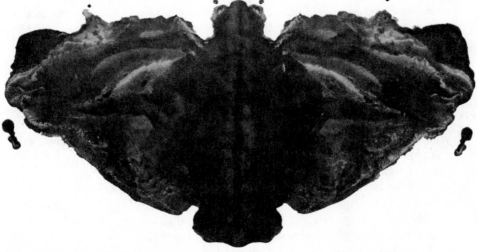

Figure 10.3 (Continued)   Holtzman Ink Blot test card

While these types differed somewhat for males and females (see Neugarten, 1968), they do suggest that individuals develop consistent patterns of dealing with biological changes and/or shifts in role-related responsibilities brought about by both age-graded, nonnormative, and history-graded events (see Chapter 1: P.B. Baltes & Willis, 1977).

Thus, neither disengagement (suggesting a *change* in the level of activity that is satisfying) or activity (suggesting *stability* in the level of activity) adequately addresses the aging and adjustment issue. The study of stability of personality style (how one relates to others) measures personality at the *level of* **socioadaptational** *processes.* Neugarten and her colleagues also found, using data gathered from projective techniques, that on an **intrapsychic** level, aged individuals utilized less energy devoted to dealing with the outer world, compared to more energy invested in one's own "impulse life." Thus, substantial *changes* toward a more inner-directed orientation-termed **interiority** seemed to occur with increasing age.

In contrast, Fox (1979) (see Siegler, 1980), using the Rorschach longitudinally, did not find an age-related pattern of increased interiority across a 12-year period, based on both cross sequential and time sequential analysis. The Duke University longitudinal study (Siegler, 1980) did, however, find evidence for a time of measurement effect in some aspects of Rorschach performance, suggesting that with time, individuals (regardless of age or cohort) tended to be more effective in mastery of their environment (Siegler, 1980). Hayslip, Panek and Stoner (1987), however, relying on projective data (Hand Test: Wagner, 1962) gathered over a 10-year interval from two samples of elderly persons, found no cohort or time of measurement differences in personality functioning. This finding reinforces Neugarten's age-related interpretation of those personality changes she termed *interiority.*

MAAS AND KUYPERS'S LONGITUDINAL RESEARCH

Maas and Kuypers (1974), in a 40-year longitudinal study of 140 people (parents in the Oakland-Berkeley longitudinal studies) measured twice—from their thirties into their seventies—also found substantial evidence for personality style continuity. Using various sources of data (an extensive interview format covering numerous life domains such as parenthood, marriage, occupation, friendship, activities, health concerns, death, as well as intensive diaries, self-concept, and life satisfaction self-ratings), these authors derived four different personality types of women and three distinct types common to men (see Table 10.3), with more continuity observed in the women than in the men. For both the "fearful-ordering" and "autonomous" women, consistency was observed across the 40-year time span, while more discontinuity (more ego disorganization later in life) was found in the "anxious-asserting" women. For men, the picture was somewhat more complicated. While "active competent" fathers both changed and remained similar (in both a positive and negative sense) (see Table 10.3), less positive personality change (more career strain) was observed in the "person-oriented" fathers. Those men who were termed "conservative-ordering" evidenced the most change; they became less relaxed and more overcontrolled in later life. In some respects, these findings bear out the findings of personality style consistency for men and women as found by Neugarten and her colleagues (1963). However, substantial evidence for change (and for sex differences in personality change) was also observed.

The studies by Maas and Kuypers (1974), Haan (1972), Block (1971), and F. Livson and her colleagues (1981) are of considerable interest

TABLE 10.3

PERSONALITY STYLES FOR MEN AND WOMEN

	Features Common Early and Late in Adult Life	Differences Early and Late in Adult Life
Fearful-ordering mothers	depressed mood and activity level low adaptive capacity low sense of self-worth health and economic disadvantage	more anxiety in old age more positive family life in early adult life
Anxious-asserting mothers	anxiety and tension assertiveness and restlessness low satisfaction high self-doubt need to share health disadvantage interpersonal conflict	more ego disorganization in late life
Autonomous mothers	aloofness high mental capacity positive sense of self cheerfulness criticalness interpersonal distance	
Person-oriented mothers	warm, close, nonconflictual interpersonal relations	
Person-oriented fathers		more unrewarding career and financial strain in young adulthood
Active-competent fathers	high capacity positive sense of self interpersonal directness	more irritability and worry in young adulthood more charm and nonconformity in late life
Conservative-ordering fathers		shyer and less demonstrative in young adulthood more relaxed and even-tempered in young adulthood more overcontrolled and conservative in late life

Source: From H. Maas & J. Kuypers. (1974). *From thirty to seventy* (p. 198). San Francisco: Josey-Bass.

to those concerned with the adult personality. While it is important to keep in mind that the above longitudinal research ignored subjects who most likely would be in young adulthood (less than 30 years old), they nevertheless cover a greater time frame than does the Neugarten research. On the other hand, one could argue that historical-cultural changes (e.g., economic fluctuations, alterations in family patterns) are in part responsible for many of the changes that were observed to occur longitudinally. However, the personality changes Maas and Kuypers observed in their sample of men do resemble what Levinson observed regarding changes in the life structure (see also Chapter 1).

In addition to personality styles, Maas and Kuypers also studied changes in *life-styles*. These changes were largely independent of those in personality. For women, being husband centered, work centered, or uncentered were dominant life-styles, while for men, being family centered, invested in hobbies, or unwell/disengaged were the most common. For life-styles, Maas and Kuypers found a great deal more continuity/sameness for men than for women, in contrast to their findings on personality. Maas and Kuypers explain this apparent contradiction via the fact that while mothers experienced more uncontrollable changes in the occupational, marital, and parenting domains of their lives, the continued demands on their coping skills made for personality continuity.

While the life-style clusters as a whole identified by Maas and Kuypers separated some mothers from others in both their thirties and seventies, the *components* of *each* life-style cluster separating women changed across age. For example, as young adults, "work-centered" mothers were more unhappily married, economically poor and dissatisfied, less intelligent, and less positive about themselves than other young women. As older women, they are unmarried and thus highly involved in their work but very satisfied with their relationships with others. On the other hand, while older widowed, uncentered mothers were more satisfied with their families and marital commitments when they were young (and still married), as older women they yearned for the family-centered life that they led earlier. Some evidence for continuity in personality type and life-style (varying by sex) was observed by Maas and Kuypers. This continuity, according to the authors, argues for the importance of early decision making and planning for the future, taking into account the many demands that may be made on one throughout the entire adult life span.

THE PARENTAL IMPERATIVE

Recall from the above discussion of the Maas and Kuypers (1974) study that there are distinct life-style and personality clusters for men and women. For the most part, therefore, whether personality and/or lifestyle varies over the adult life span also varies by sex. Neugarten (1973) and Guttman (1975, 1977) also find that these patterns differ for men and women—while "older men seemed more receptive than younger men of their affiliative, nurturant and sensual promptings; older women, more receptive than younger women of aggressive and egocentric impulses" (Neugarten, 1973, p. 320).

This trend from **active** to **passive mastery** with increased age for men, while for women a shift from passive to active mastery, has been found by Guttman (1975, 1977). Active mastery (an *instrumental-productive style*) suggests an attempt to *change the world rather than oneself* to meet one's needs, obligations, and/or the requirements of others. On the other hand, a *passive-receptive style* (passive mastery) suggests that *oneself is changed* rather than the environment to deal with demands made by others in the real world. Interestingly, in very late life (post 65 years old), a style of *magical mastery,* characterized by an unrealistic stance toward one's relationship to the world (e.g., the use of primitive defenses such as withdrawal, projection, or denial) tends to characterize both men and women. Guttman (1975, 1977), whose cross-cultural findings agree with those of Neugarten (1973), explains these shifts for each sex in terms of what he terms the **parental imperative**.

Because young boys and girls are socialized differently (to develop stereotypically sex role related skills, abilities, and characteristics) and the response of most adults to the "chronic emergency" of parenthood, men by necessity are forced to assume greater responsibility and become more dominant and aggressive (in the service of their own and their families' welfare). Women, however, develop their nurturant, caring, supportive skills out of the necessity to be physically close to their children. When the demands of parenthood are relaxed, men and women are free to revert back to that side of themselves they repressed in the service of being parents. In an evolutionary sense, Guttman argues that out of *each* parent's inability to *simultaneously* meet the physical *and* emotional needs of the infant, men (fathers) become the providers of food and physical security, whereas women (mothers) provide emotional security by staying within sight and sound of their children. These sex differences, according to Guttman, are to a certain extent innate but, more importantly, are predominantly shaped and strengthened by the culture.

Thus, with the relaxation of the cultural necessity to be competent parents, men and women revert back to what Guttman (1977) terms the "normal unisex of later life." Parenthood, rather than biological sex, determines which characteristics, feelings, and skills are expressed, according to Guttman.

HOW PERSONALITY IS ASSESSED—STABILITY VERSUS CHANGE

We must also realize that whether certain dimensions (e.g., socioadaptational, intrapsychic) of personality show stability or change is partly influenced by *how* personality is assessed. Projective tests (see Hayslip & Lowman, 1986; Panek, Wagner, & Kennedy-Zwergle, 1983), for example, often indicate *change* (e.g., interiority), while structured interviews or standardized personality inventories often portray a picture of *stability* (see Costa & McCrae, 1980a). Whether personality appears to change with age or not also depends on whether one's data are gathered *cross-sectionally* or *longitudinally.* As we learned in Chapter 3, cross-sectional studies sometimes show age effects as a function of sample homogeneity, and in cross-sectional research, age differences are confounded by cohort differences (see P. Costa, McCrae, & Arenberg, 1983). Longitudinal evidence often demonstrates age changes in personality but is potentially confounded by time of measurement effects (see Moss & Sussman, 1980).

The accurate measurement of personality can pose some unique problems for the adult developmental researcher. Lawton, Whelihan, and Belsky (1980) and K.W. Schaie and J.P. Schaie (1977) have pointed out many personality measures have not been normed on elderly persons, leading to misleading conclusions about an individual's standing relative to others. Individual differences (see Chapter 1) among older persons may make norms difficult to meaningfully use. Moreover, items on many personality scales were originally developed for the purpose of assessing psychopathology, so that their value in understanding normal or less pathological forms of personality functioning may be limited (K.W. Schaie & J.P. Schaie, 1977).

Long batteries of tests may also be fatiguing, and small print or paper that creates a glare may be difficult to read (see Chapters 4 and 5). Some persons who are poorly educated or not testwise may be easily threatened by being assessed. Instructions may be difficult to follow for persons who suffer from attentional deficits or for those who are sensorially impaired. On many personality inventories, individuals are asked to respond using computerized forms or through many different formats (ratings along a continuum, yes/no) that may be difficult to follow. In cases where an item's meaning requires an opposite response (applying versus *not* applying to oneself as representative of an individual's feelings and attitudes), unsuspecting persons may not realize that, for example, "wanting to join clubs and organizations" and "not wanting to be around others" require two different responses that may mean the same thing.

Personality inventories of a self-report nature may be subject to the effects of *response set* (e.g., guessing, choosing extreme or neutral responses, answering in socially desirable, unduly positive terms) (Carstensen & Cone, 1983; Kozma & Stones, 1987), especially when dealing with personal issues (Lawton et al., 1980). If items do not pertain to the everyday circumstances of many adults (re. dating, career goals, parental relations), they may not be taken seriously. All of these factors may detract from a measure's reliability and validity and thus lead to faulty conclusions or decisions about that person's welfare, based on one's behaviors, traits, or capabilities. Such decisions may involve (1) an individual's suitability for a new position, (2) whether an individual should be retained in the present position, (3) whether one would benefit from a training program or psychological treatment, or (4) whether that person should continue to live independently, versus living with others or being institutionalized.

K.W. Schaie and J.P. Schaie (1977) note the importance of first deciding for what *purpose* such assessments are to be made in order to enhance usefulness on an individual basis. There are advantages and disadvantages to both objective methods (P. Costa & McCrae, 1980) as well as clinical tools for assessment such as projective techniques (Hayslip & Lowman, 1986; Panek, Wagner, & Kennedy-Zwergle, 1983). The use of each depends upon the availability of appropriate, current norms and evidence for a measure's reliability and validity with the population of interest. In addition, the test administrator's interpersonal skills (honesty, supportiveness, eye contact, sensitivity to fatigue) and competence in administering and interpreting personality measures, as well as the examinee's reactions (defensiveness, anxiety) to being assessed, are important considerations. For best results, assessments should be conducted in quiet settings with adequate lighting.

It almost goes without saying that all personality test data gathered from adults should be used cautiously, considering the many influences on (older) adults' performance and the consequences of decisions based on such data. Clearly, allowances may need to be made in some cases for many of the above motivational, response, and comprehension problems that the examiner will be faced with in assessing adults of all ages and backgrounds. In this way, information gathered from each person can be used to that individual's best advantage in vocational, educational, or counseling-related situations.

Recall from Chapter 3 that cohort differences can mask what appear to be age effects in cross-sectional designs. In this light, data on the adult personality emphasizing psychological traits (recall our continuum at this chapter's outset), gathered *sequentially* (see Chapter 3), substantiates the existence of *cohort effects* in personality. It is to the work of Glenn Elder on cohort effects in personality that we now turn.

Elder's Studies of the Great Depression

The work of Elder (1979) is perhaps the best example of the influence of cohort-historical influences on personality. Elder compared two cohorts—children of the Oakland Growth samples (1920–1921 cohorts) and those of the Berkeley Guidance sample (1928–1929 cohorts) in their respective adolescent years (the Great Depression of the 1930s) and again 30 years later. Elder found that (1) the impact of the depression was specific to and more pervasive in the Berkeley cohorts, (2) males were more severely affected than were females, due to their being deprived of a father figure at this time in their lives, and (3) in Berkeley families who were experiencing marital difficulties prior to the depression, its impact on personality (e.g., submissiveness, self-inadequacy) was far more negative. Elder concluded that the earlier the depression occurred in the lives of boys, the more negative was its impact. Interestingly, the effects of the depression on girls were the opposite. Daughter-mother relationships were strengthened. When families had experienced preexisting marital difficulties, these effects on boys and girls were less strong.

Thirty years later, especially for the father-deprived boys in the Berkeley sample, psychological health was greater as reflected in their Q-sort ratings. This appeared to be due in part to their experience in the military (World War II, Korea), which caused them to marry later (hence more emotional support), and go on to become college educated (via the G.I. Bill). They were in some cases also able to escape jobs that were not satisfying and family situations that were emotionally aversive, giving them more self-confidence, stability, and a realistic set of goals to pursue, leading to greater work success later on. While the deprived Berkeley males were rated somewhat less healthy relative to others, these differences were small 30 years later. What enabled these individuals to cope with the negative effects of the depression and especially father absence and marital discord between their parents were the skills of positive comparison (things are not so bad compared to the depression) and selective ignoring (looking for the good aspects of the depression) (Elder, 1979).

Caspi and Elder (1986) studied the 1900 cohort (those of age 30 in the Berkeley Guidance sample) 40 years later and found that having had more adaptive skills (being good problem solvers, being more emotionally healthy) predicted life satisfaction depending on social class. While having had higher intellectual and social skills was crucial for working-class women, having been emotionally healthy was most important for middle-class women. For working-class women, having lived through the depression lowered life satisfaction, while the depression enhanced life satisfaction for middle-class women.

Caspi and Elder suggest that women from lower socioeconomic classes were socialized in such a way as to interfere with the learning of coping skills to deal with stress. On the other hand, many middle-class women, not having had to deal with previous stressful experiences (the depression), were ill-prepared to deal with the potentially negative impact of growing old. Not only does this study better enable us to understand cohort effects in personality, but we can also better understand the complexity of the role of personality as a mediator of an individual's response to a cohort-specific life event and its effects on adaptation to aging.

As we noted above, a great deal of literature addressing cohort effects in personality has also been gathered by those emphasizing psychological traits. Let us discuss the trait approach to personality in adulthood and the evidence regarding personality change with age within this tradition.

Trait Approaches to Personality and Aging

Trait theory (Allport, 1961; Cattell, 1950; Guilford, 1959) has provided a most promising framework for recent personality research in adulthood and aging. Allport (1961) defines a **trait** as "a neuropsychic structure having the capacity to render many stimuli functionally equivalent." Cattell (1950) assigns primary importance to "dynamic (source) traits," which are underlying factors that determine behavior. In each case, traits are inferred "mental structures" (Hall & Lindzey, 1978, 1985) that motivate and guide one's behavior across a variety of situations or across time. Traits are thus "enduring dispositions" (Kausler, 1982), particular to individuals, that structure or give meaning to their behavior. Using a trait approach, different individual(s) can be located along a continuum, in that people can be described as possessing a certain degree of a trait. This trait is *bipolar* in nature; that is, it has a negative and a positive pole.

aggressive_____passive

dominant_____ submissive

Consequently, people might be understood in terms of whether they possess a trait to a certain *degree* (e.g., very dominant————not dominant at all).

Lerner (1986) suggests that by using traits (or clusters of traits that form more general personality factors or types), one can understand whether through development people "sort themselves out" (are differentiated) along a number of bipolar trait dimensions—some people as they age become more aggressive than others. This "sorting out" process is very similar to Maddi's ideas about personality, where the "core" and "periphery" are linked through the process of development.

While this approach is often heralded as more objective for studying personality in adulthood than those relying upon clinical interviews or projective methods (see P. Costa & McCrae, 1980; P. Costa, McCrae, & Arenberg, 1983), it is an *after the fact* approach to studying personality (Lerner, 1986). That is, while it may provide us with a wealth of information *describing* individual differences in traits at a given point in time, or in changes in the levels of traits across age, it cannot provide us with an *a priori* answer to *how* (by what *processes*) people "get to be the way they are" (see Lerner, 1986; Riegel, 1977b). We still must ask questions such as, are personality changes across time qualitative or quantitative (does aggression *mean* the same thing in young adulthood as in late adulthood?) or, are such changes learned or innately determined? (See Plomin et al., 1988.)

Despite these shortcomings, using the trait approach, researchers have demonstrated *stability* with age (phenotypic persistence) for most traits. Notable exceptions to stability with age are the traits of general activity, masculinity, thoughtfulness, friendliness, and tolerance for others (all less so with age). Douglas & Arenberg (1978) obtained these findings using the Guilford Zimmerman Temperament Survey (GZTS), a personality inventory yielding scores on each of ten different traits. The GZTS was administered twice by these researchers to over 900 men, aged 18–98, over a 6 to 10 year period in the Baltimore Longitudinal Studies, using a cross sequential design (see Chapter 3). Similar evidence for general stability (in the *level* of a trait) with age for most traits using a measure of personality assessing 16 diverse traits (e.g., dominance, radicalism) (Cattell's Sixteen Personality Factor Questionnaire—16PF) has also been found in sequential studies by K.W. Schaie and Parham (1976), P. Costa and McCrae (1978), and Siegler, George, and Okun (1979) (see P. Costa & McCrae, 1980a for a review). Collectively, these studies (see also P. Costa, McCrae, & Arenberg, 1980) have also found that individuals tend to maintain their *relative* standing versus others regarding levels of a trait over time.

As we mentioned, some age differences in terms of specific traits have been noted by the above investigators. These age differences are partly due to sample differences (age range of those tested) and disparities in the time interval from initial testing to second testing (see Botwinick, 1984). One might expect more age effects when the time interval separating testings is greater and when the sample is homogeneous (Botwinick, 1984; Neugarten, 1977).

K.W. Schaie and Parham (1976) (using the 16PF), Woodruff and Birren (1972) (using the California Test of Personality), and Douglas and Arenberg (1978) (using the GZTS) have also found evidence for *cohort effects* in some personality traits (e.g., superego strength, ascendance, restraint, social adjustment) as well as some indication of *time of measurement effects* (e.g., thoughtfulness, tolerance of others, friendliness).

Costa and McCrae's NEO Model of Personality

Perhaps the most impressive evidence for stability comes from a series of investigations (see P. Costa, McCrae, & Arenberg, 1983; P. Costa & McCrae, 1980) using sequential data gathered with both the 16PF and the GZTS. P. Costa et al. (1983) have found stability in what they term the *NEO* (neuroticism-extroversion-openness to experience) trait model of personality.

Costa and McCrae's NEO model of personality (see Figure 10.4) was in part based upon Eysenck's (1960) notions of extroversion and neuroticism. In a series of studies (P. Costa & McCrae, 1976, 1978, 1980a), these three basic personality factors were defined. (This model has subsequently been expanded to five factors [see McCrae & Costa, 1987]). Neurotics (high in anxiety, depression, self-consciousness, vulnerability, impulsiveness, and hostility) tend to be more preoccupied with both their physical and mental health and have more marital and sexual difficulties. They also have more financial troubles, are unhappy, and lack self-esteem. They consequently express less life satisfaction.

Extroverts (high in attachment, assertiveness, gregariousness, activity, excitement seeking, and positive emotions) are happier, less anxious and depressed, and express more life satisfaction than do persons high in neuroticism, though introverts, being low in these qualities, are not pathological. Persons high in openness to experience (high scores on ideas, feelings, fan-

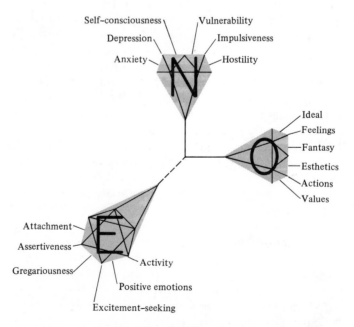

Figure 10.4. Costa and McCrae's NEO model of personality. *Source:* P. J. Costa & R. R. McCrae. (1980). Still stable after all these years: personality as a key to some issues in adulthood and old age. In P. B. Baltes & O. G. Brim (Eds.), *Life span development and behavior* (p. 71). New York: Academic Press. Reprinted by permission of Academic Press. (Note: The three-factor NEO model is now a five factor model.)

tasy, esthetics, actions, and values), interestingly, seem to have more eventful lives, full of both positive (begin a new line of work, express more positive affect) and negative (quit or are demoted, more likely to be involved in a lawsuit, more likely to be separated or divorced) aspects. While occupational choice was unrelated to neuroticism, extroverts tended to be social workers, lawyers, administrators, or advertising executives, while introverts preferred architecture, carpentry, or physics as professions.

Most recently, P. Costa, McCrae, Zonderman, Barbano, Lebowitz, and Larson (1986), in a carefully designed large-scale cross-sectional study, found substantial evidence for stability in personality, using their NEO model of personality. In addition, evidence for the negative impact of midlife crises (P. Costa & McCrae, 1980a) on personality was very scarce, consistent with previous large-scale trait research (McCrae & P. Costa, 1984). P. Costa and McCrae (1986) have validated their measures of NEO against peer and spouse ratings of these same traits. Costa and McCrae (1980b) also found neuroticism and extroversion to predict negative and positive affect 10 years later.

P. Costa and McCrae (1980a) also investigated the NEO model in relationship to the impact of various life events in adulthood. While their openness to experience factor did differentiate persons who had moved, were divorced or separated, and who had undergone job changes, no information as to how persons varying along the continuum of openness to experience coped with such changes was provided. As the authors note, it could be that being more open enables one to better prepare for or cope with change. Alternatively, experiencing such changes and coping with them successfully could lead one to become more open. Future work in this respect with the NEO model will prove more revealing.

P. Costa and McCrae (1980a) have found that the structure of personality itself remains basically the same across age, regardless of time of measurement and/or cohort variation. Using such a replicable structure (meaning that the cluster of traits defining the *NEO* model of personality is itself stable over time), individuals can be meaningfully compared in terms of changes in the *level* of each factor. As Costa and McCrae (1980a) argue, we can then assume that we are measuring "more or less" of the *same* factor—a great advantage in understanding people in the *same* terms over time. It may be helpful to recall our discussion of Maddi's system of understanding personality, which attempted to spell out this aspect of personality in terms of *core* characteristics. Overall, evidence for stability across age in adulthood (measured longitudinally) seems to be the rule for most traits.

NARROWER ASPECTS OF THE ADULT PERSONALITY

While we have attempted to answer the basic questions of what we mean by the term *personality,* whether personality varies with age, and how one's personality affects the experience of aging in this chapter, much research in somewhat narrower areas has been conducted that is also of interest to the adult personality theorist. We mention three areas in passing only, in that they are somewhat more specialized in their focus: *self-concept* (Bengston,

Reedy, & Gordon, 1985; Breyspraak, 1984; Hayslip, 1985b; Suls, 1982), *locus of control and learned helplessness* (Garber & Seligman, 1980; E. Langer, 1983; Lefcourt, 1981; Seligman, 1975), and *anxiety* (Nesselroade, 1988).

The study of these areas within personality, while as yet not fully integrated into the field of personality theory, nevertheless has implications for adult personality theorists. For example, it may be important to understand the effects of having averted a stressful life transition (divorce) or successfully coped with a normative life event (retirement) on self-esteem, anxiety, or one's sense of personal control over the environment. We can also see the importance that anxiety, control, and self-esteem play in defining both Neugarten's and Maas and Kuypers's personality "types," and in Levinson's (see Chapter 1) and Gould's discussions of the transformations in the life structure.

These aspects of personality have come to play a central role in our understanding of how individuals deal with their own aging and thus relate to the personality-aging issue we raised earlier. For example, those with high levels of self-esteem should also experience greater life satisfaction, less anxiety, and enjoy more control over events in their lives (see George, 1981; Larson, 1978; Lawton, 1983) and thus have a more positive view of their own development and aging (Brubaker & Powers, 1976).

Adequate self-concept has been seen as pivotal in defining the aging experience (Brubaker & Powers, 1976; Bultena & Powers, 1978) and in contributing to longevity (see B. Bell, Rose, & Damon, 1972, Chapter 2). Having a positive self-concept can also help reduce the negative effects of relocation from one's home to a nursing home (Bennett & Eckman, 1973; Lieberman, 1975). Moreover, self-esteem has been identified as an important dimension of change in the assessment of counseling interventions with adults of all ages (Levy, Derogatis, Gallagher, & Gatz, 1980).

Some theorists (Breyspraak, 1984; M. Lewis, 1979; Smith, 1979) feel that one's self-concept is *constructed* out of experience. In other words, our self evolves out of, yet shapes, our feelings about ourselves as adults and our relationships with others. This approach is more consistent with the dialectical tradition we discussed earlier. Others (Dickstein, 1977) are of the opinion that the self-concept develops in discrete stages. According to this view, the self passes through five distinct stages: (1) the *dynamic* self (infancy—coordination of others' demands with those of one's conscience or those stemming from biological drives); (2) self as *object* (childhood—self awareness via interaction with others); (3) self as *knower* (adolescence—the self as real or unique); (4) self as an *integrated whole* (a balance between our unique needs and abilities and the demands of the environment); and (5) *selfless* self (the self as perpetually changing, striving toward increased acceptance and improvement). According to Dickstein (1977), these latter two levels in the development of the self are characteristic of adulthood.

Mortimer, Finch, and Kumka (1982) assessed the stability of a number of dimensions of self-concept over a 14-year period in a sample of college students, using a self-rating technique known as the **semantic differential** (C.E. Osgood, Suci, & Tannenbaum, 1957), where persons rate themselves along a number of bipolar (e.g., happy-sad) continua. The dimensions of self-concept derived from these self-ratings were well-being, sociability, competence, and unconventionality. In many ways, these dimensions of self-concept were quite stable over time: (1) they retained their meaning (structure); (2) individuals maintained their relative ordering on each dimension; (3) intraindividual rank ordering of importance was constant; and (4) levels of each were similar across the 14-year period. Interestingly, however, Mortimer et al. (1982) found differences between persons' responses to various life events (reactions to work and career progress, marriage, and life as a whole) depending upon whether their self-ratings had increased over the 14-year period. Those who were classified as "stable lows" or "decreasers" responded less positively to these life events. The investigators concluded that the relationship between the experience of life events and self-concept was reciprocal—each affected and was influenced by the other. This reciprocal relationship is consistent with the process approach to personality (Thomae, 1980) and to a dialectical approach to dealing with developmental tasks (Riegel, 1977b) that we discussed earlier.

Comparisons of adults regarding self-concept have yielded inconsistent results, with some cross-sectional studies reporting declines with age (K. L. Bloom, 1961) and others reporting no differences or slight increases (Hess & Bradshaw, 1970; Nehrke, 1974; Nehrke, Hulicka, & Morganti, 1980). Some studies (Monge, 1975; Pierce & Chiriboga, 1979) have found some aspects of the self to be more variable (assertion) than others (amiability) over time. These conflicting findings (see Hayslip, 1985b) are most likely an artifact of cohort or sampling differences, different measures of self-concept, or a consequence of differential life events (experience) interacting with and changing the individual's sense of self. In light of the fact that our self-concepts are complex and change qualitatively with experience (Breyspraack, 1984; Grant, 1969; Lorr, 1978; Monge, 1975; Pierce & Chiriboga, 1979), studies comparing different components across age are bound to yield findings that are confusing and inconsistent. Most recently, however, R. Costa, Zonderman, McCrae, Cornoni-Huntley, Locke, and Barbano (1986) found no longitudinal evidence for psychological well-being, which is closely related to generalized self-concept and life satisfaction (Kausler, 1982). Bengston, Reedy, and Gordon (1985) reviewed the literature on self-concept and self-esteem in adulthood. They concluded that for the most part, cross-sectional studies indicate stability in the structure of cognitions about the self pertaining to temperament, and that mean levels of many self-concept dimensions, such as assertiveness, openness to experience, or amiability show stability across age when measured longitudinally. Other self-concept variables such as autonomy and self-competence increase well into middle age, while energy and social responsibility decrease. As a general rule, Bengston et al. (1985) found that cohort membership, sex, historical change, and life events were better predictors of self-concept than was age. Moreover, they suggest that more recent cohorts may actually begin with higher levels of self-esteem (self-evaluation) than do older cohorts. For many persons, self-esteem may either increase or be maintained as they age. These authors emphasized the fact that many studies on self-concept and self-esteem are difficult to compare due to sampling differences, diverse methods of measuring cognitions and feelings about the self, and because different designs (cross-sectional vs. longitudinal) have been used in most studies. Overall, there is little reason to believe that self-concept and self-esteem decrease as individuals age.

A number of researchers and practitioners have noted the importance of maintaining a sense of *personal control* over events as critical in determining the effects of being relocated from one's home to an institution (M.M. Baltes & P.B. Baltes, 1986; E. Langer, 1982; E. Langer & Rodin, 1976; Rodin & E. Langer, 1977, 1980; R. Schulz, 1976, 1980; R. Schulz & Brenner, 1977; Solomon, 1982; Weisz, 1983). Likewise, persons' feelings about the control they can exert over events in their daily lives may either ease or make more difficult the transition to retirement (Abel & Hayslip, 1986, 1987; Atchley, 1982, 1984). Also, older persons who are institutionalized or who are depressed (Kennelly, Hayslip, & Richardson, 1985; E. Langer, 1982; Maiden, 1987; Weisz, 1983) may have distorted ideas about their ability to control their own lives that interfere with their functioning. Interventions designed to restore accurate assessments of self-control (competence) have been successful (E. Langer & Rodin, 1976; Rodin & E. Langer, 1977; N. R. Schulz & Hanusa, 1979), leading to improved morale and health and less helplessness. Anxiety has been demonstrated to interfere with adequate levels of functioning in the learning, memory, and intelligence of elderly persons (see Chapter 6 & 7).

These narrower areas of personality functioning need to be understood in light of many of the issues we have raised in the definition and measurement of personality and adjustment to the aging process throughout adulthood. Their study may thus help us to more fully understand the process by which personality changes or remains consistent throughout adulthood. It may be that individuals who can maintain their views about themselves in the face of change, and who can retain a sense of personal control, are the very persons who live longer, happier lives.

SUMMARY

Personality can be understood along a *continuum* of emphasis, from a focus upon unobservable processes to one choosing to use observable behavior as the unit of personality. Using Maddi's *core* versus *periphery* model, one can understand the role that development plays in differentiating individuals (at the peripheral level) who also share common characteristics (the core of personality).

Several factors affect the stability of personality in adulthood. In addition to major views about adult personality (Havighurst, Gould, Erikson, Levinson, Buhler, P. Costa, & McCrae), one's biases about *activity/disengagement*, the *level* at which personality is studied, how one goes about *measuring* personality (e.g., using psychometric versus projective methods of assessment), and one's particular *developmental design* (cross-sectional, longitudinal) are all considerations in determining whether individuals change or not as they age.

While developmental stages provide us with a convenient framework within which to study adult personality, they must be viewed as *descrip-*

tive attempts to represent intraindividual change. Riegel's *dialectical* theory and Thomae's *cognitive* personality theory are consistent with the mediating role that personality plays in affecting and being influenced by experienced life events.

Relying upon data such as those of the *Berkeley-Oakland* studies and *Kansas City* studies, one can conclude that while most individuals may face age-graded sets of tasks or events, they cope (at a *socioadaptational level*) with these tasks in ways that are more or less adaptive, consistent with their established life histories. At an *intrapsychic level,* there is much evidence for increased *interiority* with age. Guttman's research dealing with sex differences in coping suggests that the pattern of personality change is specific to men and women, growing out of the cultural necessity to perform the *parental role.*

While cross-sectional data often present a picture of apparent age change, *sequential studies* of adult personality reveal cohort differences to exist for many psychological traits. Longitudinal studies paint a clear picture of stability with age in personality, relying upon psychometric scales to measure personality traits. Personality change and stability in adult years is thus a complex issue, subject to the effects of many influences.

KEY TERMS AND CONCEPTS

Personality	Illusion of Absolute Safety
Trait	Maturational ground plan
Social learning theory	Self-efficacy
Life review	Functional analysis
Reminiscence	Core
Periphery	Life tendencies
Psychosocial crises	Transformations
Stability versus change	Dialectical operations
Developmental task	Biographical versus biological life events
Personality "types"	Life satisfaction
Disengagement theory	Activity theory
Projective techniques	Interiority
Socioadaptational	Intrapsychic
Parental imperative	Active versus passive mastery
Genotypic continuity	Phenotypic persistence
Self-concept	Learned helplessness
Q-sort	Semantic differential
Life structure	Mentor

- Of what importance in adulthood is a person's selection of an occupation? Are career patterns different for men and women? What factors contribute to this?
- What are some of the major theories of occupational choice? What are some of the advantages and disadvantages of each?
- What are some of the basic rationales for the development of retirement? Are these reasons logical?
- What are the effects of retirement upon the individual? The society?
- What are some of the major reasons why leisure activities are important for the individual at all points along the life cycle?
- What types of leisure activities are characteristic of young adulthood, middle adulthood, and late adulthood?
- What are some of the major types of leisure life-styles?
- What does the term *flexible careers* mean? Why is it relevant to middle-aged and elderly persons?
- What is career indecision? How does it relate to occupational choice?

CHAPTER ▪ 11

WORK,

RETIREMENT,

AND LEISURE

▪

INTRODUCTION

Most of us spend a great deal of our time working behind a desk, at a machine, or in the home rearing our children. We may work eight to ten hours per day, five to six days a week. Moreover, we probably have spent a good deal of our high school and college careers thinking about and preparing for what we believe to be our life's work. Our work role is often critical to our identities as adults, and indeed we are socialized into this work role relatively early in our lives. After we have worked for 20 to 30 years, we may begin to consider retirement. Assuming life expectancy to increase in the future (see Chapter 2), the odds are that we will spend at least 10 to 15 years of our lives as persons who have been at one time employed. For many persons, what they have done helps them structure their lives in retirement. Others never retire in a formal sense. In other words, the world of work has a pervasive influence on many aspects of our lives *throughout* our lives. D. J. Levinson (1986), among other theorists, attaches a great deal of importance to work as an organizing principle in understanding adult development.

The focus of this chapter is to discuss this *continuum* of occupational selection, work, retirement, and leisure. Many may feel that we select an occupation, spend most of our adult years pursuing a career in that occupation, and eventually retire from the work role, which now allows us more free time to pursue our leisure activities. As we will see, this perspective on work, retirement, and leisure is quite simplistic. The topics of occupational selection, retirement, and leisure are interrelated and quite complex in themselves and have implications for our adjustment over the life cycle. While, for organizational reasons, we will discuss these topics independently, their interdependence and relationships to other areas of our lives (our marriage and roles as parents) is a reality. For example, Donald Super (1980), a prominent occupational theorist, has suggested that other roles persons play in their lives in various "theaters" (home, community, church, school, club) help to define (and are influenced by) their roles in the workplace. As these roles do change with age in many cases (see Chapters 8 and 9), the work role will also necessarily change.

OCCUPATIONAL ROLES AND THEIR SELECTION

The selection of an occupation is one of the most important decisions made by the individual during the life cycle. To some extent our occupation determines how our time is spent, who our friends will be, where we will live, and our attitudes and values, as well as our family's life-style (Tolbert, 1974). For many people, work occupies a central position for the greater part of their adult lives and serves as a basis for their self-concept, feelings of self-esteem, and often their very identity (Chown, 1977; Havighurst, 1982; J. Marshall, 1983).

This is true for both males and females (L.M. Coleman & Antonucci, 1983). In fact, research clearly indicates that work produces intrinsic satisfaction for the individual over and above that derived from its economic returns (Cohn, 1979). Hackett and Betz (1981) and Subich, Cooper, Barrett, and Arthur (1986) suggest that self-efficacy (Bandura, 1977) may underlie occupational choice for men and women. Persons with less self-efficacy may choose more traditional, less risky occupations.

Traditionally speaking, then, occupational selection is one of the major and most important developmental tasks of late adolescence and young adulthood (Havighurst, 1982). Though occupational selection is very important and critical for the individual, often it is made with little thought or assistance. In the last few years, there has been an increasing emphasis placed on career guidance and placement (Osipow, 1987). Further, career decision making is no longer considered limited to adolescence but continues throughout the life cycle (Osipow, 1983).

It is important to keep in mind that though we will discuss occupational selection as an organized life-span developmental process resulting from an interaction among specific factors, such as traits, abilities, or self-concept of the individual, many extraneous and unpredictable factors are also involved in this process (Whitbourne & Weinstock, 1979). For example, in reality, factors such as race, gender, economic factors, accessibility of educational and training opportunities, and supply and demand market conditions significantly affect an individual's occupational choice. Additionally, many individuals often get locked into jobs by accident, or jobs they thought were only temporary, and end up spending their entire lives in these jobs. As suggested by S. B. Sarason, E. K. Sarason, and Cowden (1975), many people are never able to enter the career of their first choice. This is one of the primary reasons individuals attempt midcareer life changes or pursue entirely new careers after retirement. This has been more likely due to the fact that attitudes toward work have changed dramatically in the last decade from those of materialism to those emphasizing self-fulfillment and self-actualization.

Occupational Development

Perhaps the major source of socialization during young and middle adulthood is in the work or occupational setting. Your occupation will affect (and in part result from) your identity, life-style, socioeconomic level, and friendship patterns. It will also help determine what society expects of you and your peers regarding behavior and performance in your **occupational role** (Osipow, 1983; Whitbourne & Weinstock, 1979). Such expectancies with regard to occupational role include one's dress, activities, code of conduct, values, morality, and standard of housing, to name but a few. Again, most occupations have an expected role associated with them; how well we conform to these expectancies often determines how we are viewed by society in general and by our occupational peers. S.B. Sarason et al. (1975) believe the process of making a career choice is accompanied by the individual's first awareness of the aging process, because the decision will determine how the rest of one's life will be occupied. For example, according to the United States Bureau of Labor Statistics (1983), the average male can expect to work 38 years, and the average female 28 years of their respective life spans.

Though occupational selection and choice have been usually associated with late adolescence and young adulthood, current thinking and theories of occupational choice view occupational development as a lifelong process, interwoven with other aspects of our lives (Ginzberg, 1971; Osipow, 1987; Super, 1953, 1957, 1969, 1975, 1980). For this reason, we will highlight some of the major theories of occupational selection but with a particular emphasis on theories with a life-span focus. Before discussing theories of occupational choice, we want to draw attention to the terms *career development* or **occupational development** as a necessarily semiorganized, *coherent* pattern of jobs that lead to some implicitly (subjectively) or explicitly standard level of performance or goal, reflecting a variety of decisions one has made throughout one's work life. Ideally, **careers** do progress in an orderly way, as opposed to a more or less random, unrelated series of *jobs* that one may hold just to get by financially (in the summer, while one is a full-time student, or if one lacks the requisite skills or educational background to pursue a career).

Theories of Occupational Choice

Holland One major theory of occupational choice is that of J.L. Holland (1973, 1985). Holland's theory is considered a "trait-factor" approach, since it predicts that vocational selection and satisfaction will be determined by a *congruence* or fit between the individual's attributes (such as personality traits, intelligence, skills, or special abilities) and vocational interests (similar to our person-environment interaction concept in Chapter 1). Individuals' vocational interests are viewed as an extension of their personalities. Occupations are categorized by the interpersonal settings in which the individual must function, as well as the associated life-style. It should be noted that Holland views these personal-social factors as more important to occupational selection than the performance requirements of the occupation per se.

This theory predicts individuals will choose an occupation that is a fit (consequence) between their personalities (standardized assessment scales are available for this purpose), the type of interpersonal setting in which they function, and the life-style associated with an occupation. In a sense, we choose the occupation that has the greatest similarity to our personality type. By doing this, we can express ourselves, best apply our skills (as we believe them to be), and take on work roles that are compatible with our personalities. Holland would predict that congruence between the individual and the occupation is the major factor responsible for vocational choice, stability, and satisfaction. On the other hand, dissatisfaction is the result of an incongruence (mismatch) among these factors. Spokane (1985) has recently supported the positive relationship between congruence and such factors as career persistence, career choice, career stability, and work satisfaction.

Holland's theory is somewhat limited for our purposes for two reasons. First, there is usually a significant difference between an individual's perceived and actual abilities at all points along the life span (Kidd, 1984; Panek & Sterns, 1985), and perceived ability is at the core of Holland's theory. Kidd (1984) has found that ideal self-concept in children better predicted occupational preference than did real self-concept. Second, Super's theory does not have a definite life-span focus. For example, Adler and Aranya (1984) studied career stages in accountants and found personality type–occupation congruence to vary with life stage (see Vondracek et al., 1986).

Super   Super's (1953, 1957, 1969) theory is an example of a self-concept approach to occupational development. The individual selects an occupation that allows for the expression of self-concept; this theory is presented within a life-span framework. R.H. Crook, Healy, and O'Shea (1984) suggest that career maturity is facilitated by self-concept, which in turn promotes achievement. Super describes occupational/vocational development as progressing through a series of career stages or career patterns that result from a modification of the individual's self-concept and adaptation to an occupational role. Therefore, in this theory, the major driving force behind vocational-occupational development at all points along the life cycle is the individual's self-concept. Persons are said to be located along a continuum of **vocational maturity** through their occupational lives—the more congruent individuals' vocational behaviors are with what is expected of them at different ages, the more vocationally mature they are (Super, 1980).

As proposed by Super, vocational development is seen as progressing through five distinct stages or career patterns. These are (1) implementation stage, (2) establishment stage, (3) maintenance stage, (4) deceleration stage, and (5) retirement stage.

The *implementation stage* (later adolescence) is characterized by individuals taking on a number of temporary positions (trial occupations) in which they begin to learn behaviors related to the work role, such as responsibility and productivity, and begin to develop friendship patterns and life-styles associated with the world of work. As individuals function in these jobs, they develop a more definitive identification with the occupation that is more closely related to their self-concepts, needs, and interests. Such experimentation may begin in high school (or even earlier) and is referred to as the *trial work period*, which may be very unstable (Havighurst, 1982). Grotevant and Cooper (1988) have discussed the central role that the family plays in helping the adolescent to choose a career. Parents can serve as models for career choice, and parents' work attitudes and behaviors can exert a powerful influence on children's career choice. When new or interesting career paths are opened to children in high school, the parent's own career development may be influenced as well. The family's influence, as well as individual factors (self-esteem, perceived ability) must be understood in light of cultural influences as well. Consequently cultural attitudes and expectations of individuals varying by gender, socioeconomic status, or ethnicity may well modify the family's influence on the adolescent's choice of careers (Grotevant & Cooper,

One important influence on vocational choice is our parent's own particular career pattern.

1988), as do historical changes in emphases upon what careers are "hot." For example, engineering or teaching have, at different times in the past 20 years, been desirable, while at present, social service or "high tech" careers are highly sought after.

As the individual's self-concept becomes more definite, he or she begins to move toward a specific career (occupation) choice and enters the next stage, the *establishment stage.* This usually occurs during young adulthood (ages 25 to 45 years, approximately) and is characterized by stability in the occupation, productivity, and advancement. Though individuals may change jobs or positions, they rarely change vocations. Additionally, during this stage, greater congruence is achieved between the individual's self-concept and the occupational role.

Following the establishment stage is a period of transition that usually occurs during late middle adulthood (ages 45 to 55 years), called the *maintenance stage.* This is the time when individuals prepare to decrease their occupational activity, since they feel they have already attained those occupational goals for which they have strived or else have come to realize they will never attain them. In a sense, they are no longer striving and achieving but maintaining—they are occupationally stable, yet they may be frustrated by the realization that some of their goals are unattainable.

By the mid-fifties, the individual begins to enter the *deceleration stage,* during which persons begin to prepare for retirement, foster the development of leisure activities, and begin to separate themselves from the job. This period is quite difficult for those to whom "the job" has been the most important and significant part of their lives.

Finally, there is the *retirement stage,* in which individuals formally divorce themselves from the work role. Super's theory is important because it considers vocational development as a *continuous* life-span process. Further, this theory can adequately explain specific career phenomena, such as midlife career change.

Ginzberg   Another life-span theory of occupational choice is that of Ginzberg (1971). Ginzberg's theory also suggests that over the life span individuals progress through a series of occupational periods or stages. In this case, the three stages are the *fantasy period, tentative period,* and *realistic period.* This theory integrates personal interests, values, and abilities as all being important in occupational choice.

Since the fantasy (see the study by Kidd, 1984, on page 400) and tentative periods correspond to childhood and adolescence respectively, they will not be addressed in detail here. The realistic period corresponds to the period between age 17 and the end of young adulthood, but Ginzberg believes the process of occupational choice and development is lifelong and open-ended. During this entire period, the individual constantly reaches compromises in occupational selection based on realistic factors such as job requirements, educational opportunities, and certain personal factors such as abilities and interests. Therefore, Ginzberg's theory has merits on the basis of its view of occupational selection as a dynamic life-span process, as well as its stress on the importance of environmental conditions, abilities, and preferences.

Career Patterns Among Men and Women

While we have defined careers as more or less stable, in reality this stability is an ideal. D.C. Miller and Form (1951) (see Havighurst, 1982, p. 773) identified several career patterns for men varying in terms of orderliness or stability:

    1. *Conventional*—a typical career path from *trial* (trying out several jobs) to stable employment—characteristic of managerial, skilled, and clerical workers

    2. *Stable*—common among professionals (managers, physicians, dentists, lawyers, college professors), where one goes directly from college (or graduate school) to a profession

    3. *Unstable*—characterized by trial-stable-trial career patterns common among domestic, semiskilled, or clerical workers

    4. *Multiple-trial*—characterized by frequent job changes, where no one job type is predominant; also characteristic of clerical, semiskilled, or domestic workers

While most (73 percent) of white-collar workers had stable or conventional career patterns, 46 percent of blue-collar and 29 percent of unskilled workers had stable or conventional work histories. While the occupations defining these patterns must likely have changed, and the numbers of persons in each has (and will) change, there is little reason to believe that these patterns have changed per se. Mueller (1954) (see Havighurst, 1982, p. 777) suggests that women's career patterns can be equally unstable and defines six vocational patterns for women:

    1. *Stable homemaker*—consistent involvement at home

    2. *Conventional career*—brief period of employment followed by marriage

    3. *Stable working career*—career oriented and lifelong

    4. *Double-track career*—work after completion of education, then marriage, followed by a return to work

    5. *Interrupted*—working, then homemaking, and perhaps working again, depending on the demands of children

    6. *Unstable*—alternate periods of work and homemaking, dependent on economic pressure and health—common among low-income women

Slocum and Cron (1985) found that in a sample of nearly 700 salespersons aged 21 to 60, distinct career phases (trial, stabilization, maintenance) did seem to exist, in part supporting the above-discussed career paths for men and women.

    As we have seen, women's career paths are similar to, but in some ways different from, those of men (L.S. Fitzgerald & Crites, 1980; Osipow, 1983). Much seems to depend on occupational levels, where women tend to be more similar to men as occupational levels increase.

    Attention to women's occupational development is comparatively recent (L.F. Fitzgerald & Betz, 1983), due to previous assumptions that (1) a woman's primary roles were housewife and mother, and (2) career concerns were primarily important only to single women. Due to changing societal values about men's and women's roles and to the diversity among women's career patterns (see above), L.F. Fitzgerald and Betz (1983) suggest that because women may not have the variety of career choices open to men and often are not able to fulfill their goals, theories of occupational development based on men simply do not fit women. A woman may initially have to decide whether she even wants to pursue a career, a choice that most men do not have to make.

A most recent model of women's career development is that of Astin (1984). Astin bases her approach to women's vocational choice on *motivation* for a career (needs for pleasure, survival, or contribution), *expectations* concerning alternative forms of work to satisfy her needs, *sex-role socialization* (family vs. work), and perceived *opportunities* in the work world (discrimination, job distribution, and economic constraints). Astin's (1984) career model for women has been criticized as giving too little attention to individual differences and to the force of the women's movement as a factor in career choice (L.F. Fitzgerald & Betz, 1983). For example, Osipow (1983) suggests that career-oriented women have higher achievement needs, while homemakers have higher needs for acceptance and affection.

The topic of career patterns in women has naturally been of interest as women's roles change and more women enter the work force, often in positions thought to be appropriate for men (Havighurst, 1982). Though they still lag behind men in earnings, fewer women are unemployed, and more women are pursuing their chosen careers (Harmon, 1983; Havighurst, 1982). Their career paths appear to be more complex than those of men.

Wolfson (1976) studied the career patterns of college women and found that seven patterns emerged, varying along the dimensions of *span of participation* (high, medium, low), *degree of participation* (male- versus female-dominated occupations), and *employment history* (never worked or employed). More recently, Betz (1984) followed up nearly 500 college women ten years after graduation, classifying them as:

1. never worked
2. low career commitment—traditional occupation
3. low career commitment—pioneer (nontraditional)
4. moderate career commitment—traditional
5. moderate career commitment—pioneer
6. high career commitment—traditional
7. high career commitment—pioneer

Betz found that most (two-thirds of) women were highly committed to their careers and that about 70 percent were employed in traditionally female occupations. Most had worked continuously since graduation, and only 1 percent had been full-time homemakers over the ten-year period. Most (79 percent) had successfully combined careers and homemaking. Women in traditional careers, however, were less likely to change careers and more likely to make downward (horizontal) career shifts than were pioneer women. Older women were more likely never to have worked. Relative to earlier studies, Betz found that nontraditional career patterns that would have been considered "unusual" were no longer seen this way. This study supports the optimistic yet varied picture that women's careers are taking.

Women now define their lives in terms of home, career, and continued education, and despite discrimination, stresses associated with a dual-career marriage (see Chapter 9), and less relative income, they seem to be highly committed to their chosen career paths. As interest in women's career development continues to grow, research will explore more fully the processes in career decision making for women (Osipow, 1983).

We would emphasize that diversity and flexibility in career choice are important for *both* men and women, whether one's career is homemaking or management. Reflecting this approach, Chiswick (1982) has calculated the market value of a homemaker's time on par with her "employed" peers.

Havighurst (1982) advocates **"flexible careers"** that may apply to a small number of persons in middle adulthood and prior to retirement. While persons change careers for many reasons, there is nothing necessarily wrong with such flexibility if it is pleasurable and satisfying to the individual. Moreover, as individuals age, employers might utilize their experience in a different position in the event that physical/sensory changes or health problems prevent them from doing those jobs that they have held for many years. Havighurst (1982) advocates flexible retirement plans that combine part-time work and part-time retirement. To the extent that people gain intrinsic satisfaction from their work, such flexibility could be beneficial for both the employee and the employer.

Occupational Developmental Tasks

Havighurst (1982) suggests that there are distinct **occupational developmental tasks**, similar to those espoused by life-stage theorists such as Holland and Ginzberg. The first of these developmental tasks is *preparing for an occupational career* (adolescence), where the individual begins a formal preparation for a career, perhaps by entering an apprenticeship or by attending a specific vocational training school or university. Many test their ability to function independently of their parents in these situations, and they may hold various part-time jobs or simply remain unemployed. Depending on the marketplace, specific job skills needed, or availability of career options, the "right way to go" for some persons is sometimes clearer than for others.

Even for college-bound middle-class individuals (especially for women) career options may be narrow or individuals may suffer from **career indecision** (J.L. Holland & J.E. Holland, 1977; Solomone, 1982). They may vacillate between alternatives, refuse to seek out new information, or not make any commitments whatsoever. While some colleges may forbid students to commit themselves to a given major until after they have completed two years of course work, contributing to career indecision, individual personality characteristics (indecisiveness, fear of success, anxiety, submissiveness or dependency, the tendency to avoid risks) and family dynamics (Lopez, 1983) may also contribute to (and be influenced by) career indecision. Career indecision is also affected by culturally bound sex-role or occupational stereotypes, pressures from one's family or spouse to "get established," or subcultural (racial, socioeconomic) mores and norms regarding "adulthood."

Ironically, once one has invested oneself in a given career path, these same factors may prevent an individual from switching careers. At the same time, many persons need a period of *moratorium* (Erikson, 1963; Marcia, 1966) to allow themselves time to find out what occupational path is best for them. Many times we feel pressure to become instant successes. Perhaps to avoid failing or to please others, we pursue what our parents did (Marcia calls this pattern a *foreclosed* one). In other words, there are a great number of pushes and pulls to decide or *not* to decide on a given occupation at this point in our lives. Later on, similar choices may confront us when our wives (or husbands) decide to switch careers, to return to school, having raised a family, or to retire early (or not to retire at all). Thus, the concept of career indecision is one that applies to *all* phases of the occupational work cycle. Different cohorts of individuals, based on distinct occupational histories and patterns of occupational socialization, may be more or less prone to such indecision (V.W. Gordon, 1981). In this light, Crites (1981) found the percentage of "undecided" students to vary between 5 and 61 percent over a span of 50 years.

Havighurst's second occupational developmental task is *getting started in an occupation.* Persons in this phase of the occupational life cycle are "learning the ropes," so to speak. They are being socialized into the job role regarding what skills they are expected to maintain or develop, how they are expected to dress, how much time they are to spend at home working, as well as how they are to relate to peers and to persons in positions of authority (B. Newman & P. Newman, 1986). The extent to which one's job is embedded in a career pattern, is subject to the obsolescence of skills, or is highly complex and technical determines whether more time and effort will be needed to devote to this occupational phase, often to the detriment of one's relationships with spouse, children, or friends. Of course, these decisions, while they may be occupationally justifiable, nevertheless may have repercussions for individuals, ranging from problems with one's health to mental difficulties. Ultimately, decisions and compromises need to be made regarding the relative importance of family versus work. In Chapter 9, we saw that these same conflicts may reemerge when a woman decides to enter (or return to) the work force, forcing her to balance the demands of work and family.

Havighurst (1982) suggests that the third occupational developmental task is *reaching and maintaining satisfactory performance in one's occupational career,* applying more to persons in middle adulthood.

Osipow, Doty, and Spokane (1985) feel that the pressures of work and one's *response to* these pressures varies across the life span. Such pressures, of course, affect work performance. Osipow et al. (1985) studied over 300 employed men and women of 5 age ranges (below 25, 25–34, 35–44, 45–54, 55+). While gender did not influence occupational stress, strain, or coping, younger (<25) people experienced the most psychological and interpersonal strain, while for older (>25) persons, strain in general declined consistently with age. Perhaps older persons are better at coping with strain or have left jobs that are stressful. Younger persons also reported different types of stresses (unchallenging work, conflict between values/objectives of different persons at work, aversive physical environment) than did older persons (work overload, being responsible for others at work). With increased age, persons tended to use different styles of coping that were more effective (recreational, better self-care, effective use of time) and made better use of social support to cope with job stress.

CHANGING CAREERS IN MIDLIFE

Though the above research does not single out middle adulthood as a time of **career crisis** (see P. Costa & McCrae, 1980a), middle-aged persons seem to be most vulnerable to **job loss** (Lajer, 1982). P. Murphy and Burck (1976) have suggested (as has D. Levinson, see Chapter 10) that middle adulthood can be especially pivotal occupationally. Rather than being upwardly mobile, Levinson's subjects seemed to focus on the stable, fulfilling aspects of their careers. Many other researchers (Osipow, 1983) have suggested that the midcareer phase is largely a negative one, characterized by dissatisfaction and restlessness followed by a stable period, presumably based on the notion of a male midlife crisis. On the other hand, P. Costa and McCrae (1980a) found little evidence for such disruption. Some persons do not experience a crisis or even a period of transition occupationally, and there are vast individual differences in how people *respond to* such dissatisfaction, if it is experienced at all. Given that career development cannot be understood in isolation, an emphasis on a midcareer crisis phase seems an oversimplification.

People do, however, change careers in middle adulthood; such changes may be **horizontal** (from one career to another) or **vertical** (to a higher level of responsibility) (Osipow, 1983). Many persons experience several vertical career changes in their lives. Such changes come about for a variety of reasons (Driskill & Dauw, 1975; Heddescheimer, 1976; J.D. Wright & Hamilton, 1978). Family changes (divorce, widowhood, adult children leaving home), a desire for more income, status, and security, philosophical differences with one's employer, and dissatisfaction with how one's skills are used are common reasons for such career changes. However, persons who hold jobs that are more stable (less responsive to economic changes), more complex, and who have been in a given career for many years are less likely to change careers (Gold, 1979; Gottsfredson, 1977). Vaitenas and Weiner (1977) found that such factors as a lack of interest, incongruity with one's occupation, lack of consistent and diversified interests, fear of failure, or a history of emotional problems, but *not* age, predicted career change. This suggests that some persons are more likely to change careers than others, whether or not such changes occur in middle adulthood. At present, it clearly would be premature and inaccurate to state that midlife is necessarily a period of occupational upheaval for men.

While studies in midlife for women are comparatively rare, Abush and Burkhead (1984) found that a Type A personality (see Chapter 2), less autonomy and feedback at work, less significance in one's job, and fewer friendships related positively to job stress. While the empty nest may be important for some women, it is not a universal stressor that relates to job dissatisfaction or personal unhappiness (Black & Hill, 1984). While Eadwins and Mellinger (1984) found personality (affiliation, maturity, locus of control) to influence job stress among different role groups (homemaker, married/career, single/career, returning students) of women aged 30 to 55, age was not correlated with job stress in this study. As is the case for men, there appears to be little evidence for a midlife occupational crisis in women.

THE LOSS OF ONE'S JOB

With changes in our economy brought about by inflation, competition within industries, undercutting (regarding price or quality of products) of industries in the United States by others in such countries as Japan or China, or by lessened enrollments of traditional college-age (18–22) students, even stable career patterns can be in jeopardy. College professors, middle-level managers, or research scientists can find themselves unemployed or laid off indefinitely just as easily as those who are not formally trained or who hold blue-collar skilled or semiskilled positions. In either case, significant losses in self-esteem, feelings of alienation and depression, family discord and abuse, alcoholism, and in some situations suicide are the consequences of such unforeseen "wrinkles" in the careers of many. DeFrank and Ivancevich (1986) suggest that the personal impact of job loss (unemployment) on individuals can be quite extensive—declines in physical health and self-esteem, depression, anxiety, or suicide. R.J. Estes and Wilensky (1978) found that such effects are a function of the financial stress one is under and family life cycle stage (Duvall, 1971). For example, childless couples and couples with school-age children suffered the most, while morale was higher when children were independent, had left home, or when the couple was alone again (postparental); these couples probably had more social support (adult children). Lajer (1982) found that persons were at greater risk for admission to a psychiatric unit if they were older than 45 and/or had been unemployed for a longer period of time.

According to DeFrank and Ivancevich (1986), many factors mediate individuals' responses to the loss of their jobs. While loss of a job means that the worker loses a source of income and status as a productive person, age is an important mediator of responses to job loss, with middle-aged men being more vulnerable relative to older or younger men. How persons perceive this loss, the degree of available social support, their existing coping skills, and how long they have been unemployed all contribute to how individuals respond to job loss (see Mallinckrodt & Fretz, 1988).

The last major occupational developmental task, according to Havighurst (1982), is *adjusting to retirement and reduced income.* As we mentioned above, health or physical changes may force one into considering retirement, and retirement has varying effects on individuals depending on their motives for and satisfaction with their work, relationship with their spouse (Brubaker, 1983), and attitude toward retirement (Glamser, 1976, 1981). We shall discuss retirement in depth shortly.

While there is no one generally accepted theory of occupational development, occupational/vocational development must be viewed as a lifelong *process* and as influenced by cultural, familial, and individual factors. As we noted above, most theories are limited because they focus primarily on males. As more women enter the world of work outside the home (due to economic necessity or for fulfillment), theories of occupational development will begin to address females to a greater extent. Though statistics indicate that over 50

BOX 11.1

WOMEN STILL GET SMALLER PAYCHECK

Despite 30 years of radical change—marrying later, having fewer children, and getting more schooling—American women are still bound in their traditional economic role, a government study said recently.

In an analysis tracking shifts since 1950, a Census Bureau report notes, "Women have been at the vortex of sweeping changes" in American society. No longer is a woman principally a mother, although only a handful of married women remain childless throughout their fertile years.

Only one-third of adult women worked in 1950; more than half do now. Three decades ago, women represented only 27.9 percent of the nation's workers; now they are 44.2 percent.

But while the number of women plumbers and pilots has soared, "Working women do not earn as much as working men"—averaging only 62 percent of annual pay for men in the category of over-25, college-educated workers.

The report, "American Women: Three Decades of Change," was written by Suzanne Bianchi and Daphne Spain, research associates in the bureau's Center for Demographic Studies.

Source: Women Still Get Smaller Paycheck. (1983, October 11). *Charleston Times-Courier.*

---

percent of women between the ages of 16 and 64 are currently in the work force, they suffer discrimination on the job, as reflected in discrepancies in pay, compared to males performing the same job (*Sex Equity in Education Bulletin,* 1983). This is illustrated in Box 11.1. Further, the largest group of individuals now entering the work force are women over 40 years of age.

Since our occupation and the roles associated with that occupation are significantly related to factors such as our self-concept, identity, and friendship patterns, there is an obvious need to study in greater detail the processes involved in career decision making (career indecision), particularly among persons who have not attended college. As we have previously noted, we often make career choices by accident, in haste (on the basis of inaccurate information) or due to pressure to make a career decision. In order to deal with such problems, various school systems, colleges, and state and local agencies are implementing career-planning programs for persons of varying ages. These programs can be quite successful in facilitating appropriate career decision making with persons of all age levels. For example, Franklin-Panek (1978) found that participation in a career life-span planning program could increase both self-concept and career decision making ability in adults. Stonewater and Daniels (1983) have developed a career decision making course for students, also reporting much success. Fountain (1986) and Baxter (1986) have developed specific modules for use in the classroom to aid individuals in understanding the economics of the labor market, the economy, and career choice.

RETIREMENT

It is quite likely that the majority of individuals reading this text will reach the age at which they will retire (that is, withdraw from participation in the work force) either voluntarily or involuntarily. Since most of us will experience **retirement**, it is important that we become aware of the issues and factors that will affect us at that time in order to plan appropriately for that *event* and the *role* associated with being retired (Atchley, 1984). The extent to which we do make decisions about retirement as young adults (in selecting a company with a pension plan or considering retirement packages) suggests that, like career development, retirement is a *process*. For example, Dobson and Morrow (1984) found that among college (nonfaculty) employees, career orientation (job satisfaction, work commitment, endorsing the work ethic) was related to retirement attitudes and retirement planning, as did Abel and Hayslip (1986), who studied both blue-collar and white-collar industrial workers. In both studies, age was not related to retirement attitudes.

Retirement is not easy to discuss, because the process of retirement may begin in early adulthood and have an effect on the retiree, the institution or organization from which the individual has retired, society in general, and the retiree's family. Our goal will be to briefly present the theoretical reasons behind the concept of retirement from a historical perspective and then to discuss the factors related to the retirement process and its effects upon the individual.

Theoretical Rationales for Retirement

There appear to be two basic rationales for the development of the institution of retirement. One rationale for retirement is that it allows individuals to enjoy the remaining years of their lives in pursuit of particular hobbies and leisure activities, after spending the major portion of their lives producing goods and services for the society and/or organization: in a sense, a thank-you for a job well done.

A second reason for retirement is that the process allows for a constant, predictable, and orderly flow of workers throughout the work force, that is, an orderly method of replacing older, potentially less productive and efficient workers with younger, potentially more productive and efficient workers.

Regardless of one's theoretical bias, the fact is that the number of retired individuals has been increasing dramatically in industrialized nations in the past 100 years. For example, in 1900 approximately 70 percent of American men over age 65 were employed. By 1960, the figure had dropped to 35 percent, and by 1975 to 22 percent. And, in 1984, about 11 percent of older adults were still in the work force. Interestingly, while the labor force participation has decreased steadily since 1900 for men, the participation rate for females has increased during this same period of time (Robinson, Coberly, & Paul, 1985).

Researchers and theorists have attempted to explain why the percentage of older adults who are retired continues to increase, while the percentage of older adults who remain on the job continues to decrease (American Association of Retired Persons, 1985). A number of reasons have been offered to explain this trend. First, since the beginning of this century, the United States *has progressively shifted from an agricultural to an industrial base* (Havighurst, 1982). Moreover, the United States has shifted from a nation where the majority of individuals were self-employed (farmers, craftsmen) to one where we now work for others. Since individuals were self-employed, or involved with the family business, they worked until they died or became disabled. Therefore, the decrease in the number of older adults who are still in the work force is a reflection of the shift in the percentages of individuals who work for themselves as opposed to those who work for others.

A second reason often cited for these statistics is the fact that *life expectancy has increased* substantially in this century (see Chapter 2); more individuals are alive to retire today than in previous years. The logic supporting this belief is as follows: Before 1900 very few individuals lived to be 65 years or older. Those who did live longer tended to be those who were in the best health; therefore, they were able to remain on the job longer. With increased health care and medical technology, life expectancy has increased, some (but not all) individuals' abilities and capacities may nevertheless decline in old age. Therefore, though individuals live longer, some are not physically able to continue to work, so they leave the work force. So the decrease in the percentage of older adults in the work force is just a reflection of the fact that more individuals are living longer.

A third reason cited for the increased numbers of retirees is the continued *development of formal retirement systems, pensions, as well as legal factors.* First, individuals tend to work to support themselves and their families financially. If no provision is made to support them financially when they retire, they will continue to work. Regarding this point, the United States was one of the last Western industrialized nations to provide retirement benefits for older adults. In 1935, the Social Security Act was passed that mandated that persons over 65 who had worked a certain length of time were eligible for benefits. Interestingly, some form of retirement system was in place in Germany in 1889 and in the United Kingdom in 1908.

Secondly, each year, additional financial plans (for example, pensions, tax shelters, IRAs, and so forth) become available, allowing individuals to prepare for their economic security during retirement. For this reason, more and more individuals are covered under some form of pension or retirement plan, and a greater percentage of individuals are able to leave the work force.

Moreover, since the law specifies at what age one is eligible for retirement benefits, organizations and institutions can then "legally" set mandatory retirement ages and force individuals from the work force when they reach that specified age. Therefore, since the majority of individuals tend to work for others rather than themselves, more and more come under mandatory retirement rules, causing the percentage of older workers to decrease and the percentage of retirees to increase.

A fourth reason for the decrease in the number of older workers who remain on the job has to do with increasingly high productivity due to *technological advancements.* That is, advanced technology, such as computers and industrial robots, is taking over many of the jobs originally performed by humans. This results in an oversupply of labor in many occupations and jobs.

As we indicated in our section on industrial gerontology in Chapter 5, since older workers are often viewed by business as unproductive, they are considered expendable and are encouraged to retire early. Again, the net result is a decrease in the overall number of older adults in the work force (Robinson et al., 1985).

Finally, during this century there has been a change in society's attitude toward work and the meaning of work, as well as regarding the support of nonworking members of society (Havighurst, 1982). Specifically, with successive cohorts, individuals have moved further away from the belief that the major purpose in life is to work and be active, to the attitude that the purpose of work is to attain self-actualization and/or obtain the money necessary to pursue other interests. In this light, Havighurst (1982) notes that job satisfaction has declined since 1973, reflecting different values about the meaning of work.

Further, traditional American philosophy was based on self-sufficiency and independence—taking care of yourself. Gradually, American society has adopted the philosophy that the government has some responsibility for the care and support of its citizens. Therefore, with successive cohorts, greater percentages of Americans have felt that rather than continue to work to support themselves in old age, they should retire and let others do so, for example, through social security and pension plans.

Overall, theorists have suggested a number of reasons why the percentage of older adults who retire is increasing, while the number of older adults who are still in the work force decreases. There is no one definitive explanation for this, and it is quite likely that all these factors have contributed to the growing number of retirees.

Many feel that persons experience several *phases of retirement:* the honeymoon phase, the disenchantment phase, and a stability (reorientation) phase (Atchley, 1976). Ekerdt, Bosse, and Levkoff (1985) compared retirees who had retired for three years or less by placing them in six-month intervals regarding length of time retired. Compared to men who had been retired 0 to 6 months, those retired for between 13 and 18 months expressed less optimism, saw themselves as less physically active, and had less life satisfaction. Apparently retired persons do experience a letdown of sorts shortly after this honeymoon phase.

Factors Related to the Decision to Retire

It is not easy to state why people retire. Research indicates that the decision to retire is often a personal one and due to a number of factors. In this section, those factors that have been found to be related to the decision to retire will be discussed. It should be stressed that these factors should not be considered independent; many are highly related to each other (see H. S. Parnes et al., 1985).

Major factors that influence the decision to retire are health condition, occupational level, financial situation, age, gender, work satisfaction, and personal attitude. Collectively, factors influencing the decision to retire have been separated into *personal* ones (health, economic situation, attitudes toward work/retirement, and degree of social support) and *institutional* ones (workplace conditions, employer policy, public policy regarding retirement, economic conditions, societal values regarding retirement) (Robinson et al., 1985).

Health Research clearly indicates that one of the most important factors influencing individuals' decisions to retire is their health status. In fact, a number of researchers (C.S. Kart, 1982; Schwab, 1974; Sherman, 1974) report that the main reason given for retiring by both men and women was "poor health." Further, health status plays a very important role in the decision to retire for individuals who are subject to mandatory retirement rules as well as for those who are not affected by mandatory retirement. Apparently poor health makes working burdensome and difficult.

R. Clark and Spengler (1980) report there appear to be two types of individuals who choose to retire early ($\leq$ 62 years of age). These are (1) individuals in good health and with financial resources who desire additional leisure time, and (2) individuals in poor health. Retirement frees the individual of this burden, that is, going to work each day. Interestingly, once individuals with poor health retire, they often find that their poor health affects the plans they had made for themselves for retirement. That is, their health limits their activities, travel, and leisure.

Occupational Level The individual's occupational level plays a very important factor in the decision to retire, either voluntarily or due to mandatory regulations. Further, occupational level is highly related to socioeconomic level and educational level, which have been found repeatedly to be related to a number of factors such as life expectancy and intelligence (see Chapters 2 and 6). Therefore, in the discussion of the effects of occupational level upon retirement, in a simplistic sense, high occupational level will imply high socioeconomic level and high educational level, and vice versa.

Individuals at the highest occupational levels, such as doctors, lawyers, senior executives, and other professionals, usually continue to work in some capacity and very seldom completely retire (Palmore, L.K. George, & Fillenbaum, 1982). These individuals usually continue to work at a reduced level as consultants or summer replacements or working on special assignments and cases. Further, individuals at this occupational level usually have high levels of expertise, training, and commitment to their organization or profession and choose to or are encouraged to continue working in some capacity. If individuals in this occupational category do retire, it is primarily due to poor health.

At the second occupational level are individuals who are lower-level executives and middle managers within organizations. These individuals are usually forced to retire due to organizational directives—mandatory retirement policy. Often individuals from this occupational level tend to take "early retirement," that is, retire at age 60 rather than waiting until the mandatory retirement age of 65.

These individuals often choose early retirement for two reasons. First, they may realize their careers have reached a plateau within the organization, and they will not likely advance any higher. Therefore, they choose to leave early since they have nothing to gain careerwise by staying on, plus they are still young enough and in good enough health to enjoy retirement activities. A second reason why these individuals retire early is that the company often offers an attractive retirement package to those in target positions who retire early. For example, maximum retirement benefits for retirement at age 65 result in a pension of 45 percent of the base salary. Individuals may be encouraged to retire at age 60, at which point they will receive a pension of 42 percent of their baseline plus free insurance until age 68. Therefore, the individual has little to gain by staying on the job.

This situation is quite common for positions in which younger workers are viewed as more productive than older workers, or when a younger worker can perform the same duties for significantly lower pay (cost) than older workers. The company's rationale is higher productivity for a lower cost.

The majority of workers in the United States fall into the categories of "skilled" (tool and die maker), "semiskilled" (electrician's assistant), and "unskilled" (farm laborer) labor. These individuals usually retire as a function of the mandatory retirement rules of the organization, regardless of their health status and attitude toward work.

Financial Situation Given the opportunity, the decision to choose whether one will continue to work or retire is significantly affected by one's financial situation (Ward, 1984). Since individuals will need money to maintain their life-styles after retirement, those who are enrolled in pension plans or know they have some source of funds available to them should they retire tend to have a more positive attitude toward retirement. This is due to the fact that they feel secure about their financial future. Others who do not feel secure potentially undergo stress and anxiety.

As previously reported, R. Clark and Spengler (1980) found some individuals who choose early retirement to be those in good health and with financial resources who desire additional leisure time. Therefore, in general, regardless of occupational level, health factors and financial security play the most important roles in a person's desire and decision to retire (Robinson et al., 1985).

Interestingly, it is the individuals at the lower occupational levels who tend to have the lowest retirement benefits, due to the fact that benefits are related to earnings. These are the very individuals who are subject to mandatory retirement rules. Given relatively low earnings while working, those individuals in most cases have not had extra available funds to put aside for retirement. It is this group that is usually adversely affected by retirement, especially in terms of financial resources.

In order to avoid financial crises and other retirement-related problems or changes among retirees, many companies are now implementing preretirement planning programs for workers at all levels and ages. For instance, O'Meara (1977) has reported surveys of 800 corporations representing a wide spectrum, such as manufacturing, textiles, and pharmaceuticals, and found that 88 percent provide some form of preretirement assistance to their workers from all occupational levels within the company. Such preretirement training is also viewed as desirable by workers themselves (Kalb & Kohn, 1975). Jacobson (1980) indicates that there are two major types of information that are common to all preretirement programs. First, these programs provide information regarding the company's financial benefits and social security.

Second, advice, counseling, and suggestions are made concerning such topics as health care/services, leisure activities, legal matters, and changes in life-style.

Given the positive benefits (e.g., more positive retirement attitudes, greater morale and life satisfaction) to be derived from preretirement training programs (Abel & Hayslip, 1987; Glamser & DeJong, 1975), they will most likely become more universal in the future (see Box 11.2). It should be pointed out that such programs often have only short-term results and that their primary impact seems to be that they reinforce the individual's *perception* of preparing for retirement (Abel & Hayslip, 1986; Glamser, 1981). In other words, doing something often makes us feel positive. Research has yet to demonstrate the long-term benefits of such programs, however. If unexpected changes in health or economic status were to occur, it would be difficult to have prepared for these changes.

Age   As one would expect, research suggests that as age increases, the individual is more likely to retire (L.K. George, Fillenbaum, & Palmore, 1984). There are many reasons why age affects the decision to retire. Some of these include poor health, job boredom, and mandatory retirement rules, to name a few. In a sense, though age has been found to be related to the decision to retire, it is not age per se that causes the decision to retire but factors usually associated with aging and deteriorating health.

BOX 11.2

CONTENT OF A TYPICAL PRERETIREMENT TRAINING PROGRAM

I. Individual Needs
   A. Feelings about retirement
   B. Factors in retirement—satisfactory and unsatisfactory
II. Finances
   A. Social Security
      1. Earnings restrictions
      2. Provisions for widow(er) and disabled
      3. Medicare registration and benefits
   B. Pension benefits
   C. Financial planning
   D. Consumer education
   E. Community agencies
   F. Insurance and investments
   G. Estate planning and wills
III. Health
   A. Hospital and insurance benefits
   B. Physical examinations
   C. Mental health—coping with retirement
   D. Effect of aging on health

IV. Changing Roles
   A. Planning for leisure time
   B. Retirement adjustment—T-groups
   C. Death and dying
V. Living Arrangements
   A. Housing
      1. Repairs
      2. Mortgages
      3. Rent or buy
      4. Relocation considerations
VI. Leisure Time
   A. Part-time work
   B. Travel
   C. Hobbies
   D. Volunteer work
   E. Joining clubs
   F. Meaningful use of time

Source: From Crane, Donald P. (1986). *Personnel: the management of human resources*, p. 350. Boston: Kent Publishing Company.

Gender Research indicates the predictors or reasons for retirement as somewhat different for males and females. For example, L.K. George et al. (1984) found for males there were six predictors of retirement, while for females there was only one.

Specifically, for males, George et al. (1984) found: age—the older, the more likely to retire; educational level—the lower, the more likely to retire; occupational status—the lower, the more likely to retire; health condition—the more health limitations, the more likely to retire; financial situation—those enrolled in pension programs are more likely to retire; and job tenure—the longer employed, the more likely to retire. For females, the only predictor of retirement was found to be age, with the older more likely to retire.

Therefore, for females, the decision to retire is highly related to the characteristics of the husband, such as the husband's health condition, pension plan, leisure activities, and so forth. For instance, women may retire early in order to care for a sick and infirm husband.

Work Satisfaction Since research indicates that work produces satisfaction over and above that derived from its financial benefits (Cohn, 1979), it is not surprising that many individuals enjoy working and wish to remain working as long as they can, particularly if they are in good health. As previously stated, a person's job contributes to self-esteem and self-concept, provides a social network and activities, and is related to life satisfaction. Therefore, when one retires, not only does one give up the economic benefits of working but these additional benefits as well.

For these reasons, research indicates that individuals who are satisfied with their jobs continue to work longer than individuals who are dissatisfied.

Many older persons, despite having retired, continue to practice their trades with enthusiasm and skill.

Further, job satisfaction is positively related to occupational level. That is, high occupational level is related to having high work satisfaction. Therefore, it is quite difficult to discuss job satisfaction without keeping in mind its relationship to occupational level.

Interestingly, Cohn (1979) has found that just prior to retirement, work satisfaction begins to decrease in its relationship to overall life satisfaction. This may be attributed to individuals beginning to disassociate or disengage themselves from their job. Additionally, they may anticipate adequate income in retirement (Burkhouser & Turner, 1980). Adequate income in retirement via social security benefits does seem to influence the decision to retire (D. Reynolds, Masters, & Moser, 1987), particularly for persons in poorer health (Quinn, 1977).

Personal Attitudes Toward Retirement Often, regardless of the other factors we have discussed that have been found to be related to the decision to retire, the individual's personal attitude toward retirement plays a very important role in the decision to retire (Glamser, 1976, 1981). For example, McGee, Hall, & Lutes-Dunckley (1979) investigated factors related to attitudes toward retirement with male middle to upper level managers ranging in age from 28 to 61 years. McGee et al. found that managers anticipating a change in life-style in retirement were more likely to have negative attitudes toward retirement than managers anticipating a continuity of life-style. That is, those who expected similar economic situations, continuity of leisure activities, and continuity of health status had more positive attitudes toward retirement. Interestingly, no significant relationship was found between attitude toward retirement and present commitment to work. This indicates that individuals with a high degree of commitment to the job can have a positive attitude toward leaving the job (retirement), and vice versa (Abel & Hayslip, 1986).

McGee et al. (1979) suggest their results support Atchley's (1971) hypothesis that a positive attitude toward retirement is influenced by the extent to which continuity of life-style is anticipated. This study is limited by the fact that individuals investigated were all males and of middle to high occupational status.

McPherson and Guppy (1979), with male participants ranging in age from 55 to 64 years, investigated factors related to preretirement attitudes and decision making. These researchers found socioeconomic status (occupation, income, educational level), perceived health, organizational involvement (clubs), job satisfaction, and degree of leisure activities were all positively related to preretirement attitudes and decision making. Basically, the higher one's income level, the more leisure and organizational activity involvement existed. This tended to be accompanied by better perceived health and more positive preretirement attitudes. Similar results have been found by Abel and Hayslip (1986). Again, the study by McPherson and Guppy was limited in that only males were investigated, but it does highlight the importance of many of the factors we have previously discussed that have been found to be related to the decision to retire.

Atchley (1979) suggests that persons anticipating retirement engage in a decision-making process where they compare their financial and social situation while working to that anticipated during retirement. Dependent upon one's attitudes toward work and retirement, the degree of preretirement planning, the spouse's support and job situation, financial inducements by the government or one's employer to remain employed or to retire, the availability of flexible work options, and the general economic climate (Robinson et. al., 1985), one may or may not elect to retire.

Overall, one's attitude toward retirement varies as a function of a number of factors, such as income, educational level, and occupational level. Therefore, it should be kept in mind that causal statements about why people retire are not always easy to make. For instance, though individuals with higher educational and occupational levels tend to have positive attitudes toward retirement, these individuals are also less likely to retire since they are committed to their job and find work interesting. Individuals with low occupational and income levels may want to retire but are not in the economic position to do so.

It should be noted that there is very little data available regarding retirement among women. What is available is often ambiguous. Due to the fact that more women are entering the work force, we need to learn more about female decisions to retire. In the next section, we will discuss the effects of retirement upon the individual, the organization/industry, others, and society. As this discussion will indicate, retirement has many negative and positive factors for the individual and society.

Effects of Retirement

THE INDIVIDUAL

It is commonly assumed that retirement has many significant effects upon the individual, many of them negative (Parnes et al., 1985; Robinson et al., 1985). Adjustment to retirement may often be difficult for individuals, since it requires adjustment to a new life-style characterized by decreased income and required activity and increased free time (McGee et al., 1979; National Council on the Aging, 1981; Streib & Schneider, 1971). Further, there is potential for decreased psychological well-being, since one's self-concept often revolves around one's work role. A number of theorists (such as Havighurst, 1982) suggest retirement causes extreme stress in males because a significant part of their identity lies with their jobs. The loss of this job due to retirement results in a loss of self-esteem and self-worth. If we view retirement as an ongoing process, however, such a negative view seems unjustified; all studies fail to support such a loss-oriented view of retirement (Robinson et al., 1985).

For example, Streib and Schneider (1971) report that studies indicate approximately 30 percent of retired people encounter difficulties in adjusting to retirement. Of these individuals, 40 percent stated that the major reason they were having difficulty in adjusting to retirement was due to financial problems; 28 percent claimed difficulties due to health reasons, 22 percent missed their jobs, and 10 percent suffered loneliness due to the death of their spouse.

At a commonsense level, it would appear that retirement would cause a number of adjustment problems, because the retired individual has to make many adjustments simultaneously. These include many losses: work role, personal and social associations related to the job, status, income, and a sense of accomplishment and productivity (L.K. George, Fillenbaum, & Palmore, 1984).

But does the research support this assumption that retirement results in many negative consequences for the individual? As we noted above, it does not. Interestingly, research data (L.K. George, Fillenbaum, & Palmore, 1984; Gratton & Haug, 1983) are often incongruent with our commonsense assumptions regarding the negative aspects of retirement. For example, poor health may be the cause rather than the result of retirement; health may even improve for some individuals after retirement.

The majority of research studies investigating the impact of retirement upon retirees suggests retirement may have little effect upon the individual and what changes do occur as a result of retirement may be positive as well as negative for both men and women (Gratton & Haug, 1983; L.K. George et al., 1984). For instance, L.K. George et al. (1984) found retirement had no adverse effects upon life satisfaction for either males or females. Further, there are vast individual differences in the perception of retirement and the consequences of retirement as a function of factors such as gender, availability of social support and friendship networks, race, health status, commitment to work (Hooker & Ventis, 1984), occupational level, income level, marital status, hobbies, and leisure activities (Robinson et al., 1985; Rowland, 1977). Therefore, it is difficult to discuss the effects of retirement in general terms. Simply put, some individuals experience difficulties in retiring while others do not.

One of the major positive aspects of retirement is that it allows increased time for social and hobby-related activities, especially if the individual has adequate economic resources and health to engage in these activities (Glamser & Hayslip, 1985). In fact, feelings of self-worth may not decrease after retirement if the individual is able to transfer the self-worth/self-esteem derived from the previous job to current hobbies and activities. It appears that the most important condition for an individual to adjust well to retirement is the maintenance of activity—doing something.

Often after retirement, a number of individuals begin to undertake formal and informal educational training, for example, obtaining a college degree or enrolling in a program such as *Elderhostel* (see Chapter 7). But it must be stressed that an individual must have economic resources and good health to pursue these activities.

On the negative side, research (L.K. George et al., 1984) does indicate that two of the major negative aspects of retirement are (1) increased psychosomatic complaints for both males and females, and (2) decreased income. For example, the increase in psychosomatic complaints can be attributed to stress resulting from worry over one's economic situation, one's health, a lack of satisfying social/interpersonal relationships, and missing one's previous job. A study by C. W. Aldwin, Levenson, and Ekerdt (1987) suggests that even when physical health is accounted for, retirees report more negative psychological symptoms than do those working, with older workers reporting the fewest symptoms. Moreover, those who retired both early and late reported more symptoms than those who retired at age 65. It must be remembered that these findings are adjusted for the effects of physical health, and thus this study suggests that retirement may pose problems for many men. That older workers reported the fewest mental health difficulties suggests that they may underestimate the impact retirement has on them, highlighting the importance of preretirement education as a means of identifying potential problems in adjusting to retirement.

Often, reasons for adjustment problems after retirement differ as a function of previous occupational level. For example, Riley, Foner, and Associates (1968) found that former managers and executives have difficulty in adjusting to retirement at first, because they feel a significant loss of power and status. On the other hand, even though blue-collar workers report a greater readiness to retire since they are not emotionally tied to their jobs, they are less likely to want to retire and have extreme difficulties in adjusting to retirement. There are two primary reasons for this. First, their income level while working generally does not allow them to save large amounts of funds for use during their retirement years, and second, they do not often develop hobbies and leisure activities during adulthood.

In this respect, retirement can create a number of difficulties. While working in retirement may be satisfying and enable persons to maintain a higher income, if they receive social security benefits, they are penalized for earning extra income up to a certain point (regarding level and age). On the other hand, they may literally not be able to *not* work in retirement; such pressures force persons to keep working while retired (Boaz, 1987) or to delay retirement altogether, particularly if they are self-employed or hold lower-paying jobs. Robinson et al. (1985) note that persons who are unemployed (more common among blacks and minorities) become discouraged and often "retire" from this unemployed state rather than from a job. This may apply to as many as 20 percent of all early retirees (Lauriant & Rabin, 1976; V. Reno, 1976; Robinson et al., 1985).

In conclusion, for some individuals, retirement can be a difficult and stressful event. For others, retirement can be extremely positive, a time that they can dedicate full-time to hobbies and leisure activities. In general, individuals with economic security, in good health, who have a positive attitude toward retirement and a willingness to retire live out a life-style they enjoy, and adjustment comes much easier.

Next, our discussion will center on the effects of retirement upon society. Society in this case refers to other individuals in society, other workers in the company, and society's institutions.

SOCIETY

As was the case in our discussion of the effects of retirement upon the individual, the decision to retire has implications for the overall society and members of that society, both positive and negative. Our goal will be to highlight some of these implications. Many of these are similar to those discussed with regard to increased longevity.

One of the major implications retirement has upon society is in the area of allocation of economic resources within the society. In general, retirees draw upon the pension system, such as the company retirement plan or social security, while they do not contribute funds into the system (Reynolds, Masters, & Moser, 1987). Further, retired individuals have needs for goods and services (senior centers, recreational facilities, housing) that often require a reallocation of goods and services from other groups or programs in the society, for example, preschool programs and educational institutions/programs.

Another societal aspect of retirement is that it affects the industry or company both positively and negatively. On the positive side, it allows the company a somewhat objective yet arbitrary method (chronological age) of replacing higher-paid, older employees with lower-paid, younger employees (Robinson et al., 1985). Further, chronological age as the sole criteria for a retirement decision affects all workers equally, since they will all eventually reach that age. This has an advantage for the company in that it provides a practical administrative procedure that is objective, impersonal, and impartial and that avoids potential charges of discrimination, favoritism, and bias (Donahue, Orbach, & Pollack, 1960).

On the negative side, organizations must provide economic support in terms of contributions to the pension plan, medical insurance, and life insurance for individuals who are no longer producing for the company. From the company's perspective, retirees are taking from the system but are not contributing to it. Employers may offer early retirement programs, but such programs can be costly. They may be faced with workers whose skills have become obsolete or feel pressure from older and younger workers for such programs (Robinson et al., 1985).

With regard to others in society, there are also advantages and disadvantages to retirement. For other employees within the retiree's organization, retirement allows for upward mobility in terms of position and pay increases and allows for orderly and planned progression of workers throughout all levels of the organization.

At the same time, these younger workers who have occupied the positions vacated by the retirees now have the greater responsibility and demands of these higher positions. Further, they must contribute to the pension system and benefits system in order to support the retirees. The same can be said regarding other workers in society. That is, as they are working, they are contributing to the support of individuals who are not working.

A good exercise to facilitate discussion about retirement might be to list all the possible implications, advantages, and disadvantages of your own eventual retirement for others and society in general. Then have the entire class discuss everyone's ideas. Perhaps we should abolish retirement . . . or should we?

Retirement affects not only the individual retiring but also many other individuals (friends, family—see Chapter 9) and society as well. For both men and women, retirement does not result in as many negative consequences as is usually thought, though the major negative effect of retirement appears to be in terms of decreased economic resources. Finally, there are many individual differences in reasons why people decide to retire, as well as in adjustment to retirement. In the next section of this chapter, our discussion will focus on a related topic—leisure activities along the life span and life-styles among the retired. Many assume that these two issues go together—that when one retires, leisure activities become more important to help "fill up" one's time. This is clearly inaccurate, as we shall see.

LEISURE

One of the major consequences thought to accompany retirement is a dramatic increase in the amount of time potentially available for leisure pursuits and activities (Burrus-Bammel & Bammel, 1985; Glamser & Hayslip, 1985; Robinson et al., 1985). Sessions and discussions of leisure activities are often part of many companies' retirement preparation programs (see Box 11.2).

In this section, we shall define leisure and discuss the life-span trends in leisure activities and the relationship of leisure to retirement. In order to discuss leisure meaningfully, we must first define the term.

Definition of Leisure   Defining **leisure** adequately has been a major roadblock in research to date; it is difficult to define leisure, since one person's leisure activity may be an occupation to another (Burrus-Bammel & Bammel, 1985). Leisure may be a state of mind—relaxation. For example, let's suppose someone's primary occupation is that of bank manager, whose hobby or leisure activity is being a coin collector and dealer. Should this be considered a leisure activity, since it is related both to the primary occupation and involves making money? Or, consider a lawyer who for leisure activity travels around the country visiting law schools—is this leisure? Leisure may be inherently **(intrinsically)** satisfying, or it may lead to the attainment of some other goal **(instrumental)**.

For our purposes, we will define leisure activity as any activity in which individuals engage during their free time (Kubanoff, 1980). These activities may or may not involve relaxation in an obvious sense. Moreover, this definition does not distinguish between activities that are related to the job and those that are not—nor whether the activity involves purely self-enjoyment (intrinsic) or earning money (instrumental). Further, the definition does not distinguish between one's choosing to have leisure time (such as taking time off from work or spending weekends or evenings engaged in an activity) or whether the leisure time was imposed (the result of being laid off from work or being forcibly retired). As work becomes more intrinsically meaningful, the distinction between leisure and work is more difficult to make.

Types of Leisure Activities   Though almost any activity one engages in can be considered a leisure activity, researchers generally group leisure activities into one of four major categories (Bosse & Ekerdt, 1981; Glamser & Hayslip, 1985;

Gordon, Gaitz, & Scott, 1976). These are (1) *cultural,* such as attendance at sporting events, church and religious meetings, clubs, and going to the movies; (2) *physical,* including bowling, camping, fishing, gardening, golf, hunting, odd jobs around the home; (3) *social,* such as playing cards, drinking with friends at a bar/club, visiting with family or relatives, visiting with friends or neighbors, going to parties; and (4) *solitary,* including reading the Bible, books, magazines, newspapers, listening to the radio, and watching television.

Learning to Live with Leisure   Americans have generally subscribed to what is often described as the **Protestant work ethic,** which views work as sacred and something to be engaged in and enjoyed. Basically, one is expected to be a working and contributing member of society. For this reason, leisure and leisure activities have generally been equated with idleness or something that can only be engaged in by the young and retirees. For example, Hooker and Ventis (1984) found a commitment to the work ethic to relate negatively to life satisfaction in retirees. Therefore, we have been made to feel guilty about actively engaging in leisure activities—that is, not working and enjoying ourselves. In fact, many Americans do not know how to relax when they are not working at their jobs. (Nor do many know how to relax while *on* the job!) For example, on their days off, they mow the lawn, paint the house, and so forth.

As life expectancy increases, the number of individuals who take early retirement increases, and the work week shortens for adults, leisure activities and their development will become of greater importance (Burrus-Bammel & Bammel, 1985). In fact, Ripley and O'Brien (1976) believe that future generations will have to learn how to "live with leisure."

The Importance of Leisure Competence

Leisure competence implies understanding the meaning of leisure for you personally as well as acting on (becoming involved in meaningful leisure activities) that understanding. As with retirement, it is perhaps best to state that the development of leisure competence (Peacock & Talley, 1985) is itself a learning *process.* People do not suddenly become aware of leisure in retirement. This process approach has the advantage of reframing retirement more positively, rather than seeing the "problem" of retirement as one of developing leisure activities.

YOUNG ADULTHOOD

During young adulthood, leisure activities are important because they provide a means of relaxation from the daily pressures experienced on the job, at home, and in the family. For instance, consider an individual who works as a stockbroker in a high-pressure situation for eight hours a day, followed by a one-hour commute home every evening through high-density traffic. This individual may enjoy getting away from those pressures by engaging in fishing at a quiet pond.

Another reason leisure is important is because it may allow the individual a means of self-actualization or fulfillment. Since individuals often enter fields or jobs that they may not be interested in, leisure activities may serve as a method of compensation for the lack of self-fulfillment attainable on the job. An example of this would be an individual who always wanted to be an artist but was constantly told he or she could not achieve economic security in that endeavor. This individual, in order to achieve some economic security, obtains a degree in a field such as accounting or engineering but spends leisure time painting.

Leisure activities provide a social outlet for meeting others with similar interests, such as stamp collecting, flying, bowling, and dancing. It should be noted that this function of leisure activities may be especially important for females, primarily due to the fact that in most instances women outlive their husbands. For this reason it may be especially important that females develop leisure activities and friendship networks independent of their husbands during adulthood that can be maintained after the death of their spouses.

MIDDLE ADULTHOOD

In addition to those factors that are important during adulthood, during middle adulthood leisure activities begin to assume other purposes. Leisure activities begin to fill in time and allow for the development of other roles, while previous roles and activities such as those related to the job may be lessening (J.R. Kelly, Steinkamp, & J.R. Kelly, 1986).

Further, leisure may provide opportunities for meaningful and purposeful activities in the middle-aged years if work and family commitments have lessened. For instance, rather than having to take children to their activities, such as Little League, ballet class, and so forth, individuals now have the time to pursue their own activities.

Leisure activities may also provide an outlet where social relationships can be developed and maintained. It is important that individuals develop and maintain leisure activities during young and middle adulthood. As we shall discuss in later sections of this chapter, there are a number of positive relationships between finding fulfilling leisure activities, life satisfaction, and adjustment to retirement in older adults (Palmore, 1979). For these reasons, it is important to at least begin to develop leisure activities in adulthood that can be continued into retirement.

LATE ADULTHOOD

In order to discuss the importance of leisure activities during later adulthood, it is important to discuss briefly two theories that have differing views regarding activity level during old age. These are **disengagement theory** and **activity theory**. These theories have also been identified in Chapter 10 as crucial to the understanding of the relationship between personality and adjustment to aging.

Disengagement Theory This theory, which was formulated by Cumming and Henry (1961), proposes that as individuals approach and enter later maturity, there is a natural tendency to psychologically and socially withdraw (or disengage) from the environment. This withdrawal is stimulated by increased awareness of our own mortality. In a sense, individuals begin to prepare for ultimate disengagement, that is, death.

Cumming and Henry assumed this tendency to withdraw or disengage was natural and mutual (society withdraws from the aging individual) and resulted from changes in certain internal processes that were inherent factors of aging, implying that the need to disengage is almost intrinsic. Moreover, they assumed that in order to successfully age, one had to disengage. Disengagement was assumed to begin for females with the departure of the last child from the home and for males with retirement. Since its original formulation, the theory has been reformulated somewhat to accommodate individual differences in the extent of disengagement (see Chapter 10).

Activity Theory   Activity theory stands in a direct juxtaposition to disengagement theory and assumes there is a positive relationship between activity and life satisfaction. That is, while aging individuals confront inevitable physiological, anatomical, and health changes, their sociopsychological needs remain essentially unchanged. Therefore, the older individual who manages to resist withdrawal from the social world and remains active will maintain life satisfaction. This theory proclaims that the individual who is able to maintain activities for as long as possible will be well adjusted and satisfied with life in later years. For example, one substitutes hobbies for occupation, or new friends for lost friends.

Though activity theory sounds appealing, it has some inherent problems (as does disengagement theory). For example, activity theory views individuals as having a great deal of control over their situation, which is not always the case. That is, the theory assumes all individuals have the ability to construct or reconstruct their lives by substituting new roles and activities for lost ones.

When we discuss life-span trends in activities, it will be interesting to note which theory receives more experimental support.

Life-span Trends in Leisure Activities

Prior to discussing leisure activities during the various segments of the life cycle, it is important to note that the factors that affect leisure activities are complex and varied (J.R. Kelly, Steinkamp, & J.R. Kelly, 1986). Thus, we will first highlight some of the major factors that affect an individual's choice and ability in engaging in leisure activities across the life span.

FACTORS THAT AFFECT LEISURE ACTIVITIES

Research indicates that (1) leisure activities vary according to age or period of the life cycle and (2) these activities are at all points of the life cycle related to a number of factors. The major factors affecting leisure behavior are income level, personality, interest, health condition, ability level, transportation, education level, and a number of social characteristics (Burrus-Bammel & Bammel, 1985; J.R. Kelly, 1975; 1983a, 1983b).

Each of these factors can play a significant role in the selection of and participation in leisure activities. For instance, you may wish to spend your leisure time vacationing at the seashore. However, if you cannot afford a trip of this nature nor have the means of transportation to get to the seashore, it will be extremely doubtful that you can undertake such activity.

Though often overlooked, transportation has a profound impact on an individual's quality of life, life-style, and participation in a variety of activities, especially for older adults. Adequate transportation allows the individual access to shopping facilities, medical services, social contacts with others, and participation in activities of all types. A lack of available transportation affects a large percentage of older adults (Carp, 1970).

Over the course of the life span, leisure activities change according to the current needs, abilities, and health condition of the individual (Burrus-Bammel & Bammel, 1985). It must always be remembered that there are vast individual differences in personal choice of leisure activities at all points along the life cycle. Overall, the three most important factors in determining leisure activities appear to be health, economic resources, and time available (Kaplan, 1975). Having someone to do something with and viewing leisure positively are also very important.

There appear to be common types of leisure activities individuals engage in unique to each phase of the life cycle (Gordon et al., 1976; H.S. Kaplan, 1975; Moran, 1979). There are also some forms of leisure activities common at all points along the life cycle (J.R. Kelly, 1983a).

YOUNG ADULTHOOD

During adulthood the majority of leisure activities tend to be **active** in nature and focus outside the home. These include such activities as exercising, jogging, playing sports, and going to movies, bars, and restaurants. The primary focus of these leisure activities is active "doing" and/or participation.

Many adults also spend time in **passive** leisure activities such as reading, watching television, or just relaxing. But the majority of the types of activities in which adults participate are of the active type.

Adults report that they engage in leisure activities for various reasons. These include personal interest, a means of coping with pressure and stress, and a source of meeting individuals with similar interests. Overall, adults stress the importance of interest and meaningfulness in the selection of their leisure activities (J.R. Kelly, 1983a).

MIDDLE ADULTHOOD

Middle age serves as a transition stage between the *active leisure* orientation of young adulthood and the *passive leisure* style of later adulthood. Individuals begin reducing the frequency of action-oriented activities, such as participation in sports, and increasing the frequency of passive-oriented activities, such as reading.

There are two primary reasons for this change. First, decreasing physical and health conditions may limit participation in action-oriented activities for some persons. Second, individuals begin to select activities that they can continue into later adulthood. Often, these new activities are somewhat related to the activities of young adulthood. For example, instead of playing softball, the individual now spends leisure time being an umpire; instead of long-distance jogging, the individual takes up walking or hiking.

Further, middle-aged individuals often engage in leisure activities such as participation in civil organizations or social clubs, or enroll in adult education courses. These adult education courses often deal with subjects and topics such individuals have always had an interest in but have never had the time or opportunity to explore. These topics range from academic areas to genealogy and astrology.

LATER ADULTHOOD

Though some older adults are engaged in active leisure activities, such as jogging and exercising, the majority of older adults are primarily engaged in passive leisure activities (C. Gordon, Gaitz, & Scott, 1976). These include activities such as watching television, reading, or socializing with friends (Glamser & Hayslip, 1985). In many instances older adults must develop new leisure activities because of economic and physical/health factors that reduce the opportunity for the continuation of their former leisure activities (Moran, 1979).

It is important to note that participation in activities is critical to the maintenance of positive feelings toward the "self" (Cottrell, 1962). This implies that leisure competence is itself an important construct in understanding adulthood. In order to facilitate positive self-identity and adjustment, there must be some interest, commitment, and personal investment in these activities. That is, the activity must be viewed as worthwhile rather than as simply something to occupy time. As we discussed above, such a perspective on one's leisure defines leisure competence (see Box 11.3).

LEISURE RESEARCH IN ADULTHOOD

Though individuals at all stages of the life cycle participate in similar types of leisure activities, the overall frequency of participation decreases with age. Additionally, there is a general shift from action-oriented activities to passive-oriented activities with age.

Glamser and Hayslip (1985) conducted a longitudinal investigation of the impact of retirement on participation in leisure activities. One hundred and thirty-two male workers aged 60 years plus (most were employed in semiskilled positions) were surveyed with regard to the types and frequency of their leisure activities participation. Activities were arranged into one of four major categories (see above): (1) cultural, (2) physical, (3) social, and (4) solitary. A follow-up survey was conducted 6 years later among the 110 surviving retirees from the original sample; a total of 82 individuals completed the follow-up survey.

Glamser and Hayslip (1985) found that during the six-year period, the overall level of leisure activity declined. However, there was a substantial amount of individual change in leisure activity and substantial social disengagement following retirement. Further, results indicated that the greatest decline was in social activities, followed by cultural, then physical activities. Interestingly, stability across time was found for the physical category. The most common pattern was continued *non*participation.

Similar results were reported by Mobily, Leslie, Lemke, Wallace, and Kohout (1986) in a cross-sectional study of rural elderly. That is, males and females over age 74 engaged in fewer activities than those under age 74. Further, there were significant gender differences in activity participation. Females engaged primarily in home-centered activities such as baking or sewing; males tended to report outdoor activities such as fishing and hunting.

J.R. Kelly et al. (1986) investigated leisure activities in four age-groups—40 to 54 years, 55 to 64 years, 65 to 74 years, and 75 years plus—in a small midwestern city. These researchers identified 28 kinds of leisure, which were reduced to 8 major types, as well as assessing overall activity level. These types of leisure were cultural leisure, travel, exercise and sport, family leisure, outdoor recreation, social activities, community organizations, and home-based activities.

Results are graphically represented in Figure 11.1. As this figure indicates, there was both continuity and change in leisure activities with age. In terms of change, there was a decline in overall activity level, sport and exercise, and outdoor recreation with age. Furthermore, there was continuity in a number of core activities such as family, social, and home-based activity.

BOX 11.3

RELIGION

One commonly held belief about the aging population is that as we get older, we get more religious, and that older adults spend a significant segment of their leisure time in religious activities. Research is unclear on this issue due to an inherent confound in the most frequently used measure of religiousness (level of religious feelings or beliefs), which is church attendance. That is, though frequency of church attendance would appear to be a reliable indicator of religiousness, it may not be for older adults. Such a measure is unreliable for older adults due to the fact that poor health, physical disabilities, or lack of transportation may prevent them from attending church services at all. Therefore, using church attendance as the measure of religiousness may give an inaccurate (underestimated) picture of religiousness in older adults.

For example, Moberg (1972) found that in old age there was a noticeable decline in religious activities outside the home, but self-reported "religious feelings" increased with age. Additionally, Moberg found religious involvement was positively related to life satisfaction and morale in old age.

Aware of the potential confound of using church attendance as an indicator of religiousness in older adults, Markides (1983a) conducted a longitudinal study to examine age changes in religiousness among two cultural groups, Mexican Americans and Anglos. Religiousness was measured using three separate factors: church attendance, self-rated religiousness, and the practice of prayer. Results indicated older Mexican Americans were "more religious" on all three variables than older Anglo adults; females were more religious than males in both ethnic groups. For both ethnic groups, church attendance declined with age, but the other two measures of religiousness were somewhat stable over time (four years). Therefore, Markides (1983a) and others suggest religiousness remains fairly constant across the life span, rather than increasing or decreasing substantially with advancing age, despite ethnic, individual, and denominational differences in religiousness in old age.

Finally, results indicated that for the 40 to 54 and 55 to 64 age-groups, the most common types of leisure activities were travel and cultural activities. For the 65 to 74 age-group, social and travel activities predominated, and for the oldest age-group (75 years plus), the most common leisure activities were family and home-based activities.

While these studies all support to some extent the basic tenets of disengagement theory, one cannot underestimate the importance of individ-

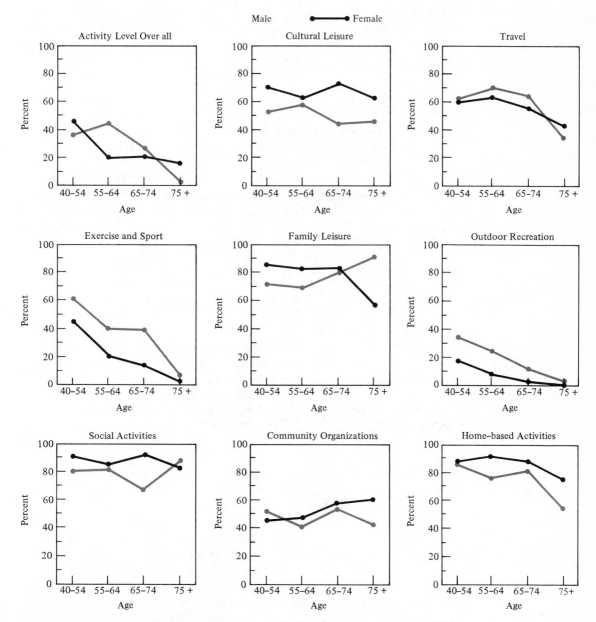

Figure 11.1 Percentages of individuals engaging in high levels of activity. *Source:* J. R. Kelly, M. W. Steinkamp, & J. R. Kelly. (1986). Later life leisure: how they play in Peoria. *The Gerontologist, 26,* 533. Reprinted with permission of the publisher.

ual differences in the amount of disengagement among older adults. Further, one must assume that current leisure involvement is satisfying. McGuire, Dottavio, & O'Leary (1986) identified *limiting* factors and *prohibitory* factors in a study of outdoor recreational activities across the life span. Limiting factors reduce participation while prohibiting factors block it altogether. Most persons, regardless of age, stressed that lack of time, people, and poor health were the major leisure constraints both limiting and prohibiting activities, with health taking on more importance with age. Interestingly, income, safety, access to transportation, and lack of information did not change across age levels. While lack of money seemed to affect most, time was an issue especially to middle-aged persons, and not having a companion increased as a barrier among older adults.

Patterns of Leisure During Retirement

Recently, there has been interest in studying life-styles of individuals during retirement since a number of investigations have documented that later-life adaptation is strongly related to activity and social contexts outside the home (Palmore, 1979). These life-styles are often referred to as **leisure life-styles**.

This area of research is relatively new. We are only beginning to scratch the surface in obtaining information about life-styles in retirement. It should be remembered that life-styles are affected by individual differences in health, social support, education, and economic resources (Burrus-Bammel & Bammel, 1985).

TYPES OF LEISURE LIFE-STYLES

Perhaps one of the most extensive studies of life-styles among retired persons was conducted by N.J. Osgood (1983), who studied the types (patterns) of retirement life-styles found in residents of age-segregated retirement communities in Florida and Arizona. Data was obtained from in-depth interviews in three retirement communities: a mobile home community in Florida populated primarily by blue-collar workers, a condominium complex of all Jewish upper middle class retirees in Florida, and a self-sufficient community of detached dwelling units (private houses) in Arizona comprised primarily of retired workers from the West and Midwest.

Six major types or patterns of residents were found within these communities. These types are presented in Table 11.1. As this table indicates, the majority of residents were classified as either *joiners, socializers, humanitarians,* or *recreationalists*.

Though results of this study should be considered tentative and could vary as a function of geographic regions and socioeconomic status, they do begin to build an important data base for future leisure programming, of which there is great need (Burrus-Bammel & Bammel, 1985). This information regarding the life-styles and interests of residents of retirement communities is also important because as more people live to advanced old age and move to retirement communities, planners and developers will require information for appropriate planning and design, as well as knowledge of what types of services and activities should be available for residents.

Fontana (1977) classified individuals from varied socioeconomic levels at a senior citizens center in a small city as relaxers, joiners, do-gooders, and waiters. These types basically correspond to Osgood's classification of recreationalists, joiners or socializers, humanitarians, and retirees. Fontana also classified elderly poor from the inner city as waiters, sitters, and drifters.

Obviously while there are many characteristic life-styles during retire-

TABLE 11.1

PATTERNS OF RETIREMENT FOUND IN THREE AGE-SEGREGATED RETIREMENT COMMUNITIES

Pattern/Type	Approximate Percentage	Characteristics
Organizers	10–15%	1. devote all their time and energy to formally organizing various clubs, organizations, activities, projects, classes, and meetings 2. extremely dedicated to community and want to make the community the kind of place they can be proud of and enjoy living in 3. busy and active all day 4. usually healthier and younger members of the community
Joiners		1. join and take part in formal activities developed by the "organizers" 2. very active; plan their day around preferred activities, clubs, meetings, etc.
Socializers		1. gregarious, friendly, spend days informally socializing with friends and neighbors 2. not active in formal clubs, activities, and organizations 3. respected for their friendliness and helpfulness
Humanitarians	70–80%	1. constantly assisting and helping others in the community, usually older and in worse health 2. overall, devote all their time and energy to helping the less fortunate
Recreationalists		1. constantly engaging in numerous and various leisure-time activities such as golf, swimming, fishing, etc. 2. primarily associated with others who share similar recreational interests 3. recreation is the central focus around which their time is organized
Retirees	10–15%	1. retired from active participation in the community 2. characterized by lack of any social role 3. usually older and in worse health than other members of the community 4. with advancing age and failing health, individuals who were once in other patterns; withdrawn

Source: From N.J. Osgood. (1983). Patterns of aging in retirement communities: Typology of residents. *Journal of Applied Gerontology, 2,* 28–43.

ment, research is at present descriptive. Moreover, it has yet to incorporate other factors such as personality and family influences (see Chapters 9 and 10). However, as in the case of leisure activities, life-style after retirement seems to be affected substantially by both health and economic resources.

Comparatively speaking, little research has been conducted regarding leisure activities at all points along the life cycle; most of what is available is cross-sectional and focuses on the *level* of leisure activities versus their *meaningfulness.* One major reason for this is the fact that leisure tends to be in opposition to the traditional ethic of work in our society. The primary thrust of leisure activities during young adulthood seems to be active; middle adulthood is thought to be a transition between active and passive leisure activities. Later adulthood is characterized by primarily passive leisure activities.

SUMMARY

The focus of this chapter was on *occupational choice* and *career development, retirement,* and *leisure* across the life span. To think that we select an occupation, spend our adult years in that occupation, and eventually retire from that occupation, allowing us the free time to pursue leisure activities, is overly simplistic. Occupational selection, retirement, and leisure are quiet complex and affected by many factors such as *personality, health, education, attitudes toward work and retirement,* and *sex role expectations.*

The major theories of occupational choice are those of *Super, Holland,* and *Ginzberg.* While Super's theory is the most developmental, available work has little to say about the career development of women. A notable exception is the theory of *Astin.*

While men and women differ in career patterns, each is highly *complex* and subject to the influence of *opportunity, economic constraints, family influences,* and *decision-making skills.* While many advocate *occupational developmental tasks* particular to distinct life stages, occupational/career development (a coherent pattern of jobs) is a lifelong process, influencing and being influenced by events in other areas of one's life. While young adulthood is often an upwardly mobile occupational period, middle adulthood may or may not be occupationally stable. Some persons are more likely to change careers than are others; *flexibility* is common for some persons.

While *retirement* usually implies *disengagement* from the work role, individuals seem to go through distinct phases *(honeymoon, disenchantment, stabilization)* of adjustment to retirement. As with occupational development, the decision to retire and the impact of retirement are mediated by a number of factors.

Retirement—withdrawal either voluntarily or involuntarily from the work force—was discussed from both a theoretical and practical perspective. The major factors that influence the *decision to retire* voluntarily are both *personal* and *institutional* in nature: *health status, occupational level, economic climate, personal financial situation, age, gender, work satisfaction,* and *personal attitudes.* There are many *individual differences* in reasons for retirement, and such differences mediate the effects of retirement upon the individual, and society.

Leisure activities were operationally defined as any activities in which individuals engage during their free time, though defining leisure clearly is difficult. Developing *leisure competence* is a lifelong process. There are numerous ways to classify leisure activities, and the selection of and participation in leisure activities is affected by many factors such as personal interest, health, and economic resources. Participation in leisure activities during all segments of the life cycle seems to be important to well-being, and research indicates there are certain types of leisure activities that are characteristically engaged in by persons varying in age. Moreover, with increasing age there is a general decrease in the overall frequency of participation in activities, with a shift away *from active to more passive activities.* These patterns of leisure activity as well as *leisure life-styles* seem to be influenced by numerous factors.

KEY TERMS AND CONCEPTS

Occupational role	Occupational developmental tasks
Occupation development	Job loss
Retirement	Career crisis in midlife
Leisure	Horizontal versus vertical career moves
Disengagement theory	Institutional versus personal factors
Activity theory	in the decision to retire
Active leisure activity	Intrinsic versus instrumental leisure
Passive leisure activity	activities
Leisure life-styles	Protestant work ethic
Flexible careers	Career
Career indecision	Vocational maturity
Leisure competence	

After reading this chapter you should be able to answer the following questions:

- What is the basis for the presumed association between aging and death? What are some of the consequences of this association?
- What approaches have been taken in defining death?
- When someone says he or she is fearful of death, what might that person mean? What factors are associated with death anxiety?
- What are the various meanings of death?
- Are widows/widowers more at risk as a consequence of being bereaved? What explanations for the phenomenon have been proposed?
- What are the unique problems bereaved persons experience? Are there different sets of problems for the young adult versus the older adult?
- How has Kubler-Ross's work helped us in communicating with the dying? How has it impeded such communication?
- What is hospice? In what ways does it differ from the hospital as an alternative to the care of the terminally ill?
- Are there common factors underlying the suicides of adults of all ages? Are there unique sets of factors associated with elderly suicides?
- What is ISDB? What is its significance for the older person?

C H A P T E R · 12

DEATH AND

DYING

■

INTRODUCTION

"We all have to go sometime!"; "There are only two things for certain in this life—death and taxes!"; "Drop dead!"; "I'm dying to go."

Most of us have made these statements at one time or another. In some cases, we may have been vaguely serious about death; in others we may have been angry, depressed, or apprehensive. Perhaps we were trying to be humorous.

All of these statements and others like them, as well as the situations in which we use them, reflect the curiosity *and* repulsion we feel at the thought of our own or others' deaths. This ambivalence about death that many feel can be likened to what we might call the "wet-paint phenomenon." As we might want to touch the paint without getting our hands dirty or sticky, so too do many of us want to touch or see death but without getting too close (we may slow down to get a good look at an accident). Many (DeSpelder & Strickland, 1983; Kalish, 1985a, 1985b; R. Kastenbaum, 1978a; Kübler-Ross, 1969) have advocated confronting death and dying on a personal level so that its avoidance can be replaced by at the least an acknowledgment of the role that death plays in our daily lives.

We may be literally forced to confront death as a reality of daily life—on radio and TV and in the newspaper. It is this basic fact of our existence (that we know we will die because we are human) that argues for getting in touch with how we feel about our own and others' deaths. While death may seem distant, as something that is outside us, there is much value in not only reading and talking about death and dying but also in simply thinking about, feeling, or contemplating our death. In spite of the fact that, except in the case of suicide, we ultimately have no control over the fact or timing of our death, coming to terms with our feelings about its certainty in our lives and in the lives of those we love may gain us a measure of comfort, if not control. With these thoughts in mind, let us discuss what death is. Being able to define death per se is not only important in understanding age differences in persons' reactions to death but also relates to concerns about *life* (e.g., abortion, the death penalty, organ transplants, living wills, and euthanasia). Discussing definitions of death is also an important issue in that it may help us to understand how and why younger adults respond to both their own and others' deaths differently.

DEFINITIONS OF DEATH

What is death? In a sense, this seems an obvious enough question, yet it is a difficult notion to "pin down." Death means different things to different people. The most widely held definition of death in the United States is broadly known as the *legal-medical* definition of death. This definition is the one used by many courts of law today pertaining to whether a person is dead or alive. According to the legal-medical view, there are two types of death, and each type is based on the presence of certain criteria. The first type of death, according to the legal-medical definition, is called **clinical death**. The criteria for being considered clinically dead are having one's heart and breathing cease spontaneously; resuscitation is, however, possible. There are no reflexes. The second type of death is called **brain death,** and the criterion for being brain dead is having one's brain cells die, perhaps reflected in a flat EEG for a certain period of time (24 hours) (R. Schulz, 1978; Wass, 1979).

To these definitions, R. Schulz (1978) adds **biological** and **cerebral death**. Biological death is defined as the deterioration of various organ systems to the point where they cannot be regenerated, while cerebral death refers to the cessation of function in higher brain centers, leading to unconsciousness. Yet the individual who is cerebrally dead can breathe unaided. Memory, thought, the ability to experience, and action are, however, destroyed. Veatch (1979) talks of cerebral death in terms of the ability to think, reason, feel, and interact with others "consciously." Veatch uses the term *brain death* to refer to the loss of the brain's ability to integrate bodily systems (heart, lung) based upon the central nervous system's loss of functioning.

Pattison's Four Types of Death

Pattison (1977) has discussed a variety of definitions for death. According to Pattison, there are four types of death, each of which is independent, and, from this point of view, individuals may take weeks, months, or years before they actually die.

Pattison's first type of death is called **social death**. This type of death occurs when the person, young or old, is abandoned or isolated from others.

The second type of death, according to Pattison, which often follows social death, is **psychic death**. Here, the individual accepts his fate or impending death and seriously regresses, a very severe and personal form of withdrawal. In a sense, such persons will think themselves to death. Perhaps the best example of this form of death is what is called voodoo death; it is similar to *learned helplessness* (Seligman, 1975). Thus, in this sense, the individual is literally thought to bring about his or her own death, and severe feelings of depression and a lack of control are common among those who have died a psychic death. Pattison's definitions of *biological* and *physiological* death are similar to those discussed above.

Implications of Varying Criteria for Death

The multiple classifications of death lead to some perplexing legal and moral issues, as evidenced by a number of cases recently presented in the newspapers and on television, most notably that of Karen Ann Quinlan, who went into an irreversible coma after mixing alcohol and drugs. These legal and moral issues are beyond the scope of this text but do suggest some complex value judgments about who is dead and who is not. They, at the very least, should cause us to question that primary quality or qualities that define what *life* is.

The difficulties principally created by these definitions are that the criteria for death obviously do not provide any universal basis for a scientific decision about death. Moreover, the criteria vary by state; they may also be interpreted differently by different persons (physicians, family). For example, a person thought to be in an irreversible coma can be revived (the coma could be drug induced) or can breathe independently, as in the Karen Ann Quinlan case. (Karen Quinlan lived for *ten* years after being disconnected from her respirator.) By one standard (brain death), the individual is dead. By another (clinical death), the person is alive.

In 1968, the *Harvard Ad Hoc Committee to Examine the Definition of Brain Death* was formed and defined death to include (1) unresponsivity, (2) no movements or breathing, (3) no reflexes, and (4) a flat EEG for 24 hours. By these standards (i.e., brain death), the person who is in a deep coma could be considered dead!

The multiple definitions of death also raise "gray" issues as to *who* should make the decision about when a life has ceased to exist. Given that death is *not* an all-or-nothing phenomenon (see Pattison, 1977), the *point* at which death is defined as occurring is a *moral* decision, *not* a *technical* or scientific one (see Veatch, 1979). It is at this point that the *value* that a person's life has comes into play. At what point has the individual's life reached the point where that person is not worth reviving by extraordinary means?

Beyond the purely physiological level, when we are forced to make such decisions, we thus bring into play the worth that we place on an individual's life, particularly if that person is elderly. Do persons near death look forward to it? Would they sooner live than die? What does death subjectively mean to them? It is to these topics that we now turn.

PERSONAL MEANINGS OF DEATH

As noted above, death may be seen as the ultimate loss in our lives. One might ask, what does one lose through death?

Death As Loss   As Kalish (1976, 1985a) has noted, death per se may involve losses of several kinds:

1. loss of ability to have experiences
2. loss of ability to predict subsequent events (after death)
3. loss of the body
4. loss of the ability to care for dependents
5. losses suffered by family and friends
6. loss of the opportunity to complete plans and projects
7. loss of being in a relatively painful state

Punishment and Release   In addition to seeing death in terms of losses (some of which can be seen in a positive light, e.g., losing a painful existence), Kalish discusses several other meanings that death may take on for elderly persons in particular. Punishment for one's sins is one of these, presumably linked to one's feelings about the afterlife, though as we discussed above, concerns about the afterlife seem to be fairly infrequent among older, terminally ill persons. Reynolds and Kalish (1976) found that while older persons generally equated moral goodness with a longer life span, a majority of those surveyed (regardless of age) saw death (particularly accidental death) as retribution, rather than seeing a long life as a reward. Obviously, when the older person who is dying has suffered a great deal, sudden death may be seen as a release from unbearable or protracted pain (Kalish & Reynolds, 1976).

Death As Transition   Death in this sense may mean that the person sees death as a "stopping off point"; that what may or may not happen afterwards is really more important. Reynolds and Kalish (1976) have also found that older persons, relative to the young, expected and wanted to live longer, possibly indicating that their feelings about the afterlife were negative, perhaps mediated by religiousness. Kalish (1976) suggests that those elderly who are more religious have *lower* death anxiety; Wass, Christian, Myers, & M. Murphy (1978–1979) concur. Wass (1979) and R. Kastenbaum and P. Costa (1977), however, point out that religiousness–fear of death relations are likely to be *complex*, dependent upon how each concept is measured. If, for example, persons are highly religious, they may fear death as anticipated punishment for sin or see death as a reward for a good life (see above). However, persons who are not religious presumably have nothing to fear in this sense. Nevertheless, the fact that they will not exist in any meaningful way may evoke a great deal of anxiety in these persons.

Death and the Use of Time   In addition to death as loss and as punishment for one's sins, Kalish (1976) sees death as an event that makes the dimension of *time* meaningful, as well as helping us to order our lives. Without such a marker, nothing would be any more important than anything else! Thus, goals/accomplishments—indeed, our whole sense of the past, present, and future as it reflects on our sense of who we are and our relationships with others—become meaningful to the extent that we know we will not live forever.

For some elderly persons, simply living life on a day-to-day basis may become more important than being preoccupied with future goals/plans, as we often are prone to be, especially when our lives seem to stretch out before us. Many aged persons seem to be able to balance the past-future aspects of their lives (Stevens-Long, 1984). Stevens-Long (1984) has also noted that available literature definitely rejects the notion that as one ages, time, supposedly representing a smaller portion of one's total life, passes more quickly. While J. A. Peterson (1980) speculates that a sense of time pressure creates a great deal of stress for many middle-aged persons, Bascue and Lawrence (1977) have found older persons *turn away* from the future; they interpret this as a means of coping with death anxiety.

RESPONSES TO DEATH

Fear of Death

We have alluded to **death anxiety** in our above discussion of the meanings that death may have. Persons respond to death differently in part because death means different things to them. We will now explore a *response to* death that is of central concern to researchers and laypersons alike, reflected in the meaning of the statement, "I am afraid of death." While fear and anxiety are not the only ways in which we respond to our death (R. Kastenbaum & Aisenberg, 1976), these reactions have received considerable research attention within the last 15 years. They are certainly responses to death that psychologists and counselors have invested a great deal of time and energy in understanding.

What might persons mean when they say they are fearful of death? While some might express anxiety over the variety of losses thought to accompany death (see above), others may value the loss of *control* over their everyday lives that may come about as a function of *dying* (see Kalish, 1976; Wass, 1979), or being isolated from others in an institutional setting (nursing home, hospital). While institutional care may be the only option for some families, dying in such situations can be very depersonalizing, and everyday decisions persons are accustomed to making on their own may no longer be possible (how one's time is to be spent, what possessions one is permitted to keep). This issue of control has important implications in the development of alternatives to traditional hospital care for dying older persons, as we shall see later on in our discussion.

Multiple Death Fears

Research on the meaning of death, as well as responses to death, suggests that both are *multidimensional* (many-faceted). Thus, *death* issues must be separated from those relating to the *dying process*. Furthermore, fears about one's *own* death may differ from those surrounding significant *others'* deaths per se and/or *dying* (see R. Schulz, 1978; R. Kastenbaum & P. Costa, 1977; Simpson, 1979). These concerns *may* or *may not* surface at a conscious level of awareness. Thus, as R. Kastenbaum and P. Costa (1977) have noted, an absence of death fear at a conscious level of awareness may simply reflect the person's success at denial, in which case such anxieties may surface at a covert, unconscious level (Hayslip & Stewart-Bussey, 1986). The individual may have physical complaints, have difficulty sleeping, experience changes in eating habits, have difficulty in completing a task, or show an overconcern with the welfare of others (R. Kastenbaum, 1985). In such cases, individuals do not report being anxious or concerned about death or dying but inexplicably experience a number of these difficulties (Wass, 1979). Moreover, a change may occur in an individual's behavior (an easy-to-get-along-with person becomes difficult to relate to). What may underlie many of these behaviors in older persons (R. Kastenbaum, 1978a) is an awareness that death is near; such feelings may create inner turmoil or evoke behavior designed to finish "unfinished business" (Kübler-Ross, 1974a).

Quite possibly, an individual's inability to explain these symptoms can create other difficulties, themselves secondary to death but nonetheless disturbing. For example, physical complaints and sleeplessness can be interpreted as symptomatic of a genuine physical illness (Eisdorfer & Stotsky, 1977). These symptoms ironically resist treatment because they fulfill a psychic function—they allow one to express concerns or fears in an acceptable manner to oneself or to others.

Research reviewed by Wass (1977), Neimeyer (1987) and by R. Kastenbaum and P. Costa (1977) suggests that, in spite of the usual assumption to the contrary, elderly persons do not *report* fearing **death** per se. They do, however, fear to a great degree the **dying** *process*—dying in pain, dying alone, loss of control over everyday events or bodily functions. Where these fears are clearly apparent, ending one's own life may be seen as preferable for some individuals to suffering a painful, lonely death, as we shall see later.

Recent findings on the complex nature of death fear and age support the view that fear of death may reflect *many* concerns. Hayslip, Pinder, and Lumsden (1981), Fiefel and Branscomb (1973), Fiefel and Nagy (1981), and Pinder and Hayslip (1981) have found that while older persons *and* younger persons did not differ in consciously expressed death fear, there were substantial age differences in covertly measured death concerns (fears of losing others, pain/suffering, loss of goals/achievements, loss of control). In this case, the differences suggested that older persons expressed more covert death fear than did the young but less overt fear.

Findings indicating an accepting attitude toward death by the aged (a lack of self-reported fear) have been found by Jeffers, Nichols, and Eisdorfer (1961), Rhudick and Dibner (1961), J. Roberts, Kimsey, Logan, and Shaw (1970), Swenson (1961), Fiefel and Branscomb (1973), and Templer, Ruff, and Frank (1971).

More recently, Conte, Weiner, and Plutchik (1982) have attempted to construct an easily administered, short measure of death anxiety. In so doing, they found no age differences utilizing items that were straightforward in their intent (e.g., "Do you worry about dying?" "Do you worry that you may be alone when you are dying?"). Assuming that fears about death are complex and may or may not be expressed in an open, overt manner, one must view such attempts to get at one's fears with suspicion. The question seems to revolve around how threatening death/dying actually is and how able and/or willing someone would be to communicate feelings about death. This is obviously not an easy question to answer and certainly reflects a belief in the influence of unconscious processes on our behavior. If, therefore, one's conscious fears about death and dying cannot be admitted, they may be denied altogether and "show up" somewhere else (displaced) (e.g., wanting things to be in order, difficulty in finishing a task, physical complaints).

Factors That Influence Death Anxiety

Rather than age per se, factors such as *health status* (reflected in one's perceived *distance from death*) or *anxiety* may play a more important role in explaining death concerns in the aged (R. Kastenbaum, 1985; McCrae, Bartone, & P. Costa, 1976). While a variety of other factors, in addition to health and anxiety, interact with the age–death anxiety relationship, findings do not always present a consistent picture. Persons who are *alone* and/or *institutionalized,* living in an *urban* setting, who have *poor mental health,* who are *female,* and who are *poorly educated* are all likely to *report* fearing death (Mullins and Lopez, 1982; Wass et al., 1978–1979). Studies by B. Bell and Patterson (1979), Christ (1961), and Swenson (1961), however, indicate an *absence* of a relationship between death fears and such factors as *retirement, life satisfaction, religiousness, socioeconomic status,* and *sex.* Moreover, *ethnic* variations in the expression of death fears have been observed by Kalish and Reynolds (1976) and by Bengston, Cuellar, and Ragan (1977).

As noted earlier, older persons' feelings related to death are sometimes an outgrowth of specific occurrences in their lives, such as being relocated from one's home to a nursing home, failing health, or the loss of one's spouse.

Kalish (1985a) suggests that a number of aspects of death awareness increase as one ages. Older persons are likely to have had more death experiences (parents, siblings, friends) than younger persons. This has several consequences: (1) the future seems more definite rather than being infinite (when we are very young, being 60 seems a long way off!); (2) older persons may see themselves as less worthy *because* their future is more limited; (3) desirable roles are closed off to them; and (4) not knowing what to do with one's "bonus time" on earth, one may think that one has already "used up" what years were available. Research reviewed by R. Kastenbaum (1985) tends to support a relationship between more death anxiety and an uneasiness with time. Lastly, as more friends and relatives die, older persons become more attuned to sadness and loneliness and to signals from their bodies that say that death is near (Kalish, 1985a).

P. Keith (1979) examined the relationship between life changes (marital status, health, church involvement, informal family or friendship contacts) and elderly persons' response patterns toward life and death. Persons' responses to such changes were classified as (1) *positivists*—those whose life goals were fulfilled and for whom death was not to be feared; (2) *negativists*—those who feared death and saw it as something that cut short their time on earth, (3) *activists*—who saw death as a foreclosing of ambition, even though valued goals had been achieved, and (4) *passivists*—who saw death as a respite from life's disappointments and for whom death was actually a positive adjustment to life. P. Keith (1979) found those experiencing the *most discontinuity* to be more frequently *negativists* or *passivists.* Women tended to be more accepting of death than did men. Changes in marital status and in health tended to elicit negativism in men only. Religiousness tended to produce positivist responses in women. Those with higher incomes tended to be positivists, whereas those with lower incomes tended to be passivists (especially where the spouse was ill) or negativists. Less formal/informal activity was associated with passivism. Given the fact that a substantial proportion of older persons favor euthanasia (see Wass, 1979; Mathieu & Peterson, 1970), such feelings may reflect the value they place on ending their own lives.

It is interesting to note here that, contrary to much research in this area, Ward (1980) did *not* find elderly people to generally favor euthanasia. Those who did so, however, tended to be in poorer health, more dissatisfied with their lives, and more anomic (feeling estranged from others, giving up). Those with less formal education and more religiousness tended to be the most rejecting of active euthanasia. Ward postulated that age (nearness to death) differences contributed to fears of death (though they were not measured in his study), while *cohort effects* bear on the acceptance of euthanasia. (We will again discuss the issue of euthanasia later in this chapter.) Sill (1980) did, however, find that in an institutionalized sample of aged persons, *awareness of finitude* positively predicted the degree to which persons disengaged from others (see Kalish, 1985a).

We can conclude from the above discussion that interpreting self-reported fears of death of an individual is not as straightforward as it may seem at first. The problems in this case seem to relate to how death is interpreted; that is, what does the term *mean* to *each individual,* and how *responses to* death are best conceived or measured. Such fears must be understood in light of current life circumstances (health, whether one is alone or not), the individual's own value systems, and what it is about death and dying that the individual is fearful of. Whether older persons are fearful or not, death seems to be more visible in the lives of most aged persons, according to Kalish (1985a).

Overcoming and Participating

One's feelings about one's own death are thought by many to determine the quality of life left to live. In addition to anxiety, one's response to death or dying may range from what R. Kastenbaum and Aisenberg (1976) have termed **overcoming** (seeing death as the enemy, as external, as failure) to **participating** (seeing death as internal, as a reunion, as a natural consequence of having lived). Interestingly, as one approaches death, one is thought to shift from an overcoming to a participating mode, according to these authors.

DEATH AND AGING—SYNONYMOUS?

Late adulthood is often a period in our lives that we unfortunately often come to think of in terms of loss. Many, for example, tend to assume that with aging comes the giving up of those things that we value in our culture (e.g., good health, relationships with others, status in the community as independent and productive persons) (R. Kastenbaum, 1985). Perhaps the most obvious of the losses thought to accompany getting older are those of losing one's spouse, and ultimately, the loss of one's own life.

Perhaps much of the mistreatment and/or avoidance of older persons in our society has as its basis the implicit link between aging and death (R. Kastenbaum, 1978a). Saying that persons die because "they are old" makes loss more predictable and less stressful (R. Kastenbaum, 1985). This association poses an interesting problem for many of us. As R. Kastenbaum (1978a, p. 1) has pointed out regarding aging and death, "Together they have posed for many a classic ambivalence: one does not want to die, yet one does not want to grow old."

Regarding perceptions of death as more or less appropriate for the young or old, R. Kastenbaum (1985) suggests that younger persons may adopt the **principle of compensation** to preserve a sense of continuity and fairness about life and death. This principle implies that just as we may have been left a penny (or perhaps with inflation, a dime) to compensate for a lost tooth as children, older or terminally ill persons are compensated for the losses of health and ultimately life by the promise of eternity. Near death, persons are assumed to acquire a kind of spiritual wisdom that lets them view death more positively. This approach has many psychological advantages for the dying or older person and survivors. For example (R. Kastenbaum, 1985, p. 624), it may enable survivors and the dying person to share a common view about the afterlife, reduce guilt about not "having done right by" the deceased person, or minimize the social disruption of death by lessening the sadness of grieving through the assumption that "she is so much happier now." Kastenbaum also asserts that this compensation reinforces the practice of **regressive intervention** (there is nothing more that could have been done for her). Unfortunately, a study of nearly 400 terminally ill (84 percent over age 60) persons receiving terminal care in a hospice indicated that only 3 percent of them mentioned the afterlife as a compensation for dying (R. Kastenbaum, B. Kastenbaum, & Morris, in preparation). According to R. Kastenbaum, this approach coexists with negative attitudes toward aged persons, but both points of view have a similar impact on dying persons.

Another consequence of this principle of compensation is to see older persons as teachers of death. The assumption that "old means incompetent" has been replaced by "old means wise." Both of these assumptions have in common a control technique that serves the interests of their advocates as well as the "knack of ignoring individual reality in favor of generalized expectancies" (R. Kastenbaum, 1985, p. 625). R. Kastenbaum asserts that while this principle of compensation may apply to some persons, it needs to be empirically tested "against reality."

Assuming that ours is a death-denying culture (Kübler-Ross, 1969), it may make sense to many to avoid that which threatens or disturbs us the most. This may be especially adaptive in an environment that tends to "sensationalize" death (by focusing on mass death, deaths of famous people, crime, violence) (Wass, 1979). Our culture also dissociates us from natural death, death on an everyday level, or the deaths of specific persons, particularly if they are old (DeSpelder & Strickland, 1983; R. Kastenbaum, 1978a). It is the very belief that death is more appropriate for the aged (and, by inference, less so for the young) that, according to J. A. Peterson (1980), accounts for the lack of research in this area. We are left to rely on our own experiences (or lack of them) and on our own biases in dealing with issues regarding death and dying of adults of all ages. We may feel prepared to deal with the death of someone elderly, whereas we are caught off guard when someone young dies. As R. Kastenbaum (1985) suggests, this expectation has been strengthened by comparatively recent lower infant/childhood mortality rates, though high infant mortality in colonial times served to prevent parents from getting close to their children lest they die (Stannard, 1977).

More tragic consequences for the aged have been documented by Sundow (1967), who found, in an observational study of general hospital emergency-room procedures, staff to make a greater effort to save the life of a young person than that of an old person. Presumably the lives of the old were somehow seen as less worthy of saving than those of the young. Blauner (1966) has also noted the lack of importance given to the lives of the aged in our culture: "The aged not only have become disengaged from significant family, economic, and community responsibilities in the present, but their future status (politely never referred to in our humane culture) is among the company of the powerless, anonymous, and virtually ignored dead" (p. 29).

R. Kastenbaum (1978a) summarizes many of the prevalent attitudes toward aging and death (p. 4):

1. The old person is thought to be "ready" if not actually "longing" to see the final curtain descend.

2. On a more philosophical level, death is "natural" and "timely" for the old person. Biologists make this point with emphasis on the preservation of the vigor of our species through the "necessary elimination" of weakened and impaired specimens.

3. On the pragmatic level, it is inappropriate to attempt to extend the life of a person who is conspicuously old and ailing; such an action is described as "indignity" or "not cost-effective," depending on the speaker's preferred vocabulary.

4. The "social loss" (Glaser, 1966) when an old person dies is minimal and is not a factor that must be taken seriously.

5. Memorialization and rituals associated with the death also are not of particular importance; they may even extend the "morbid" aura of death over the surviving elders—in any event, the death has been expected so long that there is little need to prolong the scene with rituals of mourning and memorialization.

6. Little could be done to extend the life of a sick and imperiled elder.

7. Limited social and medical resources should be applied to care of the young, who still have so much life ahead of them.

445

Death and
Aging—Synonymous?

R. Kastenbaum (1978a) states, "So long as we can believe that old people are ready for death and that it is high time for them to leave the scene, we can also hold our emotional responses and professional services within acceptable limits. . . . There is little need to explore precisely what this old man or woman is thinking or feeling" (p. 3)

Do People Die of Old Age?

We might note that statistics on death are often cited to support the aging-death association (see Chapter 2). Persons do not "die of old age," they die because of *age-related* processes that eventually cause their bodies to cease functioning (e.g., cardiovascular problems—strokes, heart disease, high blood pressure—or cancer; see Chapters 1 and 2). As R. Kastenbaum (1978a) points out, the mortality *rate* for the aged has actually declined over the past 50 years plus, in spite of the fact that there are more 65-year-olds and thus more deaths in an absolute sense. Paradoxically, the latter fact enhances the aging-death link, whereas the former tends to weaken this association, according to Kastenbaum (see also Hayslip & Martin, 1988).

Many prominent, apparently well-accepted ideas about aging tend to reinforce the association between older persons and death, leading to the conclusion that death/dying is "more natural" or "more appropriate" for older persons versus the young.

Integrity and Death

Integrity (implying a sense of completeness) is said to result in an acceptance of death, while despair implies a fear of death as a premature end to an unsatisfying life. According to Butler (1963), the realization of one's mortality brings about the process of pulling together one's life experiences, righting wrongs, and reaching closure about one's relationships with significant others (see Butler & Lewis, 1981). What both integrity and **life review** have in common is a process described as *introspection* (B. Newman & P. Newman, 1979). While such a process can be potentially very satisfying, it can also have serious consequences for the older person who is unable or unwilling to attempt a reintegration/reinterpretation of life's successes, failures, joys, and disappointments. For these persons, introspection can precipitate a depressive crisis, anxiety, anger, or ultimately cause one to decide to end one's life.

Disengagement Theory and Death

Perhaps the most widespread idea held by many, leading to the death-aging relationship, is that of **disengagement** among the aged, originally proposed by Cumming and Henry (1961). In this sense, disengaging from others (who are also thought to withdraw from the aged person) allows one to "prepare" oneself in making ready for death (see Chapters 10 and 11). Thus, older persons, although they are very much biologically *alive*, are treated *as if* they were dead. They therefore die what R. Schulz (1978) and Pattison (1977) have termed a *social death.* Simply put, they are written off by others; this may manifest itself in the form of hostility and avoidance or, worse still, involve physical abuse or emotional cruelty by others (Hayslip & Martin, 1988).

Sill (1980) and Kalish (1985a) have concluded that institutionalized elderly who estimated that they had less time to live disengaged more from others. While Sill (1980) suggests that the relationship between awareness of one's own mortality and disengagement comes about privately, in cases it is possible that others in the immediate environment (staff) implicitly socialize elders to withdraw from others, who in turn focus on their own death. While many situations (e.g., retirement centers, nursing homes, hospitals) (see Wass, 1979; V. Marshall, 1979) can create an open, facilitating atmosphere that encourages a sharing of feelings, thus "legitimizing" the discussion of death, they also (see above) have the potential to "dehumanize" care, leading to a lessening of self-esteem, isolation from others (see Watson & Maxwell, 1977), or simply giving up on life. However, S. Stein, Linn, and E. M. Stein (1985), in measuring the anticipation of stress in nursing home care, argue that if proper interpersonal care is available to the elder, adjustment and survival are more likely. Vickio and Cavanaugh (1985) found that increased contact with death among nursing home staff led to less death anxiety and more comfort in talking about death.

As we noted in Chapter 10, instead of seeing disengagement or integrity/life review as characteristic of *all* elderly, we might instead view such processes as being characteristic of some persons (*irrespective* of age) more than others, consistent with personality traits or specific life experiences. Disengagement and life review may sometimes, but not always, signal a preparation for death.

Appreciating the continuity of the life cycle is one of the hallmarks of integrity.

We thus see the double-edged effects that seeing older persons and death as "going together" can have. We can view an older person's concerns about death/dying as really very *life* oriented. On the other hand, a neglect of our *own* feelings perhaps born out of reduced contact or heightened anxiety over our own deaths can lessen the quality and quantity of the aged person's life.

Talking with Older Persons About Death

Because of the presumed link between older people and death, we may avoid discussing those very things that some older people have a real need to confront, under the assumption that these issues are either already settled, private, or simply too terrible to talk about (R. Kastenbaum, 1978a, 1985). These issues may relate to making funeral arrangements, writing a will, reviewing a treasured relationship, or simply talking out one's own fears surrounding death itself, the dying process, or the afterlife.

It is commonly assumed by the young that given the closeness of the aged to death, elderly people must be more fearful of it (Kalish, 1976, 1985a, 1985b). The young themselves often see death as something that happens to others; when young persons are asked if they think that they will die at all, their deaths are often perceived to be violent in nature, and therefore premature (Kalish, 1976). They often project this sensitivity about death onto the aged; such tendencies are encompassed by the term *countertransference* (Wilensky & Weiner, 1977) (see Chapter 14). While we may devalue older people and deny our feelings about death, we can view death as an *opportunity* to get to know ourselves as well as the aged individual.

Rather than concluding that just because one is older, he or she is necessarily more fearful of, prepared for, or preoccupied with death, the needs of each person (elderly or not) are better served by exploring what death personally *means* to him or her. This approach is particularly important in that chronological age is a poor predictor of death concerns (R. Kastenbaum, 1985). What in life does this individual value? How important are such things as family, health, religion, or work? What does retirement mean to the individual? How important are friends?

Communicating with Others About Death and Dying

While loss is often equated with death for some, it is important to note these same issues might not be important to others. Young persons who have many plans for the future may fear death because it represents an interruption of valued goals and achievements, whereas elderly persons may sorrow over the loss of their ability to care for others (R. Kastenbaum, 1985). Some may be concerned over the impact of their death on loved ones, while others fear the loss of their bodies (or what may happen to the body after death). As we noted above, each person's feelings are unique, and thus, loss may *mean* different things to different persons, causing them to respond to death in a variety of ways. Unfortunately, there are no easy solutions to the question of what to say to those facing death, or when to say it. In most cases, going with "what is in your gut" may be best—a hug or a squeeze may be more comforting than anything you can say.

Kalish (1976) and Wass (1979) conclude that relative to the young, most elderly think about death at least "occasionally." This may reflect their experiences with the deaths of others (spouse, friends). While a preoccupation with death can be harmful, it can have positive benefits in facilitating funeral planning and the writing of a will and can encourage the sharing of feelings essential to *open* communication. Kalish (1976) and Kastenbaum and Alsenberg (1976) have noted that older persons personalize death more often than do the young. This **personalization**, for example, may take the form of wanting to be reunited with a departed loved one. Such a point of view may reflect one's religious beliefs or simply represent a wish to be with those with whom one has shared a long life. It almost goes without saying that family, professionals, and others interested in helping adults of all ages should develop helping skills that facilitate the expression of each individual's feelings about such issues (Wass & Corr, 1984).

What are these skills that we are referring to? Perhaps most important, they involve an *openness* to others' experiences and points of view. Regardless of one's own personal convictions, allowing each person to express those beliefs most important to him or her, listening in a *nonjudgmental* way, in effect provides what Carl Rogers (1961) has termed **unconditional positive regard**. What we mean by this is that *anything* is permissible to talk about (or to *not* talk about). Furthermore, unconditional positive regard means that the speaker will be listened to in an *empathetic, uncritical* manner. For many persons (young and old), simply being taken seriously and listened to is a long-forgotten experience. As such, this open attitude can provide the dying person with the opportunity to make choices at a very important moment in life, and give that person a sense of dignity, control, and importance attached to personal decisions and opinions (R. Kastenbaum, 1978a).

In this light, Wass (1979) and Kalish (1985a) have provided us with some insight into the nature of death from the perspective of older persons—those persons whom we often avoid *as if* they were dying, who indeed have much to tell us. Wass (1979) speaks of "the death taboo," referring to the avoidance of death, specifically working against the older person's willingness to discuss very personal concerns, having lost a trusted confidant (e.g., a spouse, child, or close friend). As noted above, depression in the aged in some cases can be an outcome of the introspection accompanying the life review. Equally likely, however, it can reflect the *lack* of an opportunity to share one's thoughts or work through previous conflicts with others. Thus, an unwillingness to listen or an inability to understand can contribute to death-related depression in the aged. Depression, or an unwillingness to talk, could ironically easily be misinterpreted as part of the older person's "preparations" for death (R. Kastenbaum, 1978a).

Individual Differences in Responses to Death

Perhaps one of the major themes implicit in this discussion of helping is the recognition of *individual differences* in views about death and dying and adjusting to loss. As Hayslip and Martin (1988) point out, imposing a number of "shoulds" on each person can discourage wanting to share concerns about that person's or another's death, the writing of a will, funeral planning, wishing to die at home, euthanasia, bodily disposal, the fate of survivors, etc. In so doing, one communicates to each person that one is either *not willing and/or not able* to accept the elder as an *individual.* Being aware of available family or community resources (Compassionate Friends, Widow to Widow programs) is also an invaluable skill. While some feel that these programs may have the effect of stigmatizing the bereaved, they appear to be a valuable source of comfort and support at a time when such support is scarce. In fact, informal support may be more acceptable than professional help to persons who value family or neighborhood ties.

Overall, it seems safe to conclude that there is a great deal of *variability* among people in their feelings about death as well as their willingness to discuss such feelings. Recognizing this variability is important in communicating with others about death and dying.

We now turn to several comparatively new topics in the study of death and dying: hospice care, euthanasia, and suicide.

HOSPICE CARE

Within the past decade, **hospice** care for the terminally ill has emerged as a viable alternative to hospital deaths, which are often depersonalizing, lonely, painful experiences for both dying persons and their families.

While the term *hospice* originally referred to a "way station" to care for travelers on their journey, in modern times it has come to represent an approach, a concept, or an attitude toward making persons' lives as full as possible *until* they die (Kubler-Ross, 1978), thus avoiding the social death we discussed earlier.

Hospice care, originally popularized in England by Cecily Saunders at St. Christopher's Hospice in London, spread to the United States in the early 1970s in the form of the New Haven Hospice, located in New Haven, Connecticut. Since then, literally thousands of hospices have sprung up around the country. Many hospice patients (most of whom have cancer) are elderly, and hospice care can take on many forms (home care based, hospital based, a freestanding unit, wholly volunteer).

Characteristics of hospice care include: (1) pain/symptom control, (2) lessening isolation, (3) physician-directed services, (4) treatment on a 24-hour-per-day basis of *both* the patient and the family, (5) the involvement of an interdisciplinary team, (6) bereavement follow-up of the family after death, (7) the use of volunteers, and (8) the opportunity for staff support (of one another) to lessen burnout and facilitate their own grief when a patient dies (G. Davidson, 1978; Dubois, 1980; Mor & Masterson-Allen, 1987; Wass, 1979). Patients in a hospice have the same "rights" to quality care (see Box 12.1) as do those receiving care in a hospital.

Most importantly for the persons who are dying, hospice permits them to make decisions and exercise control over their lives in a warm, caring, and

BOX 12.1

THE DYING PERSON'S BILL OF RIGHTS

I have the right to be treated as a living human being until I die.

I have the right to maintain a sense of hopefulness, however changing its focus may be.

I have the right to be cared for by those who can maintain a sense of hopefulness, however changing this might be.

I have the right to express my feelings and emotions about my approaching death in my own way.

I have the right to participate in decisions concerning my care.

I have the right to expect continuing medical and nursing attention even though "cure" goals must be changed to "comfort" goals.

I have the right not to die alone.

I have the right to be free from pain.

I have the right to have my questions answered honestly.

I have the right not to be deceived.

I have the right to have help from and for my family in accepting my death.

I have the right to die in peace and dignity.

I have the right to retain my individuality and not be judged for my decisions, which may be contrary to beliefs of others.

I have the right to discuss and enlarge my religious or spiritual experiences, whatever these may mean to others.

I have the right to expect that the sanctity of the human body will be respected after death.

I have the right to be cared for by caring, sensitive, knowledgeable people who will attempt to understand my needs and will be able to gain some satisfaction in helping me face my death.

Source: M. I. Donovan & S. G. Pierce. (1976). *Cancer care nursing.* Newton, MA: Allyn & Bacon Inc.

comparatively pain-free atmosphere. Thus hospice, in many cases, simply supports each patient and family in making all types of decisions related to family matters, funeral planning, wills, grieving, *where* death will occur, and most importantly, with *whom,* under *what* conditions, and *how* death will happen (Hayslip & Leon, 1988). For many persons who value personal control or wish to be close to their loved ones, hospice care is a viable alternative. For others, perhaps, who need the security of a hospital or who have always depended on others to make decisions for them, hospice would likely be inappropriate. In spite of its emphasis on the dignity and self-worth of the dying person, it is not a panacea for the problems many dying face on a daily basis. Further, as Hine (1979–1980) has discussed, responsibilities associated with hospice–home care are such that all families may not wish to or cannot bear. While hospice purportedly deals with dying persons and their families, its real value, perhaps, is to teach us to cherish and nurture our relationships with others while we can.

EUTHANASIA

Euthanasia literally translated means "good death" (DeSpelder & Strickland, 1983). Given the comparatively recent advances in medical technology allowing for the extension of life, concerns about potentially fatal illnesses such as AIDS, Alzheimer's disease, and certain forms of cancer, as well as drug-related birth defects, are heightened. The dying person, the family, and physicians may agonize over whose wishes are to be respected if or when the patient is near death, in pain, or on life-supportive machinery. If that person is a newborn, and cannot speak up—who decides? What if the person should recover from a "fatal" illness or come out of a coma?

The issues regarding the ethics of euthanasia are complex (Hafen & Frandsen, 1983). While some may object to **active euthanasia** (cutting someone's life short to relieve needless suffering or to preserve individual dignity), **passive euthanasia** (failing to use lifesaving measures that might otherwise prolong someone's life) might be equally repulsive to other persons, based on individual philosophical or religious beliefs. Terminal care is costly; a family's finances and insurance coverage can be sapped over an extended period of time.

The individual can state his/her *right to die* by writing a **living will**. The living will is a directive (not universally legally binding, but first passed into law in California in 1976) that impells the physician to cease using artificial means of prolonging life when there is no realistic hope for recovery, thus allowing the individual to die naturally. In California, if a certain amount of time (more than two weeks) has passed since the signer was diagnosed as terminally ill, then the physician is not legally bound to execute the document (though it may be in force for five years after signing) and can exercise his or her best professional judgment. In such cases, the living will may be reexecuted. Perhaps one might change one's mind when death is imminent.

Alternatively, one may not be competent to sign a living will when one is seriously ill. Persons write living wills for many reasons—due to financial pressure or out of the wish to make death and grieving easier or more predictable for themselves or their families. Fear of prosecution or legal action may cause the physician to not support the patient's wishes or discourage a living will altogether. Wanting to speed up the dying process and end suffering, the physician could take matters into his or her own hands. What is dignified or merciful to one person may not be acceptable to another. While living wills are not legally binding in all states, frank, open discussion with one's physician and family can heighten the chances of one's wishes being carried out.

Euthanasia is obviously a moral, ethical, and legal-medical gray area. No legal penalties await the physician who fails to carry out the patient's wishes, which may conflict with those of the family. As Hafen and Frandsen (1983) suggest, the arguments for and against euthanasia are many. Several problems complicate each point of view: death isn't usually instantaneous, medical ethics are not well-defined, conflicts of interest are inevitable, and ultimately decisions about the quality, value, or worth of human life are involved. What if euthanasia got out of hand and was used to eliminate "inferior" people? Who decides when to end a life? As we noted above, older persons are less likely to favor euthanasia, as are women and nonwhites (Ward, 1980).

SUICIDE

J. Coleman, Butcher, and Carson (1984) note that *depression* is the single most common element in suicide, regardless of age. Most persons attempt suicide following a depressive episode, though it is certainly not true that all persons who are depressed will attempt suicide. Depression, however, predisposes persons toward feelings of helplessness, loss, and vulnerability, all critical elements in suicide.

Among male teenagers and the aged, rates of completed (successful) suicides are increasing most rapidly (M. Miller, 1979; Pfeffer, 1981; Wells & Stuart, 1981). While the relative frequency is low, suicide among young children has also gained increasing attention (Peck, 1984; Pfeffer, 1984).

Pfeffer (1984) notes that it is very difficult to get accurate figures regarding the extent of suicide among children. The warning signs that the child may exhibit are not often recognized or heeded by those close to that child, based on ignorance or denial of the problem. Pfeffer (1984) suggests that one must understand the *whole* child in order to deal with potentially suicidal behavior. The family situation (e.g., a death, divorce, parental pathology [depression], or presence of violence in the family) may predispose the

Depression often precipitates a suicide attempt among adults of all ages.

child to loss or abandonment, causing a loss of self-worth ("I am expend-able"). The child's resulting depression, preoccupation with ideas and fanta-sies about death, and/or aggressive behavior toward others may symbolize a wish to die. Taking one's life may be an expression of anger toward a parent, or be seen as an end to psychological pain. Peck (1984) suggests that among adolescents, a "loner" personality type and depression (often brought on by family conflicts complicated by substance abuse) are important causal factors in suicide. Moreover, for some adolescents, suicide is a manifestation of psychosis or a response to a crisis (failure in school, loss of a love relation-ship). For others, suicide attempts are a message that one is intensely unhappy or desperate—a cry for help, a response to a crisis, or a reflection of an ongoing problem.

J. Coleman et al. (1984) also note that other factors (marital status, occupation, sex), in addition to age, are correlated with the incidence of suicide. Those who are living alone, divorced or separated, are male (regard-ing successful attempts), or are lawyers, psychologists, dentists, or physicians seem to be most "at risk."

Seiden (1985–1986) suggests that nonwhite suicide rates are lower than those of whites because they (nonwhites) are less vulnerable to the loss of status that accompanies aging, having had less all their lives, while Robins, West, and G.E. Murphy (1977) did not find such racial differences. Boldt (1982) has found a cohort effect in acceptance of suicide, where younger generations were *more* positive than were older ones. Moreover, even older cohorts reported being more accepting than when they were young. Such generational shifts, if they exist, pose special challenges for those in the field of suicide prevention.

In evaluating the seriousness of suicide potential, the Los Angeles Suicide Prevention Center uses a **lethality scale** (see Box 12.2). While this scale cannot be expected to be 100 percent accurate, it does help hot-line workers' to understand more clearly whom they are dealing with in crisis situations. Perhaps a suicidal individual conceivably could see such question-ing by the hot-line worker as an indication that someone *is* interested in whether he or she lives or dies.

One should not misinterpret these findings as an indication that younger persons and females just want attention or that older persons and males do not want to be prevented from killing themselves. Over and above the moral and ethical issue of whether anyone has the "right" to take his or her own life, the simple fact is that if one truly wishes to kill oneself, one can do so without ever doing anything that might help others to prevent that person from committing suicide. Many persons who leave notes or contact suicide prevention services, however, *do* want help. Consequently, *all* refer-ences to an individual's killing himself should be taken seriously—the costs of not doing so are too great (J. Coleman et al., 1984; M. Miller, 1979).

Dealing with Suicidal Persons

Many skills are important in dealing with potential suicides. Providing sup-port and alternatives to suicide and making people aware of how their distress is impairing their ability to *realistically* assess and solve their problems are very important (J. Coleman et al., 1984). It may be particularly important to ask persons who may be depressed if they are considering suicide. Being assertive and directive when necessary and simply being with those who are at risk are the most important elements in averting a suicide attempt (J. Coleman et al., 1984; Hipple, 1986). At the worst, though it may be temporarily embarrassing, taking initiative and demonstrating that you care by asking questions cannot help but draw you closer to those who are isolated or depressed and possibly suicidal. At best, you may save the life of someone who may really need to talk about his or her feelings.

BOX 12.2

"LETHALITY SCALE" FOR ASSESSMENT OF SUICIDE POTENTIALITY

In assessing "suicide potentiality," or the probability that a person might carry out his threat to take his own life, the Los Angeles Suicide Prevention Center uses a "lethality scale" consisting of ten categories:

1. Age and sex. The potentiality is greater if the individual is male rather than female and is over 50 years of age. (The probability of suicide is also increasing for youths.)
2. Symptoms. The potentiality is greater if the individual manifests such symptoms as sleep disturbances, depression, feelings of hopelessness, or alcoholism.
3. Stress. The potentiality is greater if the individual is subject to such stress as the loss of a loved one through death or divorce, the loss of employment, increased responsibilities, or serious illness.
4. Acute vs. chronic aspects. The potentiality is greater when there is a sudden onset of specific symptoms, a recurrent outbreak of similar symptoms, or a recent increase in long-standing maladaptive traits.
5. Suicidal plan. The potentiality is greater in proportion to the lethality of the proposed method and the organizational clarity and detail of the plan.
6. Resources. The potentiality is greater if the person has no family or friends or if his family and friends are unwilling to help.
7. Prior suicidal behavior. The potentiality is greater if the individual has evidenced one or more prior attempts of a lethal nature or has a history of repeated threats and depression.
8. Medical status. The potentiality is greater when there is chronic, debilitating illness or the individual has had many unsuccessful experiences with physicians.
9. Communication aspects. The potentiality is greater if communication between the individual and his relatives has been broken off, and they reject efforts by the individual or others to reestablish communication.
10. Reaction of significant others. Potentiality is greater if a significant other, such as the husband or wife, evidences a defensive, rejecting, punishing attitude, and denies that the individual needs help.

The final suicide potentiality rating is a composite score based on the weighting of each of the ten individual items.

Another interesting approach to the assessment of suicide potentiality involves the use of computers and actuarial methods to predict not only the risk of suicide but also of assaultive and other dangerous behaviors. Clinicians find this information helpful in making decisions regarding treatment for individuals who are potentially suicidal—e.g., decisions regarding the amount of controls needed or the amount of freedom that can safely be allowed.

Source: From J. Coleman, J.N. Butcher, & R.C. Carson. (1984). *Abnormal psychology and modern life* (7th Edition) (p. 338). Glenview, IL: Scott Foresman.

Types of Suicidal Persons

Farberow and Litman (1970) separate suicidal behavior into three categories. There are those who are in the *to be* group (two-thirds of the suicidal population); these persons do not wish to die and may make several halfhearted attempts at suicide to communicate their distress to others. Those who wish *not to be* (3–5 percent of suicides) give little or no warning and genuinely wish to die; their means of suicide are designed to avoid being stopped by others. Those who are in the *to be or not to be* group (30 percent of all suicides) are ambivalent about death and leave their death "to chance," so to speak. They may be moderately serious about killing themselves and use slow-acting means of doing so, but they still hope that they can work things through and that they will be stopped before it is too late. They may make several attempts at suicide, each of which is followed by a period of relative calm. As J. Coleman et al. (1984, p. 332) states, persons in the "to be or not to be" category feel that "If I die, the conflict is settled, but if I am rescued, that is what is meant to be." As we noted above, generalizations are very harmful. Yet, most suicides of the young probably fall into the "to be" or "to be or not to be" categories, while older suicides fall into the "not to be" category.

Suicide and Aging

Relative to the suicides of the young or of the rich and famous, suicide is one form of "abnormal" behavior (see Chapter 13) of older adults that may receive little attention or publicity. While suicide may be repugnant to many, when one observes the statistics, the harsh reality of the situation comes into focus. Data of this type are illustrated in Figure 12.1 and indicate there are significant trends in suicide by age and sex.

That is, suicide rates for white females reach a peak in middle age and then decline. For males, the rate continues to rise into advanced old age. It should be pointed out that these rates are for whites; the trends among minority group members are less distinct. Figure 12.1 suggests that the highest rates of suicide occur among white males in their eighties. Additionally, suicide statistics indicate that older adults, who constitute approximately 20 percent of the population, account for approximately 25 percent of the reported suicides (M. Miller, 1979; N.J. Osgood, 1985).

It is important to note that experts in the field believe these figures for older adults to be low. For example, given the same set of circumstances and events, what is ruled a suicide for someone in his or her thirties may not be deemed a suicide for an older adult. Assume someone aged 35 is found dead next to an empty bottle of pills. In this case, the police and medical examiner suspect suicide. Alternatively, let us assume this individual is 75 years of age. The police and medical examiner may not consider this a potential suicide but instead may attribute the event to the forgetfulness that may accompany increased age. That is, "Old Harry just forgot how many medications he was supposed to take."

This point was made quite clear via a routine letter from one of the authors' mother-in-law to his wife. The mother-in-law mentioned that one of her neighbors shot himself in the head because he was in ill health and his wife had died recently. In the newspaper clipping, sent by the mother-in-law, describing the event, the obituary read this way: "Robert ———, 67, of R.D. 1, ———, Ohio, died Tuesday at his home following a sudden illness." This example illustrates this point clearly—even in situations where suicide is almost a certainty, many people purposefully overlook the facts when the individual involved is old, when they feel they have failed, or when they wish to avoid the stigma of suicide or to collect insurance benefits (see Kalish, 1985a; R. Kastenbaum, 1985; N.J. Osgood, 1985).

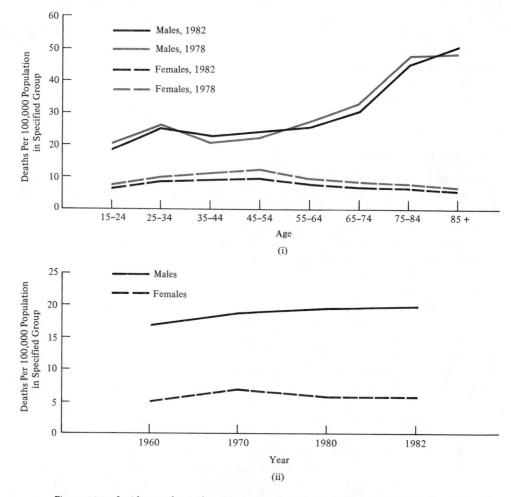

Figure 12.1 Incidence of suicide across age and sex 1960–1982 (age adjusted) (lower graph); 1978 versus 1982 (upper graph). *Source:* U.S. Bureau of the Census. 1986. *Statistical Abstract of the United States;* and J.L. McIntosh (1983, November), *Elderly suicide data bases: levels, availability and omissions (p. 19). Paper presented at the Annual Meeting of the Gerontological Society, San Francisco, CA. Reprinted by permission of the author.*

What are some of the reasons older adults commit suicide? Research indicates some of the major correlates of suicide in older adults are such factors as poor and failing health, widowhood/widowerhood, diminishing social roles, loss of friends, social isolation, and depression (see R. Kastenbaum, 1985; M. Miller, 1978, 1979; N.J. Osgood, 1985). We recommend that you exercise *caution* here in drawing conclusions as to their *causal* importance in elderly suicides. While the importance of living alone is paramount among the widowed, particularly for elderly widowers, widowed elderly are not only more prone to suicide within the first year of bereavement, but as Stenback (1980) notes, those who attempt suicide are more likely to have suffered the loss of a close relative in the past than otherwise. It is important to note that not widowhood per se but the *inability* to *replace* confidant relationships are what make the loss of a spouse pivotal (Stenback, 1980).

While retirement is typically considered to be a crisis for most elderly men, there is little direct evidence to support the notion that it is *causally* linked to suicide among the aged. Many elderly persons who enjoy good health and who have adequate retirement income may in fact see retirement positively, and particularly for men, the benefits of being released from work commitments can be a very positive aspect of retirement (see Chapter 11). Rowland (1977) concluded that widowhood and the death of a "significant other" (husband, wife, close friend), but *not* retirement, predicted death for elderly persons. For some elders, ageism, poor health, isolation, or marital conflict accompanying the withdrawal from the work force, not retirement per se, may contribute to lessened self-esteem and depression (N.J. Osgood, 1985). Much depends on the *value* attached to retirement by the older person, which, of course, varies with one's perceived preparation for retirement as well as what one expects from it (Glamser, 1976, 1981).

Death within institutions (nursing homes, mental hospitals, geriatric wards) is commonplace for many elderly (see Wass, 1979). Institutions such as these are seen (accurately or not) by many aged as depersonalizing, dehumanizing, lonely places (see E. Kahana, 1973). In contrast to retirement, the gerontological literature generally supports (see Rowland, 1977; R. Schulz & Brenner, 1977) relocation as a predictor of death among the elderly, particularly if they are less competent (Nirenberg, 1983). M. Miller (1979) states that the *mere prospect* of being institutionalized was enough to precipitate suicide for some elderly men. When overt, quick means of taking one's life are not available, many elderly persons resort to other methods: starving themselves, refusing to follow physicians' orders, voluntary isolation, behaving dangerously, excessive drinking/drug abuse, or smoking. These behaviors may be regarded by staff and other nursing home residents as "problems" in themselves (Hayslip & Martin, 1988).

Nelson and Farberow (1980) have termed such covert methods of death **indirect self-destructive behavior (ISDB)**. According to these authors, ISDB differs from suicide in that it does not have immediate fatal consequences but is thought to ultimately lead to the individual's premature death. While these behaviors may have a self-destructive component and stem from isolation or depression, they may also serve to lessen feelings of powerlessness or low self-esteem. Further research seems to be necessary to clarify the distinction between the self-destructive and adaptive components of ISDB (Nelson & Farberow, 1980). At present, research suggests that institutionalization clearly has the *potential* for eliciting suicidelike behavior in those older persons who do not see relocation in a positive way or who may already feel depressed and hopeless. When alternatives to nursing home care become more available, and when residents perceive themselves to be in more control of their lives, it is likely that the relationship between institutionalization and ISDB will lessen.

Breed and Huffine (1979) and Gerner (1979) point out that it is not exactly clear why suicide rates continue to increase into old age for males but not for females. One possible explanation for these life-span sex differences has to do with the reason for the suicide. The primary reason for suicide in females seems to be interpersonal (boyfriend, girlfriend, spouse) problems (Gerner, 1979). With increasing age, these types of problems decrease, and the result is a decreasing suicide rate. On the other hand, males appear to commit suicide for self-esteem/self-concept related reasons. Threats to one's self-esteem *may* become more frequent with aging (e.g., retirement, loss of income, etc.). This may explain the rate of suicide increases for males with age but not for females, according to Gerner (1979). Current levels of stress, loneliness, morale, and depression are likely concerns in predicting elderly suicide, which may be prevented via the judicious use of drug therapy, group or life review therapy, and creative (music, art) interventions (N.J. Osgood, 1985).

For many persons, young and old, taking their own lives may be a final expression of the wish to control the little that they have that is valued. They may desire "death with dignity," rather than die alone, or in pain. Elderly suicides have been described by Stenback (1980) as *egoistic*. Egoistic suicides involve few commitments to interpersonal or cultural values, often resulting in or stemming from social *isolation* (see Durkheim, 1951). Hence, relative to suicide among younger adults, for some elderly persons, the suicide act is highly individualistic and very serious in its intent. This makes it particularly difficult to mobilize effective support upon which the older person can rely in crisis when dealing with stress and/or loss (M. Miller, 1979). The egoistic elderly suicide unfortunately also frequently encourages a "we can't do anything about the problem" approach to treatment (M. Miller, 1979). This attitude in turn may reinforce the older person's sense of isolation and hopelessness; one sees oneself as someone whose life *is* worthless in that no one seems to want one to *not* take it.

Another consequence of this attitude is the ignorance of both the scope and seriousness of suicidal threats by older persons. Often, greater efforts are made to save the lives of those who are perceived to have a life that is *worth saving* (see Blauner, 1966; Sundow, 1967), as noted earlier in this chapter.

The diversity among aged persons, as well as the variety and potential for interaction among the many factors correlated with (but not necessarily causing) elderly suicides, would seem to argue against the construction of "suicide-proneness" (lethality) scales (see Box 12.2) for use with elderly clients. While theories about suicide-prone elderly are attractive, it is again the recognition of each aged person as a *unique individual* that best facilitates the prevention of suicide. Again, beliefs in the "appropriateness of death" for the elderly, valuing youth and power, and myths about older persons contribute to our neglect of this very important issue with the aged.

While data on attempted suicides is of questionable validity, as noted above, the ratio of committed to attempted suicides seems to increase inversely with chronological age (Stenbeck, 1980). Perhaps the most intensive study of the older white male (who is at risk, relative to other elderly) has been carried out by M. Miller (1978, 1979). Miller conducted a systematic examination of 301 white, elderly male suicides in Arizona during 1970 to 1975, interviewing the widows of 30 of these men. His analyses suggest that a "profile" of the suicide-prone older man could be constructed (see above, however). According to Miller's data, the "typical" older white male who takes his life:

1. seldom attended church
2. was not visited by (or did not visit) friends or relatives at least once a week
3. left a suicide note for someone
4. left a will
5. was experiencing chronic sleeping problems the year before his death
6. was addicted to, or had a strong reliance on, drugs
7. had a relative with an emotional or mental illness
8. killed himself in the bedroom of his house

In addition, the elderly suicide victim was described as a "loner" who had few close friends, had suffered the death of a friend or relative (who served as a confidant) during the last two years of his life, owned a firearm (pistol) that was used to kill himself and was purchased a month prior to his death, saw his physician a month prior to his death, and suffered a serious, painful physical illness during the last year of his life. He also frequently was described as seeing himself as inadequate or useless, being unhappy or depressed (Robins et al., 1977), and giving at least verbal/behavioral cues to his impending suicide.

While this "profile" is purely descriptive and *not* prescriptive (as M. Miller notes), and seems to present viable diagnostic possibilities for those working with elderly persons, it should *never* be taken as evidence of a "guarantee" that someone who is older will or will not commit suicide.

M. Miller (1979) states, regarding causes of elderly suicide, "The crucial factor seems to be how well developed and efficacious are the person's coping abilities" (p. 7). Similar findings regarding coping skills have been obtained by Robins et al. (1977).

CONDUCTING RESEARCH ON OLDER SUICIDES

Conclusions about causative factors in aged suicides are often based on interviews with survivors, and/or frequently rest on research that lacks control groups (see M. Miller, 1979). R. Kastenbaum and P. Costa (1977), moreover, have pointed out that the withholding of treatment (constituting these controls) would be considered unethical by most. Client confidentiality makes evaluation of suicide prevention efforts difficult. It is also important to note that the motivations of those (regardless of age) who attempt suicide in fact may differ from those who are successful.

M. Miller (1979) noted that aged men who committed suicide visited their physicians a month prior to their deaths. Perhaps these physicians were not skilled in "picking up on" the cues these men were providing them. What would have happened had these physicians been more skilled in confronting these men about the reasons for the visit? In light of our above discussion of helping skills, simply being able to acknowledge suicidal thoughts could have been of vital importance to these elderly men, whose value systems often stress self-reliance and independence. Accordingly, Miller (1979) found 60 percent of his sample to have given a clue as to their impending suicide; over a third of their family had admitted to acknowledging such clues! Twenty-three percent did not recognize such clues; many did nothing even when they were given advance notice! "In one case, the deceased told his wife and daughter every night for two weeks that he wanted to take his life, yet his family failed to secure the professional attention he so desperately needed. . . . In at least two of the cases . . . wives found suicide notes in advance of the men's deaths—one, one week in advance and the other the day before— but totally discounted the credibility of the notes" (p. 294). Miller speculates that it is possible that the wives in these cases were implicitly *cooperating* with their husbands, who wanted to end their lives.

Miller (1979) states, regarding suicide prevention, "Although they [the research team] emphasized outreach services are imperative to reach depressed people who may have become withdrawn and isolated, they felt *the ultimate answer would be for old age itself* to offer the elderly something worthwhile for which to live" (p. 19).

Quality of Life and Suicide

Some factors that seem to push older persons to take their own lives (see also Stenbeck, 1980) are interpersonal or social in nature; others seem to lie *within* the older person (e.g., personality traits long since established). We can view individual differences in the likelihood of an older person attempting suicide to be a function of the extent to which individuals feel they have a sense of *control* over factors that could otherwise "push" them to take their own lives.

It is important to note that the above factors must be *interpreted* by not only elderly persons but indeed by all persons in such a way as to suggest that taking one's own life is seen by the suicidal person as the *only* solution. Some persons become overwhelmed by a loss; others who have more positive coping skills react to the same loss with resilience and are able to "bounce back."

M. Miller (1979) discusses the balance between the "quality" and "quantity" of life. According to this view, each person forms his own *personal equation* whereby when the **line of unbearability** is crossed, the person determines that the *quality* of his life is more important than its *quantity*. Thus, individual evaluations of what it takes to be pushed beyond the line of unbearability are likely to differ across people. For some, this invisible line is defined by the mere prospect of growing old and dying in an institution (M. Miller, 1979). For others, it may be living in pain, the loss of a girlfriend/boyfriend or husband/wife, the loss of one's work affiliation through retirement, having failed in school or as a spouse/parent, or simply feeling unloved by one's parents or children or feeling *alone*.

Obviously, more attention needs to be given to education about suicide per se directed toward elderly persons, their families, physicians, and the general public.

THE WORK OF ELISABETH KÜBLER-ROSS

If we assume that persons who are terminally ill are "ready to die," we may tragically deny them the opportunity to deal with what Kübler-Ross (1974a) terms *unfinished business*. Quite often, discussions about death and dying are seen as depressing or sad and consequently avoided with others who are dying, regardless of age. Acknowledging *any* and *all* needs is the key to helping those adults who are struggling with their mortality or who are dying (Kübler-Ross, 1969, 1974a, 1974b).

Since the publication in 1969 of *On Death and Dying*, where Kübler-Ross's **stages** through which persons progress in reacting to their impending deaths are outlined, her theories have been interpreted too rigidly (R. Kastenbaum, 1975), and accepted uncritically, lacking consistent research support. Despite these uneven responses and criticisms, Kübler-Ross's work has been a great stimulus to improve the quality of dying persons' lives, as well as in drawing our attention to the feelings and needs of dying persons as *real people*. These "stages" consist of (1) *denial* (no, not me), (2) *anger* (directed at doctors, nurses, or those who will go on living), (3) *bargaining* with others (God) in order to prolong life, (4) *depression* (a reaction to one's worsening symptoms or deterioration, knowing that death will follow), and (5) *acceptance* (a sense of readiness about death, but without a loss of hope that life could be prolonged if a cure were found) (see also R. Kastenbaum, 1975; R. Kastenbaum & Aisenberg, 1976).

Using Kübler-Ross's Stage Theory Productively

Staff or family may feel compelled to "push" the dying person through each stage until he or she is "accepting"; anything else is seen as a failure. Kubler-Ross's stages have often been interpreted to mean that *every* person should experience these stages in a given order. However, prolonged reactions such as denial or anger can have positive emotional consequences for many terminally ill (see discussion below about grieving) even though they may make others uncomfortable. There is a great deal of moving back and forth between stages (Kalish, 1976; Kastenbaum, 1975; J.A. Peterson, 1980; Rodabough, 1980). Despite this variability, research demonstrates that *depression* seems to be a common experience for those who are dying (Wass, 1979). Dismissing a person's behavior as "just anger" may ignore very important external reasons (family conflicts, poor quality of care) for that anger, as noted by Hayslip and Martin (1988). A patient's purported "denial" may also reflect a "mutual pretense" regarding discussing death that the patient and the medical staff or family have agreed upon during the course of care (J.A. Peterson, 1980). While this may reinforce the family's or staff's own needs to deny both their own and the individual's death, it robs the dying person of the opportunity to draw others closer as well as to finish unfinished business (make up for past sins and hurts, say the unsaid). It also denies those who are in a position to help the opportunity to learn about *life* from someone else (Hayslip & Martin, 1988).

Funerals, despite their positive aspects (see below) in helping "structure" the grieving process (K.W. Schale & Geiwitz, 1982), often reinforce this denial of the person or his apparent "acceptance" of death by the use of such terms as "passed on," or "slumber room," reconstructive efforts to make the deceased look "alive," or ceremonies that do not reflect the real values of the person when he or she was alive. Quite often immediate family are physically separated from those who attend the funeral—further isolating them from others as well as from their own feelings about the death. They may feel that they must maintain an air of respect or an image of strength in the face of their loss. For example, anger is often a perfectly legitimate response to death and loss (one's own or another's) (Kalish, 1985a, 1985b). If suppressed or internalized (as might be appropriate at a funeral), it often is manifest as depression (Lindemann, 1944), further complicating adjustment to the death and making communication more difficult later on with the bereaved person.

We can conclude from this discussion about Kübler-Ross's work that whatever its methodological deficiencies, it teaches us to deal with dying persons "where they happen to be (emotionally speaking) at the moment." The same can certainly be said of those who are experiencing **anticipatory grief** prior to a loved one's expected death.

As Hayslip and Martin (1988) have discussed, to fail to recognize that *every* person's feelings about his or her own (or another's) impending death are unique is to deny that person the right to make (or not make) decisions about life as well as death. These may be decisions that one may desperately want and *need* to make in order that one (or one's loved ones) may die "an appropriate death" (DeSpelder & Strickland, 1983; Kalish, 1985). Relating to those who are bereaved and grieving demands that we recognize that grief is very *personal,* that widows and widowers may grieve in various ways (Lopata, 1973; J. Peterson & Briley, 1977) consistent with their feelings about the death. For example, it might be useful to explore whether the grieving person believed that the death was preventable or not, evaluate the strength of the relationship to the deceased, and take stock of what interpersonal/emotional resources the survivor has available (Bugen, 1979; Norris & Murrell, 1987).

BEREAVEMENT—SURVIVING DEATH

Regardless of age, the loss of a "significant other" in our lives, whether that person is a child, parent, sibling, or spouse, is likely to be one of the most disruptive events that we can experience (Holmes & Rahe, 1967; Rowland, 1977). R. Kastenbaum and Costa (1977) suggest that referring to someone as **bereaved** simply indicates that that person has survived another person's death. **Grief** is the term we use to refer to the manner in which one deals with/responds to this loss. **Mourning** simply indicates a socially condoned way of expressing one's grief (i.e., at a funeral) or acknowledging that a life has ended. While we might assume that older people are especially prone to the negative effects of having lost a "significant other" (most likely a husband or wife), research does not consistently bear this out.

Statistics do suggest that older people clearly must deal more frequently with the loss of a spouse. By the age of 65, 50 percent of women have lost their husbands; by the age of 75, two-thirds are widowed (Botwinick, 1984). Anyone (and in particular older persons) may have to deal with several closely spaced deaths, never having the opportunity to do the *grief work* necessary to "work through" each loss (R. Kastenbaum, 1978a). These persons may be literally overwhelmed by grief. They suffer from **bereavement overload**, and may appear depressed, apathetic, or suffer from physical problems (R. Kastenbaum, 1978a).

Are Widows at Risk?

R. Schulz (1978) concurs that the aged are at risk, both physically and psychologically, as a consequence of widowhood but, however, questions the assumption that such negative effects are a consequence of widow(er)hood per se. In other words, what exactly is it about being widowed that makes death or illness more likely? Is widowhood necessarily causal? According to R. Schulz (1978), there are many reasons why widow(er)s die more frequently than do nonwidows. These include:

1. Those who are in better health tend to remarry, leaving those who are in poorer health behind.

2. Those who are fit tend to marry those who are also fit.

3. Both widows/spouses live in a high-risk environment.

4. The loss of a spouse creates a sense of hopelessness and depression, leading to lowered resistance to disease and/or stress.

5. The death of one's spouse robs one of the support and/or cues required in order to take one's medicine on time, eat balanced meals, keep doctors' appointments, etc. (see R. Schulz, 1978).

Rowland (1977) concludes that widows have a greater chance of developing either a physical or psychological illness. They also are more likely to die within the first six months to one year after the deaths of their husbands than are nonwidows in this same time interval, according to Rowland. This risk factor was even higher when the spouse's death was sudden (Rowland, 1977). Given the strong emotional bond that years of marriage can create, we must not fail to realize that *the broken-heart syndrome* probably accounts for a certain degree of illness or death experienced by widows.

Similarly, stressful environments (relocation stress; see Parkes, 1973; R. Schulz & Brenner, 1977), or a loss of support, even if that "support" falls into the category of "nagging" (e.g., "Have you taken your medicine yet?"), seem to be associated with an increased probability of death in elderly persons who are widowed (Rowland, 1977). Nirenberg (1983) has found that while relocation stress was greatest for less competent older persons, being able to acquire appropriate behavioral skills and gradual exposure to relocation stimuli (physical, spatial aspects of the nursing home) predicted postmove (three months) adjustment.

Contrary to the above, Carey (1979–1980) concluded that widowers were significantly *better* adjusted than were widows during the first year of bereavement. While being "forewarned" (allowing one to grieve in an anticipatory sense) was important for widows, it was not for widowers, according to Carey's (1979–1980) research. Younger widowed elderly (less than 56) were less worse off (better adjusted) than older ones. Widows who were more *highly educated,* had *higher incomes,* and lived *alone* (with no children to care for or live with) made better adjustments after death; this was not the case for widowers. Interestingly, those with stable, *happy* marriages *and* those with constant, pervasive marital *problems* appeared to be *better* adjusted. *Not* facing the death and/or deterioration prior to death and *uncertainty* about what life would be like after the death (who would care for them, manage their personal/financial affairs, personal safety, concerns over the care of dependent children) were the major problems seen to be overcome by the widows and widowers in Carey's study. Again, we see the importance of *control* (or at least *perceived* control) in the lives of elderly persons, in that uncertainty about or denial of impending death was negatively related to postdeath adjustment. Recently, a two-year longitudinal study by Lund, Caserta, and Dimond (1986) suggested that widows *and* widowers tended to face universal problems in bereavement, suggesting that grief over the loss of one's spouse is a universal experience for both men and women.

Grieving in Children

The effects of the death of a parent on a child can also have short-term and long-term consequences, for example, emotional and school (interpersonal, academic) difficulties, physical illness, and influence upon the choice of mate later on in life based upon the image of the dead parent (Furman, 1984; Wass, 1979).

Furman (1984) stresses the supportive, accepting role that the parent must play in helping a grieving child and the importance of the child's assurance of being cared for in a continuing relationship with the surviving parent. Questions about the death of a parent (how? why? where?) should be answered openly and reactions to and feelings about the loss observed in an accepting home atmosphere. Additionally the distinction between temporary and permanent absences should be made clear to the child.

Furman (1984) does indicate that even young children can cope with the death of a parent, grandparent, or sibling with appropriate support from loved ones (e.g., a surviving parent or a parent substitute). Much depends on the level at which the child understands death, what caused the death, and how the body is to be disposed of. In this light, Speece and Brent (1984) found that, on the whole, most children between the ages of five and seven understand that death is final, that life functions end when someone dies, and that all living things die. At the same time, even older children, depending upon their own unique personalities and emotional relationship and extent of their dependency on the person who has died, can have problems (e.g., sleeping, eating, behavioral, or academic problems at school) stemming from their difficulty in coping with their parent's death. Some younger children seem to deal with their parent's death without difficulty, given the support of others. At the same time, others experience difficulties of a more pervasive, far-reaching nature (e.g., toilet training, fighting with others, nightmares, low self-esteem, unrealistically high expectations of self). Thus, there are vast differences between children in the grieving process, and each child's own uniqueness must be taken into consideration in helping him or her to grieve the loss of a parent or sibling.

Divorce, as well as death, also often has severe, long-term effects on children (see Chapters 8 and 9). Papalia and Olds (1982) note that children of divorce mourn or express grief over the loss of the relationship with their parents just as they might if one or both of the parents had died. As we noted above, they become depressed, angry, or may experience guilt, assuming that the breakup is somehow their fault. They may express fears over the future, who will care for them, and be generally anxious about what will happen to them (Hetherington, 1979). Parents, alternatively, may have more difficulty in communicating with their children and caring for and supporting them and may seem to be more inconsistent in their demands. They, in spite of the divorce, also need to hold down jobs and satisfy their need for heterosexual companionship and contact. The immediate effects of divorce on both parent and child discussed here seem to lessen in severity after approximately two years, but it seems logical to assume that long-term effects may exist for *some* children and for *some* parents as well in terms of relationships with the opposite sex, marital quality, and personal happiness. Recent longitudinal (two years +) studies by Hetherington, M. Cox, and R. Cox (1982, 1985), Guidubaldi, Cleminshaw, Perry, and McLaughlin (1983), and Guidubaldi and Perry (1985) bear out the negative effects of divorce on children's emotional health and school performance (see Chapters 8 & 9).

Grieving Over the Loss of a Child

When the death of a grown child was experienced by elderly parents, grief reactions were often very intense and prolonged (Owen, Fulton, & Markusen, 1983; Sanders, 1979–1980). Older persons who lose adult children through death experience a special sense of failure that is difficult to deal with in that being a parent involves a sense of omnipotence about one's ability to care for a child that is formed very early in life (see Miles, 1984; Osterweis et al., 1984; Stevens-Long, 1984). Very few adults expect to bury their children.

Likewise, younger adults who lose children through death, particularly if those children die at a relatively young age, grieve for long periods of time (Miles, 1984). Just as children are often protected from death because we assume that they should not/cannot understand the nature of death, parents of young children who have died are often forced to be physically and emotionally separated from their dead child, especially if the child has died in childbirth or shortly thereafter. The woman may be sedated, or the father may be given the "job" of telling his wife that their child has died (Hildebrand & Schreiner, 1980). Funerals may be avoided because it is assumed that they would be too upsetting, further interfering with the healthy expression of feelings. Many times parents assume that *they* are responsible— they did not prepare themselves adequately or they should have done something to prevent their child's death, even though they may not know what this "something" may be (Share, 1978). They often feel alone—isolated from friends, family, and one another. They may feel angry and resentful toward others—family, friends, medical staff. They may be disappointed in one another (Share, 1978). Ultimately, perhaps, the child's death challenges their feelings of "parental omnipotence"—that feeling that because they are parents, they *should* be able to "fix" everything in their child's life.

These feelings of having failed as a parent *and* having lost a part of oneself when an infant dies are intensified by the fact that in many cases a miscarriage, stillbirth, or neonatal or infant death (referred to as **sudden infant death syndrome [SIDS]**) cannot be prevented or predicted (G. W. Davidson, 1984; Donnelly, 1982; Naeye, 1980). In spite of the tremendous publicity SIDS has received recently, researchers are still unable to say what causes infants to stop breathing without warning (see G. W. Davidson, 1984; Papalia & Olds, 1982). At best, the parent might purchase a respiratory monitor to keep aware of the infant's breathing. In the long run, however, one's greatest fear as a young parent is that one's child may die suddenly and that one will be powerless to prevent it. The death of a very young child can have serious consequences for the family as a whole (see G. W. Davidson, 1984; E. Lewis, 1979; Osterweis et al., 1984; Share, 1978), often leading to divorce, physical/mental illness, or school difficulties. Clearly, for families where an atmosphere of *open* communication between husband and wife and between parents and children exists, the grief work is easier to accomplish in that the parents can communicate their feelings to one another *without* feeling that they must "put up a front" for the sake of their remaining children (Share, 1978; Osterweis et al., 1984). Information and communication are not something to be managed but instead are shared with *all* family members in an atmosphere of love, care, and respect for one another's feelings, whether those feelings are acceptable (sadness, sorrow) or not (anger, guilt, jealousy, relief) (Furman, 1984; Kübler-Ross, 1969; Share, 1978; Wass, 1979). Kotch and Cohen (1985–1986), for example, found that sharing the autopsy report with bereaved parents was helpful in aiding them to cope with the loss of their infant.

Grieving in Young and Elderly Adults

Whether older persons "grieve" in different ways in the process of adjusting to loss versus the young is a matter of some disagreement. Some authors, notably Kalish (1976), R. Schulz (1978), and E. Jackson (1979), discuss "stages" of grief: (1) initial shock/disbelief, (2) a working through of one's feelings and a review of one's relationship with the deceased, and (3) a restructuring phase, where "life moves on," which may last for varying periods of time. Research by C. Barrett and Schneweis (1980–1981), however, does not support the notion that one's reactions to being bereaved change consistently with the passage of time widowed.

Sanders (1979–1980), on the other hand, found the younger widow to initially experience intense grief reactions (denial, anger, guilt, feelings of aloneness, physical illness or sleep disturbances, being preoccupied with the death) followed by a lessening of these reactions 18 months later, while the reverse was true for older widows and widowers. While being able to anticipate one's feelings in order to prepare oneself for a spouse's death may have had beneficial effects on later adjustment for a limited amount of time, the long-term effects of the loss of one's spouse were clearly evident. *Loneliness* was, for all bereaved, the chief long-term problem (Sanders, 1979–1980). Lund, Dimond, Caserta, Johnson, Poulton, and Connelly (1985–1986) have found that elderly persons who had difficulty coping with a death two years later differed from those who were "good copers." Poor copers expressed lower self-esteem prior to bereavement and had more confusion, a greater desire to die, cried more, and were less able to keep busy shortly after the death. This suggests that elderly persons who experience particularly strong emotions and who have poor self-images are likely to have problems in adjusting to death later on. In a recent study of elderly persons' adjustment to death, Norris and Murrell (1987) interviewed over 400 older adults, 25 percent of whom had experienced the death of a spouse, child, or parent, while the remainder were not bereaved. At both pre- and post-bereavement, measures of health and psychological distress were taken. Contrary to expectations, Norris and Murrell found that bereavement did *not* affect health. Moreover, there was poorer health and psychological distress (depression) among the bereaved *only* when accompanied by prior family stress (illness, family conflicts). After the death, health worsened *if* there had been no family stress preceding death; for the bereaved group with prior stress, health *improved* after the death. Family stress worsened as death approached, but decreased thereafter (one year later).

These findings indicate that while bereavement may be stressful, it does not necessarily result in poorer health. While family stress preceded death rather than resulted from it, the authors suggested that the physical and emotional difficulties in caring for a loved one who is dying, rather than that person's death per se, accounts for this distress. In fact, for persons who had experienced some sort of family stress who were *not* yet bereaved, health declined somewhat.

The Norris and Murrell (1987) findings should alert us to the complexity of the relationship between bereavement and subsequent psychological/physical health; whether one has experienced prior family stress or not seems to influence this relationship. Helping interventions should be redesigned and targeted to vulnerable elderly caring for a dying loved one *before,* rather than after bereavement (Norris & Murrell, 1987).

Surprisingly, perhaps, M. Moss and D. Moss (1980) have discussed the impact that investing oneself emotionally in a marital relationship has in the subsequent remarriage of those elderly who are widowed. Many older women attempt to relate to their new husbands in terms of their former relationships with a *deceased* husband (Lopata, 1973). In many cases, this "sanctification" of the deceased spouse can interfere with the new relationship, and in order to move on, ties with the first spouse must be worked through by both parties (see Hayslip & Martin, 1988).

Grief Work

As many of those who have lost a loved one know, grief is a very complex yet private experience. While we often *grieve anticipatorily* (before a person actually dies), some of our grief can also be experienced at a funeral or memorial service honoring the life of the person who has died. Funerals and other forms of ritual serve to structure our emotions at a time when we might otherwise be overwhelmed. We may busy ourselves making funeral arrangements or entertaining relatives with little or no time to really be alone and reflect on how we are feeling.

Funerals' major functions are (1) to provide a socially acceptable, healthy means by which to prepare the body for burial (its *secular* function) (R. Schulz, 1978) and (2) to provide a symbolic rite of passage from the state of living to the state of being dead (its *sacred* function) (R. Schulz, 1978). Moreover, funerals provide *psychological support* to the bereaved family and others who have suffered the loss. In a sense, funerals are a final symbol of the fact that a person has lived, and they as well reaffirm the group identity of the survivors (Lopata, 1973) so that they can continue to function after the death. Thus, funerals can help those who mourn to work through their grief

Funerals serve a valuable psychological function in structuring the grieving process.

immediately after a death. Whether or not funerals are helpful in this sense in the long run, however, has yet to be explored.

Grief may take years to be fully resolved, or it may never be worked through. One might ask, *"Should* grief be 'worked through'?" The answer to this question is complex. If "working through" implies taking away what little is left of that person (memories of a relationship) in someone's life, then the answer to this question is definitely no. It is often out of our wish to avoid pain that we do not permit others to experience the pain that is necessary in order to do what has come to be known as *grief work.* Consequently, avoiding talking about the obvious and "managing" communication (by changing the subject) can only serve to make the loss more hurtful and most likely will make postdeath adjustment more difficult (Share, 1978). Since widowed persons (regardless of age) may have built their lives on a primary relationship with a significant other, extreme caution needs to be exercised in judging extended grief reactions as "abnormal" (E. Jackson, 1979). Indeed, having support from others (Hafer, 1981), acknowledging the wish to be alone (Kübler-Ross, 1982), and encouraging the immediate expression of feelings (C.M. Parkes & Weiss, 1983) seem to be helpful in grief resolution.

When the surviving spouse has no other source of emotional support (is isolated from others) or has other children to support with little financial/psychological resources (Bankoff, 1983; Raphael, 1983; Rowland, 1977; Silverman & Cooperband, 1984), bereavement seems to be more difficult. Grief is often composed of many different types of responses (affective, behavioral, physical) and seemingly contradictory emotions (an intense desire to hold on to the image/memory of the dead spouse, guilt, anger, relief) (E. Jackson, 1979). Accepting such emotions seems to positively predict bereavement outcome (C.M. Parkes & Weiss, 1983; Worden, 1982).

The importance of remaining *in touch* with someone as a crucial element in the surviving spouse's ultimate survival has been emphasized (Botwinick, 1984). Those who are bereaved are often avoided and treated as if they are *sick* (Kalish, 1985a). Allowing themselves to become isolated from others robs grieving persons (especially older widows and widowers) of an important source of support and feedback about their emotions (anger, guilt, sadness, anxiety, depression). On the other hand, it is common to observe in those who are grieving a desire for a certain amount of time to be alone. Self-imposed isolation over an extended period of time, out of a desire to *deny* that a death has occurred, *may,* however, indicate that the grieving person is experiencing difficulty in coping with the loss.

What is crucial is the *quality* (harmful, self-destructive, unrealistic) of one's behavior, not its *quantity* (length of time grieving), in making judgments about whether the grief is abnormal or not (Lindemann, 1944). Thus, abnormal (maladaptive) grief frequently involves a change in the individual's behavior (e.g., chronic depression, extended denial of the death, self-abusive/self-destructive behavior, and isolation from others) (E. Jackson, 1979).

Normal adaptive grief may or may not last for an extended time period (e.g., two to three years), depending upon a number of factors (personality, health, relationship with the deceased person, support from others). Just because after two years persons continue to feel sad from time to time about a loved one's death does *not* necessarily suggest that they are having trouble completing the grief process. Balkwell (1985) and Stevenson (1985) have found that widowers are more likely to be socially isolated and less apt to express their feelings, perhaps indicating that men may have a more difficult bereavement than do women, though there are wide individual differences in grieving among widows (Bankoff, 1983; Silverman & Cooperband, 1984).

Davis and Klopfer (1977), in a discussion of psychotherapy with the aged, note that "too many (therapists) . . . are seeking for *something to do to their clients,* rather than being concerned about how *to be somebody with them. . . .*" (p. 345). It is, perhaps, this essential aloneness, an *inability to communicate,* that prevents helpers, families, and friends from "getting through" to the older person who is considering taking his own life, who faces life without a husband or wife, or who is coping with a terminal illness. While this is certainly true for the aged, it is *no less true* for younger adults. A respect for the individuality of *every* life is perhaps the most important quality to recognize and develop in dealing with adults of all ages and death. To be permitted to make choices, unhampered by the biases of others, to be told that one's life still counts, is all that many old or young persons ask. Being sensitive to these wishes is perhaps the essential skill that we can nurture in helping adults deal with their own deaths and in counseling those who are coping with the loss of a significant other.

While this chapter has dealt often with death, dying, and aging, the issues discussed here are those that *persons of all ages face:* desiring control over their lives, wanting to be loved and cared for, being treated with respect and dignity as individuals who are growing older, and perhaps most importantly, appreciating the intertwining of life and death. As Wass and Corr (1981) have so cogently noted, "We cannot grasp or evaluate the proportions and the significance of life if we do not bring death into the picture. Just as death must be construed through life, so also life must eventually be seen in the context of death. Certainly death is not the only perspective from which to understand life, but . . . it is indispensable as a constitutive element of human existence" (p. 7).

SUMMARY

The association between death and aging has a number of negative consequences for the young and the old. Defining death is a complex process, as is the understanding of what one means when one states that one is fearful of death. Individuals can be said to die at various levels, and fears about *death* need to be separated from those about the *dying process* or the *afterlife.* These fears may or may not be expressed *consciously.*

Older persons think about death more often than do younger persons and personalize it more frequently as well. Their responses to death are highly variable but do seem to be related to a number of factors, most notably health status and institutionalization. While *grief* and *bereavement* are distinct from one another, research does not support the thesis that older persons are more prone to physical/emotional illness or death simply because they are bereaved. Rather, it seems more important to examine factors that influence whether the surviving individual interprets the loss as replaceable or not. While older versus younger widows and widowers may cope with different short-term and long-term issues, loneliness remains the chief problem for those who are bereaved. In working with grieving persons, as *Kübler-Ross*'s stage theory implies, it is most important to recognize each person's feelings as unique and to deal with each individual in a nonjudgmental manner.

Hospice has provided many terminally ill persons and their families with alternatives to dying in an institution. Its chief characteristics are pain/symptom control, 24-hour care, treatment of the patient and family as a unit, and bereavement follow-up.

Euthanasia is a highly controversial area regarding the quality versus the quantity of life. Distinctions between *active* and *passive* euthanasia can be made, and there are age, sex, and racial differences regarding its acceptance. While *living wills* have helped structure decisions regarding euthanasia, there remain numerous issues that complicate their utility in many situations.

Suicide and *depression* seem to be associated in that most attempted suicides follow a bout of depression. While younger suicides can be described as having an ambivalent character, older suicides have a definite *egoistic*, intentional quality to them. Among teenagers and older men, suicide rates are increasing at the greatest rate. Deaths within institutions are becoming a more prevalent problem for many elderly who wish to exercise control over their lives. For all adults, *clear, empathic communication* is the key to preventing suicides among those who wish to end their lives.

KEY TERMS AND CONCEPTS

Clinical death	Bereavement overload
Biological death	Sudden infant death syndrome (SIDS)
Cerebral death	Personalization of death
Social death	Hospice
Psychic death	Lethality scale
Death anxiety	Line of unbearability
Death versus dying	ISDB
Overcoming	Principle of compensation
Participating	Active versus passive euthanasia
Integrity	Stage theory of dying
Disengagement	Living will
Life review	Unconditional positive regard
Grief versus bereavement	Right to die
Anticipatory grief	Death with dignity
Regressive intervention	

- What are some of the problems in getting an accurate picture of abnormal behavior across adulthood?
- What is mental health? How can it be defined among the aged? What are the advantages of viewing mental health and mental illness along a continuum?
- What seem to be prerequisites for positive mental health among the aged?
- What models of mental illness does Zarit use in understanding abnormal behavior among the aged? What are each model's strengths and weaknesses?
- What is dementia? Of what value is it regarding diagnosis?
- What is the distinction between irreversible and reversible organic conditions? Why is this distinction important?
- What is pseudodementia? How is it different from dementia?
- What guidelines need to be kept in mind in assessing elderly persons?

CHAPTER 13

MENTAL HEALTH

AND

PSYCHOPATHOLOGY

■

INTRODUCTION

Getting an Accurate Picture

Despite the interest in psychopathology (abnormal behavior) and aging (Birren & Sloane, 1980; Busse & Blazer, 1980; Storandt, 1983; Verwoerdt, 1981), there is not much factual information regarding the frequency of the various forms of abnormal behavior during the later phases of the adult life cycle. Thus, statements about psychopathology and aging, reflecting this lack of a firm base, are often vague.

For example, a recent (1984) study by the National Institute of Mental Health (J. K. Myers et al., 1984) based upon interviews with nearly 10,000 adults found that 1 in 5 Americans suffered from some form of mental illness. Only a fifth of those, however, had sought help for these problems, and most of these helpers were physicians. Within a six-month period (see Table 13.1), anxiety disorders (phobias, panic disorders, obsessive-compulsive disorders) were the most common problems found. Women were more prone to suffer from phobias and depression, while men suffered more from alcohol abuse/ drug dependence and chronic antisocial behaviors. Character disorders were more common for those younger than 45. However, drug and alcohol abuse and antisocial behavior were rare after the age of 45. Those more highly educated were less prone to be troubled, and schizophrenia was rare (1 percent) among those studied.

These figures not only tell us that many types of mental disorders are less common than believed (depression), but also that most Americans rarely seek help for their problems (see Chapter 14). Most importantly for our purposes, they could suggest the middle-aged and elderly to be at *less* risk for some forms of psychological disorders, while more prone to others.

Other data, however, reported by D. W. Kay and Bergmann (1980), and by J. M. Murphy et al. (1984) (see Figure 13.1) suggest a *varied* pattern of incidence across age for various disorders. Moreover, high levels of referrals were found for *all* types of disorders throughout adulthood, with referrals for depression being *more* common among those over 65 years of age (D.W. Kay & Bergmann, 1980; J.M. Murphy et al., 1984).

Blazer (1980) suggests the frequency of neurosis and schizophrenia to

TABLE 13.1

RESULTS FROM 1984 NIMH STUDY ON MENTAL ILLNESS IN AMERICA

Four Most Frequent DIS/*DSM-III* Psychiatric Disorders by Sex and Age Based on Six-Month Prevalence Rates*

Rank	18–24 Yr.	25–44 Yr.	45–64 Yr.	65+ Yr.	Total
			Men		
1	Alcohol abuse/dependence	Alcohol abuse/dependence	Alcohol abuse/dependence	Severe cognitive impairment	Alcohol abuse/dependence
2	Drug abuse/dependence	Phobia	Phobia	Phobia	Phobia
3	Phobia	Drug abuse/dependence	Dysthymia	Alcohol abuse/dependence	Drug abuse/dependence
4	Antisocial personality	Antisocial personality	Major depressive episode without grief	Dysthymia	Dysthymia
			Women		
1	Phobia	Phobia	Phobia	Phobia	Phobia
2	Drug abuse/dependence	Major depressive episode without grief	Dysthymia	Severe cognitive impairment	Major depressive episode without grief
3	Major depressive episode without grief	Dysthymia	Major depressive episode without grief	Dysthymia	Dysthymia
4	Alcohol abuse/dependence	Obsessive-compulsive disorder	Obsessive-compulsive disorder	Major depressive episode without grief	Obsessive-compulsive disorder

*Dysthmia included. The basis for ranking was the mean six-month prevalence rates for New Haven, Baltimore, and St. Louis combined. DIS indicates Diagnostic Interview Schedule.

Source: From J. K. Myers, M. M. Weissman, G. L. Tischler, C. E. Holzer III, P. J. Leaf, H. Orvaschel, J. C. Anthony, J. H. Boyd, J. D. Burke, M. Kramer, & R. Stoltzmann. (1984). Six-month prevalence of psychiatric disorders in three communities. *Archives of General Psychiatry, 41,* 965.

decline with age, while organic mental disorders and psychosomatic complaints (preoccupation with one's bodily functions in the absence of a real problem) increase among the aged. While we cannot dismiss this information entirely, it should be viewed cautiously for several reasons: (1) older persons may need to be diagnosed by different means than younger persons (for example, by relying on observations of behavior rather than test scores); (2) symptoms (sleeplessness) versus diagnoses (depression) being reported yield different conclusions; (3) clinicians' biases about the elderly or about women may cause them to misdiagnose; and (4) how our data are gathered affects our conclusions about mental health and mental illness across the life span. For example, one might rely on actual chart reviews, referrals from mental-health personnel, reports of frequency of symptoms, or self-administered questionnaires.

All of these factors will affect conclusions we come to about the prevalence of mental illness in adulthood. For example, are older persons more prone to depression or schizophrenia than younger persons?

While studies do not always agree, the information they provide can be helpful in supplying a rough estimate of the incidence of disorders across the age continuum, important for research and planning purposes. Such information can also be valuable in alerting mental-health personnel to the disorders older or younger persons are especially prone to or be helpful in affecting the design and implementation of services directed to individuals who are "at risk" psychologically (e.g., those who are ill or isolated).

This chapter focuses upon the *continuum* of **mental health–mental illness**, with a particular emphasis upon late adulthood. Indeed, the figures

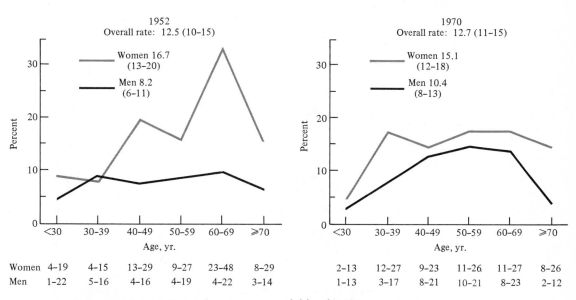

Figure 13.1 Prevalence of depression and anxiety across adulthood: 1952 versus 1970.
Source: J. M. Murphy, A. M. Sobol, R. K. Neff, D. C. Olivier, & A. H. Leighton. (1984). Stability of prevalence: depression and anxiety disorders. *Archives of General Psychiatry, 41,* 995. Copyright 1984, American Medical Association. Reprinted with permission.

we cited above suggest some forms of mental illness to be *less* prevalent among the middle-aged and elderly. Assuming, however, that older adults are less likely to seek help for their problems, we could easily argue that they are *more* vulnerable to most types of psychological disorders. Either they are less prone to see themselves in need of help or they are regarded as less likely to benefit from help by others (see Chapter 14). While a comprehensive discussion of all types of abnormal behavior is clearly beyond the scope of this chapter, you may consult J. Coleman, Butcher, and Carson (1984), Ullmann and Krasner (1975), Davison and Neale (1978), or Suinn (1975) for a thorough treatment of all forms of aberrant behavior.

Though the terms *mental health* and its purported opposite *mental illness* mean many things to many people, we will attempt to define them operationally in this chapter.

Additionally, one of our goals in this chapter is to define what factors contribute to *positive mental health* in elderly persons and to make recommendations about how we can best facilitate a positive sense of self in old age.

Older Persons' Use of Mental-Health Services: Relationship to Perceptions of Mental Health

Older persons not only often see themselves in a more positive light than do younger persons (L. Harris and Associates, 1975), but, moreover, rampant ageism (see Chapter 9) works against older persons regarding the attitudes mental-health service providers hold toward their elderly would-be clients (R. Davis & Klopfer, 1977; Ford & Sbordone, 1980; Gatz, Smyer, & Lawton, 1980; Ray, McKinney, & Ford, 1987). These negative expectations have many roots: unresolved conflicts about one's own aging, one's parents, or about death (see Chapter 12). A lack of experience with aged patients leads to even more negative evaluations about their prognosis.

In addition to negative attitudes toward older clients, many physical-emotional problems are often *mistakenly* seen as a direct consequence of aging (e.g., isolation from others, inadequate income, lessened access to health care, and limited educational and recreational opportunities). These factors work against older persons getting the kind of mental-health care they want and need.

Gatz et al. (1980) and G. Cohen (1980) have highlighted many of the problems associated with mental-health services to aged persons; these are (1) untimely use, (2) lack of information, (3) rejection of services that compete with elderly value systems that stress independence, (4) cost of services, (5) accessibility (lack of transportation), (6) gaps in service, and (7) attitudes and training of staff.

Until these barriers are dealt with, what we know about mental health and aging is likely to continue to be very limited and based on a biased sample of the potential would-be elderly counselees, perhaps those with the fewest resources and in the poorest health. Lawton (1978) has suggested that the use of mental-health services will increase as future cohorts of elderly persons become more highly educated and thus more psychologically sophisticated. Others (Lieberman, 1978; Sargent, 1980) have also noted that current services might be more fully used if they were more nontraditional in nature. Such help could be provided by persons such as paraprofessionals, nurses, friends, and volunteers or those in the "natural helping network" of the aged persons such as druggists, beauticians, mailmen, custodians, or peers. From our discussion, it should be clear that one's ideas about the mental health of older persons versus younger persons are heavily influenced by one's beliefs and attitudes regarding aging and development (see Chapters 1 and 9). A service provider's lack of contact with older clients may be both a cause for and a result of that provider's ideas about mental health and mental illness in adults.

DEFINING MENTAL HEALTH AND ABNORMALITY IN ADULTHOOD

It is probably accurate to say that we know more about what mental health is *not* than about those qualities *positively* defining mental health in adulthood.

Birren and Renner (1980) have noted that the terms *normal* and *abnormal* are difficult to define precisely, in that the criteria for each change with time and society's expectation. Thus, as society's standards for what constitutes acceptable, "normal" behavior change, so too will our ideas about defining as normal or abnormal those behaviors particular to aged persons. This is because, as Ullman and Krasner (1975) have noted, once a behavior is *labeled* abnormal or deviant, it immediately becomes the concern of a qualified professional (i.e., a psychologist, psychotherapist, or a psychiatrist) and implies that the behavior is disruptive, unlawful, or harmful to oneself or others. It is at this point that our attitudes toward the aged (as individuals and as consumers of psychological services) come into play.

Birren and Renner (1979, 1980) suggest that mental health is an exceedingly difficult concept to define, regardless of whether we are referring to the young or the aged person. They note that Jahoda (1958) suggests mentally healthy people to possess the following characteristics: (1) a positive self-attitude, (2) an accurate perception of reality, (3) environmental mastery, (4) autonomy, (5) personality balance, and (6) growth/self-actualization.

We might argue that behaviors that are harmful to individuals and take away from their sense of well-being are considered abnormal (J. Coleman, Butcher, & Carson, 1984). Thus, behaviors that bring one into conflict (within oneself or with others) and are perceived as distressing or disruptive to one's own well-being are deemed maladaptive. However, behaviors that most laypersons and professionals would define as abnormal by this standard are often quite adaptive for many aged persons, (e.g., depression, aggressiveness, obsessive-compulsive behavior, isolation, passivity, or anxiety) (Birren & Renner, 1979; Gurland, 1973; Lieberman, 1975). Such behaviors would *not* provide a good standard for determining whether an older person's behaviors are abnormal. Gurland (1973) notes that this is especially a problem if such behaviors are considered singly rather than in combination. Moreover, when the environment or society is perceived to be the cause of the behavior, it is less likely to be judged as abnormal, since the individual is not at fault.

Applying these standards to the aged presents some difficulties. Due to lessened income, poor health, enforced isolation, retirement, widowhood, or the effects of drugs, many older persons simply do not have the opportunity to be autonomous or master their environments (Gurland, 1973). They may be legitimately depressed or hostile and may turn away from what appears to be a bleak future to focus on the past. They may not have the financial or interpersonal resources to make decisions about their lives or to plan ahead. For some individuals, in some situations, depression, apathy, anxiety, or hostility may actually *help* one adjust to events over which one has little control (isolation from others, institutionalization) (Gurland, 1973). Thus, there is much merit in stating that everyone behaves "abnormally" in certain situations, while in other situations, the same behavior may clearly be inappropriate (e.g., yelling in class vs. yelling at a ballgame) (see Chapter 10).

ABNORMAL BEHAVIOR IN THE AGED

As with mental health, defining pathology in aged persons is complex. In many cases, those signs and symptoms of pathology in the aged are not the same as those in the young. Individual and situation-specific differences are substantial (see Gurland, 1973). As noted above, when clinicians have more extensive experience with a variety of disturbed elderly persons, inconsistencies that currently exist are likely to lessen.

The emphasis on individual variability is particularly important in light of the current reliance on diagnostic typologies such as DSM-III-R (*Diagnostic and Statistical Manual of Mental Disorders,* 4th Edition, developed by the American Psychiatric Association, 1987).

DSM-III-R

The *Diagnostic and Statistical Manual of Mental Disorders* (1987, 4th ed.) **(DSM-III-R)** of the American Psychiatric Association serves as a framework for diagnostic assessment of a variety of mental disorders in that it both clearly defines such disorders and is useful as a working language tool about abnormality for clinicians, researchers, and practitioners. Thus, it provides professionals with a working set of definitions that aid in communication. DSM-III-R in some cases also provides information about etiology and specifies diagnostic criteria (yet to be validated) as guides for making a diagnosis.

DSM-III-R uses a multiaxial (multidimensional) system so that each individual can be comprehensively evaluated for purposes of either planning a treatment program or predicting therapeutic outcome.

Axes I and II encompass all of the mental disorders. Axis II deals with personality disorders and specific developmental disorders, and Axis I includes all other mental disorders. Axis III includes physical disorders and conditions. Each axis forms a dimension that refers to a unique bit of information about the individual. Each individual is assessed along each axis, and the first three axes represent the official diagnostic assessment. Axes IV and V supplement the first three and are useful in arriving at a more complete understanding of the individual for treatment purposes. Axis IV deals with severity of psychosocial stresses and Axis V focuses upon highest level of adaptive functioning in the past year. Multiple diagnoses within axes are possible. Usually, the clinician, using the DSM-III-R, can reach a *principal* diagnosis (usually on Axis I), referring to the condition for which the individual was recommended to be assessed or admitted to care. Each entry within the five axes is accompanied by information about its (1) essential features, (2) associated (sometimes, but not always present) features, (3) age at onset, (4) cause, (5) expected impairments in functioning, (6) complications, (7) predisposing factors, (8) prevalence, (9) sex ratio, (10) familial pattern, and (11) disorders that should be distinguished from the one being presented. Specific diagnostic criteria follow after each disorder has been described in the above terms.

Relative to DSM-I (1952) and DSM-II (1968), DSM-III (1980) and DSM-III-R represent major improvements as aids in diagnosis with the aged (see Butler & Lewis, 1981; Gatz et al., 1980). DSM-III (and DSM-III-R) have "more specific criteria, an expanded description of disorders, and a multilevel or multiaxial approach to evaluation" (Butler & Lewis, 1981, p. 65). Despite these improvements, we recommend its use with *caution;* it is to be used *conservatively.* Diagnoses utilizing DSM with other age-groups have been proven to be somewhat unreliable (see Davison & Neale, 1978). While practitioners need to refer to the DSM-III-R for hospital diagnoses or insurance forms, they should evaluate the definitions and classifications carefully since these may not always clearly reflect reality for the older person. This is not to imply that DSM-III-R is useless but it does suggest that we not let such criteria blind us to what our clinical experience, psychological tests, interviews with family, etc. tell us about the older person we are treating.

Current Models of Abnormal Behavior in the Aged

Raskin (1979) chooses to focus on those unique forms of functional abnormal behavior in the aged, that is, depression, anxiety, dementia, schizophrenia, and sleep disturbances. To this list Pfeiffer (1977) adds organic brain syndrome, suicide, manic reactions, hypochondriasis, paranoid reactions, social pathology (sexuality, family problems, loneliness, isolation) and alcoholism. Simon (1980), still further, adds drug abuse.

Beyond the "cataloging" of the above varieties of abnormal behavior, in what *general* terms can we see psychopathology in the aged? S. Zarit (1980) (see also Eisdorfer, 1983) has discussed several: the *medical model, aging as illness model,* and the *behavioral model.* In addition, he notes *legal, statistical, humanistic,* and *social deprivational* models.

Briefly stated (see S. Zarit, 1980), the **medical model** assumes an underlying "cause" (usually of a physical or structural nature), that is, a disease state, to be responsible for the behavior. The outward symptoms are simply a manifestation of this disease. Alleviation of these symptoms via some form of treatment assumes that the disease process has been reversed. The **aging as illness model** stems from the medical model and assumes that the underlying illness is the aging process itself. The **behavioral model** focuses on the learning history of the person and those factors in the environment (or a person's perception of those factors) that serve to cause and maintain behaviors, which due to their consequences for the person are seen as maladaptive. This model is problem or symptom oriented, rather than one that attributes the person's difficulties to some unobserved process or state (see S. Zarit, 1980 for an extensive discussion).

While each approach has its advantages and disadvantages, we must remember (see Chapter 1) that, strictly speaking, they cannot be compared in that they rest on entirely different assumptions, that is, what causes abnormal behavior (Reese & Overton, 1970). On the one hand, the medical model leads us to focus on single internal (exclusive of the outside environment) disease entities (implying a single best treatment for each) that are organic in nature. Alternatively, it has led to a more finely tuned approach to the identification of organic disorders in the aged persons (chronic, irreversible OBS) (S. Zarit, 1980). The application of a *behavioral* strategy to defining abnormal behavior can be used to identify and change those aspects of the *environment* responsible for the maintenance of maladaptive behavior (organically caused or not). It does, however, not rely on a judgment about the presence of what may be a vaguely defined condition.

Legal criteria (S. Zarit, 1980) rest on assumed *competence. Humanistic* ideas about abnormality stress a lack of individual efforts at growth and *self-actualization. Statistical* criteria imply that differences from others, expressed in behaviors that are rare in their *frequency,* create difficulties for the person. The *social deprivation* approach suggests that factors such as stress and isolation in and of themselves create pathology in the aged.

Zarit (1980) suggests that each of these models taken singly is problematical when applied to the aged. How should competence be defined? How is one to evaluate departures from "optimal growth"? Are behaviors that are infrequent necessarily abnormal? Who is to define what stress is? Is stress necessarily bad? Are events generally seen as stressful (e.g., retirement) always viewed as such by all aged? (see Eisdorfer & Wilkie, 1977, 1979a, 1979b). When we attribute pathology to such factors as isolation (see G. Cohen, 1980), we are confusing the "problem" with the aged person. While some elderly are isolated, they are not necessarily abnormal simply *because* they are isolated (or older, for that matter!).

Many of those who hold the most negative attitudes toward the aged also believe in the aging as illness model. The central issue here is what we mean by anything being caused by "old age." We generally view chronological age (see Chapters 1 and 2) as *not* being causal. Instead, age-related changes in behavior are *dependent* on other factors (e.g., cardiovascular status, life-style, number and spacing of individual stressors). When persons approach later adulthood (whether it be defined as 65 or 70), they do not suddenly, by virtue of being 65 or 70 per se, become more abnormal. For example, it is one thing to say that age and depression are related; it is quite another to say *why* they are related. An older person may be depressed over factors that have nothing to do with aging per se (e.g., marital difficulties). This view contributes to the use of such nondescript terms as *senility,* which are of little value diagnostically (Hayslip, 1982a). Moreover, they encourage a "we cannot treat this older person because he or she is old" approach, which is at worst no effort at treatment and often at best custodial care in an institution (S. Zarit, 1980).

It is likely that none of these models discussed by Zarit is sufficient to define abnormal behavior adequately in aged persons. Each contributes to a piece of the puzzle. Thus, it is important to recognize how they differ and that they may be combined in a meaningful way to aid one in understanding maladaptive behavior.

SPECIFIC FORMS OF PSYCHOPATHOLOGY COMMON AMONG THE AGED

We will, in examining the major forms of psychopathology in the aged, concentrate on those manifestations *unique* to older persons. We must not forget, however, that many of the factors contributing to these syndromes are *not* age related. This very sensitivity is perhaps the most important issue in best deciding how to treat the disturbed elderly person (see Gallagher, Thompson, & Levy, 1980; Raskin, 1979).

Organic Disorders

ALZHEIMER'S DISEASE, PICK'S DISEASE, MULTI-INFARCT DEMENTIA, AND OTHER DEMENTIAS

Of considerable importance of late, both professionally and from a lay point of view, is the diagnosis of **dementia** in the aged. The causes of dementia receiving the most attention at present are **multi-infarct dementia** (multiple cerebral lesions [infarcts]) and **Alzheimer's disease** (see Box 13.1), in part due to organizations such as the Alzheimer's Disease and Related Disease Association (ADRDA) in the United States and the Alzheimer's Disease Society (ADS) in Great Britain. The dominant feature of dementia is *brain cell* (neuronal) *loss* or *impairment* (see Pfeiffer, 1977; Sloane, 1980) (see Chapter 2). It is important to note that in dementia such brain cell loss is *correlated* with a number of behavioral changes (see below). Definitive answers on *why* brain cells degenerate have yet to be discovered. Whitbourne (1985), for example, discusses several possible theories that try to explain the loss of brain cells (termed *neurons*) with age (see Chapter 2). While many neurons may serve overlapping functions, only when (1) certain critical connections between neurons (termed *synapses*) are severed through the loss of certain neurons, or (2) when neuronal loss reaches a given threshold, do persons evidence changes in their behavior (e.g., memory loss, learning difficulties). The classical *global* symptoms associated with dementia include disorientation to time and place, short-term and long-term memory loss, eye-hand coordination disturbances, impairment of intellect (deficits in calculation, learning of new material, and abstraction) and impaired judgment (Gilhooly, S. Zarit, & Birren, 1986). Mental slowing is also frequently present (Nebes & Madden,

BOX 13.1

ALZHEIMER'S DISEASE

Alzheimer's is a disease of brain dysfunction named for its discoverer, Alois Alzheimer, in 1907. Many adults of normal intelligence become afflicted with Alzheimer's disease, which causes changes in their thinking and behavior from accustomed patterns to bizarre and disoriented confusion.

Individuals with Alzheimer's disease may act confused, paranoid, drunk, tired, or depressed, depending on their own personality. Their judgment will be poor, and they may compensate for their inabilities for a period of time when they can realize their shortcomings. Sometimes, however, they appear quite normal and in the early stages of the disease often deny that they are experiencing any problem whatsoever.

Long known incorrectly as "senility" and as inevitable if one lived long enough, Alzheimer's disease is now thought to be a specific disease, not simply normal aging. There are other types of dementia (see Table 13.2), and careful diagnosis should be sought, though this is difficult to do in many cases, particularly in the early stages. Some of these patients have reversible problems, though true Alzheimer patients, who have been diagnosed correctly, usually do not.

A diagnosis of Alzheimer's disease can be positively verified only by a histological exam. Early-onset dementia of the Alzheimer's type is more rapid and progressive than late-onset Alzheimer's disease. Currently, DSM-III-R (see text) puts Alzheimer's disease within a category of primary degenerative dementia that is late-onset (senile) type. In practice, though, the presence of higher than normal concentrations of plaques or tangles in the cerebral cortex (see text) is adequate to identify the dementia as being caused by Alzheimer's disease. Persons with Down's syndrome who survive into adulthood also have elevated concentrations of plaques and tangles.

There are a variety of biochemical, electrophysiological, and neural changes associated with Alzheimer's disease that are often, upon analysis after death, confounded with vascular damage due to multiple cerebral infarcts (Bondareff, 1986; Gilhooly et al., 1986). Certain structures of the brain (hippocampus, amygdala, brain stem) seem to be especially affected by the presence of plaques and tangles, and in addition, persons with Alzheimer's disease commonly evidence decreased levels of cortical neurotransmitters (acetylcholine, norepinephrine) (Bondareff, 1986). There is a suspected link between increased levels of aluminum and the formation of tangles (Bondareff, 1986). Many persons believe that there exist distinct subtypes of Alzheimer's disease (American Psychiatric Association, 1987).

Often, persons who are injured and taken to emergency rooms or are in jail or in intensive care (particularly if they have been drinking or are on medication) may act confused and have difficulty answering questions, contributing to falsely diagnosed dementia.

Personality changes (depression and withdrawal, anxiety, agitation, loss of interest in work, inability to concentrate, denial of problem) may act as first signals regarding the onset of Alzheimer's disease. Memory loss is the major symptom and may be the cause of many behavior and personality changes that coincide with the early development of the disease. From an occasional absentmindedness, Alzheimer's disease worsens to a point where the individual loses memory for all remembered and learned routines, facts, and information (e.g., one's name or the name of a spouse).

Many everyday activities depend on memory, so daily life eventually becomes chaotic and confusing when one cannot remember how to put on a jacket, tune the TV, or brush one's teeth. Personality and behavioral changes may involve disregard for habitual manners and morals, unforeseen senseless mood swings from laughter to tears, or a sudden turnabout from love to hate. As noted above, the individual may not recognize those whom he or she has loved deeply for years.

Controls over physical functions are also impaired. Walking becomes an unsteady shuffle. Posture sags. Appetite decreases. Hallucinations of sight and sound occur. Bowel and bladder control is lost. Disorientation in space and time is pervasive. The individual may wander aimlessly and eventually become unable to communicate. Death usually occurs within seven to ten years of diagnosis. The Alzheimer's patient becomes increasingly difficult for others to relate to, understand, and care for. Those who do care for and support Alzheimer's patients find it a most devastating and frustrating experience. Most families feel totally isolated. Frequently these adults (termed "the sandwiched

(continued)

(continued)

generation," caring for older parents *and* children) and their children are subject to other stresses at home, school, or in the workplace as a consequence of the emotional, physical, and financial strain accompanying caring for an older parent with Alzheimer's (see also Chapters 8 and 9). Depression is especially common among spouses of dementia patients (Goldman & Luchins, 1984).

Relatives and friends of Alzheimer's victims have organized to form groups known as *Alzheimer support groups*. Their principal aims are to offer mutual emotional support to all families caring for an Alz-

heimer's patient, to provide information about the disease to the general public, to encourage establishment of long-term care facilities, and to help solve some of the mysteries of Alzheimer's disease through research. Within the last several years, organizations such as the Alzheimer's Disease and Related Disorders Association (ADRDA) and more recently journals such as *The American Journal of Alzheimer's Care* have focused our attention on the need for research and public support of Alzheimer's disease victims and their families.

1988). Specific forms of dementia do, however, manifest themselves somewhat differently (see Table 13.2).

Dementia affects about 4 percent of those over 65 (S. Zarit & J. Zarit, 1983); 20 percent of those aged 80 or older exhibit signs of dementia. In some cases emotional lability (shallow or rapidly changing emotions) may be present (Butler & Lewis, 1981), but Pfeiffer (1977) notes that such symptoms do not always accompany dementia. In many cases, existing personality traits may be intensified (Whanger & Myers, 1984). Anxiety, hostility and aggression, depression, or withdrawal may or may not accompany dementia.

Such symptoms (particularly regarding Alzheimer's disease), when they are present, are often most obvious in the early stages of the disorder, when individuals are still intact enough to realize that they are not as functional as they once were. As time passes, the above symptoms worsen, even-

TABLE 13.2

MAJOR DISORDERS ASSOCIATED WITH DEMENTIA SYMPTOMS

	Cause
Alzheimer's disease	?
Pick's disease	genetic?
Huntington's chorea	genetic
Creutzfeld-Jacob disease	viral
Neurosyphilis	infection
Normal pressure hydrocephalus	intracranial mass
Multi-infarct dementia	vascular
Depression	functional
Subdural hematoma	intracranial mass
B12 deficiency	dietary
Hyper/hypothyroidism	metabolic/endocrine
Alcohol dementia (Korsakoff's syndrome)	toxicity
Parkinson's disease	?

Source: Adapted from M. Gilhooly, S. Zarit, & J. Birren. (1986). *The dementias: Policy and management* (p. 15). Englewood Cliffs, NJ: Prentice-Hall.

tuating in incontinence, complete disorientation, the loss of overlearned information (one's name), the individual's total dependence on others for care,
coma, and eventual death.

Pfeiffer (1977) suggests that the severity of impairment in dementia
varies with *chronicity* and the *diffuse* nature of damage throughout the cerebral
cortex. Those persons with the fewest personality resources (e.g., fewest
existing coping skills) and the least support from others, whose damage is
diffuse and whose onset of symptoms is sudden, decline the most quickly.

Sloane (1980) notes that the *primary* (cognitive) features of dementia
are often impossible to separate from those that are *secondary* (emotional) to
the behavioral changes correlated with structural losses in brain cells with
age. Indeed, a true *functional* disorder (one that creates difficulties in everyday
functioning for the aged individual *despite* intact brain function) may coexist
with dementia.

The terms *delirium* (Sloane, 1980) or *dementia* are often used inter-
changeably to refer to generalized organicity. Whether we separate delirium
from other diseases causing dementia, the important issue is to separate those
causes of dementia that are *treatable* (formerly termed **reversible** or *acute* in
nature), such as malnutrition, drug side effects, vitamin deficiencies, from
those that are *not treatable* (formerly termed **irreversible** or *chronic*) (see Butler
& Lewis, 1981; Sloane, 1980).

Upon death, patients who have manifested true dementialike symptoms (not caused by functional disorders or reversible conditions) typically
show evidence of organic deterioration (particularly in Alzheimer's disease):
brain cells filled with *senile plaques* (collections of dead or dying neurons) and
neurofibrillary tangles (twisted nerve fibers). Moreover, the brain may appear
smaller, with convolutions being smaller and fissures being wider than normal (see photos). As we noted above, the *causes* of such changes in the brain
are largely unknown (see Chapter 2). However, work in this area continues,
for example, the identification of deficits in certain neurotransmitters inhibiting communication between neurons (acetylcholine, norepinephrine) or toxic
accumulations of aluminum (contributing to the formation of neurofibrillary
tangles) among those who have experienced dementia symptoms.

Terms such as *Alzheimer's disease* are best viewed *descriptively*. At present,
they are *symptomatic* and tell us little if anything about *etiology* (underlying
cause) of organic deterioration and moreover do not suggest any specific
treatment. Again, it is to be noted that many forms of dementia (Alzheimer's
disease and Pick's disease) (see Table 13.2) are virtually indistinguishable,
although there is some disagreement on this point (see Sloane, 1980). For
example, Strub and Black (1981) feel that those with Pick's disease are socially inappropriate, slovenly, and unconcerned despite cognitive intactness,
whereas Alzheimer's patients are neat and quite social but have substantial
intellectual loss. Usually a diagnosis of dementia is made only after other
causes for the individual's difficulties in concentration, memory, or abstract
reasoning (Gilhooly et al., 1986) have been explored. Clinically, the symptoms of all forms of dementia are similar and overlap with those of the normal
aging process (see Chapter 2) (Gilhooly et al., 1986), though it would be

inaccurate to conclude that dementia is an inevitable consequence of the aging process.

Among the other dementias (see Table 13.2) (Sloane, 1980) that have been defined symptomatically fall *Huntington's chorea,* which is comparatively rare and thought to be genetic in origin, *Parkinson's disease* (a degenerative neuromuscular disease involving the progressive loss of motor control), and *normal pressure hydrocephalus* (a treatable accumulation of cerebrospinal fluid producing dementialike symptoms).

In addition to senile dementia of the Alzheimer's type is arteriosclerotic dementia (as of DSM-III-R termed *repeated (multi-) infarct dementia*), consisting of intellectual impairment brought on by a series of *strokes* of varying intensity. Senile plaques, and neurofibrillary tangles are typically absent (Bondareff, 1986). Multi-infarct dementia comprises 10 to 20 percent of all dementias (Bondareff, 1986; S. Zarit & J. Zarit, 1983). Its onset is somewhat earlier yet more irregular than that of Alzheimer's disease, and definite cerebrovascular lesions (infarcts) (loss of brain tissue that results in a softening of the brain from impaired blood flow) are present. In multi-infarct dementia, personality and insight into one's behavior are relatively unimpaired until late in the disorder, and emotional lability is common (see Sloane, 1980). While memory loss is thought to be "spotty," high blood pressure often is present. A variety of other symptoms such as limb weakness and acalculia (inability to perform calculations) are exhibited. Wernicke's aphasia (loss of ability to comprehend language, inappropriate language), and agnosia (inability to recognize objects) may accompany multi-infarct dementia. It is considerably less common than often believed; there are even those who doubt the

Relative to a normal aged brain (A), the brains of persons diagnosed with Alzheimer's disease (B) are disproportionately small and have experienced alternations in both the fissures and sulci of the cerebral cortex.

role that impaired blood flow to the brain plays in accounting for its symptoms (see Marsden, 1978). With hypertensive medication and/or surgery, vascular disorders leading to multi-infarct dementia can be prevented. Moreover, changes in diet and exercise, treatment of diabetes mellitus, and discouraging the use of alcohol and tobacco (Bondareff, 1986) can be quite helpful.

B. Gurland, Dean, Copeland, R. Gurland, and Golden (1982) have developed what they feel is a reliable set of criteria by which to diagnose chronic **organic brain syndrome** (OBS) ("pervasive" dementia) among community aged that can be used by professionals (psychiatrists, psychologists, social workers) and nonprofessionals (nonpsychiatrists) alike. The criteria encompass many of the symptoms discussed above: memory loss, pervasive dependency, incontinence/regression (lack of self-care), inability to communicate one's needs, and apathy (see B. Gurland, Kuriansky, Sharpe, Simon, Stiller, & Birkett [1977] for a detailed discussion). Such an effort represents a real step forward to the extent that being able to reliably separate chronic versus acute (referring to onset) organicity, or to separate organic from functional disorders, can lead to improved care for elderly persons.

Helping Dementia Patients and Their Families

While some forms of dementia are commonly believed to be irreversible, to suggest nevertheless that such memory loss is beyond help would be incorrect. Thus, the decrement with compensation approach (Chapters 1 and 9) can be quite helpful in designing a supportive environment that can lessen the effects of such losses. Such a perspective is exemplified in a study by S. Zarit, J. Zarit, and Reever (1982). In this case, a cognitive training approach (didactic visual imagery, practical problem solving) facilitated to some degree memory performance (recall and recognition of several types of paired associates) in a group of community living elderly with memory impairments characteristic of diagnosable senile dementia. These gains were, however, small and not training specific; variability across persons was great. Recognition measures showed more general improvement than did recall. The authors state that while caregivers (family) were on the average more depressed after the training, the sessions did illuminate the extent of their patients' memory loss to them. Many sought further help with their feelings. These findings do suggest that even some severely impaired elderly can use memory improvement strategies, and that individual differences in such are great. Moreover, they can be of help to families, who can then provide more emotional support and care. These efforts are without question of great benefit to normal aged (S. Zarit, Gallagher, & Kramer, 1981) if they choose to use such aids. We must note in the S. Zarit et al. (1982) study that we do not know whether or not these impaired elders' lessened expectations of themselves (or those of their families) or their unwillingness to use the imagery techniques provided for them accounted for the limited success of memory training in this group. Work in this area continues.

Indeed the burdens borne by the families of those aged with diagnosed dementia are great. S. Zarit, Reever, and Bach-Peterson (1980) found such feelings of burden to be *greater* when the aged person was *not* visited by other family relatives. Interestingly, they found that the severity of behavior problems accompanying dementia (memory loss, mood swings, lessened ability to care for self) were unrelated to family caregivers' feelings of stress in caring for the impaired aged relative (primarily a spouse). These findings highlight the importance of social supports (respite care) being made available in the community (discussion groups, home visitation) to lessen feelings of helplessness, anger, and depression that family members often experience in caring for an aged relative (M. P. Burtz, Eaton, & Bond, 1988).

Lazarus, Stafford, Cooper, Cohler, and Dysken (1981) have documented the beneficial effects of a relatives' discussion group on family members of an elderly relative with Alzheimer's disease. Participants became more knowledgeable about the course of the illness and were able to be more realistic and accepting about what they could and could not expect from the elder. Consequently, they were able to cope with their own feelings of ambivalence about the ill relative. Similar success has been reported by Hausman (1979) in dealing with feelings about (1) the dependence of an elderly parent upon an adult, and (2) the childrens' fears of their own (and their parents') aging and death brought about by the realities of having to care for an elderly parent. In these small discussion groups, issues such as their parents' grief, self-centeredness, and communication problems involving the adult children and others (including other relatives and professionals) were successfully brought out in the open, shared, and solutions reached. Hausman (1979) suggests that these children learned to be more in touch with their parents' feelings. Such responses might help them cope with their own (as well as their parents') feelings precipitated much later on by institutionalization, retirement, ill health, or death. A "coming together" can be brought about by such changes. However, the task of coping with these events is made *easier* if preestablished patterns of relating to one another in an open, honest, yet supportive manner are available to both parent and child.

In this light, it is noteworthy to discuss briefly a recent study by Reifler, Cox, and Hanley (1981), who have identified a difference in opinion between the elderly patient and the family regarding the severity of the patient's problems in a variety of areas (self-care, physical/emotional stability, day-to-day routines). The elderly in this case were either diagnosed as being depressed or as having Alzheimer's disease. The authors suggest that those aged who are demented/depressed tend to *under* estimate the extent of their illness and that family are often a valuable source of information. We might note here that such denial is often adaptive; it may represent an attempt to cope with a situation over which the elder has no control or may be a response to the family's lessened expectation of them as older persons. Thus, such a discrepancy may result from an "ageist" mind-set that family and staff have toward the elder who has been diagnosed as depressed or demented. More extensive discussions of interventions for the caregivers of persons with dementia can be found in Cicirelli (1986), Gwyther and George (1986), S. Zarit and Anthony (1986), W. E. Haley et al. (1987), and S. Zarit et al. (1987).

For the present, however, we would note that behavioral interventions, reality orientation, individual and group therapy (see Chapter 14), relatively straightforward changes in furniture arrangement, carefully defining areas within the institution (to lessen random wandering) and orienting persons via signs can not only make life more predictable but also lessen anxiety and agitation for the demented elder (S. Zarit & Anthony, 1986). Weldon and Yesavage (1982) found both relaxation and imagery training to lessen confusion and increase self-care skills by helping dementia patients to focus their attention on the environment.

We will have more to say about interventions with caregivers in this regard as a form of family therapy in Chapter 14.

SEPARATING DEMENTIA FROM OTHER DISORDERS IN THE AGED

Of primary importance in the diagnosis of dementia is a sensitivity to those conditions that symptomatically *mimic* irreversible organicity but *are* treatable and reversible (see Eisdorfer & Cohen, 1978; Pfeiffer, 1977; Sloane, 1980) (see also Table 13.2).

This distinction has tremendous importance for elderly persons. Writing them off as "senile" or "organic" may overlook a variety of conditions that, if left untreated, can deteriorate to the point where they become in fact irreversible. Diagnosis should be based upon a comprehensive exam of the older person. Such an examination should include a complete physical, drug history, CAT scan, a careful personal history from the older person and the family, and a psychometric evaluation of cognitive functioning. If this reveals the absence of such dementialike conditions, then the elderly person can be treated for the symptoms that are truly characteristic of organically based dementia. Reversible dementialike conditions may be caused by prescription drug toxicity, the side effects of drugs (e.g., sedatives, antiagitation drugs) (see LaRue, Dessonville, & Jarvik, 1985), drug interactions *(polypharmacy)* (see LaRue et al., 1985), infections, neurosyphilis, cerebral tumors, metastatic cancerous tumors (those that have spread to the brain from the lungs), and alcohol or drug abuse.

Delirium

Sloane (1980) discusses the differentiation of *dementia* and *delirium,* which may appear dementialike but be in fact treatable. Delirium, if treated, is generally short-lived (less than a week), but if left untreated, can result in permanent cerebral damage and death. It, too, may result from drug toxicity, simple exhaustion, a blow to the head, heart disease, malnutrition, anemia, diabetes, fluid (electrolyte) disturbances, hepatitis, fever, or acute alcoholic intoxication (Butler & Lewis, 1981; Sloane, 1980). Symptoms such as agitation, paranoia, depression, disorientation, incontinence, lethargy, and sleeplessness have been documented (Hicks, Funkenstein, Dysken, & Davis, 1980; Kapnick, 1978; Krupa & Venar, 1979; Salzman & Shader, 1979) as consequences of drug toxicity or drug interactions in the aged (particularly with barbiturate use). Such problems can easily be misinterpreted as reflecting organicity or a functional disorder.

Alcoholism and Dementia

Sloane (1980) (see also W.G. Wood, 1978) has extensively discussed the role that alcoholism can play in leading to the misdiagnosis of dementia in the aged. In alcoholism, cognitive losses are much less severe, as is disorientation, but emotional lability is often present; delirium tremens (DTs) and hallucinations are common during withdrawal. Treatment is definitely possible but may take up to two years. If left untreated, an "alcoholic dementia" characterized by memory loss and falsification to fill in gaps (Korsakoff's syndrome) that is indistinguishable from other dementias usually appears after chronic alcohol abuse (J. Coleman et al., 1984). The symptoms of barbiturate use (and withdrawal) are similar to that of alcohol abuse over a continued length of time (Sloane, 1980).

Indeed, alcoholism has become a significant mental-health problem among adults of all ages. While many of us are familiar with the negative impact of chronic alcohol use on individual relationships with fellow workers, job performance, or family (J. Coleman et al., 1984), alcohol abuse among the aged has (comparatively speaking) only recently been recognized as a significant mental-health problem. Schuckit and Pastor (1979) and Zimberg (1979) point out that there are really two types of older alcoholics: those who were younger alcoholics and who simply grew old and those who began to abuse alcohol later in life.

Alcoholism in the aged is often characterized by either depression or disorientation/confusion and occasionally schizophrenia. Schuckit and Pastor (1979) found older alcoholics to be drinking six to seven days a week and at least four times a day. Older alcoholics often are malnourished and often have been in chronically poor health for some time. They frequently are poverty-stricken and live in run-down areas with little access to adequate health care.

COMMON FUNCTIONAL DISORDERS

In examining **functional disorders** in the aged, we will confine our discussion to depression, paranoia, schizophrenia, and anxiety. Sleep disturbances and hypochondriasis are more properly thought of as *outgrowths* of the above functional problems; suicide in the aged is discussed in Chapter 12.

Depression

According to available epidemiological data (D. W. Kay & Bergmann, 1980), *depression* is the most common functional disorder in aged persons. We must be careful to separate transient depressive reactions from prolonged dysfunctional depressions in aged persons; Pfeiffer sees the latter as "pathological responses to loss" (1977, p. 653). By this we mean that such a response is *out of proportion* (unrealistic, self-destructive, harmful to oneself or others) to the loss. Salzman and Shader (1979) note that older persons are reluctant to admit feeling depressed, "and may mask their depression through a variety of ego defense mechanisms and use denial, counterphobic defenses (overcompensation) or express depressive symptoms through somatic complaints and hypochondriasis" (p. 39). It is important to separate depression-related somatic (bodily) disturbances from genuine physical complaints; the same can be said of sleep disturbances, which may or may not be symptomatic of depression or anxiety (see Salzman & Shader, 1979; Stenback, 1980). Salzman and Shader (1979) also note that depression may precede or result from a serious illness or may be a by-product of drug effects in aged persons.

It is very important to separate normal depression accompanying loss and grief (see Chapter 12) from that which is pathological. For those (1) who are in poor health, (2) who have the fewest and most limited range of existing coping skills, (3) who are isolated from others, or (4) who are in situations they feel are beyond their control (being institutionalized or forcibly retired), pathological depression in later life as a response to loss is more likely (see Salzman & Shader, 1979; Stenback, 1980; J. A. Peterson, 1980).

Stenback (1980) and Salzman and Shader (1979) note the importance of losses that are "narcissistic" in character (valued aspects of oneself) in old-age depressions (e.g., health, a significant person, one's status at work or in the community, one's cognitive abilities, or a part of one's body through illness or surgery). What is critical is not the loss per se but the *perception* that this loss *cannot be replaced.*

Older persons who are depressed manifest two major symptoms (Stenback, 1980): *depressive mood* (sadness, guilt, hopelessness, helplessness) and subsequent *reduced behavior* (giving up, apathy). Those who are depressed often feel excessively guilty, are aggressive, or feel anxious. Negativism and other cognitive disturbances (limited attention, disorganized thought, short-term memory loss) in addition to a variety of physical complaints (indigestion, sleeplessness) and suicidal self-references are also often present. Gallagher and Thompson (1983) have defined *major depression* in terms of *five* major components, according to the *Research Diagnostic Criteria* (RDC; Spitzer, Endicott, & Robins, 1978), which they maintain is more discriminating (regarding *types* of depression) and more stringent than those specified by DSM-III-R (see above). According to these standards, the following components must be present for a major depressive episode to be diagnosed:

1. mood disturbance
2. five of eight related symptoms (psychomotor agitation, recurrent

thoughts of suicide, weight loss, sleep difficulty, loss of energy, loss of interest in pleasurable activity, feelings of worthlessness/guilt, diminished concentration)

3. a duration of two weeks or more

4. no evidence of schizophrenia

5. evidence of impaired functioning (e.g., at work, school, home, taking medication)

While some elderly who report somatic distress are genuinely ill, many *choose* to represent their depression somatically (loss of appetite, sleep disturbances).

While estimates for depression have ranged as high as 15 percent based upon less stringent criteria, when using the RDC, the true prevalence rate among the aged for depression is closer to 4 to 6 percent (Gallagher & Thompson, 1983). Reflecting their perspective of depression as the "final common pathway" for a number of more narrowly defined disorders, Gallagher and Thompson (1983) recommend a comprehensive multidimensional assessment procedure to positively diagnose depression in the aged, in much the same fashion as that which has been used in the diagnosis of dementia (see above).

Biological factors (biochemical disturbances) and social/cultural factors (loss, cultural views regarding the worth of the aged person, isolation, death, retirement, institutionalization) can contribute to depression in aged persons (LaRue et al., 1985). Psychological factors (reactions to physical change, perceived loss of sexuality and material possessions, failures, inability to replace loss of others) contribute as well to depression in the older person. This depression can be mild (transient, reactive) and characterized by a hypochondriacal preoccupation. Depressions may also be neurotic, in that they represent an attempt to cope with early childhood conflicts (Stenback, 1980). Severe depressions are characterized by excessive guilt, a great deal of anxiety (as well as hypochondriasis), delusions, excessive fatigue, dysphoria (a general feeling of not being well), excessive use of alcohol, and suicidal thoughts. When manic behavior accompanies this depression, the latter is termed **bipolar;** if no mania is present, depression is termed **unipolar.**

Interestingly, though one might think that depressed persons might recognize that learning new techniques for coping with their problems can be helpful, depression seems to feed upon itself. Foster and Gallagher (1986) compared older persons who were being treated for major depressive disorder and nondepressed aged in terms of perceived helpfulness in coping with various life events and in coping with feeling "down." These authors found that depressed elders made less use of information seeking (finding out more, seeking advice from others) and of problem solving (taking specific action) than did younger depressives (Billings, Cronkite, & Moos, 1983). Elderly depressed persons, relative to nondepressed ones, were more likely to use emotional discharge (verbal outbursts, drug use, eating, smoking) as coping techniques. Despite the fact that depressed and nondepressed aged used similar types of coping strategies, depressed aged rated these effects as less helpful; perhaps they had already deemed the situation to be beyond hope and consequently experienced any coping skills as less helpful (Foster & Gallagher, 1986). Similarly, Maiden (1987) found elderly depressed women to experience "personal helplessness" ("I will fail at this task") while nondepressed women expressed a more generalized (and less devastating) type of "universal helplessness" ("Everyone would fail at this task").

Pseudodementia

In order for accurate diagnosis and treatment, physical causes for depression must be ruled out. The treatment of depression may consist of providing support in time of loss, drug therapy (lithium, tricyclics), individual psychotherapy, cognitive "restructuring" of the environment, or lessening isolation (Gallagher & Thompson, 1983). Depression (with affective symptoms predominating) must also be separated from dementia (where cognitive symptoms are most characteristic); such misdiagnosed depression has been termed **pseudodementia** (Salzman & Shader, 1979) (see Tables 13.3 and 13.4).

Depressive equivalents are important in the diagnosis of depression as well (Pfeiffer, 1977; Salzman & Shader, 1979; Stenback, 1980). In these cases, the depression is "masked" via physical complaints (fatigue, loss of appetite, constipation, sleeplessness). Anger and guilt are turned inward instead of being expressed overtly. The "symptoms" help persons *deny* the fact that they are depressed yet permit them to legitimately ask for help. Again, social or interpersonal factors or real physical losses may precipitate this process. What is important is *how* this problem is expressed. Ironically, because these symptoms serve a useful function in "protecting" the person, they are often not given up and thus resist treatment (Pfeiffer, 1977).

Anxiety

Persons who are chronically anxious often appear tense and hyperactive and are apprehensive and vigilant about what terrible thing might happen next; such symptoms must exist for a month and other disorders such as depression or schizophrenia must be ruled out for a diagnosis to be made (American Psychiatric Association, 1987). While we know comparatively little about chronic **anxiety** in later adulthood, Himmelfarb (1984) found, in a sample of over 2,000 adults aged 55 to 90, that scores on a self-report measure of anxiety generally decreased across age up to age 69 and accelerated thereafter; additionally, women were more anxious than men. This suggests that poor health, relocation stress, isolation, or fears about loss of control may precipitate anxiety reactions that may be dysfunctional among the very old (75+), who are predominantly women. We see the influence of these factors in Himmelfarb's study. When the relationship between age and anxiety (as well as the relationship between sex and anxiety) was adjusted statistically for factors such as perceived health, quality of housing, and social support, these relationships were lessened considerably or eliminated altogether.

TABLE 13.3

MAJOR CLINICAL FEATURES DIFFERENTIATING PSEUDODEMENTIA (DEPRESSION) FROM DEMENTIA

Clinical Features	Pseudodementia	Dementia
1. Onset of illness	Usually specific	Determined only within broad limits
2. Duration	Brief duration before requesting help	Usually long duration
3. Progression	Symptoms develop rapidly.	Symptoms develop slowly through course of illness.
4. History	Prior psychiatric problems are common.	Psychiatric dysfunction uncommon
5. Complaints	Frequent and detailed complaint of cognitive loss. Disability is emphasized; failures are highlighted.	Infrequent and vague complaint of cognitive loss. Disabilities are overlooked or concealed. Satisfaction with accomplishment is frequently noted, however trivial.
6. Efforts	Minimal effort on even simple tasks	Patients usually struggle to perform tasks.
7. Affect	Change often pervasive with strong sense of distress	A frequent lack of concern with labile and shallow affect.
8. Social skills	Notable loss, usually early in course of illness	Often retained in early stages
9. Nocturnal dysfunction	Uncommon	Often accentuated
10. Attention and concentration	Often intact	Usually faulty
11. Memory loss	Occurs equally for recent and remote events, but "memory gaps" for specific periods are common.	Loss for recent events usually more severe than remote, but "gaps" for other specific periods are infrequent.
12. Variability in performance	Usually marked	Consistently poor

Source: From D. Gallagher & L. Thompson. 1983. Cognitive impairment. In P. Lewisohn & L. Teri (Eds.), *Clinical geropsychology: New directions in assessment and treatment* (p. 12). Elmsford, NY: Pergamon Press. Adapted from C. Wells. (1979). Pseudodementia. *American Journal of Psychiatry.*

Paranoid Reactions

Post (1980) has provided an extensive discussion of **paranoid** reactions (second-most frequent after depression) and schizophrenia in elderly persons. Paranoid symptoms (delusional or hallucinatory persecutory ideas) *may* accompany dementia, coexist with severe depression, or simply be a response

TABLE 13.4

SEPARATING DEMENTIA AND DEPRESSION

Characteristics	Depressed	Dementia
Depression	++++	++
Sleep and appetite disturbance	+++	++
Suicidal thoughts	++	±
Emotional lability	+	+++
Anxiety	+++	++
Hostility-irritability	++	+++
Confusion	++	++++
Disorientation	+	++++
Impaired recent memory	+	++++
Decreased mental alertness	++	++++
Unsociability	++	++++
Uncooperativeness	++	++++

Note: Plus sign refers to positive indicator for the disorder; Minus sign refers to negative indicator (contraindicative) for the disorder. More pluses, for example, indicate that greater weight needs to be given characteristic defining either dementia or depression.

Adapted from C. Salzman & R. Shader. (1979). Clinical evaluation of depression in the elderly. In A. Raskin & L. Jarvik (Eds.), *Psychiatric symptoms and cognitive loss in the elderly* (p. 50). New York: Hemisphere Publishing.

to isolation or to sensory or cognitive losses (accusations of being talked about, one's food being poisoned/mail being stolen). They must be viewed in light of older persons' attempts to "make sense" of their everyday environment via *projection* of hostile or persecutory intent onto others, rather than wildly bizarre delusions. Such accusations are somewhat logical, and in these cases providing cues (a system to keep track of when the "forgotten" letter was written), treating the sensory deficit (more seasoning on food, a hearing aid), explaining major changes (relocation) before they occur, and communicating clearly with those who are sensorily impaired (Kermis, 1986) often improve matters greatly for all concerned. Paranoia in such cases certainly should *not* be interpreted as a reason for institutionalizing an older individual.

For obvious reasons, older paranoiacs are difficult to treat (e.g., with drugs) because of their intense distrust of others. In many cases, older persons with such ideas live their lives out in an isolated, undisturbed fashion and may simply seem "odd" to others. These "simple paranoid psychotic" types are distinct from those suffering "schizophrenialike" illnesses/paranoid schizophrenia, where delusions are more systematic, organized, and bizarre (e.g., one is being plotted against by the police, poisonous gasses are being pumped into one's room). Severe speech disturbances and catatonic behaviors are not, however, common (Post, 1980) in older paranoiacs, though paranoid reactions sometimes accompany dementia.

Kermis (1986) notes that if one accepts the irrationality of the paranoid's initial delusions, subsequent delusional ideas often make sense logically. Older paranoiacs have delusions of grandeur (superiority), reference (others are following them), or persecution. Paranoid reactions must last for at least a week, and schizophrenia and organicity must be ruled out before a diagnosis is made (American Psychiatric Association, 1987). Paranoid reactions may also be acute, short-term responses to being hospitalized or transferred to a nursing home (Kermis, 1986). As Kermis (1986) states, paranoid reactions in older persons appear to be exaggerations of existing personality characteristics (the normally withdrawn person develops delusions of passivity or influence by others).

Schizophrenia

Schizophrenia, such as that discussed above, is comparatively rare in late adulthood and has not received a great deal of attention (Blazer, 1980). Pfeiffer (1977) suggests that most older "schizophrenics" were most likely diagnosed much earlier in life and simply grew old in an institution. Older chronic paranoid schizophrenics, while more upset by their symptoms, actually seem to make better social adjustments than when they were younger (Kermis, 1986).

Schizophrenics (American Psychiatric Association, 1987) have a well-developed severe delusionary system, loosely strung together thinking, and bizarre speech and hallucinations. Additionally, catatonic (frozen in one place) or maniclike behavior may be present, accompanied by a withdrawal into a private world that severely interferes with relationships with others and makes functioning on an everyday basis impossible. Schizophrenics typically do not react emotionally to their symptoms. If they have grown old in an institution, they have a characteristic "burned out" appearance—they walk around in a stupor or simply lie on the floor. They may utter incoherent, animallike sounds or be mute; they may smack their lips, grimace, or slobber like infants. They show little or no evidence of cognitive activity (stemming from years of medications to control outbursts of anger brought on by delusions or the dull sameness of institutional life) and often have a fixed stare with dark circles under the eyes accompanied by a ploddinglike gait (see J. Coleman et al., 1984).

Post (1980) even suggests that we know as little about what causes the schizophrenia that develops in late life (termed **paraphrenia**) as we do about the disorder in early adulthood or childhood.

Extensive schizophrenialike paranoid delusions do, however, sometimes accompany dementia. The schizophrenic (when observed among the aged) often manifests "ideas of reference" (others are looking at/talking about him or her), severe hypochondriacal delusions (cancer, syphilis), or manic behavior (having extraordinary amounts of energy that must be released). When the disease is organic (again, this is rare), they may be delusionally jealous, but the classic symptoms of dementia often predominate (Post, 1980; see above). Post (1980), however, feels the underlying organic degeneration typical of dementia has little to do with late-life paraphrenia; they simply coexist. Cognitive losses are usually minimal in these cases and paranoia (often preceding the illness) is easily observed in the early stages of dementia. In these cases, those persons with more interpersonal problems earlier in life tend to be worst off in this regard; their delusions are more severe. Elderly persons with paranoid delusions that are narrower in scope than those of younger paranoiacs (Post, 1980) can be treated with tranquilizing drugs.

Miscellaneous Functional Disorders

Simon (1980) has discussed a variety of disorders, for example, hypochondriasis, alcoholism, "personality/character" disorders, and neuroticism, in later life. Comparatively little is known about these topics. Simon (1980) does note that aging tends to intensify those dominant patterns established early on in life typical of the "character" disorder (the dependent personality becomes more so); the same is true of many other character disorders.

Symptoms such as transient, acute anxiety (not accompanied by dementia or psychosis, or not chronic [a carryover from childhood]), alcoholism (exclusive of organic loss brought on by excessive use), and drug misuse may all be seen as attempts by the aged person to cope with loss, stress, physical illness, or disfigurement. They may also represent attempts to manage one's grief at the death of a spouse or child (see Chapter 12).

Transient or acute depression and anxiety may also define what has been termed *relocation shock* (Aldrich & Mendkoff, 1963; Butler & Lewis, 1981; Miller & Lieberman, 1965), where an older person is moved (often involuntarily) from the home to an institution or from one institution to another. The older person may no longer be able to care for himself or herself, the family may no longer be able to care for the aged person, or the nursing home may be closing for economic reasons. Depression or anxiety is often a reaction to feelings of abandonment, feelings about the loss of control over one's life, feelings about the inability to care for oneself, or a sense that the move is a permanent one. These feelings can be lessened or avoided altogether by sharing information about the move with older persons beforehand, involving them to the greatest extent possible in decision making and planning, and continuing to visit regularly. Most importantly, older persons in these situations must feel that they are *still* persons. Each family must continue to be loving and supportive and communicate these feelings *clearly* to the older family member. In addition to relocation, acute depression or anxiety in older persons may accompany serious illness, injury, or impending surgery (Butler & Lewis, 1981; Stenback, 1980).

ASSESSMENT WITH OLDER PERSONS

A comprehensive discussion of all forms of assessment with the aged clearly is beyond our scope. However, thorough discussions of the assessment of mental health (Gurland, 1980), depression (Gallagher & Thompson, 1983), organicity/cognitive functioning (E. Miller, 1980; Raskin & Jarvik, 1979; Sloane, 1980; S. Zarit & J. Zarit, 1983), and personality functioning (Lawton, Whelihan, & Belsky, 1980; Hayslip & Lowman, 1986) are available.

As a general rule, K. W. Schaie and J. P. Schaie (1977) state that before conducting an assessment, one should be clear in defining for what *purpose* an interview, questionnaire, psychological test, or clinical examination is being done. For example, assessments might be used to measure the effects of a given intervention to aid a counselor in reaching a decision about an individual's adjustment to changed life roles (for instance, the viability of retirement). Assessment might also be used to establish job-related competence/retraining or to determine levels of competence or self-care regarding relocation.

Whatever the specific assessment technique utilized, its *purpose* should be clearly explained to the older individual and the family. The *pace* of the interview or test procedure should be slowed (see Chapter 7), and materials should reflect the existing level of sensory-motor capacities of the individual (see Chapter 4). Wherever possible, as an adjunct to standard non-age-related assessments, techniques especially developed for the aged and/or for which current age (cohort) norms exist should be relied upon (see Table 13.5 and Figure 13.2) (e.g., **mental status questionnaires** [see Gurland, 1980] for the assessment of cognitive status; *Beck depression inventory* to assess depression) (see Gallagher & Thompson, 1983). In using such scales, we must be cautious about adhering rigidly to "cutoff scores". As measures of a person's relative competence or degree of pathology, such scores should be avoided, given the variability among elderly persons (K. W. Schaie & J. P. Schaie, 1977).

Scales with demonstrated **reliability** and **validity** (see Anastasi, 1982) with the aged should be utilized. Briefly, a scale is *reliable* (stable) if it yields similar scores (scores that correlate highly with one another) at two occasions for a given individual. A test's reliability may also be ascertained by correlating scores from odd-numbered items with those from even-numbered ones (or scores from the first half of the scale with scores from the second half).

On this questionnaire there are groups of statements. Please read the entire group of statements in each category. Then pick out the one statement in that group that best describes the way you feel today, that is <u>right now</u>! Circle the number beside the statement you have chosen. If several statements in the group seem to apply equally well, circle each one. Be sure to read all the statements in each group before making your choice.

A   0   I do not feel sad.
      1   I feel sad.
      2   I am sad all the time and can't snap out of it.
      3   I am so sad or unhappy that I can't stand it.

B   0   I get as much satisfaction out of things as I used to.
      1   I don't enjoy things the way I used to.
      2   I don't get real satisfaction out of anything anymore.
      3   I am dissatisfied or bored with everything.

Figure 13.2   Selected items from the Beck Depression Inventory. *Source:* A. T. Beck, C. H. Ward, M. Mendelson, J. E. Mock, & J. Erbaugh. (1961). An inventory for measuring depression. *Archives of General Psychiatry, 4,* 569–570. Beck Depression Inventory. Copyright 1987 by The Psychological Corporation. Reproduced by permission. All rights reserved.

TABLE 13.5

REPRESENTATIVE MENTAL STATUS EXAM ITEMS

Mental Status Questionnaire (MSQ)	Disorientation Factor from a Dementia Rating Scale	Short Portable Mental Status Questionnaire (SPMSQ)	The Orientation Test	A Simplified MSQ	An Abbreviated Mental Test Score	Clifton Assessment Schedule
			Common Items			
1. What is the name of this place?	Where are you now? Are you in a school, a church, a hospital, or a house?	What is the name of this place?	What is the name of this place? What is the name of the ward you are on?	What is the name of this place?	Name of hospital?	Hospital address? Ward place? City?
2. Where is it located? (address)		What is your street address? OR What is your telephone number?				
3. What is today's date?	What is the day of the week?	What is the date today? What day of the week is it?	What day is it?	What day is it?		Day?
4. What is the month now?	What is the month?		What month is it?	What month is it?		Month?
5. What is the year?	What is the year?		What year is it?	What year is it?	Year?	Year?
6. How old are you now?	Disorientation to age (error of at least 5 years)	How old are you?	How old are you?	What age are you? (error more than 1 year)	Age?	Age?

7. When were you born (month)?	When were you born?	In what month is your birthday?	Date of birth?	Date of birth?	
8. When were you born (year)?		In what year were you born?			
9. Who is the president of the United States?	Who is the president of the United States now?	Name of present monarch?	Name of present monarch?	Prime minister? U.S. president?	
10. Who was the president before him?	Who was the president before him?				

Items Not Held in Common

What is the time of day (morning, afternoon, or evening)?	What was your mother's maiden name?	What time is it?	What time is it? (error more than 1 hour)	Time to nearest hour?	Name?
Inability to find bathroom	Subtract 3 from 20 and keep subtracting 3 from each new number all the way down	What were you doing before coming to this room?	How long have you been here? (error more than 25%)	Address given and recall at end of test	Color of British flag?
Wandering		What is my name? (as given at beginning of interview)		Year of World War I	
Disorientation to people: Inability to distinguish patients from staff		What did you have for breakfast? Lunch?		Count backwards 20–1	
		When did you last have a visitor?		Recognition of two persons	

Source: Adapted from B. Gurland. (1980). The assessment of mental health status in older adults. In J. E. Birren & R. B. Sloane (Eds.), *Handbook of mental health and aging* (p. 679). Englewood Cliffs, NJ: Prentice-Hall.

The extent to which a scale measures some quality consistently that is associated with the person and not a function of random error indicates whether or not it is a reliable scale.

A *valid* scale measures what it intends to measure when judged against some external criterion of that quality. The scale may correlate highly with some accepted measure of that quality, may differentiate individuals who are presumed to possess levels of that quality, or may accurately predict future performance of individuals who possess that quality to a certain degree. In general, measures that are valid are almost always reliable, but the opposite need not be the case. A measure can be quite reliable (we know it measures *something* consistently) but not valid (that "something" that the scale is designed to measure cannot be identified). K. W. Schaie and J. P. Schaie (1977) note that age-corrected norms (based on cross-sectional studies) are unlikely to be of help in the absence of reliability and validity data for an assessment technique. Scales that possess adequate norms for elderly persons are rare and, when available, need to be supplemented by reliability and validity data.

Above all, assessments should be *comprehensive.* Such assessments are quite thorough and thereby provide the examiner with information from a *variety* of sources upon which to make a judgment regarding the individual's functional status or candidacy for intervention. They should preferably be conducted at least *twice* by *different* examiners. At the minimum, broad-based assessments in the areas of neurological functioning, learning, memory, intelligence, personality and psychopathology, self-care, morale, social/interpersonal skills, stress, and coping should be made and interpreted in light of the individual's health, level of education, and family history (Raskin & Jarvik, 1979). These factors assume a *great* deal of importance in influencing older person's responses to psychological tests and assessments. Thorough familiarity with the individual's goals, interests, family, and other resources will aid one not only in the selection of which scales to administer but also in their interpretation and intelligent use. Obviously, we should be as interested in what individuals are *capable* of (their functional skills) as in the assessment of decline.

Assessment of older persons in the above domains may be accomplished via standardized testing, though such procedures that rely on well-defined instructions and alternatives may obscure the true range of the elder's function or personality resources (Hayslip & Lowman, 1986). Self-ratings or interviews as single sources of information, due to the influences of current health, medications, or tendencies to deny or represent one's symptoms more positively, should be viewed with caution.

Extensive *functional behavioral assessment* procedures that involve structured interviews have been developed and productively used for some time (Older Americans Resources and Services questionnaire; Pfeiffer, 1976), as has the interview procedure described above (Comprehensive Assessment and Referral Evaluation; Gurland et al., 1977). These interviews (1) identify the problem, and (2) understand its history and relationship to the older person's current social, occupational, or familial situation. Older persons may not interpret self-rated items as they were intended or may choose items that are confounded by health (physical) status (e.g., sleeplessness, changes in eating habits). For example, acknowledging such symptoms may lead to a diagnosis of depression (see Addington & Fry, 1986) that may or may not be accurate.

When a diagnosis of depression or dementia is falsely made, it is termed a **false positive** error. When such conditions are assumed not to exist when they in fact are present, a **false negative** error has been made. Regardless of whether the disorder will deteriorate further and harm the individual irreversibly if left untreated or what effects falsly diagnosing a problem that is not present may have, each error in judgment can result in serious consequences for older persons and their families. Moreover, diagnoses based on quantitative scores may miss important qualitative changes in individuals' responses to test items (e.g., mental status questionnaires; see S. Zarit, J. Eiler, & M. Hassinger, 1985). Diagnosing someone as depressed rather than as demented makes it more likely that the individual will receive treatment. On the other hand, falsely diagnosing someone as having a primary degenerative condition (Alzheimer's disease, multi-infarct dementia) may overlook a disorder that, if left untreated, produces irreversible damage. Interestingly, in this light, Perlick and Atkins (1984) found clinicians to be more likely to make a diagnosis of dementia versus depression, *given the same symptoms,* if the "patient" was described as old as opposed to young. Personal interviews supplemented by interviews with family and friends, as well as the judicious use of individualized personality assessment techniques called *projective* techniques (see Chapter 10), may prove invaluable in understanding a particular older individual in the context of his or her unique life situation (Hayslip & Lowman, 1986; S. Zarit et al., 1985).

Whenever possible, instructions should be personalized, and care should be taken to first establish trust and rapport in order to allay fears and anxiety about the assessment itself or the consequences of the assessment. Particular care should be taken to use materials and techniques that are concrete, clear, and easily seen and heard. Preferably assessments should be done in a relaxed, nonthreatening, familiar atmosphere. If possible, they should not be so long as to needlessly fatigue or irritate the individual. Due to the influence of such *noncognitive* factors on performance (see Chapter 7), we should perhaps be especially cautious about relying too heavily on performance or structured interview data to the extent that our own common sense and observations tell us something else may be wrong (or that things really are not as bad as our assessments indicate). Simply put, we should strive for a *balanced* yet *realistic* assessment of the elder's behavioral skills, abilities, or personality characteristics in light of what we know about that person's reaction to being depressed, background, family, daily living situation, and health. As S. Zarit et al. (1985) note, gerontological assessment is not developed to the extent that "a cookbook that can sort out the multiple influences on test behavior" (p. 733) is available. Mounds of information do not compensate for good clinical judgment, sensitivity, experience, and inter-personal skills.

MENTAL HEALTH IN LATER LIFE

Birren and Renner (1980) suggest that mental health *at any age* involves "the ability to respond to other individuals, to love, to be loved, and to cope with others in give-and-take relationships" (p. 29). They add that the mentally healthy elder "should have the essential quality of being able to cope with loneliness, aggression, and frustration without being overwhelmed" (p. 29), since they are likely to encounter these as part of the normal aging process (e.g., death of a spouse or friend or physical decline). Again, "coping" with these changes can involve a whole *range* of responses.

Those qualities Birren and Renner discuss that are *especially* pertinent to mental health in later adulthood are *relevance* to a set of values, *reverence* (self-esteem) for one's own values, life *review,* and a *release* from stress in that one's own life accomplishments and values are *reconciled* with one's ideals.

It was stated at this chapter's outset that we probably know more about what mental health in adulthood is *not* than what it *is.* Consequently, we are drawn to the "problems" older persons sometimes experience (i.e., depression, paranoia, organicity, hypochondriasis, suicide). This often leads to the development of mental-health services that are *remedial* rather than *preventative.* That is, they do not encourage a "positive" orientation toward "wellness." Instead, they encourage us to find out what is wrong; we make a "diagnosis."

Optimally Mentally Healthy Aged Persons

Hellebrandt (1980) has written of those characteristics associated with what are called the *advantaged aged.* This term refers to the well-educated, reasonably healthy, financially secure, independent-living elderly person. She talks of these individuals not *feeling* old, accepting their physical/health-related limitations, and being preoccupied with meaningful activities of their *own* choosing. Moreover, they held very *individualistic* feelings about work and retirement and about religion (or a personally meaningful set of values). Lastly, they exhibited a notable lack of fears about death (see Chapter 12). While we do not want to imply that reviewing one's life cannot be helpful (see our discussion of life review therapy in Chapter 14), these individuals rarely reminisced about the past. What transcends all of these qualities is what we might call "sitting loose in the saddle." In other words, we are talking about an attitude of *flexibility* about life in general as well as about aging. While the specific qualities are not important in and of themselves, the emphasis on flexibility in adapting to life's pleasures and problems is important in being mentally healthy *at any age.*

Even institutionalized aged persons can experience positive mental health, contrary to common belief. Noelker and Harel (1978) found that nursing home residents who had the highest morale and life satisfaction (1) had more favorable attitudes about entry into a long-term care situation, (2) held more positive perceptions of the facility and the staff, (3) had their preference met for visitors, (4) saw their life there as permanent, and (5) had higher self-rated health. They also lived the longest! We see here the importance of *perceived control* (Solomon, 1982) as a factor contributing to positive mental health among older persons who are institutionalized.

Harel, Aollod, and Bogner (1982) found that if rural elderly had ample social resources (not being lonely, having someone to depend on), felt that their financial resources were adequate, and saw themselves as healthy or active, they enjoyed mental health. Birren and Renner (1980) have noted that it is only when poor health, social isolation, inadequate income, and substandard housing are experienced *simultaneously* that older persons report low morale. Indeed, seriously chronically ill aged may have the most difficulty (Felton & Revenson, 1987).

Why are some elders more adaptive than others? A longitudinal study by Mussen et al. (1982) suggests that the seeds for positive mental health in old age may have been sown years earlier. Mussen et al. (1982) found that women who were life satisfied at age 70 were described at age 30 as "mentally alert, cheerful, satisfied with their life, self-assured, and neither worrisome or fatigued" (p. 321). Strong concerns of the *husbands* for their own wives' health, the quality of their marriage, and both income and leisure time were also important predictors of life satisfaction at age 70. For men, their own physical and emotional well-being *and* their wives' personality characteristics predicted life satisfaction at age 70. Again, we see the importance that developing a flexible attitude toward life early on plays in contributing to mental health in old age.

Snow and Crapo (1982) found that being emotionally bonded to a "significant other" (sibling, spouse, friend) contributed to emotional stability in old age. Persons who are ill or isolated often lack this special person, who serves as a "buffer" or **confidant** (Botwinick, 1984).

It is important to note that research of this kind helps foster *positive* mental health in old age through the identification of its correlates and causal factors, providing the basis for either changing the environment and/or some aspect of the person in such a way as to make it likely that he or she will continue to prosper *throughout* life. Thus, the "counseling" that we would provide here is of a *preventive* rather than a remedial nature (see Chapter 14). Such skills/changes can be made *early on* in life; one need *not* wait to develop them until the latter phase of life. Often what appears to be a consequence of old age upon closer scrutiny really emerges as an individualized lifelong pattern of coping (Neugarten, 1977). Of course, this pattern of adjustment may be very adaptive, or it may be very ineffective (see Chapter 10).

Increased self-confidence and self-reliance, healthy attitudes about one's strengths and weaknesses, learning and maintaining effective coping skills, and an active approach toward the environment are prerequisites for mental health in elderly persons. Obviously, such assets benefit the young as well! Unrealistic expectations of self, narrowness of experience, emotional fragility, resistance to criticism, and a restrictive environment encourage *unhealthy* styles of coping in *both* the young and the old (Hayslip, 1982a).

In closing our discussion of mental health and psychopathology, we again point out the importance of looking at each of these topics as opposite ends of a single *continuum,* whose definition is, therefore, *relative* rather than absolute. Under these conditions, we can interpret both our own and others' behavior in a realistic, flexible manner. Moreover, our assessment procedures, therapeutic efforts, and design of mental-health services for both the mentally healthy and the pathological adult can more fully be geared to the needs of the individual, in light of current circumstances, unique life history, and personal experiences.

SUMMARY

Information about *mental health* and mental illness across the adult life span is scarce and must be viewed with caution for a number of reasons. Mental health and mental illness are best thought of as ends of a *continuum.* This is particularly important in that mental health has rarely been defined, especially with the aged, and has been traditionally seen as the absence of mental illness. A variety of models have been proposed to understand this continuum with the aged; each has strengths and weaknesses that must be kept in mind in defining mental illness and in planning mental-health interventions with the aged.

Of major importance is separating *reversible* and *irreversible* forms of *dementia* as well as separating *dementia* and *depression* in the aged. The confusion of these categories often leads to improper treatment or no treatment at all for aged persons and their families. While forms of dementia such as *Alzheimer's disease* and *multi-infarct* dementia and depression have received the most attention, other disorders such as *anxiety, paranoia,* and *schizophrenia* are less well understood.

The *assessment* of mental health–mental illness should be *purposeful* and as *comprehensive* as possible, in order to enable one to make as *reasonable* an interpretation as possible in light of the older person's goals, needs, resources, and capabilities.

KEY TERMS AND CONCEPTS

Mental health–mental illness

Confidant

Abnormal behavior

Medical model

Aging as illness model

Behavioral model

Organic brain syndrome (OBS)

Dementia

Alzheimer's disease

Multi-infarct dementia

Reversible versus irreversible
dementia

Pseudodementia

Functional disorders

Bipolar versus unipolar
depression

Depressive equivalent

Schizophrenia

Paranoia

Anxiety

Mental status questionnaire

Beck Depression Inventory

Reliability

Validity

False positives

False negatives

DSM-III-R

Paraphrenia

After reading this chapter you should be able to answer the following questions:

- How important is age in the treatment of psychological disorders?
- How does age seem to affect access to mental-health services? What barriers exist regarding older versus younger adults' access to treatment?
- What are transference and countertransference? How do they affect the therapist-client relationship?
- What factors need to be taken into account when designing a treatment plan, according to Gottesman et al. (1973)?
- What objections to the treatment of older clients did Freud have? What changes in psychodynamic therapy with the aged have taken place since Freud's time?
- What are the advantages and disadvantages of group therapy with aged clients?
- What is family systems theory? How might it be used with the aged?
- What are the advantages and disadvantages of behavioral interventions with the aged?
- What general goals can be achieved in the treatment of older persons?
- What specialized treatment techniques have been developed for elderly persons? Are they successful? For what types of elderly persons are they best suited?
- What is meant by the concept of levels of intervention? How might it be applied to older persons?

CHAPTER 14

INTERVENTION

AND THERAPY

▪

MENTAL-HEALTH SERVICES—EQUALLY HELPFUL ACROSS ADULTHOOD?

All of us most likely turn to others (friends, relatives, clergy, paraprofessionals, professionals of many types) in times of severe stress. It is the mental-health professional that we often turn to when we experience emotional problems that are beyond our own resources to handle effectively. In this chapter, we will examine the psychological treatment of adults as well as more specific questions relating to the importance of chronological age in treating mental illness. In addition, we will discuss ways of handling difficulties, which may or may not be long-standing in nature, in coping with life on a daily basis.

Well-Being and Mental-Health Services

In perhaps the most comprehensive study dealing with mental-health services to date, Veroff, Douvan, and Kulka (1981a, 1981b) asked over 2500 adults a wide variety of questions regarding their mental health and where they sought help for emotional problems, as well as how effective this help was. These individuals were compared with a similar sample of adults who had been interviewed in 1957. While comparisons within persons were not possible, *intracohort estimates* of age changes (see Chapter 3) in the use of mental-health services *were* possible, based on data from individuals ranging in age from 21 to 65+ over a 20-year period of time.

Not only were these investigators able to determine age-related shifts

507

in how persons viewed their mental health and in their use of mental-health services, they were also able to examine the role that *cultural changes* played in persons' views about mental health and the use of mental-health services. Understanding the *relationship* between mental health and **well-being** and help-seeking can lead to a better understanding of the *reasons why* adults of all ages do or do not seek help for mental/emotional problems.

Influences on Well-Being: Sex, Income, and Level of Education

In general, these investigators found not only *age,* but *sex* and *level of education* influenced persons' feelings of subjective well-being.

In both 1957 and 1976, women tended to report more distress in their daily lives, with the exception of men finding their work more stressful in 1957, but not in 1976. This difference is explained by the fact that women actually confront more difficulties than do men—they are required to take more responsibility for the success of their marriages and the socialization of their children. Women, therefore, have less control over their own lives in that their well-being depends upon others' success and happiness in life. Relative to others, women in their forties reported less happiness, while older men reported less happiness, presumably due to the decreased importance of their work.

Those who were more educated felt best about their lives; their higher levels of education led to higher-paying, higher-status positions, permitting them more influence and control over their lives. They also enjoyed the benefits of having "reference groups which tell how to proceed with life and how to evaluate experience" (1981a p. 381). Those who were less educated were, simply put, "more demoralized." The authors point out, "Demoralization may also lie behind the finding that less educated people clearly less often see professional help as relevant to their problems" (p. 382). Less highly educated persons reported health, rather than relationships with others, as a major source of happiness—they have, so to speak, learned to value the little that they have. Those with higher incomes and those who attended church regularly reported higher levels of well-being.

We discuss these findings for sex and education because they enable us to better understand the age effects (see Chapter 3) found for well-being and awareness of mental-health services in the Veroff et al. (1981a, 1981b) studies. Many of the age effects found in well-being can be explained via sex differences and/or educational differences in well-being and help-seeking that are correlated with age.

Age Effects in Well-Being: Relationship to Help-Seeking

Regarding *well-being,* younger versus older people (within the same cohorts) were found to differ in four major ways. *First,* younger persons focused on the interpersonal joys and sorrows of their lives, while older persons, on the other hand, tended to focus upon more "spiritual" or community-oriented sources of happiness and well-being. Rather than being caught up in how their lives *might be,* older persons tended to appreciate things for what they *were.* While the basis for their feelings of well-being differed, older versus younger persons seemed equally happy. *Second,* younger people reported being more overwhelmed with life. *Third,* older persons were more past oriented, in that the past was more often seen as a source of happiness; the future was seen less often as a time for "positive change." *Fourth,* younger people defined well-being more innovatively.

In both 1957 and 1976, *fewer* older people reported having problems for which they could have used professional help. In 1976 older people less often reported feeling "overwhelmed" when "bad things" happened to them. Because they had confronted illness and death, they were able to put other problems into perspective.

Cohort Differences in Help-Seeking

Over and above age, sex, education, or income level, those in 1976 were more likely to see talking with others as sources of help when worried; less "institutional" (memberships in groups such as churches) and more "intimate" means of solving personally distressing problems were being sought. This implies that older (versus younger) cohorts will be *less* likely to deal with their problems by seeking out a mental-health professional. On the other hand, what are considered "personal or family matters" by the old are dealt with in a more "outside" help-seeking manner by younger persons. These 20-year differences also suggest that future cohorts of older persons will be more likely to turn to others in times of trouble in the future, in that a historical shift toward more professional help-seeking has occurred.

Regarding the 1957–1976 findings, the authors concluded:

1. In 1976, younger persons in particular expressed more anxiety and worry versus those in 1957. There was, however, overall consistency in levels of well-being.

2. In 1957, well-being was defined socially, whereas in 1976, it was defined more personally—this was reflected in (1) less importance being assigned to role standards for defining adjustment, (2) more focus on self-directedness, and (3) a shift to interpersonal intimacy as a basis for well-being.

3. People in 1976 were *more* prone to seek expert help and thus less likely to deny their problems.

4. *Within* cohorts (on the average), there was much *consistency* in help-seeking. Those who were younger in 1957 versus those who were middle-aged or older in 1976 were just as likely to seek informal help. Moreover, those who were middle-aged in 1957 and elderly in 1976 were consistent in their tendency to seek out a mental-health professional.

These results imply that it is those who are *younger* (in a relative sense) who are more likely to evince more positive attitudes toward receiving professional help, according to the authors. Thus, younger (versus middle-aged and elderly) persons tended to be more "psychological" in their orientation toward asking for assistance from some professionally trained person (psychologist, social worker, clergy, doctor, lawyer, psychiatrist). Interestingly, a *third* of the 1976 adult sample could *not* see themselves as *ever* having difficulties requiring professional assistance. On the brighter side, those who did seek help in 1976 versus 1957 were more likely to select a "specialized" mental-health professional (psychologist/psychiatrist, counselor) over a general help source (doctor, lawyer) and be more appreciative of the value of referrals from family and friends.

IMPLICATIONS OF THE VEROFF ET AL. FINDINGS ON WELL-BEING AND HELP-SEEKING

While these national surveys on mental health and help-seeking behavior are revealing, we must be cautious in interpreting the findings regarding younger versus older persons in that *different* people were interviewed in 1957 versus 1976. Thus, we have no longitudinal information dealing with age changes in well-being and help-seeking, and the effects of age, education, income, or sex on these factors are undoubtedly influenced by the gross cultural shifts (1957 versus 1976) noted above. At best, we can make some very tentative statements about age-related changes in well-being and help-seeking behavior. When these two sets of findings do not overlap, age effects are more likely to be interpreted as being better explained by cohort/historical effects on well-being or attitudes toward seeking mental-health care. Recall that the same individuals were *not* reinterviewed in 1976 (see Chapter 3 for a discussion of the measurement of cohort effects).

Other reports by the President's Commission on Mental Health (1978) and the White House Conference on Aging (1981) have documented the relatively high prevalence of mental-health disorders in the aged (depression, suicide, treatable dementia, anxiety—see Chapter 13) versus the meager support for (1.5 percent of funds for mental health go to elderly would-be clients) and access to mental-health services directed to older adults. For example, older persons comprise 6 percent of all clients at community mental-health centers, 3 percent of all clients seen in private practice, and 1 percent of clients seen by psychologists working within nursing homes (American Psychological Association, 1984). A recent survey by Knesper, Pagnucco, and Wheeler (1985) confirmed this trend. These authors surveyed over 9000 mental-health service providers and found older persons to be underrepresented, with more elderly being seen by primary care physicians than by other mental-health personnel (psychologists, psychiatrists, social workers). Persons who could not pay for services were less likely to receive private help. Unfortunately, those who are poor are also likely to have more severe mental-health problems.

A discussion of all possible forms of treatment with adults of all ages is beyond our scope (see Garfield & Bergin, 1986, for in-depth treatments of major approaches to psychotherapy and counseling). We will focus on the variety of treatment approaches with older adults, given the age bias in treatment and referral (Gatz et al., 1980; S. Zarit, 1980) and their relative lack of contact with mental-health professionals (see Felton, 1982). Fortunately, a great deal of research, stemming from the life-span tradition (see Chapter

Older persons are equally viable candidates for successful counseling interventions.

1), has shown that older adults are *equally* amenable to change (P. B. Baltes, Reese, & Lipsitt, 1980). This should provide additional impetus for counselors to treat elderly clients. In this light, let us discuss factors that influence the elderly's access to mental health services.

BARRIERS TO MENTAL-HEALTH SERVICES

Many researchers and practitioners have expressed considerable concern about the underutilization of available mental-health services by elderly adults (Gatz, Popkin, Pino, & VandenBos, 1985; Gatz et al., 1980; Smyer & Gatz, 1979; Storandt, 1983; Storandt, Siegler, & Elias, 1978; J. E. Myers & Salmon, 1984). In some cases, services that exist are based on an *irreversible decrement* model of aging (see Chapter 1). Until recently, this model has dominated gerontological research and practice (R. Kastenbaum, 1978b).

Felton (1982) also points out that while many older adults seek "basic services" (housing, meals, income assistance), what are offered are often "life-enhancing" services (socialization, growth experiences, activity programs). Clearly, this suggests that mental-health service providers need to more carefully design and implement their programs so that they will be perceived as acceptable by would-be older clients.

Many types of services could be provided at multiple levels (Danish, 1981), depending upon the individual's need in a variety of settings, by both professionals, paraprofessionals, and peers (Myers & Salmon, 1984; Sargent,

1980; Waters, 1984). *Coordination* among services (Smyer & Gatz, 1979) of both a community-based, institutionalized, and individual nature is essential (Felton, 1982; J. E. Myers & Salmon, 1984) (see Figure 14.1). *Transportation* to where services are offered may be a problem for older persons who cannot drive or afford transportation. Mass transit may not be available, or the older person may be isolated from others (living in a rural area). Moreover, providing services that are *affordable* could remove a major barrier to their use by older adults. For example, raising Medicare ceilings on reimbursement for mental-health services provided by *all* professionals qualified to deliver such services (see J. E. Hagebak & R. R. Hagebak, 1983; Santos & Vandenbos, 1982) would help matters greatly.

Thus, lower expectations of change for aged clients, lack of coordination, cost, ignorance of the potential of psychological interventions by the aged, and services that are narrow in scope emerge as major factors in the underutilization of mental-health services by older persons.

Santos, Hubbard, McIntosh, and Eisner (1984) point out that existing services may be already overburdened, personnel may be poorly trained, or services may not be geared to deal with elderly patients (making home visits, offering services in other contexts [senior center, church, public housing]). These factors further lessen the use of existing mental-health services by older persons.

Why do we see such a lack of interest in the treatment of elderly adults? One reason lies in the feelings and attitudes of therapists regarding treating the aged patient, often based on a lack of professional experience with elders and personal contact with aged persons (e.g., death, parental conflicts, fears of aging) (Goodstein, 1982). A number of persons (Gatz et al., 1980; Butler & Lewis, 1981) have discussed the professional ageism (see Chapter 9) that pervades treatment of the aged, often resulting in no care at all or at best, poor quality of care. Another factor behind the lack of mental-

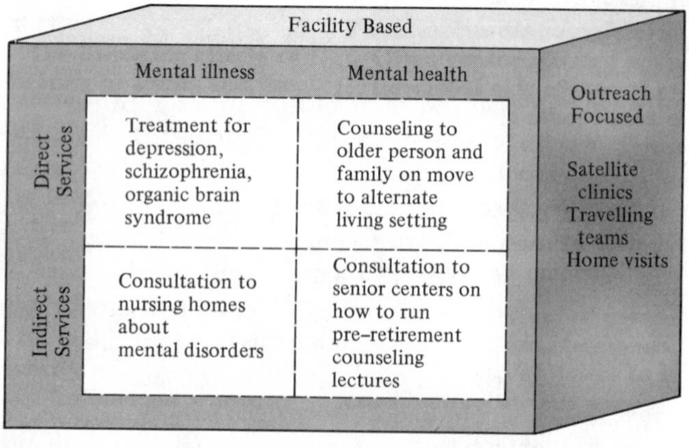

Figure 14.1 NIMH scheme for the reorganization of mental-health services for the aged. *Source:* National Institute of Mental Health. (1979). *Issues in mental health and aging: Vol. 3. Services* (p. ix). Rockville, MD: DHEW.

health care elderly patients sometimes receive is **countertransference** (Blum & Tallmer, 1977; Goodstein, 1982), wherein the therapist projects personal negative feelings about aging, death, or loss onto the elderly client, interfering with diagnosis and treatment. Both caring for one's elderly parents and for one's children intensifies the therapist's countertransference, leading to (1) unrealistic demands for a cure, (2) a parental "know-it-all" attitude, and (3) hostility, pity, or sympathy toward the elderly persons as persons who cannot care for themselves (Goodstein, 1982). What sometimes complicates this situation is the older person's **transference** to the counselor. The patient may see the therapist as a parent or a child figure. Transferences may thus cause the client to see the helper as the one who is to be "taught," as an authority figure, or as a long-lost sexual object.

Recognizing and handling these feelings requires both honesty and objectivity. Goals for therapy must be set and adhered to in light of the client's needs, abilities, and resources but with a large measure of empathy for both the physical and the interpersonal losses the older person may have experienced. Respecting the older person *as an individual,* encouraging independent decision making and a knowledge of community resources (Lawton & Gottesman, 1974; Smyer & Gatz, 1979) are also crucial. Ultimately, the individual's sense of dignity and self-respect must be preserved throughout the course of therapy. These factors are especially important given the sense of suspicion and distrust with which some older clients may approach therapy, particularly if they have been referred by a trusted family member or physician. Many elderly prefer to help themselves (Butler, Gertman, Overlander, & Shindler, 1979–1980) rather than turn to others, an attitude based on a work ethic that emphasizes independence at all costs.

Narrow ideas about older persons as "crazy, senile, or depressed," limited experience with elderly, and professional backgrounds that are conceptually narrow also work against the development of interventions with older persons (Eisdorfer, 1983). A flexible approach is not only more likely to succeed in helping older clients but also generates more knowledge about the processes of development and aging (P. B. Baltes & Danish, 1980), providing an even broader basis for future treatment efforts. Quite often we expect younger persons to "fit the mold" for the ideal patient/client who can be helped. They are more likely to fulfill our expectations of being *young, attractive, verbal, intelligent,* and *successful* (YAVIS), and are thus seen as having more therapeutic potential. Thinking of older adults evokes images of decline, loss, or death, clearly issues that many would just as soon ignore.

In many cases, services are organized around age-related themes or life events (widowhood, death, retirement, disability, illness) (see Smyer, 1984). These services unfortunately ultimately increase ageist notions of what older persons' problems really are (Lieberman, 1978; Neugarten, 1983; S. Zarit, 1980) or mediate the effects of being isolated or institutionalized (S. Zarit, 1980). While these programs provide structure and a source of identity for many aged and are easily identified targets for support (Danish, Smyer, & Nowak, 1980), they may "turn off" other older persons, in addition to the age segregation they often unfortunately promote. Programs that are age heterogeneous or issue oriented (coping, loss or change, career counseling, self-help, maintaining decision making and independence) may be more beneficial to participants, lessen age segregation, and remove the stigma of seeing a mental-health professional (Sargent, 1980, 1982).

Gottesman, Quarterman, and Cohn (1973) note that with older persons, one's choice of treatment should *always* involve (1) the *capacities* (physical, emotional, cognitive) of the elderly individual, (2) *societal demands* regarding "appropriate" behavior for the aged, (3) *expectations of significant others,* and (4) what the elderly person expects of *himself.* While they focus on the aged, these seem to be equally important concerns for adults of all ages.

APPROACHES TO THERAPY AND COUNSELING WITH OLDER ADULTS

In spite of Freud's (1924) contention to the contrary, research does not bear out age as a predictor of therapeutic success (Garfield, 1978; Luborsky, Chandler, Averback, Cohen, & Bachrach, 1971; M. Smith & Glass, 1977). Gotestam (1980) and Eisdorfer (1983) suggest that we should be primarily concerned with improving the *quality* of life, not necessarily just its quantity, *regardless* of our client's age. Goodstein (1982) highlights building "adaptive resources" through psychotherapy. More specific goals in therapy, as noted by Wellman and McCormack (1984) and by Gotestam (1980) with the aged are:

1. insight into one's behavior
2. symptom (anxiety or depression) relief
3. relief to relatives
4. delaying deterioration (psychic or physical)
5. adaptation to a present situation
6. improving self-care skills
7. encouraging activity
8. facilitating independence
9. becoming more self-accepting
10. improving interpersonal relationships

In most cases, these are also goals for adults of *all* ages! Each goal will be more or less important depending on the physical health, strengths, and resources each elderly person has, as well as the therapist's own biases. Eisdorfer and Stotsky (1977) note that relying on a single approach virtually *guarantees* an unsatisfying helping experience for *both* the counselor and the client.

While many treatment approaches are all quite commonly used with younger and middle-aged adults, a specialized literature has evolved in recent years to explore the range of approaches with the aged, in an effort to undo negative expectations of their potential to be helped by such techniques. However, we are unsure as to whether a given approach works better with younger versus older adults. Gatz et al. (1985) highlight the importance of diagnosis (organicity, chronicity, situationality) and patient types (community living vs. institutionalized) as factors in evaluating outcome research with elderly persons—different therapies work better with different types of older persons, as we shall see. Additionally, we are not, at present, certain about whether particular approaches are more effective for younger versus older adults, or for older adults versus younger ones with certain disorders.

Garfield (1986), however, in a review of the psychotherapy and counseling literature, asserts that the correlation between age and outcome is extremely low, if not absent altogether. Wherever possible, we will discuss these issues in an effort to put the treatment of adults who vary in age into an adult developmental perspective. Many therapeutic approaches, it must be pointed out, have been developed for older persons (life review) in certain situations (reality orientation). In that many therapies are closely derived from a more basic theory of personality, we recommend rereading Chapter 10 on personality development as well as a comprehensive text on personality and psychotherapy (Corsini, 1977; Hall & Lindzey, 1978, 1985; Maddi, 1980; Rychlak, 1973) in order to achieve a fuller understanding of the relationship between personality theory and psychotherapy/counseling.

In addition to what might be termed generalized approaches to helping older persons (e.g., individual psychoanalytic therapy, behavioral approaches), more specific techniques geared to the aged person's capabilities and environment have become popular in recent years. While it is tempting to focus upon these specialized techniques, serious consideration must be given to the therapeutic *options* open to the aged person in distress. Unfortunately, given that the area of gerontology is relatively new, interest in and discussion of specific treatment modalities with the aged persons have in most cases preceded an evaluation of their effectiveness.

INDIVIDUAL PSYCHOTHERAPY/PSYCHOANALYSIS

Recall in Chapter 10 that we discussed the work of psychoanalyst Roger Gould (1980a, 1980b), whose discussion of "transformations" were extensions of the infantlike "illusion of absolute safety." Brammer (1984) suggests that psychoanalytic terminology may be difficult for older persons but that "the overriding argument against psychoanalysis in my opinion, is that it takes too long and is too inaccessible" (p. 29). While therapists such as Abraham and Goldfarb (see Gotestam, 1980) were much more optimistic in their analytic work with aged adults, **psychodynamic** theory has had its prime impact on work with older persons via such concepts as introspection, life review, and reminiscence (Butler, 1963). Psychoanalysis (Freud, 1924) is based on the assumption that through insight (aided by the guidance of a therapist) one may come to grips with troublesome emotions that have been reprised via unconscious defense mechanisms. While such defenses ordinarily operate very efficiently, a breakdown in one's defenses leads to the expression of anxiety, a sign that the control that may be exercised by the ego (being reality oriented) over the id (composed of instincts, wishes, drives) and the superego (referring to one's morals, ideals) is weakening. Through free association, such conflicts between the ego, id, and superego, normally unconscious, are made conscious, and their meaning interpreted to the client by the therapist (Hall & Lindzey, 1978, 1985). Unfortunately, Freud saw very few older clients (or even clients in their forties and fifties) and was skeptical about his techniques' success with elderly persons, under the assumption that the effort required to change persons whose defenses had been overused for years was not worth the limited time left to them. Gotestam (1980), however, refers to such Freudian therapists as Abraham and Goldfarb, who were instrumental in pioneering changes in psychoanalytic therapy with the aged. For example, the therapist may be more supportive and make use of the aged person's defense mechanisms. The older person's needs to be dependent on the therapist (transference) would be encouraged.

As we noted above, much of the skepticism about older persons as clients is based on a biological decline model of aging. Not only are older persons' biological drives thought to be less strong, but their ego strength (based upon their preoccupation with loss) is less, impairing their ability to respond to therapy (see Birren & Renner, 1979). Some advocate brief psychoanalytic therapy with the aged, where more realistic goals of reducing anxiety and restoring the person to a more functional state can be achieved. Lesser, Lazarus, Frankel, & Havasy (1981) have found that psychoanalytic approaches do not work well with severely confused and/or disturbed aged. In these cases, behavioral or life review (reminiscence) approaches perhaps are more effective, according to these authors.

Reports of classic psychoanalysis are rare with older clients (see discussion by Newton, Brauer, Gutmann, & Grunes, 1986), often being poorly designed and documented (Gotestam, 1980; Wellman & McCormack, 1984). Certainly, psychoanalysis should not be dismissed but perhaps reserved for highly verbal, insightful older clients.

Life Review Therapy

An extension of psychoanalytic thought is to be found in **life review** therapy. As Butler and Lewis (1981) point out, life review therapy is more extensive than a simple recall of the past, although reminiscence is important in this approach. Butler and Lewis also point out that obtaining an extensive autobiography from the elderly person is important, allowing that elder the opportunity to put his life in order. Thus, conflict resolution, improved relationships with one's family, making decisions about success and failure, resolving guilt, clarifying one's own values, and simply "getting out" one's feelings about painful experiences in the past (Newton et al., 1986) are benefits to be gained through the life review, which may be conducted individually or in a group setting. However, the life review can be a frustrating, painful experience for many aged, who may require emotional support from a counselor for an extended period of time in order to deal with the by-products of this process. Many older persons have led hard, frustrating lives that forced them to make choices that they regretted (e.g., not finishing high school). Many lack someone to confide in, with whom such confidences may be shared.

Despite its potential for some types of people, Brammer (1984) suggests that the life review falsely assumes that problems in adulthood rest upon childhood experiences. Moreover, M. Romaniuk and J. Romaniuk (1981) have pointed out that reminiscence (underlying life review) is not particular to older persons but is triggered by many events throughout *all*

The life review can be a valuable therapeutic experience for many adults.

phases of the adult life cycle. Thus, all persons engage in life review from time to time. Butler and Lewis (1981), Birren (1982), Lesser et al. (1981), and E. Wheeler and Knight (1981) have all reported success with life review/ reminiscence therapy (less depression, memory complaints) but found that more structured versions and work with more intact elderly were more successful.

GROUP THERAPY

The distinguishing feature of **group therapy** with the aged is that dependency needs can be used to their best advantage (Hayslip & Kooken, 1982). In some cases, simply being with others evokes a feeling of safety. Group therapy can take many forms (Hartford, 1980; Parham, Priddy, McGovern, & Rickman, 1982; Waters, 1984) ranging from issue-oriented (life event) discussion groups (see Smyer, 1984) to groups designed to stimulate interaction among group members, to groups specifically geared to promoting independence and a positive sense of self. Groups are typically short-term (when used within the institution) and informal in nature. Group therapy is often used in a variety of settings in combination with art therapy, dance therapy, or music therapy for elderly persons.

Waters (1984) and Hartford (1980) discuss the variety of settings within which group methods have been used with the aged: nursing homes, hospitals, private homes, day-care centers, retirement communities, senior centers.

Waters (1984) stresses that while basic helping skills may be a bit more difficult to accomplish with the aged without special training, the skills necessary to conduct group therapy are similar for clients of *all* ages. These skills are: communicating clearly, establishing trust, openness to thoughts and feelings, goal setting, confrontation (when necessary), empathy, respect for the client's wishes, and knowing when to make decisions (Waters, 1984). In working with the aged, however, one needs to realize that physical or sensory losses may dictate slower-paced, shorter counseling sessions. Moreover, using properly designed written materials (large, clear, bold print, nonglare paper) and having adequate lighting are very important. Sessions must be held at locations that are easily accessible for those who have difficulty walking. Conducting sessions in areas that lack background noises that would interfere with hearing is essential. Groups may need to be smaller to lessen the elder's confusion and fatigue, and plans need to be made with each group member as to what to do when the group ends. While group work may not be advisable for older adults who are severely disturbed, aggressive, extremely introverted, or disoriented (see Burnside, 1984), Waters (1984) suggests that all forms of group therapy provide many benefits for older persons. These benefits include:

1. enabling people to see that their problems are not unique and thus lessening their sense of isolation
2. providing individuals with the opportunity to learn new social and communicative skills
3. being able to give support, guidance, or insight to one another
4. allowing for an airing of feelings about being old, ill, or alone

Parham, Priddy, McGovern, and Richman (1982) note that well-designed research demonstrating that group therapy is effective with the aged is lacking. Its effectiveness seems to rest upon an accurate *assessment* (see Chapter 13) of each prospective group member to identify persons who may interfere with the sharing process or fail to profit from feedback from the group leader as well as one another. In the role as group leader, the helper may facilitate discussion, provide structure, define goals, clarify what is being said, or simply be supportive. Wellman and McCormack (1984) suggest that group therapy, in its many forms, has been effective but that results are clouded by methodological shortcomings (e.g., no control groups, disability among group members as an impediment to group progress).

FAMILY THERAPY

Family therapy is another attractive alternative in treating older persons whose difficulties are communicative in nature (Hayslip & Kooken, 1982). Family therapy can aid in adjustment to roles such as retirement or grandparenthood and help resolve problems accompanying caring for an ill spouse, institutionalizing one's parent(s) or spouse, or conflicts arising when an older parent is being cared for at home by a middle-aged child (see discussion of family caregiving in Chapter 13). Each family member can be involved in setting up clear expectations for behavior, improving communication, lessening distrust and guilt, or dealing with hostility and anxiety.

Family therapy is also appropriate in dealing with parent-child conflicts centering on remarriage, struggles for power within the home, or restrictions on the aged person brought about by ill health or by the divorce of an adult child. In these cases, allowing each person to express his or her own feelings, explore options, and increase sensitivity to others' points of view are the major benefits of family therapy.

Sterns, Weis, and Perkins (1984) suggest that family therapy can be more effective if supplemented by individual counseling, depending upon the *level* of functioning of the family as a whole and of the individuals within the family, ranging from panic to mastery. As Figure 14.2 illustrates, depending upon how effectively the family is functioning, different methods of treatment will be necessary.

Herr and Weakland (1979) have applied **family systems theory**

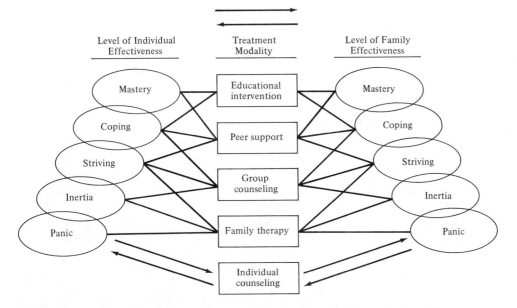

Figure 14.2 Levels of family functioning and suggested interventions for each. *Source:* H. Sterns, D. M. Weis, & S. E. Perkins. A conceptual approach to counseling older adults and their families. *Counseling Psychologist, 12,* (1984), p. 58. Copyright © 1984 Reprinted by permission of Sage Publications, Inc. and by permission of the author.

(Haley, 1963, 1971) to work with families where there is an elder. Systems theory treats the family in terms of a working *system* of relationships between family members. Each set of relationships is influenced by and influences one another. This approach, then, stresses the here-and-now nature of the *interaction* among family members. The therapist concentrates on how a problem is being handled by the family as a whole. Several problematic interactions involving elder family members may exist, according to Herr and Weakland:

1. *scapegoating* of the older person (e.g., the elder is blamed for the family's problems)
2. *parent-child role reversal* (the elder is forced into the role of child)
3. *dyadic alliances* (mother and daughter join forces against father)
4. *symbiotic* relationships (where the older parents cannot "let go" of their adult children)
5. *incongruencies* between what the older person expects and what the adult children expect of their parent(s)
6. *role inversion* (due to the husband's illness, the wife assumes his former duties)
7. *fearful withdrawal* of the older person from the younger family members

Such difficulties may be brought on by events such as illness, death, retirement, or institutionalization, or they may be long-standing in nature. Herr and Weakland (1979) specify the framework within which the family counseling process takes place:

1. the establishment of an initial contact with the client(s)
2. inquiry and definition of the problematic interaction
3. inquiries into the handling of the problem by family members
4. goal setting
5. perceptions of the problem by the family
6. an analysis of how the problem is being maintained and the construction of a strategy for its avoidance in the future
7. further interventions and their evaluation
8. termination of a therapeutic relationship

Keller and Hughston (1981), who also take a systems approach, emphasize that opportunities for communication/sharing must be "scheduled." Other techniques, such as reminiscence and "contracting" (defining and agreeing upon the consequences of a behavior pattern), can be used to deal with many types of unproductive behavior within the family: attention gaining, being bossy, counter hurting (striking back), and disablement (not taking responsibility). S. Zarit (1980) notes the importance of **relabeling** problems so that they can be more effectively solved (relabeling a problem in terms of the *relationship* rather than the characteristics of individuals). He also advocates using *specific directives* with family members to set ground rules for resolving conflict. The therapist may use *straightforward* direction (changing who is responsible for certain tasks) or he or she may use a **paradoxical** intervention technique (directing the family to continue engaging in the behavior that brought them to therapy; for example, to keep fighting over who is to care for an elder parent).

More recently, Cicirelli (1986), Dye and Richards (1980), Dye (1982), M. M. Cohen (1982), Smyer (1984), Ware and Carper (1982), S. H. Zarit and J. M. Zarit (1982), and S. Zarit and Anthony (1986) have successfully applied family therapy to a number of problems and choices families with older members often face, for example, pluses and minuses to institutionalization, alternatives to institutionalization (day care, home care), coping with the terminal illness of an older family member, and managing and caring for an aging parent or for a parent who has been diagnosed as having Alzheimer's disease (see Chapter 13). For example, S. Zarit and Anthony (1986) suggest that giving information, active problem solving, support, and one-on-one counseling techniques can help families make decisions about caring for a family member with dementia. When feelings of isolation and burdening are dealt with, the stress of coping with the death of a loved one or in caring for a family member who has Alzheimer's disease can be relieved (see Gwyther & L. K. George, 1986; Robins, Lucas, & Eastham, 1986; S. Zarit, Todd, & J. Zarit, 1986). Moreover, feelings of guilt and isolation that often accompany the decision to institutionalize an older parent can be lessened, leaving the family intact. In many cases, if properly handled, such issues can actually strengthen feelings of closeness, love, and interdependence. One need not give up control over one's life. Thus, families can avoid feeling overwhelmed by guilt, anger, or a sense of hopelessness or helplessness.

BEHAVIORAL INTERVENTIONS

As with psychodynamic psychotherapy and both group and family therapy, the use of behavioral methods of intervention is not unique to older persons (see S. L. Garfield & Bergin, 1978, 1986). As opposed to psychodynamic approaches, **behaviorally oriented therapy** focuses on the immediate, observable consequences of stimulus-response contingencies in the environment (Hoyer, 1973). According to this approach, application of a behavioral strategy requires three primary tasks be carried out:

1. a definition and assessment prior to intervention of the desired *target behavior*,

2. a *reinforcer* (defined as a stimulus whose impact makes the desired behavior *more frequent* or of *longer duration*) must be identified. This reinforcer may be self-administered or administered by the therapist, and

3. the establishment of specific *behavior-reinforcer contingencies*.

Positive (leading to pleasurable events) and *negative* (providing relief from aversive events) *reinforcing stimuli* (decreasing the frequency of a behavior by providing unpleasant consequences) may be used for the purpose of defining such contingencies. A variation on this theme is the *token economy,* where patients can earn tokens for desired behaviors, which can later be exchanged for appropriate rewards (see S. Zarit, 1980). Another technique that can be utilized by the behavior modifier involves positively reinforcing a behavior that *competes* with the unwanted target behavior (e.g., rewarding self-care behaviors that compete with aggressive behaviors) (see Vaccaro, 1988).

Contracting is a form of behavior modification that deserves mention. In contracting the client and therapist arrive at a mutually agreed upon, clearly specified goal. Being able to jointly define this goal may in itself promote a sense of control and independence for some elderly (Hayslip & Kooken, 1982).

Extensive discussions of the use of behavioral techniques with the aged can be found in Levy et al. (1980), Rosenstein and Swenson (1980), and Richards and Thorpe (1978). Of all the forms of intervention we will discuss, it is perhaps easiest to document and there is ample, well-designed research (e.g., P. B. Baltes & Zerbe, 1976; Hussian, 1981; Mishara, 1978) to support its efficacy in dealing with the modification of a variety of behavior problems, for example, dependent interactions with other elderly and staff, incontinence, assertive behavior, withdrawal, inappropriate sexual behavior, wandering, anxiety, and self-care. Many of these behaviors are a consequence of being institutionalized and have been termed *excess disabilities* (Kahn & Miller, 1978b). Moreover, behavioral methodologies have been utilized to successfully modify staff attitudes toward elderly patients (see Hussian, 1981; LaRue et al., 1985; Richards & Thorpe, 1978, for extensive reviews).

Behavioral technology with the aged possesses a number of advantages. It can be readily measured and its effects easily assessed, goals can be readily defined, and it can be carried out and understood by staff at all levels of training. Moreover, it can be tailored to the individual patient, and behavioral procedures are relatively brief and economical. However, it requires a great deal of expertise to use effectively, and its use can raise some ethical questions, particularly when it is used with institutionalized or isolated older adults.

Hoyer (1973) and Levy et al. (1980) have discussed a number of these ethical issues in behavioral work with the aged:

1. the long-term (versus the positive short-term) effects of such interventions (which may be harmful when such techniques are discontinued)
2. whether the reinforced behavior is actually within the person's capacities or will be supported by the immediate environment/staff (withdrawal of control over daily activities)
3. careful selection of the behavior itself, for example, discouraging (via negative reinforcement) the eating of foreign objects, which may generalize to the eating of food, leading to malnutrition or death

As Hayslip (1988) has noted, "Intervention for intervention's sake is not always in the older person's best interests. . . . In many cases, it may be more feasible to change the environment per se or to leave things as they are"

(p. 27). These concerns are very important if one is unsure of the consequences of a given treatment (see P. B. Baltes & Danish, 1980; Danish, 1981; Harshberger, 1973).

COGNITIVE THERAPIES

Closely related to behavioral approaches is **cognitive behavior therapy** (Ellis, 1962; Meichenbaum, 1974, 1977; A. Beck, 1976). While Ellis and Beck focus on a rational analysis of the client's belief system, Meichenbaum alters the "inner dialogue" of the individual. In general, however, cognitive behavior therapists believe that the way a person *thinks* largely determines the way he or she feels. In other words, thought causes emotional response. Cognitive behavior therapy is an attempt to help the client change his or her maladaptive thinking habits to relieve emotional disturbances such as depression, anger, and anxiety. Ellis (1962) views this process in an *A-B-C* fashion. *A* is designated as the event that the client thinks is causing the anxiety, depression, etc. The emotional disturbance lies at point *C*. A client might believe that, for example, her depression *(C)* is being caused by her getting old *(A)*. Ellis insists that age *(A)* is not causing the depression *(C)*. Instead, the depression *(C)* is attributed, not to aging *(A)*, but to the woman's *belief (B)* about her own aging; this belief about aging is the culprit. In this case, the woman might erroneously believe that being old means that she is a horrible person, unworthy of respect or love (see Hayslip & Kooken, 1982).

Elderly persons, perhaps lacking realistic feedback about themselves from others, often make "thinking errors" that in reality are quite inaccurate (Hayslip & Caraway, 1988). Irrational assumptions about one's age or about the loss of skills one once had may lead to feelings of self-deprecation in many aged persons. These feelings can lead to anger, guilt, and depression. Cognitive techniques are available to instruct the elder to substitute more rational thoughts for these irrational ones (Caraway & Hayslip, 1985).

Cognitive-behavioral approaches to therapy have been successfully utilized to treat a variety of cognitive and emotional problems in the aged, for example, depression (Gallagher & Thompson, 1982; Thompson & Gallagher, 1983), memory loss, test anxiety, performance on intellectual tasks, and response speed (Labouvie-Vief & Gonda, 1976; Richards & Thorpe, 1978; Reidl, 1981). Kooken and Hayslip (1984) and Hayslip (1989) have used a cognitive-behavioral approach (employing programs using both stress inoculation [cognitive] and relaxation training) to modify test anxiety and intellectual performance in older students. Recent research by Beutler, Scogin, Kirkish, Schetlan, Corbishley, Hamblin, Meredith, Potter, Bomford, & Levenson (1987) and Thompson, Gallagher, & Breckenridge (1987) reinforces the effectiveness of cognitive therapies with clinically depressed older adults. Wellman and McCormack (1984) note that while cognitive-behavioral research has recently begun to catch on with geropsychologists, much of the work is limited to groups, and not individuals. However, sampling issues, placebo (expectancy) effects, and measurement problems remain to be addressed in this area (Hayslip & Caraway, 1988). The research by Thompson and Gallagher (1983) and by Gallagher and Thompson (1982) is perhaps the best example of the potential of cognitive-behavioral interventions with elderly persons in dealing with depression. These authors, however, qualify their support for this method in noting that it works more effectively with aged persons who experience a major depressive episode that is exogenous—reaction to recent stress—versus endogenously depressed (depression that is life-long) elderly persons.

SPECIALIZED TREATMENTS FOR THE ELDERLY PERSON

In addition to life review therapy, reality orientation (Folsom, 1968), remotivation therapy, pet therapy, and milieu therapy (Barns, Sack, & Shore, 1973) have become popular alternatives to treatment for the institutionalized aged.

Reality Orientation

Reality orientation (RO) stresses the lessening of confusion/disorientation (primarily within the institution) and may be highly structured, stressing orientation to time, place, and person, or be more intensive. As Sherwood and Mor (1980) note, studies dealing with RO tend to be primarily descriptive, where generalized improvement or discharge from the institution have been the goals of choice. This research is methodologically flawed in many respects, for example, not controlling for staff expectancy of improvement. Zeplin, Wolfe, and Kleinplatz (1981), for example, found that RO is effective in reducing disorientation but that this effectiveness is limited to those elderly who are not severely disoriented or who are younger. The authors conclude that "the limited effectiveness of RO notwithstanding, it is useful as a vehicle to organize attention to the disoriented, thereby guarding against unjustified custodial policies" (p. 77). Zeplin et al. (1981) and Storandt (1978) both point out that an adherence to a rigid treatment regimen often limits the effectiveness of RO. Its use should be flexible and probably limited to those aged who are not profoundly deteriorated. On the other hand, Storandt (1983) notes that the less disoriented patient may become hostile if needlessly exposed to RO, requiring more staff time and effort to deal with this anger.

Waters (1984), Wellman and McCormack (1984), and Gatz et al. (1985) review the evidence for the effectiveness of RO and conclude that while it does temporarily improve orientation to time and place, more permanent, "deeper" changes in mood and cognitive status do not follow from reality orientation. However, it may be more appropriate and effective for moderately but not severely impaired elderly (Gatz et al., 1985). A similar but more intensive approach is remotivation therapy (RT), designed to improve the individual's reality contact and social skills.

Remotivation Therapy

Remotivation therapy (RT), which can be employed by nursing aides, assumes that the "healthy" portions of the person's personality can be activated (see Storandt, 1978). Remotivation therapy stresses acceptance by the therapist and other (structured) group members, "bridging" the client with reality, and a "rediscovery" of previous satisfying activities. Increased social competence and self-care skills and greater levels of activity are the goals of RT. Reviews of remotivation therapy (Storandt, 1978; Sherwood & Mor, 1980; Waters, 1984; Wellman & McCormack, 1984) suggest it to be moderately effective but varying with patient status (favoring the more deteriorated). Like RO, remotivation therapy is very popular. However, consistent evidence is lacking regarding its effectiveness (Storandt, 1983). S. Zarit (1980) even suggests that such techniques are designed to stimulate patients who have been *under*stimulated via institutionalization. Such techniques are therefore designed to correct deficits that may not have otherwise occurred, according to Zarit. Storandt (1983) notes that remotivation may have its greatest impact early on, where enthusiasm for remotivation groups is highest in staff and patients.

Milieu Therapy

Milieu therapy involves the creation of a "therapeutic community," where all phases of the elderly patient's interactions with the staff are redesigned to benefit the patient. Milieu therapy makes three assumptions (see Sherwood & Mor, 1980):

1. that patient care shall be humane and noncustodial
2. that its use enhances ward management
3. that it relies upon the immediate interpersonal resources of the environment in which it is utilized

Therapeutic goals in this case may be increased social skills, greater responsibility for one's own actions, deeper involvement in structured activities, or greater self-esteem (see Barns et al., 1973); new skills can be learned in a relatively safe environment. Milieu therapy also relies on peer support to achieve such goals. Milieu therapy varies from one "environment" to the other and is often used in combination with other approaches (behavioral, group methods).

Storandt (1983) notes that while milieu therapy has several drawbacks (minimal responsibility being placed on patients per se for change, patient-staff discrepancies in goals), it may nevertheless benefit those elderly who have become very apathetic and unresponsive, while it is not recommended for hostile, acting-out elderly persons.

In addition to the above approaches, a number of what may be termed "environmental manipulations" may be appropriate and helpful in some situations (see Waters, 1984). Fozard and Popkin (1978) note many such changes that may be helpful—simply clarifying or highlighting (making more discriminable) aspects of the environment may lessen anxiety, disorientation, and confusion in the elderly person. Additionally, Rodin and Langer (1976), Langer and Rodin (1977), R. Schulz (1976), and R. Schulz and Hanusa (1978) have noted the positive benefits (improved physical health, morale, and enhanced self-esteem) when older persons are given control over certain aspects of their everyday environment (visiting hours, being able to have plants in one's room, being able to choose from a variety of foods for one's dinner). While these approaches would certainly not seem to be "therapy" in a traditional sense, they do possess a great deal of promise in this regard as "environmental" approaches to treatment.

Pet Therapy

While not unique in its use with other individuals (e.g., abused children, the physically handicapped, mentally retarded) (Angier, 1983), a great deal of recent interest has emerged in the therapeutic use of **pets** in the treatment of older persons who are institutionalized, isolated, or cognitively impaired (Arkow, 1982). While studies of pet therapy are few in number, they indicate some *short-term* benefits to be gained, for example, more positive feelings about oneself, more interaction with others, less depression, and improved cognitive functioning. Their long-term benefits, however, remain to be established.

Not only are dogs, cats, birds (even turtles!) lovable and affectionate, but their care demands a certain amount of responsibility and thus allows one to shift this focus from personal anxieties or dissatisfactions with life to the welfare of an animal who wants and needs love and care. The older person may gain a sense of control over his or her own feelings as well as over the immediate situation. Pets (see Brickel, 1984) can also be used to elicit life history information from the individual that may be of importance (childhood experiences with pets). Such information can be obtained in a nonthreatening way. Feelings about one's past (life events where a pet was present) or about the present (feelings of depression, suicidal ideation) can be discussed in a situation where the animal provides a sense of security and both psychological/tactile comfort. The individual must "come out of himself" to interact with a pet. Other aspects of the individual's life can be explored with the aid of a pet that can be stroked and hugged.

Obviously, some commonsense decisions need to be made regarding the appropriate level of responsibility for care with a given older person (caring for gerbils vs. dogs), whether pets can be integrated into institutional life or not (permanent vs. temporary residence), and whether the animal is too active or can bring on allergies. Nevertheless, these are minor problems (see Brickel, 1979, 1984) compared to the therapeutic gains that can be achieved. Francis (1984) has advocated the use of plush animals, with similar positive results. While most of us react positively to small animals, their use with the aged, who in many cases have no one to whom they feel close, can be quite beneficial.

Pet therapy is a viable option for many aged and who are isolated or institutionalized.

ROGERS'S SELF-THERAPY

As Brammer (1984) points out, Rogerian self-theory is a popular framework for therapists working with the aged in that it provides insight into the world of the older person. The older person can experience what Rogers has termed *unconditional positive regard*—his feelings of self-worth are reaffirmed by the therapist. Especially for those who are lonely, dependent, or isolated, simply being listened to can be very important. As Brammer (1984) notes, a person-centered approach challenges the age bias of the counselor, and it may be difficult to implement with noncommunicative elderly or with those who have multiple sensory deficits. Despite these difficulties, simply *being with* the older person, making eye contact, touching and expressing your support and empathy for that person as an *individual* first can capture the essence of what Rogerian therapy expresses. In view of the skepticism about counseling often expressed by the aged and their reluctance to contact mental-health personnel, counselors with these qualities can truly perform a valuable service.

PSYCHOPHARMACOLOGICAL TREATMENTS

While drug treatment with adults has been a clear option in the treatment of such disorders as schizophrenia, anxiety, or depression (J. Coleman et al., 1984), its use with the aged has been more critical, though psychotropic medications are more widely used with the aged (Hicks & Davis, 1980). While some (Gallagher & Thompson, 1982, 1983) have abandoned drug treatment as too risky, others (T. Crook, Ferris, & Bartus, 1983) advocate **psychopharmacological treatments** with the aged. G.D. Cohen (1984) suggests that we not abandon drug treatment with the aged entirely but instead see it as an intervention to complement individual and/or group counseling (Eisdorfer, 1975).

Several major categories of drugs have been utilized with the aged. They include:

1. *antidepressants* (tricyclics, MAO inhibitors, lithium carbonate, electroconvulsive therapy, estrogens)

2. *antipsychotic* agents and "anti-Parkinsonian" drugs (chlorpromazine)

3. *antimanics* (antipsychotics, lithium carbonate)

4. *antianxiety* agents/hypnotics (barbiturates, chloral hydrate, meprobamate, benzodiazepines, chlordiazepoxide, propranolol)

5. *cognitive-acting* drugs (cerebral vasodilators, CNS stimulants, gerovital, anabolic substances, cholinomimetic agents (Kapnick, 1978; Hicks et al., 1980).

Problems with Drug Treatment of Elderly Persons

Antipsychotic drugs are commonly used to treat agitation, violent behavior, irrational behavior, and perceptual disturbances (hallucinations) accompanying paranoid state/late-life schizophrenia. Predictable side effects include extrapyramidal motor signs (tremors) for which anti-Parkinson (anticholinergic) medication is often incorrectly prescribed as a remedy. Other side effects include tardive dyskinesia (involuntary facial, mandibular finger movements) with prolonged use, and akathisia (uncontrolled restlessness/agitation). Occasionally, glaucoma, constipation, and retention of urine are seen as side effects of antipsychotic medications with the aged. *Major tranquilizers* used to treat psychosis produce similar side effects. Most often, reduced dosage levels and/or "drug holidays" are recommended in these cases. *Antidepressant drugs* (tricyclics, MAO inhibitors) often interact with a variety of foods (e.g., cheese, caffeine). Tricyclics can create many problems (arrhythmia, strokes, myocardial infarction, tachycardia) for those aged with cardiovascular disorders. Amitriptyline, and imipramine are the recommended antidepressant compounds for use with the aged. *Antimanics* (lithium) often produce side effects of nausea, central nervous system toxicity, and confusion. *Antianxiety drugs* (barbiturates) often produce "paradoxical" symptoms (excitement), and negatively affect enzyme action. Other minor tranquilizers (benzodiazepine) can be both physiologically/psychologically addictive. A variety of "cognitive-acting" drugs (e.g., hydrergine) are used to supposedly reverse cognitive impairment, though their use in this regard has been questioned (see Hicks et al., 1980). Older persons are particularly sensitive to drug effects; wide individual differences exist regarding response to psychopharmacological agents (Hicks & Davis, 1980).

Polypharmacy (the use of and interaction among many drugs) is a pervasive problem with the aged (Cadwallader, 1979). Furthermore, older persons are not as capable of metabolizing and excreting drugs as are the young (e.g., lithium carbonate) (Vestal, 1979). Most drugs (prescription or not) have a longer half-life in older persons; they build up in concentration when fixed dosage intervals are used (due to age-related changes in fat-to-muscle tissue). Those that do so are not being used by the body and are thus ineffective. This, in addition, makes their interactions with other drugs, medicines (anticoagulants, antacids), as well as with many foods more likely, producing a variety of side effects (Ziance, 1979) that may not only be harmful and intensify previous health problems (e.g., impairment of renal, liver, cardiovascular functioning), but also be misdiagnosed as irreversible organic brain syndrome (OBS) (e.g., confusion, loss of memory, agitation, depression, paranoid delusions, hallucinations) thought to be untreatable by the unsuspecting clinician (see Chapter 13). Drug treatment may also produce a variety of side effects that produce management problems in themselves, ranging from mild confusion, depression, and urinary or cardiac dysfunction to hallucinations or seizures.

Drug Misuse and Abuse Among the Aged

More recently, attention has been drawn to the problem of drug abuse among the aged: alcohol (Schuckit & Pastor, 1979; W. G. Wood, 1978; Zimberg, 1979), hypnotics, sedatives, or opiates (Whanger, 1984). In discussing drug use among elderly persons, Whanger (1984) specifies the criteria for substance abuse:

1. *pathologic pattern of use*—pathological use includes the lack of ability to alter one's pattern of use, regular use to maintain adequate functioning, and complications (blackouts or overdose),

2. *impairment* of *social* or *cognitive functioning* due to substance use (e.g., work difficulties, accidents, violent behavior at home)

3. *duration* of use over one month.

Whanger (1984) also notes that abuse of prescription/over-the-counter drugs and caffeine are becoming more recognized as problems among the aged. Overmedication by physicians in the form of inaccurate diagnosis, improper drug treatment, and arbitrary medication or overmedication are also serious problems for many aged, often leading to *more* medications to deal with side effects or to treat the condition for which the drug(s) was prescribed (incorrectly) in the first place (Whanger, 1984). The problems are further complicated when older persons inappropriately self-medicate themselves, mixing medications and/or taking medications that may no longer be appropriate or effective in an effort to avoid a costly prescription.

Kapnick (1978) lists simple rules that should guide both the therapist and layperson in the use of drugs with the aged:

1. Understand the pharmacological action of the drug used—how it is metabolized (absorbed) and excreted.

2. Use the *lowest* dose possible that is effective, on an *individual* basis; drug dose should be titrated with patient response.

3. Use the *fewest* drugs the person needs.

4. Do not use drugs to treat symptoms without first discovering the causes of those symptoms.

5. Do not withhold medication on the basis of age per se.

6. Do not use a drug if its effects are worse than the symptoms it is prescribed to cure.

7. Discontinue the use of a drug when it is no longer necessary.

8. Review repeat prescriptions.

9. Encourage the aged person to contact the physician (who should be willing to listen) if any adverse effects are experienced (Kapnick, 1978, pp. 248–249). This is especially important if the older person is seeing several physicians and several drugs are being prescribed.

Regardless of the age of the client, but especially so with the aged, one should *always* have an extensive drug history and an accurate record of *what* drugs the elderly person is taking, in what *dosage,* and *how often.* Drug usage needs to be monitored conscientiously. An extensive list of common prescribed psychoactive drugs for the aged, to include total dosage levels (in milligrams per day), can be found in Whanger (1984), who suggests that the best rule of thumb is to "start low and go slow."

SOCIETAL INTERVENTION AS THERAPY

In addition to changing the individual, we might also want to alter the environment or context in which that person functions. Smyer (1984) has argued that interventions at the *physical/social environment* level can be quite effective, in place of or in combination with treatment at the individual family level (see also Gatz et al., 1985). Attention needs to be given to both the *micro*environment (home, institution, activities programs, rehabilitation [Hartford, 1980]), as well as the *macro*environment (neighborhood, community, subculture) as targets for intervention. The *adult in context* approach we presented in Chapter 1 is very consistent with the idea of societal intervention as therapy. Smyer also discusses the *intergenerational* relationships (see Chapters 8 and 9) that affect older persons' sense of independence, demographic shifts ("the graying" of America) that influence worker-retiree ratios, and the experience of retirement as targets for societal change. Moreover, increasing divorce rates may affect older parents' sense of failure in raising their children. Additionally, the changing work involvement of women affects how they define their roles (motherhood vs. career?) as well as decisions regarding child care and parenting. Clearly these broader social influences will affect future cohorts of older persons. Not only will their role commitments and relationships to those younger change, but what they expect of themselves, as well as what others expect of them, will be altered as our culture changes. Counselors and therapists need to be aware of these influences, much as they need to be skilled in various therapeutic techniques in order to best facilitate the "fit" (Lawton & Nahemow, 1973) between the older person and that person's microenvironment and macroenvironment.

As many (Beattie, 1976; Gatz et al., 1985; Lowy, 1980) have pointed out, intervention at a broader societal level may be helpful and necessary. Altering attitudes toward the aged and increasing the older person's reliance on the community, family, and friends are examples of such intervention. Moreover, the development of services (home-based care, outreach, hospice care, foster grandparent programs, widow-to-widow programs) geared to older persons may prove to be as effective as intervention at the individual level. The counselor will often utilize the above resources as well as many of the various treatments discussed earlier in combination (pharmacological treatment and individual psychotherapy, individual and group therapy) to achieve a more effective solution for the patient and family/staff. Such a person thus acts not only as counselor but also as advocate and psychosocial care planner (Lawton & Gottesman, 1974).

CONCLUSIONS

In light of the issues about development and aging we raised in Chapter 1, counselors who deal with adults of *all* ages should have come to terms with what they expect from younger versus older clients. What kinds of assumptions are made about them? Are they dealt with on an age-related basis or are other factors taken into account in assessment and therapy? Clearly, counselors' views about human development across the life span, based upon comparisons between the young and the old and their own recollections of youth, play an important role in how effective they will be with clients of all ages. Moreover, beliefs about personality change (see Chapter 10) are likely to have an important bearing on whether one chooses to work with adults of all ages (or with older clients at all) and which approach(es) is (are) selected for use with a particular client. As we noted in Chapter 10, while many feel existing personality theory has little to offer the gerontological counselor, one's beliefs about "what makes people tick" will certainly influence one's choice of therapy with elderly persons.

In light of the questions we raised at the beginning of this chapter, we would recommend striking a balance between acquiring specialized knowledge about the assessment and therapy of adults of a given age range versus a more flexible, *individualized* approach, where basic competence in assessment, therapeutic approaches, and community psychology are developed (see Lawton, 1976; Lawton & Gottesman, 1974; Smyer & Gatz, 1979). Indeed, such a view has characterized our approach to adulthood. The adult counselor, moreover, should be prepared to call on other professionals (social workers, physicians) when necessary as well as intervene at multiple levels (individual, family, societal) simultaneously (Gottesman et al., 1973) in both a *preventive* and a *remedial* sense. Perhaps many of the difficulties adults of all ages experience could be headed off by this dual emphasis on prevention and remediation.

Above all, the *integrity* and *humanity* of the person must be maintained to ensure that regardless of the quantity of the years the individual has accrued, the *quality* of his or her life can be improved. New skills can be learned, insight about self can be gained, and pent-up feelings can be expressed (Gatz et al., 1985). Most of us can benefit in these ways from help of many kinds. Given these advantages, the counselor can then become an important change agent, on par with the individual himself, in facilitating personal growth and development *throughout* the adult years.

SUMMARY

A number of individual and cultural factors have converged to create more interest in the treatment of older clients. Despite this interest, a variety of barriers currently exist regarding older adults' access to the **mental-health system** (e.g., beliefs in untreatability, cost, and resistance to help, borne out of ignorance or pride). Evidence does not suggest age to be a factor in the efficacy of various therapies.

Several therapeutic options currently exist for elderly persons once they gain access to a therapist. These options include *psychodynamic, behavioral, cognitive, group, family, and pharmacological* treatments. More specialized approaches include *life review, remotivation, reality orientation, milieu,* and *pet therapy.* Not only should one examine the feasibility with different types of older clients, but their efficacy should be established. More recently, many have advocated *self-help* or psychotherapy in *nontraditional* settings as alternatives to more formal types of interventions with the aged. Regardless of the nature of the help provided, it should be directed at *multiple levels* (individual, family, community, subcultural) and be geared to the needs, interests, capabilities, and goals of the individual.

KEY TERMS AND CONCEPTS

Mental-health system

Well-being

Countertransference

Transference

Psychodynamic therapy

Behavior therapy

Cognitive behavior therapy

Group therapy

Life review

Remotivation therapy

Reality orientation (RO)

Pet therapy

Family systems theory

Relabeling

Paradoxical directives

Psychopharmacological treatment

Milieu therapy

· GLOSSARY ·

Abnormal behavior Behavior that is at odds with reality or injurious to oneself or others.

Absolute threshold The minimum level of stimulus energy/intensity required for the individual to detect stimulation.

Accommodation The process whereby the eye adjusts itself to attain maximal image resolution (clarity).

Active euthanasia Doing something to cut life short for those who are in pain or suffering. Failing to do something (passive) that would otherwise extend life.

Active leisure activity Refers to activities such as exercising, jogging, playing sports, or going to restaurants. The primary focus of these leisure activities is active "doing" and/or participation.

Active mastery A style of relating to the environment that changes with age in different ways for men and women, according to Guttman. Imposing oneself on the environment to change it.

Active versus passive role of the organism Developmental issue concerned with whether the developing organism plays an active or a passive role in its own developmental process.

Activity theory Theory that suggests that the older individual who manages to resist withdrawal from the social world and remains active will maintain life satisfaction.

Adaptation The change in sensitivity of the eye as a function of change in illumination. There are two types: dark adaptation—improvement in sensitivity to light in a dark environment; and light adaptation—increased sensitivity to light in a light environment.

Adaptation level The process whereby individual receptor processes (hearing, vision) tend to function at a comfortable level relative to the external stimulation, so that a stimulus of a given magnitude is perceived as neither strong nor weak.

Age credit Adding IQ points to the score of an older person under the assumption of age decline to equate that person's average score with that of someone younger.

Age debit Subtracting IQ points from the score of a younger person under the assumption of age decline to equate that person's score with that of someone older.

Age Discrimination in Employment Act (ADEA) Federal law enacted in 1967 to prohibit age discrimination in employment. Amended in 1974 and 1978 to provide more comprehensive coverage.

Age function A statement of the relationship between a given variable and chronological age.

Ageism Discrimination or bias against persons due to their age.

Ageism in employment Discrimination against workers on the basis of their age.

Age-normative influences Factors that are general to development, are highly related to chronological age, and are presumed to affect everyone of a given chronological age range similarly.

Aging The biological, psychological, and sociological aspects of growth and development across the life span.

Aging as illness model A variation of the medical model ascribing aging-related changes (decrements) to physical causes.

Aging process The process of aging emphasizing change. The aging process is complex and affected by many biological, psychological, sociological, and environmental factors.

Alzheimer's disease A form of dementia characterized by a higher than normal incidence of senile plaques and neurofibrillary tangles in brain tissue.

Androgyny Refers to a change in the traditional gender roles associated with males and females toward the integration of the characteristics, traits, and behaviors of both genders.

Anticipation interval The time interval taken to encode and rehearse a paired-associate prior to the next item-pair.

Anticipatory grief Preparation or rehearsal for death prior to its actual occurrence.

Anxiety A sense of impending dread or apprehension that is amorphous in character.

Arteriosclerosis Progressive hardening of blood vessel walls with age.

Atherosclerosis Progressive narrowing of blood vessel walls with age.

Attachment An emotional bond that develops between children and their parents. Often viewed as the foundation upon which other interpersonal relationships are built.

Audition   The hearing sense.

Auditory training   A procedure used by individuals with hearing impairments to comprehend what others are saying. Involves attending to certain key sounds and words in the conversation while at the same time watching the speaker's lips move.

Baby boom period   The period from approximately 1940 to 1957 during which there was a high birthrate in the United States.

Beck Depression Inventory   A widely used test for the diagnosis of depression in adulthood.

Behavior therapy   Form of therapy where rewarding and punishing stimuli in the environment are manipulated to bring about a desired behavior(s).

Behavioral model   Approach to personality and mental illness emphasizing behavioral responses to distinct situations that vary in their requirements for adaptive behavior.

Bereavement overload   The inability to work through the deaths of loved ones that occur close to one another in time.

Bifactorial designs   Baltes's two factor (age and cohort) approach to describing developmental change.

Biographical life events   One of Buhler's dimensions of change that is experiential and stable.

Biological age   Biological age has two aspects. It can be considered to be the relative age or condition of the individual's organ and body systems. Also, it refers to individuals' present position relative to their potential life span, which varies from species to species.

Biological death   The cessation of function or irreversible damage to certain critical organs or organ systems.

Biological life events   One of Buhler's dimensions of change that is independent of experience and declines with age.

Bipolar vs. unipolar depression   Depression characterized by mood swings (bipolar) versus predominately sad affect (feeling low) (unipolar).

Bona fide occupational qualification (BFOQ) An ability, trait, or factor that is considered to be related to job performance.

Brain plasticity   The capacity of the brain to regenerate or compensate for losses in brain cells.

Career   A planned, coherent, organized sequence of positions that have meaning for the individual.

Career crisis in midlife   During midlife a number of individuals become dissatisfied with their current occupation, which often leads to stress.

Career indecision   The inability to choose a particular occupation, or difficulty in deciding whether to change occupations or remain in the same occupation.

Cautiousness   Being conservative in decision making and with respect to many aspects of behavior.

Central explanations for RT slowdown Central (brain and spinal cord) explanations for reaction time (RT) view the slowdown in behavior/performance with age as being due to some higher level internal process.

Cerebral death   The cessation of brain activity for a given period of time (e.g., 24 hrs.), often termed brain death.

Childless marriage   A marriage in which both partners decide not to have children. This decision can be based on a number of reasons such as personal concerns, economic costs, and career demands.

Clinical death   The cessation of spontaneous heart and respiratory activity.

Cognitive behavior therapy   Form of therapy emphasizing internal cognitions or ideas about oneself or the environment as key concepts in bringing about behavior change.

Cognitive personality theory   Approach to personality emphasizing one's perceptions or cognitions about experiences or events.

Cognitive versus noncognitive influences Referring to the distinction between factors (noncognitive) that influence performance on tests of learning or memory (e.g., fatigue) and those processes that the tests are designed to reflect (i.e., cognition [learning, memory]).

Cohort   A group of individuals sharing a common set of experiences (e.g., individuals born at a given point in history who, by virtue of their birth data, experience certain sets of events at roughly the same time in their development).

Cohort/generation effects   Sociocultural influences that are particular to a group of persons sharing a common set of experiences due to being born at a certain point in history.

Cohort sequential   Developmental design permitting the separation of age and cohort effects, where time of measurement is confounded.

Collagen   A fibrous protein present in connective tissue (ligaments, muscles, joints, bones).

Colleague marriage   In the colleague marriage, the partners recognize role and responsibility differences. Each partner assumes responsibility and authority for specific duties and tasks within the family, and these are generally stable, rather than constantly changing.

Color vision The faculty by which colors are perceived and distinguished.

Companionship marriage A marriage in which there is no differentiation between male and female roles. Each partner can take on the rights, obligations, and duties of the other. In fact, each may exchange duties and responsibilities with the other on some prearranged agreement (e.g., each week or month).

Competition at recall When old S-R associations interfere with the learning of new associations.

Complementarity Theory of mate selection that suggests that opposites attract.

Complexity explanation for RT Central theory used to explain response slowing with age. Views the psychomotor slowdown with increasing age as due to the increased difficulty of older adults to respond as tasks become more complex.

Confidant One with whom intimate moments, secrets, etc., can be shared, who provides emotional support through life.

Confounding When the effects of at least two factors cannot be disentangled, they are said to be confounded.

Convoy Personal network of friends and family members who accompany us throughout the life cycle.

Core Core constructs are central overriding ideas or assumptions about personality, according to Maddi.

Correlation vs. causation The distinction between relationships among variables that descriptively covary with one another (correlation) versus statements that explain the influence of one variable on another (causation).

Countertransference The difficulties experienced by a younger therapist who is treating an older client (e.g., feelings about one's parents may be projected upon the older client).

Crossover effect The fact that for more recent cohorts black females' life expectancy will exceed that of white males.

Cross-sectional Design in which the behavior or performance of several groups of persons who differ in age, sex, etc., are compared at one point in time.

Cross-sectional sequences A design within P.B. Baltes's bifactorial model where at least two independent cross-sectional age samples are drawn at each level of cohort.

Cross sequential Developmental design permitting the separation of time of measurement and cohort effects, where age is confounded.

Crystallized ability Acculturated skills that build

upon one another and remain stable across most of adulthood.

Cult of the adult Refers to the period of the 1980s in the United States during which society believes that you can still be over 30 and enjoy life.

Cult of the aged Refers to the Colonial period in America during which it was considered acceptable and positive to be old. Older adults were viewed with respect and occupied places of honor, prestige, and leadership in society and business.

Cult of the young Refers to the period of the 1960s in America when being young was considered good and positive, and being old was considered bad and negative.

Cultural ethics Prevailing attitudes of a society at a particular point in time that determine how individuals view their relationship with society and others at all points in the life span.

Death anxiety Fear of death, dying, or the afterlife that may or may not be consciously expressed.

Death versus dying The moment of death versus the process of days' or weeks' duration leading up to death.

Death with dignity Death that is "appropriate" (of the individual's choosing) and that preserves the person's sense of respect and honor.

Decision making The ability to make or the process of making decisions—may be affected by personal characteristics or task demands.

Decision/premotor time In a perceptual-motor reaction time task, the time lapsed from the onset of the stimulus to the initiation of the response to that stimulus.

Decrement with compensation model Model of aging emphasizing interventions that can compensate for age-related declines in functioning.

Deep friendships Friendships based on intimate feelings between individuals.

Deep processing Material that is encoded at the meaning level is deeply processed.

Dementia A cluster of behaviors or characteristics (e.g., disorientation) common to many diagnostic entities ranging from depression to Alzheimer's disease.

Depressive equivalent A form of depression whereby persons complain of physical ailments, etc., yet consciously deny that they feel depressed.

Determinism versus nondeterminism The issue of whether one's behavior is dictated by

r="537">

Glossary

various factors (e.g., heredity, past experience) or whether behavior is independent (free) of these controlling factors.

Developmental stages Developmental issue that revolves around the question of whether higher order behaviors and activities, such as motor skills or cognitive skills, develop in a qualitative manner, incorporating earlier (preceding) and simpler forms of behavior (stages of development).

Developmental tasks Behaviors, activities, skills, or milestones that individuals are expected to accomplish by their culture during specific stages of the life cycle. For instance, in our culture these include activities for the adult such as obtaining a driver's license and voting.

Developmental versus nondevelopmental research Developmental research seeks to explore relationships between age (or age-related factors) and some variable of interest. Nondevelopmental research, on the other hand, explores relationships between variables that are age-irrelevant.

Deviation IQ A method of computing an intelligence quotient based upon deviations from the mean.

Dialectical operations Theory of Riegel that suggests internal factors (genetically preprogrammed instinctual behaviors, traits, characteristics, physiological state) and external factors (aspects of the physical environment, cultural components) continuously influence and are influenced by each other.

Difference threshold The degree to which a stimulus (e.g., sound, light) must be louder or brighter to be perceived as such.

Differentiation of abilities The hypothesis that the relationship between distinct abilities becomes more differentiated or spreads out (lessens) with age.

Disengagement theory Theory that suggests that with increasing age individuals withdraw (disengage) from society and society withdraws (disengages) from the individual. There are two types of disengagement, psychological and social. The theory has been reformulated to account for individual differences.

Double jeopardy The notion that the black aged suffer a dual cultural disadvantage because they are both old and black.

DSM-III-R The *Diagnostic and Statistical Manual* of the American Psychiatric Association. It serves as the major framework for the classification and treatment of mental disorders in the United States today.

Ecological validity Refers to the ability of tasks or tests to reflect everyday requirements (e.g., the real-life ecology of learning).

Ecology of mental health Applying real-world criteria in defining mental health for adults of varying ages.

Elder abuse Psychological, physical, or financial neglect or active harm of older persons by others.

Empty nest Refers to the time when all the children have left the home. Its impact may be positive or negative.

Encoding The interpretation or giving of meaning to information so that it may be stored and retrieved.

Errors of omission versus errors of commission On numerous real-world and laboratory tasks the performance of older adults is marked by more errors of omission (omitting an answer) than errors of commission (giving an incorrect answer). Often interpreted as an indication of cautiousness.

Exchange theory Theory that has been adapted to help explain negative attitudes toward aging. Suggests individuals attempt to maximize rewards and reduce costs in interpersonal relationships.

Exercised versus unexercised abilities Denny's notion that abilities maintain themselves with age if they are used; those that are not used (unexercised) decline.

Existential questioning Self-examination of the meaning of one's existence.

Expectancy/set theory Central theory used to explain response slowing with age. Views the slowdown in responding with age as the result of older individuals' inability or difficulty in preparing their response to a stimulus.

Experimental versus control group The experimental group is typically the one that is the object of a treatment program or manipulation. The control group generally lacks such a treatment and serves as a baseline against which the effects of the treatment can be measured.

Experimental versus correlational approach Two approaches to research, one of which emphasizes control and the manipulation of independent-dependent variable relationships (experimental), while the other emphasizes corelationships between variables, where inferences about causality are not possible (correlational).

Exposure factor Term used in the study of accidents. Refers to amount of time individual is in a situation when an accident can occur—for example, number of miles driven or number of hours worked.

Extended family Close relatives such as aunts, uncles, cousins, and grandparents. See *kinship network*.

External validity The extent to which the results of a study generalize to other samples, tests, procedures, etc.

Extrinsic factors related to sexual behavior External, environmental, and/or social factors that affect an individual's sexual behavior. These include factors such as religious beliefs and cultural attitudes.

Factor analysis Statistical technique to reduce a matrix of intercorrelations among variables down to fewer factors that are more interpretable.

False negatives Error of diagnosis where a disorder is diagnosed as absent when it is, in fact, present.

False positives Error of diagnosis where a disorder is falsely diagnosed as present when it is not (false positive).

Family systems theory An approach to understanding and treating families that emphasizes the entire family as a system of interrelating individuals.

Field dependence/independence A construct developed to explain individual differences in perception. Persons who are field dependent make judgments that are heavily influenced by the surrounding, immediate environment, while field independent persons' judgments are not influenced by the immediate environment.

Filial maturity When adult children no longer view their parents as only parents but as real people who need their help.

Filial responsibility Refers to the perceived obligation (frequently determined by law, custom, or personal preference) with regard to the various types of services and social support that children should provide for their older parents.

Filter theory of mate selection Theory of mate selection that suggests that in selecting a mate people do so via the use of a hierarchical set of "filters." The person who passes through each of these filters is the person we marry.

Flexible careers Careers or occupations that allow the individual flexibility in working hours, working days, etc.

Fluid ability Cognitive skills that are independent of acculturated influences and that decline with increased age.

Functional ability An individual's ability to care for himself/herself or the ability to cope in a given situation.

Functional age (industrial) Judging workers on their ability to function or perform a job adequately as opposed to their chronological age.

Functional analysis An analysis of an individual's behavior in relation to the function it serves in managing the environment.

Functional (definition of age) An index of a person's level of capacities or abilities relative to those of others of similar age.

Functional disorders Behavioral changes that are problematic, whose cause can be attributed to psychogenic versus organic factors. Functional disorders can coexist with organicity.

Gender roles Those behavior patterns (culture specific) that are considered appropriate and often specific to each gender, which are formed (acquired) early in life and are maintained until death.

General adaptation syndrome Selye's notion of the body's three-phase reaction to stress or illness (alarm, resistance, exhaustion).

Generalizability The dimension(s) along which the results of a study might be externally valid (e.g., generalization to other samples, tasks, or procedures).

Genetic biological theories of aging Theories of aging that emphasize the formation of genetic structures as explanations for the aging process.

Genotypic continuity Genotypic continuity suggests that persons with certain clusters of traits change in certain ways.

Glare sensitivity Sensitivity to bright light that results in unpleasantness or discomfort and/or that interferes with optimum vision.

Global perception Perception based on a response to the "whole" stimulus rather than the separate parts of the stimulus.

Grandparental styles Modes of interacting with one's adult children and grandchildren (e.g., formal versus involved styles) and the meaning attached to the grandparent role.

"Graying" of the American work force Refers to the fact that more and more individuals are remaining on the job for a longer time. Therefore, the average age of the average worker is increasing.

Grief versus bereavement Grief refers to the expression of feelings about a loss, while bereavement simply indicates that one has experienced a loss.

Group marriage A marriage in which a number of couples are legally married in a traditional manner (a husband to a wife), but these individuals share living arrangements, duties, responsibilities, and sexual partners.

Group therapy A form of therapy where individuals in a group setting share experiences under the guidance of a group leader.

History-normative influences Factors or events that occur at a specific point in time (day, year, month) and theoretically impart upon everyone in that society or culture.

Homogeneous versus heterogeneous samples Persons who are to a large extent like one another define a homogeneous sample; heterogeneous samples are composed of persons who are very different from one another.

Homosexual partnership A relationship where two gay individuals make a personal commitment to each other to live together as married partners. Each partner shares or takes individual responsibility for specific roles and duties within the relationship.

Horizontal career move A move from one career to another.

Hospice A philosophy of caring for the terminally ill and their families emphasizing individualized care over cure and bereavement counseling.

Hypothetical constructs Ideas, definitions, and concepts that only have meaning and relevance within a particular theory. They do not have any physical or material existence outside the theory.

Illusion of absolute safety Gould's concept stressing the false myth of safety learned during childhood, that one eventually gives up in adulthood.

Independent versus dependent samples In a cross-sectional study, persons in different age-groups are selected independently of one another. In a longitudinal study, however, samples at later points in time are dependent upon those with which the study began.

Independent versus dependent variables Independent variables are those that are manipulated by the experimenter. Dependent variables' effects depend upon some manipulation of the independent variable.

Indirect self-destructive behavior (ISDB) Taking one's life covertly or indirectly within an institution by becoming combative, not taking medication, not eating, etc.

Individual differences Refers to differences between persons on any trait, behavior, ability, or performance skill at any given point in time. See *interindividual differences.*

Informal role types According to Rosow, informal role types assume no institutional status but have definite roles attached to them. These include family scapegoat, heroes, criminals, etc.

Information overload Central theory used to explain response slowing with age. Assumes that as stimulus information from the environment increases, the individual's information processing systems may be overloaded and consequently will not be able to perform quickly and correctly.

Information processing approach to aging A framework within which to structure the implications of age changes in various abilities. This approach suggests that once a person has received stimulation from the environment, this stimulation (information) must pass through four distinct information processing stages before a response in the form of observable behavior occurs. A breakdown in function in any of these stages can affect the relationship between stimuli (input) and responses (output).

Informed consent The process by which a research participant voluntarily agrees to participate in a study, having been fully informed of the risks and benefits associated with such participation.

Inspection intervals In a paired associates task, the inspection interval is the lapse of time taken to inspect (read) the item pair.

Institutional role types According to Rosow, an institutional role type assumes a given status for a person who has defined roles. These include such factors as social class, gender, race, and age.

Instrumental leisure activity Leisure activity that is in the service of attaining a goal or producing a result.

Integrity A sense of completeness about one's life characterized by an acceptance of death (Erikson).

Intellectual plasticity The view that suggests older adults' intellectual skills are quite plastic or malleable with training or intervention.

Intelligence General index of an individual's ability to behave intelligently in situations or in tests designed to elicit such behaviors.

Interest-related friendships Friendships that are based on some similarity of life-style or interest. These may include plants, pets, hobbies, or sports.

Interference The process by which learning or memory is interfered with via unlearning (new associations interfere with already learned ones) or competition at recall (where new and old associations compete or interfere with one another).

Interindividual differences Refers to differences between persons on any trait, behavior, ability, or performance skill at any given point in time. See *individual differences.*

Interiority Neugarten's term for the tendency to become preoccupied with one's inner experiences (intrapsychic level) with increased age.

Internal validity Validity as it applies to independent-dependent variable relationships (i.e., that only the independent variable is casually related to the dependent variable).

Interpersonal relationships Relationships with others. These include friends, spouse, family members, and so forth.

Intraindividual changes Refers to changes within an individual over time on any trait, behavior, ability, or performance skill.

Intraindividual differences Refers to differences between traits, behaviors, abilities, or performance levels within a person at any one point in time.

Intrapsychic Refers to internal personality dynamics.

Intrinsic factors related to sexual behavior Biological-physiological changes in the body structures and organ systems that are part of the normal aging processes and are related to sexual behavior.

Intrinsic leisure activity Intrinsic leisure activities are those that are inherently satisfying to the individual.

Intrinsic (primary) versus extrinsic (secondary) influences on life expectancy Intrinsic factors (e.g., genetic inheritance, race) contribute directly to life expectancy, while extrinsic factors' (smoking, exercise) influence on life expectancy is indirect.

IQ An index of an individual's ability to perform on a test of intelligence, relative to age peers.

Irreversible decrement model Model of aging emphasizing the parallel between biological decline and social-psychological change.

Job loss The loss of one's position due to a number of factors. These include factory closing, a position being phased out, or being replaced by industrial robots, etc.

Kinship network The extended family—aunts, uncles, and cousins. See *extended family.*

Learned helplessness The perception that the correlation between one's behavior and desired outcomes is minimal.

Learning Learning is the acquisition of information and facts via experience.

Legal age The age, defined by law, governing certain behaviors or responsibilities (e.g., drinking, voting, service in the military, being legally responsible for damages one might cause).

Leisure Typically refers to a person's activities during free time. Leisure can include work or may simply be a state of mind.

Leisure competence The development of satisfying leisure activities—implies understanding the meaning of leisure for you personally.

Leisure life-styles Patterns of activity among

retirees. Researchers classify these individuals into categories on the basis of their primary leisure activities.

Lethality scale A method of assessing potential suicide risk via gathering information about age, sex, etc.

Life expectancy How long on the average one is expected to live; it is species specific.

Life review The internal process by which the individual comes to terms with crises, problems, conflicts, etc., in an effort to make sense out of personal life experiences via reminiscence.

Life satisfaction Overall perception or feeling about the quality of one's life.

Life-span developmental model A view that sees development as the result of an interdependence between internal and external factors throughout the course of the life span.

Life structure Levinson's concept emphasizing the overall plan of one's life, composed of many interrelated aspects (e.g., work vs. family).

Life tendencies Buhler's set of motivating forces that organize behavior at various points in one's development.

Line of unbearability One's personal equation governing suicide as an end to life where life's quality is emphasized over its quantity.

Lipofuscin Aging pigment that accumulates in certain organ systems with age.

Living will A provision by which the individual directs the physician or family not to needlessly sustain that individual's life if such acts would prolong suffering.

Longevity The theoretical upper limit of the life span; it is species specific.

Longitudinal design Study in which the changes in behavior or performance of a group of persons is studied by repeatedly assessing them at several points in time.

Longitudinal sequences A design within P.B. Baltes's bifactorial model where at least two dependent samples of cohorts are followed at several (at least two) levels of age.

Maturational ground plan The biologically determined sequence one progresses through, according to Erikson's psychosocial stages.

Mechanics versus pragmatics of intelligence Distinction by P. B. Baltes emphasizing basic fundamental intellectual skills (mechanics) versus the use of intellectual skills that are more applied or adaptive (e.g., wisdom) (pragmatics).

Mechanistic model Stimulus-response or

behavioral models of development. Human development is seen as progressive, continuous, quantitative improvement in the levels of abilities and behavior.

Medical model   Model of abnormal behavior emphasizing distinct diagnostic categories with presumed physical causes.

Memory   The storage and retrieval of facts over time. May also be defined functionally.

Menopause   The cessation of menstruation and the ability to bear children. Usually occurs in one's late forties or early fifties.

Mental age   An index of an individual's having accumulated a certain degree of age credits (in months) relative to chronological age to yield an IQ.

Mental health–mental illness   The concept of adjustment lying on a continuum emphasizing the presence of adaptive qualities (mental health) or their absence, implying the presence of maladaptive qualities (mental illness).

Mental-health system   The system of inpatient, outpatient, formal, and informal mental-health service providers.

Mental status questionnaire   Screening instrument composed of questions regarding orientation to time and place (e.g., one's residence, month, day, year, etc.) designed to identify individuals who may have some form of organicity.

Mentor   One who guides or advises another in terms of either occupational or personal goals, behaviors, etc.

Metamemory   One's memory for what is in one's memory, to include self-assessment or self-estimates of one's memory capacity or efficiency.

Midlife crisis   A personal sense of upheaval experienced by some men and women in their forties, fifties, and sixties.

Milieu therapy   A form of therapy often used within institutions where all aspects of the interpersonal environment are changed to facilitate the individual's adaptation or adjustment (e.g., interactions with staff).

Mnemonic devices   Referring to a variety of techniques by which learning and memory performance may be improved.

Motor-cognitive rigidity   Refers to the degree to which an individual can shift without difficulty from one activity to another.

Motor time   In a perceptual-motor reaction time task, the time lapse from the initiation of the response to the stimulus to the completion of that response. Sometimes called *movement time*.

Multidimensional change   Refers to numerous changes in different types of ability, skill, and behavior simultaneously within an individual over time.

Multidirectional change   Numerous behaviors and traits that exhibit different types of change (e.g., increases and decreases in functioning) along the course of development.

Multi-infarct dementia   Dementia produced by small strokes producing clusters of dead neurons or infarcts that create disturbances in the flow of blood to the brain.

Myth   A belief based more on fiction or imagination than fact.

Nature versus nurture   Developmental issue concerned with whether development is the result of genetically determined hereditary forces (nature), or of learning and/or other environmental influences (nurture).

Negative versus positive transfer   Negative transfer occurs when two tasks interfere with each other's learning or recall, whereas positive transfer occurs when each task facilitates the other.

Neural noise   Central theory used to explain response slowing with age. It is thought to be either random background neural activity or irregularities in the action of the cells carrying the signals that interfere with information passing from one part of the brain to another.

Neurofibrillary tangles   Intertwined nerve fibers that interfere with brain cell function.

Neurotransmitter substances   Various chemicals (e.g., acetylcholine) that make possible communication across synapses between brain cells.

Noise   Background interference. Stimuli that interfere with the individual's ability to detect a relevant signal or stimulus.

Nongenetic biological theories of aging   Theories of aging that emphasize changes in cells and tissues with age after they have been formed.

Nonnormative influences   Factors that are not related to age or history and that affect specific individuals during the life cycle. These factors cannot be attributed to the normal process of development or to the impact of environmental, cultural-societal events.

Nontraditional student   Student who is older than the "traditional" 18 to 22-year-old, often involved in very diverse forms of adult education.

Nuclear family   The traditional nuclear family in American society is one in which there is a husband, wife, and children.

Occupational development   Refers to the selection and choice of an occupation during the life course. Often called *career development*.

Occupational developmental tasks   The particular goals, activities, or skills associated with a specific occupation.

Occupational role   The behaviors, status, and traits associated with a specific occupation. Occupations vary in terms of the expectancies of society and others with regard to behaviors and activities.

Old age dependency ratio   The ratio of older persons who are receiving retirement or health care benefits relative to the number of younger persons whose earnings support such funds.

Older worker   Designation varies substantially as a function of specific occupation. It can be applied as early as age 40.

Open marriage   A marriage that is based on a legally sanctioned union between a husband and a wife, but in which partners feel it is perfectly acceptable to have intimate and/or sexual relations with other partners.

Organic brain syndrome   General term implying that some structural organic change is responsible for one's behavior. Often termed *dementia*.

Organismic model   Views the course of development as being genetically programmed. Development is seen as qualitative and progresses through a series of discontinuous stages.

Orthogenetic principle   Suggests that the perception of shapes, forms, objects, and stimuli follows a specific and predictable life-span trend. Early in life children perceive the world in a diffuse or global manner; as they get older, they learn to integrate the parts of the stimulus pattern with the whole stimulus pattern simultaneously in relation to each other.

Outer, middle, inner ears   Sections of the ear (see Chapter 4). Changes in the inner ear, and to a lesser extent in the middle ear, are responsible for losses in hearing with age.

Overcoming   A style of dealing with death that emphasizes death as failure.

Paired associates task   Task where the learner is to associate and recall certain stimuli (S) that have been paired with specific responses (R).

Paradoxical directives   Suggestions by the therapist to the client not to engage in a behavior designed to reveal its self-defeating nature and establish control over that behavior.

Paranoia   Feelings of persecution or suspiciousness.

Paraphrenia   Term given to schizophrenia when it appears for the first time in later life.

Parental imperative   The notion that biological and cultural factors cause men and women to suppress certain behaviors or characteristics. When the demands of parenthood cease, these suppressed characteristics can surface.

Participating   A style of dealing with death that emphasizes the interrelatedness of life and death as natural partners.

Passive euthanasia   Failing to do something that would otherwise extend the life of a terminally ill person.

Passive leisure activity   Refers to activities such as reading or watching television in the home.

Passive mastery   A style of coping which emphasizes the molding of oneself to the environment that varies by age and sex, according to Guttman.

Pattern recognition   Involves recognizing a specific stimulus pattern from a group of stimulus patterns or displays.

Perception   The interpretation of sensory stimulation.

Perceptual inference   Theory that suggests that older adults do not utilize incomplete information as effectively as young adults.

Perceptual information processing model   Model of driving behavior that suggests the abilities of perceptual style, selective attention, and perceptual motor reaction time are related to behavior or performance.

Perceptual information processing tasks   Laboratory tasks that serve as a method of accurately determining the condition and efficiency of our perceptual processes. These include tasks such as geometric illusions.

Perceptual-motor reaction time   A reaction time task.

Perceptual noise theory   Central theory used to explain response slowing with age. Views slowdown in performance as due to an age decrement in ability to suppress irrelevant stimuli.

Peripheral explanations for RT slowing   View the loss of response speed with age as due to decrements in the sense organs and/or peripheral nervous system.

Peripheral field   The outer areas of the visual field. The visual field is the extent of physical space visible to an eye in a given position—that whole area you see.

Periphery   That aspect of personality that is situational and behavioral, according to Maddi.

Personality   Cohesive organization of traits or qualities that give behavior meaning or consistency.

Personality-perceptual rigidity Refers to an individual's ability to adjust readily to new surroundings and changes in cognitive and environmental patterns.

Personality "types" Neugarten's clusters of personalities whose styles differ and who vary regarding life satisfaction.

Personalization of death Giving death a personal meaning (e.g., death means being reunited with loved ones).

Person-environment interaction Theory that suggests that all aspects of behavior and performance can be conceived of as a result of the interaction or transaction between the individual and the environment.

Pet therapy Form of therapy using real or plush animals as aids in reestablishing caring relationships with others.

Phenotypic persistence Stability of certain traits over time.

Physiological theories of aging Theories of biological aging that emphasize breakdown of certain organs or organ systems.

Pitch discrimination The ability to detect changes in the pitch of sounds.

Pluralism Refers to the fact that development takes on many forms.

Poverty level index A dollar figure set by the government to officially designate individuals as living below the poverty line, for purposes of eligibility for federal assistance.

Practice effects The fact that individuals typically improve with practice, independent of the effects of aging.

Premature presbycusis The damaging effects of repeated exposure upon hearing in adults and the middle-aged.

Presbycusis The most common hearing disorder of older adults. It is characterized by a progressive bilateral loss of hearing for tones of high frequency due to degenerative physiological changes in the auditory system as a function of age.

Presbyopia The progressive decline with age in the eye's ability to focus on near objects. Results mainly from a loss of elasticity in the lens.

Primary memory Memory for material whose limit is five to seven bits of information.

Primary mental abilities Theory of intelligence hypothesizing seven major abilities—the focus of Schaie's work on the aging of intelligence.

Prime age Designation varies substantially as a function of specific occupation. The United States Bureau of Labor Statistics considers the ages between 25 and 54 to be "prime age" for a worker.

Principle of compensation The perception that terminally ill persons are compensated for the loss of life by the promise of eternity.

Progeria A disease process that rapidly accelerates the physical signs and symptoms of aging.

Projective techniques Unstructured techniques for personality assessment that tap unconscious processes.

Protestant work ethic Traditional work value that views work as sacred and something to be engaged in and enjoyed.

Pseudodementia The misdiagnosis of depression as dementia in older persons.

Psychic death Extreme withdrawal from others, often characterized by giving up.

Psychoanalytic model Views development as instinctual and biologically based, progressing through a series of discontinuous psychosexual stages that are quantitatively different.

Psychodynamic therapy Freud's psychoanalytic therapy emphasizing free association, insights provided by the therapist, and the uncovering of unconscious material embedded in one's childhood experiences.

Psychological age Refers to the adaptive capacities of the individual, such as coping ability or intelligence.

Psychometric tradition Perspective emphasizing the construction of empirically derived tests with established reliability and validity to assess intelligence or personality.

Psychomotor speed rigidity Refers to the individual's rate of emission of familiar cognitive responses.

Psychopharmacological therapy Drug therapy. Often contraindicated with elderly persons due to unwanted side effects of many medications. Can be used with other forms of therapy.

Psychosocial crises Erikson's sequence of individual-social choices that face all persons at various points in their lives (e.g., intimacy vs. isolation).

Q-sort A method of personality assessment where individuals sort statements about themselves along a continuum of "most to least like me."

Qualitative versus quantitative change Developmental issue concerned with the question of whether behavior change is the result of the continuous accumulation of small improvements in similar behaviors or processes (quantitative), or the acquisition of new processes or behaviors (qualitative).

Random assignment Procedure by which subjects have an equal chance of being assigned to a treatment versus a control group; a means of experimental control to equate the groups at an experiment's outset.

Reality orientation (RO) Form of therapy stressing reorientation of self to time and place on a daily basis.

Recognition versus recall Methods of studying memory processes (retrieval, encoding), presenting tasks where cues for the information exist (recognition) versus those where such cues must be generated (recall).

Reductionist versus holist approach to development Developmental issue concerned with whether all aspects of development and behavior can be reduced to an observable stimulus-response connection (reductionist), or whether to understand behavior and development, we must view the total situation (holist).

Registration The process of taking in information or stimulation so that it may be processed.

Regression to the mean The fact that individuals whose scores place them at the extremes of the sample distribution will "regress to the mean" upon retesting, independent of any genuine developmental change.

Regressive intervention Doing little or nothing for someone who is terminally ill because that person is beyond all help.

Relabeling A technique frequently used in cognitive or family therapies where the "problem" is redefined so as to enable the client to see things from a new perspective.

Reliability The repeatability or internal consistency of a scale or test.

Reminiscence The process of looking back on one's life, central to the life review.

Remotivation therapy A form of therapy assuming that the healthy portion of the person's personality can be activated via restructuring the real environment with the help of the therapist and others.

Response bias Term used in laboratory investigation of cautiousness. Refers to the particular response characteristics of individuals—their criteria for making a response.

Retirement Voluntary or mandated withdrawal from an occupation or the work force.

Retrieval The "getting out" of information from memory storage.

Reversible (acute) versus irreversible (chronic) dementia Referring to the distinction between dementias whose cause can be identified and whose symptoms can be reversed (e.g., malnutrition) versus those whose causes are organic and presumed irreversible (e.g., brain cell loss).

Rigidity hypothesis Assumption that as we become older we become more rigid or less flexible in our behavior, attitudes, habits, and personality.

Rites of passage Rites, rituals, or milestones that mark the transition from one stage of the life cycle to another. For example, a "rite of passage" from the stage of adolescent to adulthood might be obtaining a job or getting married. These rites vary from culture to culture.

Role change A role shift that involves the complete shifting from one type of role to another. An example would be a change from student to teacher.

Role transition A role shift that involves the evolution of one form of a specific role to another form of that same role. An example would be a shift from mother to grandmother.

Roles Roles are the behaviors, traits, and characteristics expected by others for individuals who occupy a specific social position in society.

Rote versus mediated learning Rote learning is learning via simple repetition, whereas mediated learning relies on a scheme or mnemonic (e.g., *i* before *e* except after *c*). Some tasks and some persons tend to favor one type of learning over the other.

Schizophrenia General term suggesting symptoms that imply a break with reality (e.g., delusions or hallucinations).

Secondary memory Memory for material whose span exceeds the capacity of primary memory (5–7 digits). Often referred to as short-term memory. Requires active rehearsal.

Selective attention The control of information processing so that a particular source of information is processed more fully than any other simultaneous sources of information.

Selective dropout The fact that certain individuals are not available or choose not to participate in retesting due to illness, schedule conflicts, lack of interest, etc., producing a biased sample of retestees.

Selective exposure The formulation of a belief or attitude on the basis of limited information—not having observed all possible instances.

Selective sampling The fact that not all persons who are contacted for a study choose to volunteer, often producing a biased sample of individuals that may not generalize to nonvolunteers.

Selective survival The fact that not all members

of a given cohort survive into adulthood, yielding a sample that is no longer representative of its original cohort.

Self-concept   Our view of ourselves, often defined to include self-esteem (what we think of this view of self).

Self-efficacy   The sense of one's ability to succeed or accomplish a task.

Semantic differential   Technique of personality assessment where individuals rate themselves along a continuum defined by opposites (e.g., happy-sad).

Semantic versus episodic memory   Refers to the distinction between the recall of general information (e.g., what a plane is) and the recall of specific details (e.g., dates, places; for instance, the date and destination of your last plane trip).

Senile plaques   Clusters of dead or dying neurons that interfere with brain function and that are especially present in the brains of persons with Alzheimer's disease.

Sensation   The reception of physical stimulation and the translation of this stimulation into neural impulses.

Sensory information processing tasks   Laboratory tasks that serve as a method of accurately determining the condition and efficiency of our sensory system. These include tasks such as critical flicker fusion and click fusion.

Sensory memory   Memory that is preattentive—it requires no conscious effort or attention. Material is processed solely in terms of its physical (visual, aural) features.

Sensory receptors   Structures that receive and register stimulation from the environment. Each primary sense has specific receptors.

Serial learning task   Task where the learner is required to learn and recall items in a given order (e.g., as presented).

Shallow processing   Material that is processed at the sensory level (visually, aurally).

Shifting roles   As we progress along the life span we are constantly shifting roles. Role shifts may occur in two ways, via role transitions or role changes.

Signal   A specific cue or stimulus that the individual must respond to, observe, or detect.

Similarity   Theory of mate selection that suggests that individuals who are similar on a number of factors are attracted to each other.

Social age   Refers to the social habits and roles of the individual relative to the expectations of society.

Social clock   Expectations about the timing of various events, behaviors, and activities along the life cycle with regard to their being "on" or "off" time.

Social death   The death of meaningful relationships with others.

Social learning theory   Personality theory that emphasizes the role of models who serve as guides for the construction of internal standards of behavior.

Socialization   The process that molds each of us into a member of a particular society or subculture through our acquisition of the roles appropriate to our age, gender, social class, or ethnic group.

Socioadaptational   Refers to adaptation at the level of roles and relationships with others.

Somesthesis   Our sensitivities to touch, vibration, temperature, kinesthesis, and pain are collectively referred to as "somesthesis" since they arise from normal and intensive stimulations of the skin and viscera.

Spearman's two-factor theory   Theory of intelligence specifying a general ability factor (G) complemented by several test-specific ability factors (s).

Speechreading   Another name for lipreading. A procedure used by individuals with hearing impairments to comprehend what others are saying.

Speed versus accuracy trade-off   Accuracy is stressed at the expense of speed in performing a psychomotor task; often characteristic of older persons.

Stability versus change   The issue of whether personality remains stable or changes with increased age.

Stage theory of dying   Kübler-Ross's notion that dying patients go through discrete stages (denial, anger, bargaining, depression, acceptance) in their reactions to impending death.

Stage theory of intellectual development   The notion that the quality or function of intelligence changes with age, according to such theorists as Schaie or Piaget.

Stage theory of mate selection   The process by which individuals are attracted to one another, fall in love, and marry. This process is defined in terms of discrete stages corresponding to the deepening and stability of the relationship, and in part by stimulus variables and social role expectations.

Stanford-Binet intelligence test   Major test of intelligence applying to children and adults; yields an IQ via the accumulation of mental age credits.

Status   The relative position of a person within society. This status is often effected by factors such as age, gender, occupation, education level, and so forth. Often considered social position.

Stereotype Beliefs, attitudes, or expectations about individuals from a specific group that are presumed solely on the basis of the individual's membership in that group.

Stimulus persistence theory A theory based on the assumption that stimulus traces persist longer in the nervous system of older people than in that of younger ones, accounting for slowness of behavior.

Storage Memory process whereby information is organized in some fashion—storehouse of information that has been encoded and that will be retrieved.

Structure-function versus antecedent-consequent Developmental issue concerned with whether a theory analyzes behavior and development in terms of structure-function (organism) or antecedent-consequent relationships (mechanism).

Structure of intellect Guilford's theory of intelligence hypothesizing 120 separate abilities.

Styles of child rearing Distinct patterns of relating to, disciplining, and educating one's children, yielding very different personality patterns (e.g., authoritarian, permissive).

Styles of grandparenting Different approaches taken by middle-aged and elderly persons toward defining the role of grandparent (e.g., reservoir of family wisdom, parent surrogate).

Sudden infant death syndrome (SIDS) The spontaneous cessation of breathing via a cerebral shutdown among infants from birth through approximately a year of age.

Sustained and transient visual channels Relates to the assumption that different types of visual stimuli are processed by different neural channels in the visual system. Sustained channels detect stable high spatial frequency stimuli, with little contrast, and respond more slowly yet more persistently over a longer span of time. Transient neural channels, on the other hand, respond to low spatial frequency stimuli that are moving and respond more quickly for shorter periods of time.

Task pacing The slowing down of presentation rates so that learning and memory can be improved.

Tenuous role types According to Rosow, tenuous role types reflect persons in definite social positions (status) who do not have well-defined functions or roles. These include the aged and the unemployed.

Terminal change (drop) The decline in functioning that precedes death by three to five years.

Tertiary memory Memory for overlearned, meaningful material that is relatively permanent and whose capacity is unlimited. Often termed long-term memory.

Time lag Study in which the effects of cultural change are assessed by comparing at least two samples of persons who are of similar ages.

Time of measurement effects Influences that affect all persons, regardless of age or cohort, at a given point in time.

Time perspective A shift in one's definition of life in terms of time since birth versus time left to live.

Time sequential A sequential design separating the effects of age and time of measurement where the cohort is confounded. The replication of a cross-sectional design at another time of measurement.

Traditional marriage A relationship between a husband and a wife. In the classic traditional marriage, the husband is considered the head of the family and the decision maker. The wife's role is usually limited to child care and household matters. This type of marriage relationship is decreasing in relative frequency.

Trait An internal quality or characteristic reflected in behavior that is consistent across situations.

Transactional model Point of view stressing the individual's interaction or transaction with the environment, as a means of understanding how persons adapt to or cope with change.

Transference The attribution to the therapist of positive or negative qualities by the client.

Transformations Gould's notion that through experience we are transformed into adults, having shed several myths about the world, ourselves, and our parents collectively referred to as the *myth of absolute safety.*

Trifactorial designs Schaie's three-factor (age, cohort, time of measurement) scheme for measuring and explaining developmental change.

Type A versus Type B individuals Type A individuals are hard driving and achievement oriented, whereas Type B individuals are more relaxed, less hurried, and less preoccupied with success.

Types of widows Research by Lopata indicating that there are a number of types of widows; each type has a specific set of characteristics. These types include liberated women, merry widows, working women, widow's widows, traditional widows, and grieving women.

Unconditional positive regard Rogers's concept emphasizing uncritical acceptance of another person.

Universals of aging   Eight factors identified by Cowgill and Holmes that are assumed to be present and similar in all cultures/societies regarding the aged.

Unlearning   When new S-R associations interfere with the maintenance of previously learned associations.

Validity   The extent to which a test or scale measures what it purports to measure.

Variations of aging   Twenty-two variations or differences between cultures/societies in terms of the aging experience, identified by Cowgill and Holmes.

Vertical career move   A move to a higher level of responsibility within a specific career.

Vigilance   The ability to maintain attention to a task for a sustained period.

Visual acuity   The eye's ability to resolve detail. It is most often equated with accuracy of distance vision compared to the "hypothetical normal person."

Visual search behavior   How an individual searches, scans, or processes a visual scene.

Vocational maturity   Super's index of the congruence between one's vocational behaviors and societal expectations. Varies by stage of the occupational life cycle.

Wechsler Adult Intelligence Scale (WAIS)   Major test of adult intelligence yielding both verbal and performance IQs; termed a point scale.

Well-being   Referring to the subjective state of being well (i.e., self-esteem, morale, life satisfaction).

Wisdom factor   The use of one's experience or life perspective to aid in adaptation to the aging process.

· REFERENCES ·

Abel, B. J., & Hayslip, B. (1983, August). *Locus of control and adjustment to retirement.* Paper presented at the 91st annual meeting of the American Psychological Association, Anaheim, CA.

Abel, B. J., & Hayslip, B. (1986). Locus of control and attitudes toward work and retirement. *Journal of Psychology, 120,* 479–488.

Abel, B., & Hayslip, B. (1987). Locus of control and preparation for retirement. *Journal of Gerontology, 42,* 162–165.

Abrahams, J. P. (1976). Health status as a variable in aging research. *Experimental Aging Research, 2,* 63–71.

Abramson, L., Seligman, M., & Teasdale, J. (1978). Learned helplessness in humans: Critique and reformulation. *Journal of Abnormal Psychology, 87,* 49–74.

Abush, R., & Burkhead, E. J. (1984). Job stress in midlife working women: Relationships among personality type, job characteristics, and job tension. *Journal of Counseling Psychology, 31,* 36–44.

Achenbach, T. M. (1978). *Research in developmental psychology: Concepts, strategies, methods.* New York: Free Press.

Adam, J. (1977). Statistical bias in cross-sequential studies of aging. *Experimental Aging Research, 3,* 325–333.

Adam, J. (1978). Sequential strategies and the separation of age, cohort, and time of measurement contributions to developmental data. *Psychological Bulletin, 85,* 1309–1316.

Adams, B. N. (1968). *Kinship in an urban setting.* Chicago: Markham.

Adams, D. L. (1969). Analysis of a life satisfaction index. *Journal of Gerontology, 24,* 470–474.

Adams, R. D. (1980). The morphological aspects of aging in the human nervous system. In J. E. Birren & R. B. Sloane (Eds.), *Handbook of mental health and aging* (pp. 149–160). Englewood Cliffs, NJ: Prentice-Hall.

Addington, J., & Fry, P. S. (1986). Directions for clinical-psychosocial assessment of depression in the elderly. In T. L. Brink (Ed.), *Clinical gerontology* (pp. 97–118). New York: Haworth Press.

Adler, S., & Aranya, N. (1984). A comparison of the work needs, attitudes, and preferences of professional accountants at different career stages. *Journal of Vocational Behavior, 25,* 574–580.

Ahammer, I. M. (1973). Social learning theory as a framework for the study of adult personality development. In P. B. Baltes & K. W. Schaie (Eds.), *Life-span developmental psychology: Personality and socialization* (pp. 253–284). New York: Academic Press.

Ahammer, I. M., & Baltes, P. B. (1972). Objective versus perceived age differences in personality: How do adolescents, adults and older people view themselves and each other? *Journal of Gerontology, 27,* 41–46.

Ainsworth, M. (1973). The development of infant-mother attachment. In B. M. Caldwell & H. N. Riciuti (Eds.), *Review of Child Development Research III.* Chicago: University of Chicago Press.

Ainsworth, M., & Bell, S. (1970). Attachment, exploration, and separation: Illustrated by the behavior of one-year-olds in a strange situation. *Child Development, 41,* 49–67.

Aizenberg, R., & Treas, J. (1985). The family in late life: Psychosocial and demographic considerations. In J. E. Birren & K. W. Schaie (2nd ed.), *Handbook of the psychology of aging* (pp. 169–189). New York: Van Nostrand Reinhold.

Albaugh, P., & Birren, J. (1977). Variables affecting creative contributions across the adult life span. *Human Development, 20,* 240–248.

Albaugh, P., Parham, I., Cole, K., & Birren, J. (1982). Creativity in adulthood and old age: An exploratory study. *Educational Gerontology, 8,* 101–116.

Albrecht, G. L., & Gift, H. C. (1975). Adult socialization: Ambiguity and adult life crises. In N. Datan & L. Ginsburg (Eds.), *Life span developmental psychology: Normative life crises* (pp. 237–251). New York: Academic Press.

Aldag, R. J. & Brief, A. P. (1977). Age, work values and employee relations. *Industrial Gerontology, 4,* 192–197.

Aldrich, C. & Mendkoff, B. (1963). Relocation of the aged and disabled, a mortality study. *Journal of the American Geriatrics Society, 11,* 185–194.

Allan, C., & Bortman, H. (1981). *Chartbook on aging in America.* Washington, DC: White House Conference on Aging.

Allport, G. W. (1961). *Pattern and growth in personality.* New York: Holt, Rinehart & Winston.

Alpert, J. L., & Richardson, M. S. (1980). Parenting. In L. Poon (Ed.), *Aging in the 1980s: Psychological* issues (pp. 441–454). Washington, DC: American Psychological Association.

American Association of Retired Persons. (1985). *A profile of older Americans: 1985.* Washington, DC.

American Association of Retired Persons. (1986). *A profile of older Americans: 1986.* Washington, DC.

American Association of Retired Persons. (1987). *A profile of older Americans: 1987.* Washington, DC.

American Psychiatric Association. (1987). *Diagnostic and statistical manual of mental disorders* (4th rev. ed.). Washington, DC.

American Psychological Association. (1982). *Ethical principles in the conduct of research with human participants.* Washington, DC.

American Psychological Association. (1984, November). Mental health added to Older Americans Act. *APA Monitor, 19,* 121–128.

Anastasi, A. (1982). *Psychological testing* (5th ed.). New York: Macmillan.

Anderson, C., Porrata, E., Lore, J., Alexander, S., & Mercer, M. (1969). A multidisciplinary study of psychogenetic patients. *Geriatrics, 23,* 105–113.

Angier, N. (1983, November). Four-legged therapists. *Discover,* pp. 87–89.

Ansello, E. F. (1977). Age and ageism in children's first literature. *Educational Gerontology, 2,* 255–274.

Ansello, E. F., & Hayslip, B. (1979). Older adult higher education: Stepchild and Cinderella. In H. Sterns, E. Ansello, B. Sprouse, & R. Layfield-Faux (Eds.), *Gerontology in Higher Education* (pp. 262–273). Belmont, CA: Wadsworth.

Antonucci, T. C. (1985). Personal characteristics, social support, and social behavior. In R. Binstock & E. Shanas, (Eds.), *Handbook of aging and the social sciences* (pp. 94–128). New York: Van Nostrand Reinhold.

Arena, J. G., Hightower, N. E., & Chong, G. C. (1988). Relaxation therapy for tension headache in the elderly: A prospective study. *Psychology and Aging, 3,* 96–98.

Arenberg, D. (1965). Anticipation interval and age differences in verbal learning. *Journal of Abnormal Psychology, 70,* 419–425.

Arenberg, D. (1976). The effects of input condition on free recall in young and old adults. *Journal of Gerontology, 31,* 551–555.

Arenberg, D. (1980). Comments on the processes that account for memory declines with age. In L. Poon, J. Fozard, L. Cermak, D. Arenberg, & L. Thompson (Eds.), *New directions in memory and aging* (pp. 67–72). Hillsdale, NJ: Lawrence Erlbaum.

Arenberg, D. (1982). Learning from our mistakes in aging research. *Experimental Aging Research, 8,* 73–75.

Arenberg, D., & Robertson-Tchabo, E. (1977). Learning and aging. In J. E. Birren & K. W. Schaie (Eds.), *Handbook of the psychology of aging* (p. 482). New York: Van Nostrand Reinhold.

Arkow, P. (1982). *Pet therapy: A study of the use of companion animals: Selected therapies.* Colorado Springs: Humane Society of Pikes Peak Region.

Arlin, P. K. (1975). Cognitive development in adulthood: A fifth stage? *Developmental Psychology, 11,* 602–606.

Arlin, P. K. (1984). Adolescent and adult thought: A structural interpretation. In M. L. Commons, F. A. Richards, & C. Armon (Eds.), *Beyond formal operations: Late adolescent and adult cognitive development* (pp. 258–271). New York: Praeger.

Arvey, R. D., & Mussio, S. (1973). Test discrimination, job performance and age. *Industrial Gerontology, 16,* 22–29.

Astin, H. S. (1984). The meaning of work in women's lives: A sociopsychological model of career choice and work behavior. *Counseling Psychologist, 12,* 117–126.

Atchley, R. C. (1971). Retirement and work orientation. *The Gerontologist, 2,* 29–32.

Atchley, R. (1975). The life course, age grading, and age-linked demands for decision making. In N. Datan & L. Ginsburg (Eds.), *Life-span developmental psychology: Normative life crises* (pp. 261–278). New York: Academic Press.

Atchley, R. C. (1976). *The sociology of retirement.* Cambridge, MA: Schenkman.

Atchley, R. C. (1977). *The social forces in later life.* Belmont, CA: Wadsworth.

Atchley, R. C. (1979). Issues in retirement research. *The Gerontologist, 19,* 44–54.

Atchley, R. C. (1982). The aging self. *Psychotherapy: Theory, Research and Practice, 19,* 388–396.

Atchley, R. C. (1983). *Aging: Continuity and change.* Belmont, CA: Wadsworth.

Atchley, R. C. (1984). *The social forces in later life.* Belmont, CA: Wadsworth.

Atchley, R. C. (1987). Disengagement theory. In G. Maddox (Ed.), *The encyclopedia of aging* (pp. 186–187). New York: Springer.

Atkeson, B. M. (1978). Differences in the magnitude of the simultaneous and successive Muller-Lyer illusions from age twenty to seventy-nine years. *Experimental Aging Research, 4,* 55–66.

Atkinson, R. C., & Shiffrin, R. M. (1968). Human memory: A proposal system and its control processes. In K. W. Spence & J. T. Spence (Eds.), *The psychology of learning and motivation* (Vol. 2, pp. 90–196). New York: Academic Press.

Auerbach, D. N. & Levinson, R. L., Jr. (1977). Second impressions: Attitudes in college students toward the elderly. *The Gerontologist, 17,* 362–366.

Austin, D. R. (1985). Attitudes toward old age: A hierarchical study. *The Gerontologist, 25,* 431–434.

Avolio, B. J., Alexander, R. A., Barrett, G. V., & Sterns, H. L. (1979). Analyzing preference for pace as a component of task performance. *Perceptual and Motor Skills, 49,* 667–674.

Avolio, B. J., & Barrett, G. V. (1987). Effects of age stereotyping in a simulated interview. *Psychology and Aging, 2,* 56–63.

Avolio, B. J., Barrett, G. V., & Sterns, H. L. (1984). Alternatives to chronological age for assessing occupational performance capacity. *Experimental Aging Research, 10,* 101–105.

Avolio, B. J., & Panek, P. E. (1981, November). Assessing changes in levels of capacity and preferences across the working life span. Paper presented at the symposium *Industrial Gerontological Psychology: Why survive?* at the 34th annual meeting of the Gerontological Society, Toronto.

Avolio, B. J., & Panek, P. E. (1983, August). *Automobile accidents characteristic of young and old female drivers.* Paper presented at the 91st annual meeting of the American Psychological Association, Anaheim, CA.

Axelrod, S. (1963). Cognitive tasks in several modalities. In R. H. Williams, C. Tibbitts, and W. Donahue (Eds.), *Processes of aging* (Vol. 1, pp. 132–145). New York: Atherton Press.

Axelrod, S., Thompson, L. W., & Cohen, L. D. (1968). Effects of senescence on the temporal resolution of somesthetic stimuli presented to one hand or both. *Journal of Gerontology, 23,* 191–195.

Backman, C. W., & Secord, P. F. (1959). The effect of perceived liking on interpersonal attraction. *Human Relations, 12,* 379–384.

Baker, S. P., & Deitz, P. E. (1979). Injury prevention. In Department of Health, Education, and Welfare (PHS), *Healthy people—the surgeon general's report on health promotion and disease prevention background papers,* (Publication No. 79–55071A, pp. 53–80). Rockville, MD: Department of Health, Education, and Welfare.

Balkwell, C. (1985). Transition to widowhood: A review of the literature. In L. Cargan (Ed.), *Marriage and family: Coping with change* (pp. 312–322). Belmont, CA: Wadsworth.

Baltes, M., & Zerbe, M. (1976). Independence training in nursing home residents. *The Gerontologist, 16,* 428–432.

Baltes, M. M., & Baltes, P. B. (1986). *The psychology of control and aging.* Hillsdale, NJ: Lawrence Erlbaum.

Baltes, P. B. (1968). Cross-sectional and longitudinal sequences in the study of age and generation effects. *Human Development, 11,* 145–171.

Baltes, P. B. (1973). Prototypical paradigms and questions in life span research on development and aging. *The Gerontologist, 13,* 458–467.

Baltes, P. B. (1987). Theoretical propositions of life-span developmental psychology: On the dynamics between growth and decline. *Developmental Psychology, 23,* 611–626.

Baltes, P. B., Cornelius, S. W., & Nesselroade, J. R. (1978). Cohort effects in behavioral development: Theoretical and methodological perspectives. *Minnesota Symposium on Child Psychology, 11,* 1–63.

Baltes, P. B., Cornelius, S., & Nesselroade, J. (1979). Cohort effects in developmental psychology. In J. Nesselroade & P. B. Baltes (Eds.), *Longitudinal research in the study of behavior and development* (pp. 61–87). New York: Academic Press.

Baltes, P. B., Cornelius, S., Spiro, A., Nesselroade, J., & Willis, S. (1980). Integration vs. differentiation of fluid-crystallized intelligence in old age. *Developmental Psychology, 16,* 625–635.

Baltes, P. B., & Danish, S. (1980). Intervention in life-span development and aging. In R. R. Turner & H. W. Reese (Eds.), *Life-span developmental psychology: Intervention* (pp. 49–78). New York: Academic Press.

Baltes, P. B., Dittmann-Kohli, F., & Dixon, R. (1984). New perspectives on the development of intelligence in adulthood: Toward a dual process conception and a model of selective optimization with compensation. In P. Baltes & O. Brim (Eds.), *Life-span development and behavior* (Vol. 6, pp. 33–76). New York: Academic Press.

Baltes, P. B., & Goulet, L. R. (1970). Status and issues of a life-span developmental psychology. In L. R. Goulet and P. B. Baltes (Eds.), *Life-span developmental psychology: Research and theory* (pp. 4–21). New York: Academic Press.

Baltes, P. B. & Labouvie, G. V. (1973). Adult development of intellectual performance: Description, explanation, modification. In C. Eisdorfer & M. P. Lawton (Eds.), *The psychology of adult development and aging* (pp. 157–219). Washington, DC: American Psychological Association.

Baltes, P. B. & Nesselroade, J. (1973). The developmental analysis of individual differences on multiple measures. In J. R. Nesselroade & H. W. Reese (Eds.), *Life-span developmental psychology: Methodological issues* (pp. 214–251). New York: Academic Press.

Baltes, P. B., Nesselroade, J. R., Schaie, K. W., & Labouvie, G. V. (1972). On the dilemma of regression effects in examining ability-related differentials in ontogenetic patterns of intelligence. *Developmental Psychology, 6,* 78–84.

Baltes, P. B., Reese, H. W., & Lipsitt, L. P. (1980).

References

Life-span developmental psychology. *Annual Review of Psychology, 31,* 65–111.

Baltes, P. B., Reese, H., & Nesselroade, J. (1977). *Life-span developmental psychology: Introduction to research methods.* Belmont, CA: Wadsworth.

Baltes, P. B., & Schaie, K. W. (1973). On life-span developmental research paradigms: Retrospects and prospects. In P. B. Baltes and K. W. Schaie (Eds.), *Life-span developmental psychology: Personality and socialization* (pp. 365–395). New York: Academic Press.

Baltes, P. B., & Schaie, K. W. (1976). On the plasticity of intelligence in adulthood and old age: Where Horn and Donaldson fail. *American Psychologist, 31,* 720–725.

Baltes, P. B., Schaie, K. W., & Nardi, A. (1971). Age and experimental mortality in a seven-year longitudinal study of cognitive behavior. *Developmental Psychology, 5,* 18–26.

Baltes, P. B., & Willis, S. L., (1977). Toward psychological theories of aging and development. In J. E. Birren & K. W. Schaie (Eds.), *Handbook of the psychology of aging* (pp. 128–154). New York: Van Nostrand Reinhold.

Baltes, P. B., & Willis, S. L. (1982). Plasticity and enhancement of intellectual functioning in old age: Penn State's Adult Development and Enrichment Program (ADEPT). In F. I. M. Craik & S. E. Trehub (Eds.), *Aging and cognitive processes* (pp. 353–389). New York: Plenum.

Bandura, A. (1977). Self-efficacy: Toward a unifying theory of behavioral change. *Psychological Review, 84,* 191–215.

Bankoff, E. A. (1983). Social support and adaptation to widowhood. *Journal of Marriage and the Family, 45,* 827–840.

Banziger, G., & Drevenstedt, J. (1982). Achievement attributions by young and old judges as a function of perceived age of stimulus person. *Journal of Gerontology, 37,* 468–474.

Barnes-Farrell, J. L. (1983, March). *Perceptions of age-typed occupations: A preliminary investigation* (Interim report N00014–82–K–0449). West Lafayette, IN: Purdue University, Department of Psychological Sciences.

Barns, E. K., Sack, A., & Shore, H. (1973). Guidelines to treatment approaches. *The Gerontologist, 13,* 513–527.

Barrett, C., & Schneweis, K. (1980–1981). An empirical search for stages of widowhood. *Omega, 11,* 97–104.

Barrett, G. V. (1976, October). *Task design, individual attributes, work satisfaction, and productivity.* Paper presented at the Comparative Administration Research Institute Conference, Berlin, West Germany.

Barrett, G. V., Alexander, R. A., & Forbes, J. B. (1977). Analysis of performance measurement and training requirements for driving decision making in emergency situations. *JSAS Catalogue of Selected Documents in Psychology, 7* (Ms. No. 1623), 126.

Barrett, G. V., & Jorgensen, C. (1986, November). Employment decisions and the older worker: Personnel practices and the Age Discrimination in Employment Act. Paper presented at the symposium on aging and work, *Gerontological research and legal decisions,* at the 39th annual meeting of the Gerontological Society, Chicago, IL.

Barrett, G. V., Mihal, W. L., Panek, P. E., Sterns, H. L. & Alexander, R. A. (1977). Information processing skills predictive of accident involvement for young and older commercial drivers. *Industrial Gerontology, 4,* 173–182.

Barrett, G. V., & Thornton, C. L. (1978). Relationship between perceptual style and driver reaction to an emergency situation. *Journal of Applied Psychology, 52,* 169–176.

Barrett, G. V., Thornton, C. L., & Cabe, P. A. (1969). Relation between embedded figures test performance and simulator behavior. *Journal of Applied Psychology, 53,* 253–254.

Barrow, G. M., & Smith, P. A. (1983). *Aging, the individual, and society* (2nd ed.). New York: West.

Baruch, G., Barnett, R., & Rivers, C. (1983). *Lifeprints: New patterns of love and work for today's woman.* New York: McGraw-Hill.

Bascue, L. O., & Lawrence, R. (1977). A study of subjective time and death anxiety in the elderly. *Omega, 8,* 81–89.

Basowitz, H., & Korchin, S. J. (1957). Age differences in the perception of closure. *Journal of Abnormal and Social Psychology, 54,* 93–97.

Baumrind, D. (1971). Current patterns of parental authority. *Developmental Psychology Monographs, 1,* 1–103.

Baxter, N. (1986). Career information in the classroom. *Occupational Outlook Quarterly, 30,* 32–33.

Beattie, W. (1976). Aging and the social services. In R. Binstock & E. Shanas (Eds.), *Handbook of aging and the social sciences* (pp. 619–642). New York: Van Nostrand Reinhold.

Beck, A. (1976). *Cognitive therapy and the emotional disorders.* New York: International Universities Press.

Beck, A. T., Ward, C. H., Mendelson, M., Mock, J. E., & Erbaugh, J. (1961). An inventory for measuring depression. *Archives of General Psychiatry, 4,* 569–570.

Beck, P. (1982). Two successful interventions in nursing homes: The therapeutic effects of cognitive activity. *The Gerontologist, 22,* 378–383.

Bell, B., & Patterson, C. (1979). The death attitudes of older adults: A path-analytical exploration. *Omega, 10,* 59–71.

Bell, B., Rose, C. L., & Damon, A. (1972). The normative aging study: An interdisciplinary and longitudinal study of healthy aging. *International Journal of Aging and Human Development, 3,* 5–17.

Bell, B., Wolf, E., & Bernolz, C. D. (1972). Depth perception as a function of age. *Aging and Human Development, 3,* 77–88.

Bell, R. R. (1981). *Worlds of friendship.* Beverly Hills, CA: Sage.

Bem, S. (1981). Gender scheme theory: A cognitive account of sex typing. *Psychological Review, 88,* 354–364.

Benedict, R. (1972). A profile of Indian aged. In *Minority aged in America.* Occasional Papers in Gerontology, No. 10. Wayne State Institute of Gerontology (pp. 51–57), Ann Arbor.

Bengston, V. L. (1970). The generation gap. A review and typology of social-psychological perspectives. *Youth and Society, 2,* 7–32.

Bengston, V. L., Cuellar, J. B., & Ragan, P. K. (1977). Stratum contrasts and similarities in attitudes toward death. *Journal of Gerontology, 32,* 76–88.

Bengston, V. L., Dowd, J. J., Smith, D. H., & Inkeles, A. (1975). Modernization, modernity, and perceptions of aging: A cross-cultural study. *Journal of Gerontology, 30,* 688–695.

Bengston, V., Kasschau, P. L., & Ragan, P. K. (1977). The impact of social structure on aging individuals. In J. E. Birren & K. W. Schaie (Eds.), *Handbook of the psychology of aging* (pp. 327–353). New York: Van Nostrand Reinhold.

Bengston, V. L., Reedy, M. N., & Gordon, C. (1985). Aging and self-conceptions: Personality processes and social contexts. In J. E. Birren & K. W. Schaie (Eds.), *Handbook of the psychology of aging* (pp. 544–593). New York: Van Nostrand Reinhold.

Bengston, V., & Treas, J. (1980). The changing family context of mental health and aging. In J. E. Birren & R. B. Sloane (Eds.), *Handbook of mental health and aging* (pp. 400–428). Englewood Cliffs, NJ: Prentice-Hall.

Bengston, V., & Troll, L. (1978). Youth and their parents: Feedback and intergenerational influence in socialization. In R. Lerner & G. Spanier (Eds.), *Child influences on marital and family interaction: A life-span perspective* (pp. 215–240). New York: Academic Press.

Benjamin, B. J. (1981). Frequency variability in the aged voice. *Journal of Gerontology, 36,* 722–726.

Benjamin, B. J. (1982). Phonological performance in gerontological speech. *Journal of Psycholinguistic Research, 11,* 159–167.

Bennett R., & Eckman, J. (1973). Attitudes toward aging: A critical examination of recent literature and implications for future research. In C. Eisdorfer & M. P. Lawton (Eds.), *The psychology of adult development and aging* (pp. 575–597). Washington, DC: American Psychological Association.

Bensman, J., & Lilienfeld, R. (1979, October). Friendship and alienation. *Psychology Today,* pp. 56–66.

Bentler, P. M., & Newcomb, M. D. (1978). Longitudinal study of marital success and failure. *Journal of Consulting and Clinical Psychology, 46,* 1053–1070.

Bergman, M. (1971a). Changes in hearing with age. *The Gerontologist, 11,* 148–151.

Bergman, M. (1971b). Hearing and aging: Implications of recent research findings. *Audiology, 10,* 164–171.

Bergman, M. (1980). *Aging and the perception of speech.* Baltimore: University Park Press.

Berkowitz, L. (1986). *A survey of social psychology* (2nd ed.). New York: Holt, Rinehart & Winston.

Betz, E. L. (1984). A study of career patterns of women college graduates. *Journal of Vocational Behavior, 24,* 249–263.

Beutell, N. J., & Brenner, O. C. (1986). Sex differences in work values. *Journal of Vocational Behavior, 28,* 29–41.

Beutler, L. E., Scogin, F., Kirkish, P., Schetlan, D., Corbishley, A., Hamblin, D., Meredith, K., Potter, R., Bomford, C. R., & Levenson, A. I. (1987). Group cognitive therapy and Alprazolam in the treatment of depression in older adults. *Journal of Consulting and Clinical Psychology, 55,* 550–556.

Biller, H. B. (1982). Fatherhood: Implications for child and adult development. In B. Wolman (Ed.), *Handbook of developmental psychology* (pp. 702–725). Englewood Cliffs, NJ: Prentice-Hall.

Billings, A., Cronkite, R. C., & Moos, R. H. (1983). Social-environmental factors in unipolar depression: Comparisons of depressed patients and nondepressed controls. *Journal of Abnormal Psychology, 92,* 119–133.

Binet, A. (1905). [Review of C. Spearman: The proof and measurement of association between two things; General intelligence objectively defined and measured.] *Annee Psychologie, 11,* 623–624.

Binstock, R. (1983). The aged as scapegoat. *The Gerontologist, 23,* 136–143.

Birkhill, W., & Schaie, K. W. (1975). The effect of differential reinforcement of cautiousness in intellectual performance among the elderly. *Journal of Gerontology, 30,* 578–583.

Birren, J. E. (1964). *The psychology of aging.* Englewood Cliffs, NJ: Prentice-Hall.

References

Birren, J. E. (1965). Age changes in speed of behavior: Its central nature and physiological correlates. In A. T. Welford & J. E. Birren (Eds.), *Behavior, aging and the nervous system* (pp. 191–216). Springfield, IL: Thomas.

Birren, J. E. (1969). An introduction to contemporary gerontology. In J. E. Birren (Ed.), *Contemporary gerontology—concepts and issues* (pp. 3–42). Summer Institute for Advanced Study in Gerontology. UCLA.

Birren, J. E. (1970). Toward the experimental psychology of aging. *American Psychologist, 25,* 124–135.

Birren, J. E. (1982, November). *A review of the development of the self.* Paper presented at the annual meeting of the Gerontological Society, Boston, MA.

Birren, J. E., & Cunningham, W. (1985). Research on the psychology of aging: Principles, concepts, and theory. In J. E. Birren & K. W. Schaie (Eds.), *Handbook of the psychology of aging* (2nd ed, pp. 3–34). New York: Van Nostrand Reinhold.

Birren, J. E., Cunningham, W., & Yamamoto, K. (1983). Psychology of adult development and aging. *Annual Review of Psychology, 34,* 543–576.

Birren, J. E., & Renner, V. J. (1977). Research on the psychology of aging: Principles and experimentation. In J. E. Birren & K. W. Schaie (Eds.), *Handbook of the psychology of aging* (pp. 3–38). New York: Van Nostrand Reinhold.

Birren, J. E., & Renner, V. J. (1979). A brief history of mental health and aging. In *Issues in mental health and aging: Volume 1. Research* (pp. 1–26). Washington, DC: National Institute of Mental Health, Department of Health, Education, and Welfare.

Birren, J. E., & Renner, V. J. (1980). Concepts and issues of mental health and aging. In J. E. Birren & R. B. Sloane (Eds.), *Handbook of mental health and aging* (pp. 3–33). Englewood Cliffs, NJ: Prentice-Hall.

Birren, J. E., & Schaie, K. W. (1977). *Handbook of the psychology of aging.* New York: Van Nostrand Reinhold.

Birren, J. E., & Sloane, R. B. (1980). *Handbook of mental health and aging.* Englewood, NJ: Prentice-Hall.

Birren, J., & Woodruff, D. S. (1973a). Academic and professional training in the psychology of aging. In C. Eisdorfer & M. P. Lawton (Eds.), *The psychology of adult development and aging* (pp. 11–36). Washington, DC: American Psychological Association.

Birren, J. E., & Woodruff, D. S. (1973b). Human development over the life span through education.

In P. B. Baltes & K. W. Schaie (Eds.), *Life-span developmental psychology: Personality and socialization* (pp. 305–337). New York: Academic Press.

Birren, J. E., Woods, A. M., & Williams, M. V. (1980). Behavioral slowing with age: Causes, organization, and consequences. In L. W. Poon (Ed.), *Aging in the 1980s: Psychological issues* (pp. 293–308). Washington, DC: American Psychological Association.

Bishop, J. M., & Krause, D. R. (1984). Depictions of aging and old age on Saturday morning television. *The Gerontologist, 24,* 91–94.

Black, S. M., & Hill, C. E. (1984). The psychological well-being of women in their middle years. *Psychology of Women Quarterly, 8,* 282–292.

Blakely, A. E. (1979). OAA amendments remember the forgotten Americans. *Perspective on aging, 8*(1), 4–5.

Blauner, R. (1966). Death and social structure. *Psychiatry, 28,* 378–394.

Blazer, D. (1980). Epidemiology of mental illness in late life. In E. Busse & D. Blazer (Eds.), *Handbook of geriatric psychiatry* (pp. 249–272). New York: Van Nostrand Reinhold.

Blenkner, M. (1965). Social work and family relationships in later life with some thoughts on filial maturity. In E. Shanas & G. Streib (Eds.), *Social structure and the family: Generational relations* (pp. 46–59). Englewood Cliffs, NJ: Prentice-Hall.

Block, J. (1962). *The Q-sort method in personality assessment and psychiatric research.* Springfield, IL: C. C. Thomas.

Block, J. (1971). *Lives through time.* Berkeley, CA: Bancroft Books.

Block, M. (1979). Exiled Americans: The plight of Indian aged in the United States. In D. Gelfand and A. Kutzik (Eds.), *Ethnicity and aging: Theory, research, and policy* (pp. 184–192). New York: Springer.

Bloom, B. L., Hodges, W. F., & Caldwell, R. A. (1983). Marital separation: The first eight months. In E. J. Callahan & K. A. McCluskey (Eds.), *Life-span developmental psychology: Nonnormative life events* (pp. 217–239). New York: Academic Press.

Bloom, K. L. (1961). Age and the self concept. *American Journal of Psychiatry, 118,* 534–538.

Blum, J., & Tallmer, M. (1977). The therapist vis-à-vis the older patient. *Psychotherapy: Theory, Research, and Practice, 14,* 361–367.

Blumenthal, H. T., & Birns, A. W. (1964). Autoimmunity and aging. In B. L. Strebler (Ed.), *Advances in gerontological research* v. 1 (pp. 289–342). New York: Academic Press.

Boaz, R. F. (1987). Work as a response to low and decreasing real income during retirement. *Research on Aging, 9,* 428–440.

Boldt, M. (1982). Normative evaluation of suicide

and death: A cross-generational study. *Omega, 10,* 145–158.

Bondareff, W. (1980). Neurobiology of aging. In J. E. Birren & R. B. Sloane (Eds.), *Handbook of mental health and aging* (pp. 75–99). Englewood Cliffs, NJ: Prentice-Hall.

Bondareff, W. (1985). The neural basis of aging. In J. E. Birren & K. W. Schaie (Eds.), *Handbook of the psychology of aging* (pp. 157–176). New York: Van Nostrand Reinhold.

Bondareff, W. (1986). Biomedical perspective of Alzheimer's disease and dementia in the elderly. In M. Gilhooly, S. Zarit, & J. E. Birren (Eds.), *The dementias: Policy and management* (pp. 1–24). Englewood Cliffs, NJ: Prentice-Hall.

Borges, M. A. & Dutton, L. J. (1976). Attitudes toward aging: Increasing optimism found with age. *The Gerontologist, 16,* 220–224.

Bornstein, R., & Smircina, M. (1982). The status and support for the hypothesis of increased variability in aging populations. *The Gerontologist, 22,* 258–260.

Bortman, H. B. (1977a). Income and poverty in the older population in 1975. *The Gerontologist, 17,* 23–26.

Bortman, H. B. (1977b). Life expectancy: Comparison of national levels in 1900 and 1974 and variations in state levels, 1969–1977. *The Gerontologist, 17,* 12–22.

Bosse, R., Aldwin, C. M., Levenson, M. R., & Ekerdt, D. J. (1987). Mental health differences among retirees and workers: Findings from the normative aging study. *Psychology and Aging, 2,* 383–389.

Bosse, R., & Ekerdt, D. J. (1981). Change in self-perception of leisure activities with retirement. *The Gerontologist, 21,* 650–654.

Botwinick, J. (1966). Cautiousness in advanced age. *Journal of Gerontology, 21,* 347–353.

Botwinick, J. (1967). *Cognitive processes in maturity and old age.* New York: Springer.

Botwinick, J. (1969). Disinclination to venture response versus cautiousness in responding: A difference. *Journal of Genetic Psychology, 115,* 55–62.

Botwinick, J. (1970a). *Aging and cognitive processes.* New York: Springer.

Botwinick, J. (1970b). Learning in children and in older adults. In L. R. Goulet and P. B. Baltes (Eds.), *Life-span developmental psychology: Research and theory* (pp. 257–284). New York: Academic Press.

Botwinick, J. (1971). Sensory-set factors in age differences in reaction time. *Journal of Genetic Psychology, 119,* 241–249.

Botwinick, J. (1972). Sensory-perceptual factors in reaction time in relation to age. *Journal of Genetic Psychology, 121,* 173–177.

Botwinick, J. (1973). *Aging and behavior.* New York: Springer.

Botwinick, J. (1977). Intellectual abilities. In J. E. Birren & K. W. Schaie (Eds.), *Handbook of the psychology of aging* (pp. 580–605). New York: Van Nostrand Reinhold.

Botwinick, J. (1978). *Aging and behavior* (2nd ed.). New York: Springer.

Botwinick, J. (1984). *Aging and behavior* (3rd ed.). New York: Springer.

Botwinick, J., & Arenberg, D. (1976). Disparate time spans in sequential studies of aging. *Experimental Aging Research, 1,* 55–61.

Botwinick, J., Robbin, J. S., & Brinley, J. F. (1959). Reorganization of perception with age. *Journal of Gerontology, 14,* 85–88.

Botwinick, J., & Siegler, I. (1980). Intellectual ability among the elderly: Simultaneous cross-sectional and longitudinal comparisons. *Developmental Psychology, 16,* 49–53.

Botwinick, J., & Storandt, M. (1972). Sensation and set in reaction time. *Perceptual and Motor Skills, 34,* 103–106.

Botwinick, J., & Storandt, M. (1974a). Cardiovascular status, depressive affect, and other factors in reaction time. *Journal of Gerontology, 29,* 543–548.

Botwinick, J., & Storandt, M. (1974b). *Memory, related functions, and age.* St. Louis, MO: Mosby.

Botwinick, J., & Thompson, L. W. (1966). Components of reaction time in relation to age and sex. *Journal of Genetic Psychology, 108,* 175–183.

Botwinick, J., West, R., & Storandt, M. (1978). Predicting death from behavioral test performance. *Journal of Gerontology, 33,* 755–762.

Bowlby, J. (1969). *Attachment and loss: Vol. 1. Attachment.* New York: Basic Books.

Brackbill, Y., & Broman, S. (1979). *Obstetrical medication and development in the first year of life.* Unpublished manuscript.

Brainerd, C. J. (1978). *Piaget's theory of intelligence.* Englewood Cliffs, NJ: Prentice-Hall.

Braken, M., Holford, T., White, C., & Kelsey, J. (1980). Role of oral contraception in congenital malformations of offspring. *International Journal of Epidemiology, 7,* 309–317.

Brammer, L. M. (1984). Counseling theory and the older adult. *Counseling Psychologist, 12,* 29–38.

Breed, W., & Huffine, L. L. (1979). Sex differences in suicide among older white Americans: A role and developmental approach. In O. J. Kaplan (Ed.), *Psychopathology of aging* (pp. 289–309). New York: Academic Press.

Breslau, L., & Haug, M. (1983). *Depression and aging: Causes, care, and consequences.* New York: Springer-Verlag.

References

Breytspraak, L. (1984). *The development of the self in later life.* Boston: Little, Brown.

Breytspraak, L., & George, L. K. (1979). Measurement of self-concept and self-esteem in older people: State of the art. *Experimental Aging Research, 5,* 137–155.

Brickel, C. M. (1979). The therapeutic roles of cat mascots with a hospital-based geriatric population: A staff survey. *The Gerontologist, 19,* 368–372.

Brickel, C. M. (1984). The clinical use of pets with the aged. *Clinical Gerontologist, 2,* 72–74.

Brim, O. G. (1966). Socialization through the life cycle. In O. G. Brim & S. Wheeler (Eds.), *Socialization after childhood: Two Essays.* New York: John Wiley.

Brim, O. G. (1976). Theories of the male mid-life crisis. *The Counseling Psychologist, 6,* 2–9.

Brim, O. G., & Ryff, C. (1978). On the properties of life events. In P. Baltes & U. Brim (Eds.), *Life-span development and behavior* (pp. 368–387). New York: Academic Press.

Brinley, J. F. (1965). Cognitive sets, speed and accuracy of performance in the elderly. In A. T. Welford & J. E. Birren (Eds.), *Behavior, aging, and the nervous system* (pp. 114–149). Springfield, IL: Thomas.

Broadbent, D. E. (1958). *Perception and communication.* London: Pergamon Press.

Broadbent, D. E. (1971). *Decision and stress.* London: Academic Press.

Broadbent, D. E., & Heron, A. (1962). Effects of a subsidiary task on performance involving immediate memory by younger and older men. *British Journal of Psychology, 53,* 189–198.

Broderick, C. B. (1982). Adult sexual development. In J. Wolman (Ed.), *Handbook of developmental psychology* (pp. 726–733). Englewood Cliffs, NJ: Prentice-Hall.

Brody, E. M. (1979). Aging parents and aging children. In P. K. Kagan (Ed.), *Aging parents* (pp. 267–287). Los Angeles, CA: University of Southern California Press.

Brody, E. M., & Brody, N. (1976). *Intelligence: Nature, determinants and consequences.* New York: Academic Press.

Brody, E. M., Johnson, P. T., & Fulcomer, M. C. (1984). What should adult children do for elderly parents? Opinions and preferences of three generations of women. *Journal of Gerontology, 39,* 736–746.

Brubaker, T. (1983). *The family in later life.* Beverly Hills, CA: Sage.

Brubaker, T. H., & Powers, E. A. (1976). The stereotype of "old": A review and alternative approach. *Journal of Gerontology, 31,* 441–447.

Bruce, P., Coyne, A., & Botwinick, J. (1982). Adult age differences in metamemory. *Journal of Gerontology, 37,* 354–357.

Buck, P. (1966). *The people of Japan.* New York: Simon & Schuster.

Bugen, L. (1979). *Death and dying: Theory, research and practice.* Dubuque, IA: Brown.

Buhler, C. (1953). The curve of life as studied in biographies. *Journal of Applied Science, 19,* 405–409.

Buhler, C. (1961). Meaningful living in the mature years. In R. W. Kleemeier (Ed.), *Aging and leisure* (pp. 345–388). New York: Oxford University Press.

Buhler, C. (1962). Genetic aspects of the self. *Annals of the New York Academy of Sciences, 96,* 730–764.

Buhler, C. (1982). Meaningfulness of the biographical approach. In L. R. Allman & D. I. Jaffe (Eds.), *Readings in adult psychology: Contemporary perspectives* (pp. 30–37). New York: Harper & Row.

Bultena, G. L., & Powers, E. (1978). Denial of aging: Age identification and reference group orientations. *Journal of Gerontology, 33,* 748–754.

Burdz, M. P., Eaton, W. O., & Bond, J. B. (1988). Effect of respite care on dementia and nondementia patients and their caregivers. *Psychology and Aging, 3,* 38–42.

Burg, A. (1967). Light sensitivity as related to age and sex. *Perceptual and Motor Skills, 24,* 1279–1288.

Burke, D. M., & Light, L. L. (1981). Memory and aging: The role of retrieval processes. *Psychological Bulletin, 90,* 513–546.

Burkhouser, R. V., & Turner, J. A. (1980). The effects of pension policy through life. In R. L. Clark (Ed.), *Retirement policy in an aging society* (pp. 12–31). Durham, NC: Duke University Press.

Burnside, I. (1984). *Working with the elderly: Group processes and techniques.* Belmont, CA: Wadsworth.

Burrus-Bammel, L., & Bammel, G. (1985). Leisure and recreation. In J. E. Birren & K. W. Schaie (Eds.), *Handbook of the psychology of aging* (2nd ed, pp. 848–863). New York: Van Nostrand Reinhold.

Burt, C. (1909). Experimental tests of human intelligence. *British Journal of Psychology, 3,* 94–177.

Buskirk, E. R. (1985). Health maintenance and longevity: Exercise. In C. E. Finch & E. L. Schneider (Eds.), *Handbook of the biology of aging* (2nd ed., pp. 894–931). New York. Van Nostrand Reinhold.

Buss, A. (1979). Dialectics, history and development: The historical roots of the individual-society dialectic. In P. B. Baltes & O. G. Brim (Eds.), *Life-span development and behavior* (pp. 313–333). New York: Academic Press.

Busse, E., & Blazer, D. (1980). *Handbook of geriatric psychiatry.* New York: Van Nostrand Reinhold.

Butcher, H. J. (1968). *Human intelligence: Its nature and assessment.* New York: Harper & Row.

Butler, R. (1963). The life review: An interpretation of reminiscence in the aged. *Psychiatry, 26,* 65–76.

Butler, R. N. (1969). Ageism: Another form of bigotry. *The Gerontologist, 9,* 243–246.

Butler, R. N. (1975). *Why survive? Being old in America.* New York: Harper & Row.

Butler, R. N. (1983, July/August). A generation at risk. *Across the Board,* pp. 37–45.

Butler, R. N., Gertman, J., Overlander, C., & Shindler, L. (1979–1980). Self-help, self-care, and the elderly. *International Journal of Aging and Human Development, 10,* 95–117.

Butler, R. N., & Lewis, M. I. (1977). *Aging and mental health: Positive psychosocial approaches.* St. Louis, MO: Mosby.

Butler, R. N., & Lewis, M. I. (1981). *Aging and mental health: Positive psychosocial approaches.* (2nd ed.). St. Louis, MO: Mosby.

Cadwallader, D. E. (1979). Drug interactions in the elderly. In D. M. Peterson, F. J. Whittington, & B. P. Payne (Eds.), *Drugs and the elderly* (pp. 80–93). Springfield, IL: Thomas.

Calhoun, R., & Gounard, B. (1979). Meaningfulness, presentation rate, list length, and age in elderly adults' paired associate learning. *Educational Gerontology, 4,* 49–56.

Cameron, P. (1970a). The generation gap: Beliefs about sexuality and self-report sexuality. *Developmental Psychology, 3,* 272.

Cameron, P. (1970b). The generation gap: Which generation is believed powerful versus generational members' self-appraisal of power? *Developmental Psychology, 3,* 403–404.

Cameron, P. (1972). Stereotypes about generational fun and happiness vs. self-appraised fun and happiness. *The Gerontologist, 12,* 120–123.

Cameron, P. (1973). Which generation is believed to be intellectually superior and which generation believes itself intellectually superior? *International Journal of Aging and Human Development, 4,* 157–170.

Cameron, P. (1975). Mood as an indicant of happiness: Age, sex, social class and situational differences. *Journal of Gerontology, 30,* 216–224.

Campanelli, P. A. (1968). Audiological perspectives in presbycusis. *Eye, Ear, Nose and Throat Monthly, 47,* 3–9, 81–86.

Campbell, D. T., & Stanley, J. C. (1963). *Experimental and quasi-experimental designs for research.* Chicago: Rand McNally.

Canestrari, R. E. (1963). Paced and self-paced learning in young and elderly adults. *Journal of Gerontology, 18,* 165–168.

Canestrari, R. E. (1968). Age changes in acquisition. In G. A. Talland (Ed.), *Human aging and behavior* (pp. 169–187). New York: Academic Press.

Cantor, M. H. (1979). Effect of ethnicity on life-styles of the inner-city elderly. In A. Monk (Ed.), *The age of aging* (pp. 241–264). Buffalo, NY: Prometheus Books.

Cantor, M., & Little, V. (1985). Aging and social care. In R. Binstock & E. Shanas (Eds.), *Handbook of aging and the social sciences* (pp. 745–781). New York: Van Nostrand Reinhold.

Caraway, M., & Hayslip, B. (1985). Facilitating rational thinking in older persons. *Clinical Gerontologist, 4,* 48–50.

Carey, R. (1979–1980). Weathering widowhood: Problems and adjustments of the widowed during the first year. *Omega, 10,* 163–175.

Carlson, N. R. (1986). *Physiology of behavior.* Boston: Allyn & Bacon.

Carp, F. M. (1970). The mobility of retired people. In E. J. Cantilli and J. L. Shmelzer (Eds.), *Transportation and aging: Selected issues.* Washington, DC: U.S. Government Printing Office.

Carroll, J. (1976). Psychometric tests as cognitive tasks: A new "Structure of Intellect." In L. Resnick (Ed.), *The nature of intelligence* (pp. 27–56). Hillsdale, NJ: Lawrence Erlbaum.

Carroll, J. B. (1979). How shall we study individual differences in cognitive abilities? In R. Sternberg & D. Detterman (Eds.), *Human intelligence: Perspectives on its theory and measurement* (pp. 3–31). Norwood, NJ: Ablex.

Carstensen, L., & Cone, J. (1983). Social desirability and the measurement of well-being in elderly persons. *Journal of Gerontology, 38,* 713–715.

Caspi, A., & Elder, G. (1986). Life satisfaction in old age: Linking social psychology and history. *Psychology and Aging, 1,* 18–26.

Cater, J., & Easton, P. (1980, May 3). Separation and other stress in childhood. *Cancel,* pp. 972–974.

Cattell, R. B. (1950). *Personality: A systematic, theoretical and factual study.* New York: McGraw-Hill.

Cavanaugh, J. C., Grady, J. G., & Perlmutter, M. P. (1983). Forgetting and the use of memory aids in 20 and 70-year-old's everyday life. *International Journal of Aging and Human Development, 19,* 140–148.

Cerella, J., & Lowe, D. (1984, November). *Age deficits and practice: 27 studies reconsidered.* Paper presented at the annual meeting of the Gerontological Society, Washington, DC.

Cerella, J., Poon, L. W., & Williams, D. M. (1980). Age and the complexity hypothesis. In L. W. Poon (Ed.), *Aging in the 1980s: Psychological issues* (pp. 332–340). Washington, DC: American Psychological Association.

Chen, Y. P. (1985). Economic status of the aging. In

References

R. Binstock & E. Shanas (Eds.), *Handbook of aging and the social sciences* (pp. 641–665). New York: Van Nostrand Reinhold.

Cherlin, A. (1981). *Marriage, divorce, remarriage.* Cambridge, MA: Harvard University Press.

Chiswick, C. (1982, Summer). The value of a housewife's time. *Journal of Human Resources,* pp. 413–425.

Chown, S. (1959). Rigidity—a flexible concept. *Psychological Bulletin, 56,* 195–223.

Chown, S. (1961). Age and the rigidities. *Journal of Gerontology, 16,* 353–362.

Chown, S. M. (1977). Morale, careers and personal potentials. In J. E. Birren & K. W. Schaie (Eds.), *Handbook of the Psychology of Aging* (pp. 672–691). New York: Van Nostrand Reinhold.

Christ, A. (1961). Attitudes toward death among a group of acute geriatric psychiatric patients. *Journal of Gerontology, 16,* 56–59.

Circirelli, V. G. (1980). Sibling relationships in adulthood: A lifespan perspective. In L. W. Poon (Ed.), *Aging in the 1980s* (pp. 455–474). Washington, DC: American Psychological Association.

Circirelli, V. G. (1986). Family relationships and care/management of the dementing elderly. In M. Gilhooly, S. Zarit, & J. E. Birren (Eds.), *The dementias: Policy and management* (pp. 89–103). Englewood Cliffs, NJ: Prentice-Hall.

Clark, L. E., and Knowles, J. B. (1973). Age differences in dichotic listening performance. *Journal of Gerontology, 28,* 173–178.

Clark, M., & Anderson, B. (1967). *Culture and aging.* Springfield, IL: Thomas.

Clark, R., & Spengler, J. (1980). *The economics of individual and population aging.* Cambridge, MA: Cambridge University Press.

Clayton, V. (1975). Erikson's theory of human development as it applies to the aged: Wisdom as contraindicative cognition. *Human Development, 18,* 119–128.

Clayton, V., & Birren, J. E. (1980). The development of wisdom across the life span: A reexamination of an ancient topic. In P. B. Baltes & O. G. Brim (Eds.), *Life-span development and behavior* (pp. 104–135). New York: Academic Press.

Clingempeel, W. G., & Repucci, N. D. (1982). Joint custody after divorce: Major issues and goals for research. *Psychological Bulletin, 91,* 102–127.

Cobb, S. (1976). Social support as a moderator of life stress. *Psychosomatic Medicine, 38,* 300–314.

Cockerham, W. C., Sharp, K., & Wilcox, J. A. (1983). Aging and perceived health status. *Journal of Gerontology, 38,* 349–355.

Cohen, C. I., & Rajkowski, H. (1982). What's a friend? Substantive and theoretical issues. *The Gerontologist, 22,* 261–266.

Cohen, G. (1979). Language and comprehension in old age. *Cognitive Psychology, 11,* 412–429.

Cohen, G. (1980). Prospects for mental health and aging. In J. E. Birren & R. B. Sloane (Eds.), *Handbook of mental health and aging* (pp. 971–993). Englewood Cliffs, NJ: Prentice-Hall.

Cohen, G. D. (1984). Counseling interventions for the late twentieth century elderly. *Counseling Psychologist, 12,* 97–100.

Cohen, J. (1957). The factorial structure of the WAIS between early adulthood and old age. *Journal of Consulting Psychology, 21,* 283–290.

Cohen, M. M. (1982). In the presence of your absence: The treatment of older families with a cancer patient. *Psychotherapy: Theory, Research and Practice, 19,* 453–460.

Cohn, R. M. (1979). Age and the satisfaction from work. *Journal of Gerontology, 34,* 264–272.

Colavita, F. B. (1978). *Sensory changes in the elderly.* Springfield, IL: Thomas.

Coleman, J. C. (1976). *Abnormal psychology and modern life.* Glenview, IL: Scott, Foresman.

Coleman, J., Butcher, J. N., & Carson, R. C. (1984). *Abnormal psychology and modern life* (7th ed.). Glenview, IL: Scott, Foresman.

Coleman, L. M., & Antonucci, T. C. (1983). Impact of work on women at midlife. *Developmental Psychology, 19,* 290–294.

Comalli, P. E., Jr. (1970). Life-span changes in visual perception. In L. R. Goulet and P. B. Baltes (Eds.), *Life-span development psychology: Research and theory* (pp. 211–226). New York: Academic Press.

Comalli, P. E., Jr., Krus, D. M., & Wapner, S. (1965). Cognitive functioning in two groups of aged: One institutionalized, the other living in the community. *Journal of Gerontology, 20,* 9–13.

Comalli, P. E., Jr., Wapner, S., & Werner, H. (1962). Interference of Stroop-Color-Word Test in childhood, adulthood, and aging. *The Journal of Genetic Psychology, 100,* 47–53.

Comfort, A. (1964). *Aging: The biology of senescence.* New York: Holt, Rinehart & Winston.

Comfort, A. (1980). Sexuality in later life. In J. E. Birren & R. B. Sloane (Eds.), *Handbook of mental health and aging* (pp. 885–892). Englewood Cliffs, NJ: Prentice-Hall.

Commons, M. L., Richards, F. A., & Armon, C. (1984). *Beyond formal operations: Late adolescent and adult cognitive development.* New York: Praeger.

Conte, H., Weiner, M., & Plutchik, R. (1982). Measuring death anxiety: Conceptual, psychometric, and factor-analytic aspects. *Journal of Personality and Social Psychology, 43,* 775–785.

Corby, N., & Solnick, R. (1980). Psychosocial and physiological influences on sexuality in the older adult. In J. E. Birren & R. B. Sloane (Eds.),

Handbook of mental health and aging (pp. 893–921). Englewood Cliffs, NJ: Prentice-Hall.

Cornelius, S. W. (1984). Classic pattern of intellectual aging: Test familiarity, difficulty, and performance. *Journal of Gerontology, 39,* 201–206.

Cornelius, S., Caspi, A., & Harnum, J. (1983, November). *Intelligence adaptation.* Paper presented at the annual meeting of the Gerontological Society, San Francisco, CA.

Corsini, R. J. (1977). *Current personality theories.* Itasca, IL: F. Peacock.

Corso, J. F. (1971). Sensory processes and age effects in normal adults. *Journal of Gerontology, 26,* 90–105.

Corso, J. F. (1977). Auditory perception and communication. In J. E. Birren & K. W. Schaie (Eds.), *Handbook of the psychology of aging* (pp. 535–553). New York: Van Nostrand Reinhold.

Costa, J. J. (1984). *Abuse of the elderly.* Lexington, MA: Heath.

Costa, P., & McCrae, R. (1976). Age differences in personality structure: a cluster analytic approach. *Journal of Gerontology, 31,* 663–669.

Costa, P., & McCrae, R. (1978). Objective personality assessment. In M. Storandt, I. Siegler, & M. Elias (Eds.), *The clinical psychology of aging* (pp. 119–143). New York: Plenum.

Costa, P., & McCrae, R. (1980a). Still stable after all these years: Personality as a key to some issues in adulthood and old age. In P. Baltes & O. Brim (Eds.), *Life-span development and behavior* (pp. 66–103). New York: Academic Press.

Costa, P. J., Jr., & McCrae, R. R. (1980b). Functional age: A conceptual empirical critique. In S. G. Haynes and M. Feinleib (Eds.), *Second Conference on the Epidemiology of Aging* (Publication No. 80–969, pp. 23–46). Washington, DC: U.S. Government Printing Office, National Institute of Health.

Costa, P., & McCrae, R. (1982). An approach to the attribution of aging period, and cohort effects. *Psychological Bulletin, 92,* 238–250.

Costa, P., & McCrae, R. (1986). Cross-sectional studies of personality in a national sample: 1. Development and validation of survey measures. *Psychology and Aging, 1,* 140–143.

Costa, P., McCrae, R., & Arenberg, D. (1980). Enduring dispositions in adult males. *Journal of Personality and Social Psychology, 38,* 793–800.

Costa, P., McCrae, R., & Arenberg, D. (1983). Recent longitudinal research on personality and aging. In K. W. Schaie (Ed.), *Longitudinal studies of adult psychological development* (pp. 222–265). New York: Guilford Press.

Costa, P., McCrae, R., Zonderman, A., Barbano, H., Leibowitz, B., & Larson, D. (1986). Cross-sectional studies of personality in a national sample: Stability in neuroticism, extraversion and openness. *Psychology and Aging, 1,* 144–149.

Costa, P., Zonderman, A., McCrae, R.,

Cornoni-Huntley, J., Locke, B., & Barbano, H. (1986). Longitudinal analyses of psychological well-being in a national sample: Stability of mean levels. *Journal of Gerontology, 42,* 50–55.

Cottrell, L. (1962). The adjustment of the individual to his age and sex roles. *American Sociological Review, 7,* 617–620.

Cowgill, D. (1974). Aging and modernization: A revision of the theory. In J. Gubrium (Ed.), *Late life: Communities and environmental policy* (pp. 123–146). Springfield, IL: Thomas.

Cowgill, D. O., & Holmes, L. D. (1972). *Aging and Modernization.* New York: Appleton-Century-Crofts.

Coyne, A. C. (1981, November). *Age and response uncertainty.* Paper presented at the 34th annual scientific meeting of the Gerontological Society of America, Toronto.

Craik, F. I. M. (1965). The nature of the age decrementive performance on dichotic listening tasks. *Quarterly Journal of Experimental Psychology, 17,* 227–240.

Craik, F. I. M. (1977). Age differences in human memory. In J. E. Birren & K. W. Schaie (Eds.), *Handbook of the psychology of aging* (pp. 384–420). New York: Van Nostrand Reinhold.

Craik, F. I. M., & Lockhart, R. S. (1972). Levels of processing: A framework for memory research. *Journal of Verbal Learning and Verbal Behavior, 11,* 671–684.

Craik, F. I. M., & Simon, E. (1980). Age differences in memory: The roles of attention and depth of processing. In L. Poon, J. Fozard, L. Cermak, D. Arenberg, & L. Thompson (Eds.), *New directions in memory and aging* (pp. 95–112). Hillsdale, NJ: Lawrence Erlbaum.

Crane, D. P. (1986). *Personnel: The management of human resources.* Boston: Kent.

Crites, J. O. (1981). *Career counseling.* New York: McGraw-Hill.

Cronbach, L. J. (1984). *Essentials of psychological testing* (4th ed.). New York: Harper & Row.

Crook, R. H., Healy, C. C., & O'Shea, D. W. (1984). The linkage of work achievement to self esteem, career maturity, and college achievement. *Journal of Vocational Behavior, 25,* 70–79.

Crook, T., Ferris, S., & Bartus, R. (1983). *Assessment in geriatric psychopharmacology.* New Canaan, CT: Mark Powley Associates.

Crooks, R., & Bauer, K. (1980). *Our sexuality.* Reading, MA: Benjamin/Cummings.

Crouse, J. S., Cobb, D. C., Harris, B. B., Kopecky, F. J., Poertner, J., Edwards, V. L., Ham, R. J., Sophos, J. (1984, September). *Abuse and neglect of the elderly: Incidence and characteristics, legislation and policy* recommendations. Springfield, IL: Sangamon State University, Illinois, Department on Aging.

Cuellar, J. (1978). El Senior Citizens Club. In B. Myerhoff & A. Simic (Eds.), *Life's career: Aging* (pp. 207–230). Beverly Hills, CA: Sage.

Cumming, E. (1963). Further thoughts on the theory of disengagement. *International Social Science Journal, 15,* 377–393.

Cumming, E. (1975). Engagement with an old theory. *International Journal of Aging and Human Development, 6,* 187–191.

Cumming, E., & Henry, W. E. (1961). *Growing old: The process of disengagement.* New York: Basic Books.

Cunningham, W., Clayton, V., & Overton, W. (1975). Fluid and crystallized intelligence in young adulthood and old age. *Journal of Gerontology, 30,* 53–55.

Cunningham, W., Sepkowski, C., & Opel, M. (1978). Fatigue effects on intelligence test performance in the elderly. *Journal of Gerontology, 33,* 541–545.

Cusack, O., & Smith, E. (1984). *Pets and the elderly: The therapeutic bond.* New York: Haworth Press.

Cutrona, C., Russell, D., & Rose, J. (1986). Social support and adaptation to stress in the elderly. *Psychology and Aging, 1,* 47–54.

Cytrynbaum, S., Blum, L., Patrick, R., Stein, J., Wadner, P., & Wilk, C. (1980). Midlife development: A personality and social systems perspective. In L. W. Poon (Ed.), *Aging in the 1980s: Psychological Issues* (pp. 463–474). Washington, DC: American Psychological Association.

Dancy, J., Jr. (1977). *The black elderly: A guide for practitioners.* Ann Arbor: University of Michigan.

Daniel, D., Templin, R., & Shearon, R. (1977). The value orientations of older adults toward education. *Educational Gerontology, 2,* 33–42.

Danish, S. (1981). Life-span development and intervention: A necessary link. *Counseling Psychologist, 9,* 40–43.

Danish, S., Smyer, M., & Nowak, C. (1980). Developmental intervention: Enhancing life event processes. In P. B. Baltes & O. G. Brim (Eds.), *Life-span development and behavior* (pp. 340–366). New York: Academic Press.

Danziger, W. L. (1980). Measurement of response bias in aging research. In L. N. Poon (Ed.), *Aging in the 1980s: Psychological issues* (pp. 552–557). Washington, DC: American Psychological Association.

Danziger, W. L., & Salthouse, T. A. (1978). Age and the perception of incomplete figures. *Experimental Aging Research, 4,* 67–80.

Datan, N., Green, A. L., & Reese, H. W. (1986). *Life span developmental psychology: Intergenerational relations.* Hillsdale, NJ: Lawrence Erlbaum.

Davenport, J. (1986). Learning style and its relationship to gender and age among Elderhostel participants. *Educational Gerontology, 12,* 205–217.

Davidson, G. (1978). *The hospice: Development and administration.* Washington, DC: Hemisphere.

Davidson, G. W. (1984). Stillbirth, neonatal death, and sudden infant death syndrome. In H. Wass & C. Corr (Eds.), *Childhood and death* (pp. 243–257). Washington, DC: Hemisphere/McGraw-Hill.

Davidson, M. J., & Cooper, C. L. (1986). Executive women under pressure. *International Review of Applied Psychology, 35,* 301–326.

Davies, D. R. (1968). Age differences in paced inspection tasks. In G. A. Tallard (Ed.), *Human aging and behavior: Recent advances in research and theory* (pp. 217–238). New York: Academic Press.

Davis, K. (1985). Health care policies and the aged: Observations from the United States. In R. Binstock & E. Shanas (Eds.), *Handbook of aging and the social sciences* (pp. 727–744). New York: Van Nostrand Reinhold.

Davis, R. W. M., & Klopfer, W. (1977). Issues in psychotherapy with the aged. *Psychotherapy: Theory, Research & Practice, 14,* 343–348.

Davison, G. C., & Neale, J. M. (1978). *Abnormal psychology: An experimental clinical approach.* New York: Wiley.

de Beauvoir, S. (1972). *The coming of age.* New York: Putnam.

DeFrank, R. S., & Ivancevich, J. M. (1986). Job loss: An individual level review and model. *Journal of Vocational Behavior, 28,* 1–20.

Demographic Yearbook (31st ed., pp. 450–471). (1979). New York: United Nations.

Denny, N. (1974). Clustering in middle and old age. *Developmental Psychology, 10,* 471–475.

Denny, N. (1982). Aging and cognitive changes. In B. Wolman (Ed.), *Handbook of developmental psychology* (pp. 807–827). Englewood Cliffs, NJ: Prentice-Hall.

DeSpelder, L. A., & Strickland, A. L. (1983). *The last dance: Encountering death and dying.* Palo Alto, CA: Mayfield Publishing Co.

Detterman, D. (1979). A job half done: The road to intelligence testing in the year 2000. In R. Sternberg & D. Detterman (Eds.), *Human intelligence: Perspectives on its theory and measurement* (pp. 245–256). Norwood, NJ: Ablex.

Diamond, M. D. (1978). The aging brain: Some enlightening and optimistic results. *American Scientist, 66,* 66–71.

Dickens, W. J., & Perlman, D. (1981). Friendship over the life cycle. In S. Duck & R. Gilmour (Eds.), *Personal relationships: 2. Developing personal relationships* (pp. 91–122). New York: Academic Press.

Dickstein, E. (1977). Self and self esteem: Theoretical foundations and their implications for research. *Human Development, 20,* 149–140.

Dirken, J. M. (1972). *Functional age of industrial workers.* Groningen: Wolters-Moorhoff.

Dixon, R., Simon, E., Nowak, C., & Hultsch, D. (1982). Text recall in adulthood as a function of level of information, input modality and delay interval. *Journal of Gerontology, 37,* 358–364.

Dobson, C., & Morrow, P. C. (1984). Effects of career orientation on retirement planning. *Journal of Vocational Behavior, 24,* 73–83.

Doherty, W. J., & Jacobson, N. S. (1982). Marriage and the family. In J. Wolman (Ed.), *Handbook of developmental psychology* (pp. 667–680). Englewood Cliffs, NJ: Prentice-Hall.

Dollard, J., & Miller, N. E. (1950). *Personality and psychotherapy: An analysis in terms of learning, thinking, and culture.* New York: McGraw-Hill.

Donahue, W., Orback, H., & Pollack, O. (1960). Retirement: The emerging social pattern. In C. Tibbitts (Ed.), *Handbook of social gerontology* (pp. 330–406). Chicago: University of Chicago Press.

Donaldson, G. (1981). [Letter to the editor.] *Journal of Gerontology, 36,* 634–638.

Donnan, H. H., & Mitchell, H. (1979). Preferences for older versus younger counselors among a group of elderly persons. *Journal of Counseling Psychology, 26,* 514–418.

Donnelly, K. (1982). *Recovering from the loss of a child.* New York: Macmillan.

Doppelt, J. E., & Wallace, W. L. (1955). Standardization of the Wechsler Adult Intelligence Scale for older persons. *Journal of Abnormal and Social Psychology, 51,* 312–330.

Douglas, K., & Arenberg, D. (1978). Age changes, age differences, and cultural change on the Guilford-Zimmerman Temperament Survey. *Journal of Gerontology, 33,* 737–747.

Dowd, J. J., & Bengston, V. (1978). Aging in minority populations: An examination of the double jeopardy hypothesis. *Journal of Gerontology, 33,* 427–436.

Drachman, D. A. (1980). An approach to the neurology of aging. In J. E. Birren & R. B. Sloane (Eds.), *Handbook of mental health and aging* (pp. 501–519). Englewood Cliffs, NJ: Prentice-Hall.

Drake, J. T. (1957). Some factors influencing student attitudes toward older people. *Social Forces, 35,* 266–271.

Drevenstedt, J. (1981). Age bias in the evaluation of achievement: What determines? *Journal of Gerontology, 36,* 453–454.

Driskill, T., & Dauw, D. C. (1975). Executive mid-career job change. *Personnel and Guidance Journal, 54,* 562–567.

Duberman, L. (1974). *Marriage and its alternatives.* New York: Praeger.

Dubois, P. M. (1980). *Hospice way of death.* New York: Human Sciences Press.

Dunham, C. C., & Bengston, V. (1986). Conceptual and theoretical perspectives on generational relations. In N. Datan, A. L. Greene, & H. Reese (Eds.), *Life-span developmental psychology: Intergenerational relations* (pp. 1–27). Hillsdale, NJ: Lawrence Erlbaum.

Durkheim, E. (1951). *Suicide.* New York: Free Press.

Duvall, E. (1971). *Family development.* Philadelphia, PA: Lippincott.

Dye, C. (1982). The experience of separation at the time of placement in long-term care facilities. *Psychotherapy: Theory, Research and Practice, 19,* 532–537.

Dye, C. J., & Koziatek, D. A. (1981). Age and diabetes effects on threshold and hedonic perception of sucrose solutions. *Journal of Gerontology, 36,* 310–315.

Dye, C., & Richards, C. (1980). Facilitating the transition to nursing homes. In S. S. Sargent (Ed.), *Nontraditional counseling and therapy with the aging* (pp. 100–15). New York: Springer.

Eadwins, C. J., & Mellinger, J. C. (1984). Mid-life women: Relationship of age and role to personality. *Journal of Personality and Social Psychology, 47,* 390–395.

Eisdorfer, C. (1960). Rorschach rigidity and sensory decrement in a senescent population. *Journal of Gerontology, 15,* 188–190.

Eisdorfer, C. (1975). Observations on the psychopharmacology of aging. *Journal of the American Geriatrics Society, 23,* 53–57.

Eisdorfer, C. (1968). Arousal and performance: Experiments in verbal learning and a tentative theory. In G. A. Tolland (Ed.), *Human aging and behavior* (pp. 189–216). New York: Academic Press.

Eisdorfer, C. (1983). Conceptual models of aging: The challenge of a new frontier. *American Psychologist, 39,* 197–202.

Eisdorfer, C., Axelrod, S., & Wilkie, F. L. (1963). Stimulus exposure time as a factor in serial learning in an aged sample. *Journal of Abnormal and Social Psychology, 67,* 597–600.

Eisdorfer, C., & Cohen, D. (1978). The cognitively impaired elderly: Differential diagnosis. In M. Storandt, I. C. Siegler & M. F. Elias (Eds.), *The clinical psychology of aging* (pp. 7–42). New York: Plenum.

Eisdorfer, C., & Stotsky, B. (1977). Intervention, treatment, and rehabilitation of psychiatric

References

disorders. In J. E. Birren & K. W. Schaie (Eds.), *Handbook of the psychology of aging* (pp. 724–748). New York: Van Nostrand Reinhold.

Eisdorfer, C., & Wilkie, F. (1977). Stress, disease, aging and behavior. In J. E. Birren & K. W. Schaie (Eds.), *Handbook of the psychology of aging* (pp. 251–275). New York: Van Nostrand Reinhold.

Eisdorfer, C., & Wilkie, F. (1979a). Stress and behavior in the aging. *Issues in mental health and aging: Research* (Vol. 3). Rockville, MD: Department of Health, Education, and Welfare.

Eisdorfer, C., & Wilkie, F. (1979b). Research on crisis and stress in aging. In H. Pardes (Ed.), *Issues in mental health and aging: Research* (Vol. 3). Rockville, MD: Department of Health, Education, and Welfare.

Eisner, D. A. (1972). Life-span differences in visual perception. *Perceptual and Motor Skills, 34,* 857–858.

Eisner, D. A., & Schaie, K. W. (1971). Age change in response to visual illusions from middle to old age. *Journal of Gerontology, 26,* 146–150.

Ekerdt, D. J., Bosse, R., & Levkoff, S. (1985). An empirical test for phases of retirement: Findings from the normative aging study. *Journal of Gerontology, 40,* 95–101.

El-Baradi, A. F., & Bourne, G. H. (1951). Theory of tastes and odors. *Science, 113,* 660–661.

Elder, G. H. (1979). Historical change in life patterns and personality. In P. B. Baltes & O. G. Brim (Eds.), *Life-span development and behavior* (pp. 117–159). New York: Academic Press.

Elias, M. F., & Streeten, D. H. P. (Eds.). (1980). *Hypertension and cognitive processes.* Mount Desert, ME: Beech Hill.

Elkind, D., Koegler, R. R., & Go, E. (1964). Studies in perceptual development: 2. Part-whole perception. *Child Development, 35,* 81–90.

Ellis, A. (1962). *Reason and emotion in psychotherapy.* New York: Lyle Stuart.

Emery, G., & Lesher, E. (1982). Treatment of depression in older adults: Personality considerations. *Psychotherapy: Theory, Research and Practice, 19,* 500–505.

Emmerich, W. (1973). Socialization and sex role development. In P. B. Baltes & K. W. Schaie (Eds.), *Life-span developmental psychology: Personality and socialization* (pp. 123–144). New York: Academic Press.

Engen, T. (1977). Taste and smell. In J. E. Birren & K. W. Schaie (Eds.), *Handbook of the psychology of aging* (pp. 554–561). New York: Van Nostrand Reinhold.

Engen, T. (1982). *The perception of odors.* New York: Academic Press.

Eriksen, C. W., Hamlin, R. M., & Breitmeyer, R. G. (1970). Temporal factors in visual perception as related to aging. *Perception and Psychophysics, 7,* 354–356.

Erikson, E. H. (1959). Identity and the life cycle. *Psychological Issues, 1* (Whole No. 1).

Erikson, E. H. (1963). *Childhood and society* (2nd ed.). New York: W. W. Norton.

Estes, R. J., & Wilensky, H. L. (1978). Life cycle squeeze and the morale curve. *Social Problems, 25,* 277–292.

Estes, W. K. (1975). The state of the field: General problems and issues of theory and metatheory. In W. Estes (Ed.), *Handbook of learning and cognitive processes* (Vol. 1, pp. 1–24) Hillsdale, NJ: Lawrence Erlbaum.

Estes, W. K. (1976). Intelligence and cognitive psychology. In L. Resnick (Ed.), *The nature of intelligence* (pp. 295–305). Hillsdale, NJ: Lawrence Erlbaum.

Facing up to the high cost of kids. (1983, April). *Changing Times,* pp. 28–33.

Fairchild, T., & Burton, B. (1982). Aging in the year 2000. In N. Ernst & H. Glazer-Waldman (Eds.), *The aged patient* (pp. 84–100). New York: Year Book Medical Publishers.

Farberow, N. L., & Litman, R. E. (1970). *A comprehensive suicide prevention program* (Suicide Prevention Center, Los Angeles, 1958–1969. Unpublished final report DHEW, NIMH Grants No. 14946 and No. 00128). Los Angeles: Suicide Prevention Center.

Farberow, N., & Moriwaki, S. (1975). Self-destructive crises in the older person. *The Gerontologist, 15,* 333–337.

Featherman, D. L. (1983). Life-span perspectives in social science research. In P. B. Baltes & O. G. Brim, Jr. (Eds.), *Life-span development and behavior* (Vol. 5). New York: Academic Press.

Feifel, H., & Branscomb, A. (1973). Who's afraid of death? *Journal of Abnormal Psychology, 81,* 282–288.

Feifel, H., & Nagy, V. T. (1981). Another look at fear of death. *Journal of Consulting and Clinical Psychology, 49,* 278–286.

Felton, B. J. (1982). The aged: Settings, services and needs. In L. R. Snowden (Ed.), *Reaching the underserved* (pp. 23–42). Beverly Hills, CA: Sage.

Felton, B. J., & Revenson, T. A. (1987). Age differences in coping with chronic illness. *Psychology and Aging, 2,* 164–170.

Ferraro, K. F. (1987). Double jeopardy to health for black older adults? *Journal of Gerontology, 42,* 528–533.

Festinger, L., Schachter, S., & Back, K. (1950). *Social pressures in informal groups: A study of a housing community.* New York: Harper & Row.

Field, T. M., & Widmayer, S. M. (1982).

Motherhood. In B. Wolman (Ed.), *Handbook of developmental psychology* (pp. 681–701). Englewood Cliffs, NJ: Prentice-Hall.

Fillenbaum, G., George, L. K., & Palmore, E. (1985). Determinants and consequences of retirement among men of different races and economic levels. *Journal of Gerontology, 40,* 85–94.

Filsinger, E., & Sauer, W. (1978). An empirical typology of adjustment to aging. *Journal of Gerontology, 33,* 437–445.

Finch, C. E., & Hayflick, L. (Eds.) (1977). *Handbook of the biology of aging.* New York: Van Nostrand Reinhold.

Fischer, D. H. (1977). *Growing old in America.* New York: Oxford.

Fitting, M., Rabins, P., Lucas, M. J., & Eastham, J. (1986). Caregivers for dementia patients: A comparison of husbands and wives. *The Gerontologist, 26,* 248–252.

Fitzgerald, L. F., & Betz, N. E. (1983). Issues in the vocational psychology of women. In W. B. Walsh & S. H. Osipow (Eds.), *Handbook of vocational psychology: Vol. 1. Foundations* (pp. 83–160). Hillsdale, NJ: Lawrence Erlbaum.

Fitzgerald, L. S., & Crites, J. O. (1980). Toward a career psychology of women: What do we know? What do we need to know? *Journal of Counseling Psychology, 27,* 44–68.

Flanagan, J. C., & Russ-Eft, D. (1976). *An empirical study aid in formulating educational goals.* Palo Alto, CA: American Institutes for Research.

Flavell, J. H. (1970). Cognitive changes in adulthood. In L. R. Goulet and P. B. Baltes (Eds.), *Life-span developmental psychology: Research and theory* (pp. 248–253). New York: Academic Press.

Folkman, S., Lazarus, R. S., Pimley, S., & Novacek, J. (1987). Age differences in stress and coping processes. *Psychology and Aging, 2,* 171–184.

Folsom, J. (1968). Reality orientation for the elderly mental patient. *Journal of Geriatric Psychiatry, 1,* 291–307.

Fontana, A. (1977). *The last frontier: The social meaning of growing old.* Beverly Hills, CA: Sage.

Ford, C., & Sbordone, R. (1980). Attitudes of psychiatrists toward elderly patients. *American Journal of Psychiatry, 137,* 571–577.

Foster, J., & Gallagher, D. (1986). An exploratory study comparing depressed and nondepressed elders' coping strategies. *Journal of Gerontology, 41,* 91–93.

Fountain, M. (1986). Matching yourself with the world of work: 1986 edition. *Occupational Outlook Quarterly, 30,* 2–12.

Fox, C. F. (1979). *A cross-sequential study of age changes in personality in an aged population.* Unpublished doctoral dissertation, University of Florida. *Dissertation Abstracts International, 4,* 4461.

Fozard, J. L. (1980). The time for remembering. In L. Poon (Ed.), *Aging in the 1980s: Psychological issues* (pp. 273–287). Washington, DC: American Psychological Association.

Fozard, J. L., Nuttal, R. J., & Waugh, N. C. (1972). Age-related differences in mental performance. *Aging and Human Development, 3,* 19–43.

Fozard, J. L., & Popkin, S. (1978). Optimizing adult development: Ends and means of an applied psychology of aging. *American Psychologist, 33,* 975–989.

Fozard, J. L., Wolf, E., Bell, B., McFarland, R. A., & Podolsky, D. (1977). Visual perception and communication. In J. E. Birren & K. W. Schaie (Eds.), *Handbook of the psychology of aging* (pp. 497–534). New York: Van Nostrand Reinhold.

Francher, J. S., & Henkin, J. (1973). The menopausal queen: Adjustment to aging and the male homosexual. *American Journal of Orthopsychiatry, 43,* 670–674.

Francis, G. M. (1984). Plush animals as therapy in a nursing home. *Clinical Gerontologist, 2,* 75–76.

Franklin-Panek, C. E. (1978). Effects of personal growth groups on the self-concept and decision-making ability of normal adults. *Psychology: A Quarterly Journal of Human Behavior, 15,* 25–29.

Freedman, J. L., Sears, D. O., & Carlsmith, J. M. (1981). *Social psychology.* Englewood Cliffs, NJ: Prentice-Hall.

Freedman, D. X. (1984). Psychiatric epidemiology counts. *Archives of General Psychiatry, 41,* 931–933.

Freud, S. (1924). On psychotherapy. *Collected papers of Sigmund Freud: Vol. 1* (pp. 249–263). London: Hogarth Press.

Friedman, M., & Rosenman, R. H. (1974). *Type A behavior and your heart.* New York: Knopf.

Friedrich, D. (1972). *A primer of developmental methodology.* Minneapolis: Burgess.

Fries, J. F., & Crapo, L. M. (1981). *Vitality and aging.* San Francisco: Freeman.

Furman, E. (1984). Children's patterns in mourning the death of a loved one. In H. Wass & C. Corr (Eds.), *Childhood and death* (pp. 185–203). Washington, DC: Hemisphere/McGraw-Hill.

Furry, C., & Baltes, P. B. (1973). The effect of age differences in ability-extraneous performance variables on the assessment of intelligence in children, adults, and the elderly. *Journal of Gerontology, 28,* 73–80.

Furry, C., & Schaie, K. W. (1979). Pretest activity and intellectual performance in middle aged and elderly persons. *Experimental Aging Research, 3,* 413–421.

Furstenberg, F. F. (1982). Conjugal succession: Reentering marriage after divorce. In P. B. Baltes & O. G. Brim, Jr. (Eds.), *Life-span development and behavior* (Vol. 4, pp. 107–146). New York: Academic Press.

Gaitz, C., & Varner, R. (1980). Preventative aspects of mental illness in late life. In J. E. Birren & R. B. Sloane (Eds.), *Handbook of mental health and aging* (pp. 959–970). Englewood Cliffs, NJ: Prentice-Hall.

Gallagher, D. E., Breckenridge, J. N., Thompson, L. W., & Peterson, J. A. (1983). Effects of bereavement on indicators of mental health in elderly widows and widowers. *Journal of Gerontology, 38,* 565–571.

Gallagher, D., & Thompson, L. (1982). Treatment of major depressive disorder in older adult outpatients with brief psychotherapies. *Psychotherapy: Theory, Research and Practice, 19,* 482–490.

Gallagher, D., & Thompson, L. (1983). Depression. In P. Lewinsohn & L. Teri (Eds.), *Clinical geropsychology: New directions in assessment and treatment* (pp. 7–37). New York: Pergamon Press.

Gallagher, D., Thompson, L., & Levy, S. (1980). Clinical psychological assessment of older adults. In L. Poon (Ed.), *Aging in the 1980s: Psychological issues* (pp. 19–40). Washington, DC: American Psychological Association.

Garber, J., & Seligman, M. E. P. (1980). *Human helplessness.* New York: Academic Press.

Gardner, H. (1983). *Frames of mind: The theory of multiple intelligences.* New York: Basic Books.

Garfield, S. L. (1978). Research on client variables in psychotherapy. In S. Garfield & A. Bergin (Eds.), *Handbook of psychotherapy and behavior change* (pp. 271–298). New York: Wiley.

Garfield, S. L. (1986). Research on client variables in psychotherapy. In S. L. Garfield & A. E. Bergin (Eds.), *Handbook of psychotherapy and behavior change* (pp. 271–298). New York: Wiley.

Garfield, S., & Bergin, A. E. (1986). *Handbook of psychotherapy and behavior change* (3rd ed.). New York: Wiley.

Garn, S. M. (1975). Bone loss and aging. In R. Goldman and M. Rockstein (Eds.), *The physiology and pathology of aging* (pp. 39–57). New York: Academic Press.

Garrett, H. E. (1946). A developmental theory of intelligence. *American Psychologist, 1,* 372–378.

Gatz, M., Popkin, S., Pino, C., & VandenBos, G. (1985). Psychological interventions with older adults. In J. E. Birren & K. W. Schaie (Eds.), *Handbook of the psychology of aging* (pp. 755–788). New York: Van Nostrand Reinhold.

Gatz, M., Smyer, M., & Lawton, M. P. (1980). The mental health system and the older adult. In L.

Poon (Ed.), *Aging in the 1980s: Psychological issues* (pp. 5–18). Washington, DC: American Psychological Association.

Gekoski, W. L., & Knox, V. J. (1983, November). *Identifying age stereotypes in adolescents: An attributional approach.* Paper presented at the annual scientific meeting of the Gerontological Society, San Francisco, CA.

Gelfand, D. (1982). *Aging: The ethnic factor.* Boston: Little, Brown.

Gentry, W. D. (1978). Psychosomatic issues in assessment. In M. Storandt, I. Siegler, & M. Elias (Eds.), *The clinical psychology of aging* (pp. 181–194). New York: Plenum.

George, C., & Maim, M. (1979). Social interactions of young abused children: Approach, avoidance, and aggression. *Child Development, 50,* 306–318.

George, L. K. (1981). *Role transitions in later life.* Monterey, CA: Wadsworth.

George, L. K., Fillenbaum, G. G., & Palmore, E. (1984). Sex differences in the antecedents and consequences of retirement. *Journal of Gerontology, 39,* 364–371.

Gerner, R. H. (1979). Depression in the elderly. In O. J. Kaplan (Ed.), *Psychopathology of aging* (pp. 97–148). New York: Academic Press.

Gerson, L. W., Jarjoura, D., & McCord, G. (1987). Factors related to impaired mental health in urban elderly. *Research on Aging, 9,* 356–371.

Giambra, L. M., & Quilter, R. E. (1988). Sustained attention in adulthood: A unique, large-sample, longitudinal and multicohort analysis using the Mackworth Clock-Test. *Psychology and Aging, 3,* 75–83.

Gibb, G. D., & Bailey, J. R. (1983). Attitude toward equal rights amendment scale: An objective measurement look at attitudes toward equal rights legislation. *Psychological Reports, 53,* 804–806.

Gilford, R. (1984). Contrasts in marital satisfaction throughout old age: An exchange theory analysis. *Journal of Gerontology, 39,* 325–333.

Gilhooly, M., Zarit, S., & Birren, J. (1986). *The dementias: Policy and management.* Englewood Cliffs, NJ: Prentice-Hall.

Ginzberg, E. (1971). *Career guidance.* New York: McGraw-Hill.

Glamser, F. D. (1976). Determinants of a positive attitude toward retirement. *Journal of Gerontology, 31,* 104–107.

Glamser, F. D. (1981). The impact of preretirement programs on the retirement experience. *Journal of Gerontology, 36,* 244–250.

Glamser, F. D., & DeJong, G. F. (1975). The efficacy of preretirement preparation programs for industrial workers. *Journal of Gerontology, 30,* 595–600.

Glamser, F. D., & Hayslip, B. J. (1985). The impact of retirement on participation in leisure activities. *Therapeutic Recreation Journal, 19,* 28–38.

Glasser, B. G. (1966). The social loss of aged dying patients. *The Gerontologist, 6,* 77–80.

Glenn, N. D., & McLanahan, S. (1981). The effects of offspring on the psychological well-being of older adults. *Journal of Marriage and the Family, 43,* 409–421.

Glenn, N. D., & McLanahan, S. (1982). Children and marital happiness: A further specification of the relationship. *Journal of Marriage and the Family, 44,* 63–72.

Glenn, N. D., & Supancic, M. (1984). The social and demographic correlates of divorce and separation in the United States: An update and reconsideration. *Journal of Marriage and the Family, 46,* 563–575.

Glenn, N. D., & Weaver, C. N. (1977). The marital happiness of remarried divorced persons. *Journal of Marriage and the Family, 39,* 331–337.

Glenn, N. D., & Weaver, C. N. (1978). A multivariate, multisurvey study of marital happiness. *Journal of Marriage and the Family, 40,* 269–282.

Glick, R. C. (1977). Updating life cycle of the family. *Journal of Marriage and the Family, 39,* 5–15.

Golan, N. (1986). *The perilous bridge: Helping clients through mid-life transitions.* New York: Free Press.

Gold, A. R. (1979). Re-examining barriers to women's career development. *American Journal of Orthopsychiatry, 48,* 690–702.

Goldman, L. S., & Luchins, D. J. (1984). Depression in spouses of demented patients. *American Journal of Psychiatry, 141,* 1467–1468.

Goodstein, R. K. (1982). Individual psychotherapy and the elderly. *Psychotherapy: Theory, Research and Practice, 19,* 412–418.

Gopher, D., & Kahneman, D. (1971). Individual differences in attention and the prediction of flight criterion. *Perceptual and Motor Skills, 33,* 1335–1342.

Gordon, C., Gaitz, C. M., & Scott, J. (1976). Leisure and lives: Personal expressivity across the lifespan. In R. Binstock & E. Shanas (Eds.), *Handbook of aging and the social sciences* (pp. 310–400). New York: Van Nostrand Reinhold.

Gordon, V. W. (1981). The undecided student: A developmental perspective. *Personnel and Guidance Journal, 59,* 433–439.

Gotestam, K. (1980). Behavioral and dynamic psychotherapy with the elderly. In J. E. Birren & R. B. Sloane (Eds.), *Handbook of mental health and aging* (pp. 775–805). Englewood Cliffs, NJ: Prentice-Hall.

Gottesman, L., Quarterman, C., & Cohn, G. (1973). Psychosocial treatment of the aged. In C. Eisdorfer & M. P. Lawton (Eds.), *The psychology of adult development and aging* (pp. 378–427). Washington, DC: American Psychological Association.

Gottsfredson, G. D. (1977). Career stability and redirection in adulthood. *Journal of Applied Psychology, 62,* 436–445.

Gould, R. (1972). The phases of adult life: A study in developmental psychology. *American Journal of Psychiatry, 129,* 521–531.

Gould, R. (1975, February). Adult life stages: Growth toward self-tolerance. *Psychology Today,* pp. 74–78.

Gould, R. (1978). *Transformations: Growth and change in adult life.* New York: Simon and Schuster.

Gould, R. (1979). Transformations in midlife. *New York University Education Quarterly, 10*(2), 2–9.

Gould, R. (1980a). Transformational tasks in adulthood. In S. I. Greenspan & G. H. Pollock (Eds.), *The course of life: Psychoanalytic contributions toward understanding personality development* (pp. 55–90). Washington, DC: National Institute of Mental Health.

Gould, R. (1980b). Transformational tasks in adulthood. In *The course of life: Volume 3. Adulthood and aging process* (pp. 55–90). Bethesda, MD: National Institute of Mental Health.

Goulet, L. (1972). New directions in research on aging and retention. *Journal of Gerontology, 27,* 52–60.

Granick, S., Kleban, M. H., & Weiss, A. D. (1976). Relationships between hearing loss and cognition in normally hearing aged persons. *Journal of Gerontology, 31,* 434–440.

Grant, C. R. H. (1969). Age differences in self concept from early adulthood through old age. *Proceedings of the American Psychological Association, 7,* 717–718.

Gratton, B., & Haug, M. R. (1983). Decision and adaptation: Research on female retirement. *Research on Aging, 5,* 59–76.

Green, S. K. (1981). Attitudes and perceptions about the elderly: Current and future perspectives. *International Journal of Aging and Human Development, 13,* 99–115.

Gribbin, K., & Schaie, K. W. (1978, November). *Performance factors and age group ability differences: Practice in the face of fatigue.* Paper presented at the annual meeting of the Gerontological Society, Dallas, TX.

Griew, S., & Davies, D. R. (1962). The affects of aging on auditory vigilance performance. *Journal of Gerontology, 17,* 88–90.

Griew, S., & Lynn, R. (1960). Constructive "reaction inhibition" in the interpretation of age changes in performance. *Nature, 186,* 182.

Grotevant, H. D., & Cooper, C. R. (1988). The role of family experience in career exploration: A life-span perspective. In P. B. Baltes, D. L. Featherman, & R. L. Lerner (Eds.), *Life-span development and behavior* (Vol. 8, pp. 231–258). Hillsdale, NJ: Lawrence Erlbaum.

Gubrium, J. (1973). *The myth of the golden years: A socio-environmental theory of aging.* Springfield, IL: Thomas.

Guidubaldi, J., Cleminshaw, H. K., Perry, J. D., & McLoughlin, C. S. (1983). The impact of parental divorce on children: Report of the nationwide NASP study. *School Psychology Review, 12,* 300–323.

Guidubaldi, J., & Perry, J. (1985). Divorce and mental health sequelae for children: A two year follow-up of a nationwide sample. *Journal of the American Academy of Child Psychiatry, 24,* 531–537.

Guilford, J. P. (1959). *Personality.* New York: McGraw-Hill.

Guilford, J.. P. (1967). *The nature of human intelligence.* New York: McGraw-Hill.

Gurland, B. J. (1973). A broad clinical assessment of psychopathology in the aged. In C. Eisdorfer & M. P. Lawton (Eds.), *The psychology of adult development and aging* (pp. 343–377). Washington, DC: American Psychological Association.

Gurland, B. J. (1980). The assessment of mental health status in older adults. In J. E. Birren & R. B. Sloane (Eds.), *Handbook of mental health and aging* (pp.671–700). Englewood Cliffs, NJ: Prentice-Hall.

Gurland, B. J., Dean, L., Copeland, J., Gurland, R., & Golden, R. (1982). Criteria for the diagnosis of dementia in community elderly. *The Gerontologist, 22,* 180–186.

Gurland, B. J., Kuriansky, J., Sharpe, L., Simon, R., Stiller, P., & Birkett, P. (1977). The comprehensive assessment and referral evaluation (CARE): Rationale, development, and reliability. *Internation Journal of Aging and Human Development, 8,* 9–42.

Guttman, D. (1975). Parenthood: A key to the comparative study of the life cycle. In N. Datan & L. Ginsburg (Eds.), *Life-span developmental psychology: Normative life crises* (pp. 167–184). New York: Academic Press.

Guttman, D. (1977). The cross cultural perspective: Notes toward a comparative psychology of aging. In J. E. Birren & K. W. Schaie (Eds.), *Handbook of the psychology of aging* (pp. 302–326). New York: Van Nostrand Reinhold.

Gwenwald, M. (1975). The SAGE model for serving older lesbians and gay men. *Journal of Social Work and Sexuality, 2,* 53–61.

Gwyther, L., & George, L. K. (1986). Introduction: Symposium on caregivers for dementia patients. *The Gerontologist, 26,* 245–247.

Haan, N. (1972). Personality development from adolescence to adulthood in the Oakland growth and guidance studies. *Seminars in Psychiatry, 4,* 399–414.

Haan, N., Millsap, R., & Hartka, E. (1986). As time goes by: Change and stability in personality over 50 years. *Psychology and Aging, 1,* 220–232.

Habib, J. (1985). The economy and the aged. In R. Binstock & E. Shanas (Eds.), *Handbook of aging and the social sciences* (pp. 479–502). New York: Van Nostrand Reinhold.

Hackett, G., & Betz, N. (1981). A self-efficacy approach to the career development of women. *Journal of Vocational Behavior, 3,* 326–329.

Hafen, B. Q., & Frandsen, K. J. (1983). *Faces of death: Grief, dying, euthanasia, and suicide.* Englewood, CO: Morton.

Hafer, W. K. (1981). *Coping with bereavement.* Englewood Cliffs, NJ: Prentice-Hall.

Hagebak, J. E., & Hagebak, B. R. (1983, January–February). Meeting the mental health needs of the elderly: Issues and action steps. *Aging,* pp. 26–31.

Hagestad, G. (1978). *Patterns of communication and influence between grandparents and grandchildren.* Paper presented at the World Conference of Sociology, Helsinki, Finland.

Hagestad, G. O., & Neugarten, B. L. (1985). Age and the life course. In R. Binstock & E. Shanas (Eds.), *Handbook of aging and the social sciences* (pp. 35–61). New York: Van Nostrand Reinhold.

Haley, J. (1963). *Strategies of psychotherapy.* New York: Grune & Stratton.

Haley, J. (1971). Family therapy. *International Journal of Psychiatry, 9,* 233–242.

Haley, J. (1974). A review of the family therapy field. In J. Haley (Ed.), *Changing families: A family therapy reader* (pp. 1–12). New York: Grune & Stratton.

Haley, W. E., Levine, E. G., Brown, S. L., & Bartolucci, A. A. (1987). Sress, appraisal, coping, and social supports as predictors of adaptational outcome among dementia caregivers. *Psychology and Aging, 2,* 323–330.

Hall, G. S., & Lindzey, G. (1978). *Theories of personality* (3rd ed.). New York: Wiley.

Hall, G. S., & Lindzey, G. (1985). *Introduction to theories of personality.* New York: Wiley.

Hanson, S. L., Sauer, W. J., & Seelbach, W. C. (1983). Racial and cohort variations in filial responsibility norms. *The Gerontologist, 23,* 626–631.

Harel, Z., Aollod, R., & Bognar, B. (1982). Predictors of mental health among semi-rural aged. *The Gerontologist, 22,* 499–504.

Harel, Z., & Noelker, L. S. (1982). Social integration, health, and choice: Their impact on the well-being of institutionalized aged. *Research on Aging, 4,* 97–111.

Harkins, S. W., Price, D. D., & Martelli, M. (1986). Effects of age on pain perception: Termonociception. *Journal of Gerontology, 41,* 58–63.

Harlan, W. H. (1968). Social status of the aged in three Indian villages. In B. Neugarten (Ed.), *Middle age and aging* (pp. 469–485). Chicago: University of Chicago Press.

Harman, D. (1968). Free radical theory of aging: Effect of free radical reaction inhibitors on themortality rate of male LAF, mice. *Journal of Gerontology, 23,* 476–482.

Harmon, L. W. (1983). *Testing some models of women's career development with longtitudinal data.* Unpublished address. College Park, MD. University of Maryland.

Harper, L. V. (1975). The scope of offspring effects: From caregiver to culture. *Psychological Bulletin, 82,* 784–801.

Harris, D. K., & Cole, W. E. (1980). *Sociology of Aging.* Boston: Houghton Mifflin.

Harris, L., & Associates. (1975). *The myth and reality of aging in America.* Washington, DC: National Council on Aging.

Harris, L., & Associates. (1981). *Aging in the eighties: America in transition.* Washington, DC: National Council on Aging.

Harris, W. (1952). Fifth and seventh cranial nerves in relation to the nervous mechanism of taste sensation: A new approach. *British Medical Journal, 1,* 831–836.

Harshberger, D. (1973). Some ecological implications for the organization of human intervention throughout the life span. In P. B. Baltes & K. W. Schaie (Eds.), *Life-span developmental psychology: Personality and socialization* (pp. 339–364). New York: Academic Press.

Hartford, M. E. (1980). The use of group methods for work with the aged. In J. E. Birren & R. B. Sloane (Eds.), *Handbook of mental health and aging* (pp. 806–826). Englewood Cliffs, NJ: Prentice-Hall.

Hartley, J. T. (1986). Reader and text variables as determinants of discourse memory in adulthood. *Psychology and Aging, 1,* 150–158.

Hartley, J. T., Harker, J. O., & Walsh, D. (1980). Contemporary issues and new directions in adult development of learning and memory. In L. Poon (Ed.), *Aging in the 1980s: Contemporary issues* (pp. 239–252). Washington, DC: American Psychological Association.

Hartup, W. H., & Lempers, J. (1973). A problem in life-span development: The interactional analysis of family attachments. In P. B. Baltes & K. W. Schaie (Eds.), *Life-span developmental psychology: Personality and socialization* (pp. 235–252). New York: Academic Press.

Hasher, L., & Zacks, R. T. (1979). Automatic and effortful processes in memory. *Journal of Experimental Psychology: General, 108,* 356–388.

Hassett, J. (1984). *Psychology in perspective.* New York: Harper & Row.

Hausman, C. (1979). Short-term counseling groups for people with elderly parents. *The Gerontologist, 19,* 102–107.

Havighurst, R. J. (1952). *Developmental tasks and education.* New York: David McKay.

Havighurst, R. J. (1953). *Human development and education.* New York: Longman.

Havighurst, R. J. (1972). *Developmental tasks and education* (3rd ed.). New York: McKay.

Havighurst, R. J. (1973). History of developmental psychology: Socialization and personality development through the life span. In P. B. Baltes & K. W. Schaie (Eds.), *Life span developmental psychology: Personality and socialization* (pp. 4–24). New York: Academic Press.

Havighurst, R. J. (1982). The world of work. In J. Wolman (Ed.), *Handbook of developmental psychology* (pp. 771–787). Englewood Cliffs, NJ: Prentice-Hall.

Havighurst, R. J., & Albrecht, R. (1953). *Older people.* New York: Longmans, Green.

Havighurst, R. J., Neugarten, B., & Tobin, S. (1961). The measurement of life satisfaction. *Journal of Gerontology, 16,* 134–143.

Havighurst, R. J., Neugarten, B., & Tobin, S. (1968). *Disengagement and patterns of aging.* In B. L. Neugarten (Ed.), *Middle age and aging* (pp. 161–177). Chicago: University of Chicago Press.

Hayflick, L. (1965). The limited in vitro lifetime of human diploid cell strains. *Experimental Cell Research, 37,* 614–636.

Hayflick, L. (1977). The cellular basis for biological aging. In L. E. Finch & L. Hayflick (Eds.), *Handbook of the biology of aging* (pp. 159–186). New York: Van Nostrand Reinhold.

Hayghe, H. (1984, December) Working mothers reach record numbers in 1984. *Monthly Labor Review,* pp. 21–34.

Hayslip, B. (1982). Mental health and aging. In N. S. Ernst & H. Glazer-Waldman (Eds.), *The aged patient: A sourcebook for the allied health professional* (pp. 158–181). New York: Year Book Medical Publishers.

Hayslip, B. (1984). The elderly—emergency care considerations. In S. Lewis and & H. Weinman (Eds.), *Emergency care dynamics* (pp. 315–337). New York: Wiley.

Hayslip, B. (1985). Idiographic assessment of the self in the aged: A case for the use of the Q-sort. *International Journal of Aging and Human Development, 20,* 293–311.

Hayslip, B. (1986a, January). *Modification of fluid intelligence in the elderly* (Final Report to the National Institute on Aging, Grant No. AG 02726–01A2).

References

Hayslip, B. (1986b). *Alternative mechanisms for improvements in fluid ability among elderly persons.* Paper presented at the annual convention of the American Psychological Association, New York, NY.

Hayslip, B. (in press). *Alternative mechanisms for improvements in fluid ability among the aged. Psychology and Aging.*

Hayslip, B. (1988a). Personality-ability relationships in the aged. *Journal of Gerontology, 43,* pp. 79–84.

Hayslip, B. (1988b). Treatment modalities. In K. Esberger & S. Hughs (Eds.), *Nursing care of the aged.* Bowie, MD: Brady.

Hayslip, B., & Caraway, M. (in press). Cognitive therapy with aged persons: Implication of research design for its implementation and evaluation. *International Journal of Cognitive Psychotherapy.*

Hayslip, B., & Kennelly, K. (1982). Short-term memory and crystallized-fluid intelligence in adulthood. *Research on Aging, 4,* 314–332.

Hayslip, B., & Kennelly, K. (1985). Cognitive and non-cognitive factors affecting learning among older adults. In B. Lumsden (Ed.), *The older adult as learner* (pp. 73–98). Washington, DC: Hemisphere.

Hayslip, B., & Kooken, R. (1982). Therapeutic interventions—mental health. In N. Ernst & H. Glazer-Waldman (Eds.), *The aged patient: A sourcebook for the allied health professional* (pp. 282–303). New York: Yearbook Medical Publishers.

Hayslip, B., & Leon, J. (1988). *Geriatric case practice in hospice settings.* Beverly Hills, CA: Sage.

Hayslip, B., & Lowman, R. (1986). The clinical use of projective techniques with the aged: A critical review and synthesis. *Clinical Gerontologist, 5,* 63–94.

Hayslip, B., & Martin, C. (1988). Approaching death. In K. Esberger & S. Hughs (Eds.), *Nursing care of the aged.* Bowie, MD: Brady.

Hayslip, B., & Panek, P. (1987, August). *Cohort differences in hand test perfomance: A time lagged analysis.* Paper presented at the Annual Covention of the American Psychological Association.

Hayslip, B., Pinder, M., & Lumsden, B. (1981). The measurement of death anxiety in adulthood: Implications for counseling. In R. Pacholski & C. Corr (Eds.), *Proceedings of the forum for death education and counseling* (pp. 201–211). Arlington, VA: Forum for Death Education and Counseling.

Hayslip, B., & Sterns, H. (1979). Age differences in relationships between crystallized and fluid intelligences and problem solving. *Journal of Gerontology, 34,* 404–414.

Hayslip, B., & Stewart-Bussey, D. (1986). Locus of control-death anxiety relationships. *Omega, 17,* 41–50.

Heddescheimer, J. (1976). Modal motivations for mid-career changes. *Personnel and Guidance Journal, 55,* 109–111.

Heglin, H. J. (1956). Problem solving set in different age groups. *Journal of Gerontology, 11,* 310–317.

Hellebrandt, F. (1980). Aging among the advantaged: A new look at the stereotype of the elderly. *The Gerontologist, 20,* 404–417.

Helson, H. (1964). *Adaptation level theory.* New York: Harper & Row.

Hendricks, J., & Hendricks, C. D. (1981). *Aging in mass society: Myths and realities* (2nd ed.). Cambridge, MA: Winthrop.

Herr, J., & Weakland, J. (1979). *Counseling elders and their families: Practical techniques for applied gerontology.* New York: Springer.

Hertzog, C., Schaie, K. W., & Gribbin, N. (1978). Cardiovascular disease and changes in intellectual function from middle to old age. *Journal of Gerontology, 33,* 872–883.

Hess, A., & Bradshaw, H. L. (1970). Positiveness of self concept and ideal self as a function of age. *Journal of Genetic Psychology, 117,* 56–57.

Hess, B. B., & Waring, J. M. (1978). Parent and child in later life. In R. M. Lerner & G. B. Spanier (Eds.), *Child influences on marital and family interaction: A life-span perspective* (pp. 241–273). New York: Academic Press.

Hetherington, E. M. (1979). Divorce: A child's perspective. *American Psychologist, 34,* 851–858.

Hetherington, E. M., Cox, M., & Cox, R. (1982). Effects of divorce on parents and children. In M. E. Lamb (Ed.), *Nontraditional families: Parenting and child development,* Hillsdale, NJ: Lawrence Erlbaum.

Hetherington, E. M., Cox, M., & Cox, R. (1985). Long term effects of divorce and remarriage on the adjustment of children. *Journal of the American Academy of Child Psychiatry, 24,* 518–530.

Hickey, T. (1974). Simulating age-related sensory impairments for practitioner education. *The Gerontologist, 15,* 452–456.

Hickey, T. (1980). *Health and aging.* Monterey, CA: Brooks/Cole.

Hickey, T., & Douglass, R. L. (1981). Neglect and abuse of older family members: Professionals' perspectives and case experiences. *The Gerontologist, 21,* 171–176.

Hickey, T., Rakowski, W., Hultsch, D. F., & Fatula, B. J. (1976). Attitudes toward aging as a function of in-service training and practitioner age. *Journal of Gerontology, 31,* 681–686.

Hicks, R., & Davis, J. M. (1980). Pharmacokinetics in geriatric psychopharmacology. In C. Eisdorfer & W. E. Fann (Eds.), *Psychopharmacology of aging* (pp. 169–212). Jamaica, NY: Spectrum.

Hicks, R., Funkenstein, H., & Dysken, J., & Dovis, M. (1980). Geriatric psychopharmacology. In J. E. Birren & R. B. Sloane (Eds.), *Handbook of mental health and aging* (pp. 745–774). Englewood Cliffs, NJ: Prentice-Hall.

Hiemstra, R. (1976). Older adult learning: Instrumental and expressive categories. *Educational Gerontology, 1,* 227–236.

Hiemstra, R. (1985). The older adult's learning projects. In D. B. Lumsden (Ed.), *The older adult as learner* (pp. 165–196). Washington, DC: Hemisphere.

Hildebrand, W. L., & Schreiner, R. L. (1980). Helping parents cope with perinatal death. *American Journal of Pediatrics, 22,* 121–125.

Hill, R. (1965). Decision making and the family cycle. In E. Shanas and G. Streib (Eds.), *Social structure and the family: Generational relations.* Englewood Cliffs, NJ: Prentice-Hall.

Hill, R., & Mattessich, P. (1979). Family development theory and life-span development. In P. B. Baltes & O. G. Brim, Jr. (Eds.), *Life-span development and behavior* (Vol. 2, pp. 161–204). New York: Academic Press.

Hill, C. T., & Stuhl, D. E. (1981). Sex differences in effects of social and value similarity in same-sex friendship. *Journal of Personality and Social Psychology, 41,* 488–502.

Himmelfarb, S. (1984). Age and sex differences in the mental health of older persons. *Journal of Consulting and Clinical Psychology, 52,* 844–856.

Hine, V. (1979–1980). Dying at home: Can families cope? *Omega, 10,* 175–187.

Hipple, J. (1986). *Suicide: The preventable tragedy.* Unpublished manuscript.

Hochschild, A. R. (1975). Disengagement theory: A critique and proposal. *American Sociological Review, 40,* 553–569.

Hogue, C. C. (1980). Epidemiology of injury in older age. In S. G. Haynes & M. Feinleib (Eds.), *Second conference on the epidemiology of aging* (NIH Publication No. 80–969, pp. 127–138). Hyattsville, MD: U.S. Department of Health and Human Services.

Hogue, C. C. (1982a). Injury in late life: Epidemiology. *Journal of the American Geriatrics Society, 30,* 183–190.

Hogue, C. C. (1982b). Injury in late life: Prevention. *Journal of the American Geriatrics Society, 30,* 276–280.

Holland, J. L. (1973). *Making vocational choices.* Englewood Cliffs, NJ: Prentice-Hall.

Holland, J. L. (1985). *Making vocational choices: A theory of vocational personalities and work environments* (2nd ed.). Englewood Cliffs, NJ: Prentice-Hall.

Holland, J. L., & Holland, J. E. (1977). Vocational indecision: More evidence and speculation. *Journal of Counseling Psychology, 24,* 404–414.

Holmes, J. H., & Rahe, R. H. (1967). The social readjustment rating scale. *Journal of Personality and Social Psychology, 11,* 213–218.

Holt, G. L. & Matson, J. L. (1974). Necker cube reversals as a function of age and IQ. *Bulletin of the Psychonomic Society, 4,* 519–521.

Holt, G. L. & Matson, J. L. (1976). The effects of age on perceptual changes using two new perspectives of the Necker cube. *Bulletin of the Psychonomic Society, 8,* 560–652.

Holtzman, J. M., & Akiyama, H. (1985). What children see: The aged on television in Japan and the United States. *The Gerontologist, 25,* 62–68.

Holzberg, C. (1982). Ethnicity and aging: Anthropological perspectives on more than just minority elderly. *The Gerontologist, 22,* 249–257.

Hooker, K., & Ventis, D. G. (1984). Work ethic, daily activities, and retirement satisfaction. *Journal of Gerontology, 39,* 478–484.

Hooper, F. H., Hooper, J. O., & Colbert, K. (1984). *Personality and memory correlates of intellectual functioning: Young adulthood to old age.* Switzerland: Basel-Karger.

Horn, J. L. (1970). Organization of data on life-span development of human abilities. In L. Goulet & P. Baltes (Eds.), *Life-span developmental psychology: Research and theory* (pp. 424–466). New York: Academic Press.

Horn, J. L. (1976). Human abilities: A review of research and theory in the early 1970s. *Annual Review of Psychology, 27,* 437–486.

Horn, J. L. (1978). Human ability systems. In P. Baltes (Ed.), *Life-span development and behavior* (Vol. 1, pp. 211–256). New York: Academic Press.

Horn, J. L. (1979). Trends in the measurement of intelligence. In R. Sternberg & D. Detterman (Eds.), *Human intelligence: Perspectives on its theory and measurement* (pp. 191–201). Norwood, NJ: Ablex.

Horn, J. L. (1982). The aging of human abilities. In B. Wolman (Ed.), *Handbook of developmental psychology* (pp. 847–870). Englewood Cliffs, NJ: Prentice-Hall.

Horn, J. L. (1985). Remodeling old models of intelligence. In B. B. Wolman (Ed.), *Handbook of intelligence: Theories, measurements, and applications* (pp. 267–300). New York: Wiley Interscience.

Horn, J. L., & Cattell, R. B. (1966). Refinement and test of the theory of fluid and crystallized general intelligence. *Journal of Educational Psychology, 53,* 253–270.

Horn, J. L., & Cattell, R. B. (1967). Age differences in fluid and crystallized intelligence. *Acta Psychologica, 26,* 107–129.

Horn; J. L., & Donaldson, G. (1976). On the myth of intellectual decline in adulthood. *American Psychologist, 31,* 701–719.

References

Horn, J. L., & Donaldson, G. (1977). Faith is not enough: A response to the Baltes-Schaie claim that intelligence does not wane. *American Psychologist, 32,* 369–373.

Hornblum, J. N., & Overton, W. F. (1976). Area and volume conservation among the elderly: Assessment and training. *Developmental Psychology, 12,* 68–74.

Hoyer, W. J. (1973). Application of operant techniques to the modification of elderly behavior. *The Gerontologist, 13,* 18–22.

Hoyer, W. J. (1974). Aging and intraindividual change. *Developmental Psychology, 10,* 821–826.

Hoyer, W. J., Labouvie, G., & Baltes, P. B. (1973). Modification of response speed deficits and intellectual performance in the elderly. *Human Development, 16,* 233–242.

Hoyer, W. J., & Plude, D. J. (1980). Attentional and perceptual processes in the study of cognitive aging. In L. W. Poon (Ed.), *Aging in the 1980s: Psychological issues* (pp. 227–238). Washington, DC: American Psychological Association.

Hoyer, W., Raskind, C., & Abrahams, J. (1984). Research practices in the psychology of aging. A survey of research published in the *Journal of Gerontology,* 1975–1982. *Journal of Gerontology, 39,* 44–48.

Hudson, R. B., & Strate, J. (1985). Aging and political systems. In R. Binstock & E. Shanas (Eds.), *Handbook of aging and the social sciences* (pp. 554–585). New York: Van Nostrand Reinhold.

Hulicka, I. (1967). Age changes and age differences in memory functioning. *The Gerontologist, 7,* 46–54.

Hulicka, I., & Grossman, J. (1967). Age group comparisons for the use of mediators in paired-associate learning. *Journal of Gerontology, 22,* 46–51.

Hulse, S., Egeth, H., & Deese, J. (1980). *The psychology of learning.* New York: McGraw-Hill.

Hultsch, D. F. (1969). Adult age differences in the organization of free recall. *Developmental Psychology, 1,* 673–678.

Hultsch, D. F. (1971). Adult age differences in free classification and free recall. *Developmental Psychology, 4,* 338–342.

Hultsch, D. F. (1974). Learning to learn in adulthood. *Journal of Gerontology, 29,* 302–308.

Hultsch, D. F. (1975). Adult age differences in retrieval: Trace-dependent and cue-dependent forgetting. *Developmental Psychology, 11,* 197–201.

Hultsch, D. F., & Dixon, R. (1983). The role of pre-experimental knowledge in text processing adulthood. *Experimental Aging Research, 9,* 17–22.

Hultsch, D. F., & Dixon, R. (1984). Memory for text materials in adulthood. In P. Baltes & O. Brim (Eds.), *Life-span development and behavior* (Vol. 6, pp. 77–108). New York: Academic Press.

Hultsch, D. F., & Hickey, T. (1978). External validity in the study of human development: Theoretical and methodological issues. *Human Development, 21,* 76–91.

Hultsch, D. F., Hickey, T., Rakowski, W., & Fatula, B. (1975). Research on adult learning: The individual. *The Gerontologist, 15,* 424–430.

Hultsch, D. F., & Plemons, J. (1979). Life events and life-span development. In P. B. Baltes & O. Brin (Eds.), *Life-span development and behavior* (pp. 1–36). New York: Academic Press.

Hussian, R. (1981). *Geriatric psychology: A behavioral perspective.* New York: Van Nostrand Reinhold.

Huston-Stein, A., & Baltes, P. B. (1976). Theory and method in life-span developmental psychology: Implications for child development. In H. W. Reese (Ed.), *Advances in child development and behavior* (Vol. 11, pp. 169–189). New York: Academic Press.

Hwalek, M. A., & Richter, F. (1983, November). *Measuring alcoholism among the elderly.* Paper presented at the annual meeting of the Gerontological Society, Boston, MA.

Hyde, J. S. (1982). *Understanding Human Sexuality* (2nd ed.). New York: McGraw-Hill.

Ikels, C. (1982). *Final progress report on cultural factors in family support for the elderly.* Mimeo. Cited in J. Keith. (1985). Age in anthropological research. In R. Binstock & E. Shanas (Eds.), *Handbook of aging and the social sciences* (p. 247). New York: Van Nostrand Reinhold.

Ivester, C., & King, K. (1977). Attitudes of adolescents toward the aged. *The Gerontologist, 17,* 85–89.

Jackson, E. (1979). Bereavement and grief. In H. Wass (Ed.), *Dying: Facing the facts* (pp. 279–298). Washington, DC: Hemisphere.

Jackson, J. J. (1967). Social gerontology and the Negro: A review. *The Gerontologist, 7,* 168–178.

Jackson, J. J. (1970). Aged Negros: Their cultural departures from statistical stereotypes and rural-urban differences. *The Gerontologist, 10,* 140–145.

Jackson, J. J. (1985). Race, national origin, ethnicity, and aging. In R. Binstock & E. Shanas (Eds.), *Handbook of aging and the social sciences* (pp. 264–303). New York: Van Nostrand Reinhold.

Jackson, M., & Wood, J. L. (1976). *Aging in America: No. 5. Implications for the black aged.* Washington, DC: National Council on the Aging.

Jacobson, B. (1980). *Young programs for older workers: Case studies in progressive personal policies.* New York: Van Nostrand Reinhold.

Jahoda, M. (1958). *Current concepts of positive mental health.* New York: Basic Books.

Jahoda, M. (1961). A social-psychological approach to the study of culture. *Human Relations, 14,* 23–30.

Janson, P., & Ryder, L. K. (1983). Crime and the elderly: The relationship between risk and fear. *The Gerontologist, 23,* 207–212.

Jacques, E. (1965). Death and the midlife crisis. *International Journal of Psychoanalysis, 46,* 502–514.

Jacques, E. (1980). The midlife crisis. In S. Greenspan & G. Pollock (Eds.), *The course of life: Volume 3. Adulthood and aging process* (pp. 1–24). Bethesda, MD: National Institute of Mental Health.

Jarvik, L. F. (1975). Thoughts on the psychobiology of aging. *American Psychologist, 30,* 576–583.

Jarvik, L. F. (1976). Aging and depression: Some unanswered questions. *Journal of Gerontology, 31,* 324–326.

Jarvik, L. F., & Blum, J. E. (1971). Cognitive declines as predictors of mortality in twin pairs: A twenty-year longitudinal study of aging. In E. Palmer and F. Jeffers (Eds.), *Prediction of life-span* (pp. 144–211). Lexington, MA: Heath.

Jarvik, L., Blum, J., & Varma, O. (1972). Genetic components and intellectual functioning during senescence: A 20-year study of aging twins. *Behavior Genetics, 2,* 159–171.

Jarvik, L. F., & Falek, A. (1963). Intellectual stability and survival in the aged. *Journal of Gerontology, 18,* 173–176.

Jeffers, F. C., Nichols, C. R., & Eisdorfer, C. (1961). Attitudes of older persons toward death: A preliminary study. *Journal of Gerontology, 16,* 53–56.

Jeffko, W. (1979). Redefining death. *Commonwealth, 6,* 394–397.

Jenkins, J. J. (1979). Four points to remember: A tetrahedral model of memory experiments. In L. S. Cermal & F. I. M. Craik (Eds.), *Levels of processing in human memory* (pp. 429–446). Hillsdale, NJ: Erlbaum.

Jensen, A. R. (1969). How much can we boost IQ and scholastic achievement? *Harvard Education Review, 39,* 1–123.

Johnson, D. R., & Johnson, J. T. (1982). Managing the older worker. *Journal of Applied Gerontology, 1,* 58–66.

Jourard, S. (1987). *The transparent self* (2nd ed.). New York: Van Nostrand Reinhold.

Jung, C. (1960). The stages of life. In *Collected works* (Vol. 8). Princeton, NJ: Princeton University Press. (First German edition, 1931)

Kabanoff, B. (1980). Work and nonwork: A review of models. *Psychological Bulletin, 88,* 60–77.

Kahana, E. (1973). The humane treatment of old people in institutions. *The Gerontologist, 13,* 31–35.

Kahana, E., & Kahana, B. (1970, August). *Theoretical and research perspectives on grandparenthood.* Paper presented at the 78th annual meeting of the American Psychological Association, Miami, FL.

Kahana, E., & Midlarsky, E. (1982, November). *Is there help beyond exchange? Contributory options in late life adaptation.* Paper presented at the 35th annual meeting of the Gerontological Society, Boston, MA.

Kahn, R., & Antonucci, T. (1980). Convoys over the life course: Attachment, roles and social support. In P. B. Baltes and O. G. Brim, Jr. (Eds.), *Life-span development and behavior* (Vol. 3, pp. 254–286). New York: Academic Press.

Kahn, R., & Miller, N. (1978a). Assessment of altered brain function in the aged. In M. Storandt, I. Siegler, & M. Elias (Eds.), *The clinical psychology of aging* (pp. 43–69). New York: Plenum.

Kahn, R., & Miller, N. (1978b). Adaptational factors in memory function in the aged. *Experimental Aging Research, 4,* 273–290.

Kahneman, D. (1973). *Attention and effort.* Englewood Cliffs, NJ: Prentice-Hall.

Kahneman, D., Ben-Ishai, R., & Lotan, M. (1973). Relation of a test of attention to road accidents. *Journal of Applied Psychology, 58,* 113–115.

Kalb, N., & Kohn, M. (1975). Pre-retirement counseling: Characteristics of programs and preferences of retirees. *The Gerontologist, 15,* 179–181.

Kalish, R. A. (1975). *Late adulthood: Perspectives on human development.* Monterey, CA: Brooks/Cole.

Kalish, R. (1976). Death and dying in a social context. In R. Binstock & E. Shanas (Eds.), *Handbook of aging and the social sciences* (pp. 483–507). New York: Van Nostrand Reinhold.

Kalish, R. (1985a). The social context of death and dying. In R. Binstock & E. Shanas (Eds.), *Handbook of aging and the social sciences* (pp. 149–172). New York: Van Nostrand Reinhold.

Kalish, R. (1985b). *Death, grief, and caring relationships* (2nd ed.). Monterey, CA: Wadsworth.

Kalish, R., & Reynolds, D. (1976). *Death and ethnicity: A psychocultural study.* Los Angeles: University of Southern California Press.

Kaplan, H. S. (1974). *The new sex therapy.* New York: Brunner/Mazel.

Kaplan, H. S. (1975). *The illustrated manual of sex therapy.* New York: Quadrangle.

Kaplan, M. (1975). *Leisure: Theory and policy.* New York: Wiley.

Kapnick, P. (1978). Organic treatment of the elderly. In M. Storandt, I. Siegler, & M. Elias (Eds.), *The clinical psychology of aging* (pp. 225–251). New York: Plenum.

Kart, C. S. (1982). Explaining changes in labor force participation rates of aged men. *Journal of Applied Gerontology, 1,* 34–44.

Kasl, S. V., & Rosenfield, S. (1980). The residential environment and its impact on the mental health of the aged. In J. E. Birren & R. B. Sloane (Eds.), *Handbook of mental health and aging* (pp. 468–498). Englewood Cliffs, NJ: Prentice-Hall.

Kastenbaum, R. (1975). Is death a life crisis? On the confrontation with death in theory and practice. In N. Datan & L. Ginsburg (Eds.), *Life-span developmental psychology: Normative life crises* (pp. 19–50). New York: Academic Press.

Kastenbaum, R. (1978a). Death, dying, and bereavement in old age: New developments and their possible implications for psychosocial care. *Aged Care and Services Review, 1,* 1–10.

Kastenbaum, R. (1978b). Personality theory, therapeutic approaches, and the elderly client. In M. Storandt, I. Siegler, & M. Elias (Eds.), *The clinical psychology of aging* (pp. 199–224). New York: Plenum.

Kastenbaum, R. (1985). Dying and death: A life-span approach. In J. E. Birren and K. W. Schaie (Eds.), *Handbook of the psychology of aging* (pp. 619–643). New York: Van Nostrand Reinhold.

Kastenbaum, R., & Aisenberg, R. (1976). *The psychology of death.* New York: Springer.

Kastenbaum, R., & Costa, P. (1977). Psychological perspectives on death. *Annual Review of Psychology, 28,* 225–249.

Kastenbaum, R., Kastenbaum, B., & Morris, J. (In preparation). Strengths and preferences of the terminally ill [Data from the National Hospice Demonstration Study].

Kausler, D. H. (1970). Retention-forgetting as a nomological network for developmental research. In L. R. Goulet and P. B. Baltes (Eds.), *Life-span developmental psychology: Research and theory* (pp. 305–353). New York: Academic Press.

Kausler, D. H. (1982). *Experimental psychology and human aging.* New York: Wiley.

Kay, D. W., & Bergman, K. (1980). Epidemiology of mental disorders among the aged in the community. In J. E. Birren & R. B. Sloane (Eds.), *Handbook of mental health and aging* (pp. 34–56). Englewood Cliffs, NJ: Prentice-Hall.

Kay, H. (1951). Learning of a serial task by different age groups. *Quarterly Journal of Experimental Psychology, 3,* 166–183.

Kaye, L., Stuen, C., & Monk, A. (1985). The learning and retention of teaching skills by older adults: A time series analysis. *Educational Gerontology, 11,* 113–125.

Keating, D. (1982). The emperor's new clothes: The "new look" in intelligence research. In R. J. Sternberg (Ed.), *Advances in the psychology of human intelligence* (Vol. 2, pp. 1–46). Hillsdale, NJ: Lawrence Erlbaum.

Keith, J. (1985). Age in anthropological research. In R. Binstock & E. Shanas (Eds.), *Handbook of aging and the social sciences* (pp. 231–263). New York: Van Nostrand Reinhold.

Keith, P. M. (1977). An exploratory study of sources of stereotypes of old age among administrators. *Journal of Gerontology, 32,* 463–469.

Keith, P. (1979). Life changes and perceptions of life and death among older men and women. *Journal of Gerontology, 34,* 870–878.

Keith, P. M., Hill, K., Goudy, W. J., & Powers, E. A. (1984). Confidants and well-being: A note on male friendships in old age. *The Gerontologist, 24,* 318–320.

Keller, J., & Hughston, G. (1981). *Counseling the elderly: A systems approach.* New York: Harper & Row.

Kelly, G. A. (1955). *The psychology of personal constructs.* New York: Norton.

Kelly, J. B. (1982). Divorce: The adult perspective. In J. Wolman (Ed.) *Handbook of developmental psychology* (pp. 734–750). Englewood Cliffs, NJ: Prentice-Hall.

Kelly, J. R. (1975). Life styles and leisure choices. *Family Coordinator, 24,* 185–190.

Kelly, J. R. (1983a). *Leisure identities and interactions.* London and Boston: Allen and Unwin.

Kelly, J. R. (1983b). Leisure styles: A hidden care. *Leisure Sciences, 5,* 321–328.

Kelly, J. R., Steinkamp, M. W., & Kelly, J. R. (1986). Later life leisure: How they play in Peoria. *The Gerontologist, 26,* 531–537.

Kemp, B. J. (1973). Reaction time of young and elderly subjects in relation to perceptual deprivation and signal-on versus signal-off conditions. *Developmental Psychology, 8,* 268–272.

Kennelly, K. J., Hayslip, B., & Richardson, S. K. (1985). Depression and helplessness-induced cognitive deficits in the aged. *Experimental Aging Research, 8,* 165–173.

Kenshalo, D. R. (1977). Age changes in touch, vibration, temperature, kinesthesis and pain sensitivity. In J. E. Birren and K. W. Schaie (Eds.), *Handbook of the psychology of aging* (pp. 562–579). New York: Van Nostrand Reinhold.

Kermis, M. (1986). *Mental health in late life: The adaptive process.* Boston: Jones & Bartlett.

Kidd, J. M. (1984). The relationship of self and occupational concepts to the occupational preferences of adolescents. *Journal of Vocational Behavior, 24,* 48–65.

Kiefer, C. (1974). *Changing cultures, changing lives.* San Francisco: Jossey-Bass.

Kilty, K. M. & Feld, A. (1976). Attitudes toward aging and toward the needs of older people. *Journal of Gerontology, 31,* 586–594.

Kinsbourne, M., & Berryhill, J. (1972). The nature of the interaction between pacing and the age decrement in learning. *Journal of Gerontology, 27,* 471–477.

Kirchner, W. K. (1958). Age differences in short-term retention of rapidly changing information. *Journal of Experimental Psychology, 55,* 352–358.

Kivnick, H. (1982). Grandparenthood: An overview of meaning and mental health. *The Gerontologist, 22,* 59–66.

Kivnick, H. Q. (1985). Grandparenthood and mental health: Meaning, behavior, and satisfaction. In V. L. Bengston & J. F. Robertson (Eds.), *Grandparenthood* (pp. 49–88). Beverly Hills, CA: Sage.

Kleemeier, R. W. (1962). Intellectual change in the senium. *Proceedings of the Social Statistics Section of the American Statistical Association, 1,* 290–295.

Kline, D. W., & Birren, J. E. (1975). Age differences in backward dichotic masking. *Experimental Aging Research, 1,* 17–25.

Kline, D. W., & Schieber, F. (1981). Visual aging: A transient/sustained shift? *Perception and Psychophysics, 29,* 181–182.

Kline, D. W., & Scheiber, F. (1985). Vision and aging. In J. E. Birren and K. W. Schaie (Eds.), *Handbook of the psychology of aging* (2nd ed., pp. 296–331). New York: Van Nostrand Reinhold.

Kline, D. W., & Szafran, J. (1975). Age differences in backward monoptic visual noise masking. *Journal of Gerontology, 30,* 307–311.

Klisz, D. (1978). Neuropsychological evaluation in older persons. In M. Storandt, I. C. Siegler, & M. F. Elias (Eds.), *The clinical psychology of aging* (pp. 71–95). New York: Plenum.

Klopfer, B., & Davis, R. (1977). Issues in psychotherapy with the aged. *Psychotherapy: Theory, research, and practice, 14,* 343–348.

Knesper, D. J., Pagnucco, D. J., & Wheeler, J. (1985). Similarities and differences across mental health services providers and practice settings in the United States. *American Psychologist, 40,* 1352–1369.

Knox, D. (1985). Trends in marriage and the family—the 1980s. *Family Relations, 29,* 145–150.

Kobata, F., Lockery, S., & Moriwaki, S. (1980). Minority issues in mental health and aging. In J. E. Birren & R. B. Sloane (Eds.), *Handbook of mental health and aging* (pp. 448–467). Englewood Cliffs, NJ: Prentice-Hall.

Kogan, N. (1973). Creativity and cognitive style: A life-span perspective. In P. B. Baltes and K. W. Schaie (Eds.), *Life-span developmental psychology: Personality and socialization* (pp. 145–178). New York: Academic Press.

Kogan, N. (1979). Beliefs, attitudes, and stereotypes about old people: A new look at some old issues. *Research on Aging, 1,* 11–36.

Kohlberg, L. (1966). A cognitive-developmental analysis of children's sex role concepts and attitudes. In E. E. Macoby, (Ed.), *The development of sex differences* (pp. 48–64). Stanford: Stanford University Press.

Kohlberg, L. (1973). Continuities in childhood and adult moral development revisited. In P. B. Baltes & K. W. Schaie (Eds.), *Life-span developmental psychology: Personality and socialization* (pp. 180–207). New York: Academic Press.

Kompara, D. R. (1980). Difficulties in the socialization process of stepparenting. *Family Relations, 29,* 69–73.

Kooken, R. A., & Hayslip, B. (1984). The use of stress inoculation in the treatment of test anxiety in older students. *Educational Gerontology, 11,* 39–58.

Korchin, S. J., & Basowitz, H. (1956). The judgment of ambiguous stimuli as an index of cognitive functioning in aging. *Journal of Personality, 25,* 81–95.

Kotch, J. B., & Cohen, S. R. (1985–1986). SIDS counselors' reports of own and parents' reactions to reviewing the autopsy report. *Omega, 16,* 129–139.

Kozma, A., & Stones, M. (1987). Social desirability in measures of subjective well-being: A systematic evaluation. *Journal of Gerontology, 42,* 56–57.

Kramer, D. F. (1983). Post-formal operations? A need for further conceptualization. *Human Development, 26,* 91–105.

Krauss, I. (1980). Between and within-group comparisons in aging research. In L. Poon (Ed.), *Aging in the 1980s: Psychological issues* (pp. 542–551). Washington, DC: American Psychological Association.

Krupa, L., & Vener, A. (1979). Hazards of drug use among the elderly. *The Gerontologist, 19,* 90–95.

Kryter, K. (1970). *The effects of noise on man.* New York: Academic Press.

Kubanoff, B. (1980). Work and nonwork: A review of models. *Psychological Bulletin, 88,* 60–77.

Kubler-Ross, E. (1969). *On death and dying.* New York: Macmillan.

Kubler-Ross, E. (1974a). *On death and dying* (2nd ed.). New York: Macmillan.

Kubler-Ross, E. (1974b). *Questions and answers on death and dying.* New York: Macmillan.

Kubler-Ross, E. (1978). *To live until we say goodbye.* Englewood Cliffs, NJ: Prentice-Hall.

Kubler-Ross, E. (1982). *Working it through.* New York: Macmillan.

Kuhn, M. E. (1983, July 31). We're old, not senile, Ronald. *New York Times.*

Labouvie, E. V., Bartsch, T., Nesselroade, J., & Baltes, P. (1974). On the internal and external validity of simple longitudinal designs: Dropout and retest effects. *Child Development, 45,* 282–290.

References

Labouvie-Vief, G. (1982). Dynamic development and mature autonomy: A theoretical prologue. *Human Development, 25,* 161–191.

Labouvie-Vief, G. (1985). Intelligence and cognition. In J. E. Birren & K. W. Schaie (Eds.), *Handbook of the psychology of aging* (2nd ed., pp. 500–530). New York: Van Nostrand Reinhold.

Labouvie-Vief, G., Adams, C., Hakim-Larson, J., & Hayden, M. (1983, April). *Contexts of logic: The growth of interpretation from pre-adolescence to mature adulthood.* Paper presented at the meeting of the Society for Research in Child Development, Washington, DC.

Labouvie-Vief, G. V., & Baltes, P. B. (1976). Reduction of adolescent misperceptions of the aged. *Journal of Gerontology, 31,* 68–71.

Labouvie-Vief, G. & Gonda, J. (1976). Cognitive strategy training and intellectual performance in the elderly. *Journal of Gerontology, 31,* 327–336; 372–382.

Labouvie-Vief, G., & Shell, D. (1982). Learning and memory in later life. In B. Wolman (Ed.), *Handbook of developmental psychology* (pp. 828–846). Englewood Cliffs, NJ: Prentice-Hall.

Lachman, J. L., & Lachman, R. (1980). Age and the actualization of world knowledge. In L. Poon, J. Fozard, L. Cermak, D. Arenberg, & L. Thompson (Eds.), *New directions in memory and aging* (pp. 285–311). Hillsdale, NJ: Lawrence Erlbaum.

Lachman, M., & Jelalian, E. (1984). Self-efficacy and attributions for intellectual performance in young and elderly adults. *Journal of Gerontology, 39,* 577–582.

Lachman, J. L., Lachman, R., & Thronesbery, C. (1979). Metamemory throughout the adult life span. *Developmental Psychology, 15,* 543–551.

Lachman, M. E., & McArthur, L. Z. (1986). Adult age differences in causal attributions for cognitive, physical, and social performance. *Psychology and Aging, 1,* 127–132.

Lajer, M. (1982). Unemployment and hospitalization among bricklayers. *Scandinavian Journal of Social Medicine, 10,* 3–10.

Lamb, M. (1976). The role of the father: An overview. In M. E. Lamb (Ed.), *The role of the father in child development* (pp. 1–61). New York: Wiley.

Lamb, M. E. (1981). *The role of the father in child development.* New York: Wiley.

Landahl, H. D., & Birren, J. E. (1959). Effects of age on discrimination of lifted weights. *Journal of Gerontology, 14,* 48–55.

Langer, E. (1982). Old age: An artifact? In S. Kiesler & J. McGaugh (Eds.), *Biology, behavior, and aging* (pp. 255–281) New York: National Research Council.

Langer, E. (1983). *The psychology of control.* Palo Alto, CA: Sage.

Langer, E., & Rodin, J. (1976). The effects of choice and enhanced personal responsibility: A field experiment in institutionalized setting. *Journal of Personality and Social Psychology, 34,* 191–198.

Langer, E., Rodin, J., Beck, P., Weinman, C., & Spitzer, L. (1979). Environmental determinants of memory improvement in late adulthood. *Journal of Personality and Social Psychology, 37,* 2003–2013.

Langer, J. (1969). *Theories of development.* New York: Holt, Rinehart and Winston.

Lansing, A. K. (1959). General biology of senescence. In J. E. Birren (Eds.), *Handbook of aging and the individual* (pp. 119–135). Chicago: University of Chicago Press.

Larson, R. (1978). Thirty years of research on the subjective well-being of older Americans. *Journal of Gerontology, 33,* 109–125.

Larson, R., Mannell, R., & Zuzanek, J. (1986). Daily well-being of older adults with friends and family. *Psychology and Aging, 1,* 117–126.

LaRue, A., Bank, L., Jarvik, L., & Hetland, M. (1979). Health in old age: How do physicians' ratings and self-ratings compare? *Journal of Gerontology, 34,* 687–691.

LaRue, A., Dessonville, C., & Jarvik, L. F. (1985). Aging and mental disorders. In J. E. Birren & K. W. Schaie (Eds.), *Handbook of the psychology of aging* (pp. 664–702). New York: Van Nostrand Reinhold.

Lauriant, P., & Rabin, W. (1976). Characteristics of new beneficiaries by age at entitlement. In U.S. Department of Health, Education and Welfare, Social Security Administration, *Reaching retirement age: Findings from a survey of newly entitled workers 1968–1970* (pp. 11–29). Washington, DC: U.S. Government Printing Office.

Laws, J. L. (1980). Female sexuality through the life-span. In P. B. Baltes & O. G. Brim, Jr. (Eds.), *Life-span development and behavior* (Vol. 3, pp. 208–252). New York: Academic Press.

Lawton, M. P. (1975). The Philadelphia Geriatric Morale Scale: A revision. *Journal of Gerontology, 30,* 85–89.

Lawton, M. P. (1976). Geropsychological knowledge as a background for psychotherapy with older people. *Journal of Geriatric Psychiatry, 9,* 221–233.

Lawton, M. (1977). The impact of the environment on aging and behavior. In J. E. Birren & K. W. Schaie (Eds.), *Handbook of the psychology of aging* (pp. 276–301). New York: Van Nostrand Reinhold.

Lawton, M. (1978). Clinical geropsychology: Problems and prospects. *Master lectures in the psychology of aging.* Washington, DC: American Psychological Association.

Lawton, M. P. (1980a, November). Do elderly research subjects need special protection?:

Psychological vulnerability. *Institutional Review Board.* Washington, DC: Department of Health, Education, and Welfare.

Lawton, M. P. (1980b). *Environment and aging.* Monterey, CA: Brooks/Cole.

Lawton, M. P. (1983). Environment and other determinants of well-being in older people. *The Gerontologist, 23,* 349–357.

Lawton, M. P. (1985). Housing and living environments of older people. In R. Binstock & E. Shanas (Eds.), *Handbook of aging and the social sciences* (pp. 450–478). New York: Van Nostrand Reinhold.

Lawton, M. P., & Gottesman, L. E. (1974). Psychological services to the elderly. *American Psychologist, 29,* 689–693.

Lawton, M. P., Moss, M., & Moles, E. (1984). Pet ownership: A research note. *The Gerontologist, 24,* 208–210.

Lawton, M. P., & Nahemow, L. (1973). Ecology and the aging process. In C. Eisdorfer & M. P. Lawton (Eds.), *The psychology of adult development and aging* (pp. 619–674). Washington, DC: American Psychological Association.

Lawton, M. P., Whelihan, W., & Belsky, J. K. (1980). Personality tests and their uses with older adults. In J. E. Birren & R. B. Sloane (Eds.), *Handbook of mental health and aging* (pp. 537–553). Englewood Cliffs, NJ: Prentice-Hall.

Layton, B. J. (1975). Perceptual noise and aging. *Psychological Bulletin, 82,* 875–883.

Layton, J., & Siegler, I. (1978, November). *Mid-life: Must it be a crisis?* Paper presented at the annual convention of the Gerontological Society, Dallas, TX.

Lazarus, L., Stafford, B., Cooper, K., Cohler, B., & Dysken, M. (1981). A pilot study of an Alzheimer patient's relatives discussion group. *The Gerontologist, 22,* 353–358.

Lazarus, R. S. & Delongis, A. (1983). Psychological stress and coping in aging. *American Psychologist, 38,* 245–254.

Leaf, A. (1973). Getting old. *Scientific American, 299,* 45–52.

Leech, S., & Witte, K. L. (1971). Paired-associate learning in elderly adults as related to pacing and incentive conditions. *Developmental Psychology, 5,* 180.

Leete, R. (1979, April). New directions in family life. *Population Trends,* pp. 1–9.

Lefcourt, H. M. (1981). *Research with the locus of control construct: Volume 1. Assessment methods.* New York: Academic Press.

Leifer, M. (1977). Psychological changes accompanying pregnancy and motherhood. *Genetic Psychology Monographs, 95,* 55–96.

Leitner, M. (1977). A study of reciprocity in preschool play groups. *Child Development, 48,* 1288–1295.

Lemon, B., Bengston, V., & Peterson, J. (1972). An explanation of the activity theory of aging: Activity tapes and life satisfaction among in-movers to a retirement community. *Journal of Gerontology, 27,* 511–523.

Lerner, R. M. (1984). *On the nature of human plasticity.* Cambridge, MA: Cambridge University Press.

Lerner, R. (1986). *Concepts and theories of human development.* Reading, MA: Addison-Wesley.

Lerner, R., & Ryff, C. (1978). Implementation of the life-span view of development: The sample case of attachment. In P. B. Baltes & O. G. Brim, Jr. (Eds.), *Life-span development and behavior* (Vol. 1, pp. 2–44). New York: Academic Press.

Lerner, R. M., & Spanier, G. (1978). A dynamic, interactional view of child and family development. In R. M. Lerner & G. Spanier (Eds.), *Child influences on marital and family interaction* (pp. 1–22). New York: Academic Press.

Lesser, J., Lazarus, L. W., Frankel, R., & Havasy, S. (1981). Reminiscence group therapy with psychotic geriatric inpatients. *The Gerontologist, 21,* 291–296.

Levin, J., & Levin, W. C. (1980). *Ageism: Prejudice and discrimination against the elderly.* Belmont, CA: Wadsworth.

Levinson, B. M. (1972). *Pets and human development.* Springfield, IL: Thomas.

Levinson, D. J. (1978). *The seasons of a man's life.* New York: Knopf.

Levinson, D. J. (1986). A conception of adult development. *American Psychologist, 41,* 3–13.

Levy, S. M., Derogatis, L. R., Gallagher, D., and Gatz, M. (1980). Intervention with older adults and the evaluation of outcome. In L. Poon (Ed.), *Aging in the 1980's: Psychological issues* (pp. 41–64). Washington, DC: American Psychological Association.

Lewis, E. (1979). Mourning by the family after a stillbirth or neonatal death. *Archives of Disease in Childhood, 54,* 303–306.

Lewis, M. (1979). The self as a developmental concept. *Human Development, 22,* 416–419.

Lewis, R. A., & Spanier, G. B. (1979). Theorizing about the quality and stability of marriage. In W. Burr, R. Hill, F. Nye, & I. Reiss (Eds.), *Contemporary theories about the family* (Vol. 1, pp. 268–294). New York: Free Press.

Lieberman, M. A. (1965). Psychological correlates of impending death: Some preliminary observations. *Journal of Gerontology, 20,* 181–190.

Lieberman, M. A. (1975). Adaptive processes in later life. In N. Datan and L. Ginsburg (Eds.), *Life-span*

References

developmental psychology: Normative life events (pp. 135–159). New York: Academic Press.

Lieberman, M. A. (1978, November). *Methodological issues in the evaluation of psychotherapy with older adults.* Paper presented at the annual meeting of the Gerontological Society, Dallas, TX.

Lindemann, E. (1944). The symptomatology and management of acute grief. *American Journal of Psychiatry, 101,* 141–148.

Lipinski, M. A. (1979, October 21). Relationships boom despite gap of age. *Chicago Tribune,* Sect. 12, pp. 1–3.

Lippmann, W. (1922). *Public opinion.* New York: Harcourt, Brace.

Liss, L., & Gomez, F. (1958). The nature of senile changes of the human olfactory bulb and tract. *Archives of Otolaryngology, 67,* 167–171.

Liu, W. T., & Yu, E. (1985). Asian/Pacific American Elderly: Mortality differentials, health status, and use of health services. *Journal of Applied Gerontology, 4,* 35–64.

Livson, F. B. (1981). Paths to psychological health in the middle years: Sex differences. In D. Eichorn, N. Haan, J. Clausen, M. Honzik, & P. Mussen (Eds.), *Present and past in middle life* (pp. 195–221). New York: Academic Press.

Livson, N. (1973). Developmental dimensions of personality: A lifespan formulation. In P. B. Baltes & K. W. Schaie (Eds.), *Life-span developmental psychology: Personality and socialization* (pp. 98–122). New York: Academic Press.

Livson, N., & Peskin, H. (1981). Psychological health at age 40: Prediction from adolescent personality. In D. Eichorn, N. Haan, J. Clausen, M. Honzik, & P. Mussen (Eds.), *Present and past in middle life* (pp. 183–194). New York: Academic Press.

Long, G. M. (1974). Reported correlates of perceptual style: A review of the field dependency-independency dimension. *JSAS Catalog of Selected Documents in Psychology, 4,* 304. (Ms. No. 540).

Looft, W. R. (1973). Socialization and personality throughout the life-span. An examination of contemporary psychological approaches. In P. B. Baltes and K. W. Schaie (Eds.), *Life-span developmental psychology: Personality and socialization* (pp. 25–52). New York: Academic Press.

Lopata, H. Z. (1973). *Widowhood in an American city.* Cambridge: Schenkman.

Lopata, H. Z. (1975). Widowhood: Societal factors in life-span disruptions and alternatives. In N. Datan & L. Ginsburg (Eds.), *Life-span developmental psychology: Normative life crises* (pp. 217–234). New York: Academic Press.

Lopata, H. (1979). *Women as widows: Support systems.* New York: Elsevier.

Lopez, F. G. (1983). A paradoxical approach to vocational indecision. *Personal and Guidance Journal, 59,* 433–439.

Lorr, M. (1978). The structure of the California Q-set. *Multivariate Behavioral Research, 13,* 387–393.

Lorsbach, T. C., & Simpson, G. B. (1988). Dual task performance as a function of adut age and task complexity. *Psychology and Aging, 3,* 210–212.

Lowenthal, M. F. (1977). Toward a sociopsychological theory of change in adulthood and old age. In J. E. Birren & K. W. Schaie (Eds.), *Handbook of the psychology of aging* (pp. 116–127). New York: Van Nostrand Reinhold.

Lowenthal, M. F., & Chiriboga, D. (1973). Social stress and adaptation toward a life-course perspective. In C. Eisdorfer & M. P. Lawton (Eds.), *The psychology of adult development and aging* (pp. 281–310). Washington, DC: American Psychological Association.

Lowenthal, M. F., & Robinson, B. (1976). Social networks and isolation. In R. Binstock & E. Shanas (Eds.), *Handbook of aging and social sciences* (pp. 432–456). New York: Van Nostrand Reinhold.

Lowenthal, M. F., Thurnher, M., Chiriboga, D., & Associates (1975). *Four stages of life: A comparative study of women and men facing transitions.* San Francisco: Jossey-Bass.

Lowy, L. (1980). Mental health services in the community. In J. E. Birren & R. B. Sloane (Eds.), *Handbook of mental health and aging* (pp. 827–853). Englewood Cliffs, NJ: Prentice-Hall.

Luborsky, L., Chandler, M., Averback, A., Cohen, J., & Bachrach, H. (1971). Factors influencing the outcome of psychotherapy. *Psychological Bulletin, 75,* 145–185.

Ludeman, K. (1981). The sexuality of the older person: Review of the literature. *The Gerontologist, 21,* 203–208.

Lumsden, D. B. (Ed.). (1985). *The older adult as learner.* Washington, DC: Hemisphere.

Lund, D., Caserta, M. S., & Dimond, M. F. (1986). Gender differences through two years of bereavement among the elderly. *The Gerontologist, 26,* 314–320.

Lund, D. A., Dimond, M. F., Caserta, M. S., Johnson, R. J., Poulton, J. L., & Connelly, J. R. (1985–1986). Identifying elderly with coping difficulties after two years of bereavement. *Omega, 16,* 213–224.

Lupri, E., & Frideres, J. (1981). The quality of marriage and the passage of time: Marital satisfaction over the family life cycle. *Canadian Journal of Sociology, 6,* 283–305.

Lutsky, N. S. (1980). Attitudes toward old age and

elderly persons. *Annual Review of Gerontology and Geriatrics, 1,* 287–336.

Maas, H., & Kuypers, J. (1974). *From thirty to seventy.* San Francisco: Josey-Bass.

Madden, J. D. (1982). Age differences and similarities in the improvement of controlled search. *Experimental Aging Research, 8,* 91–98.

Madden, J. D. (1983). Aging and distraction by highly familiar stimuli during visual search. *Developmental Psychology, 19,* 499–507.

Madden, J. D. (1984). Date-driven and memory-driven selective attention in visual search. *Journal of Gerontology, 39,* 72–78.

Maddi, S. (1976). *Personality theories: A comparative analysis.* Homewood, IL: Dorsey Press.

Maddi, S. (1980). *Personality theories: A comparative analysis.* Homewood, IL: Dorsey.

Maddox, G. L. (1964). Disengagement theory: A critical evaluation. *The Gerontologist, 4,* 80–83.

Maddox, G. L. (1965). Fact and artifact: Evidence bearing on disengagement theory from the Duke Longitudinal Study. *Human Development, 8,* 117–130.

Maddox, G. L., & Campbell, R. T. (1985). Scope, concepts, and methods in the study of aging. In R. Binstock & E. Shanas (Eds.), *Handbook of aging and the social sciences* (2nd ed.). New York: Van Nostrand Reinhold.

Maddox, G. L., & Douglass, E. B. (1974). Aging individual differences: A longitudinal analysis of social, psychological, and physiological indicators. *Journal of Gerontology, 29,* 555–563.

Maddox, G. L., & Eisdorfer, C. (1962). Some correlates of activity and morale among the elderly. *Social Forces, 40,* 254–260.

Maeda, D. (1983). Family care in Japan. *The Gerontologist, 23,* 579–583.

Maiden, R. J. (1987). Learned helplessness and depression: A test of the reformulation model. *Journal of Gerontology, 42,* 60–64.

Maldonado, D. Jr., (1975). The Chicano aged. *Social Work, 20,* 213–216.

Maldonado, D. Jr., (1979). Aging: The Chicano context. In D. Gelfand & A. Kutzik (Eds.), *Ethnicity and aging* (pp. 175–183). New York: Springer.

Maldonado, D., Jr., (1985). The Hispanic elderly: A sociohistorical framework for public policy. *Journal of Applied Gerontology, 4,* 6–17.

Maldonado, D. Jr., & Applewhite-Lozano, S. (1986). *The Hispanic elderly: Empowerment through training.* Arlington, TX: Center for Chicano Aged.

Mallinckrodt, B., & Fretz, B. R. (1988). Social support and the impact of job loss on older professionals. *Journal of Counseling Psychology, 35,* 281–286.

Marcia, J. E. (1966). Development and validation of ego identity status. *Journal of Personality and Social Psychology, 3,* 551–558.

Marcus, S., & Hayslip, B. (1987, April). *Effects of maternal employment and family life cycle stage on the psychological well-being of women.* Paper presented at the annual convention of the Society for Research in Child Development, Baltimore, MD.

Markham, S. (1983). I can be a bum: Knowledge about abilities and lifestyle in vocational behavior. *Journal of Vocational Behavior, 23,* 72–86.

Markides, K. S. (1983a). Aging, religiosity, and adjustment: A longitudinal analysis. *Journal of Gerontology, 38,* 621–625.

Markides, K. S. (1983b). Minority aging. In M. W. Wiley, B. B. Hess, & K. Bond (Eds.), *Aging in society: Selected reviews of recent research* (pp. 115–137). Hillsdale, NJ: Lawrence Erlbaum.

Marsden, C. D. (1978). The diagnosis of dementia. In A. D. Isaacs & F. Post (Eds.), *Studies in geriatric psychiatry* (pp. 99–118). New York: Wiley.

Marsh, G. R., & Thompson, L. W. (1977). Psychophysiology of aging. In J. E. Birren & K. W. Schaie (Eds.), *Handbook of the psychology of aging* (pp. 219–248). New York: Van Nostrand Reinhold.

Marshall, J. (1983). Reducing the effects of work oriented values on the lines of male American workers. *The Vocational Guidance Quarterly, 32,* 109–115.

Marshall, V. (1975). Age and awareness of finitude in developmental gerontology. *Omega, 6,* 113–127.

Marshall, V. (1979). Socialization for impending death in a retirement village. *American Journal of Science, 80,* 1124–1144.

Marshall, V. (1980). *Last chapters: A sociology of aging and dying.* Belmont, CA: Brooks/Cole.

Masters, W. H., & Johnson, V. E. (1966). *Human sexual response.* Boston, MA: Little, Brown.

Masters, W. H., & Johnson, V. E. (1970). *Human sexual response.* (2nd ed.) Boston, MA: Little, Brown.

Masters, W. H., Johnson, V. E., & Kolodny, R. C. (1982). *Human sexuality.* Boston, MA: Little, Brown.

Matarazzo, J. D. (1972). *Wechsler's measurement and appraisal of adult intelligence.* Baltimore: Williams and Wilkins.

Matthews, R., & Matthews, A. (1986). Infertility and involuntary childlessness: The transition to nonparenthood. *Journal of Marriage and the Family, 48,* 166–178.

Matthews, S. H., & Sprey, J. (1984). The impact of divorce on parenthood: An exploratory study. *The Gerontologist, 24,* 41–47.

McCary, J. L., & McCary, S. P. (1982). *McCary's human sexuality* (4th ed.). Belmont, CA.: Wadsworth.

McCrae, R. R., Arenberg, D., & Costa, P. T. (1987).

References

Declines in divergent thinking with age: cross-sectional, longitudinal, and cross-sequential analyses. *Psychology and Aging, 2,* 130–137.

McCrae, R. R., Bartone, P., & Costa, P. T. (1976). Age, anxiety, and self-reported health. *Aging and Human Development, 7,* 49–58.

McCrae, R. R., & Costa, P. T. (1984). *Emerging lives, enduring dispositions: Personality in adulthood.* Boston: Little, Brown.

McCrae, R. R., & Costa, P. T. (1987). Validation of the five-factor model of personality across instruments and observers. *Journal of Personality and Social Psychology, 52,* 81–90.

McFarland, R. A. (1968). The sensory and perceptual processes in aging. In K. W. Schaie (Ed.), *Theory and methods of research on aging* (pp. 3–52). Morgantown, WV: West Virginia University Press.

McFarland, R. A. (1973). The need for functional age measurements in industrial gerontology. *Industrial Gerontology, 1,* 1–19.

McFarland, R. A., Tune, C. S., & Welford, A. T. (1964). On the driving of automobiles by older people. *Journal of Gerontology, 19,* 190–197.

McGee, M. G., III, Hall, J., & Lutes-Dunckley, J. L. (1979). Factors influencing attitude towards retirement. *The Journal of Psychology, 101,* 15–18.

McGuigan, F. J. (1983). *Experimental psychology: Methods of research.* Englewood Cliffs, NJ: Prentice-Hall.

McGuire, F. A., Dottavio, D., & O'Leary, J. T. (1986). Constraints to participation in outdoor recreation across the life span: A nationwide study of limitors and prohibitors. *The Gerontologist, 26,* 538–544.

McIlroy, J. H. (1984). Midlife in the 1980s: Philosophy, economy, and psychology. *The Personnel and Guidance Journal, 62,* 623–628.

McIntosh, J. L. (1983, November). *Elderly suicide data bases: Levels, availability, omission.* Paper presented at the annual meeting of the Gerontological Society, Boston, MA.

McPherson, B., & Guppy, N. (1979). Pre-retirement life-style and the degree of planning for retirement. *Journal of Gerontology, 34,* 254–263.

McTavish, D. G. (1971). Perceptions of old people: A review of research methodologies and findings. *The Gerontologist, 11,* 90–101.

Meichenbaum, D. (1974). *Cognitive behavior modification.* Morristown, PA: General Learning Press.

Meichenbaum, D. (1977). *Cognitive behavior modification.* New York: Plenum.

Meier, E. L., & Kerr, E. A. (1976). Capabilities of middle-aged and older workers: A survey of the literature. *Industrial Gerontology, 3,* 147–156.

Meredith, D. (1985, June). Mom, dad and the kids. *Psychology Today,* pp. 62–67.

Merriam, S. (1979). Middle-age: A review of the research. *New Directions for Continuing Education, 2,* 7–15.

Mihal, W. L., & Barrett, G. V. (1976). Individual differences in perceptual-information-processing and their relation to automobile accident involvement. *Journal of Applied Psychology, 61,* 229–233.

Miles, M. S. (1984). Helping adults mourn the death of a child. In H. Wass & C. Corr (Eds.), *Childhood and death* (pp. 219–240). Washington, DC: Hemisphere/McGraw-Hill.

Miller, D. C., & Form, W. H. (1951). *Industrial sociology.* New York: Harper & Row.

Miller, E. (1980). Cognitive assessment of the older adult. In J. E. Birren & R. B. Sloane (Eds.), *Handbook of mental health and aging* (pp. 520–536). Englewood Cliffs, NJ: Prentice-Hall.

Miller, M. (1978). Geriatric suicide: The Arizona study. *The Gerontologist, 18,* 488–495.

Miller, M. (1979). *Suicide after sixty: The final alternative.* New York: Springer.

Mischel, W. (1968). *Personality and assessment.* New York: Wiley.

Mischel, W. (1970). Sex-typing and socialization. In P. Mussen (Ed.), *Carmichael's handbook of child psychology* (Vol. 2, pp. 3–72) New York: Wiley.

Mischel, W. (1981). *Introduction to personality.* New York: Holt, Rinehart & Winston.

Mishara, B. L. (1978). Geriatric patients who improve in token economy and general milieu treatment programs: A multivariate analysis. *Journal of Consulting and Clinical Psychology, 46,* 1340–1348.

Moberg, D. O. (1972). Religion and the aging family. *Family Coordinator, 21,* 47–60.

Mobily, K. E., Leslie, D. K., Lemke, J. H., Wallace, R. B., & Kohout, F. J. (1986). Leisure patterns and attitudes of the rural elderly. *The Journal of Applied Gerontology, 5,* 201–214.

Monge, R. H. (1975). Structure of the self concept from adolescence through old age. *Experimental Aging Research, 1,* 281–291.

Monge, R. H., & Hultsch, D. (1971). Paired-associate learning as a function of adult age and the length of the anticipation and inspection intervals. *Journal of Gerontology, 26,* 157–162.

Monte, C. F. (1977). *Beneath the mask: An introduction to theories of personality.* New York: Praeger.

Mor, V., & Masterson-Allen, S. (1987). *Hospice care systems: Structure, process, costs, and outcome.* New York: Springer.

Moran, J. M. (1979). *Leisure activities for the mature adult.* Minneapolis, MN: Burgess.

Mortimer, J. T., Finch, M. D., & Kumka, D. (1982). Persistence and change in development: The multidimensional self concept. In P. B. Baltes & O. G. Brim (Eds.), *Life-span development and behavior* (pp. 264–313). New York: Academic Press.

Mosatche, H. S., Brady, E. M., & Noberini, M. R. (1983). A retrospective life-span study of the closest sibling relationship. *Journal of Psychology, 113,* 237–243.

Moss, H., & Sussman, E. (1980). Longitudinal study of personality development. In O. Brim & J. Kagan (Eds.), *Constancy and change in human development* (pp. 530–595). Cambridge, MA: Harvard University Press.

Moss, M., & Moss, D. (1980). *The image of the dead spouse in remarriage of elderly widow(er)s.* Paper presented at the annual meeting of the Gerontological Society, Washington, DC.

Mueller, K. H. (1954). *Educating women for a changing world.* Minneapolis: University of Minnesota Press.

Muller, H. F., Grad, B., & Engelsman, F. (1975). Biological and psychological predictors of survival in a psychogenetic population. *Journal of Gerontology, 30,* 47–52.

Mullins, L., & Lopez, M. (1982). Death anxiety among nursing home residents: A comparison of the young-old and old-old. *Death Education, 6,* 75–86.

Murphy, J. M., Sobol, A. M., Neff, R. K., Olivier, D. C., & Leighton, A. H. (1984). Stability of prevalence: Depression and anxiety disorders. *Archives of General Psychiatry, 41,* 990–997.

Murphy, M., Sanders, R. E., Gariesheski, A., & Schmitt, F. (1981). Metamemory in the aged. *Journal of Gerontology, 36,* 185–193.

Murphy, P., & Burck, H. (1976). Career development of men and mid-life. *Journal of Vocational Behavior, 9,* 337–343.

Murrell, F. H. (1970). The effect of extensive practice on age differences in reaction time. *Journal of Gerontology, 25,* 268–274.

Murrell, F. H., & Griew, S. (1965). Age, experience and speed response. In A. T. Welford & J. E. Birren (Eds.), *Behavior, aging and the nervous system* (pp. 60–66). Springfield, IL: Thomas.

Murstein, B. I. (1982). Marital choice. In J. Wolman (Ed.), *Handbook of developmental psychology* (pp. 652–666). Englewood Cliffs, NJ: Prentice-Hall.

Mussen, P. B. (1970). *Carmichael's manual of child psychology* (3rd ed.). New York: Wiley.

Mussen, P., Honzig, M., & Eichorn, D. (1980). Early adult antecedents of life satisfaction at age 70. *Journal of Gerontology, 37,* 316–322.

Mussen, P., Honzik, M. P., & Eichorn, D. H. (1982). Early adult antecedents of life satisfaction at age 70. *Journal of Gerontology, 37,* 316–322.

Myers, G. C., (1985). Aging and worldwide population change. In R. Binstock & E. Shanas (Eds.), *Handbook of aging and the social sciences* (pp. 173–198). New York: Van Nostrand Reinhold.

Myers, J. E., & Salmon, H. E. (1984). Counseling programs for older persons: Status, shortcomings and potentialities. *Counseling Psychologist, 12,* 39–54.

Myers, J. K., Weissman, M. M., Tischler, G. L., Holzer, C. E., III, Leaf, P. J., Orvaschel, H., Anthony, J. C., Boyd, J. H., Burke, J. D., Kramer, M., & Stoltzmann, R. (1984). Six-month prevalence of psychiatric disorders in three communities. *Archives of General Psychiatry, 41,* 959–967.

Nardi, A. H. (1971). *Autoperception and heteroperception of personality traits in adolescents, adults, and the aged.* Unpublished doctoral dissertation, West Virginia University. *Dissertation Abstracts International, 32,* 6624.

Nardi, A. H. (1973). Person-perception research and the perception of life-span development. In P. B. Baltes & K. W. Schaie (Eds.), *Life-span developmental psychology: Personality and socialization* (pp. 285–301). New York: Academic Press.

National Council on the Aging. (1981). *Aging in the eighties: America in transition.* Washington, DC: Author.

National Institute of Mental Health. (1979a). *Issues in mental health and aging: Volume 1. Research.* Washington, DC: Department of Health, Education, and Welfare.

National Institute of Mental Health. (1979b). *Issues in mental health and aging: Volume 2. Training.* Washington, DC: Department of Health, Education, and Welfare.

National Institute of Mental Health. (1979c). *Issues in mental health and aging: Volume 3. Services.* Washington, DC: Department of Health, Education, and Welfare.

National Institute of Mental Health. (1980, December). NIMH seeks proposals on suicide and depression among the elderly. *Aging research and training news,* pp. 5–6.

Nebes, R. D., & Madden, D. J. (1988). Different patterns of cognitive slowing produced by Alzheimer's Disease and normal aging. *Psychology and Aging, 3,* 102–104.

Nehrke, M. (1974, November). *Actual and perceived attitudes toward death and self-concept in three-generational families.* Paper presented at the annual meeting of the Gerontological Society, Washington, DC.

Nehrke, M., Hulicka, I., & Morganti, J. (1980). Age differences in life satisfaction, locus of control and self-concept. *International Journal of Aging and Human Development, 11,* 25–33.

Neimeyer, R. A. (1987). Death anxiety. In H. Wass, F. M. Berardo, & R. A. Neimeyer (Eds.), *Dying:*

References

Facing the facts (2nd ed., pp. 97–136). Washington, DC: Hemisphere.

Nelson, F., & Farberow, N. (1980). Indirect self-destructive behavior in the nursing home patient. *Journal of Gerontology, 35,* 949–957.

Nesselroade, J. R. (1988). *Some implications of the trait-state distinction for the study of development over the life-span: the case of personality.* In P. B. Baltes, D. L. Featherman, R. L. Lerner (Eds.), *Life-span development and behavior* (Vol. 8) (pp. 163–191). Hillsdale, NJ: Lawrence Erlbaum.

Nesselroade, J. R., & Baltes, P. B. (1974). Adolescent personality development and historical change: 1970–72. *Monographs of the Society for Research in Child Development, 39* (Whole No. 154).

Nesselroade, J. R., Siegler, I., & Baltes, P. B. (1980). Regression to the mean and the study of change. *Psychological Bulletin, 88,* 622–637.

Neugarten, B. L. (1964). *Personality in middle and late life.* New York: Atherton Press.

Neugarten, B. L. (1968). The awareness of middle age. In B. L. Neugarten (Ed.), *Middle-age and aging: A reader in social psychology* (pp. 93–98). Chicago: University of Chicago Press.

Neugarten, B. L. (1973). Personality change in late life: A developmental perspective. In C. Eisdorfer & M. P. Lawton (Eds.), *The Psychology of adult development and aging*. Washington, DC: American Psychological Association.

Neugarten, B. L. (1976). Adaptation and the life cycle. *Counseling Psychologist, 6,* 16–20.

Neugarten, B. L. (1977). Personality and aging. In J. E. Birren & K. W. Schaie (Eds.), *Handbook of the psychology of aging* (pp. 626–649). New York: Van Nostrand Reinhold.

Neugarten, B. (1982). *Age or need?* Belmont, CA: Sage.

Neugarten, B. L., Crotty, W. F., & Tobin, S. (1964). *Personality in middle and late life.* New York: Atherton Press.

Neugarten, B. L., & Datan, N. (1973). Sociological perspectives on the life cycle. In P. B. Baltes & K. W. Schaie (Eds.), *Life-span developmental psychology: Personality and socialization* (pp. 53–69). New York: Academic Press.

Neugarten, B. L., & Hagestad, G. (1976). Aging and the life course. In R. H. Binstock & E. Shanas (Eds.), *Handbook of aging and the social sciences* (pp. 35–57). New York: Van Nostrand Reinhold.

Neugarten, B. L., Moore, J., & Lowe, J. (1965). Age norms, age constraints and adult socialization. *American Journal of Sociology, 70,* 710–717.

Neugarten, B. L., & Weinstein, K. K. (1964). The changing American grandparent. *Journal of Marriage and the Family, 26,* 199–204.

Newman, B. M. (1982). Mid-life development. In B. Wolman (Ed.), *Handbook of developmental psychology* (pp. 617–635). Englewood Cliffs, NJ: Prentice-Hall.

Newman, B., & Newman, P. (1979). *Development through life.* Homewood, IL: Dorsey.

Newman, B., & Newman, P. (1986). *Development through life* (3rd ed.). Homewood, IL: Dorsey.

Newton, N. A., Brauer, D., Gutmann, D., & Grunes, J. (1986). Psychodynamic therapy with the aged: A review. In T. L. Brink (Ed.), *Clinical gerontology* (pp. 205–230). New York: Haworth Press.

Nirenberg, T. D. (1983). Relocation of institutionalized elderly. *Journal of Consulting and Clinical Psychology, 51,* 693–701.

Noam, G. G., Higgins-O'Connell, R., & Goethals, G. W. (1982). Psychoanalytic approaches to developmental psychology. In B. B. Wolman (Ed.), *Handbook of developmental psychology* (pp. 23–43). Englewood Cliffs, NJ: Prentice-Hall.

Nock, S. L. (1982). The life-cycle approach to family analysis. In B. Wolman (Ed.), *Handbook of developmental psychology* (pp. 636–651). Englewood Cliffs, NJ: Prentice-Hall.

Noelker, L., & Harel, Z. (1978). Predictors of well-being and survival among institutionalized aged. *The Gerontologist, 18,* 562–567.

Norris, F. H., & Murrell, S. A. (1987). Older adult family stress and adaptation before and after bereavement. *Journal of Gerontology, 42,* 606–612.

Norton, A. J., & Glick, P. E. (1979). Marital instability in America: Past, present and future. In G. Levinger & O. C. Moles (Eds.), *Divorce and separation: Context, causes, and consequences* (pp. 6–19). New York: Basic Books.

Norris, F. H., & Murrell, S. A. (1987). Older adult family stress and adaptation before and after bereavement. *Journal of Gerontology, 42,* 606–612.

Obler, L. K., & Albert, M. L. (1985). Language skills across adulthood. In J. E. Birren & K. W. Schaie (Eds.), *Handbook of the psychology of aging* (pp. 463–473). New York: Van Nostrand Reinhold.

O'Brien, J. E., & Lind, D. (1976). [Review of *The Honorable Elders*, by E. Palmore.] *The Gerontologist, 19,* 560–561.

Ochs, A. L., Newberry, J., Lenhardt, M. L., & Harkins, S. W. (1985). Neural and vestibular aging associated with falls. In J. E. Birren & K. W. Schaie (Eds.), *Handbook of the psychology of aging* (pp. 378–399). New York: Van Nostrand Reinhold.

Oerter, R. (1986). Developmental task through the life span: A new approach to an old concept. In P. Baltes, D. Featherman, & R. Lerner (Eds.), *Life-span development and behavior* (Vol. 7, pp. 233–269). Hillsdale, NJ: Lawrence Erlbaum.

O'Hara, M. W., Hinnicks, J. V., Kohout, F. J.,

Wallace, R. B., & Lemke, J. H. (1986). Memory complaint and memory performance in depressed elderly. *Psychology and Aging, 1,* 208–214.

Ohta, R. J. (1981). Spatial problem solving: The response selection tendencies of young and elderly adults. *Experimental Aging Research, 1,* 81–84.

Ohta, R. J., Carlin, M. F., & Harmon, B. M. (1981). Auditory acuity and performance on the Mental Status Questionnaire in the elderly. *Journal of the American Geriatrics Society, 29,* 476–478.

Okun, M. A. (1976). Adult age and cautiousness in decision: A review of the literature. *Human Development, 19,* 220–233.

Okun, M. A., Siegler, E. C., & George, L. K. (1978). Cautiousness and verbal learning in adulthood. *Journal of Gerontology, 33,* 94–77.

Older Americans: The aging made gains in the 1970s, outpacing the rest of the population. (1983, Febrary 17). *The Wall Street Journal,* pp. 1, 2, 24, 25.

Olsho, L. W., Harkins, S. W., & Lenhardt, M. L. (1985). Aging and the auditory system. In J. E. Birren and K. W. Schaie (Eds.), *Handbook of the psychology of aging* (2nd ed., pp. 332–377). New York: Van Nostrand Reinhold.

O'Meara, J. R. (1977). *Retirement: Reward or rejection?* New York: The Conference Board.

Omenn, G. S. (1977). Behavior genetics. In J. E. Birren and K. W. Schaie (Eds.), *Handbook of the psychology of aging* (pp. 190–218). New York: Van Nostrand Reinhold.

Osgood, C. E., Suci, G. J., & Tannenbaum, P. H. (1957). *The measurement of meaning.* Chicago: University of Illinois Press.

Osgood, N. J. (1983). Patterns of aging in retirement communities: Typology of residents. *Journal of Applied Gerontology, 2,* 28–43.

Osgood, N. J. (1985). *Suicide in the elderly.* Germantown, MD: Aspen.

Osipow, S. H. (1983). *Theories of career development.* Englewood Cliffs, NJ: Prentice-Hall.

Osipow, S. H. (1987). Counseling psychology: Theory, research, and practice in career counseling. *Annual Review of Psychology, 38,* 257–278.

Osipow, S. H., Doty, R. E., & Spokane, A. R. (1985). Occupational stress, strain, and coping across the life span. *Journal of Vocational Behavior, 27,* 98–108.

Osterweis, M., Solomon, F., & Green, M. (1984). *Bereavement: Reactions, consequences, and care.* Washington, DC: National Academy Press.

Otero-Sabogal, R., Hayslip, B., & Sabogal, F. (1987, August). *Marital strain, parental strain, and marital quality: A causal analysis.* Paper presented at the annual convention of the American Psychological Association.

Overton, W. F., & Reese, H. W. (1973). Models of development: Methodological implications. In J. R. Nesselroade & H. W. Reese (Eds.), *Life-span*

developmental psychology: Methodological issues (pp. 65–86). New York: Academic Press.

Owen, G., Fulton, R., & Markusen, E. (1983). Death at a distance: A study of family survivors. *Omega, 13,* 191–226.

Palmore, E. (1969). Physical, mental and social factors in predicting longevity. *The Gerontologist, 9,* 103–108.

Palmore, E. (1975a). What can the U.S. learn from Japan about aging? *The Gerontologist, 15,* 64–67.

Palmore, E. (1975b). *The honorable elders.* Durham, NC: Duke University Press.

Palmore, E. (1979). Predictors of successful aging. *The Gerontologist, 16,* 441–446.

Palmore, E. (Ed.). (1980). *International handbook on aging.* Westport, CT: Greenwood Press.

Palmore, E. (1984). Longevity in Abkhasia: A re-evaluation. *The Gerontologist, 24,* 95–96.

Palmore, E., & Cleveland, W. (1976). Aging, terminal decline, and terminal drop. *Journal of Gerontology, 31,* 76–81.

Palmore, E., Fillenbaum, G. G., & George, L. K. (1984). Consequences of retirement. *Journal of Gerontology, 39,* 109–116.

Palmore, E., George, L. K., & Fillenbaum, G. G. (1982). Predictors of retirement. *Journal of Gerontology, 37,* 733–742.

Panek, P. E. (1981). On the relationship between auditory and visual selective attention in young and old adults. *Experimental Aging Research, 7,* 497–499.

Panek, P. E. (1982a). Do beginning psychology of aging students believe 10 common myths of aging? *Teaching of Psychology, 9,* 104–105.

Panek, P. E. (1982b). Relationship between field-dependence/independence and personality in older adult females. *Perceptual and Motor Skills, 54,* 811–814.

Panek, P. E. (1982c, November). *Cautiousness and auditory selective attention performance of older adults.* Paper presented at the 35th annual meeting of the Gerontological Society of America, Boston, MA.

Panek, P. E. (1984, February). *Stimulating classroom discussion regarding negative attitudes toward aging.* Paper presented at the 10th annual meeting of the Association for Gerontology in Higher Education (AGHE), Indianapolis, IN.

Panek, P. E., Barrett, G. V., Alexander, R. A., & Sterns, H. L. (1979). Age and self-selected performance pace on a visual monitoring inspection task. *Aging and Work: A Journal on Age, Work and Retirement, 2,* 183–191.

Panek, P. E., Barrett, G. V., Sterns, H. L., &

582

References

Alexander, R. A. (1977). A review of age changes in perceptual information processing ability with regard to driving. *Experimental Aging Research, 3,* 387–449.

Panek, P. E., Barrett, G. V., Sterns, H. L., & Alexander, R. A. (1978). Age differences in perceptual style, selective attention, and perceptual-motor reaction time. *Experimental Aging Research, 4,* 377–387.

Panek, P. E., & McGown, W. P. (1981). Risk-taking across the life-span as measured by an intrusion-omission ratio on a selective attention task. *Perceptual and Motor Skills, 52,* 733–734.

Panek, P. E., & Merluzzi, T. V. (1983). Influence of client age on counselor trainees' assessment of case material. *Teaching of Psychology, 10,* 227–228.

Panek, P. E., & Rearden, J. (1987). Age and gender effects on accident types for rural drivers. *Journal of Applied Gerontology, 6,* 332–346.

Panek, P. E., & Rush, M. C. (1981). Simultaneous examination of age related differences in the ability to maintain and reorient auditory selective attention. *Experimental Aging Research, 7,* 405–416.

Panek, P. E., & Rush, M. C., & Greenawalt, J. P. (1977). Current sex stereotypes of 25 occupations. *Psychological Reports, 40,* 212–214.

Panek, P. E., Rush, M. C., & Slade, L. A. (1984). An exploration examination on the locus of the age-Stroop interference relationship. *Journal of Geriatric Psychology, 145,* 209–216.

Panek, P. E., & Sterns, H. L. (1985). Self-evaluation, actual performance and preference across the life span. *Experimental Aging Research, 11,* 221–223.

Panek, P. E., Stoner, S. B., & Beystehner, K. M. (1983). Behavioral rigidity in young and old adults. *Journal of Psychology, 114,* 199–206.

Panek, P. E., Wagner, E. E., Barrett, G. V., & Alexander, R. A. (1978). Selected Hand Test personality variables related to accidents in female drivers. *Journal of Personality Assessment, 42,* 355–357.

Panek, P. E., Wagner, E. E., & Kennedy-Zwergle, K. (1983). A review of projective test findings with older adults. *Journal of Personality Assessment, 47,* 562–582.

Papalia, D., & Bielby, D. D. (1974) Cognitive functioning in middle aged and elderly adults: A review of research based on Piaget's theory. *Human Development, 17,* 424–443.

Papalia, D., & Olds, S. (1982). *A child's world.* New York: McGraw-Hill.

Pardini, A. (1984, April/May). Exercise, vitality, and aging. *Aging,* pp. 19–29.

Parham, I. A., Priddy, J. M., McGovern, T. V., &

Richman, C. M. (1982). Group psychotherapy with the elderly: Problems and prospects. *Psychotherapy: Theory, Research and Practice, 19,* 437–443.

Parkes, C. (1973). *Bereavement: Studies of grief in adult life.* New York: International Universities Press.

Parkes, C. M., & Weiss, R. S. (1983). *Recovery from bereavement.* New York: Basic Books.

Parnes, H. S., Crowley, J. E., Haurin, R. J., Less, L. J., Morgan, W. R., Mott, F. L., & Nestel, G. (1985). *Retirement among American men.* Lexington, KY: Lexington Books.

Parnes, H. S., & Meyer, J. A. (1972). Withdrawal from the labor force by middle-aged men. In G. M. Shatto (Ed.), *Employment of the middle-aged* (pp. 63–86). Springfield, IL: Thomas.

Pastalan, L. A., Mantz, R. K., & Merrill, J. (1973). The simulation of age related losses: A new approach to the study of environmental barriers. In W. R. E. Presier (Ed.), *Environmental design research* (Vol. 1, pp. 383–392). Strondsberg, PA: Powder, Hutchinson & Ross.

Pasuth, P. M., & Cook, F. L. (1985). Effects of television viewing on knowledge and attitudes about older adults. *The Gerontologist, 25,* 69–77.

Pattison, E. M. (1977). *The experience of dying.* Englewood Cliffs, NJ: Prentice-Hall.

Peacock, E. W., & Talley, W. M. (1985). Developing leisure competence: A goal for late adulthood. *Educational Gerontology, 11,* 261–276.

Peck, M. (1984). Youth suicide. In H. Wass & C. Corr (Eds.), *Childhood and death* (pp. 279–290). Washington, DC: Hemisphere/McGraw-Hill.

Peck, R. C. (1968). Psychological developments in the second half of life. In B. L. Neugarten (Ed.), *Middle age and aging* (pp. 44–49). Chicago: University of Chicago Press.

Pedrick-Cornell, C., & Gelles, R. J. (1982). Elder abuse: The status of current knowledge. *Family Relations, 31,* 457–465.

Pellegrino, J., & Glaser, R. (1979). Cognitive correlates and components in the analysis of individual differences. In R. Sternberg & D. Detterman (Eds.), *Human intelligence: Perspectives on its theory and measurement* (pp. 61–88). Norwood, NJ: Ablex.

Penrod, S. (1986). *Social psychology* (2nd ed.). Engelwood Cliffs, NJ: Prentice-Hall.

Perlick, D. & Atkins, A. (1984). Variations in reported age of a patient: A source of bias in the diagnosis of depression and dementia. *Journal of Consulting and Clinical Psychology, 52,* 812–820.

Perlmutter, M. (1978). What is memory aging the memory of? *Developmental Psychology, 14,* 330–345.

Perlmutter, M. (1983). Learning and memory through adulthood. In M. W. Riley, B. B. Hess, & K. Bond (Eds.), *Aging in society* (pp. 219–242). Hillsdale, NJ: Lawrence Erlbaum.

Perlmutter, M., Metzger, R., Miller, K., & Nezevorski, T. (1980). Memory of historical events. *Experimental Aging Research, 6,* 47–60.

Perlmutter, M., & Mitchell, D. (1982). The appearance and disappearance of age difference in adult memory. In F. I. M. Cariak & S. Trehub (Eds.), *Aging and cognitive processes* (pp. 127–144). New York: Plenum.

Perosa, S. L., & Perosa, L. M. (1983). The mid-career crisis: A description of the psychological dynamics of transition and adaptation. *The Vocational Guidance Quarterly, 32,* 69–79.

Pervin, L. A. (1968). Performance and satisfaction as a function of individual-environment fit. *Psychological Bulletin, 69,* 56–68.

Peskin, H., & Livson, F. (1981). Uses of the past in psychological health. In D. Eichorn, N. Haan, J. Clausen, M. Honzik, & P. Mussen (Eds.), *Present and past in middle life* (pp. 153–181). New York: Academic Press.

Peterson, D. (1985). A history of education for older learners. In D. B. Lumsden (Ed.), *The older adult as learner* (pp. 1–24). Washington, DC: Hemisphere.

Peterson, D., & Eden, D. (1981). Cognitive style and the older learner. *Educational Gerontology, 7,* 57–66.

Peterson, J. A. (1980). Social-psychological aspects of death and dying and mental health. In J. E. Birren & R. B. Sloane (Eds.), *Handbook of mental health and aging* (pp. 922–942). Englewood Cliffs, NJ: Prentice-Hall.

Peterson, J., & Briley, M. (1977). *Widows and widowhood: A creative approach to being alone.* New York: Association Press.

Pfeffer, C. R. (1981). The family system of suicidal children. *American Journal of Psychotherapy, 35,* 330–341.

Pfeffer, C. R. (1984). Death preoccupations and suicidal behavior in children. In H. Wass & C. Corr (Eds.), *Childhood and death* (pp. 261–290). Washington, DC: Hemisphere/McGraw-Hill.

Pfeiffer, E. (1970). Survival in old age: Physical, psychological and social correlates of longevity. *Journal of the American Geriatrics Society, 18,* 273–285.

Pfeiffer, E. (1976). *Multidimensional functional assessment: The OARS methodology.* Durham, NC: Center for Study of Aging and Human Development.

Pfeiffer, E. (1977). Psychopathology and social pathology. In J. E. Birren & K. W. Schaie (Eds.), *Handbook of the psychology of aging* (pp. 650–671). New York: Van Nostrand Reinhold.

Pfeiffer, E., Verwoerdt, A., & Wang, H. S. (1968). Sexual behavior in aged men and women. *Archives of Genetic Psychiatry, 19,* 753–758.

Piaget, J., & Inhelder, B. (1969). *The psychology of the child.* New York: Basic Books.

Pierce, B., & Chiriboga, D. (1979). Dimensions of adult self concept. *Journal of Gerontology, 34,* 80–85.

Pinder, M., & Hayslip, B. (1981). Cognitive, attitudinal and affective aspects of death and dying in adulthood: Implications for care providers. *Educational Gerontology, 6,* 107–123.

Piovesana, G. K. (1979). The aged in Chinese and Japanese cultures. In J. Hendricks & L. D. Hendricks (Eds.), *Dimensions of aging: Readings* (pp. 13–20). Cambridge, MA: Winthrop.

Planek, T. W. (1982). Home accidents: a continuing social problem. *Accident Analysis and Prevention, 14,* 107–120.

Planek, T. W., & Fowler, R. C. (1971). Traffic accident problems and exposure characteristic of the aging driver. *Journal of Gerontology, 26,* 224–230.

Plath, D. W. (1973). Ecstasy years—old age in Japan. *Pacific Years, 46,* 421–428.

Plomin, R., Pederson, N. L., McClearn, G. E., Nesselroade, J. R., & Bergeman, C. S. (1988). EAS temperaments during the last half of the life span: Twins reared apart and twins reared together. *Psychology and Aging, 3,* 43–59.

Plude, D. J., & Hoyer, W. L. (1981). Adult age differences in visual search as a function of stimulus mapping and processing level. *Journal of Gerontology, 36,* 598–604.

Plude, D. J., Kaye, D. B., Hoyer, W. J., Post, T. A., Saynisch, M. J., & Hahn, M. V. (1983). Aging and visual search under consistent and varied mapping. *Developmental Psychology, 19,* 508–512.

Pollack, R. H. (1966). Temporal range of apparent movement as a function of age and intelligence. *Psychonomic Science, 5,* 243–244.

Poon, L. (1985). Differences in human memory with aging. In J. E. Birren & K. W. Schaie (Eds.), *Handbook of the psychology of aging* (pp. 427–462). New York: Van Nostrand Reinhold.

Poon, L., & Shaffer, G. (1982, August). *Prospective memory in young and elderly adults.* Paper presented at the annual convention of the American Psychological Association, Washington, DC.

Popkin, S., Schaie, K. W., & Krauss, I. (1983). Age-fair assessment of psychometric intelligence. *Educational Gerontology, 9,* 47–55.

Post, F. (1980). Paranoid, schizophrenia-like, and schizophrenic states in the aged. In J. E. Birren & R. B. Sloane (Eds.), *The handbook of mental health and aging.* Englewood Cliffs, NJ: Prentice-Hall.

Powell, L. A., & Williamson, J. B. (1985, Summer). The mass media and the aged. *Social Policy,* pp. 38–49.

Powell, S. & Berg, R. (1985). Elder abuse: A multi-case study. *Educational Gerontology, 13,* 71–83.

Powers, E. A., & Bultena, G. L. (1976). Sex

References

differences in intimate friendships of old age. *Journal of Marriage and the Family, 38,* 739–747.

President's Commission on Mental Health. (1978). *Mental health in America: 1978. Findings and assessment.* Washington, DC: U.S. Government Printing Office.

Quilter, R. E., Giambra, L. M., & Benson, P. E. (1983). Longitudinal age changes in vigilance over an eighteen-year interval. *Journal of Gerontology, 38,* 51–54.

Quinn, J. F. (1977). Microeconomic determinants of early retirement: A cross-sectional view of white married men. *Journal of Human Resources, 12,* 329–346.

Rabbitt, P. M. A. (1965). Age and discrimination between complex stimuli. In A. T. Welford & J. E. Birren (Eds.), *Behavior, aging, and the nervous system* (pp. 35–53). Springfield, IL: Thomas.

Rabbitt, P. M. A. (1968). Age and the use of structure in transmitted information. In G. A. Tallard (Ed.), *Human aging and behavior: Recent advances in research and theory* (pp. 75–92). New York: Academic Press.

Rabinowitz, J. C., Ackerman, B. P., Craik, F. I. M., & Hinchley, J. (1982). Aging and metamemory: The roles of relatedness and imagery. *Journal of Gerontology, 37,* 688–695.

Raphael, B. (1983). *The anatomy of bereavement.* New York: Basic Books.

Rapoport, R., Rapoport, R. N., & Strelitz, Z. (1977). *Fathers, mothers, and society.* New York: Basic Books.

Raskin, A. (1979). Signs and symptoms of psychopathology in the elderly. In A. Raskin & L. Jarvik (Eds.), *Psychiatric symptoms and cognitive loss in the elderly: Evaluation and assessment techniques* (pp. 3–18). New York: Halsted.

Raskin, A., & Jarvik, L. (1979). *Psychiatric symptoms and cognitive loss in the elderly: Evaluation and assessment techniques.* Washington, DC: Hemisphere Publishing.

Raskind, C. L., Hoyer, W. J., & Rebok, G. W. (1983, November). *Familiarization effects on alertness and encoding in younger and older adults.* Paper presented at the 36th annual scientific meeting of the Gerontological Society of America, San Francisco, CA.

Rawlins, M. E., Rawlins, L. D., & Rearden, J. (1985). Stresses and coping strategies of dual-career couples affiliated with a university. *Education Journal, 18,* 26–30.

Ray, D., McKinney, K., & Ford, C. (1987). Differences in psychologists' ratings of older and younger clients. *The Gerontologist, 27,* 82–86.

Redick, R. W., & Taube, C. A. (1980). Demography and mental health care of the aged. In J. E. Birren & R. B. Sloane (Eds.), *Handbook of mental health and aging* (pp. 57–71). Englewood Cliffs, NJ: Prentice-Hall.

Reedy, M. N., Birren, J. E., & Schaie, K. W. (1982). Age and sex differences in satisfying love relationships across the life span. *Human Development, 24,* 52–66.

Rees, J. N., & Botwinick, J. (1971). Detection and decision factors in auditory behavior of the elderly. *Journal of Gerontology, 26,* 133–136.

Reese, H. W., & Lippsitt, L. P. (1970). *Experimental child psychology.* New York: Academic Press.

Reese, H. W., & Overton, W. F. (1970). Models of development and theories of development. In L. R. Goulet & P. B. Baltes (Eds.), *Life-span developmental psychology: Research and theory* (pp. 116–145). New York: Academic Press.

Reese, H., & Smyer, M. (1983). The dimensionalization of life events. In E. Callahan & K. McCluskey (Eds.), *Life-span developmental psychology: Nonnormative life events* (pp. 1–33). New York: Academic Press.

Reflection on old age: I have lived my life. (1977, August). *Washington Star.*

Reichard, S., Livson, P., & Peterson, P. (1962). *Aging and personality.* New York: Wiley.

Reidl, R. (1981). Behavioral therapies. In C. Eisdorfer (Eds.), *Annual review of gerontology and geriatrics* (pp. 148–180). New York: Springer.

Reifler, B., Cox, G., & Hanley, R. (1981). Problems of mentally ill elderly as perceived by patients, families and clinicians. *The Gerontologist, 21,* 165–170.

Reinert, G. (1970). Comparative factor analytic studies of intelligence throughout the human life-span. In L. Goulet & P. Baltes (Eds.), *Life-span developmental psychology: Research and theory* (pp. 468–484). New York: Academic Press.

Reno, R. (1979). Attribution for success and failure as a function of perceived age. *Journal of Gerontology, 34,* 709–715.

Reno, V. (1976). *Why men stop working before age 65. An information paper prepared for the House Select Committee on Aging.* Washington, DC: U.S. Government Printing Office.

Resnick, L. B. (1976). Introduction: Changing conceptions of intelligence. In L. Resnick (Ed.), *The nature of intelligence* (pp. 1–10). Hillsdale, NJ: Lawrence Erlbaum.

Resnick, L. B. (1979) The future of IQ testing in education. In R. J. Sternberg & D. K. Detterman (Eds.), *Human intelligence* (pp. 203–216). Norwood, NJ: Ablex.

Reynolds, D., & Kalish, R. (1974). Anticipation of futurity as a function of ethnicity and age. *Journal of Gerontology, 29,* 224–231.

Reynolds, D., & Kalish, R. (1976). Death rates, ethnicity and the ethnic press. *Ethnicity, 3,* 305–316.

Reynolds, L. F., Masters, S. H., & Moser, C. H. (1987). *Economics of labor.* Englewood Cliffs, NJ: Prentice-Hall.

Rhodes, S. R. (1983). Age-related differences in work attitudes and behavior: a review and conceptual analysis. *Psychological Bulletin, 93,* 328–367.

Rhudick, R. J., & Dibner, A. (1961). Age, personality and health correlates of death concern in normal aged individuals. *Journal of Gerontology, 16,* 44–49.

Rhyne, D. (1981). Bases of marital satisfaction among men and women. *Journal of Marriage and the Family, 43,* 941–954.

Rice, D. P. (1981, March/April). The aging of America: Economic woes may dim the elderly's golden years. *The Review,* p. 3.

Rice, F. P. (1979). *Marriage and parenthood.* Boston: Allyn & Bacon.

Rich, B. M., & Baum, M. (1984). *The aging: A guide to public policy.* Pittsburgh, PA: University of Pittsburgh Press.

Richards, W. S., & Thorpe, G. L. (1978). Behavioral approaches to the problems of later life. In M. Storandt, I. Siegler, & M. F. Elias (Eds.), *The clinical psychology of aging* (pp. 253–276). New York: Plenum.

Riegel, K. F. (1973). Developmental psychology and society: Some historical and ethical considerations. In J. R. Nesselroade & P. B. Baltes (Eds.), *Life-span developmental psychology: Methodological issues* (pp. 1–24). New York: Academic Press.

Riegel, K. F. (1975). Adult life crises: A dialectical interpretation of development. In N. Datan & L. Ginsburg (Eds.), *Life-span development psychology: Normative life crises* (pp. 99–128). New York: Academic Press.

Riegel, K. F. (1976). The dialectics of human development. *American Psychologist, 31,* 689–700.

Riegel, K. F. (1977a). History of psychological gerontology. In J. E. Birren and K. W. Schaie (Eds.), *Handbook of the psychology of aging* (pp. 70–102). New York: Van Nostrand Reinhold.

Riegel, K. F. (1977b). The dialectics of time. In N. Datan & H. Reese (Eds.), *Life-span developmental psychology: Dialectical perspectives on experimental research* (pp. 3–45). New York: Academic Press.

Riegel, K. F., & Riegel, R. M. (1972). Development and death. *Developmental Psychology, 6,* 306–319.

Riegel, K. F., Riegel, R. M., & Meyer, G. (1967). Sociopsychological factors of aging: A cohort sequential analysis. *Human Development, 10,* 27–56.

Riley, M., Foner, A., & Associates (1968). *Aging and society: Vol. 1: An inventory of research findings.* New York: Russell Sage Foundation.

Riley, M. W., Johnson, M. W., & Foner, A. (1972). *Aging and society* (Vol. 3). New York: Russell Sage Foundation.

Ripley, T., & O'Brien, S. (1976). Career planning for leisure. *Journal of College Placement, 36,* 54–58.

Robbins, P. (1978). *Successful midlife career change.* New York: AMACON.

Roberts, J., Kimsey, L., Logan, D., & Shaw, G. (1970). How aged in nursing homes view death and dying. *Geriatrics, 25,* 115–119.

Roberts, P., & Newton, P. M. (1987). Levinsonian studies of women's adult development. *Psychology and Aging, 2,* 154–163.

Roberto, K. A., & Scott, J. P. (1986). Friendships of older men and women: Exchange patterns and satisfaction. *Psychology and Aging, 1,* 103–109.

Robertson, J. (1976). Significance of grandparents: Perceptions of young adult grandchildren. *The Gerontologist, 16,* 137–140.

Robertson, J. F. (1977). Grandmotherhood: A study of role conceptions. *Journal of Marriage and the Family, 39,* 165–174.

Robertson-Tchabo, E. A. (1980). Cognitive skill and training for the elderly: Why should "old dogs" require new tricks. In C. W. Poon, J. Fozard, L. Cermak, D. Arenberg, & L. Thompson (Eds.), *New directions in memory and aging* (pp. 511–518). Hillsdale, NJ: Lawrence Erlbaum.

Robertson-Tchabo, E., Hausman, C., & Arenberg, D. (1976). A classical mnemonic for older learners: A trip that works! *Educational Gerontology, 1,* 215–226.

Robey, B. (1984, February). Entering middle-age. *American Demographics,* p. 4.

Robins, L. N., West, P. A., & Murphy, G. E. (1977). The high rate of suicide among older white men: A study testing ten hypotheses. *Social Psychiatry, 12,* 1–20.

Robinson, P. K., Coberly, S., & Paul, C. E. (1985). Work and retirement. In R. Binstock & E. Shanas (Eds.), *Handbook of aging and the social sciences* (pp. 503–527). New York: Van Nostrand Reinhold.

Rodabough, T. (1980). Alternatives to the stages model of the dying process. *Death Education, 4,* 1–19.

Rodin, J. & Langer, E. (1977). Long-term effects of a control-relevant intervention with the institutionalized aged. *Journal of Personality and Social Psychology, 34,* 314–350.

Rodin, J. & Langer, E. (1980). Aging labels: The decline of control and the fall of self-esteem. *Journal of Social Issues, 36,* 12–29.

Rogers, C. (1961). *On becoming a person: A therapist's view of psychotherapy.* Boston: Houghton-Mifflin.

Rollins, B. C., & Cannon, K. L. (1974). Marital

satisfaction over the family life cycle: A reevaluation. *Journal of Marriage and the Family, 36,* 271–282.

Rollins, B. C., & Feldman, H. (1970). Marital satisfaction over the life cycle. *Journal of Marriage and the Family, 32,* 20–28.

Romaniuk, J., and Romaniuk, M. (1982). Participation motives of older adults in higher education: The elderhostel experience. *The Gerontologist, 22,* 364–368.

Romaniuk, M. (1981). Reminiscence and the second half of life. *Experimental Aging Research, 7,* 315–336.

Romaniuk, M. & Romaniuk, J. (1981). Looking back: An analysis of reminiscence functions and triggers. *Experimental Aging Research, 7,* 477–490.

Root, W. (1981). Injuries at work are fewer among older employees. *Monthly Labor Review, 104,* 30–34.

Rose, C. L. (1964). Social factors in longevity. *The Gerontologist, 4,* 27–37.

Roseman, I. (1980). Bodily changes with aging. In E. W. Busse & D. G. Blazer (Eds.), *Handbook of geriatric psychiatry* (pp. 125–146). New York: Van Nostrand Reinhold.

Rosen, B., & Jerdee, T. H. (1976). The nature of job-related stereotypes. *Journal of Applied Psychology, 61,* 180–183.

Rosenstein, J., & Swenson, E. (1980). Behavioral approaches to therapy with the elderly. In S. S. Sargent (Ed.), *Nontraditional therapy and counseling with the aging* (pp. 178–198). New York: Springer.

Rosenthal, R., & Rosnow, R. (1984). *Essentials of behavioral research: Methods and data analysis.* New York: McGraw-Hill.

Rosewater, L. B. (1985). On MMPI profiles of battered women. *Journal of Counseling and Development, 63,* 387.

Rosow, I. (1974). *Socialization to old age.* Berkeley: University of California Press.

Rosow, I. (1978). What is a cohort and why? *Human Development, 21,* 65–75.

Rosow, I. (1985). Status and role change through the life cycle. In R. Binstock & E. Shanas (Eds.), *Handbook of aging and the social sciences* (pp. 62–93). New York: Van Nostrand Reinhold.

Ross, E. (1968). Effects of challenging and supportive instructions on verbal learning in older persons. *Journal of Educational Psychology, 59,* 261–266.

Rossi, A. (1980). Aging and parenthood in the middle years. In P. B. Baltes & O. G. Brim (Eds.), *Life-span development and behavior.* (Vol. 3, pp. 138–205). New York: Academic Press.

Rowe, E. J., & Schnore, M. M. (1971). Item concreteness and reported strategies in paired-associate learning as a function of age. *Journal of Gerontology, 26,* 470–475.

Rowe, J. W., & Minaker, K. L. (1985). Geriatric medicine. In C. E. Finch and E. L. Schneider (Eds.), *Handbook of the biology of aging* (2nd ed., pp. 932–960). New York: Van Nostrand Reinhold.

Rowland, K. (1977). Environmental events predicting death for the elderly. *Psychological Bulletin, 84,* 349–372.

Rubin, J. (1976). *Sexual life after sixty.* New York: Basic Books.

Rubin, K. H. & Brown, I. D. R. (1975). A life-span look at person-perception and its relationship to communicative interaction. *Journal of Gerontology, 30,* 461–468.

Rust, J. O., Barnard, D., & Oster, G. D. (1979). WAIS verbal-performance differences among elderly when controlling for fatigue. *Psychological Reports, 44,* 489–490.

Rybash, J. M., Hoyer, W. J., & Roodin, P. A. (1986). *Adult cognition and aging.* New York: Pergamon Press.

Rychlak, J. F. (1973). *Introduction to personality and psychotherapy.* Boston: Houghton Mifflin.

Rychlak, J. F. (1980). *An introduction to personality and psychotherapy* (2nd ed.). Boston: Houghton Mifflin.

Ryff, C. (1984). Personality development from the inside: The subjective experience of change in adulthood and aging. In P. B. Baltes & O. G. Brim (Eds.), *Life-span development and behavior* (pp. 244–279). New York: Academic Press.

Rytina, N. F., & Bianchi, S. M. (1984, March). Occupational reclassification and changes in distribution by gender. *Monthly Labor Review* (U.S. Department of Labor, Bureau of Labor Statistics), pp. 11–17.

Salamon, M. J., & Charytan, P. (1984). *The Clinical Gerontologist, 2,* 25–35.

Salend, E., Kane, A., Satz, M., & Pynoos, J. (1984). Elder abuse reporting: Limitations of statutes. *The Gerontologist, 24,* 61–69.

Salthouse, T. A. (1980). Age and memory: Strategies for localizing the loss. In L. Poon, J. Fozard, L. Cermak, D. Arenberg, & L. Thompson (Eds.), *New directions in memory and aging* (pp. 47–65). Hillsdale, NJ: Lawrence Erlbaum.

Salthouse, T. (1982). *Adult cognition.* New York: Springer-Verlag.

Salthouse, T. A. (1984). The skill of typing. *Scientific American, 250,* 128–136.

Salthouse, T. A. (1985). Speed of behavior and its implications for cognition. In J. E. Birren and K. W. Schaie (Eds.), *Handbook of the psychology of aging* (2nd ed., pp. 400–426). New York: Van Nostrand Reinhold.

Salthouse, T. A., & Somberg, B. L. (1982a). Isolating the age deficit in speeded performance. *Journal of Gerontology, 37,* 59–63.

Salthouse, T. A., & Somberg, B. L. (1982b). Skilled performance: The effects of adult age and experience on elementary processes. *Journal of Experimental Psychology: General, 111,* 176–207.

Salvendy, G. (1974). Discrimination in performance assessments against the aged. *Perceptual and Motor Skills, 39,* 1087–1099.

Salzman, C., & Shader, R. (1979). Clinical evaluation of depression in the elderly. In A. Raskin & L. Jarvik (Eds.), *Psychiatric symptoms and cognitive loss in the elderly: Evaluation and assessment techniques* (pp. 39–74). Washington, DC: Hemisphere Publishing.

Sanders, K. (1979–1980). A comparison of older and younger spouses in bereavement outcome. *Omega, 11,* 217–232.

Sanders, K. (1980–1981). A comparison of adult bereavement in the death of a spouse, child, and parent. *Omega, 10,* 303–322.

Santos, J., Hubbard, R. W., McIntosh, J. L., & Eisner, H. R. (1984). Community mental health and the elderly: Training approaches. *Journal of Community Psychology, 12,* 359–368.

Santos, J. F., & Vandenbos, G. R. (1982). *Psychology and the older adult: Challenges for training in the 1980s.* Washington, DC: American Psychological Association.

Sarafino, E. P., & Armstrong, J. W. (1986). *Child and adolescent development.* St. Paul, MN: West.

Sarason, S. B. (1977). *Work, aging, and social change.* New York: Free Press.

Sarason, S. B., Sarason, E. K., & Cowden, P. (1975). Aging and the nature of work. *American Psychologist, 30,* 584–592.

Sargent, S. (1980). Why non-traditional therapy and counseling with the aged? In S. Sargent (Ed.), *Nontraditional therapy and counseling with the aging* (pp. 1–11). New York: Academic Press.

Sargent, S. S. (1982). Therapy and self-actualization in the later years via nontraditional approaches. *Psychotherapy: Theory, Research and Practice, 19,* 522–531.

Schaffer, G., & Poon, L. W. (1982). Individual variability in memory training with the elderly. *Educational Gerontology, 8,* 217–229.

Schaie, K. W. (1958). Rigidity-flexibility and intelligence: A cross-sectional study of the adult life-span from 20–70 years. *Psychological Monographs, 72* (9, Whole No. 462), 1–26.

Schaie, K. W. (1962). A field-theory approach to age changes in cognitive behavior. *Vita Humana, 7,* 129–141.

Schaie, K. W. (1965). A general model for the study of developmental problems. *Psychological Bulletin, 64,* 92–107.

Schaie, K. W. (1967). Age changes and age differences. *The Gerontologist, 7,* 128–132.

Schaie, K. W. (1970). A reinterpretation of age-related changes in cognitive structure and functioning. In L. Goulet & P. B. Baltes (Eds.), *Life-span developmental psychology: Research and theory* (pp. 486–508). New York: Academic Press.

Schaie, K. W. (1973). Methodological problems in descriptive developmental research on adulthood and aging. In J. R. Nesselroade & H. W. Reese (Eds.), *Life-span developmental psychology: Methodological issues* (pp. 253–280).

Schaie, K. W. (1977). Quasi-experimental designs in the psychology of aging. In J. E. Birren & K. W. Schaie (Eds.), *Handbook of the psychology of aging* (pp. 39–69). New York: Van Nostrand Reinhold.

Schaie, K. W. (1977–1978). Toward a stage theory of adult cognitive development. *Aging and Human Development, 8,* 129–138.

Schaie, K. W. (1978). External validity in the assessment of intellectual development in adulthood. *Journal of Gerontology, 33,* 696–701.

Schaie, K. W. (1979). The primary mental abilities in adulthood: An exploration in the development of psychometric intelligence. In P. Baltes & O. Brim (Eds.), *Life-span development and behavior* (Vol. 2, pp. 68–115). New York: Academic Press.

Schaie, K. W. (1983). Age changes in intelligence. In D. S. Woodruff & J. E. Birren (Eds.), *Aging: Scientific perspectives and social issues* (2nd ed., pp. 150–163). New York: Van Nostrand Reinhold.

Schaie, K. W. (1986). Beyond calendar definitions of age, time and cohort: The general developmental model revisited. *Developmental Review, 6,* 252–277.

Schaie, K. W., & Baltes, P. B. (1975). On sequential strategies in developmental research: Description or explanation? *Human Development, 18,* 384–890.

Schaie, K. W., & Baltes, P. B. (1977). Some faith helps to see the forest: A final comment on the Horn and Donaldson myth of the Baltes-Schaie position on adult intelligence. *American Psychologist, 32,* 1118–1120.

Schaie, K. W., & Geiwitz, J. (1982). *Adult development and aging.* Boston: Little, Brown.

Schaie, K. W., & Gribbin, K. (1975). Adult development and aging. *Annual Review of Psychology, 26,* 65–96.

Schaie, K. W., & Hertzog, C. (1983). Fourteen-year cohort sequential analyses of adult intellectual development. *Developmental Psychology, 19,* 531–543.

Schaie, K. W., Labouvie, G., & Barrett, T. (1973). Selective attrition effects in a fourteen-year study of adult intelligence. *Journal of Gerontology, 28,* 328–334.

Schaie, K. W., Labouvie, G. V., & Buech, B. U.

References

(1973). Generational and cohort-specific differences in adult cognitive functioning. *Developmental Psychology, 9,* 151–166.

Schaie, K. W., & Labouvie-Vief, G. (1974). Generational versus ontogenetic components of change in adult cognitive behavior: A fourteen-year cross-sequential study. *Developmental Psychology, 10,* 305–320.

Schaie, K. W. & Parham, I. A. (1960, 1975). *Test of behavioral rigidity: Manual.* Pala Alto, CA: Counsulting Psychologists Press.

Schaie, K. W. & Parham, I. (1976). Stability of adult personality traits: Fact or fable? *Journal of Personality and Social Psychology, 34,* 146–158.

Schaie, K. W., & Schaie, J. P. (1977). Clinical assessment and aging. In J. E. Birren & K. W. Schaie (Eds.), *Handbook of the psychology of aging* (pp. 692–723). New York: Van Nostrand Reinhold.

Schaie, K. W., & Strother, C. (1968a). A cross-sequential study of age changes in cognitive behavior. *Psychological Bulletin, 70,* 671–680.

Schaie, K. W., & Strother, C. (1968b). The effects of time and cohort differences on the interpretation of age changes in cognitive behavior. *Multivariate Behavioral Research, 3,* 259–294.

Schaie, K. W., & Willis, S. L. (1978). Life-span development: Implications for education. *Review of Research in Education, 6,* 120–156.

Schaie, K. W., & Willis, S. L. (1986). Can decline in intellectual functioning in the elderly be reversed? *Developmental Psychology, 22,* 223–232.

Scheidt, R. (1980). Ecologically valid inquiry: Fait accompli? *Human Development, 23,* 225–228.

Scheidt, R., & Schaie, K. W. (1978). A taxonomy of situations for an elderly population: Generating situational criteria. *Journal of Gerontology, 33,* 838–857.

Schlossberg, N. (1976). A model for analyzing human adaptation to transition. *Counseling Psychology, 9,* 2–18.

Schludermann, E., & Zubek, J. P. (1962). Effect of age on pain sensitivity. *Perceptual and Motor Skills, 14,* 295–301.

Schmeck, R. R. (1983). Learning styles of college students. In R. F. Dillon & R. R. Schmeck (Eds.), *Individual differences in cognition* (Vol. 1, pp. 233–380). New York: Academic Press.

Schmidt, D. F., & Boland, S. M. (1986). Structure of perceptions of older adults: Evidence for multiple stereotypes. *Psychology and Aging, 1,* 255–260.

Schmidt, F., Murphy, M., & Sanders, R. E. (1981). Training older adult free recall rehearsal strategies. *Journal of Gerontology, 36,* 329–337.

Schneider, D. M., & Smith, R. T. (1973). *Class differences and sex roles in American kinship and family structure.* Englewood Cliffs, NJ: Prentice-Hall.

Schneider, W., & Shiffrin, R. M. (1977). Controlled and automatic human information processing: I. Detection, search, and attention. *Psychological Review, 84,* 1–66.

Schonfield, D. (1969). *Recognition tests of dichotic listening and the age variable.* Paper presented to the International Congress of Psychology, London, UK.

Schonfield, D. (1974). Translations in gerontology: From lab to life. Utilizing information. *American Psychologist, 29,* 796–801.

Schonfield, D. (1982). Who is stereotyping whom and why? *The Gerontologist, 22,* 267–272.

Schonfield, D., Trueman, V., & Kline, D. (1972). Recognition test of dichotic listening and the age variable. *Journal of Gerontology, 27,* 487–493.

Schuckit, M. A., & Pastor, P. A. (1979). Alcohol-related psychopathology in the aged. In O. J. Kaplan (Ed.), *Psychopathology of aging* (pp. 211–227). New York: Academic Press.

Schuknecht, H. F., & Igarashi, M. (1964). Pathology of slowly progressive sensorineural deafness. *Transaction of the American Academy of Ophthalmology and Otolaryngology, 68,* 222–242.

Schulz, R. (1976). The effects of control and predictability on the psychological and physical well-being of the institutionalized aged. *Journal of Personality and Social Psychology, 33,* 563–573.

Schulz, R. (1978). *The psychology of death, dying and bereavement.* Reading, MA: Addison-Wesley.

Schulz, R. (1980). Aging and control. In J. Garber & M. E. P. Seligman (Eds.), *Human helplessness* (pp. 261–278). New York: Academic Press.

Schulz, R., & Brenner, G. (1977). Relocation of the aged: A review and theoretical analysis. *Journal of Gerontology, 32,* 323–333.

Schulz, R., & Hanusa, B. H. (1978). Long-term effects of control and predictability enhancing interventions: Findings and ethical issues. *Journal of Personality and Social Psychology, 35,* 1194–1201.

Schulz, R., & Hanusa, B. (1979). Environmental influences on the effectiveness of control and competence-enhancing interventions. In L. C. Perlmutter & R. Monty (Eds.), *Choice and perceived control* (pp. 315–337). Hillsdale, NJ: Lawrence Erlbaum.

Schwab, D. P., & Heneman, H. G. (1977). Effects of age and experience on productivity. *Industrial Gerontology, 4,* 113–117.

Schwab, K. (1974). Early labor force withdrawal of men: Participants and nonparticipants aged 58–63. *Social Security Bulletin, 37,* 24–38.

Schwartz, A. N., & Peterson, J. A. (1979). *Introduction to gerontology.* New York: Holt, Rinehart & Winston.

Schwartz, D. W., & Karp, S. A. (1967). Field dependence in geriatric population. *Perceptual and Motor Skills, 80,* 369–382.

Scott, J. P. (1962). Critical periods in behavioral development. *Science, 138,* 949–958.

Sears, D., Freedman, J., & Peplau, L. (1986). *Social psychology.* Englewood Cliffs, NJ: Prentice-Hall.

Sears, R. R. (1977). Sources of life satisfactions of the Terman gifted men. *American Psychologist, 32,* 119–128.

Seefeldt, C., Jontz, R. K., Galper, A., & Serock, K. (1977). Children's attitudes toward the elderly: Educational implications. *Educational Gerontology, 2,* 301–310.

Seiden, R. H. (1985–86). Mellowing with age: Factors influencing the nonwhite suicide rate. *Omega, 16,* 14–19.

Seligman, M. E. P. (1975). *Helplessness: On depression, development and death.* San Francisco: W. H. Freeman.

Selye, H. (1966). The future for aging research. In N. W. Shock (Ed.), *Perspectives in experimental gerontology* (pp. 375–387). Springfield, IL: Thomas.

Selye, H. (1976). *The stress of life* (rev. ed.). New York: McGraw-Hill.

Sex Equity in Education Bulletin (1983). Title IX Makes Progress. Illinois State Board of Education. Title IV Sex Desegregation Project, June.

Shanas, E. (1962). *The health of older people: A social survey.* Cambridge, MA: Cambridge University Press.

Shanas, E. (1979). The family as a social support system in old age. *The Gerontologist, 19,* 169–174.

Shanas, E., & Maddox, G. (1985). Health, health resources, and the utilization of care. In R. Binstock & E. Shanas (Eds.), *Handbook of aging and the social sciences* (pp. 697–726). New York: Van Nostrand Reinhold.

Shanas, E., Townsend, P., Wedderburn, D., Friis, H., Milhoj, P., & Stehouwer, J. (1968). *Old people in three industrial societies.* New York: Atherton Press.

Share, L. (1978). Family communication in the crisis of a child's fatal illness: A literature review and analysis. In R. Kalish (Ed.), *Caring for the dying and the bereaved.* Farmingdale, NY: Baywood.

Sheehy, G. (1976). *Passages: Predictable crises of adult life.* New York: Dutton.

Sheppard, H. (1976). Work and retirement. In R. Binstock and E. Shanas (Eds.), *Handbook of aging and the social sciences* (pp. 286–309). New York: Van Nostrand Reinhold.

Sheppard, H. L., & Rix, S. E. (1977). *The graying of working America: The coming crisis in retirement-age policy.* New York: Free Press.

Sherman, C. (1974). Labor force studies of non-married women on the threshold of retirement. *Social Security Bulletin, 37,* 3–15.

Sherwood, S., & Mor, V. (1980). Mental health institutions and the elderly. In J. E. Birren & R. B. Sloane (Eds.), *Handbook of mental health and aging* (pp. 854–884). Englewood Cliffs, NJ: Prentice-Hall.

Shock, N. W. (1977). Biological theories of aging. In J. E. Birren & K. W. Schaie (Eds.), *Handbook of the psychology of aging* (pp. 103–115). New York: Van Nostrand Reinhold.

Shore, H. (1976). Designing a training program for understanding sensory losses in aging. *The Gerontologist, 16,* 157–165.

Siefert, K. L., & Hoffnung, R. J. (1987). *Child and adolescent development.* Boston: Houghton Mifflin.

Siegler, I. (1975). The terminal drop hypothesis: Fact or artifact? *Experimental Aging Research, 1,* 169–185.

Siegler, I. C. (1980). Psychological aspects of the Duke longitudinal studies. In K. W. Schaie (Ed.), *Longitudinal studies of adult psychological development* (pp. 136–190). New York: Guilford Press.

Siegler, I., & Botwinick, J. (1979). A long-term longitudinal study of intellectual ability of older adults: The matter of selective subject attrition. *Journal of Gerontology, 34,* 242–245.

Siegler, I., & Costa, P. T., Jr. (1985). Health-behavior relationships. In J. E. Birren and K. W. Schaie (Eds.), *Handbook of the psychology of aging* (2nd ed., pp. 144–166). New York: Van Nostrand Reinhold.

Siegler, I., George, L., & Okun, M. (1979). Cross-sequential analysis of adult personality. *Developmental Psychology, 15,* 350–351.

Siegler, I., McCarty, S., & Logue, P. (1982). Wechsler Memory Scale scores, selective attrition, and distance from death. *Journal of Gerontology, 37,* 176–181.

Sigall, H., & Landy, D. (1973). Radiating beauty: The effects of having a physically attractive partner on person perception. *Journal of Personality and Social Psychology, 28,* 218–224.

Sill, J. (1980). Disengagement reconsidered: Awareness of finitude. *The Gerontologist, 20,* 457–462.

Silverman, I. (1963). Age and the tendency to withhold response. *Journal of Gerontology, 18,* 372–375.

Silverman, P. R. (1969). The widow to widow program: An experiment in preventative intervention. *Mental Hygiene, 53,* 333–337.

Simon, A. (1980). The neuroses, personality disorders, alcoholism, drug use and misuse, and crime in the aged. In J. E. Birren & R. B. Sloane (Eds.), *Handbook of mental health and aging* (pp. 653–670). Englewood Cliffs, NJ: Prentice-Hall.

Simpson, M. (1979). Social and psychological aspects

References

of dying. In H. Wass (Ed.), *Dying: Facing the facts* (pp. 108–136). Washington, DC: Hemisphere.

Sinclair, D. (1969). *Human growth after birth.* London: Oxford University Press.

Sinnott, J. (1984). Postformal reasoning: The relativistic stage. In M. L. Commons, F. A. Richards & C. Armon (Eds.), *Beyond formal operations: Late adolescent and adult cognitive development* (pp. 298–325). New York: Praeger.

Skinner, B. F. (1974). *About behaviorism.* New York: Knopf.

Skinner, B. F. (1983). Intellectual self-management in old age. *American Psychologist, 38,* 239–244.

Skolnick, A. (1986). Early attachment and personal relationships across the life course. In P. B. Baltes, D. L. Featherman, & R. M. Lerner (Eds.), *Life-span development and behavior* (Vol. 7, pp. 174–269). Hillsdale, NJ: Lawrence Erlbaum.

Slater, P. (1964). Cross-cultural views of the aged. In R. Kastenbaum (Ed.), *New thoughts on old age* (pp. 229–236). New York: Springer.

Sloane, R. B. (1980). Organic brain syndrome. In J. E. Birren & R. B. Sloane (Eds.), *Handbook of mental health and aging* (pp. 554–590). Englewood Cliffs, NJ: Prentice-Hall.

Slocum, J. W., & Cron, W. L. (1985). Job attitudes and performance during three career stages. *Journal of Vocational Behavior, 26,* 126–145.

Smith, M. B. (1979). Perspectives on selfhood. *American Psychologist, 33,* 1053–1063.

Smith, M., & Glass, G. (1977). Meta-analysis of psychotherapy outcome studies. *American Psychologist, 32,* 752–760.

Smith, R. E., Sarason, I. G., & Sarason, B. R. (1982). *Psychology: The frontiers of behavior* (2nd ed.). New York: Harper & Row.

Smyer, M. (1984). Life transitions and aging: Implications for counseling older adults. *Counseling Psychologist, 12,* 17–28.

Smyer, M., & Gatz, M. (1979). Aging and mental health: Business as usual? *American Psychologist, 34,* 240–246.

Snow, R., & Crapo, L. (1982). Emotional bondedness, subjective well-being, and health in elderly medical patients. *Journal of Gerontology, 37,* 609–615.

Sokolovsky, J. (1985). Ethnicity, culture and aging: Do differences really make a difference. *Journal of Applied Gerontology, 4,* 6–17.

Soldo, B. (1980). America's elderly in the 1980s. *Population Bulletin, 35*(4), Population Reference Bureau, Inc., Washington, D.C., 1–47.

Solomon, K. (1982). Social antecedents of learned helplessness in the health care setting. *The Gerontologist, 22,* 282–287.

Solomone, P. R. (1982). Difficult cases in career counseling II: The indecisive client. *Personnel and Guidance Journal, 60,* 496–500.

Sonnefeld, J. (1978). Dealing with the aging work force. *Harvard Business Review, 56,* 81–92.

Sontag, S. (1977). The double standard of aging. In L. R. Allman & D. T. Jaffee (Eds.), *Readings in adult psychology: Contemporary perspectives* (pp. 324–333). New York: Harper & Row.

Spearman, C. E. (1904). General intelligence objectively determined and measured. *American Journal of Psychology, 15,* 72–101.

Speece, M. W., & Brent, S. B. (1984). Children's understanding of death: A review of three components of a death concept. *Child Development, 55,* 1671–1686.

Spitzer, R. L., Endicott, J., & Robins, E. (1978). Research diagnostic criteria: Rationale and reliability. *Archives of General Psychiatry, 35,* 773–782.

Spokane, A. R. (1985). A review of research in person-environment congruence in Holland's theory of careers. *Journal of Vocational Behavior, 26,* 306–343.

Stack, C. B. (1974). *All our kin.* New York: Harper & Row.

Stagner, R. (1985). Aging in industry. In J. E. Birren and K. W. Schaie (Eds.), *Handbook of the psychology of aging* (2nd ed., pp. 789–817). New York: Van Nostrand Reinhold.

Stankov, L. (1988). Aging, attention, and intelligence. *Psychology and Aging, 3,* 59–74.

Stannard, D. E. (1977). *The puritan way of death.* New York: Oxford University Press.

Stein, S., Linn, M. W., & Stein, E. M. (1985). Patients' anticipation of stress in nursing home care. *The Gerontologist, 25,* 88–94.

Stenback, A. (1980). Depression and suicidal behavior in old age. In J. E. Birren & R. B. Sloane (Eds.), *Handbook of aging and mental health* (pp. 616–652). Englewood Cliffs, NJ: Prentice-Hall.

Stern, J. A., Oster, P. J., & Newport, K. (1980). Reaction time measures, hemispheric specialization, and age. In L. W. Poon (Ed.), *Aging in the 1980s: Psychological issues* (pp. 309–326). Washington, DC: American Psychological Association.

Stern, W. (1914). The psychological methods of testing intelligence. *Educational Psychological Monographs, 13.*

Sternberg, R. J. (1979). Intelligence research at the interface between differential and cognitive psychology: Prospects and proposals. In R. Sternberg & D. Detterman (Eds.), (1979). *Human intelligence: Perspectives on its theory and measurement* (pp. 33–60). Norwood, NJ: Ablex.

Sternberg, R. J. (1982). A componential approach to intellectual development. In R. J. Sternberg (Ed.), *Advances in the psychology of human intelligence* (Vol. 1). Hillsdale, NJ: Lawrence Erlbaum.

Sternberg, R. J. (1985). Cognitive approaches to intelligence. In B. B. Wolman (Ed.), *Handbook of human intelligence: Theories, measurements, and applications* (pp. 59–118). New York: Wiley Interscience.

Sternberg, R. J., & Detterman, D. (1979). *Human intelligence: Perspectives on its theory and measurement.* Norwood, NJ: Ablex.

Sterns, H. L., Barrett, G. V., & Alexander, R. A. (1980, November). *Older adult skills related to driving: Individual and group training.* Paper presented at the 33rd annual scientific meeting of the Gerontological Society of America, San Diego, CA.

Sterns, H. L., Barrett, G. V., & Alexander, R. A. (1985). Accidents and the aging individual. In J. E. Birren and K. W. Schaie (Eds.), *Handbook of the psychology of aging* (2nd ed., pp. 703–721). New York: Van Nostrand Reinhold.

Sterns, H. L., Barrett, G. V., Alexander, R. A., Greenawalt, J. P., Gianetta, T., & Panek, P. E. (1975, October). Improving skills of the older adult critical for effective driving performance. Paper presented at the symposium, *Maintaining the personal mobility of older persons,* at the 28th annual meeting of the Gerontological Society, Louisville, KY.

Sterns, H. L., Barrett, G. V., Alexander, R. A., Greenawalt, J. P., Gianetta, T., & Panek, P. E. (1976, July). *Improving skills of the older adult critical for effective driving performance* (Final report prepared for the Andrus Foundation of the National Retired Teachers Association and the American Association of Retired Persons). Washington, DC.

Sterns, H. L., Barrett, G. V., Alexander, R. A., Panek, P. E., Avolio, B. J., & Forbringer, L. R. (1977, August). *Training and evaluation of older adult skills critical for effective driving performance* (Final report prepared for the Andrus Foundation of the National Retired Teachers Association and the American Association of Retired Persons). Washington, DC.

Sterns, H. L., & Mitchell, S. (1979). Personal and cognitive development across the life-span. In H. Sterns, E. Ansello, B. Sprouse, & R. Layfield-Faux (Eds.), *Gerontology in higher education* (pp. 250–261). Belmont, CA: Wadsworth.

Sterns, H. L., & Sanders, R. E. (1979). Training and education in the elderly. In R. R. Turner & H. W. Reese (Eds.), *Life-span developmental psychology: Intervention* (pp. 307–330). New York: Academic Press.

Sterns, H., Weis, D. M., & Perkins, S. E. (1984). A conceptual approach to counseling older adults and their families. *Counseling Psychologist, 12,* 55–62.

Stevens-Long, J. (1984). *Adult life: Developmental processes* (2nd ed.). Palo Alto, CA: Mayfield.

Stevenson, J. (1985). *Death, grief and mourning.* New York: Free Press.

Stinnett, N., & Montgomery, J. E. (1968). Youth's perceptions of marriages of older persons. *Journal of Marriage and the Family, 32,* 1–15.

Stinnett, N., & Walters, J. (1977). *Relationships in marriage and family.* New York: Macmillan.

Stinnett, N., Walters, J., & Kaye, E. (1984). *Relationships in marriage and the family* (2nd ed.). New York: Macmillan.

Stoner, S., Panek, P. E., & Satterfield, G. T. (1982). Age and sex differences on the Hand Test. *Journal of Personality Assessment, 46,* 260–264.

Stonewater, J. K., & Daniels, M. H. (1983). Psychosocial and cognitive development in a career decision making course. *Journal of College Student Personnel, 24,* 403–410.

Storandt, M. (1977). Age, ability level, and scoring the WAIS. *Journal of Gerontology, 32,* 175–178.

Storandt, M. (1978). Other approaches to therapy. In M. Storandt, I. Siegler, & M. Elias (Eds.), *Clinical psychology of aging* (pp. 277–293). New York: Plenum.

Storandt, M. (1983). *Counseling and therapy with older adults.* Boston: Little, Brown.

Storandt, M., Grant, E. A., & Gordon, B. C. (1978). Remote memory as a function of age and sex. *Experimental Aging Research, 4,* 365–375.

Storandt, M., Siegler, E., & Elias, M. (1978). *The clinical psychology of aging.* New York: Plenum.

Strain, L., & Chappell, N. (1982). Problems and strategies: Ethical concerns in survey research with the elderly. *The Gerontologist, 22,* 526–531.

Strehler, B. (1975). Implications of aging research for society. *Federation Proceedings of American Societies for Experimental Biology, 34,* 5–8.

Streib, G. F., & Schneider, C. J. (1971). *Retirement in American Society.* Ithaca, NY: Cornell University Press.

Stroop, J. R. (1935). Studies of interference in serial verbal reaction. *Journal of Experimental Psychology, 18,* 643–662.

Strub, R. L., & Black, F. W. (1981). *The mental status examination in neurology.* Philadelphia, PA: Davis.

Subich, L., Cooper, E. A., Barrett, G. V., & Arthur, W. (1986). Occupational preferences of males and females as a function of sex ratios, salary, and availability. *Journal of Vocational Behavior, 28,* 123–134.

Suinn, R. (1975). *Fundamentals of behavior pathology.* New York: Wiley.

References

Suls, J. (1982). *Psychological perspectives on the self.* Hillsdale, NJ: Lawrence Erlbaum.

Sundow, D. (1967). *Passing on: The social organization of dying.* Englewood Cliffs, NJ: Prentice-Hall.

Super, D. E. (1953). A theory of vocational development. *American Psychologist, 8,* 198–190.

Super, D. E. (1957). *The psychology of careers.* New York: Harper & Row.

Super, D. E. (1969). Vocational development theory: Persons, positions, and processes. *The Counseling Psychologist, 1,* 2–8.

Super, D. (1975). *The psychology of careers.* New York: Harper & Row.

Super, D. (1980). A life span, life space approach to career development. *Journal of Vocational Behavior, 16,* 282–298.

Surwillo, W. W. (1964). The relation of decision time to brain wave frequency and to age. *Electroencephalography and Clinical Neurophysiology, 16,* 510–514.

Surwillo, W. W. (1968). Timing of behavior in senescence and the role of the central nervous system. In G. A. Talland (Ed.), *Human aging and behavior: Recent advances in research and theory* (pp. 1–35). New York: Academic Press.

Surwillo, W. W., & Quilter, R. E. (1964). Vigilance, age, and response time. *The American Journal of Psychology, 77,* 614–620.

Surwillo, W. W., & Quilter, R. E. (1965). The influence of age on latency time of involuntary (Galvanic skin reflex) and voluntary responses. *Journal of Gerontology, 20,* 173–176.

Sussman, M. B. (1976). The family life of old people. In R. Binstock & E. Shanas (Eds.), *Handbook of aging and the social sciences* (pp. 218–243). New York: Van Nostrand Reinhold.

Sussman, M. B. (1985). The family life of old people. In R. Binstock & E. Shanas (Eds.), *Handbook of aging and the social sciences* (pp. 415–449). New York: Van Nostrand Reinhold.

Swenson, W. M. (1961). Attitudes toward death in an aged population. *Journal of Gerontology, 16,* 49–52.

Szafran, J. (1965). Age differences in sequential decisions and cardiovascular status among pilots. *Aerospace Medicine, 36,* 303–310.

Szafran, J. (1968). Psychophysiological studies of aging in pilots. In G. A. Talland (Ed.), *Human aging and behavior: Recent advances in research and theory* (pp. 37–74). New York: Academic Press.

Szafran, J. (1970). The effects of aging on professional pilots. In J. H. Price (Ed.), *Modern trends in psychological medicine* (pp. 37–71). New York: Appleton-Century-Crofts.

Sziland, L. (1959). On the nature of the aging process. *Proceedings of the National Academy of Science, 45,* 30–45.

Taub, H. (1975). Mode of presentation, age, and short-term memory. *Journal of Gerontology, 30,* 56–59.

Taylor, R. H. (1972). Risk-taking, dogmatism and demographic characteristics of managers as correlates of information-processing and decision-making behavior. *Proceedings of the 80th Annual Convention of the American Psychological Association, 7,* 443–444.

Templer, D. I., Ruff, C., & Frank, C. (1971). Death anxiety: Age, sex and parental resemblance in diverse populations. *Developmental Psychology, 4,* 108.

Thackray, R. I., & Touchstone, R. M. (1981). *Age-related differences in complex monitoring performance.* (Technical Report FAA-AM-81-12). Washington, DC: Federal Aviation Administration.

Thomae, H. (1976). Patterns of successful aging. In H. Thomae (Ed.), *Patterns of aging: Findings from the Bonn longitudinal study of aging* (pp. 147–161). New York: Karger.

Thomae, H. (1980). Personality and adjustment to aging. In J. E. Birren & K. W. Schaie (Eds.), *Handbook of mental health and aging* (pp. 285–309). Englewood Cliffs, NJ: Prentice-Hall.

Thomas, J. L. (1986). Gender differences in satisfaction with grandparenting. *Psychology and Aging, 1,* 215–219.

Thomas, L. E. (1982). Sexuality and aging: Essential vitamin or popcorn? *The Gerontologist, 22,* 240–243.

Thomas, P. D., Hunt, W. C., Garry, P. J., Hood, R. B., Goodwin, J. M., & Goodwin, J. S. (1983). Hearing activity in a healthy population: Effects on emotional, cognitive, and social status. *Journal of Gerontology, 38,* 321–325.

Thomas, W. C., Jr. (1981). The expectation gap and the stereotype of stereotype: Images of old people. *The Gerontologist, 21,* 402–407.

Thompson, L. W., & Botwinick, J. (1968). Age differences in the relationship between EEG arousal and reaction time. *Journal of Psychology, 68,* 167–172.

Thompson, L. W., Breckenridge, J. N., Gallagher, D., & Peterson, J. (1984). Effects of bereavement on self-perceptions of physical health in elderly widows and widowers. *Journal of Gerontology, 39,* 309–314.

Thompson, L., & Gallagher, D. (1983). A psychoeducational approach for treatment of depression in elders. *Psychotherapy in Private Practice, 1,* 25–28.

Thompson, L. W., Gallagher, D., & Breckenridge, J. S. (1987). Comparative effectiveness of psychotherapies for depressed elders. *Journal of Consulting and Clinical Psychology, 55,* 385–390.

Thompson, L. W., Opton, E., Jr., & Cohen, K. D.

(1963). Effects of age, presentation speed, and sensory modality performance of a vigilance task. *Journal of Gerontology, 18,* 366–369.

Thompson, R. F. (1975). *Introduction to physiological psychology.* New York: Harper & Row.

Thorson, J., Whatley, L., & Hancock, K. (1974). Attitudes toward the aged as a function of age and education. *The Gerontologist, 14,* 316–318.

Thornton, A. (1978). Marital instability differentials and interactions: Insights from multivariate contingency table analysis. *Sociology and Social Research, 62,* 572–575.

Thurstone, L. L. (1938). *Primary mental abilities.* Chicago: University of Chicago Press.

Till, R. E. (1978). Age-related differences in binocular backward masking with visual noise. *Journal of Gerontology, 33,* 702–710.

Timiras, P. S. (1972). *Developmental physiology and aging.* New York: Macmillan.

Timiras, P. S. (1978). Biological perspectives on aging. *American Scientist, 66,* 605–613.

Tobin, S. (1975). Social and health services for the future aged. *The Gerontologist, 15,* 32–37.

Tolbert, E. L. (1974). *Counseling for career development.* Boston: Houghton Mifflin.

Treat, N., Poon, L., & Fozard, J. (1981). Age, imagery, and practice in paired-associate learning. *Experimental Aging Research, 7,* 337–342.

Treat, N., & Reese, H. (1976). Age, imagery, and pacing in paired-associate learning. *Developmental Psychology, 12,* 119–124.

Treisman, A. M. (1969). Strategies and models of selective attention. *Psychological Review, 76,* 282–299.

Troll, L. E. (1975). *Early and middle adulthood: The best is yet to be—maybe.* Monterey, CA: Brooks/Cole.

Troll, L. (1980). Grandparenting. In L. Poon (Ed.), *Aging in the 1980s: Psychological issues* (pp. 475–481). Washington, DC: American Psychological Association.

Troll, L., & Bengston, V. (1982). Intergenerational relations throughout the life span. In J. Wolman (Ed.), *Handbook of developmental psychology.* Engelwood Cliffs, NJ: Prentice-Hall.

Troll, L. E., Miller, S. J., & Atchley, R. C. (1979). *Families in later life.* Belmont, CA: Wadsworth.

Tuckman, J., & Lorge, I. (1952a). Attitudes toward older workers. *Journal of Applied Psychology, 36,* 149–153.

Tuckman, J., & Lorge, I. (1952b). The influence of a course on the psychology of the adult on attitudes toward old people and older workers. *Journal of Educational Psychology, 43,* 400–407.

Tuckman, J., & Lorge, I. (1954). Old people's appraisal of adjustment over the life span. *Journal of Personality, 22,* 417–422.

Tuckman, J., & Lorge, I. (1958). The projection of

personal symptoms into stereotypes about aging. *Journal of Gerontology, 13,* 70–73.

Tune, G. S. (1966). Errors of commission as a function of age and temperament in a type of vigilance task. *Quarterly Journal of Experimental Psychology, 18,* 358–361.

Turkoski, B. B. (1984, February). *Nurses' attitudes toward the elderly in three different case settings.* Paper presented at the 10th annual meeting of the Association for Gerontology in Higher Education (AGHE), Indianapolis, IN.

Udry, J. R. (1974). *The social context of marriage.* New York: Lippincott.

Ullman, L. P., & Krasner, L. (1975). *A psychological approach to abnormal behavior.* Englewood Cliffs, NJ: Prentice-Hall.

United Nations. (1980). *Demographic Yearbook, 1979,* (31st ed., pp. 450–471). New York: United Nations.

U.S. Bureau of the Census. (1981). *Current Population Reports* (Series P–20, No. 365). Washington, DC: U. S. Government Printing Office.

U.S. Bureau of the Census. (1986). *Statistical abstract of the United States.* Washington, DC: U.S. Government Printing Office.

U.S. Congress. House of Representatives. Select Committee on Aging. (1978). *Future directions for an aging policy—a human services model: A report by the subcommittee on human services.* Washington, DC: U.S. Government Printing Office.

U.S. Department of Labor. (1983, January). *News. Bureau of Labor Statistics* (publication number USDL 83–42). Washington, DC: U.S. Government Printing Office.

U.S. Public Health Service. National Center for Health Statistics. (1981). Current estimates from the National Health Interview Survey: United States, 1980. *Vital Health Statistics* (Series 10, No. 139). Washington, DC: U.S. Government Printing Office.

U.S. Senate Special Committee on Aging. (1985, October). *How older Americans live: An analysis of census data* (Serial No. 99–D). Washington, DC: U.S. Government Printing Office.

Usui, W. N. (1984). Homogeneity of friendship networks of elderly blacks and whites. *Journal of Gerontology, 39,* 350–356.

Vaccaro, F. J. (1988). Application of operant procedures in a group of institutionalized aggressive geriatric patients. *Psychology and Aging, 3,* 22–28.

Vaitenas, R., & Weiner, Y. (1977). Developmental, emotional, and interest factors in mid-career change. *Journal of Vocational Behavior, 11,* 291–304.

References

Valliant, G. E. (1977). *Adaptation to life.* Boston: Little, Brown.

Veatch, R. (1979). Defining death anew. In H. Wass (Ed.), *Dying: Facing the facts* (pp. 320–359). Washington, DC: Hemisphere.

Vernon, P. E. (1950). *The structure of human abilities.* London: University of London Press.

Veroff, J., Douvon, E., & Kulka, R. A. (1981a). *The inner American: A self-portrait from 1957 to 1976.* New York: Basic Books.

Veroff, J., Douvan, E., & Kulka, R. A. (1981b). *Mental health in America: Patterns of help seeking from 1957 to 1976.* New York: Basic Books.

Verrillo, R. T., & Verrillo, V. (1985). Sensory and perceptual performance. In N. Charness (Ed.), *Aging and human performance* (pp. 1–46). New York: Wiley.

Verwoerdt, A. (1981). *Clinical geropsychiatry.* Baltimore: Williams & Wilkins.

Vestal, R. E. (1979). *Drugs and the elderly.* Washington, DC: Department of Health, Education, and Welfare.

Vickio, C. J., & Cavanaugh, J. C. (1985). Relationships among death anxiety, attitudes toward aging, and experience with death in nursing home employees. *Journal of Gerontology, 40,* 347–349.

Vogel, F. S. (1977). The brain and time. In E. W. Busse & E. Pfeiffer (Eds.), *Behavior and adaptation in later life* (2nd ed., pp. 228–239). Boston: Little, Brown.

Vondracek, F. W., Lerner, R. M., & Schulenberg, J. E. (1986). *Career development: A life-span developmental approach.* Hillsdale, NJ: Erlbaum.

Wachtel, H. (1966). Hard-core unemployment in Detroit: Causes and remedies. In *Proceedings of the Industrial Relations Research Association* (pp. 233–241). Madison, WI.

Wagner, E. E. (1962). *The hand test: Manual for administration, scoring, and interpretation.* Los Angeles, CA: Western Psychological Services.

Walaskay, M., Whitbourne, S. K., & Nehrke, M. (1983–1984). Construction and validation of an ego integrity status interview. *International Journal of Aging and Human Development, 18,* 61–72.

Wall, S., & Kaltreider, N. (1977). Changing social-sexual patterns in gynecological practice. *Journal of the American Medical Association, 237,* 565–568.

Wallerstein, J. S. (1985). Children of divorce: Preliminary report of a ten-year followup of older children and adolescents. *Journal of American Academy of Child Psychiatry, 24,* 545–553.

Walsh, D. A. (1976). Age differences in central perceptual processing: A dichotic backward masking investigation. *Journal of Gerontology, 31,* 178–185.

Walsh, D. A., & Prasse, M. J. (1980). Iconic memory and attentional processes in the aged. In L. W. Poon, J. L. Fozard, L. S. Cermak, D. Arenberg, & L. W. Thompson (Eds.), *New directions in memory and aging* (pp. 153–180). Hillsdale, NJ: Lawrence Erlbaum.

Wang, H. S., & Busse, E. W. (1969). EEG of healthy persons—a longitudinal study: I. Dominant background activity and occipital rhythm. *Journal of Gerontology, 24,* 419–426.

Wantz, M. S. & Gay, J. E. (1981). *The aging process: A health perspective.* Cambridge, MA: Winthrop.

Wapner, S., Werner, H., & Comalli, P. E. (1960). Perception of part-whole relationships in middle and old age. *Journal of Gerontology, 15,* 412–416.

Ward, R. A. (1977). The impact of subjective age and stigma on older persons. *Journal of Gerontology, 32,* 227–232.

Ward, R. A. (1979). *The aging experience: An introduction to social gerontology.* New York: Lippincott.

Ward, R. H. (1980). Age and acceptance of euthanasia. *Journal of Gerontology, 35,* 421–431.

Ward, R. A. (1984). *The aging experience: An introduction to social gerontology* (2nd ed.). New York: Harper & Row.

Ware, L. A., & Carper, M. (1982). Living with Alzheimer's disease patients: Family stresses and coping mechanisms. *Psychotherapy: Theory, Research and Practice, 19,* 472–481.

Warshak, R. A., & Santrock, J. W. (1983). Children of divorce: Impact of custody disposition on social development. In E. J. Callahan & K. A. McCluskey (Eds.), *Life-span developmental psychology: Nonnormative life events* (pp. 241–263). New York: Academic Press.

Wass, H. (1979). Death and the elderly. In H. Wass (Ed.), *Dying: Facing the facts* (pp. 182–207). Washington, DC: Hemisphere.

Wass, H., Christian, M., Myers, J., & Murphy, M. (1978–1979). Similarities and dissimilarities in attitudes toward death in a population of older persons. *Omega, 9,* 337–354.

Wass, H., & Corr, C. (1981). *Helping children cope with death: Guidelines and resources.* Washington, DC: Hemisphere.

Wass, H., & Corr, C. (1984). *Childhood and death.* Washington, DC: Hemisphere/McGraw-Hill.

Waters, E. B. (1984). Building on what you know: Techniques for individual and group counseling with older people. *Counseling Psychologist, 12,* 81–96.

Watson, W., & Maxwell, R. (1977). *Human aging and dying.* New York: St. Martin's Press.

Wayner, M. J., Jr., & Emmers, R. (1958). Spinal

synaptic delay in young and aged rats. *American Journal of Physiology, 194,* 403–405.

Weale, R. A. (1965). On the eye. In A. T. Welford & J. E. Birren (Eds.), *Behavior, aging, and the individual* (pp. 307–325). Chicago: University of Chicago Press.

Weeks, G. R. & Wright, L. (1985). Dialectics of the family life cycle. *American Journal of Family Therapy, 27,* 85–91.

Weeks, J. R. (1984). *Aging: Concepts and social issues.* Belmont, CA: Wadsworth.

Weinberger, L. E. & Millham, J. (1975). A multi-dimensional multiple method analysis of attitudes toward the elderly. *Journal of Gerontology, 30,* 343–348.

Weiss, A. D. (1959). Sensory functions. In J. E. Birren (Ed.), *Handbook of aging and the individual* (pp. 503–542). Chicago: University of Chicago Press.

Weiss, A. D. (1965). The locus of reaction time change with set, motivation and age. *Journal of Gerontology, 20,* 60–64.

Weisz, J. R. (1978). Transcontextual validity in developmental research. *Child Development, 49,* 1–12.

Weisz, J. R. (1983). Can I control it? The pursuit of veridical answers across the lifespan. In P. Baltes & O. Brim (Eds.), *Life-span development and behavior* (pp. 234–300). New York: Academic Press.

Weldon, S. & Yesavage, J. (1982). Behavioral improvement with relaxation training in senile dementia. *Clinical Gerontologist, 1,* 45–49.

Welford, A. T. (1951). *Skill and age: An experimental approach.* London: Oxford University Press.

Welford, A. T. (1962). Changes in the speed of performance with age and their industrial significance. *Ergonomics, 5,* 139–145.

Welford, A. T. (1965). Performance, biological mechanisms and age: A theoretical sketch. In A. T. Welford & J. E. Birren (Eds.), *Behavior, aging and the nervous system* (pp. 3–20). Springfield, IL: Thomas.

Welford, A. T. (1977). Motor performance. In J. E. Birren & K. W. Schaie (Eds.), *Handbook of the psychology of aging* (pp. 450–496). New York: Van Nostrand Reinhold.

Wellman, F. E., & McCormack, J. (1984). Counseling with older persons: A review of outcome research. *Counseling Psychologist, 12,* 81–96.

Wells, C. F., & Stuart, I. R. (1981). *Self-destructive behavior in children and adolescents.* New York: Van Nostrand Reinhold.

Werner, H. (1948). *Comparative psychology of mental development.* New York: International Universities Press.

Wetzel, L., & Ross, M. A. (1983). Psychological and social ramifications of battering: Observations leading to counseling methodology of victims of domestic violence. *Personnel and Guidance Journal, 61,* 423–427.

Whanger, A. D. (1984). Summary of psychoactive drugs for geriatric patients. In A. D. Whanger & A. C. Myers (Eds.), *Mental health assessment and therapeutic intervention with older adults.* Germantown, MD: Aspen.

Whanger, A. D., & Myers, A. C. (1984). *Mental health assessment and therapeutic intervention with older adults.* Germantown, MD: Aspen.

What age would we like to be? Look in the mirror and see (1987, February). *USA Weekend,* p. 4.

Wheeler, E., & Knight, B. (1981). Morrie: A case study. *The Gerontologist, 21,* 323–328.

Wheeler, L., Reis, H., & Nezlek, J. (1983). Loneliness, social interaction, and sex roles. *Journal of Personality and Social Psychology, 45,* 943–953.

Whitbourne, S. K. (1985). *The aging body: Physiological changes and psychological consequences.* New York: Springer-Verlag.

Whitbourne, S. K., & Weinstock, L. S. (1979). *Adult development: The differentiation of experience.* New York: Holt, Rinehart & Winston.

White House Conference on Aging (1981). *Report on the mini-conference on the mental health of older Americans.* Washington, DC.

Wilcoxon, S. A. (1987). Grandparents and grandchildren: An often neglected relationship between significant others. *Journal of Counseling and Development, 65,* 289–290.

Wilensky, J., & Weiner, M. (1977). Facing reality in psychotherapy with the aging. *Psychotherapy: Theory, Research & Practice, 14,* 373–377.

Williams, J. G., & Solano, C. H. (1983). The social reality of feeling lonely: Friendship and reciprocation. *Personality and Social Psychology Bulletin, 9,* 237–242.

Williamson, R. C. (1966). *Marriage and family relations.* New York: Wiley.

Willis, S. (1982). *Fluid-crystallized ability correlates of real life tasks.* Unpublished manuscript.

Willis, S. (1985). Towards an educational psychology of the older adult learner: Intellectual and cognitive bases. In J. E. Birren & K. W. Schaie (Eds.), *Handbook of the psychology of aging* (2nd ed., pp. 818–847). New York: Van Nostrand Reinhold.

Wilson, A. J. E. (1984). *Social services for older persons.* Boston: Little, Brown.

Wilson, K. B., & DeShane, M. R. (1982). The legal rights of grandparents: A preliminary discussion. *The Gerontologist, 22,* 67–71.

Windley, P., & Scheidt, R. (1980). Person-environment dialectics: Implications for competent functioning in old age. In L. Poon (Ed.), *Aging in the 1980s: Psychological issues* (pp. 407–423).

References

Washington, DC: American Psychological Association.

Windley, P., & Scheidt, R. (1982). An ecological model of mental health among small-town rural elderly. *Journal of Gerontology, 37,* 235–242.

Wine, J. (1971). Test anxiety and direction of attention. *Psychological Bulletin, 76,* 92–104.

Witkin, H. A., & Goodenough, D. R. (1977). Field dependence and interpersonal behavior. *Psychological Bulletin, 84,* 661–689.

Witkin, H. A., Lewis, H. B., Hertzman, M., Machover, K., Meissner, P. B., & Wapner, S. (1954). *Personality through perception.* New York: Harper.

Wohlwill, J. R. (1966). The physical environment: A problem for a psychology of stimulation. *Journal of Social Issues, 22,* 29–38.

Wohlwill, J. R. (1970a). The age variable in psychological research. *Psychological Review, 77,* 49–64.

Wohlwill, J. R. (1970b). Methodology and research strategy in the study of developmental change. In L. R. Goulet and P. B. Baltes (Eds.), *Life-span developmental psychology: Research and theory* (pp. 150–193). New York: Academic Press.

Wolfson, K. P. (1976). Career development patterns of college women. *Journal of Counseling Psychology, 23,* 119–125.

Wood, V., & Robertson, J. F. (1976). The significance of grandparenthood. In J. F. Gubrium (Ed.), *Time, roles, and self in old age* (pp. 278–304). New York: Human Sciences Press.

Wood, W. G. (1978). The elderly alcoholic: Some diagnostic problems and considerations. In M. Storandt, I. Siegler, & M. Elias (Eds.), *The clinical psychology of aging* (pp. 97–113). New York: Plenum.

Woodruff, D. S. (1972). Biofeedback control of the EEG alpha rhythm and its effects on reaction time in the young and old. Unpublished Ph.D. thesis. University of Southern California.

Woodruff, D. S. (1977). *Can you live to be 100?* Boston: Chatham Square Press.

Woodruff, D., & Birren, J. E. (1972). Age changes and cohort differences in personality. *Developmental Psychology, 6,* 252–259.

Woodruff, D. S., & Walsh, D. A. (1975). Research in adult learning: The individual. *The Gerontologist, 15,* 424–430.

Worden, J. W. (1982). *Grief counseling and grief therapy.* New York: Springer.

Work in America Institute. (1980). *The future of older workers in America: New options for an extended working life.* Scarsdale, NY: Author.

Wright, J. D., & Hamilton, R. S. (1978). Work satisfaction and age: Some evidence for the job change hypothesis. *Social Forces, 56,* 1140–1158.

Wright, R. E. (1981). Aging, divided attention, and processing capacity. *Journal of Gerontology, 36,* 605–614.

Yankelovich, D. (1981a, April). New rules in American life: Searching for self-fulfillment in a world turned upside down. *Psychology Today,* pp. 35, 91.

Yankelovich, D. (1981b). *New rules: Searching for self-fulfillment in a world turned upside down.* New York: Random House.

Yordi, C., Chu, A., Ross, K., & Wong, S. (1982). Research and the frail elderly: Ethical and methodological issues in controlled social experiments. *The Gerontologist, 22,* 72–77.

Zajonc, R. B. (1968). Attitudinal effects of mere exposure. *Journal of Personality and Social Psychology. Monograph Supplement, 9,* 1–27.

Zarit, S. (1980). *Aging and mental disorders.* New York: Free Press.

Zarit, S., & Anthony, C. (1986). Interventions with dementia patients and their families. In M. Gilhooly, S. Zarit, & J. E. Birren (Eds.), *The dementias: Policy and management* (pp. 104–121). Englewood Cliffs, NJ: Prentice-Hall.

Zarit, S. H., Anthony, C. R., & Boutselis, M. (1987). Interventions with caregivers of dementia patients: Comparison of two approaches. *Psychology and Aging, 2,* 225–232.

Zarit, S., Cole, K. D., & Guider, R. L. (1981). Memory training strategies and subjective complaints of memory in the aged. *The Gerontologist, 21,* 158–164.

Zarit, S., Eiler, J., & Hassinger, M. (1985). Clinical assessment. In J. E. Birren & K. W. Schaie (Eds.), *Handbook of the psychology of aging* (pp. 725–754). New York: Van Nostrand Reinhold.

Zarit, S., Gallagher, D., & Kramer, N. (1981). Memory training in the community aged: Effects on depression, memory complaint, and memory performance. *Educational Gerontology, 6,* 11–27.

Zarit, S., Reever, K., & Bach-Peterson, J. (1980). Relatives of the impaired elderly: Correlates of feelings of burden. *The Gerontologist, 20,* 649–655.

Zarit, S., Todd, P., & Zarit, J. (1986). Subjective burden of husbands and wives as caregivers: A longitudinal study. *The Gerontologist, 26,* 260–266.

Zarit, S. H., & Zarit, J. M. (1982). Families under stress: Intervention for care-givers of senile dementia patients. *Psychotherapy: Theory, Research and Practice, 19,* 461–470.

Zarit, S., & Zarit, J. (1983). Cognitive impairment. In P. Lewinsohn & L. Teri (Eds.), *Clinical geropsychology:*

New directions in assessment and treatment (pp. 38–80). New York: Pergamon Press.

Zarit, S., Zarit, J., & Reever, K. (1982). Memory training for severe memory loss: Effects on senile dementia. *The Gerontologist, 22,* 373–377.

Zeits, C. R., & Prince, R. M. (1982). Child effects on parents. In B. Wolman (Ed.), *Handbook of developmental psychology* (pp. 751–770). Englewood Cliffs, NJ: Prentice-Hall.

Zelinski, E., Gilewski, M., & Thompson, L. (1980). Do laboratory tests relate to everyday remembering and forgetting? In L. Poon, J. Fozard, L. Cermack, D. Arenberg, & L. Thompson (Eds.), *New directions in memory and aging* (pp. 519–544). Hillsdale, NJ: Lawrence Erlbaum.

Zelnick, M., & Kanter, J. F. (1981). Sexual activity, contraceptive use and pregnancy among metropolitan-area teenagers: 1970–1979. *Family Planning Perspectives, 12,* 230–237.

Zimberg, S. (1979). Alcohol and the elderly. In D. M. Peterson, F. J. Whittington, & B. P. Payne (Eds.), *Drugs and the elderly* (pp. 28–40). Springfield, IL: Thomas.

Zeplin, H., Wolfe, C., & Kleinplatz, F. (1981). Evaluation of a yearlong reality orientation program. *Journal of Gerontology, 36,* 70–77.

Ziance, R. J. (1979). Side effects of drugs in the elderly. In D. M. Peterson, F. J. Whittington, & B. P. Payne (Eds.), *Drugs and the elderly* (pp. 53–79). Springfield, IL: Thomas.

· CREDITS ·

PHOTOGRAPHS (listed by page numbers)

3 Irene Bayer, Monkmeyer. 10 AP/Wide World Photos. 43 Howard Dratch/The Image Works. 50 Copyright © Abraham Menashe. 97 Dean Abramson/Stock, Boston. 120 The Picture Cube. 153 Taurus Photos. 161 The Picture Cube. 162 Frank Siteman/Stock, Boston. 181 The Picture Cube. 205 Mike Douglas/The Image Works, Inc. 237 The Picture Cube. 250 The Picture Cube. 259 Rapho/Photo Researchers, Inc. 281 Mark Antman/The Image Works, Inc. 308 Elizabeth Crews/The Image Works, Inc. 313 Mark Antman/The Image Works, Inc. 328 Judy S. Gelles/Stock, Boston. 356 Elizabeth Crews/The Image Works, Inc. 375 Photo Researchers, Inc. 401 James Holland/Stock, Boston. 416 Alan Carey/The Image Works, Inc. 446 Jean-Claude Lejeune/Stock, Boston. 452 The Picture Cube. 468 The Picture Cube. 485 Strub & Black (1981), p. 149. *Organic brain syndromes: An introduction to neurobehavioral disorders.* Reprinted by permission of F. A. Davis publishers. 511 Mark Antman/The Image Works, Inc. 517 Alan Carey/The Image Works, Inc. 527 Photo Researchers, Inc.

TABLES (listed by page numbers)

57 Table 2.2: Adapted from Birren, 1964, pp. 57, 58, 59, and Lansing, 1959. 63 Table 2.3: National Center for Health Statistics (1980). 62 Table 2.4: © by Devin-Adain, Publishers, Inc., Old Greenwich, Connecticut 06870. Permission granted to reprint "Can You Live to Be 100?" by D. S. Woodruff, 1977. All rights reserved. 63 Table 2.5: Adapted from United Nations. (1980). *Demographic Yearbook,* 1979, 31st ed., pp. 450–471. New York: United Nations. Copyright, United Nations 1980. Reproduced with permission. 80 Table 2.7: Used with permission of the author and the publisher. 104 Table 3.1: Adapted from D. Friedrich. (1972). *A primer for developmental methodology,* pp. 35–38. Minneapolis, Minn.: Burgess Publishing Co. 118 Table 4.1: R. E. Smith, I. G. Sarason, & B. R. Sarason. (1982). *Psychology: The frontiers of behavior* (2d ed.) (p. 144). New York: Harper & Row. 196 Table 6.2: Adapted from J. Cohen. (1957). The factorial structure of the WAIS between early adulthood and old age. *Journal of Consulting Psychology, 21,* p. 284. 219 Table 6.3: Reprinted with permission of the Gerontological Society of America. 233 Table 7.2: Adapted from J. Fozard. (1980). A time for remembering. In L. Poon (Ed.), *Aging in the 1980's: Psychological issues,* pp. 273–290. Washington, D. C.: American Psychological Association. Copyright 1980 by the American Psychological Association. Adapted by permission of the publisher and author. 279 Table 8.2: From *Family development,* 4th ed., by Evelyn M. Duvall. © 1957, 1962, 1967, 1971 by Harper & Row, Publishers, Inc. 314 Table 9.1: Reprinted with permission of publisher from: Panek, P. E., Rush, M. C., & Greenawalt, J. P. Current sex stereotypes of 25 occupations. *Psychological Reports,* 1977, 40, pp. 212–214. 359 Table 10.1: Buhler's biographical approach to personality. From C. Buhler, Genetic aspects of the self. *Annals of the New York Academy of Sciences,* 1962, 96, p. 756. Reprinted by permission. 383 Table 10.3: Maas and Kuypers' personality types for men and women. From Maas & Kuypers. (1974). *From thirty to seventy,* p. 198. Reprinted by permission of Jossey Bass, Inc., publishers. 431 Table 11.1: N. J. Osgood, Patterns of aging in retirement communities: Typology of residents. *Journal of Applied Gerontology,* 2 (1983), pp. 28–43. Copyright © 1983. 474 Table 13.1: Myers et al. (1984). Estimates of several common disorders by age and sex. Six-month prevalence of psychiatric disorders in three communities. *Archives of General Psychiatry, 41,* p. 965. Reprinted by permission of the American Medical Association. © 1984, American Medical Association. 483 Table 13.2: William Bondareff, "Biomedical Perspective of Alzheimer's Disease & Dementia in the Elderly," in *The Dementias,* Gilhooly/Zarit/Birren, eds., © 1986, p. 15. Adapted by permission of Prentice-Hall, Inc., Englewood Cliffs, New Jersey. 493 Table 13.3: From D. Gallagher & L. Thompson. (1983). Cognitive impairment. In P. Lewisohn & L. Teri (Eds.), *Clinical geropsychology: New directions in assessment and treatment* (p. 12). Elmsford, NY: Pergamon Press. Adapted from C. Wells. (1979). Pseudodementia, *American Journal of Psychiatry, V,* 136, p. 898. Copyright 1979, The American Psychiatric Association. Reprinted by permission. 494 Table 13.4: Adapted from C. Salzman & R. Shader. (1979). Clinical evaluation of depression in the elderly. In A. Raskin & L. Jarvik (Eds.), *Psychiatric symptoms and cognitive loss in the elderly* (p. 50). Reprinted by permission of Hemisphere Publishing Corp. NY & Washington, D. C. © 1979. 498–499 Table 13.5: Barry J. Gurland, "The Assessment of the Mental Health Status of Older Adults," in *Handbook of Mental Health and Aging,* Birren/Sloane, eds., © 1980, p. 679. Adapted by permission of Prentice-Hall, Inc., Englewood Cliffs, New Jersey. Tabular information drawn from: J. S. Lawson et al., 1977; E. Pfeiffer, 1975; G. Irving et al., 1972; A. H. Patie and C. J. Gilleard, 1975.

· NAME INDEX ·

Name Index

· SUBJECT INDEX ·

Subject Index